AIR POLLUTION

ANDERSON'S
Law School Publications

ADMINISTRATIVE LAW: CASES AND MATERIALS
by Daniel J. Gifford

APPELLATE ADVOCACY: PRINCIPLES AND PRACTICE
Cases and Materials
by Ursula Bentele and Eve Cary

CASES AND PROBLEMS IN CRIMINAL LAW
by Myron Moskovitz

COMMERCIAL TRANSACTIONS: PROBLEMS AND MATERIALS
by Louis F. Del Duca, Egon Guttman and Alphonse M. Squillante

A CONSTITUTIONAL LAW ANTHOLOGY
by Michael J. Glennon

A CONTRACTS ANTHOLOGY
by Peter Linzer

A CRIMINAL LAW ANTHOLOGY
by Arnold H. Loewy

CRIMINAL LAW: CASES AND MATERIALS
by Arnold H. Loewy

EFFECTIVE INTERVIEWING
by Fred. E. Jandt

ENDING IT: DISPUTE RESOLUTION IN AMERICA
Descriptions, Examples, Cases and Questions
by Susan M. Leeson and Bryan M. Johnston

ENVIRONMENTAL LAW
by Jackson B. Battle and Mark Squillace

FEDERAL RULES OF EVIDENCE
Rules, Legislative History, Commentary and Authority
by Glen Weissenberger

INTERNATIONAL HUMAN RIGHTS: LAW, POLICY AND PROCESS
Problems and Materials
by Frank Newman and David Weissbrodt

INTRODUCTION TO THE STUDY OF LAW: CASES AND MATERIALS
by John Makdisi

JUSTICE AND THE LEGAL SYSTEM
A Coursebook
by Anthony D'Amato and Arthur J. Jacobson

THE LAW OF DEFAMATION, PRIVACY, PUBLICITY AND "MORAL RIGHTS"
Cases and Materials on Protection of Personality Interests
by Sheldon W. Halpern

THE LAW OF MODERN PAYMENT SYSTEMS AND NOTES
by Fred H. Miller and Alvin C. Harrell

LEGAL RESEARCH, WRITING AND ADVOCACY, SECOND EDITION
by Welsey Gilmer, Jr.

PATIENTS, PSYCHIATRISTS AND LAWYERS
Law and the Mental Health System
by Raymond L. Spring, Roy B. Lacoursiere, M.D., and Glen Weissenberger

PROBLEMS AND SIMULATIONS IN EVIDENCE
by Thomas F. Guernsey

THE REGULATION OF BANKING
Cases and Materials on Depository Institutions and Their Regulators
by Michael P. Malloy

SPORTS LAW: CASES AND MATERIALS
by Raymond L. Yasser, James R. McCurdy and C. Peter Goplerud

TRIAL PRACTICE
Text by Lawrence A. Dubin and Thomas F. Guernsey
Problems and Case Files with *Video* Presentation
by Edward R. Stein and Lawrence A. Dubin

AIR POLLUTION

MARK SQUILLACE
Professor of Law
University of Wyoming

Second Edition

ENVIRONMENTAL LAW VOLUME THREE

Anderson Publishing Co. / Cincinnati, Ohio

ENVIRONMENTAL LAW VOLUME THREE: Air Pollution
Second Edition

ISBN: 0-87084-089-4

For my wife, Brenda Kelley

TABLE OF CONTENTS

Preface
Acknowledgements
Table of Cases

PART I
AN INTRODUCTION TO AIR POLLUTION LAW

Chapter 1 Air Pollution: The Case for Its Control ... 1
Wark & Warner, Air Pollution: Its Origins and Control ... 1

Chapter 2 Market Approaches to the Air Pollution Problem ... 15
Schelling, Incentives for Environmental Protection ... 15
Ackerman & Stewart, Reforming Environmental Law: The Democratic Case for Market Incentives ... 21

Chapter 3 Air Pollution and the Common Law ... 29
Boomer v. Atlantic Cement Company ... 29
International Paper Company v. Ouelette ... 37

PART II
THE CLEAN AIR ACT

Chapter 4 The Big Picture: A Summary of the Clean Air Act ... 47

Chapter 5 National Ambient Air Quality Standards ... 63
Natural Resources Defense Council v. Train ... 63
Lead Industries Association v. EPA ... 67

Chapter 6 State Implementation Plans ... 83
A. Approval and Disapproval of State Implementation Plans ... 83
State of Texas v. EPA ... 83
Kennecott Copper Corporation v. Train ... 90

B. Economic and Technological Feasibility ... 96
Union Electric Company v. EPA ... 96

C. Nonattainment Areas ... 105
Citizens Against Refinery's Effects v. EPA ... 111

D. Nonattainment Area Plans 115
National Steel Corporation v. Gorsuch 116
State of Ohio v. Ruckelshaus 121
Problem #1: State Implementation Plans and Nonattainment Areas 127

E. Transboundary Disputes 128
State of Connecticut v. EPA 128
Air Pollution Control District of Jefferson County v. EPA 140
Her Majesty the Queen in Right of Ontario v. EPA 149

F. Enforcement of State Implementation Plans 157
General Motors Corporation v. United States 158
Problem #2: The Scope of Federal Authority Under State Implementation Plans 163

G. Judicial Review of State Implementation Plans 163
Kennecott Copper Corporation v. Costle 164

H. The Right to Be Heard 169
Anaconda Company v. Ruckelshaus 169

Chapter 7 Prevention of Significant Deterioration 173
Alabama Power Company v. Costle 173
Kerr-McGee Chemical Corporation v. U.S. Department of the Interior . 189
Problem #3: Air Quality Related Values 193
Natural Resources Defense Council v. EPA 194

Visibility Protection 201
State of Vermont v. Thomas 201
Grand Canyon National Park Visibility Impairment 206
Problem #4: Visibility 215

Chapter 8 Monitoring and Modeling 217
PPG Industries v. Costle 217
Cleveland Electric Illuminating Company v. EPA 223
State of Ohio v. EPA 228

Chapter 9 Permits and Performance Standards for Stationary Sources 233
A. New Source Performance Standards 233
National Asphalt Pavement Association v. Train 233

B. New Source Review 241
Wisconsin Electric Power Company v. Reilly 241

C. The Permit Program for Stationary Sources 250
Roady, Permitting and Enforcement Under the Clean Air Act Amendments of 1990 250
Hawaiian Electric Company v. EPA 255
Problem #5: Permits for Stationary Sources 260

D. Hazardous Air Pollutants . . . 260
Natural Resources Defense Council v. EPA . . . 261
The 1990 Amendments to Section 112 . . . 270
Cross, Byrd, & Lave, Discernible Risk — A Proposed Standard for Significant Risk in Carcinogen Regulation . . . 273
Problem #6: Technology-Based Standards . . . 280

E. The Emissions Trading Program . . . 280
Chevron USA, Inc. v. Natural Resources Defense Council . . . 280
EPA Emissions Trading Policy Statement . . . 290
Problem #7: Permits, Bubbles & Visibility . . . 300

F. The Acid Precipitation Program . . . 301
Acid Rain Program: EPA Proposed Rules . . . 302

Chapter 10 Inspections and Enforcement of Stationary Sources . . . 327
A. Inspections and Recordkeeping . . . 327
Stauffer Chemical Company v. EPA . . . 327
Dow Chemical Company v. United States . . . 332

B. Enforcement . . . 337
City of Seabrook v. Costle . . . 339
Union Electric Company v. EPA . . . 343
Adamo Wrecking Company v. United States . . . 348
Duquesne Light Company v. EPA . . . 353
Problem #8: Inspection and Enforcement of Stationary Sources . . . 364

Chapter 11 Stratospheric Ozone Depletion . . . 365
Montreal Protocol on Substances that Deplete the Ozone Layer . . . 365
EPA Proposed Rules on Stratospheric Ozone Depletion . . . 376
Senate Debate: London Amendments to the Montreal Protocol . . . 382

Chapter 12 Mobile Sources . . . 387
A. Emission Standards for New Motor Vehicles . . . 387
Natural Resources Defense Council v. Ruckelshaus . . . 389
Natural Resources Defense Council v. EPA . . . 393
Center for Auto Safety v. Ruckelshaus . . . 403

B. Regulation of Fuels and Fuel Additives . . . 409
Ethyl Corporation v. EPA . . . 409

Chapter 13 Judicial Review . . . 427
A. Petitions for Review and Rulemaking Proceedings . . . 427
Harrison v. PPG Industries . . . 429

B. Citizen Suits . . . 435
Environmental Defense Fund v. Thomas . . . 436
Natural Resources Defense Council v. EPA . . . 443

PART III
BEYOND THE CLEAN AIR ACT

Chapter 14 Global Climate Change 449
Changing By Degrees — Steps to Reduce Greenhouse Gases 449
EPA, The Potential Effects of Global Climate Change on the U.S. 452
Changing By Degrees — Steps to Reduce Greenhouse Gases 467

Chapter 15 Indoor Air Pollution
Indoor Air Pollution: Federal Efforts Not Effectively Addressing a Growing Problem 473

Glossary 479

Index 485

PREFACE

In the preface to the original edition of this book, I argued that the field of environmental law had become so complex that it was virtually impossible to cover the subject matter adequately in a "traditional" three hour course. That proposition is more true today than it was in 1988, and there is perhaps no better confirmation of this fact than the Clean Air Act Amendments of 1990. What began as a complex statute before 1990 has now become virtually impenetrable to all but the most dedicated students. Thus, this second edition presents new challenges. I have not deviated from the basic approach taken in the first edition. Rather, I have attempted to update the materials to reflect the substantial changes in the federal law, and to enrich the course by offering the students various problems which allow them to test their understanding of the materials. In my experience, students have much difficulty understanding the law until they are able to see how it is applied. The problems are designed to serve this purpose.

I have included in this edition excerpts from various EPA proposed and final rules, as well as recent articles and reports on selected topics. I urge caution, however, in assigning these materials to the students. If the instructor is prepared to spend considerable class time discussing these materials they should prove pedagogically beneficial. If not, most of these materials are best treated as background for the instructor, and interested students.

I have successfully used these materials in a three-hour course that covers environmental decisionmaking (including NEPA and the Endangered Species Act), and air pollution control, as an example of a complex environmental regulatory system. For the instructor who would like to use only a portion of the materials, I recommend chapters 5, 6, 7, 9, 10, and 12. These materials form the core of air pollution control law as it has developed in the United States.

One important change from the first edition is that the statute no longer appears as an appendix. While the language of the statute is indispensable to teaching this course, environmental law statutes are available commercially from a number of outlets, and I have found that students generally prefer to have them in a separate book so that they can use their text and the statute simultaneously. For courses where a broader set of statutes is not needed, the statute is available in a separate binding from the Anderson Publishing Company. Anderson will also make it available on disk for those who prefer to receive it in that form.

I wish to acknowledge the George Hopper Research Fund for assistance during the preparation of this manuscript. I would also like to express profound gratitude to my student research assistants, Scott Skavdahl, Dan Hitchcock, and Peggy Kirk, for their substantial contribution, and to my secretaries Jane Gray, Mandy Engel and Kevin Cartie for their yeoman efforts in bringing this project to fruition.

Mark Squillace — Laramie, Wyoming
June, 1992

ACKNOWLEDGEMENTS

The author gratefully acknowledges the following authors and publishers who have graciously permitted me to reproduce portions of their copyrighted work.

Terry Anderson & Donald Leal, FREE MARKET ENVIRONMENTALISM, Pacific Research Institute (1991). Reprinted by permission of Pacific Research Institute for Public Policy, San Francisco, CA.

Bruce Ackerman & Richard Stewart, *Reforming Environmental Law: The Democratic Case for Market Incentives*, 13 COLUM. J. ENV. L. 171 (1988). Reprinted by permission of Columbia Journal of Environmental Law.

Frank Cross, Daniel Byrd & Lester Lave, *Discernible Risk — A Proposed Standard for Significant Risk in Carcinogen Regulation*, 43 ADMIN. L. REV. 61 (1991). © 1991 American Bar Association. All rights reserved. Reprinted by permission of the American Bar Association.

David P. Currie, AIR POLLUTION, FEDERAL LAW & ANALYSIS, § 1.03, Copyright © 1981 Callaghan & Co. All rights reserved. Reprinted by permission of Clark Boardman Callaghan, 1-800-221-9421.

Timothy Dyk, *The Supreme Court's Role in Not Shaping Administrative Law,* 44 ADMIN. L. REV. 429 (1992). © 1991 American Bar Association. All rights reserved. Reprinted by permission of the American Bar Association.

Richard A. Posner, ECONOMIC ANALYSIS OF THE LAW (Little, Brown & Co., 2d ed. 1977). Reprinted with permission of Little, Brown and Company.

Stephen E. Roady, *Permitting and Enforcement Under the Clean Air Act Amendments of 1990,* 21 ELR P0178 (News & Analysis) (April 1991). © 1991 Environmental Law Institute. Reprinted with permission from the Environmental Law Reporter.

Mark Sagoff, THE ECONOMY OF THE EARTH (Cambridge University Press, 1988). Reprinted with permission of Cambridge University Press.

Thomas C. Schelling, INCENTIVES FOR ENVIRONMENTAL PROTECTION (MIT Press, 1983). © 1983 by The Massachusetts Institute of Technology.

Kenneth Wark and Cecil F. Warner, AIR POLLUTION: ITS ORIGINS AND CONTROL (Harper & Row, 2d ed. 1981).

Table of Cases

Abbott Laboratories v. Gardner, 168
Action on Smoking and Health v. Civil Aeronautics Board, 477
Adamo Wrecking Company v. United States, 348, 428
Air Pollution Control District v. EPA, 139, *140*
Air Pollution Variance Board v. Western Alfalfa Corporation, 336
Alabama Power Company v. Costle, 55, 93, 95, *173*, 288, 300
American Lung Association v. EPA, 67, 108
American Methyl Corporation v. EPA, 422
American Petroleum Institute v. Costle, 66, 78
Amoco Oil Company v. EPA, 420
Anaconda Company v. Ruckelshaus, 163, *169*
ASARCO, Inc. v. EPA, 288
Ashbacker Radio Corp. v. FCC, 139
Automotive Parts Rebuilders Association v. EPA, 408
Avery v. Powell, 476

Bi-Metallic Investment Company v. Colorado, 172
Boomer v. Atlantic Cement Company, 29
Buckeye Power, Inc. v. EPA, 88, 89
Bunker Hill Co. v. EPA, 104, 331, 337

Center for Auto Safety v. Ruckelshaus, 403
Chevron, USA, Inc. v. Natural Resources Defense Council, 126, 187, *280*, 332, 407
Cincinnati Gas & Electric v. EPA, 88, 227
Citizens Against Refinery's Effects v. EPA, 111
Citizens to Preserve Overton Park v. Volpe, 89
Citizens to Save Spencer County v. EPA, 187
City of Burbank v. Lockheed Air Terminal, Inc. 36
City of Highland Park v. Train, 447
City of Seabrook v. Costle, 339
Cleveland Electric Illuminating Co. v. EPA, 104, *223*
Connecticut Fund for the Environment v. EPA, 140
Connecticut, State of v. EPA, 128, 227
Council of Commuter Organizations v. Metropolitan Transportation Authority, 339, 342

DeBlois v. Bowers, 34
Delaney v. EPA, 116
District of Columbia v. Train, 163
Dow Chemical Company v. EPA, 94
Dow Chemical Company v. United States, 332
Drummond Coal Company v. Watt, 428
Duquesne Light Company v. EPA, 353
Eisen v. Carlysle & Jacquelin, 34
Environmental Defense Fund v. EPA, 82, 201
Environmental Defense Fund v. Thomas, 66, *436*
Essex Chemical Corporation v. Ruckelshaus, 238
Ethyl Corporation v. EPA, 409
Ex Parte Young, 347

Friends of the Earth v. Potomac Electric Power Company, 447

General Motors Corporation v. Ruckelshaus, 409
General Motors Corporation v. United States, 158, 363
Georgia v. Tennessee Copper Company, 37

Gwaltney of Smithfield, Ltd. v. Chesapeake Bay Foundation, 61, 339

Hancock v. Train, 90
Harrison v. PPG Industries, 347, *429*
Hawaiian Electric Company v. EPA, 255
Hensley v. Eckerhart, 447
Her Majesty the Queen in Right of Ontario v. EPA, 149
Holmes Limestone,Inc. v. Andrus, 428

Illinois v. City of Milwaukee, 44, 140
I.N.S. v. Cardoza-Fonseca, 288
International Harvester v. Ruckelshaus, 79, 402
International Paper Company v. Ouellette, 37

Kennecott Copper Corporation v. Costle, 96, *164*
Kennecott Copper Corporation v. EPA, 79
Kennecott Copper Corporation v. Train, 90
Kerr-McGee Chemical Corporation v. U.S. Department of the Interior, 189

Lead Industries Association v. EPA, 67
Londoner v. Denver, 172
Lubrizoil Corporation v. EPA, 421

Marshall v. Barlows, 337
McCastle v. Rollins Environmental Services, 34
Metropolitan Washington Coalition for Clean Air v. District of Columbia, 447
Montgomery Environmental Coalition v. Costle, 447
Motor Vehicle Manufacturers Association v. EPA, 422
Motor Vehicle Manufacturers Association v. State Farm Insurance, 288, 407

Nance v. EPA, 192
National Asphalt Pavement Association v. Train, 233
National Lime Association v. EPA, 238, 239
National Steel Corp. v. Gorsuch, 105, *116*
National Wildlife Federation v. Hodel, 200
Natural Resources Defense Council v. EPA, 56, 94, 186, *194*, 261, 270, *393*, 403, 443, 446
Natural Resources Defense Council v. Ruckelshaus, 389, 436
Natural Resources Defense Council v. Thomas, 81
Natural Resources Defense Council v. Train, 63
Nebraska v. Wyoming, 140
New England Legal Foundation v. Costle, 45
New York v. EPA, 139
New York v. Ruckelshaus, 149
New York v. Thomas, 448
Newman v. Piggie Park Enterprises, 447
Northern Plains Resources Council v. EPA, 238

Ohio, State of v. EPA, 228
Ohio, State of v. Ruckelshaus, 121

Pennsauken County, In the Matter of, 188
Pennsylvania v. Delaware Valley Citizens Council for Clean Air, 447
PPG Industries v. Costle, 217
Public Service Company of Indiana v. EPA, 336
Puerto Rican Cement Co. v. EPA, 249

R.L. Renken v. Harvey Aluminum, 35
Robbins Resource Recovery Company, In the Matter of, 188
Ruckelshaus v. Sierra Club, 339, 447
Rylands v. Fletcher, 37

Sierra Club v. Costle, 66, 239
Sierra Club v. EPA, 94
Sierra Club v. Gorsuch, 200
Sierra Club v. Thomas, 200
Sierra Pacific Power Co. v. EPA, 238
Small Refinery Lead Phase Down Task

Force v. EPA, 422
Specialty Equipment Marketing Association v. Ruckelshaus, 408
Spur Industries v. Del E. Webb Development Company, 35
Stauffer Chemical Company v. EPA, 327
Surface Mining Regulation Litigation, In re, 200

T & E Industries, Inc. v. Safety Light Corporation, 36
Texas, State of v. EPA, 83, 88, 157
Thomas v. New York, 149
Town of Brookline v. Gorsuch, 188
Tull v. United States, 347

Union Electric Company v. EPA, 78, *96, 343*
Union Electric Company v. Train, 96

United States v. Causby, 35
United States v. City of Painesville, 238
United States v. Ethyl Corporation, 352
United States v. Narragansett Improvement Co., 238
United States v. Stauffer Chemical Company, 331
United States v. Western Pacific Railroad, 168

Vermont, State of v. Thomas, 201
Vermont Yankee Nuclear Power Corporation v. Natural Resources Defense Council, 80, 89

Warth v. Seldin, 448
West Penn Power Company v. Train, 347
Wisconsin Electric Power Company v. Reilly, 55, *241*

I
AN INTRODUCTION TO AIR POLLUTION

1 AIR POLLUTION: THE CASE FOR ITS CONTROL

The following excerpt offers a technical summary of the effects of air pollutants on human health and the environment. Refer back to this information periodically during your review of the legal materials so that you have a firm understanding of the technical basis for the regulatory controls that are imposed by law.

AIR POLLUTION: ITS ORIGIN AND CONTROL

K. WARK AND C.F. WARNER (Harper & Row, 2d. ed. 1981)

I
INTRODUCTION

Air pollution is woven throughout the fabric of our modern life. A by-product of the manner in which we build our cities, air pollution is waste remaining from the ways we produce our goods, transport ourselves and our goods, and generate the energy to heat and light the places where we live, play, and work. The major cause of all air pollution is combustion, and combustion is essential to man. When perfect or theoretical combustion occurs, the hydrogen and carbon in the fuel combine with oxygen from the air to produce heat, light, carbon dioxide, and water vapor. However, impurities in the fuel, poor fuel-to-air ratio, or too high or too low combustion temperatures cause the formation of such side products as carbon monoxide, sulfur oxides, nitrogen oxides, fly ash, and unburned hydrocarbons — all air pollutants.

Air pollution is not a recent phenomenon. King Edward I of England tried to clear the smoky sky over London in 1272 by banning the use of "sea coal." The British Parliament ordered the torturing and hanging of a man who sold and burned the outlawed coal. Under Richard II (1377-1399) and later under Henry V (1413-1422), England took steps to regulate and restrict the use of coal. One of the earliest recorded publications dealing with air pollution is a pamphlet published in 1661 by royal command of Charles II: "Fumifugium; or the Inconvenience of the Air and Smoke of London Dissipated; together with Some Remedies Humbly Proposed," written by John Evelyn, one of the founding members of the Royal Society. The use of coal in the generation of energy was a major factor in the Industrial Revolution, which formed the basis of our current technological society. Unfortunately, intimately associated with the benefits of our technological society is the fouling and degrading of our environment. One of the earliest legal attempts to control air pollution in the United States appears to be an 1895 ordinance making illegal the "showing of visible vapor" as exhaust from steam automobiles.

Such natural processes as forest fires, decaying vegetation, dust storms, and volcanic eruptions have always contaminated the air. Although the total global production of many gases and particulate matter recognized as pollutants is much greater from natural sources than from man-made sources, global distribution and dispersion of those pollutants result in low average concentrations. By precipitation, oxidation, and absorption into the oceans and the soil, the atmosphere can cleanse itself of all known pollutants given sufficient time. On the other hand, man-generated pollutants are usually concentrated in small geographic regions; hence most air pollution is truly man-made. In the United States alone, over 200 million tons of gaseous, solid, and liquid waste products are discharged annually into the atmosphere. Currently the rate at which pollutants are discharged into the atmosphere in highly populated regions at times exceeds the cleansing rate of the atmosphere.

* * *

In the past, industry, agriculture, and individual polluters have found it more economical to discharge waste products into the atmosphere than to exercise waste control. In general the organization or activity causing the pollution did not suffer the consequences of the pollution; likewise, those who benefitted from a reduction in air pollution resulting from the installation of control equipment did not directly bear the cost of the equipment. In recent years, as the public has become increasingly concerned with environmental problems, air has come to be regarded as a resource within the public domain. Hence air pollution is considered a public problem, a concern not only of those who discharge the pollution, but also of those who may suffer as a result. Thus the laws in some countries now permit an individual or group of private individuals to sue directly an organization or company which is polluting that particular part of the public domain.

The rational control of air pollution rests on four basic assumptions:

1. *Air is in the public domain.* Such an assumption is necessary if air pollution is to be treated as a public problem, of concern not only to those who discharge the pollution but also to those who may suffer as a result.

2. *Air pollution is an inevitable concomitant of modern life.* There is a conflict between man's economic and biologic concerns; in the past, this conflict was recognized only after air pollution disasters. We need a systematic development of policies and programs to conserve the atmosphere for its most essential biological function.

3. *Scientific knowledge can be applied to the shaping of public policy.* Information about the sources and effects of air pollution is far from complete, and a great deal of work must be done to develop control devices and methods. Nevertheless, sufficient information is now available to make possible substantial reductions in air pollution levels. Man does not have to abandon either his technology or his life, but he must use his knowledge.

4. *Methods of reducing air pollution must not increase pollution in other sectors of the environment.* Some industries reduce wastes in the air by dissolving them in water and by pouring the polluted water into streams. For example, one proposal to reduce the sulfur dioxide emitted by coal-burning electrical power plants results

in the formation of large quantities of either solid or liquid wastes. Such methods are not true solutions to air pollution problems.

* * *

A general classification of air pollutants is as follows:

1. Particulate matter.
2. Sulfur-containing compounds.
3. Organic compounds.
4. Nitrogen-containing compounds.
5. Carbon monoxide.
6. Halogen compounds.
7. Radioactive compounds.

Particulate matter is frequently divided into subclasses which include fine dust (less than 100 μm [micro meters] in diameter), coarse dust (above 100 μm in diameter), fumes (0.001-1 μm in diameter), and mists (0.1-10 μm in diameter). Fumes are particles formed by condensation, sublimation, or chemical reaction, and sometimes are designated as smoke. Mists are comprised of liquid particles formed by condensation and are fairly large in diameter compared to fumes or smoke. As a larger class, fumes, smoke, mist, and fog are called aerosols.

* * *

II
Particulate Matter

Particulate is a term employed to describe dispersed airborne solid and liquid particles larger than single molecules (molecules are approximately 0.0002 μm in diameter but smaller than 500 μm = 1 micron = 10-4 cm). Particles in this size range have a lifetime in suspension varying from a few seconds to several months. Particles less than 0.1 μm undergo random Brownian motions resulting from collision with individual molecules. Particles between 0.1 and 1 μm have large settling velocities and are removed from the air by gravity and other inertial processes.

A portion of the particles introduced into the atmosphere by man's activity serve as condensation nuclei that influence the formation of clouds, rain, and snow. Some cities display a definite minimum rainfall on Sundays, when particulate concentrations are the lowest. It has been observed that the precipitation at La Porte, Indiana, 30 miles east of Chicago, is significantly larger than for South Bend and Valparaiso, Indiana. These latter two cities are considerably farther east of the region of heavy particulate emissions along the southern shore of Lake Michigan.

* * *

A. Visibility and Related Atmospheric Characteristics

One of the most common effects of air pollution is the reduction in visibility resulting from the absorption and scattering of light by airborne liquid and solid materials. Visibility is principally affected by particles that are formed in the atmosphere from gas-phase reactions. Although not visible, carbon dioxide, water vapor, and ozone in increased concentrations change the absorption and transmission characteristics of the atmosphere. Much effort has been expended in recent years to relate the concentration of airborne pollutants to the optical characteristics of various plumes in the atmosphere. Reduction in visibility not only is unpleasing to an individual, but also may have strong psychological effects. In addition, certain safety hazards arise.

* * *

B. Atmospheric Absorption

In addition to a reduction in visibility caused by particulate air pollutants, certain gaseous substances, because of their radiation absorption characteristics, have the potential for causing a deterioration in our environment and in the future may come to be classified as pollutants. During the normal diurnal cycle solar radiation passes through the transparent atmosphere and is absorbed by the earth's surface areas. The heated surface areas lose energy by radiating in the infrared. When the atmosphere contains low concentrations of carbon dioxide and water vapor, the quantity of incoming solar energy is approximately equal to the outgoing terrestrial radiation, and the equilibrium temperature of the earth's surface and lower atmosphere is thereby established. With an increase in concentration of either water vapor or carbon dioxide, the atmospheric absorption of the infrared is increased whereas the transmission of short-wave radiation is unchanged. The net result, it has been argued, would be an increase in the average temperature of the earth's surface and lower atmosphere since the quantity of solar radiation during the day would be unchanged while the terrestrial radiation would be reduced. Several authors have predicted that if the current rate of increase in concentration of carbon dioxide in the atmosphere continues, by the year 2000 the surface temperature will have increased approximately 4°F. Further speculation indicates that sufficient ice would melt as a result of the increase in temperature to cause an increase of 60 feet in the level of the oceans. On the basis of the preceding argument, it has been proposed that both water vapor and carbon dioxide should be considered air pollutants.

For the sake of argument it should also be pointed out that increased concentrations of carbon dioxide have been found to stimulate the growth of selected plants. Since plants absorb CO_2 from the atmosphere in their life cycle, the increased growth could cause a corresponding increase in CO_2 absorption, and a new static balance of the CO_2 content in the environment would be established. The new concentration of CO_2 might not be greatly different from the current level.

Another factor affecting the average temperature of the earth is the absorption and reflection of solar radiation caused by particulate matter in the atmosphere. The results of certain studies seem to indicate that the average temperature of the lower atmosphere is dropping and that the reduction in solar energy reaching the surface because of the absorption by particulate matter is the cause. Thus it can be argued that rather than causing an increase in atmospheric temperature, increased air pollution will cause a reduction in temperature and a return of the ice age.

C. Effects of Atmospheric Particulate Matter on Materials, Vegetation, and Animals

Airborne particles can be chemically inert or chemically active of themselves; they may be inert but absorb chemically active substances from the atmosphere, or they may combine to form chemically active species. Depending upon its chemical composition and physical state, particulate matter causes wide damage to materials. Particles will soil painted surfaces, clothing, and curtains merely by settling on them.

The cost of repainting interior and exterior surfaces of homes and buildings and of cleaning or replacing textiles is estimated at hundreds of millions of dollars annually.

* * *

More importantly, particulate matter can cause direct chemical damage either by intrinsic corrosiveness or by the action of corrosive chemicals absorbed, or adsorbed, by inert particles emitted into the atmosphere. Metals ordinarily can resist corrosion in dry air alone or even in clean moist air. However, hydroscopic particles commonly found in the atmosphere can corrode metal surfaces with no other pollutants present. Examples of the corrosion of metallic surfaces exposed to industrial atmospheres are well documented.

Little is known of the effects of particulate matter in general on vegetation. However, several specific substances have been observed to cause some damage. Particles containing fluorides appear to cause some plant damage, and magnesium oxide falling on agricultural soils has resulted in poor plant growth. An animal's health may suffer when the animal feeds on plants covered by toxic particulate. Such toxic compounds may be absorbed into the plant tissues or may remain as a surface contaminant of the plants. Fluorosis in animals has been attributed to their ingestion of vegetation covered with a fluoride-containing particulate matter. Cattle and sheep that have ingested vegetation on which arsenic-containing particles have settled have been victims of arsenic poisoning.

D. Effects of Atmospheric Particulate Matter on Human Health

Particulate matter alone or in combination with other pollutants constitutes a very serious health hazard. The pollutants enter the human body mainly via the respiratory system. Damage to the respiratory organs may follow directly, since it has been estimated that over 50 percent of the particles between 0.01 and 0.1 μm which penetrate into the pulmonary compartment will be deposited there.

Particulate matter may exert a toxic effect in one or more of the following three ways:

1. The particle may be intrinsically toxic because of its inherent chemical and/or physical characteristics.
2. The particle may interfere with one or more of the mechanisms which normally clear the respiratory tract.
3. The particle may act as a carrier of an absorbed toxic substance.

It is extremely difficult to obtain a direct relationship between exposure to various concentrations of particulate matter and the resulting effects upon human health. The length of time of exposure is important. In some cases it has been observed that exposure to particulate in combination with other pollutants such as SO_2 produces more severe health deterioration than does exposure to each pollutant separately. It is also difficult to reproduce in the laboratory the exact conditions that prevail in the ambient atmosphere.

To date, we have had to rely upon the statistical analysis of such data as increases in hospital admissions, clinic admissions, absences from work and school, and mortality, and the limited data pertaining to the measured concentrations of atmospheric pollutants that prevailed during the subject time periods. Such data do indicate a relationship between increases in particulate concentrations and rises in the number of clinic and hospital visits for upper respiratory infections, cardiac diseases, bronchitis, asthma, pneumonia, emphysema, and the like. Deaths of elderly persons afflicted with respiratory diseases and cardiac conditions also show an increase during periods when the concentration of particulate matter is unusually high for several days. A growing volume of evidence indicates that much of the particulate matter in the atmosphere is carcinogenic in nature, especially when combined with cigarette smoking.

* * *

III
CARBON MONOXIDE

Carbon monoxide is a colorless and odorless gas. It is very stable and has a lifetime of 2 to 4 months in the atmosphere. The global emissions of carbon monoxide are large (350 million tons/yr in 1968), of which roughly 20 percent is from man-made sources. Such a quantity would result in an increase of around 1.13 ppm/yr in the ambient concentration. This increase is not observed. Soil fungi may remove a significant amount of the quantity released, and it is generally assumed that CO is oxidized to CO_2 in the atmosphere, although the rate is quite slow. There is some evidence that CO may be chemically active in smog formation.

* * *

A. Effects of Carbon Monoxide on Materials and Plants

Carbon monoxide appears to have no detrimental effects on material surfaces. The results of numerous experiments have not shown CO to produce any harmful effects on the higher plant life at concentrations below 100 ppm during exposures for 1 to 3 weeks. Ambient concentrations of CO rarely reach this level even for short periods of time.

B. Effects of Carbon Monoxide on Health

There are many studies that show that high concentrations of carbon monoxide can cause physiological and pathological changes and ultimately death. Carbon monoxide is a poisonous inhalant that deprives the body tissues of necessary oxygen.

Carbon monoxide has long been known to cause death when exposure to a high concentration (>750 ppm) is encountered. The combination of carbon monoxide with hemoglobin leads to carboxyhemoglobin, COHb; the combination of oxygen and hemoglobin leads to oxyhemoglobin, O_2Hb.

* * *

Evidence has been presented that CO concentrations in the Los Angeles basin are associated with excess mortality. The ambient 24-hr averages for CO are in the range of 10 to 15 ppm for this area. (The vast majority of this CO is due to emissions from gasoline engines.) Many other urban areas have ambient daily averages in the 5- to 20-ppm range. A value of 100 ppm generally is considered an upper limit of safety in industry for healthy persons within certain age ranges for an 8-hr exposure. At 100 ppm, most people experience dizziness, headache, and lassitude. In terms of CO exposure, it should also be noted that cigarette smoke contains 400 to 450 ppm CO. The percent of COHb in the blood of cigarette smokers increases as the number of cigarettes smoked per day increases. Blood samples from 29,000 blood donors in U.S. cities, suburbs, and rural areas revealed high concentrations of COHb. Forty-five percent of nonsmokers had blood containing 1.5 percent COHb. The blood of most smokers averaged above 5 percent COHb. One-pack-a-day smokers averaged 6.3 percent, and two-pack-a-day smokers averaged 7.7 percent. Relating either ambient air CO concentration or percent of COHb in the blood to health effects is much more difficult than relating ambient CO concentration to the percent COHb.

There is disagreement as to whether CO is a threshold pollutant. Some experts believe that even small concentrations of CO produce some undesirable effects. Most American scientists believe that carbon monoxide is not a cumulative poison. Chronic poisoning does not occur as a result of long-term exposure to relatively low concentrations. Persons particularly susceptible (those already afflicted with a disease that involves the oxygen capacity of the blood, such as anemia or cardiorespiratory disease) may be affected by CO levels existing on city streets. Exposure to low concentrations of CO (10 to 50 ppm) can impair a person's ability to estimate time intervals and affect his visual acuity with regard to brightness threshold. There is some evidence that such effects on a person driving a car increase his chances of having an accident as his abilities deteriorate.

* * *

IV
SULPHUR OXIDES

Sulfur dioxide and sulfur trioxide are the dominant oxides of sulfur present in the atmosphere. Sulfur dioxide is an inflammable, nonexplosive, colorless gas that causes a taste sensation at concentrations from 0.3 to 1.0 ppm in air. At concentrations above 3.0 ppm the gas has a pungent, irritating odor. Sulfur dioxide is partly converted to sulfur trioxide or to sulfuric acid and its salts by photochemical or catalytic processes in the atmosphere. Sulfur trioxide and moisture form sulfuric acid. The oxides of sulfur in combination with particulate and moisture produce the most damaging effects attributed to atmospheric air pollution. Unfortunately it has proven difficult to isolate the effects of sulfur dioxide alone. Brief discussions of the effects of sulfurous compounds will be presented in the following sections.

* * *

A. Effects of Sulfur Compounds on Visibility and Materials

As pointed out in Section II. A, suspended particulate in the atmosphere reduces the visual range by scattering and absorbing light. Since aerosols of sulfuric acid and other sulfates make up from 5 to 20 percent of the total suspended particulate matter in urban air, they contribute significantly to the reduction in the visibility. Investigations indicate that much atmospheric haze is caused by the formation of various aerosols resulting from the photochemical reactions between SO_2, particulate matter, oxides of nitrogen, and hydrocarbons in the atmosphere. In laboratory measurements, mixtures of NO_X and most common hydrocarbons form little or no aerosols when irradiated. However, considerable aerosol formation takes place when mixtures of olefins, NO_2, and

SO_2 are irradiated by sunlight. One of the major products of such complex photochemical reactions is light-scattering droplets of sulfuric acid mist.

* * *

Sulfur compounds are responsible for the major damage to materials. Unfortunately the relative contribution of each of the individual pollutants is difficult to evaluate precisely. Observations indicate that concentrations of 1 to 2 ppm of SO_2 in the atmosphere cause an increase of 50 to 100 percent in the drying time of a paint film, and higher concentrations — 7 to 10 ppm — increase the drying time to 2 to 3 days. The final surface is also less durable when the paint dries in the presence of SO_2. Sulfur oxides seem to have little or no effect on dry, hard paints. Paints containing metal salts react with H_2S. Newer type paints are much more resistant to H_2S.

Sulfur oxides generally accelerate metal corrosion by first forming sulfuric acid either in the atmosphere or on the metal surface. Depending upon the kind of metal exposed as well as the duration of exposure, corrosion rates in urban atmospheres have been observed to be from 1½ to 5 times the rural environments. A threefold reduction in sulfur dioxide in Pittsburgh from 0.15 to 0.05 ppm for the time period 1926 to 1960 caused almost a fourfold reduction in the corrosion rate of zinc. The most detrimental pollutant that contributes to metal corrosion generally is sulfur dioxide. Temperature, and especially relative humidity, also influence corrosion rate significantly. Aluminum is fairly resistant to SO_2 attack.

However, at relative humidities greater than 70 percent the corrosion rate is greatly increased. ASTM [American Society for Testing Materials] has reported some long-range studies of atmospheric effects on the tensile strength of aluminum. Exposure in rural areas led to a loss of 1 percent or less in tensile strength over 20 years, while industrial atmospheres led to a 14 to 17 percent loss in the same time period. The literature offers an extensive review of metal corrosion due to different atmospheric conditions through the early 1960s. Sulfurous or sulfuric acids are capable of attacking a wide variety of building materials, including limestone, marble, roofing slate, and mortar. Fairly soluble sulfates are formed which are then leached away by rain. Textiles of nylon, especially nylon hose, are also susceptible to pollutants in the atmosphere. Weakening is apparently caused by SO_2 or by sulfuric acid aerosol.

* * *

B. Effects on Human Health

Various animal species, including man, respond to sulfur dioxide by bronchoconstriction, which may be assessed in terms of a slight increase in airway resistance. Most individuals will show a response to SO_2 at concentrations of 5 ppm and above, and certain sensitive individuals show slight effects at 1 to 2 ppm. Sulfuric acid is a much more potent irritant to man than is sulfur dioxide; therefore, most studies deal with combined sulfurous materials rather than with SO_2 alone. Analysis of numerous epidemiological studies clearly indicate an association between air pollution, as measured by the concentration of SO_2 accompanied by particulate matter and moisture, and health effects of varying severity. This is especially true for short-term exposure. The association between long-term exposure and chronic disease morbidity and mortality is not so clear.

* * *

C. Acid Rain

Water droplets formed by condensation in the atmosphere normally should have a pH close to 7. However, the dissolution of atmospheric CO_2 in rainwater tends to lower the pH due to the formation of carbonic aid. This acid is very weak, and at equilibrium with CO the pH of rainwater would lie close to 5.65 in value. By the early 1970s however, individual pH values from 2 to 6 were measured in various parts of the world, with yearly averages between 4 and 5. Thus acid concentrations from 10 to 10,000 times greater than expected from natural sources were detected. Measurements in Gander, Newfoundland, since 1975 indicate pH values of 4.0 to 4.5 on a yearly basis in that region. Similar values are valid for the average pH of rainfall in the eastern half of the United States. These low values are due to the transformation of SO_2 and NO_x into acids when they are absorbed in cloud water and rain drops. A typical reaction might be

$$2SO_2 + O_2 \rightarrow 2SO_3$$
$$SO_3 + H_2O \rightarrow 2H^+ + SO_4^+$$

These acid aerosols are then deposited in significant quantities on the surface of land and water masses. Such a phenomenon is called acid rain.

* * *

The increasing presence of these acids is attributed to the increase in emissions of SO_2 and NO_x that has occurred since the 1940s through the increased use of fossil fuels in industrialized nations. Data from the eastern United States indicate that roughly 60-70 percent of the acidity is due to sulfuric acid, and 30-40 percent is due to nitric acid. A high proportion of nitric derivatives indicates mobile sources are responsible, while a high proportion of sulfuric acid derivatives suggest stationary sources. The concentrations of sulfates and nitrates formed in the atmosphere are frequently low, but the deposition effect is cumulative. the relationship between SO_2 emissions and acidification is well established; the contribution due to NO_x is somewhat less known.

Such pollutants travel in the lowest 2km of the atmosphere, and are often carried hundreds of kilometers from their source. Their presence has been observed in a qualitative sense by the remarkable increase in summer haze in a number of regions in industrialized nations. Acid rain has affected areas in Switzerland, the southern part of the Scandinavian countries, and especially in the northeastern half of North America. In the latter case, measurements indicate a severe problem in the Atlantic provinces of Canada and in the Adirondack Mountain region of the United Sates, for example. Recent data, however, indicates that the problem is increasing in the midwest and southeast parts of the United States. Even major urban areas on the West Coast are affected. The phenomenon has been under active study in Europe since the early 1950s. The problem exists in northern Europe since a major portion of the air pollution produced on the continent is transported in a northeasterly direction toward Scandinavia. Likewise, pollution produced in the central provinces of Canada and in the central and eastern states of the United States is carried in the summer and fall in a northeasterly direction.

Data taken at St. Margaret's Bay in eastern Canada indicates that upwards of 25 percent of the suspended particulate was in the form of sulfates. Higher percentages have been measured elsewhere. Although the particulate concentration has been reduced in many industrialized nations due to effective control techniques on sources of particulate, the fraction of the remaining particulate which is in the form of an acid aerosol continues to increase. Conditions in the atmosphere which favor aerosol sulfate formation include poor atmospheric dispersion and ample sunlight. Such conditions also are favorable to ozone formation. The natural acid concentration in rainwater would be less than 10 μg/1 (expressed as H^+). In the Netherlands the average pH fell below 4.0 around 1966 on yearly basis. A value around 3.7 is possible by 1985. In Sweden the pH of rainwater is changing by about 0.3 to 0.4 units per decade.

There are several effects of acid rain that are disturbing. First, there is an acidification of natural water sources. This can have a devastating effect on fish life. Trout and salmon are particularly sensitive to a low pH. Reproduction in many fish fails to occur for a pH less than around 5.5 in value. A decrease in plankton and bottom fauna is also observed as the pH is lowered, which reduces the food supply for fish. Secondly, a leaching of nutrients occurs in the soil. This demineralization can lead to loss in productivity of crops and forests, or a change in the natural vegetation. Vegetation itself can be directly damaged, and an increase in corrosion of materials is observed. The severity of damage to soils and bodies of water is partially determined by the minerals in the soil in a given region. Those areas that contain rock such as calcium carbonate or similar minerals are buffered against the onslaught of acid rain. In such regions lakes tend to maintain a pH closer to 5 or 6.

Since there is no way to alter the results of acid rain once it has occurred in a region, the only solution is the control of emissions at the source. Desulfurization of fossil fuels has been considered important in the past in order to prevent local air pollution. It is now becoming more apparent that SO_2 (and NO_x) control is needed to prevent the long-range dispersion of pollutants as well. Thus emission control takes on an international scope, since emissions from one country are affecting the nature of rain in another country. Continued monitoring and evaluation of the situation will be needed if the full extent of the problem is to be realized.

* * *

V
Effects of Hydrocarbons, Oxides of Nitrogen, Photochemical Oxidants, Asbestos, and Metals On Materials and Health

A. Hydrocarbons

Hydrocarbons do not appear to cause any appreciable corrosive damage to materials. Particulate, or soot made up of unburned hydrocarbons and carbon, soils surfaces. Of all the hydrocarbons, only ethylene has adverse effects on plants at known ambient concentrations. The principal effect of ethylene is to inhibit plant growth.

To date, studies of the effects of ambient air concentrations of gaseous hydrocarbons have not demonstrated direct adverse effects upon human health. Studies of the carcinogenicity of certain classes of hydrocarbons do indicate that some cancers appear to be caused by exposure to aromatic hydrocarbons found in soots and tars. Identifiable airborne carcinogens are mostly polynuclear aromatic hydrocarbons. Unburned hydrocarbons in combination with the oxides of nitrogen in the presence of sunlight form photochemical oxidants, components of photochemical smog, that do have adverse effects on human health and on plants.

B. Oxides of Nitrogen

Of the six or seven oxides of nitrogen, nitric oxide (NO) and nitrogen dioxide (NO_2) are important air pollutants. Although N_2O is commonly present in the lower atmosphere (formed by biological action at the earth's surface) it is not considered an air pollutant. Neither NO nor NO_2 causes direct damage to materials; however, NO_2 can react with moisture present in the atmosphere to form nitric acid, which can cause considerable corrosion of metal surfaces. Nitrogen dioxide absorbs visible light and at a concentration of 0.25 ppm will cause appreciable reduction in visibility. Nitrogen dioxide at a concentration of 0.5 ppm for a period of 10 to 12 days has suppressed growth of such plants as pinto beans and tomatoes. Experiments with navel oranges show that yield is reduced by prolonged exposure to NO_2 at concentrations from 0.25 to 1 ppm.

Nitrogen dioxide acts as an acute irritant and in equal concentrations is more injurious than NO. However, at concentrations found in the atmosphere NO_2 is only potentially irritating and potentially related to chronic pulmonary fibrosis. Some increase in bronchitis in children (2 to 3 years old) has been observed at concentrations below 0.01 ppm. In combination with unburned hydrocarbons, the oxides of nitrogen react in the presence of sunlight to form photochemical smog. It is because of this chemical activity that the primary air quality standard for the oxides of nitrogen has been set as 100 $\mu g/m^3$ annual average. The components of photochemical smog which are the most damaging to plants and detrimental to human health are the photochemical oxidants, which we discuss in the following section.

C. Photochemical Oxidants

Oxidizing agents, ozone (O_3), peroxyacetyl nitrate (PAN), peroxybenzoyl nitrate (PBN), and other trace substances which can oxidize the iodide ion of potassium iodide are termed photochemical oxidants. Ozone and PAN are present in the highest concentrations, and the damaging effects of photo chemical smog are generally related to the concentrations of these species. The aerosols formed during the chemical reactions that create smog cause a marked reduction in visibility and give the atmosphere a brownish cast. Ozone attacks synthetic rubbers, thereby reducing the life of tires, rubber insulation, and so on. Ozone inhibitors can be built into rubber products. Ozone also attacks the cellulose in textiles, reducing the strength of such items. All of the oxidants cause some fading of fabrics. Oxidants, primarily PAN and PBN, cause severe eye irritation, and in combination with ozone they irritate the nose and throat, cause chest constriction, and at high concentration (3900 $\mu g/m^3$) produce severe coughing and inability to concentrate.

D. Asbestos and Metals

Many studies have shown a higher than expected incidence of bronchial cancer among people whose occupations expose them to asbestos. In addition, asbestos has been identified as a causal factor in the development of cancers of the membranes lining the chest and abdomen. Beryllium has also proved dangerous to health, producing both acute and chronic lethal inhalation effects as well as causing damage to the skin and eyes. Most of the cases studied concern occupational exposure. Exposure to metallic mercury vapors may cause injury to the central nervous system and kidneys. And mercury can accumulate in the body system, eventually causing brain damage.

Because of these proven hazards, emission standards were established in 1973 for asbestos, beryllium, and mercury. The standard for asbestos stipulates how asbestos material is to be applied as well as the precautions to be taken in its manufacture and the demolition of buildings. The beryllium standard applies to industrial processes involving beryllium, beryllium ore, and alloys containing more than 25 percent beryllium by weight, and stipulates emission rates from such processes. The mercury standard applies to stationary sources which process mercury ore, recover mercury, and use mercury chor-alkali cells to produce chlorine gas and alkali metal hydroxide.

* * *

VI
SOURCES OF AIR POLLUTANTS

Once selected substances have been carefully studied and declared to be air pollutants on the basis of the evidence available, it is of immediate interest to ascertain the major sources of these substances. The nonviable solid particulates in the atmosphere are generated from the combustion of fuels such as coal and fuel oil in stationary furnaces and from gasoline, diesel fuel, and jet-engine fuel in mobile sources. Manufacturing processes such as grinding, smelting, crushing, and grain milling and drying also contribute to air pollution. The major source of the sulfur oxides is from the combustion of fuels containing sulfur. However, some sulfur compounds are released to the atmosphere from ore processing and manufacturing processes involving sulfuric acid. Carbon monoxide is generated primarily by incomplete combustion of carbonaceous fuels in automobile engines and space-heating units. Unburned hydrocarbons result from incomplete combustion of fuels and from petroleum refining. A relatively small portion of the hydrocarbons results from other operations such as dry cleaning, the evaporation of industrial coating, and the cleaning of manufactured parts. Oxides of nitrogen are formed in a combustion process when the nitrogen in the air or in the fuel combines with oxygen at elevated temperatures. A very small quantity of the oxides is released from plants employing or manufacturing nitric acid.

* * *

The damaging effects of air pollutants are not equivalent on an equal mass basis. That is, a given concentration of SO_2 for example, maybe more detrimental to health than an equivalent concentration of carbon monoxide. Some authors have proposed that the quantity of a pollutant should be multiplied by a "tolerance factor" to obtain a combined pollution index as a true measure of its total contribution to air pollution.

* * *

NOTES

1. Gaseous pollutants present in the ambient air are commonly measured in parts per million (ppm). The mass of a pollutant is usually expressed as micrograms of pollutant per cubic meter of air (μ/m^3). A microgram (μ) is equal to 1/1,000,000 of a gram.

2. The authors state that "[i]n the past, . . .individual polluters have found it more economical to discharge waste products into the atmosphere than exercise waste control." Compare the problem posed by air pollution with that of grazing cattle in a commons, as described by Garrett Hardin in his classic essay, *The Tragedy of the Commons*, 162 SCIENCE 1243 (1968).

3. Frequently, the harm occasioned by air pollution is substantial and quantifiable; yet the persons responsible for the pollution are, by and large, able to escape certain identity and thus, liability. Why? What relevance does this problem have for designing an effective control system?

4. Representatives of a local church in an industrial community come to your office asking your assistance in obtaining compensation for the damage to the copper roof of their church. An investigation has confirmed that the damage was caused by air pollution. The church representatives suspect that the polluter primarily responsible for the damage is a nearby steel mill which emits copious quantities of particulates and SO_2. How would you advise your prospective clients? How would you assess your chances for a successful tort action against the steel mill?

5. In Japan, persons suffering a disease which has been determined by an executive agency to be pollution-related may receive compensation without having to prove causation. *See* Gresser, *The 1973 Japanese Law for the Compensation of Pollution-Related Health Damage: An Introductory Assessment*, 8 LAW IN JAPAN 91 (1975). What relevance does a statute like the Japanese Compensation Law have for those charged with designing a regulatory system for limiting air pollution?

6. Traditionally, air pollution regulation has focused on the direct impact that the pollutant has on the public health and welfare. In recent years, scientists have come to recognize that certain types of air emissions which pose no direct threat to persons or the environment may nonetheless trigger significant adverse consequences. The two principal examples are carbon dioxide and chlorofluorocarbons. Carbon dioxide, of course, occurs in the atmosphere naturally. But excessive amounts of CO_2, which result largely from burning fossil fuels, appears to be the prime cause of the global warming phenomenon. *See* Chapter 11, *infra*. Chlorofluorocarbons also contribute to global warming and, as well, appear to be depleting the stratospheric ozone layer. How should a regulatory scheme for addressing nonconventional pollutants such as these differ from that employed for more traditional pollutants which cause direct impact?

2 MARKET APPROACHES TO THE AIR POLLUTION PROBLEM

As we turn to a study of the various schemes for controlling air pollution, the student should bear in mind the role that economics can, and sometimes does, play in the regulatory process. The following article by Thomas C. Schelling focuses on emission charges — a mechanism that has not seen much practical application in the air pollution field. What are the advantages and drawbacks of such a mechanism? What alternative market-based programs might be employed?

PRICES AS REGULATORY INSTRUMENTS

T. SCHELLING, INCENTIVES FOR ENVIRONMENTAL PROTECTION (MIT Press, 1983)

For an economist, markets and prices play a central role. Environmental effects are effects that escape the market. They are outside the price system and "external" to the accounts of participants. The economist diagnoses environmental problems, therefore, as a failure of the pricing system or the market . . .

Two things can be said confidently about extending the price system as a way of bringing environmental problems under control. One is that there is indubitably a role for prices. Numerous successes can be pointed out. A good part of the development of economic institutions has been bringing what used to be externalities into the market system by the conferring and protection of property rights and the enforcement of contracts, by the availability of better information, and by technological development that facilitates marketing. The second is that some environmental problems are bound to remain beyond the reach of even the most ingenious efforts to create or extend markets. Indeed, there is a presumption that it is going to be difficult to bring additional effects into the market system; if it were easy, it would have already been done.

* * *

There is great variety in the pricing methods that can be and have been used in regulating activities that effect the environment. In recent years, attention has focused on what are usually called *effluent charges* or *emission charges.*

* * *

Assume for illustration a charge that is not conceived as a source of revenue or as a penalty for violating some regulation. The charge is intended as a cost to the firm or individual (to simplify the image and the terminology, think of a plant belonging to a business firm) that attaches to one of the "outputs". Firms usually pay for their inputs: material fuel, electricity, labor, repair services, and the like. Sometimes they pay taxes on their output. They pay property taxes on fixed installations and they pay fees to operate. An effluent or emission charge is simply another cost that attaches to their production — this one a cost on the amount of some output the firm produces. It is an output, however, to which ordinarily no value attaches, or not enough to make the substance worth recapturing. The output or outflow is usually an avoidable byproduct.

For simplicity, imagine a large number of plants (not necessarily identical in what they produce and how they produce it) that all emit a noxious substance. The emissions of each plant are susceptible to measurement, but once in the air the emissions of all plants become mixed. Damage is not attributable to individual firms, but the emissions of every plant affect the total. How would a charge system work?

This is an easy case. We have an identified culprit (the noxious emission). We can monitor each plant. Only the total of the emissions matters, since the emissions are alike and co-mingled. All the plants are within a single jurisdiction, the same one in which the victim population resides. Our primary objective is to reduce total emissions, preferably in a manner that treats individual sources "fairly." More accurately, we want to limit the harm the emissions do; but we do that by reducing the emissions.

There are two alternatives to consider in what we know about the "damage function," about the way the severity of the damages relates to the total quantity of the noxious gas. One is that we know how much damage a unit of that noxious substance does, and we can put a money value on that damage. If we can value the damage caused by a pound of the substance without stipulating what the total is to which that pound is added, the damage function must be linear - proportionate to the total quantity. In that case we will probably want to relate the charge to the damage, perhaps charging each plant for its contribution to the damage. The other possibility is that we begin with an idea of how much of the substance we are willing to allow and then set a charge that keeps total emissions within that limit. A possibility is that damages remain moderate up to a certain concentration and thereafter mount rapidly ("nonlinearly")—perhaps after a certain concentration is reached the atmosphere can no longer be refreshed by wind and rain. Or possibly, without any knowledge of how to assess damage, a target (an aggregate allowed quantity) has simply been set, and we want whatever price will get emissions down within that predetermined limit. The price that goes with that quantity can then be estimated. Permits can be issued at that price, and if the price turns out to be too high or too low to generate that demand for permits, the price can be adjusted up or down.

Alternatively, an auction can dispose of the target number of permits. The auction is merely a way of finding the price that corresponds to that quantity of emissions. Once the price has been found, if conditions do not change abruptly the auction can be dispensed with. Prices can be adjusted up or down when the demand for emission permits exceeds or falls short of the target quantity.

In principle there should be no difference between setting a price and letting demand determine the quantity of emissions and setting a quantity and letting demand determine the price to be paid. If we knew the demand curve — the schedule of prices corresponding to different quantities, or that of quantities corresponding to different prices (which is the same thing) — we would simply pick a price-quantity combination. The difference between the two methods of price setting is significant only when the price-quantity relation is uncertain. At the outset, if one is surer of the correct quantity than of the associated price, the auction-type technique is helpful; if one is surer of the appropriate price than of the quantity that would be allowed, the price can be stipulated and the quantity allowed to emerge. When damages are nonlinear in the total of emissions and rise rapidly beyond some concentration, setting the right quantity (short of the rapid rise in damage) will be the main interest. When damages are proportionate to total emissions, a predetermined limit will usually be of less interest than finding the right level of charges . . . There are several arguments for putting a price on harmful emissions, and, although they are compatible and reinforce each other, they are quite separate.

* * *

The Market Test

As noted above, a price offers an automatic adjustment process — a decentralized decision process — not only inducing the abatement in those particular firms, uses, or production processes where abatement can most economically be carried the furthest, but also providing a measure and a "market test." All abatement that is cheaper than the price will tend to be undertaken. Abatement that is so expensive that paying the price is preferable will be avoided, but only at a cost (paying the price) no less than what any other firm is expending on actual abatement. If the price has been determined at a level that represents the economic worth of abatement (that is, if it measures the economic damages that will be produced or the costs externally inflicted by the emission in question), each firm will undertake whatever abatement saves more damage than it costs, and no abatement will be undertaken that costs more than the damage is worth.

* * *

Paying The Costs

The second and third arguments for putting a price on emissions relate not to the abatement accomplished, but to the continued charges that are paid for the abatement not accomplished. One of the arguments is simply that firms ought to be required to pay the full costs of what they produce, including the costs they impose on the public. The offending emissions are the "externalities" that in the absence of regulation were not being paid for. If what goes up a firm's smokestack deteriorates the paint on my house, reduces the productivity of my farm, requires me to install air conditioning, or increases my veterinary bill, I am contributing at my own expense to the value of the goods the firm is producing. If the firm rented my house it would pay me, but if it deteriorates my house it does not. If I provide part of my crop as raw material the firm will pay me, but if it reduces my crop by emitting something harmful the cost to me is the same but the firm does not pay. And it ought to pay. Not necessarily to me, but still it ought to pay. That is the argument.

This argument fits almost hand in glove with the market-test argument. One argument is that by paying the price on its continued emissions the firm is complying with the rule that you ought to pay for what you get, where "what you get" includes the benefits of inflicting expenses on the public. The second argument is that paying the price "keeps the firm honest"; the price paid is the guarantee that the firm has not evaded any economically reasonable opportunities to abate the substance. Thus the price (pursuant to one argument) induces abatement at the firm's expense up to where further abatement would cost more than the averted damage is worth, and (pursuant to the other argument) the firm meets its responsibilities by paying for the damage caused by its continuing emissions.

* * *

Disposition of Proceeds

Meanwhile, back at the agency, the money is coming in. Whose money is it? What should be done with it? Is it a pure byproduct of a regulatory scheme, embarrassing to an agency that has no budgetary authority to spend it and perhaps appearing to be a revenue bonus available to meet public needs?

Here is where a third argument for pricing enters. It is not the argument that pricing produces revenue; the goods produced by the emitting firms could just as well have been subjected to an excise tax if we had wanted the purchasers of those commodities to provide revenue to the government. And if we think of the money as punitive damages, we can be pleased to have transferred money from offenders to the government, like the fines collected from traffic violations; but that is not the attitude that goes with pricing in the first place. The argument instead is that these funds, generated from a regulatory mechanism that induces an "economical" level of emissions to continue, are equivalent to the costs or damages estimated to be inflicted by those emissions. They ought to be used to complete the transaction by which the emitting firms pay for what they use and what they do. Paying into a public treasury on account of emissions and paying *for* the emissions by paying to repair, indemnify, or forestall the damage are not the same. And getting the benefits to the victim is every bit as important as getting the money from the firm that produces the damage. That is the argument.

It will be the rare environmental externality that permits us, at no exorbitant administrative expense, to identify all the victims and assess their damages individually. We probably have a crude aggregate estimate of damage, and at the level of an individual victim there may be no reliable way of determining how much of any apparent costs is actually due to the regulated emissions. Still, in principle the distributional objections mentioned above could be mitigated if funds were dedicated to completing that transaction.

* * *

To recapitulate: There are at least four distinct attractions, separable but compatible, to a charge system. One is to get the abatement allocated among firms so that if some have lower abatement costs than others the cost of any given abatement can be minimized. (This statement can be turned around to read ". . . so that for any given aggregate cost the greatest aggregate abatement can be achieved.") Second, if the price is an approximation of the estimated damage per unit of emission, it offers a market test, revealing the marginal cost of further abatement and inducing the undertaking of abatement where it is no longer less expensive than the costs inflicted by emissions. Third, whoever does the emitting, or whoever purchases the goods and services produced by the emitter, "beneficiary," or "offender," pays the full "social costs" of the goods and services so produced. And fourth, revenue is available that could in principle be used for repair, reparations, and protection, in an amount sufficient to cover the costs inflicted by the emissions if the price has been approximated to those costs (with the "costs" or "damages" augmented by the costs of administering the program).

* * *

NOTES

1. A system of effluent charges will not relieve the government of the burden of enforcement. On the contrary, an effluent charge system places a premium on effective enforcement. Those paying for the right to emit a certain level of pollution must have confidence that other polluters are paying their fair share.

2. An effluent charge system also requires the government to establish an appropriate level at which such charges are set. The following discussion illustrates the difficulty in translating economic theory into practical reality.

> The difficulty of determining the level at which emission taxes or charges should be set, however, has precluded their widespread use. In order to achieve optimal pollution control, the charge should reflect the cost of the damage done by each unit of contaminant emitted. Quantifying pollution damage even in the gross has proved problematic for economists, however. The problem is exacerbated by the fact that the damage done by any given unit of contamination varies widely according to a host of factors. A stated quantity of sulfur dioxide, for example, may not do detectable harm at all if emitted in an area where there are no other emissions; yet when it is added to existing discharges of the same pollutant in a heavily contaminated area, it could mean the difference between life and death. Moreover, the identical quantity discharged may have a more acute effect on air quality, and thus do more damage, if emitted at ground level rather than through a high stack, or during calm rather than windy weather, or in a confined river valley rather than on a plain. The same quantity of hydrocarbon emissions may cause a more serious oxidant problem in Denver than in Minneapolis because of the higher altitude and greater prevalence of sunlight. Identical sulfur dioxide emissions may be more harmful in the presence of high particulate concentrations. Further, even the same levels of ambient air quality may do more harm in New York City, where there are many people and much valuable property, than an uninhabited desert. Pollution will do more harm to the elderly and ill than to healthy young adults, and least of all to those who take precautions against it.
>
> Given these uncertainties, any tax that is set would probably be highly arbitrary, and the likelihood that it would result in anything resembling an optimal degree of control is slim. Most legislative bodies have therefore understandably placed primary reliance on subjective but candid efforts to determine optimal levels of pollution by direct governmental prescription.

CURRIE, AIR POLLUTION, FEDERAL LAW AND ANALYSIS, § 1.03 (Callaghan & Co. 1981).

3. One of the most difficult areas of pollution control is that involving sources that are too numerous to regulate effectively. Automobiles and wood stoves are major contributors of air pollution in some parts of the country, yet they seem to defy effective regulation. The Clean Air Act addresses the automobile problem, primarily at the manufacturing stage. It requires manufacturers to limit air emissions for the "useful life" of the vehicle. Several years ago, EPA announced plans to develop new source performance standards for controlling particulate emissions from residential wood heaters, primarily wood stoves. 50 Fed. Reg. 31,504 (1985). Existing stoves would not be subject to regulation under the proposed rules. 52 Fed. Reg. 4994 (1987). EPA has yet to follow through on its proposal. Are there any market mechanisms that might be employed to further reduce pollution from these sources? Can the "transaction costs," that is, the costs of negotiating the effective use of such mechanisms, be kept at a level that is low enough to make the market systems worthwhile?

4. Suppose the government of Shangri La recognizes the right of polluters to discharge emissions freely into the air. The injury to the citizens of Shangri La from uncontrolled emissions far outweighs the benefits from the industry. One economic solution to the problem is for the citizens to join together and pay the polluters a sufficient amount to obtain a reduction in pollution to the point where the total benefits exceed the total costs. Assuming that transaction costs are the same, will the quantity of pollution or economic positions of the parties be any different if, rather than recognizing the rights of polluters to pollute, the government recognized the right of its citizens to demand clean air? For an argument that the result is the same, *see* Coase, *The Problem of Social Cost*, 3 J. LAW & ECON. 1 (1960). Note, however, that the transaction costs under either scenario may be prohibitive. R. POSNER, ECONOMIC ANALYSIS OF THE LAW, 44-46 (Little, Brown & Co. 2d ed. 1977). Posner describes the transaction costs in our hypothetical problem along with the related problem of the "free rider" as follows:

> If there are significant elements of bilateral monopoly in a two-party transaction — i.e., if neither party has good alternatives to dealing with the other — the transaction costs may be quite high . . .
>
> The costs of transacting are highest where elements of bilateral monopoly coincide with a large number of parties to the transaction — a quite possible conjunction. For example, if homeowners have a right to be free from pollution, the factory that wishes to acquire the right to pollute must acquire it from every homeowner. If only one out of a thousand refuses to come to terms, the rights that the factory has purchased from the other 999 are worth nothing. (Why?) Because the holdout can extract an exorbitant price . . . each homeowner has an incentive to delay coming to terms with the factory; the process of negotiation may therefore be endlessly protracted.
>
> If instead of the homeowners having the right to be free from pollution, the factory has the right to pollute, the homeowners must get together and purchase the factory's right if they wish to be free from pollution. Transaction costs will again be high. Each homeowner will again have an incentive to drag his feet in coming to terms with the factory. He will think: "If I refuse to contribute my fair share of the purchase price, others, who care more deeply about pollution than I do, will make up the difference. The factory will be induced to stop polluting. I will benefit along with the others but at zero cost." The costs of overcoming this foot-dragging by negotiations among the affected homeowners will be high if there are many of them, so again a transaction may be infeasible.

Id. at 45-46. What mechanisms are available to avoid high transaction costs and thus promote the most efficient result?

5. Another market tool for regulating air pollution, which is best described as freely marketable pollution rights, has begun to receive broad acceptance at the federal level. In its purest form, the scheme operates as follows: First, the agency determines the maximum amount of emissions that will be permitted in a given area. Then, an auction or other method for distributing those rights is established. Thereafter, the owners of such rights are free to sell their pollution rights to others for whatever the market will bear. A set-aside program can be established if necessary to assure that small businesses or other special groups are not left out of the distribution. Unlike the effluent charge system, the system of transferable pollution rights will not generate income for the government for the mitigation of damages caused by pollution. The 1990 Amendments introduce what may be the most ambitious experiment with marketable pollution rights ever adopted. The Acid Deposition Program contained in Title IV of the Amendments establishes a ceiling on SO_2 emissions nationwide, and provides for the distribution of "allowances" for each ton of SO_2 emitted to electric utilities, the chief source of SO_2 emissions in the United States. These allowances are freely marketable. The Acid Deposition Program is described in greater detail in Chapter 9, *infra*.

6. Well before the 1990 Amendments, EPA developed an emissions trading policy which, among other things, established a mechanism for trading pollution rights in areas where existing pollution levels were too high to otherwise allow the construction of new sources in an area. EPA's current emissions trading policy is reproduced, in part, in Chapter 9. A thorough review of the development of emissions trading in the United States is set forth in Dudek & Palmisano, *Emissions Trading: Why is This Thoroughbred Hobbled?*, 13 COLUM. J. OF ENV. L. 217 (1988).

7. The Clean Air Act employs economics in its enforcement program as well as its regulatory program. Under § 120 of the Act penalties for violations of the law are imposed based on the economic value of noncompliance. Is such penalty necessary to assure compliance with the law? Is it sufficient? What problems would you anticipate in administering such a program? *See* Chapter 10, *infra*.

8. Despite the increasing acceptance of market approaches to air pollution problems, "command and control" strategies continue to dominate the law. Consider the following criticism of the command and control approach to regulation, and its comparison to a marketable permit approach.

REFORMING ENVIRONMENTAL LAW: THE DEMOCRATIC CASE FOR MARKET INCENTIVES

ACKERMAN & STEWART, 13 COLUM. J. OF ENV. L. 171 (1988).

* * *

II. THE EXISTING SYSTEM

The existing system of pollution regulation is primarily based on a best available control technology (BAT) strategy. If an industrial process generates some non-trivial risk, the responsible plant or industry must install whatever technology is available to reduce or eliminate the risk, so long as the costs of doing so will not shut down the relevant plant or industry. BAT requirements are largely determined through centralized uniform federal regulation. Under the Clean Water Act's BAT strategy, EPA adopts nationally uniform effluent limitations for some 500 different industries. A similar BAT strategy is used in the Clean Air Act for new industrial sources of toxic air pollutants.

BAT strategies are also widely used in many fields of environmental regulation other than air and water pollution.

BAT was embraced by Congress and administrators in the early 1970s in order to impose immediate, readily-enforceable, federal controls on a relatively few, widespread pollutants, while avoiding widespread industrial shutdowns. Subsequent experience and analysis has demonstrated:

1. Uniform BAT requirements waste many billions of dollars annually by ignoring variations among plants and industries in the costs of reducing pollution and by ignoring geographic variations in pollution effects. A more cost-effective strategy of risk reduction could free up enormous resources for additional pollution reduction or other purposes.

2. BAT controls, and the litigation which they provoke, impose disproportionate penalties on new products and processes. A BAT strategy typically imposes far more stringent controls on new sources because there is no risk of shutdown. Also, new plants and products must run the gauntlet of lengthy regulatory and legal proceedings to win approval; the resulting uncertainty and delay discourage new investment. By contrast, existing products and processes can use the legal process to postpone or water down compliance requirements. Also, BAT strategies impose disproportionate burdens on more productive and profitable industries because they can "afford" more stringent controls. This "soak the rich" approach penalizes growth and international competitiveness.

3. BAT controls can ensure the diffusion of established control technologies. But they do not provide strong incentives for the development of new, environmentally superior strategies and may actually discourage their development. Such innovations are essential if we are to maintain economic growth in the long run without simultaneously increasing pollution and other forms of environmental degradation.

4. BAT involves centralized, uniform determination of complex scientific, engineering and economic issues involving the feasibility of controls on hundreds of thousands of pollution sources. Such determinations impose massive information gathering burdens on administrators and provide a fertile ground for litigation, producing reams of technical data, complex adversary rulemaking proceedings and protracted judicial review. Given the high cost of regulatory requirements, it is often more cost effective for industry to invest in litigation rather than compliance.

5. A BAT strategy is inconsistent with intelligent priority setting. Simply regulating to the hilt whatever pollutants or problems happen to get on the regulatory agenda may preclude an agency from dealing adequately with other more serious problems that come to scientific attention later. The BAT strategy also tends to reinforce regulatory inertia. Foreseeing that "all or nothing' regulation of a given substance under BAT will involve very large administrative and compliance costs, and recognizing that resources are limited, agencies will seek to limit the number of substances on the agenda for regulatory action.

This indictment is not a piece of idle speculation but the product of years of patient study by lawyers, economists and political scientists. There are, for example, no less than fifteen careful efforts to estimate this extra cost burden generated by a wide variety of traditional bureaucratic systems used to control a variety of air and water pollutants in different parts of the country. Of the twelve studies of different air pollutants — ranging from particulates to chlorofluorocarbons — seven indicated that traditional forms of regulation were more than four times more expensive than the least-cost solution; four indicated that they were about seventy-five percent more expensive;

and only one suggested a modest cost-overrun of seven percent. Three studies of water pollution control in five different watersheds also indicate the serious inefficiency of traditional forms of command and control regulation. These careful studies of selected problems cannot be sued to estimate precisely the total amount traditional forms of regulation are costing the American people. Nonetheless, very large sums are at stake. Even if a reformed system could cut costs by "only" one-third, it could save more than $15 billion a year from the nation's annual expenditure of $50 billion on air and water pollution control.

* * *

III. Reform is Realistic

A BAT system has an implicit environmental goal: achievement of the environmental quality level that would result if all sources installed BAT controls on their discharges. The usual means for implementing this goal are centralized, uniform regulations that command specific amounts of cleanup from specific polluters. When a polluter receives an air or water permit under existing law, the piece of paper does not content itself, in the manner of Polonius, with the vague advice that he "use the best available technology." Instead, the permit tries to be as quantitatively precise as possible, telling each discharger how much of each of the regulated pollutants he may discharge.

Reformers propose to build upon, and do not abandon, this basic permit system. Indeed, they have only two, albeit far-reaching, objections to the existing permit mechanism. First, existing permits are free. This is bad because it gives the polluter no incentive to reduce his wastes below the permitted amount. Second, permits are not transferable. This is bad because polluter A is obliged to cut back his own wastes even if it is cheaper for him to pay his neighbor B to undertake the extra cleanup instead.

The basic reform would respond to these deficiencies by allowing polluters to buy and sell each other's permits — thereby creating a powerful financial incentive for those who can clean up most cheaply to sell their permits to those whose treatment costs are highest. This reform will, at one stroke, cure many of the basic defects with existing command-and-control regulation. A system of tradeable rights will tend to bring about a least-cost allocation of control burdens, saving billions of dollars annually. It will eliminate the disproportionate burdens that BAT imposes on new industries and more productive industries by treating all sources of the same pollutant on the same basis. It will provide positive economic rewards for the development by those regulated of environmentally superior products and processes. It will, as we show below, reduce the incentives for litigation and simplify the issues in controversy.

But would allowing the sale of permits lead to a bureaucratic nightmare? Before proceeding to the new administrative burdens marketability will generate, it is wise to pause to consider marketability's great administrative advantages.

First, it would immediately eliminate most of the information processing tasks that are presently overwhelming the federal and state bureaucracies. No longer would the EPA be required endlessly to hold hearings to determine the best available control technologies in each major industry of the United States, and defend its determinations before the courts; nor would federal and state officials be required to spend vast amounts of time and energy to adapt these changing national guidelines to suit the particular conditions of every important pollution source in the United States. Instead of giving the job of economic and technological assessment to bureaucrats, the marketable rights mechanism would put this information-processing burden precisely where it belongs: upon business managers and engineers who are in the best position to figure out how to cut back on their plant's pollution costs. If the managers operating plant A think they can clean up a pollutant more cheaply than those in charge of plant B, they should be expected to sell some of their pollution rights to B at a mutually advantageous price; cleanup will tend to occur at least cost without the need for constant bureaucratic decisions about the best available technology. While the reformed system may impose new regulatory tasks, it removes the greatest roadblock to administrative efficiency: it allows inevitably ill-informed bureaucrats to avoid technological and economic decisions best made by the people operating the plants.

Second, marketable permits would open up enormous financial resources for effective and informed regulation. While polluters would have the right to trade their permits among themselves during the *n* years they are valid, they would be obliged to buy new ones when their permits expired at an auction held by the EPA in each watershed and air quality control region. These auctions would raise substantial sums of money for the government on a continuing basis. While no study has yet attempted to make global estimates for the United States as a whole, existing work suggests that auction revenues could well equal the amount polluters would spend in cost-minimizing control activities. Even if revenues turned out to be a third of this amount, the government would still be collecting more than $6-$10 billion a year. Moreover, it seems reasonable to suppose that Congress would allow the EPA (and associated state agencies) to retain a share of these revenues. Since the current EPA operating budget is $1.3 billion, using even a fraction of the auction fund to improve regulatory analysis, research and monitoring would allow a great leap forward in the sophistication of the regulatory effort. Given its revenue-raising potential, environmental reform is hardly a politically unrealistic pipe dream. To the contrary, it is only a matter of time before the enormous federal deficit forces Congress and the President to consider the fiscal advantages of an auction scheme.

Third, the auction system would help correct one of the worst weaknesses of the present system: the egregious failure of the EPA and associated state agencies to enforce the laws on the books in a timely and effective way. Part of the problem stems from the ability of existing polluters to delay regulatory implementation by using legal proceedings to challenge the economic and engineering bases of BAT regulations and permit conditions. But agencies also invest so little on monitoring that they must rely on polluters for the bulk of their data on discharges. Since polluters are predictably reluctant to report their own violations, EPA systematically generates a Panglossian view of regulatory reality. For example, a General Accounting Office investigation of 921 major air polluters officially deemed in compliance revealed 200, or twenty-two percent were out of compliance. Even when illegal polluters are identified, they are not effectively sanctioned. For example, the EPA's Inspector General in 1984 found that it was a common practice for water pollution officials to respond to violations by issuing administrative orders which effectively legitimize excess discharges. Thus, while the system may, after protracted litigation, eventually "work" to force the slow installation of expensive control machinery, there is no reason to think this machinery is being run well when it is eventually installed. Although there are many reasons for this appalling weakness in enforcement, one stands out above all others: the present system does not put the pressure on agency policymakers to make the large investments in monitoring and personnel that are required to make the tedious and unending work of credible enforcement a bureaucratic reality.

The auction system would change existing compliance incentives dramatically. It would reduce the opportunity and incentive of polluters to use the legal system for delay and obstruction by finessing the complex BAT issues, and it would limit dispute to the question whether a source's discharges exceeded its permits. It would also eliminate the possibility of using the legal system to postpone implementation of regulatory requirements by requiring the polluter that lost its legal challenge to pay for the permits it would have been obliged to buy during the entire intervening period of noncompliance (plus interest).

The marketable permit system would also provide much stronger incentives for effective monitoring and enforcement. If polluters did not expect rigorous enforcement for the term of their permits, this fact would show up at the auction in dramatically lower bids: Why pay a lot for the right to pollute legally when one can pollute illegally without serious risk of detection? Under a marketable permit approach, this problem would be at the center of bureaucratic attention. For if, as we envisage, the size of the budget available to the EPA and state agencies would depend on total auction revenues, the bureaucracy's failure to invest adequately in enforcement would soon show up in a potentially dramatic drop in auction income available in the next budgetary period. This is not a prospect that EPA administrators will take lightly. Monitoring and enforcement will become agency priorities of the first importance. Moreover, permit holders may themselves support strong enforcement in order to ensure that cheating by others does not depreciate the value of the permit holders' investments.

A system of marketable permits, then, not only promises to save Americans billions of dollars a year, to reward innovative improvements in existing cleanup techniques and to eliminate the BAT system's penalty on new, productive investment. It also offers formidable administrative advantages. It relieves agencies of the enormous information-processing burdens that overwhelm them under the BAT system; it greatly reduces litigation and delay; it offers a rich source of budgetary revenue in a period of general budgetary stringency; and it forces agencies to give new importance to the critical business of enforcing the law in a way that America's polluters will take seriously. But, of course, there is no such thing as a free lunch in bureaucracy-land. Against these formidable advantages, the new system will generate new tasks. Are these new functions more or less onerous than the command-and-control operations that have been reformed away?

Begin by isolating four distinct bureaucratic functions required by the new system. First, the agency must estimate how much pollution is presently permitted by law in each watershed and each air quality region. Second, it must run a system of fair and efficient auctions in which polluters can regularly buy rights for limited terms. Third, it must run an efficient title registry in each region that will allow buyers and sellers to transfer rights in a legally effective way. Fourth, it must consistently penalize polluters who discharge more than their permitted amounts.

And that's that. So far as the fourth bureaucratic task is concerned, we have already given reasons to believe that the EPA would enforce the law far more effectively under the new regime than it does at present. So far as the first three management functions are concerned, we think that they are, in the aggregate, far *less* demanding than those they displace under the BAT system.

* * *

NOTES

1. The Acid Deposition Program contained in Title IV of the 1990 Amendments and described previously, essentially tracks the recommendations made by Ackerman and Stewart and thus will offer a useful experiment for gauging the success of their approach.

2. Underlying the approach advocated by Ackerman and Stewart is the assumption that pollution rights are fungible — i.e., that a ton of SO_2 from one point source is equivalent to a ton of SO_2 at any other source within a defined region. Ackerman and Stewart suggest, for example, that the agency could limit trades to pollution rights within the same watershed or air quality region. Is this necessary in all cases? Consider, for example, carbon dioxide (CO_2), a gas emitted as a result of fossil fuel combustion. CO_2 is currently unregulated but it is thought to be the most important global warming gas. Assuming a market system for global warming gases, over what portion of the world could such gases be traded?

3. Conversely, is it sufficient in all cases to allow trading within a watershed or defined region? Suppose, for example, that all of the pollution rights for total suspended particulates within a watershed were discharged at one point along a stream, rather than 40 different points.

4. Assuming that the problems inherent in a marketable pollution rights program can be solved, does such a program go far enough? Should economic principles be used, in the first instance, to help determine the number of rights to put on the market? Some economists argue that this decision should itself be subject to market forces — that persons who pollute should bargain with persons who bear the costs of pollution to efficiently determine how much pollution should be allowed. *See e.g.*, T. ANDERSON & D. LEAL, FREE MARKET ENVIRONMENTALISM, 17-23 (Westview Press 1991). What is the alternative to this approach? What problems exist with each approach? *See* Symposium, *Free Market Environmentalism*, 15 Harv. J.L. & Pub. Policy (Spring 1992).

5. A basic assumption of the "free market environmentalists" is that the market is capable of allocating goods based on a "willingness to pay" theory. Is the assumption correct? Consider Mark Sagoff's criticism of this approach. Sagoff argues that the market approach ignores the fact that individuals play different roles in society. M. SAGOFF, THE ECONOMY OF THE EARTH (Cambridge Univ. Press 1988). Of particular relevance to the issue of "environmental" choices are the individual's role as a citizen on the one hand, and a consumer on the other:

> As a *citizen*, I am concerned with the public interest, rather than my own interest; with the good of the community, rather than simply the well-being of my family . . . .
>
> In my role as a *consumer* . . . I concern myself with personal or self-regarding wants and interests; I pursue the goals I have as an individual. I put aside the community-regarding values I take seriously as a citizen, and I look out for Number One instead.

Id. at 8. (Emphasis in original). Recognition of this distinction leads Sagoff to observe that citizen values and the social regulation that follows from those values help to define a nation:

> The positive thesis of this book is that social regulation expresses what we believe, what we are, what we stand for as a nation, not simply what we wish to buy as individuals. Social regulation reflects public values we

> choose collectively, and these may conflict with wants and interests we pursue individually . . . .
>
> Social regulation most fundamentally has to do with the identity of a nation — a nation committed historically, for example, to appreciate and preserve a fabulous natural heritage and to pass it on reasonably undisturbed to future generations. This is not a question of what we *want*; it is not exactly a question of what we *believe in*; it is a question of what we *are*.

Id. at 16-17. (Emphasis in original.) This observation leads to Sagoff's conclusion that market theory is not an appropriate vehicle for making social choices:

> Cost-benefit analysis does not, because it cannot, judge opinions and beliefs on these merits but asks instead how much might be paid for them, as if a conflict of views could be settled in the same way as a conflict of interests. Analysts who take this approach, of course, tend to confuse views with interests. They do this by giving political, ethical and cultural convictions technical names — "bequest values," "existence values," "intangibles," "fragile values," or "soft variables" — as if by the nomenclature they could transform beliefs that have carried the day before legislatures into the data of economic methodology . . . .
>
> . . . [W]hen cost-benefit analysis attempts to do the work of ethical and political judgment, it loses whatever objectivity it might have had and becomes a tool of partisan politics. . . . [W]hen cost-benefit analysis assigns "shadow" prices to "amenity," "option," "bequest," and other citizen beliefs and values, theoretical "breakthroughs" replace sound judgment and common sense. At that point, economic analysis deteriorates into storytelling and hand-waving likely to convince no one except those partisans who agree with — and possibly have paid for — its results.

Id. at 38-39. Who is correct — Sagoff or Anderson and Leal?

3 Air Pollution and the Common Law

The case that follows should be familiar to many law students. Consider its particular relevance to the problem of air pollution.

Boomer v. Atlantic Cement Company
26 N.Y. 2d 219, 309 N.Y.S.2d 312, 257 N.E.2d 870 (1970)

BERGAN, Judge.

Defendant operates a large cement plant near Albany. These are actions for injunction and damages by neighboring land owners alleging injury to property from dirt, smoke and vibration emanating from the plant. A nuisance has been found after trial, temporary damages have been allowed; but an injunction has been denied.

The public concern with air pollution arising from many sources in industry and in transportation is currently accorded ever wider recognition accompanied by a growing sense of responsibility in State and Federal Governments to control it. Cement plants are obvious sources of air pollution in the neighborhoods where they operate.

But there is now before the court private litigation in which individual property owners have sought specific relief from a single plant operation. The threshold question raised by the division of view on this appeal is whether the court should resolve the litigation between the parties now before it as equitably as seems possible; or whether, seeking promotion of the general public welfare, it should channel private litigation into broad public objectives.

* * *

Effective control of air pollution is a problem presently far from solution even with the full public and financial powers of government. In large measure adequate technical procedures are yet to be developed and some that appear possible may be economically impracticable.

It seems apparent that the amelioration of air pollution will depend on technical research in great depth; on a carefully balanced consideration of the economic impact of close regulation; and of the actual effect on public health. It is likely to require massive public expenditure and to demand more than any local community can accomplish and to depend on regional and interstate controls.

A court should not try to do this on its own as a by-product of private litigation and it seems manifest that the judicial establishment is neither equipped in the limited nature of any judgment it can pronounce nor prepared to lay down and implement an effective policy for the elimination of air pollution. This is an area beyond the circumference of one private lawsuit. It is a direct responsibility for government and should not thus be undertaken as an incident to solving a dispute between property owners and a single cement plant — one of many — in the Hudson River valley.

The cement making operations of defendant have been found by the court of Special Term to have damaged the nearby properties of plaintiffs in these two actions. That court, as it has been noted, accordingly found defendant maintained a nuisance and this has been affirmed at the Appellate Division. The total damage to plaintiffs' properties is, however, relatively small in comparison with the value of defendant's operation and with the consequences of the injunction which plaintiffs seek.

The ground for the denial of injunction, notwithstanding the finding both that there is a nuisance and that plaintiffs have been damaged substantially, is the large disparity in economic consequences of the nuisance and of the injunction. This theory cannot, however, be sustained without overruling a doctrine which has been consistently reaffirmed in several leading cases in this court and which has never been disavowed here, namely that where a nuisance has been found and where there has been any substantial damage shown by the party complaining an injunction will be granted.

The rule in New York has been that such a nuisance will be enjoined although marked disparity be shown in economic consequence between the effect of the injunction and the effect of the nuisance.

The problem of disparity in economic consequence was sharply in focus in *Whalen v. Union Bag & Paper Co.*, 101 N.E. 805. A pulp mill entailing an investment of more than a million dollars polluted a stream in which plaintiff, who owned a farm, was "a lower riparian owner". The economic loss to plaintiff from this pollution was small. This court, reversing the Appellate Division, reinstated the injunction granted by the Special Term against the argument of the mill owner that in view of the slight advantage to plaintiff and the great loss that will be inflicted on defendant an injunction should not be granted. "Such a balancing of injuries cannot be justified by the circumstances of this case," Judge Werner noted. He continued: "Although the damage to the plaintiff may be slight as compared with the defendant's expense of abating the condition, that is not a good reason for refusing an injunction".

* * *

Although the court at Special Term and the Appellate Division held that injunction should be denied, it was found that plaintiffs had been damaged in various specific amounts up to the time of the trial and damages to the respective plaintiffs were awarded for those amounts. The effect of this was, injunction having been denied, plaintiffs could maintain successive actions at law for damages thereafter as further damage was incurred.

The court at Special Term also found the amount of permanent damage attributable to each plaintiff, for the guidance of the parties in the event both sides stipulated to the payment and acceptance of such permanent damage as a settlement of all the controversies among the parties. The total of permanent damages to all plaintiffs thus found was $185,000. This basis of adjustment has not resulted in any stipulation by the parties.

This result at Special Term and at the Appellate Division is a departure from a rule that has become settled; but to follow the rule literally in these cases would be to close down the plant at once. This court is fully agreed to avoid that immediately drastic remedy; the difference in view is how best to avoid it.[1]

---

[1] Respondent's investment in the plant is in excess of $45,000,000. There are over 300 people employed there.

One alternative is to grant the injunction but postpone its effect to a specified future date to give opportunity for technical advances to permit defendant to eliminate the nuisance; another is to grant the injunction conditioned on the payment of permanent damages to plaintiffs which would compensate them for the total economic loss to their property present and future caused by defendant's operations. For reasons which will be developed the court chooses the latter alternative.

If the injunction were to be granted unless within a short period — e.g., 18 months — the nuisance be abated by improved methods, there would be no assurance that any significant technical improvement would occur.

The parties could settle this private litigation at any time if defendant paid enough money and the imminent threat of closing the plant would build up the pressure on defendant. If there were no improved techniques found, there would inevitably be applications to the court at Special Term for extensions of time to perform on showing of good faith efforts to find such techniques.

Moreover, techniques to eliminate dust and other annoying by-products of cement making are unlikely to be developed by any research the defendant can undertake within any short period, but will depend on the total resources of the cement industry nationwide and throughout the world. The problem is universal wherever cement is made.

For obvious reasons the rate of the research is beyond control of defendant. If at the end of 18 months the whole industry has not found a technical solution a court would be hard put to close down this one cement plant if due regard be given to equitable principles.

On the other hand, to grant the injunction unless defendant pays plaintiffs such permanent damages as may be fixed by the court seems to do justice between the contending parties. All of the attributions of economic loss to the properties on which plaintiffs' complaints are based will have been redressed.

The nuisance complained of by these plaintiffs may have other public or private consequences, but these particular parties are the only ones who have sought remedies and the judgment proposed will fully redress them. The limitation of relief granted is a limitation only within the four corners of these actions and does not foreclose public health or other public agencies from seeking proper relief in a proper court.

It seems reasonable to think that the risk of being required to pay permanent damages to injured property owners by cement plant owners would itself be a reasonable effective spur to research for improved techniques to minimize nuisance.

The power of the court to condition on equitable grounds the continuance of an injunction on the payment of permanent damages seems undoubted. (*See, e.g.*, the alternatives considered in *McCarty v. Natural Carbonic Gas Co.*, *supra*, as well as *Strobel v. Kerr Salt Co.*, *supra*.)

The damage base here suggested is consistent with the general rule in those nuisance cases where damages are allowed. "Where a nuisance is of such a permanent and unabatable character that a single recovery can be had, including the whole damage past and future resulting therefrom, there can be but one recovery" (66 C.J.S. Nuisances § 140, p. 947). It has been said that permanent damages are allowed where the loss recoverable would obviously be small as compared with the cost of removal of the nuisance (*Kentucky-Ohio Gas Co. v. Bowling*, 264 Ky. 470, 477, 95 S.W.2d 1).

* * *

There is some parallel to the conditioning of an injunction on the payment of permanent damages in the noted "elevated railway cases" (*Pappenheim v. Metropolitan*

El. Ry. Co., 28 N.E. 518 and others which followed). Decisions in these cases were based on the finding that the railways created a nuisance as to adjacent property owners, but in lieu of enjoining their operation, the court allowed permanent damages.

* * *

Thus it seems fair to both sides to grant permanent damages to plaintiffs which will terminate this private litigation. The theory of damage is the "servitude on land" of plaintiffs imposed by defendant's nuisance. (*See United States v. Causby*, 328 U.S. 256, 261, 262, 267, where the term "servitude" addressed to the land was used by Justice Douglas relating to the effect of airplane noise on property near an airport.)

The judgment, by allowance of permanent damages imposing a servitude on land, which is the basis of the actions, would preclude future recovery by plaintiffs or their grantees (*See* Northern Indiana Public Serv. Co. v. W. J. & M. S. Vesey, 200 N.E. 620).

This should be placed beyond debate by a provision of the judgment that the payment by defendant and the acceptance by plaintiffs of permanent damages found by the court shall be in compensation for a servitude on the land.

* * *

The orders should be reversed, without costs, and the cases remitted to Supreme Court, Albany County to grant an injunction which shall be vacated upon payment by defendant of such amounts of permanent damage to the respective plaintiffs as shall for this purpose be determined by the court.

JASEN, Judge (dissenting).

I agree with the majority that a reversal is required here, but I do not subscribe to the newly enunciated doctrine of assessment of permanent damages, in lieu of an injunction, where substantial property rights have been impaired by the creation of a nuisance.

It has long been the rule in this State, as the majority acknowledges, that a nuisance which results in substantial continuing damage to neighbors must be enjoined. (*Whalen v. Union Bag & Paper Co.*, 208 N.Y. 1, 101 N.E. 805; *Campbell v. Seaman*, 63 N.Y. 568; *see, also, Kennedy v. Moog Servocontrols*, 21 N.Y.2d 966, 237 N.E.2d 356.) To now change the rule to permit the cement company to continue polluting the air indefinitely upon the payment of permanent damages is, in my opinion, compounding the magnitude of a very serious problem in our State and Nation today.

In recognition of this problem, the Legislature of this State has enacted the Air Pollution Control Act (Public Health Law, Consol.Laws, c. 45, §§ 1264 to 1299-m) declaring that it is the State policy to require the use of all available and reasonable methods to prevent and control air pollution (Public Health Law § 1265).

The harmful nature and widespread occurrence of air pollution have been extensively documented. Congressional hearings have revealed that air pollution causes substantial property damage, as well as being a contributing factor to a rising incidence of lung cancer, emphysema, bronchitis and asthma.

The specific problem faced here is known as particulate contamination because of the fine dust particles emanating from defendant's cement plant. The particular type of nuisance is not new, having appeared in many cases for at least the past 60 years. (*See Hulbert v. California Portland Cement Co.*, 161 Cal. 239, 118 P. 928 (1911).) It is interesting to note that cement production has recently been identified as a significant source of particulate contamination in the Hudson Valley. This type of pollution, wherein very small particles escape and stay in the atmosphere, has been denominated as the type of air pollution which produces the greatest hazard to human health. We have thus a nuisance which not only is damaging to the plaintiffs, but also is decidedly harmful to the general public.

I see grave dangers in overruling our long-established rule of granting an injunction where a nuisance results in substantial continuing damage. In permitting the injunction to become inoperative upon the payment of permanent damages, the majority is, in effect, licensing a continuing wrong. It is the same as saying to the cement company, you may continue to do harm to your neighbors so long as you pay a fee for it. Furthermore, once such permanent damages are assessed and paid, the incentive to alleviate the wrong would be eliminated, thereby continuing air pollution of an area without abatement.

It is true that some courts have sanctioned the remedy here proposed by the majority in a number of cases, but none of the authorities relied upon by the majority are analogous to the situation before us. In those cases, the courts, in denying an injunction and awarding money damages, grounded their decision on a showing that the use to which the property was intended to be put was primarily for the public benefit. Here, on the other hand, it is clearly established that the cement company is creating a continuing air pollution nuisance primarily for its own private interest with no public benefit.

This kind of inverse condemnation (*Ferguson v. Village of Hamburg*, 272 N.Y. 234, 5 N.E.2d 801) may not be invoked by a private person or corporation for private gain or advantage. Inverse condemnation should only be permitted when the public is primarily served in the taking or impairment of property. (*Matter of New York City Housing Auth. v. Muller*, 270 N.Y. 333, 343, 1 N.E.2d 153, 156; *Pocantico Water Works Co. v. Bird*, 130 N.Y. 249, 258, 29 N.E. 246, 248). The promotion of the interests of the polluting cement company has, in my opinion, no public use or benefit.

Nor is it constitutionally permissible to impose servitude on land, without consent of the owner, by payment of permanent damages where the continuing impairment of the land is for a private use. (*See Fifth Ave. Coach Lines v. City of New York*, 229 N.Y.S.2d 400, 403, 183 N.E.2d 684, 686; *Walker v. City of Hutchinson*, 352 U.S. 112) This is made clear by the State Constitution (art. I, § 7, subd.(a)) which provides that private property shall not be taken for *public use* without just compensation (emphasis added). It is, of course, significant that the section makes no mention of taking for a *private* use.

In sum, then, by constitutional mandate as well as by judicial pronouncement, the permanent impairment of private property for private purposes is not authorized in the absence of clearly demonstrated public benefit and use.

I would enjoin the defendant cement company from continuing the discharge of dust particles upon its neighbors' properties unless, within 18 months, the cement company abated this nuisance.

It is not my intention to cause the removal of the cement plant from the Albany area, but to recognize the urgency of the problem stemming from this stationary source of air pollution, and to allow the company a specified period of time to develop a means to alleviate this nuisance.

I am aware that the trial court found that the most modern dust control devices available have been installed in defendant's plant, but, I submit, this does not mean that *better* and more effective dust control devices could not be developed within the time allowed to abate the pollution.

Moreover, I believe it is incumbent upon the defendant to develop such devices, since the cement company, at the time the plant commenced production (1962), was well aware of the plaintiffs' presence in the area, as well as the probable consequences of its contemplated operation. Yet, it still chose to build and operate the plant at this site.

In a day when there is a growing concern for clean air, highly developed industry should not expect acquiescence by the courts, but should, instead, plan its operations to eliminate contamination of our air and damage to its neighbors.

Accordingly, the orders of the Appellate Division, insofar as they denied the injunction, should be reversed, and the actions remitted to Supreme Court, Albany County to grant an injunction to take effect 18 months hence, unless the nuisance is abated by improved techniques prior to said date.

NOTES

1. The majority decision in *Boomer* imposed a "servitude" on the land. Is Judge Jasen's dissenting opinion correct in arguing that the majority grants to Atlantic Cement Company a private right of condemnation in violation of the State Constitution?

2. Suppose that following the payment of permanent damages, Congress enacts a law that effectively requires Atlantic Cement Company to abate the nuisance by reducing its emissions substantially. Is the Company entitled to recoup part of its damages? Suppose, in the alternative, that the Company increases its emissions substantially. Can the plaintiffs or their successors in interest take further legal action against the Company?

3. The *Boomer* decision has been criticized in testimony before Congress on the Clean Air Act for taking away all incentives for the Company to reduce emissions. *Hearings Before the Subcommittee on Air and Water of the Senate Committee on Public Works*, 91st Cong., 2d Sess., part 2 at 849 (1970). Some courts have addressed this "incentives" problem by requiring the polluter to use the best available technology to control the pollution. *See e.g., DeBlois v. Bowers*, 44 F.2d 621,623 (D. Mass. 1930). Congress has imposed similar technology-based standards on new sources of pollution under the Clean Air Act. *See e.g.*, §§ 111(a)(i); 165(a)(4). What happens, however, where, as in *Boomer*, the polluter claims to have installed the best available technology, but injury still occurs?

4. The dissenting opinion in *Boomer* suggests that the Court should grant an injunction where a nuisance causes a substantial continuing injury, notwithstanding the possible impacts that an injunction might have on the local economy. Note, however, that Judge Jasen would have structured the relief so as to attempt to force the development of better technological controls, thereby making an injunction unnecessary. "Technology forcing" provisions are another important feature of the Clean Air Act. They have been employed most effectively in the establishment of emissions standards for mobile sources. 42 U.S.C. 7521(B). *See* Currie, *The Mobile Source Provisions of the Clean Air Act*, 46 U. CHI. L.REV. 811, 816-818 (1979).

5. In *McCastle v. Rollins Environmental Services*, 456 So.2d 612 (La. 1984) plaintiffs commenced a class action suit seeking injunctive relief and monetary damages on behalf of approximately 4,000 persons who resided near defendant's hazardous waste and land farming facility. The court determined that chemical fumes from the site "greatly increased the risk of diseases such as asthma, cancer and heart disease." What problems will the plaintiffs encounter being certified as a class? *See e.g., Eisen v. Carlysle & Jacquelin*, 417 U.S. 156 (1974) requiring "the best practical notice" to each member of the class. On the merits, are plaintiffs entitled to monetary damages? Injunctive relief?

6. *Spur Industries, Inc. v. Del E. Webb Development Co.*, 108 Ariz. 178, 494 P.2d 700 (1972), is the classical illustration of the "coming to the nuisance" problem. In *Spur Industries*, the court permanently enjoined the owner of a feedlot from operating near a recently built subdivision under the theory that it was a public nuisance. Nonetheless, as a condition of enforcement of the injunction, the court forced the subdeveloper to indemnify the feedlot operator for the cost of moving his operation. The plaintiff was aware of the feedlot's existence and repugnant odor at the time that he commenced building, and, as a result, would have received a windfall if the feedlot operation was abated. At common law, a plaintiff who "came to the nuisance" was unable to obtain any relief. *Id.* at 184, 494 P.2d at 706. Today, however, "coming to the nuisance" is merely one element that a court must examine in a nuisance cause of action. Compare the RESTATEMENT (SECOND) OF TORTS § 840D: "The fact that plaintiff has acquired or improved his land after a nuisance interfering with it has come into existence is not itself sufficient to bar his (nuisance) action, but it is a factor to be considered in determining whether the nuisance is actionable."

7. Trespass is another possible basis for controlling air pollution through a common law action. In *R.L. Renken v. Harvey Aluminum, Inc.*, 226 F. Supp. 169 (D. Or. 1963), the defendant's aluminum plant was emitting fluoride and particulates which settled on the plaintiff's land and fruit trees, causing considerable damage. The court determined that "the continued settling of the fluorides from defendant's property constituted a continuing trespass as a matter of law", and the court ordered the defendant to install technology, used in similar facilities, to limit the emissions. Unlike the polluter in *Boomer*, the polluter in the *Renken* case was unable to demonstrate that he was using the best technology. Moreover, the court found that the nearby Reynolds Aluminum plant was using a much more effective pollution control system. The court order essentially required Harvey Aluminum to employ the same kind of system. Note the court's concern that anything less would put "a premium on air pollution" by giving Harvey a competitive advantage over Reynolds. Suppose the Reynolds technology does not abate the injury to plaintiffs. Should the court require more?

8. Compare the order in *Renken* with the requirement at § 173(2) of the Clean Air Act that major new stationary sources of air pollution in areas that exceed current air quality standards meet the "lowest achievable emission rate." The "lowest achievable emission rate" is defined by law to mean "that rate of emissions which reflects — (A) the most stringent emission limit which is contained in the implementation plan of any State for such . . . source . . ., or (B) *the most stringent emission limitation which is achieved in practice* by such . . . source, whichever is more stringent." (Emphasis added.) § 171(3); 42 U.S.C. § 7501(3).

9. Most of the common law air pollution cases are nuisance actions. In *Renken*, the court found that the settling of pollutants on plaintiff's property constituted a "continuing trespass." Which do you think is the better legal theory?

10. Trespass is a common plea in cases involving invasion of air space. The most famous case is *United States v. Causby*, 328 U.S. 256 (1946). In that case the federal government operated a military airport near the plaintiff's chicken farm. The noise from the planes and the glare from their lights at night so frightened plaintiff's chickens that they killed themselves flying into the walls of the chicken coop. The chicken farm was destroyed. In awarding damages to the plaintiff for the government's wrongful invasion of property, the Court expressly rejected the common law notion that ownership of real property extends from the center of the earth to the sky:

> It is ancient doctrine that at common law ownership of the land extended to the periphery of the universe — *cujus est solum est usque ad coelum*. But that doctrine has no place in the modern world. The air is a public highway....Were that not true, every transcontinental flight would subject the operator to countless trespass suits. Common sense revolts at the idea.

Id. at 260-261. The court found, nonetheless, that this principle did not govern the *Causby* case:

> We have said that the airspace is a public highway. Yet it is obvious that if the landowner is to have full enjoyment of the land he must have exclusive control of the immediate reaches of the enveloping atmosphere. Otherwise, buildings could not be erected, trees could not be planted, and even fences could not be run. The principle is recognized when the law gives a remedy in a case where overhanging structures are erected on adjoining land. The landowner owns at least as much of the space above the ground as he can occupy or use in connection with the land.... The fact that he does not occupy it in a physical sense — by the erection of buildings and the like — is not material. As we have said, the flight of airplanes which skim the surface but do not touch it, is as much an appropriation of the use of land as a more conventional entry upon it. We would not doubt that, if the United States erected an elevated railway over respondent's land at the precise altitude where its planes now fly, there would be a partial taking, even though none of the supports of the structure rested on the land. The reason is that there would be an intrusion so immediate and direct as to subtract from the owner's full enjoyment of the property and to limit his exploitation of it. While the owner does not in any physical manner occupy that stratum of airspace or make use of it in a conventional sense, he does use it in somewhat the same sense that space left between buildings for the purpose of light and air is used. The superadjacent airspace at this low altitude is so close to the land that continuous invasions of it affect the use of the surface of the land itself. We think the land owner, as an incident to his ownership, has a claim to it and that invasions of it are in the same category as invasions of the surface.

Id. at 264.

11. Airplane noise control is now governed by statute under the joint responsibility of the Federal Aviation Administration and the Environmental Protection Agency. *See* Federal Aviation Act of 1958, 49 U.S.C. § 1431; The Noise Control Act of 1972, 42 U.S.C. §§ 4901 *et seq.* The Clean Air Act also provides for the establishment of an Office of Noise Abatement and Control within the EPA to investigate and study noise and its effect on the public health and welfare. 42 U.S.C. §§ 7641 *et seq.* The Supreme Court has held that these statutes preempt state and local controls over airplane noise. *City of Burbank v. Lockheed Air Terminal Inc.*, 411 U.S. 624 (1973).

12. Strict liability for carrying on abnormally dangerous activities is another common law legal theory upon which a pollution action might be based. In *T&E Industries, Inc. v. Safety Light Corporation*, 123 N.J. 371, 587 A.2d 1249 (1991), the plaintiff purchased property on which radioactive waste had been discarded by a predecessor in title. The plaintiff sued the prior owner under a theory of strict liability. The Supreme Court of New Jersey held that depositing a dangerous product such as radium was an abnormally dangerous activity within the meaning of *Rylands v. Fletcher*, L.R. 3 H.L. 330 (1868). Thus the prior owner of the property was liable for the damages to the plaintiff, including clean-up costs. How might this theory be used in the context of air pollution?

13. A *federal* common law right to abate air pollution crossing state boundaries was established in *Georgia v. Tennessee Copper Co.*, 206 U.S. 230 (1907). In that case, Georgia complained that the discharges from the defendant copper companies were fouling her air and damaging her forests. In enjoining the nuisance, the Court attached great importance to the fact that this was not a dispute between private parties, but was rather an action to abate a public nuisance brought by the State of Georgia acting in a quasi-sovereign capacity:

> This is a suit by a state for an injury to it in its capacity of quasi-sovereign. In that capacity the state has an interest independent of and beyond the titles of its citizens, in all the earth and air within its domain. It has the last word as to whether its mountains shall be stripped of their forests and its inhabitants shall breathe pure air.

Id. at 237.

14. Consider the applicability of the following water pollution case to air pollution problems.

INTERNATIONAL PAPER COMPANY V. OUELLETTE

479 U.S. 481 (1987)

Justice POWELL delivered the opinion of the Court.

This case involves the preemptive scope of the Clean Water Act, 33 U.S.C. § 1251 *et seq.* (CWA or Act). The question presented is whether the Act preempts a common-law nuisance suit filed in a Vermont court under Vermont law, when the source of the alleged injury is located in New York.

I

Lake Champlain forms part of the border between the states of New York and Vermont. Petitioner International Paper Company (IPC) operates a pulp and paper mill on the New York side of the lake. In the course of its business, IPC discharges a variety of effluents into the lake through a diffusion pipe. The pipe runs from the mill through the water toward Vermont, ending a short distance before the state boundary line that divides the lake.

Respondents are a group of property owners who reside or lease land on the Vermont shore. In 1978 the owners filed a class action suit against IPC, claiming, *inter alia*, that the discharge of effluents constituted a "continuing nuisance" under Vermont common law. Respondents alleged that the pollutants made the water "foul, unhealthy, smelly, and . . . unfit for recreational use," thereby diminishing the value of their property. App. 29. The owners asked for $20 million in compensatory damages, $100 million in punitive damages, and injunctive relief that would require IPC to restructure part of its water treatment system. The action was filed in State Superior Court, and then later removed to Federal District Court for the District of Vermont.

IPC moved for summary judgment and judgment on the pleadings, claiming that the Clean Water Act preempted respondents' state law suit. With the parties' consent, the District Judge deferred a ruling on the motion pending the decision by the Court of Appeals for the Seventh Circuit in a similar case involving Illinois and the city of Milwaukee. In that dispute, Illinois filed a nuisance action against the city under Illinois statutory and common law, seeking to abate the alleged pollution of Lake Michigan. *Illinois v. Milwaukee*, 731 F.2d 403 (1984) (*Milwaukee III*), *cert. denied*, 469 U.S. 1196 (1985). The Court of Appeals ultimately remanded the case for dismissal of Illinois' claim, finding that the CWA precluded the application of one State's law against a pollution source located in a different State. The decision was based in part on the Court's conclusion that the application of different state laws to a single "point source"[4] would interfere with the carefully devised regulatory system established by the CWA. 731 F.2d, at 414. The Court also concluded that the only suits that were *not* preempted were those alleging violations of the laws of the polluting, or "source," State. *Id.*, at 413-414.

IPC argued that the holding in *Milwaukee III* was dispositive in this case. The Vermont District Court disagreed and denied the motion to dismiss. 602 F.Supp. 264 (1985). The Court acknowledged that federal law normally governs interstate water pollution. It found, however, that two sections of the CWA explicitly preserve state-law rights of action. First, § 510 of the Act provides:

> "Except as expressly provided ..., nothing in this chapter shall ... be construed as impairing or in any manner affecting any right or jurisdiction of the States with respect to the waters (including boundary waters) of such States." 33 U.S.C. § 1370.

In addition, § 505(e) states:

> "Nothing in this section shall restrict any right which any person (or class of persons) may have under any statute or common law to seek enforcement of any effluent standard or limitation or to seek any other relief. . ." 33 U.S.C. § 1365(e).

The District Court held that these two provisions (together, "the saving clause") made it clear that federal law did not preempt entirely the rights of States to control pollution. Therefore the question presented, said the court, was which *types* of state suits Congress intended to preserve. It considered three possibilities: first, the saving clause could be construed to preserve state law only as it applied to waters not covered by the CWA. But since the Act applies to virtually all surface water in the country,[6] the District Court rejected this possibility. Second, the saving clause might preserve state nuisance law only as it applies to discharges occurring within the source State; under

---

[4] A "point source" is defined by the CWA as "any discernible, confined and discrete conveyance ... from which pollutants are or may be discharged." 33 U.S.C. § 1362(14); see 40 CFR § 122.2 (1986). It is not disputed that IPC is a point source within the meaning of the Act.

[6] While the Act purports to regulate only "navigable waters," this term has been construed expansively to cover waters that are not navigable in the traditional sense. See *United States v. Riverside Bayview Homes*, 474 U.S. 121 (1985); 33 U.S.C. § 1362(7) (defining navigable waters as "waters of the United States"); 118 Cong.Rec. 33756-33757 (1972), 1 Legislative History of Water Pollution Control Act Amendments of 1972 (Committee Print compiled for the Senate Committee on Public Works by the Library of Congress), Ser. No. 93-1, p. 250 (1973) (hereinafter Leg.Hist.).

this view a claim could be filed against IPC under New York common law, but not under Vermont law. This was the position adopted by the Court of Appeals for the Seventh Circuit in *Milwaukee III*. The Vermont Court nevertheless rejected this option, finding that "there is simply nothing in the Act which suggests that Congress intended to impose such limitations on the use of state law." 602 F.Supp., at 269.

The District Court therefore adopted the third interpretation of the saving clause, and held that a state action to redress interstate water pollution could be maintained under the law of the State in which the injury occurred. *Ibid.* The Court was unpersuaded by the concern expressed in *Milwaukee III* that the application of out-of-state law to a point source would conflict with the CWA. It said there was no interference with the procedures established by Congress because a State's "imposition of compensatory damage awards and other equitable relief for injuries caused ... merely *supplement* the standards and limitations imposed by the Act." 602 F.Supp., at 271 (emphasis in original). The Court also found that the use of state law did not conflict with the ultimate goal of the CWA, since in each case the objective was to decrease the level of pollution. *Ibid.*

The District Court certified its decision for interlocutory appeal, *see* 28 U.S.C. § 1292(b) (1982 ed., Supp. III), and the Court of Appeals for the Second Circuit affirmed for the reasons stated by the District Court. 776 F.2d 55, 56 (1985) (*per curiam*). We granted certiorari to resolve the Circuit conflict on this important issue of federal preemption. 475 U.S. 1081 (1986). We now affirm the denial of IPC's motion to dismiss, but reverse the decision below to the extent it permits the application of Vermont law to this litigation. We hold that when a court considers a state-law claim concerning interstate water pollution that is subject to the CWA, the court must apply the law of the State in which the point source is located.

II

A brief review of the regulatory framework is necessary to set the stage for this case. Until fairly recently, federal common law governed the use and misuse of interstate water. *See, e.g., Hinderlider v. La Plata River & Cherry Creek Ditch Co.*, 304 U.S. 92, 110 (1938) (water apportionment); *Missouri v. Illinois*, 200 U.S. 496 (1906) (water pollution). This principle was called into question in the context of water pollution in 1971, when the Court suggested in dicta that an interstate dispute between a state and a private company should be resolved by reference to state nuisance law. *Ohio v. Wyandotte Chemicals Corp.*, 401 U.S. 493, 499, n. 3 (1971) ("[A]n action such as this, if otherwise cognizable in federal district court, would have to be adjudicated under state law") (*citing Erie R. Co. v. Tompkins*, 304 U.S. 64 (1938)).

We had occasion to address this issue in the first of two Supreme Court cases involving the dispute between Illinois and Milwaukee. In *Milwaukee I*, the State moved for leave to file an original action in this Court, seeking to enjoin the city from discharging sewage into Lake Michigan. *Illinois v. Milwaukee*, 406 U.S. 91 (1972). The Court's opinion in that case affirmed the view that the regulation of interstate water pollution is a matter of federal, not state, law, thus overruling the contrary suggestion in *Wyandotte*. 406 U.S., at 102, n. 3. The Court was concerned, however, that the existing version of the Act was not sufficiently comprehensive to resolve all interstate disputes that were likely to arise. *Milwaukee I* therefore held that these cases should be resolved by reference to federal common law; the implicit corollary of this ruling was that state common law was preempted. *See id.*, at 107, n. 9; *Milwaukee III*, 731 F.2d, at 407. The Court noted, though, that future action by Congress to regulate water pollution might preempt federal common law as well. 406 U.S., at 107.

Congress thereafter adopted comprehensive amendments to the Act. We considered the impact of the new legislation when Illinois and Milwaukee returned to the Court several years later. *Milwaukee v. Illinois*, 451 U.S. 304 (1981) (*Milwaukee II*). There the Court noted that the amendments were a " 'complete rewriting' " of the statute considered in *Milwaukee I*, and that they were " 'the most comprehensive and far reaching' " provisions that Congress ever had passed in this area. 451 U.S., at 317-318 (citations to legislative history omitted). Consequently, the Court held that federal legislation now occupied the field, preempting all *federal* common law. The Court left open the question of whether injured parties still had a cause of action under *state* law. *Id.*, at 310, n. 4. The case was remanded for further consideration; the result on remand was the decision of the Court of Appeals for the Seventh Circuit in *Milwaukee III*, discussed *supra*.

One of the primary features of the 1972 amendments is the establishment of the National Pollutant Discharge Elimination System (NPDES), a federal permit program designed to regulate the discharge of polluting effluents. 33 U.S.C. § 1342; *see generally EPA v. California ex rel. State Water Resources Control Board*, 426 U.S. 200, 205-208 (1976) (describing NPDES system). Section 301(a) of the Act, 33 U.S.C. § 1311(a), generally prohibits the discharge of any effluent into a navigable body of water unless the point source has obtained an NPDES permit from the Environmental Protection Agency (EPA). The permits contain detailed effluent limitations, and a compliance schedule for the attainment of these limitations.

The amendments also recognize that the States should have a significant role in protecting their own natural resources. 33 U.S.C. § 1251(b). The Act provides that the Federal Government may delegate to a State the authority to administer the NPDES program with respect to point sources located within the State, if the EPA Administrator determines that the proposed state program complies with the requirements set forth at 33 U.S.C. § 1342(b). The Administrator retains authority, however, to block the issuance of any permit to which he objects. § 1342(d). Even if the Federal Government administers the permit program, the source State may require discharge limitations more stringent than those required by the Federal Government. *See* 40 CFR § 122.1(f) (1986). Before the Federal Government may issue an NPDES permit, the Administrator must obtain certification from the source State that the proposed discharge complies with the State's technology-based standards and water quality-based standards. 33 U.S.C. § 1341(a)(1). The CWA therefore establishes a regulatory "partnership" between the Federal Government and the source State.

While source States have a strong voice in regulating their own pollution, the CWA contemplates a much lesser role for States that share an interstate waterway with the source (the affected States). Even though it may be harmed by the discharges, an affected State only has an advisory role in regulating pollution that originates beyond its borders. Before a federal permit may be issued, each affected State is given notice and the opportunity to object to the proposed standards at a public hearing. 33 U.S.C. § 1341(a)(2); *Milwaukee III*, *supra*, at 412. An affected State has similar rights to be consulted before the source State issues its own permit; the source State must send notification, and must consider the objections and recommendations submitted by other States before taking action. § 1342(b). Significantly, however, an affected State does not have the authority to block the issuance of the permit if it is dissatisfied with the proposed standards. An affected State's only recourse is to apply to the EPA

Administrator, who then has the discretion to disapprove the permit if he concludes that the discharges will have an undue impact on interstate waters. § 1342(d)(2). Also, an affected State may not establish a separate permit system to regulate an out-of-state source. *See* § 1342(b) (State may establish permit system for waters "within its jurisdiction") (emphasis added). Thus the Act makes it clear that affected States occupy a subordinate position to source States in the federal regulatory program.

III

With this regulatory framework in mind, we turn to the question presented: whether the Act preempts Vermont common law to the extent that law may impose liability on a New York point source. We begin the analysis by noting that it is not necessary for a federal statute to provide explicitly that particular state laws are preempted. *Hillsborough County v. Automated Medical Laboratories, Inc.*, 471 U.S. 707, 713 (1985). Although courts should not lightly infer pre-emption, it may be presumed when the federal legislation is "sufficiently comprehensive to make reasonable the inference that Congress 'left no room' for supplementary state regulation." *Ibid.* (*quoting Rice v. Sante Fe Elevator Corp.*, 331 U.S. 218, 230 (1947)). In addition to express or implied pre-emption, a state law also is invalid to the extent that it "actually conflicts with a ... federal statute." *Ray v. Atlantic Richfield Co.*, 435 U.S. 151, 158 (1978). Such a conflict will be found when the state law " 'stands as an obstacle to the accomplishment and execution of the full purposes and objectives of Congress.' " *Hillsborough County v. Automated Medical Laboratories, supra*, 471 U.S., at 713 (*quoting Hines v. Davidowitz*, 312 U.S. 52, 67 (1941)).

A

* * *

Although Congress intended to dominate the field of pollution regulation, the saving clause negates the inference that Congress "left no room" for state causes of action. Respondents read the language of the saving clause broadly to preserve both a State's right to regulate its waters, 33 U.S.C. § 1370, and an injured party's right to seek relief under "any statute or *common law*," § 1365(e) (emphasis added). They claim that this language and selected portions of the legislative history compel the inference that Congress intended to preserve the right to bring suit under the law of any affected-state. We cannot accept this reading of the Act.

To begin with, the plain language of the provisions on which respondents rely by no means compels the result they seek. Section 505(e) merely says that "nothing *in this section*," *i.e.*, the citizen-suit provisions, shall affect an injured party's right to seek relief under state law; it does not purport to preclude preemption of state law by other provisions of the Act. Section 510, moreover, preserves the authority of a State "with respect to the waters (including boundary waters) of such Stat[e]." This language arguably limits the effect of the clause to discharges flowing directly into a State's own waters, i.e., discharges from within the State. The savings clause then, does not preclude preemption of the law of an affected State.

Given that the Act itself does not speak directly to the issue, the Court must be guided by the goals and policies of the Act in determining whether it in fact preempts an action based on the law of an affected State. *Cf. City of Rome v. United States*, 446 U.S. 156, 199 (1980) (POWELL, J., dissenting) ("We resort to legislative materials only when the congressional mandate is unclear on its face"). After examining the CWA as a whole, its purposes and its history, we are convinced that if affected States were allowed to impose separate discharge standards on a single point source, the inevitable result would be a serious interference with the achievement of the "full purposes and objectives of Congress." *See Hillsborough County v. Automated Medical Laboratories, supra*, 471 U.S. at 713. Because we do not believe Congress intended to undermine this carefully drawn statute through a general saving clause, we conclude that the CWA precludes a court from applying the law of an affected State against an out-of-state source.

B

In determining whether Vermont nuisance law "stands as an obstacle" to the full implementation of the CWA, it is not enough to say that the ultimate goal of both federal and state law is to eliminate water pollution. A state law also is preempted if it interferes with the methods by which the federal statute was designed to reach this goal. *See Michigan Canners & Freezers Assn. v. Agricultural Marketing & Bargaining Bd.*, 467 U.S. 461, 477 (1984). In this case the application of Vermont law against IPC would allow respondents to circumvent the NPDES permit system, thereby upsetting the balance of public and private interests so carefully addressed by the Act.

By establishing a permit system for effluent discharges, Congress implicitly has recognized that the goal of the CWA - elimination of water pollution - cannot be achieved immediately, and that it cannot be realized without incurring costs. The EPA Administrator issues permits according to established effluent standards and water quality standards, that in turn are based upon available technology, 33 U.S.C. § 1314, and competing public and industrial uses, § 1312(a). The Administrator must consider the impact of the discharges on the waterway, the types of effluents, and the schedule for compliance, each of which may vary widely among sources. If a State elects to impose its own standards, it also must consider the technological feasibility of more stringent controls. Given the nature of these complex decisions, it is not surprising that the Act limits the right to administer the permit system to the EPA and the source States. *See* § 1342(b).

An interpretation of the saving clause that preserved actions brought under an affected State's law would disrupt this balance of interests. If a New York source were liable for violations of Vermont law, that law could effectively override both the permit requirements and the policy choices made by the source State. The affected State's nuisance laws would subject the point source to the threat of legal and equitable penalties if the permit standards were less stringent than those imposed by the affected State. Such penalties would compel the source to adopt different control standards and a different compliance schedule from those approved by the EPA, even though the affected State had not engaged in the same weighing of the costs and benefits. This case illustrates the problems with such a rule. If the Vermont Court ruled that respondents were entitled to the full amount of damages and injunctive relief sought in the complaint, at a minimum IPC would have to change its methods of doing business and controlling pollution to avoid the threat of ongoing liability. In suits such as this, an affected-state court also could require the source to cease operations by ordering immediate abatement. Critically, these liabilities would attach even though the source had complied fully with its state and federal permit obligations. The inevitable result of such suits would be that Vermont and other States could do indirectly what they could not do directly — regulate the conduct of out-of-state sources.

Application of an affected State's law to an out-of-state source also would undermine the important goals of efficiency and predictability in the permit system. The history of the 1972 amendments shows that Congress intended to establish "clear and identifiable" discharge standards. *See* S. Rep. No. 92-414, p. 81 (1971), 2 Leg. Hist. 1499, U.S. Code Cong. & Admin. News 1972, p. 3747. As noted above, under the reading of the saving clause proposed by respondents, a source would be subject to a variety of common-law rules established by the different States along the interstate waterways. These nuisance standards often are "vague" and "indeterminate." The application of numerous States' laws would only exacerbate the vagueness and resulting uncertainty. The Court of Appeals in *Milwaukee III* identified the problem with such an irrational system of regulation:

> "For a number of different states to have independent and plenary regulatory authority over a single discharge would lead to chaotic confrontation between sovereign states. Dischargers would be forced to meet not only the statutory limitations of all states potentially affected by their discharges but also the common law standards developed through case law of those states. It would be virtually impossible to predict the standard for a lawful discharge into an interstate body of water. Any permit issued under the Act would be rendered meaningless." 731 F.2d, at 414.

It is unlikely — to say the least — that Congress intended to establish such a chaotic regulatory structure.

Nothing in the Act gives each affected State this power to regulate discharges. The CWA carefully defines the role of both the source and affected States, and specifically provides for a process whereby their interests will be considered and balanced by the source State and the EPA. This delineation of authority represents Congress' considered judgment as to the best method of serving the public interest and reconciling the often competing concerns of those affected by the pollution. It would be extraordinary for Congress, after devising an elaborate permit system that sets clear standards, to tolerate common-law suits that have the potential to undermine this regulatory structure.

C

Our conclusion that Vermont nuisance law is inapplicable to a New York point source does not leave respondents without a remedy. The CWA precludes only those suits that may require standards of effluent control that are incompatible with those established by the procedures set forth in the Act. The saving clause specifically preserves other state actions, and therefore nothing in the Act bars aggrieved individuals from bringing a nuisance claim pursuant to the law of the source State. By its terms the CWA allows States such as New York to impose higher standards on its own point sources, and in *Milwaukee II* we recognized that this authority may include the right to impose higher common-law as well as higher statutory restrictions. 451 U.S., at 328 (suggesting that "States may adopt more stringent limitations ... through state nuisance law, and apply them to in-state dischargers"); *see also Committee for Jones Falls Sewage System v. Train*, 539 F.2d 1006, 1009, and n. 9 (CA4 1976) (CWA preserves common law suits filed in source State).

An action brought against IPC under New York nuisance law would not frustrate the goals of the CWA as would a suit governed by Vermont law. First, application of the source State's law does not disturb the balance among federal, source-state, and affected-state interests. Because the Act specifically allows source States to impose stricter standards, the imposition of source-state law does not disrupt the regulatory partnership established by the permit system. Second, the restriction of suits to those brought under source-state nuisance law prevents a source from being subject to an indeterminate number of potential regulations. Although New York nuisance law may impose separate standards and thus create some tension with the permit system, a source only is required to look to a single additional authority, whose rules should be relatively predictable. Moreover, States can be expected to take into account their own nuisance laws in setting permit requirements.

IPC asks the Court to go one step further and hold that all state-law suits also must be brought in source-state *courts*. As petitioner cites little authority or justification for this position, we find no basis for holding that Vermont is an improper forum. Simply because a cause of action is preempted does not mean that judicial jurisdiction over the claim is affected as well; the Act preempts laws, not courts. In the absence of statutory authority to the contrary, the rule is settled that a district court sitting in diversity is competent to apply the law of a foreign State.

IV

The District Court correctly denied IPC's motion for summary judgment and judgment on the pleadings. Nothing in the Act prevents a court sitting in an affected State from hearing a common-law nuisance suit, provided that jurisdiction otherwise is proper. Both the District Court and the Court of Appeals erred, however, in concluding that Vermont law governs this litigation. The application of affected-state laws would be incompatible with the Act's delegation of authority and its comprehensive regulation of water pollution. The Act preempts state law to the extent that the state law is applied to an out-of-state point source.

The decision of the Court of Appeals is affirmed in part and reversed in part. The case is remanded for further proceedings consistent with this opinion.

It is so ordered.

NOTES

1. The *International Paper* decision was an attempt to resolve a conflict in the circuit courts between the lower court decision in *International Paper* and the Seventh Circuit's decision following the second remand in *Illinois v. City of Milwaukee*. *See Illinois v. City of Milwaukee*, 731 F.2d 403 (7th Cir. 1984). What was the conflict between the circuit courts that the Supreme Court had to resolve? As a result of the decision in *International Paper* what continuing role do common law remedies, both state and federal, play in interstate pollution disputes?

2. It is important to recognize that the difficulties created by the *Milwaukee* and *International Paper* decisions have no relevance for common law actions involving purely *intrastate* disputes. Both the Clean Water Act and the Clean Air Act (as well as a host of other environmental statutes) expressly preserve the rights of persons to maintain common law actions for harm caused by pollution. *Compare* § 505(e) of the Clean Water Act, 33 U.S.C. § 1365(e), *with* § 304(e) of the Clean Air Act, 42 U.S.C. § 7604(e). Common law remedies will, however, continue to pose problems for plaintiffs where the defendant's conduct is consistent with specific government standards. The difficult task for the plaintiff's lawyer will be to convince a court that a company which maintains its operation in strict compliance with costly environmental, health, and safety laws, and which provides substantial income and employment for the community, is nonetheless maintaining a nuisance. *See e.g.*, *New England Legal Foundation v. Costle*, 666 F.2d 30, 33 (2d Cir. 1981) ("Courts traditionally have been reluctant to enjoin as a public nuisance activities which have been considered and specifically authorized by the government.")

3. After the Supreme Court's decision, International Paper moved for the trial court to dismiss the plaintiff's state common law nuisance claims for the interstate air pollution from the mill. Applying the Supreme Court's reasoning on the water claims, the trial court held that the plaintiff's nuisance claim for air pollution was not preempted by the Clean Air Act, insofar as it was based on New York law. *Ouellette v. International Paper Co.*, 666 F. Supp. 58 (D.Vt. 1987).

4. As described above, the Clean Water Act and the Clean Air Act both contain provisions expressly preserving common law remedies. Section 304(e) of the Clean Air Act provides as follows:

> Nothing in this section shall restrict any right which any person (or class of persons) may have under any statute or common law to seek enforcement of any emission standard or limitation *or to seek any other relief* (including relief against the Administrator or State agency) . . . (Emphasis added.)

Considering this provision, how did the Supreme Court conclude that the federal common law remedy had been preempted?

5. The Clean Air Act follows a permitting scheme not unlike the scheme for NPDES permits under the Clean Water Act. Under the Clean Air Act, all regulated sources of air pollution are required to obtain permits. § 502(a). States are encouraged to establish their own permitting program, but EPA retains the right to veto a state decision granting a permit. § 505(b) and (c). Furthermore, for all stationary sources of air pollution, states retain the authority to adopt more stringent standards than those required by federal law. § 116. Thus it seems that common law nuisance actions for air pollution problems remain viable. Nonetheless, as the Clean Air Act Amendments of 1990 are implemented, it will become much more difficult to demonstrate that any single source contributes a sufficient amount of air pollution to the atmosphere to support a nuisance claim.

II
THE CLEAN AIR ACT

4 THE BIG PICTURE: A SUMMARY OF THE CLEAN AIR ACT

Before the 1990 Amendments the Clean Air Act was sufficiently complex to overwhelm all but the most persistent students. The 1990 Amendments make the previous law seem simple. Just reading the Clean Air Act is a daunting task. Set forth below is a brief review of the Clean Air Act, its history and its most salient features. This summary is by no means comprehensive. Rather it is intended to provide the student with a general understanding of the framework and key components of the law. Because the law forms an intricate web of legal requirements, such an understanding should prove helpful as individual aspects of the law are examined in the ensuing chapters.

I. INTRODUCTION AND HISTORY

The Air Pollution Control Act of 1955 was the first federal foray into the air pollution field. It was designed to promote air pollution research under the auspices of the former Department of Health, Education and Welfare (HEW). Regulation of air pollution remained with the states. The Clean Air Act of 1963 provided the Secretary of HEW with limited jurisdiction to regulate interstate air pollution problems, and a full-scale regulatory program was eventually authorized by the Air Quality Act of 1967. It was this law that first focused regulatory efforts on ambient air quality. Implementation of the law , however, remained with the states. Compliance was erratic. *See* CURRIE, AIR POLLUTION: FEDERAL LAW AND ANALYSIS, § 8.01 (1981).

The forerunner to the present Clean Air Act was passed in 1970 and coincided with the establishment of the Environmental Protection Agency by the executive order of President Nixon. The 1970 Act entrusted the new agency with the authority to develop and administer plans for achieving compliance with ambient air quality standards in those states lacking adequate plans of their own. Point source controls were also adopted, but applied only to new or modified facilities. Significant amendments were enacted in 1977. Among other things, these amendments provided for the prevention of significant deterioration of clean air areas, and tougher standards for those "nonattainment areas" that remained out of compliance with the ambient air quality standards. Point source standards, particularly for large stationary sources, were strengthened, but remained largely inapplicable to existing sources of air pollution.

The 1990 Amendments ushered in a whole new era of regulation. While compliance with ambient air quality standards remains a significant goal of the law, that program is now overshadowed by massive new programs for new and existing point sources that greatly expand the number of facilities subject to point source regulation. Set forth below is a brief summary of the current law. It is divided into six parts. First, National Ambient Air Quality Standards (NAAQS) are described. These standards are designed to insure that air quality throughout the United States is adequate to protect public health and the public welfare. Part two focuses on the program for preventing the significant deterioration of air quality in those areas of the country which are currently clean. Part three describes the law's complex requirements for stationary sources of air pollution. Part four discusses the strict inspection and enforcement program for stationary sources. Part five concerns tailpipe emission standards for mobile sources of air pollution, and the regulation of fuels which are burned by such sources. Part six describes the program for limiting the production of air pollutants which are depleting the stratospheric ozone layer.

II. Ambient Air Quality Standards and the State Implementation Plan Process

A. Background

As originally enacted in 1970, the Clean Air Act required EPA to establish ambient air quality standards for air pollutants that may endanger public health or welfare and which result from numerous and diverse sources. § 108(a)(1). Primary standards are set to protect public health, allowing an adequate margin of safety; secondary standards are established to protect the public welfare. § 109(b). The pollutants regulated under this program are commonly referred to as "criteria pollutants" because they are established following the publication of air quality criteria which are supposed to reflect "the latest scientific knowledge" about the pollutants and their impact on the public health and welfare. § 108(a)(2).

Congress intended that states assume the primary responsibility for meeting the ambient air quality standards. Accordingly, the 1970 law required states to submit for EPA approval a state implementation plan (SIP) which was to provide for the attainment of the primary ambient air quality standards as expeditiously as practicable (but no later than three years after the plan was approved) and of the secondary standards within a reasonable time. § 110(a)(2)(A). States were allowed to adopt whatever mix of controls they desired so long as they were sufficient to attain the ambient air quality standards within the time set out in the statute.

By the time of the 1977 Amendments to the Clean Air Act, it became apparent that the goal of achieving the primary standards as expeditiously as practicable was not being met. In 1977, Congress imposed substantially new requirements for "nonattainment areas" in an effort to gain compliance. Implementation plans for states with nonattainment areas were required to be revised and, among other things, to (1) incorporate all reasonably available control measures; (2) require "reasonable further progress" (RFP) (then defined to mean annual incremental reductions of the relevant pollutant); and (3) require existing sources in the area to install reasonable available control technology. § 172(b). In addition, the Act prohibited the construction of major new sources in nonattainment areas unless these sources offset their emissions by obtaining emissions reductions greater than their contributions. Furthermore, the new source had to employ technology that would meet the lowest achievable emission rate

(LAER), which was stringently defined to mean the lower of either the lowest rate achieved by any source or the lowest required by any other state program. §§ 171(3), 173.

B. 1990 Amendments

1. Nonattainment Areas. Under the original law the ambient air quality standards were supposed to be achieved by about 1975; under the 1977 Amendments, by 1982, or in the case of carbon monoxide and ozone, by 1987. Unfortunately, these goals have not been met. Under the 1990 Amendments, the time for achieving the standards depends upon the pollutant involved and the degree of the problem; for Los Angeles, the biggest problem area for ozone, attainment is not required until 2010. The new law separately addresses the three pollutants that have caused the most problems for regulators: ozone, carbon monoxide, and particulate matter. Of these, ozone has been the most problematic and receives the most attention.

All *ozone nonattainment areas* under the 1990 Amendments are designated as "marginal", "moderate", "serious", "severe" or "extreme" § 181(a). Each area is given a certain period of time (from 3-20 years) to achieve the ozone standards and each area is subject to more or less stringent standards depending on the level of noncompliance. The provisions contained in the 1990 Amendments are complex and will be considered in greater detail in Chapter 6. Several examples, however, will help to illustrate how the law works. Moderate ozone nonattainment areas must achieve a 15% reduction in Volatile Organic Compound (VOC) emissions by 1996 (§ 182(b))[1]; serious areas must achieve the same reduction, plus a reduction of an additional 3% each year thereafter. § 182(c). (Also, a state can combine VOC/NO_X reductions if the same level of ozone reductions will result.) Severe areas must meet the same standards as serious areas. In addition, however, transportation control standards must be implemented as specified in the law, and major new sources must achieve offsets of not less than 1.3 to 1. § 182(d). This means that for every additional pound of VOC contributed by a new source, 1.3 pounds of VOCs must be eliminated generally from the same area. Extreme areas must meet the same standards as severe areas and in addition are subject to offsets for major new sources of not less than 1.5 to 1. § 182(e).

Similar though less onerous standards are established for *CO nonattainment areas* and *PM-10 nonattainment areas*. All CO nonattainment areas are designated by law as either moderate or serious. § 186. Moderate areas must achieve the ambient air quality standards by 1996; serious areas must be in compliance by 2001. All PM-10 nonattainment areas are designated in the law as moderate (NAAQS to be achieved by 1995), but they can be redesignated as serious by the Administrator (NAAQS to be achieved by 2002). § 188(a)(b).

2. The RACT/BACT/LAER Clearinghouse. The Amendments establish a central data bank of information about various technologies that may qualify as RACT, BACT and/or LAER for particular types of sources. This data bank should assist both the regulated community, the regulators, and the interested public in understanding the current state of air pollution control technology. § 108(h). Moreover, in addition to providing information about what constitutes RACT, BACT, or LAER for a given

---

[1] This essentially becomes the RFP requirement for moderate areas. *See* § 171(1).

source, the clearinghouse will provide useful information as EPA attempts to define MACT for various sources of hazardous air pollutants.

III. PREVENTION OF SIGNIFICANT DETERIORATION

The 1977 Amendments followed the lead of the Supreme Court in mandating the implementation of a program to prevent the significant deterioration of air quality in those areas that currently exceed the NAAQSs. Under this program, all areas in attainment for one or more of the criteria pollutant areas are designated as a Class I, II, or III area for that pollutant. The total additional pollution allowed in these areas is an increment beyond a baseline level which is established at the time of the location of the first major emitting facility in the regulated area. Class I areas are allowed the smallest incremental pollution increases; Class III areas are allowed the largest increases. (Currently, however, PSD standards have been set for only three of the six criteria pollutants — SO_2, NO_X, and particulate matter.)

Under the Act, all areas of a state which meet the NAAQSs are initially designated as Class II except for certain national parks and wilderness areas which are specially designated as Class I areas. Class III areas allow the greatest additional increments of pollution. § 163(b)(3). Under no circumstances, of course, is additional pollution allowed if it will cause the NAAQSs to be exceeded. Lands may be redesignated by the states, or in the case of Indian reservations, by the appropriate indian governing body. § 164. Certain national resource lands that exceed 10,000 acres in size, including national parks, wilderness areas, and recreation areas may only be redesignated as Class I or Class II areas. § 164(a). Before an area may be redesignated Class III, the local governing bodies representing the majority of the residents in the area must concur in the redesignation. *Id.* Major new facilities in PSD areas must meet special permitting requirements, including the requirement that they use the best available control technology. §§ 162-165. These requirements are described in greater detail below. The PSD provisions were left essentially unchanged by the 1990 Amendments.

A. Baseline Data

As described above, the PSD areas operate to allow an additional increment of pollutants beyond that which is in the ambient air, so long as the addition of such pollutants will not exceed the NAAQSs. Under the statutory definition of "baseline concentration" at § 169(4), the ambient concentration levels from which the increments will be measured are determined as of the date of the first application for a "major emitting facility" in the PSD area. Because the first permit applicant must collect the data necessary to ascertain the ambient concentration levels, this data can be used to establish an accurate baseline. (Note that each applicant must furnish a minimum of one year of continuous monitoring data. § 165(e)(2). The initial applicant may, of course, have to produce more than this amount of data if that is necessary to assure reasonable accuracy in the baseline calculations.)

In setting these ambient "baseline" concentration levels, EPA must take into account all projected emissions from any major emitting facility on which construction commenced prior to January 6, 1975, the date that the EPA initially promulgated PSD rules. However, SO_2 and particulate emissions from these facilities are *not* included in the baseline and thus are counted against the maximum allowable increases in pollution concentrations. § 169(4).

B. Visibility Protection

The Secretary of the Interior, in consultation with other federal land managers, is required to review all mandatory Federal Class I areas and identify those for which visibility is an important value. Such areas have been identified in 35 states, and the Virgin Islands. The Roosevelt Campobello International Park in New Brunswick, Canada has also been identified for protection under this provision by the Secretary of the Interior. 40 CFR Part 81, Subpart D.

"Major stationary sources" which adversely affect visibility in designated Federal Class I areas, and which commenced operations any time after August 7, 1962, must install and maintain, as expeditiously as practicable, the "best available retrofit technology" (BART) to reduce visibility impairment. New sources that would impact visibility in an identified Federal Class I area are subject to a visibility review. 40 CFR § 51.307. In addition, federal land managers have an affirmative duty to protect the "air quality related values" (AQRVs) (including visibility) of Federal Class I areas. § 165(d)(2)(B). This responsibility could lead to a federal land manager objecting to a new facility even where that facility would not violate the Class I increment. Conversely, a federal land manager may concur in a decision to construct a new facility even where Class I increments are not met, so long as AQRVs are protected and specific increments slightly more stringent than the Class II increments are not violated. *Compare* § 165(d)(2)(c)(ii) and (iii).

C. Visibility Transport Regions

Although there was considerable debate over visibility protection in the discussions leading to the 1990 Amendments, the changes in the law were minimal. The most important change provides for the establishment of interstate visibility transport regions with commissions to study and report on visibility problems associated with these regions. § 169B(c) and (d). The law also provides substantial funding for studies relating to visibility impairment. § 169B(a).

IV. PERMITS AND OTHER REQUIREMENTS FOR STATIONARY SOURCES

A. General Permitting Authority

Various provisions under prior law insured that most large stationary sources held some type of permit. Permit requirements were particularly detailed for major new stationary sources in nonattainment areas (§ 173) and PSD areas (§ 165) and indeed, most large facilities must meet the requirements of both of these programs.[2] A "permit

---

[2] The designation of an area as a nonattainment area or a PSD area is pollutant specific. Since no area of the country is out of compliance for all of the criteria pollutants, all facilities in a nonattainment area are also in PSD areas. Thus, a facility that meets the definitions of "major emitting facility" for purposes of PSD regulation, and "major stationary source" for purposes of nonattainment area regulation, will generally have to meet the requirements applicable to nonattainment areas for those pollutants for which the area is

or equivalent program" was also required as part of every SIP for major existing sources, but these permits were not subject to any particular requirements or standards (formerly § 110(a)(2)(d).)

The 1990 Amendments add an entirely new and comprehensive permitting program that will affect virtually all stationary sources subject to regulation under the Act.[3] The National Association of Manufacturers has estimated that approximately 134,000 sources that are currently unpermitted will require permits under the new law. *See The Legal Winds of Change, Business and the New Clean Air Act* (PBS Videoconference broadcast, 1990). The estimated cost of such permits for smaller sources is between $8,000 and $22,000. *Id.* Set forth below are the basic permitting requirements of the law.

1. **Scope.** Every source regulated under the Act must have a permit. This will include major stationary sources, any regulated hazardous air pollution source, sources subject to new source performance standards (NSPS), and any other class of sources that EPA determines, by rule, should be included in the permit program. § 502(a). Permit terms are limited to five years.

2. **Standards.** Permits must contain enforceable emission limitations and/or standards to ensure compliance with all aspects of the law. If a source will not be in full compliance upon issuance of the permit, then the permit must include a compliance plan that includes an enforceable schedule of compliance. § 504(a).

3. **Monitoring.** Permits must include monitoring and reporting requirements, and reports must be filed every six months. Continuous emissions monitoring is not necessarily required, unless required elsewhere under the law as, for example, for sources subject to the acid deposition control program. § 504(b).

4. **Permit Fees.** All permitted sources must pay substantial annual fees to the regulatory authority. Fees are initially set at a minimum level of $25/ton of each regulated pollutant, not to exceed 4,000 tons. Thus, the annual fee may not exceed $100,000 per pollutant. § 502(b)(3). These fees can be increased if necessary to meet program costs, or decreased if costs for funding the program are lower than the income generated by the fees. Fees will rise over time with the consumer price index.

5. **Permit Shield.** Compliance with a lawful permit is deemed to be compliance with the Act. § 504(f). Nonetheless, any permit for major sources issued for three or more years is subject to revision to reflect new requirements that will become effective before the permit expires. § 502(b)(9). Revisions must be made no later than 18 months after the new requirements become effective.

6. **EPA Rulemaking.** EPA must publish final rules establishing minimum standards for state permitting programs by November 15, 1991. Among other things, these rules must include: (a) a standard application form; (b) monitoring and reporting requirements; (c) permit fee requirements; (d) requirements for adequate personnel and funding; (e) requirements to ensure adequate authority to issue permits and assure

---

out of compliance, and PSD areas for those pollutants for which compliance has been achieved.

[3] Similar sources that exist in large numbers may be covered by a general permit. § 504(d). General permits, however, must meet all requirements of the law, and do not relieve the permittee of the application requirements contained in § 503.

compliance; (f) adequate procedures for processing applications, including public notice and an opportunity to comment. § 502(b).

7. EPA must object to the issuance of any permit that is not in compliance with the law. If EPA fails to object, a private party can petition EPA to object on any grounds raised during the public comment period. § 505(b)(2). EPA must grant or deny any such petition within 60 days. EPA must deny any permit where its objections have not been met. § 505(c).

B. New Source Performance Standards

1. The Clean Air Act provides for the establishment of emission standards for *categories or classes* of facilities which the EPA Administrator determines cause or contribute significantly to air pollution. § 111(b)(1)(A).[4] These requirements apply only to *new sources* which are defined in the Act to mean any *stationary* source, the construction *or modification*[5] of which was commenced after the promulgation of regulations prescribing "standards of performance" for such source. Thus, a primary lead smelter is considered a *new* source under the law if the construction or modification of that smelter began after October 16, 1974, the date the EPA first promulgated standards of performance for primary lead smelters. 40 CFR Part 60, Subpart R.

These "standards of performance" are established by EPA to reflect the degree of emission limitations (and for fossil fuel plants, a percentage reduction of emissions) achievable through the application of the best technological system of continuous emission reduction which EPA determines has been adequately demonstrated. In making this determination, EPA must take into account the cost of achieving such emission reduction, any nonair quality health and environmental impacts, and energy requirements. § 111(a)(1). If EPA determines that it is not feasible to prescribe a standard of performance then it may impose a design, equipment, work practice, or operational standard. § 111(h).

2. Fossil Fuel Fired Stationary Sources. In order to promote the use of higher sulfur Eastern coal, Congress amended the Clean Air Act in 1977 to provide a dual standard of performance for fossil fuel-fired stationary sources. In addition to the normal "emission limit," the Act also requires a percentage reduction of the emissions from these sources. This served to promote the high sulfur coal industry (primarily in the Eastern United States) by essentially requiring all such facilities to install flue gas desulfurization systems or "scrubbers," even where they might meet the emission standards without such technology by burning low sulfur coal. The 1990 Amendments

---

[4] Thus, for example, EPA has set different standards for iron and steel plants (40 CFR Part 60, Subpart N), primary copper smelters (40 CFR Part 60, Subpart P), and coal preparation plants (40 CFR Part 60, Subpart Y). The NSPS for any particular category of facility may limit its application to facilities of a certain size but NSPS are *not* limited to major emitting facilities or major stationary sources as are some other provisions of the law. As of July 1, 1991, EPA had established NSPS for 70 categories or classes of facilities. 40 CFR Part 60.

[5] "The term 'modification' means any physical change in, or change in the method of operation of, a stationary source which increases the amount of any air pollutant emitted by such source, or which results in the emission of any air pollutant not previously emitted." § 111(a)(4).

repealed the percentage reduction requirement. Clean Air Act Amendments of 1990, § 403.

C. New Source Review — Major Stationary Sources and Major Emitting Facilities

1. Definitions. Before proceeding with this discussion, it is necessary to describe what is certainly one of the more confusing aspects of the law — that is, the definitions of, and occasional distinction between, "major stationary sources" and "major emitting facilities." Section 302(j) of the Act provides:

> Except as otherwise expressly provided, the terms "major stationary source" and "major emitting facility" mean any stationary facility or source of air pollutants which directly emits, or has the potential to emit, one hundred tons per year or more of any air pollutant . . . .

Such sources and facilities include fugitive sources, *i.e.*, non-point sources, as determined by rule by EPA. *Id.* While this definition seems straightforward enough, the Act employs different definitions for each term in certain contexts so as to limit the applicability of the general definition. Specifically, the term "major emitting facility" is defined for purposes of the prevention of significant deterioration standards at § 169(1) of the Act to mean any of 27 enumerated plants that emit more than 100 tons/year of any air pollutant, or any other plant that emits more than 250 tons/year of any air pollutant. For purposes of visibility degradation the term "major stationary source" is defined at § 169A to mean any of the same 27 enumerated plants described at § 169(1) but only where such plants emit more than 250 tons/year of any pollutant. No other plants are included in this definition regardless of the amount of their emissions. The principal portion of the law where the general definition at § 302(j) remains relevant is with regard to performance standards for major stationary sources in nonattainment areas.

The 1990 Amendments further add to this confusion by defining the term "major stationary source" to mean a source that emits something less than 100 tons per year for certain classes of ozone and PM-10 nonattainment areas. For example, a major stationary source in a serious ozone nonattainment area is one that emits 50 tons or more per year of VOCs. § 182(c). Also, the statute now employs another similar term, "major source", which refers to a certain category of sources regulated under the hazardous air pollution program. § 112(a)(1). Having defined these key terms, we can now turn to the special standards that apply to these facilities.

2. PSD Areas. New or modified "major emitting facilities" in PSD areas must obtain a PSD permit. As described previously, such sources must use the "best available control technology" (BACT) to control air pollution. BACT is defined as an *emission limitation* "based on the maximum degree of reduction of each pollutant . . . which the permitting authority, on a case-by-case basis, taking into account energy, environmental, and economic impacts and other costs, determines is achievable . . . ." § 169(3).

In order that the agency might make these determinations, *preconstruction review* of the facility is required. § 165. This review is preceded by the applicant's submission of a minimum of one year of continuous monitoring data. The EPA must then use modeling techniques to make its predictions regarding PSD compliance. Strict timing and public participation standards apply to the PSD permitting process. Among other things, the PSD permit applicant must demonstrate, and the regulatory agency (either the State or EPA) must find, that the proposed facility will meet all emissions standards, utilize BACT, assure maintenance of the NAAQSs, and assure that the applicable PSD increments are not violated.

3. Nonattainment Areas. A "major (new or modified) stationary source" located in a nonattainment area, that is, an area that does not meet the NAAQSs for one or more criteria pollutants, must meet the lowest achievable emission rate (LAER). LAER is defined to mean a rate of emissions which reflects either the most stringent emission limit contained in an implementation plan of *any* state for such class or category of source (unless the owner demonstrates that such limits are not achievable), *or* the most stringent emission limit achieved in practice by that category or class, whichever is more stringent. § 171(3). Note that any given plant may have to meet BACT for certain pollutants, and LAER for others. This should occur only where the plant is located in a nonattainment area for some, but not all, of the criteria pollutants. The impact that emissions from the plant will have on other areas may not be considered in determining the applicable standards. *See Alabama Power Co. v. Costle*, 636 F.2d 323 (D.C. Cir. 1979).

In addition to LAER, major new stationary sources in nonattainment areas must offset their emissions by obtaining permanent reductions in emissions from other sources in the area. § 173(a)(1). Also, they must demonstrate that construction of the new source will not interfere with attainment of the NAAQS.

4. Modifications. Although the Act appears to employ the same definition for modifications for purposes of the PSD and nonattainment area programs (*see e.g.*, § 171(4)), in practice, EPA takes a different approach. For purposes of the NSPS program, EPA compares the *hourly* emissions of a facility at its current maximum capacity with its potential emissions at maximum capacity after the change. If the comparison shows an increase, then the change is treated as a modification for purposes of the NSPS program. Under EPA's regulations, the permit requirements for major stationary sources and major emitting facilities in PSD and nonattainment areas, apply only to new sources and *major modifications* of existing sources. *See* 40 CFR §§ 51.165, 51.166 (1991). The determination as to whether a change constitutes a major modification is based upon a comparison of total *annual* emissions before and after the change. If the change would result in "significant" increases in pollutants as defined under EPA's rules (40 CFR §§ 51.165(a)(1)(x), 51.166(b)(23)) then it is deemed a major modification subject to the PSD and nonattainment area permitting programs. *See Wisconsin Electric Power Company v. Reilly*, 893 F.2d 901 (7th Cir. 1990).

D. Existing Sources

1. SIP Requirements. There is no specific requirement that existing sources meet any particular emission level for "criteria pollutants." Reductions may, however, be required by the SIP as necessary to achieve or maintain the NAAQS. Moreover, in nonattainment areas the SIP must require all existing sources to achieve emissions reductions based on reasonably available control technology (RACT). RACT is defined as devices, systems process modifications, or other apparatus or techniques that are reasonably available taking into account (1) the necessity of imposing such controls in order to attain and maintain a national ambient air quality standard, (2) the social, environmental, and economic impact of such controls, and (3) alternative means of providing for attainment and maintenance of such standard. 40 CFR (1991) § 51.100(o)(1991).

2. Designated Pollutants. Both new and existing sources must meet emission limits for "designated pollutants" which are established for each class or category of facility under the NSPS program. § 111(a)(1)(B) and (C). The state plan may set more lenient emission limits for existing sources, however, than those established for new sources. § 111(d)(1). Thus, for example, new source primary aluminum reduction plants must meet standards for fluoride emissions, a designated pollutant for aluminum reduction plants. 40 CFR § 60.192. The state plan must, accordingly, make some provision for regulating fluoride emissions from existing aluminum reduction plants although it need not be the same as the NSPS for such plants.

3. Hazardous Air Pollutants. Existing sources must also meet standards for hazardous pollutants as described below.

E. Hazardous Air Pollution Regulation

1. Background. Section 112 of the Act provides for the regulation of hazardous air pollutants (HAP). Before its amendment in 1990, this provision required EPA to list as a hazardous air pollutant any air pollutant which might reasonably be anticipated to result in an increase in mortality or an increase in serious and irreversible or incapacitating but reversible illness. Once listed all stationary sources were required to meet health-based emission standards, which were supposed to be set with an ample margin of safety. These standards had to be met regardless of cost. *But see Natural Resources Defense Council v. EPA*, 824 F.2d 1146 (D.C. Cir. 1987), which allowed considerations of cost in setting an ample margin of safety, but not in initially determining a level that was safe. Despite substantial pressure from Congress, EPA was reluctant to list pollutants under this section because of the anticipated economic impacts of such decisions. As described below, the 1990 Amendments overhaul this provision entirely.

2. Current Program. Under the prior law, EPA had listed only seven hazardous air pollutants. The 1990 Amendments list 189 such pollutants but establish a very different approach to their regulation. § 112(b)(1). (The government was able to compile this list largely as a result of information about hazardous materials which companies furnished in accordance with the Emergency Planning and Community Right to Know Act. 42 U.S.C. § 11001 *et seq.*) This list may be revised at EPA's own discretion or as a result of a petition by "any person". § 112(b)(2),(3). EPA must grant or deny a petition within 18 months. EPA "shall add" a pollutant to the list if it "present[s], or may present, ... a threat of adverse human health effects ... or adverse environmental effects." § 112(b)(2). Thus, hazardous pollutants are no longer limited to those that may cause a serious illness in humans.

While the 1990 Amendments significantly broadened the coverage of the hazardous air pollutant section, they also changed the manner in which HAP standards are set. Instead of setting standards based upon adverse impacts on health, the new legislation requires standards to be set for categories or classes of sources of the 189 pollutants, based initially, at least, on feasibility. A two-phase approach to air toxics regulation is employed.

Phase I involves technology-based standards. Within one year after passage of the law EPA must list all categories or classes of sources which emit one or more pollutant on the list of 189 pollutants. § 112(c). Standards for major sources in each of these categories must then be set at MACT — the maximum achievable control technology. For new sources, the emissions standards established under MACT must be at least as stringent as the "best controlled similar source." For existing sources, MACT must be set at the level of pollution that has been achieved by the best 12% of currently operating similar sources. EPA must promulgate MACT standards for 41 sources within two years; 25% of the remaining sources within four years; an additional 25% of the remaining sources within seven years; and all of the remaining sources within ten years.

Under Phase II, if the residual risk of cancer to the most exposed individual is greater than one in one million after the implementation of MACT standards, EPA must impose more stringent standards to reduce the risk below that level. § 112(f)(1). This must be done within eight years after the promulgation of the original standards.

EPA may limit the application of MACT standards to "major sources" which are defined as sources (or groups of sources) with the potential to emit ten tons per year of any single HAP, or 25 tons per year of any combination of HAPs. §112 (a)(1). Moreover, EPA has the discretion to differentiate between sizes, classes and types of sources within a particular source category.

Smaller "area sources," which EPA chooses not to regulate under the MACT standards, remain subject to generally available control technology (GACT). § 112(d)(5). EPA is required to list categories of area sources whenever it finds that such categories present "a threat of adverse effects to human health and the environment . . . warranting regulation under this section." § 112(c)(3). (It will be interesting to see if this last phrase is construed to give EPA broad discretion to eschew listing even where adverse effects are shown.) In any event, EPA must list categories of area sources representing 90% of area source emissions of the 30 HAPs presenting the greater threat to public health in urban areas within five years. Regulations controlling emissions from these sources must be promulgated by the year 2000.

3. **Early Reduction Program**. Any source that achieves a 90% reduction of gaseous HAPs, or a 95% reduction of particulate HAPs (based on 1987 emission levels) before new standards are proposed, can obtain a six year extension on compliance. § 112(i)(5). Air pollution lawyers from around the country are now busy advising their clients about the need to consider the desirability of obtaining this extension before it is too late.

4. **Accidental Release Program.** The 1990 Amendments create two new programs to address accidental releases of extremely hazardous air pollutants. Section 112(r)(6) provides for establishment of an independent Chemical Safety and Hazard Investigation Board for the purposes of investigating and reporting on any accidental release of extremely hazardous air pollutants that results in death, serious injury or substantial property damage. The Board is also authorized to conduct research and make recommendations to EPA regarding methods for preventing the occurrence and minimizing the consequences of accidental release of extremely hazardous air pollutants.

In addition to the Chemical Safety Board's activities, EPA is required to list at least 100 substances which qualify as extremely hazardous air pollutants (EHAP) and promulgate rules to require certain owners and operators of sources which might release these pollutants to prepare and implement risk management plans to address accidental releases of these substances. § 112(r)(7)(B)(ii).

A second program requires the Occupational Safety and Health Administration, in conjunction with EPA, to establish a program to protect workers from accidental release of "highly hazardous chemicals" in the work place. § 304 (a).

F. Emissions Trading Policy

The Clean Air Act has served as a model for programs designed to achieve more efficient and economical pollution control. Perhaps the most ambitious example of this phenomenon is the Acid Deposition Program incorporated into the 1990 Amendments and described in detail below. Well before the 1990 Amendments, however, EPA had developed an emissions trading policy designed to control the costs of pollution control while at the same time encouraging faster compliance. The emissions trading policy has four components; bubbles, netting, emission offsets, and emission reduction credits. The bubble policy allows existing plants with more than one emission source to treat all such sources as if they were under a bubble encompassing the entire facility with only one stack emanating from the bubble. The bubble policy allows individual sources under the *bubble* to change their emissions levels without being treated as a *modification* so long as total emissions from the bubble are not increased. This policy of increasing emissions from one source under the bubble while simultaneously decreasing at least as much of the same pollution from another source is called *netting* and a plant that is able to achieve such a trade is said to "net out" of certain new source review requirements. *See* Emissions Trading Policy, 51 Fed. Reg. 43,814 (1986), *infra* at Chapter 9.

Emission offsets are used to allow the construction of major stationary sources in nonattainment areas or major emitting facilities in PSD areas where the new facility would exceed the applicable PSD increment for that area. *Emission reduction credits* (ERCs) are "the common currency of all trading activity." Only those ERCs which are surplus, enforceable, permanent and quantifiable may be used in emission trades. ERCs may also be banked for future sale or use.

G. Acid Deposition Control

1. Background. One of the chief flaws in the pre-1990 law was its failure to adequately address pre-existing sources of air pollution. Most of the significant air pollution control provisions of the law applied only to major new or modified sources. States through their SIPs could impose controls on existing sources, but rarely did so to any significant degree. This gave companies a tremendous incentive to keep their old facilities on line, since it was clear that any new facilities would have to meet strict anti-pollution standards. The failure of the state and federal governments to regulate existing sources of air pollution was a substantial cause of the entire acid deposition problem.

Before the 1990 Amendments, existing sources, whether major or minor, were subject to only limited controls. Those located in nonattainment areas were required to employ reasonably available control technology (RACT), but this is the least restrictive of the technology based standards under the law. Moreover, for sources in PSD areas (and indeed for all pollutants for which the area is in attainment) the only controls imposed are those required at the state's discretion under the SIP.[6] Herein lies the fundamental problem with the pre-existing law.

The failure to address existing sources of air pollution was particularly troublesome as it related to electric utilities. Many utilities had gone on line before the Clean Air Act requirements became applicable to them, and the prospect of strict regulation under the Clean Air Act provided a powerful incentive against modernization. Moreover, transboundary air pollution problems, which were becoming increasingly serious, were largely a product of the SO_2 and NO_X pollution from these large utilities.

2. 1990 Amendments. The goal of the law is a 10 million ton/year reduction of SO_2 emissions, and a 2 million ton/year reduction in NO_X emissions from 1980 levels. All of this is supposed to be achieved by reductions at electric utilities. This goal is to be achieved in two phases.

a. SO_2 Reductions

1. "Affected units" are those facilities subject to the emission reduction provisions of Title IV. During Phase I this includes 111 existing utility sources of SO_2 which exceed 2.5 lbs/mmBtu as set out in Table A of § 404 of the Act. During Phase II, this includes all commercial facilities (of 25 MW or more) in existence when the law was passed.

2. Phase I: Sets allowances (one ton of pollution per each allowance) for 111 existing sources in the east and midwest (Kansas is the farthest West) at a level of 2.5 lbs/mmBtu. § 404. (This is more than double the long-standing NSPS for fossil fuel fired power plants. *See* 40 CFR § 60.43a(a)(1990)) These allowances may not be exceeded after 1995.

3. Phase II: By the year 2000, existing sources of 25 MW or more will receive allowances based upon a maximum rate of 1.2 lbs/mmBtu. (This is the current maximum NSPS for fossil fuel-fired steam generators. 40 CFR § 60.43a(a)(1990).) Power plants with lower emissions will generally be awarded allowances based upon their 1985 emissions. EPA may not issue allowances that will allow annual emissions to exceed 8.9 million tons of SO_2 (subject to certain provisions for bonus allowances).

4. All sources must hold allowances equal to emissions and source operators will be fined $2,000 for each ton of emissions in excess of the allowance. But an elaborate market system is established for buying and selling allowances. EPA also holds auctions for allowances. Companies can get energy conservation and renewable energy allowances. States can get bonus allowances if their average emissions are below .8 lbs/mmBtu. § 406. Cleaner plants (better than 1.2 lbs/mmBtu) will get 20% more allowances than their baseline. § 405(d).

5. Continuous emission monitoring systems (CEMS) are required on all units that are subject to the acid deposition control program. (The availability of CEMS data should make citizen suits for enforcement of violations much easier to bring. In this way, the CEMS data will serve the function of discharge monitoring reports under the Clean Water Act.)

---

[6] Existing sources were also subject to hazardous air pollution standards and to controls on designated pollutants — those that were neither hazardous air pollutants nor criteria pollutants, but which were regulated under the NSPS program. *See* § 111(d). An example of a designated pollutant is fluoride from aluminum reduction plants. Fluoride is not listed as a hazardous air pollutant in the list of 189 HAPs in § 112. Nonetheless, it plainly qualifies as such a pollutant under the expanded definition of that term, and it will be interesting to see whether the hazardous air pollution section eventually renders § 111(d) superfluous.

6. New units cannot go on line until they have acquired sufficient allowances to account for their emissions. § 403(c).

b. NO_X Reductions. The proposed NO_X reductions will be handled under more conventional provisions. The 1990 Amendments require EPA to revise the NSPS for fossil fuel fired steam generators based upon low NO_X burner technology by 1994. § 407(c). Standards must be adopted for all types of boilers by 1997. § 407(b)(2). In addition, existing facilities which are affected units for purposes of the SO_2 reduction program must meet certain emission limits set out in the law. § 407(b)(1).

V. INSPECTIONS AND ENFORCEMENT

A. Background

Long before the 1990 Amendments, the enforcement provisions of the Clean Air Act had proved inadequate. In particular, the EPA was hampered by its inability to seek civil penalties for violations of the law, without either going to court or engaging in the cumbersome process of assessing "economic benefit" "noncompliance" penalties under § 120. The 1990 Amendments corrected this problem, and added substantial new weapons to EPA's enforcement arsenal.

B. 1990 Amendments

1. **Inspections.** Section 114(a)(2) grants EPA broad authority to inspect sites subject to the Act. EPA's inspection authority has not changed significantly as a result of the 1990 Amendments with one important exception. Under §114 (a)(3), major stationary source operators are required to perform enhanced monitoring and submit "compliance certifications" which provide assurance that the facility is meeting applicable performance standards. Persons concerned about noncompliance will, for the first time, have ready access to compliance information.

2. **Civil Penalties.** Under new § 113(b), EPA may assess civil penalties of up to $25,000 per day for certain specified violations of the Act. (Total penalties under this provision, however, may not exceed $200,000 unless a joint determination is made by EPA and the Attorney General to exceed that amount.) Penalties may be assessed for both present and past violations that occurred not more than 12 months prior to the assessment date. All penalties assessed under § 113(b) are in addition to penalties that may be assessed under § 120 (which is designed solely to remove any economic benefit that an operator may receive from noncompliance). The criteria for penalty assessment are set out at § 133(e). EPA may initiate civil actions and recover penalties for past violations that are no older than five years.

If any person fails to pay a final assessment, EPA must ask the Attorney General to collect the assessment. The alleged violator may not challenge the fact of the violation or the assessment amount in this proceeding. Furthermore, the violator is subject to payment of the assessment, appropriate interest, a 10% "failure to pay" penalty, and the government's costs and expenses incurred in collecting the penalty, including attorney fees.

3. **Field Citations.** EPA is authorized to implement a field citation program that would allow federal inspectors to issue "traffic tickets" for minor violations of the Act.

Fines for such citations may not exceed $5,000. Rules must be promulgated before this authority can be exercised.

4. Criminal Penalties. The 1990 Amendments make it much easier to impose criminal sanctions on violators. Any person who "knowingly" violates one of several enumerated provisions of the law may be punished by a fine and imprisonment not to exceed five years. Knowing the releases of hazardous air pollutants, however, can lead to a fine and prison sentence of up to 15 years. Negligent releases of HAPs may result in a fine and imprisonment for up to one year.

The legislative history makes clear that "responsible corporate officers" can be held liable for "knowing" violations simply by showing that the officer was aware that the act or omission was committed. The government need not show that the officer knew that the act was unlawful. (A responsible employee, by contrast, can be held liable only if the government can show that the employee knew that the act was unlawful.)

The strict standards to which corporate officers are held could be construed by some to discourage self-audits. The legislative history makes clear, however, that information obtained through a self-audit should not ordinarily form the basis for a criminal action. 136 Cong. Rec. 13,201.

5. "Bounties". The 1990 Amendments allow rewards to persons who furnish information leading to a criminal conviction or a criminal or civil penalty. The reward may not exceed $10,000.

6. Public Participation in Settlements. The Amendments afford the public a 30 day comment period on consent orders or settlement agreements before such documents are allowed to become final.

7. Citizen Suits. The Amendments allow citizens to sue for past violations if the violation has been repeated. This was previously not allowed as a result of the Supreme Court's decision in *Gwaltney of Smithfield Ltd. v. Chesapeake Bay Foundation*, 108 S.Ct. 376 (1987).

8. Government Contractors. Under prior law, the government could not contract for the procurement of goods or services from a facility in violation of the law. The 1990 Amendments extend this provision to any facility owned or operated by the violator. § 306(a).

9. Permit Fees. Although it is not found in the enforcement provisions, the most significant enforcement provision contained in the law may very well be the fee provisions for permits imposed by the 1990 Amendments. Since the law requires the regulatory agency to recoup the costs of administering and enforcing the program, state agencies should receive a significant boost in funding. As a result, more aggressive enforcement of the law seems inevitable.

VI. Mobile Sources and Fuel Standards

A. Background

1. Section 202 of the Act sets tailpipe emission standards for motor vehicles which must be met during their useful life. Elaborate testing procedures are also established to be certain that new and used vehicles meet these standards. Manufacturers must pay nonconformance penalties for vehicles that fail to meet federal standards. Among other things, these penalties must be high enough to remove any competitive advantage received by the company for non-compliance. § 206(g).

2. EPA may require the registration and testing of fuels and fuel additives before their introduction into commerce, and may regulate, control or prohibit fuels on the market that may endanger public health or impair the operation of emission control devices. § 211.

B. 1990 Amendments

The Amendments establish more stringent tailpipe emission standards for hydrocarbons and NO_X. They also — (1) require the use of reformulated (clean) gasoline in the nine worst ozone nonattainment areas (extreme and severe areas) by January 1, 1995 (§ 219); (2) ban the sale of leaded gasoline by 1996; and (3) provide for the regulation of toxic air pollutants from motor vehicles (particularly benzene and formaldehyde). In addition, the useful life of vehicles is extended, in most cases, from five years and 50,000 miles to ten years or 100,000 miles for any new requirements that are imposed after the 1990 Amendments. §202(d)(1). Testing, however, will be limited to seven years or 75,000 miles, whichever occurs first. *Id.*

VII. STRATOSPHERIC OZONE

The 1977 Amendments supported research and studies that were deemed necessary to understand the causes and effects of ozone layer depletion. Since that time a large number of countries, including the United States, have signed a treaty known as the "Montreal Protocol" which establishes international standards for controlling the emission of ozone depleting substances. Title VI of the 1990 Amendments was basically intended to implement the Montreal Protocol as it relates to U.S. emissions. Essentially, this title requires that the production of all substances listed as Class I substances be phased out by the year 2000. Methyl chloride production must be phased out by 2002. Class II substances (which are thought to be less significant ozone depleters) must be phased out by 2030. In addition, the 1990 Amendments establish requirements for warning labels for products containing ozone depleting substances, federal procurement of ozone depleting substances, and recycling of such substances. Recent new evidence suggests that ozone depletion is more serious than previously believed. President Bush prompted that the United States will ban the manufacture of Class I substances by the end of 1995, five years earlier than required under the Montreal Protocol. *See* 22 ENV. REP. (Current Developments) 2408 (Feb. 21, 1992).

5 NATIONAL AMBIENT AIR QUALITY STANDARDS

NATURAL RESOURCES DEFENSE COUNCIL, INC. V. TRAIN
545 F.2d 320 (2d Cir. 1976)

J. JOSEPH SMITH, Circuit Judge:

The Environmental Protection Agency, ("EPA"), and its Administrator, Russell Train, appeal from an order of the United States District Court for the Southern District of New York, Charles E. Stewart, Jr., Judge,. . . .requiring the Administrator of the EPA, within thirty days, to place lead on a list of air pollutants under § 108(a)(1) of the Clean Air Act, as amended, ("the Act"). We affirm the order of the district court.

The 1970 Clean Air Act Amendments provide two different approaches for controlling pollutants in the air. One approach, incorporated in §§ 108-110, provides for the publication of a list of pollutants adverse to public health or welfare, derived from "numerous or diverse" sources, the promulgation of national ambient air quality standards for listed pollutants, and subsequent implementation of these standards by the states. The second approach of the Act provides for control of certain pollutants at the source, pursuant to §§ 111, 112, 202, 211 and 231.

The relevant part of § 108 reads as follows:

> (a)(1) For the purpose of establishing national primary and secondary ambient air quality standards, the Administrator shall within 30 days after December 31, 1970, publish, and shall from time to time thereafter revise, a list which includes each air pollutant —
>
> (A) which in his judgment has an adverse effect on public health or welfare;
>
> (B) the presence of which in the ambient air results from numerous or diverse mobile or stationary sources; and
>
> (C) for which air quality criteria had not been issued before December 31, 1970, but for which he plans to issue air quality criteria under this section.

Once a pollutant has been listed under § 108(a)(1), §§ 109 and 110 of the Act are automatically invoked. These sections require that for any pollutant for which air quality criteria are issued under § 108(a)(1)(C) after the date of enactment of the Clean Air Amendments of 1970, the Administrator must simultaneously issue air quality standards. Within nine months of the promulgation of such standards, states are required to submit implementation plans to the Administrator. § 110(a)(1). The Administrator must approve or disapprove a state plan within four months. § 110(a)(2). If a state fails to submit an acceptable plan, the Administrator is required to prepare and publish such a plan himself. § 110(c). State implementation plans must provide for the attainment of primary ambient air quality standards no later than three years from the date of approval of a plan. § 110(a)(2)(A)(i). Extension of the three-year period for attaining the primary standard may be granted by the Administrator only in very limited circumstances, and in no case for more than two years. § 110(e).

The EPA concedes that lead meets the conditions of §§ 108(a)(1)(A) and (B) that it has an adverse effect on public health and welfare, and that the presence of lead in the ambient air results from numerous or diverse mobile or stationary sources. The EPA maintains, however, that under § 108(a)(1)(C) of the Act, the Administrator retains discretion whether to list a pollutant, even though the pollutant meets the criteria of §§ 108(a)(1)(A) and (B). The EPA regards the listing of lead under § 108(a)(1) and the issuance of ambient air quality standards as one of numerous alternative control strategies for lead available to it. Listing of substances is mandatory, the EPA argues, only for those pollutants for which the Administrator "plans to issue air quality criteria." He may, it is contended, choose not to issue, i. e., not "plan to issue" such criteria, and decide to control lead solely by regulating emission at the source, regardless of the total concentration of lead in the ambient air. The Administrator argues that if he chooses to control lead (or other pollutants) under § 211, he is not required to list the pollutant under § 108(a)(1) or to set air quality standards.

The EPA advances three reasons for the position that the Administrator has discretion whether to list a pollutant even when the conditions of § 108(a)(1) (A) and (B) have been met: the plain meaning of § 108(a)(1)(C); the structure of the Clean Air Act as a whole; and the legislative history of the Act.

The issue is one of statutory construction. We agree with the district court and with appellees, National Resources Defense Council, Inc., et al., that the interpretation of the Clean Air Act advanced by the EPA is contrary to the structure of the Act as a whole, and that if accepted, it would vitiate the public policy underlying the enactment of the 1970 Amendments as set forth in the Act and in its legislative history.

* * *

I
Section 108(a)(1) and the Structure of the Clean Air Act

Section 108(a)(1) contains mandatory language. It provides that "the Administrator shall . . . publish . . . a list . . . ." (Emphasis added.) If the EPA interpretation were accepted and listing were mandatory only for substances "for which (the Administrator) plans to issue air quality criteria . . . ", then the mandatory language of § 108(a)(1)(A) would become mere surplusage. The determination to list a pollutant and to issue air quality criteria would remain discretionary with the Administrator, and the rigid deadlines of § 108(a)(2), § 109, and § 110 for attaining air quality standards could be bypassed by him at will. If Congress had enacted § 211 as an alternative to, rather than as a supplement to, §§ 108-110, then one would expect a similar fixed timetable for implementation of the fuel control section. The absence of such a timetable for the enforcement of § 211 lends support to the view that fuel controls were intended by Congress as a means for attaining primary air quality standards rather than as an alternative to the promulgation of such standards.

* * *

The EPA contention that the language of § 108(a)(1)(C) "for which [the Administrator] plans to issue air quality criteria" is a separate and third criterion to be met before § 108 requires listing lead and issuing air quality standards, thereby leaving the decision to list lead within the discretion of the Administrator, finds no support in the legislative history of the 1970 Amendments to the Act. The summary of the provisions of the conference agreement furnished the Senate by Senator Muskie contain the following language:

> The agreement requires issuance of remaining air quality criteria for major pollutants within 13 months of date of enactment.

and

> Within the 13-month deadline, the Congress expects criteria to be issued for nitrogen oxides, fluorides, lead, polynuclear organic matter, and odors, though others may be necessary.

* * *

Language relating to the issuance of new source performance standards makes it clear that the Senate intended these standards to be supplementary to, not in lieu of, ambient air quality standards.

* * *

While the literal language of § 108(a)(1)(C) is somewhat ambiguous, this ambiguity is resolved when this section is placed in the context of the Act as a whole and in its legislative history. The deliberate inclusion of a specific timetable for the attainment of ambient air quality standards incorporated by Congress in §§ 108-110 would become an exercise in futility if the Administrator could avoid listing pollutants simply by choosing not to issue air quality criteria. The discretion given to the Administrator under the Act pertains to the review of state implementation plans under § 110, and to § 211 which authorizes but does not mandate the regulation of fuel or fuel additives. It does not extend to the issuance of air quality standards for substances derived from specified sources which the Administrator had already adjudged injurious to health.

* * *

The structure of the Clean Air Act as amended in 1970, its legislative history, and the judicial gloss placed upon the Act leave no room for an interpretation which makes the issuance of air quality standards for lead under § 108 discretionary. The Congress sought to eliminate, not perpetuate, opportunity for administrative foot-dragging. Once the conditions of §§ 108(a) (1)(A) and (B) have been met, the listing of lead and the issuance of air quality standards for lead become mandatory.

The order of the district court is affirmed.

NOTES

1. In the *NRDC* case, EPA argued that testing lead under the ambient air quality standards was "one of numerous control strategies for lead available to it." What are the other principal control strategies available to EPA under the Act? *See* §§ 202, 211. Consider that, according to EPA estimates, 88 percent of the total lead emissions in this country come from motor vehicle exhaust.

2. Although national ambient air quality standards are "rules" within the meaning of the Administrative Procedure Act (5 U.S.C. §§ 551 *et seq.)*, the rulemaking requirements of the APA do not apply generally to the promulgation or revision of such standards. Rather, the Clean Air Act sets its own procedural requirements, which are much more detailed than those in the APA, for a wide variety of rulemaking-type actions, including the promulgation and revision of ambient air quality standards. § 307(d). Among other things, proposed rules must contain: (a) a statement of basis and purpose which must include a summary of the factual data upon which the rules are based; (b) the methodology used in obtaining and analyzing the data; and (c) the major legal interpretations and policy considerations underlying the proposed rule. *Id.* (A similar requirement is made only for final rules under the APA. *See* 5 U.S.C. § 553.) The rulemaking docket must include all documents and comments pertinent to the rule, including all written comments, data and other information that may be submitted by any person. The final rule must be accompanied by responses to significant comments and data (§ 307(d)(6)(B)), and cannot be based on any information or data not placed in the rulemaking docket as of the date of promulgation. § 307(d)(6)(C). *See American Petroleum Institute v. Costle*, 609 F.2d 20 (D.C. Cir. 1979). (The "date of promulgation" means the date the rule is signed and announced and not the date it is published in the Federal Register.) Further, the record for judicial review is limited to the material in the docket, and only those objections to the rule raised during the public comment period for the rulemaking may be raised during judicial review. § 307(d)(7). Note that these special rulemaking requirements of the Clean Air Act were adopted in 1977, and thus, were not applicable to the proceedings at issue in the *NRDC* case.

3. Despite the strict procedural requirements for rulemaking proceedings under the Clean Air Act, it may be difficult to overturn a rule on the grounds that EPA failed to follow those requirements. Section 307(d)(8) states that "a court may invalidate [a] rule only if the [procedural] errors were so serious and related to matters of such central relevance to the rule that there is a substantial likelihood that the rule would have been significantly changed if such errors had not been made." This provision was invoked by the court to sustain a rule in *Sierra Club v. Costle,* 657 F.2d 298, 396 (D.C. Cir. 1981).

4. The 1977 Amendments added § 109(d) which requires the Administrator to review and, if necessary, revise the NAAQS every five years. 42 U.S.C. § 7409(d). In *Environmental Defense Fund v. Thomas*, 870 F.2d 892 (2d Cir. 1989), *cert. denied, sub nom., Alabama Power v. EDF*, 110 S. Ct. 537 (1989), the plaintiffs challenged the Administrator's failure to revise the NAAQS for sulfur oxides (SO_X), the major cause of acid deposition. The plaintiffs originally brought their action, under § 304 of the Clean Air Act, which allows citizens to bring suits in a district court against the Administrator for a "failure of the Administrator to perform any act or duty . . . which is not discretionary. . .." 42 U.S.C. § 7604(a)(2). The U.S District Court for the Southern District of New York dismissed the plaintiff's action for lack of jurisdiction, holding that the revision of NAAQS by the Administrator was a discretionary function, and thus, the Court of Appeals for the District of Columbia had exclusive jurisdiction over the matter under § 307. Section 307 vests the Court of Appeals for the District of Columbia Circuit with exclusive jurisdiction to review final rules and other "final actions" by the Administrator. 42 U.S.C. § 7607(b). On appeal, the Court of Appeals for the Second Circuit reversed, holding that the duty to make some decision regarding the revision of the NAAQS was non-discretionary, and thus was enforceable by the District Court in accordance with § 304. Nonetheless, the court found that the District Court could not order the Administrator to revise the NAAQS, because the decision to revise was discretionary. The holding of the Second Circuit allows a plaintiff to shop for a convenient forum to force the Administrator to make a decision regarding the revision of the NAAQS within the statutory time limits set out in § 109(d). Challenges to the Administrator's decision itself, however, will have to be filed in Court of Appeals for the District of Columbia Circuit.

5. In 1991, the American Lung Association, and others, filed a lawsuit challenging EPA's failure to review the ozone standard as required by § 109(d).

American Lung Association v. EPA, No. 91-4114, (E.D. N.Y.). A settlement agreement, approved by the Court on February 28, 1992, requires EPA to publish a proposal in the Federal Register by August 1, 1992 to retain or revise the current ozone standards. Final rules must be promulgated by March 1, 1993. Robert Abrams, Attorney General for the State of New York, which was a party to the lawsuit, claimed in a post-settlement press statement that the evidence "clearly shows that a tougher [ozone] standard is needed." 22 ENV. REP. (Current Developments) 2461 (March 6, 1992). If the evidence was clear, why would the plaintiffs settle for a rulemaking where the agency may decide to retain its existing standard?

6. Currently, there are six "criteria" pollutants for which national ambient air quality standards have been established. They are: sulfur dioxide (40 CFR §§ 50.4 - 50.5); particulates (40 CFR §§ 50.6 - 50.7); carbon monoxide (40 CFR § 50.8); ozone (40 CFR § 50.9); nitrogen dioxide (40 CFR § 50.11); and lead (40 CFR § 50.12). Ozone was formerly regulated within the broader category of "photochemical oxidants." Hydrocarbons had been listed separately, but are now controlled through the ozone standard because their health impact results from ozone formation which is caused by the mixture of nitrous oxides and hydrocarbons in sunlight.

7. What does it mean to say that an area or region is violating an ambient air quality standard? The answer will depend upon the standard involved but the question is best understood by illustration. The primary NAAQS for sulfur dioxide has been set at 80 $\mu g/m^3$ annual arithmetic mean, and 365 $\mu g/m^3$ maximum 24-hour concentration, the latter standard not to be exceeded more than once per year. 40 CFR § 50.4 (1985). Air quality monitors sample air throughout all regions of the country. Using models and the information from these monitors, all violations of the NAAQS can theoretically be determined. A violation of the primary SO_2 standard exists whenever: (1) the annual arithmetic mean (computed by dividing the sum of all samples, and adjusted for the time period of the sample by the number of samples) exceeds 80 $\mu g/m^3$, or (2) where more than one 24-hour air sample exceeds 365 $\mu g/m^3$.

8. EPA's eventual listing of lead as a "criteria" pollutant did not end the controversy. The *Lead Industries* case which follows offers the reader a glimpse at the complexity behind government decisions under the Clean Air Act.

LEAD INDUSTRIES ASSOCIATION V. EPA

647 F.2d 1130 (D.C. Cir. 1980), *cert. denied*, 449 U.S. 1042 (1980)

J. SKELLY WRIGHT, Chief Judge:

This is the third occasion on which this court has been asked to review Environmental Protection Agency (EPA or Agency) regulations promulgated under authority of the Clean Air Act, as amended, 42 U.S.C. § 7401 *et seq.* (Supp. I 1977) (the Act), and specifically designed to deal with the health problems associated with lead in the ambient air. In *Amoco Oil Co. v. EPA*, 501 F.2d 722 (D.C.Cir.1974), we upheld regulations prohibiting the sale of leaded gasoline for use in automobiles equipped with "catalytic converter" devices for controlling exhaust emissions and requiring widespread retail marketing of at least one grade of unleaded gasoline. And in Ethyl Corp. v. EPA, 541 F.2d 1 (D.C.Cir.) (*en banc*), *cert. denied*, 426 U.S. 941 (1976), we affirmed an EPA order requiring annual reductions in the lead content of leaded gasoline. In the present consolidated cases we are asked to review EPA regulations establishing national ambient air quality standards for lead. These air quality standards prescribe the maximum concentrations of lead that will be permitted in the air of our country. We must decide whether EPA's Administrator acted within the scope of his statutory authority in promulgating these regulations and, if so, whether the evidence adduced at the rulemaking proceeding supports his final determinations. In addition, we must examine the petitioners' claims that infirmities in the procedures employed by EPA in this rulemaking warrant remand of the regulations to the Agency. Petitioners are the Lead Industry Association, Inc. (LIA), a nonprofit trade association whose 78 members include most of the country's producers and commercial consumers of lead (No. 78-2201), and St. Joe Minerals Corporation (St. Joe) (No. 78-2220).

I. BACKGROUND

Man's ability to alter his environment to achieve perceived goals has undoubtedly made an enormous contribution to his economic and social well-being. This undertaking is not, however, without attendant costs. One of these costs is the toll that these alterations may exact on the environment itself and, in turn, the dangers that this may pose for the public health and welfare. Unfortunately, man's ability to alter the environment often far outstrips his ability to foresee with any degree of certainty what untoward effects these changes may bring. The issues presented by these cases illustrate this sad fact.

Lead's environmental significance is a consequence of both its abundance and its utility. The relative abundance of lead in the earth's crust makes it unique among the toxic heavy metals. EPA's "Air Quality Criteria For Lead". And centuries of mining and smelting, and the use of lead in a variety of human activities, have increased the natural background concentration of lead in the environment. But it is only since the industrial age and the use of lead as a gasoline additive that lead has become pervasive. Today lead is ubiquitous. It is found in almost every medium with which we come into contact — food, water, air, soil, dust, and paint, each of which represents a potential pathway for human lead exposure through ingestion or inhalation. The widespread presence of this toxic metal in the environment poses a significant health risk. Lead is a poison which has no known beneficial function in the body, but when present in the body in sufficient concentrations lead attacks the blood, kidneys, and central nervous and other systems and can cause anemia, kidney damage, severe brain damage, and death.

There are three major sources of the body's lead burden. In most people the largest source is diet. Another source, particularly in children, is the habit of placing hands, objects, and materials in the mouth. The third major source is the ambient air; airborne lead is deposited in the respiratory tract as a person breathes lead-contaminated air and is subsequently absorbed into the bloodstream. Once the lead is in the bloodstream its source is immaterial; total lead intake is the sum of the intake from all these sources. The multiplicity of sources of lead intake increases the difficulty of controlling human lead exposure. Much of the protective activity in this area has focused on limiting the amount of lead in the ambient air, the most controllable source of lead exposure. In this country, by far the largest source of lead emissions accounting for 88 percent of total lead emissions according to EPA estimates is the exhaust of motor vehicles powered by gasoline containing lead additives. Another eight percent of lead emissions is the result of solid waste incineration and combustion of waste oil. Industrial facilities account for the remaining four percent of total lead emissions.

Acting pursuant to authority conferred on it by Congress in the Clean Air Act, as amended, 42 U.S.C. 7401 *et seq.*, EPA has been involved in regulation of lead emissions almost since the Agency's inception. Its initial approach to controlling the amount of lead in the ambient air was to limit lead emissions from automobiles by restricting the amount of lead in gasoline. To this end it promulgated the regulations which we upheld in *Amoco Oil Corp. v. EPA*, *supra*, and *Ethyl Corp. v. EPA*, *supra*. However, in 1975 the Natural Resources Defense Council, Inc. (NRDC), and others brought suit against EPA claiming that the Agency was required by Section 108 of the Clean Air Act, 42 U.S.C. § 7408, to list lead as a pollutant for which an air quality criteria document would be prepared, and for which national ambient air quality standards should be promulgated under Section 109 of the Act, 42 U.S.C. § 7409. The District Court agreed with NRDC and directed the Administrator to list lead as a pollutant under Section 108 of the Act, by March 31, 1976. *Natural Resources Defense Council, Inc. v. Train*, 411 F.Supp. 864 (S.D.N.Y.1976). The Second Circuit affirmed, 545 F.2d 320 (2d Cir. 1976), and EPA initiated the proceedings outlined in the statute which are under review here.

II. THE STATUTORY SCHEME

The first step toward establishing national ambient air quality standards for a particular pollutant is its addition to a list, compiled by EPA's Administrator, of pollutants that cause or contribute to air pollution "which may reasonably be anticipated to endanger public health or welfare[.]" Section 108(a)(1), 42 U.S.C. § 7408(a)(1). Within twelve months of the listing of a pollutant under Section 108(a) the Administrator must issue "air quality criteria" for the pollutant. Section 108 makes it clear that the term "air quality criteria" means something different from the conventional meaning of "criterion"; such "criteria" do not constitute "standards" or "guidelines," but rather refer to a document to be prepared by EPA which is to provide the scientific basis for promulgation of air quality standards for the pollutant. This criteria document must "accurately reflect the latest scientific knowledge useful in indicating the kind and extent of all identifiable effects on public health or welfare which may be expected from the presence of such pollutant in the ambient air, in varying quantities." Section 108(a)(2), 42 U.S.C. § 7408(a)(2).

At the same time as he issues air quality criteria for a pollutant, the Administrator must also publish proposed national primary and secondary air quality standards for the pollutant. Section 109(a)(2), 42 U.S.C. § 7409(a)(2). National primary ambient air quality standards are standards "the attainment and maintenance of which in the judgment of the Administrator, based on such criteria and allowing an adequate margin of safety, are requisite to protect the public health." Section 109(b)(1), 42 U.S.C. § 7409(b)(1). Secondary air quality standards "specify a level of air quality the attainment and maintenance of which in the judgment of the Administrator, based on such criteria, is requisite to protect the public welfare from any known or anticipated adverse effects associated with the presence of such air pollutant in the ambient air." Section 109(b)(2), 42 U.S.C. § 7409(b)(2). Effects on "the public welfare" include "effects on soils, water, crops, vegetation, manmade materials, animals, wildlife, weather, visibility, and climate, damage to and deterioration of property, and hazards to transportation, as well as effects on economic values and on personal comfort and well-being." Section 302(h), 42 U.S.C. § 7602(h). The Administrator is required to submit the proposed air quality standards for public comment in a rulemaking proceeding, the procedure for which is prescribed by Section 307(d) of the Act, 42 U.S.C. § 7607(d).

Within six months of publication of the proposed standards the Administrator must promulgate final primary and secondary ambient air quality standards for the pollutant. Section 307(d)(10), 42 U.S.C. § 7607(d)(10). Once EPA has promulgated national ambient air quality standards, responsibility under the Act shifts from the federal government to the states. Within nine months of promulgation of the standards each state must prepare and submit to EPA for approval a state implementation plan. Section 110(a)(1), 42 U.S.C. § 7410(a) (1). These state implementation plans must contain emission limitations and all other measures necessary to attain the primary standards "as expeditiously as practicable," but no later than three years after EPA approval of the plan, and to attain the secondary standards within a reasonable period of time. Section 110(a)(2)(A) & (B), 42 U.S.C. § 7410(a)(2)(A) & (B). The Administrator is authorized to extend the deadline for attainment of the primary air quality standards by two years, but thereafter it must be met. Section 110(e), 42 U.S.C. § 7410(e).

III. THE LEAD STANDARDS RULE MAKING PROCEEDINGS

As required by statute, EPA's first step toward promulgating air quality standards for lead was to prepare a criteria document. The Lead Criteria Document was the culmination of a process of rigorous scientific and public review, and thus is a comprehensive and thoughtful analysis of the most current scientific information on the subject. The Lead Criteria Document went through three major drafts, and three separate reviews, including public meetings by the Subcommittee on Scientific Criteria for Environmental Lead of EPA's Science Advisory Board (SAB Lead Subcommittee). The Agency reviewed over 280 public comments, most of a sophisticated scientific nature, before it issued the final Criteria Document. Members of the public, industry (including the petitioners in these cases), environmental groups, the scientific community, and state and federal government agencies actively participated in the review of the drafts. Notice of the meetings of the SAB Lead Subcommittee was published in the *Federal Register*, and the drafts of the Criteria Document which were to be reviewed were available before the meetings. A formal record and a transcript of the proceedings were kept, and a review of the transcript shows that scientists with differing views could and did exchange ideas with each other as well as agency staff, and that all were questioned by the members of the Subcommittee.

A. *The Lead Criteria Document*

EPA released its "Air Quality Criteria For Lead" on December 14, 1977. 42 Fed.Reg. 63076. The document was "prepared to reflect the current state of knowledge about lead specifically, those issues that are most relevant to establishing the objective scientific data base that will be used to recommend an air quality standard for lead that will adequately safeguard the public health." Accordingly, the Criteria Document examined a large number of issues raised by the problem of lead in the environment. One of these was the effects of lead exposure on human health. The Criteria Document concluded that, among the major organ systems, the hematopoietic (blood-forming) and neurological systems are the areas of prime concern.

* * *

The Criteria Document also examined other more subtle effects on the blood-forming system, associated with lower levels of lead exposure. The most pertinent of these "subclinical" effects for purposes of these cases is lead-related elevation of erythrocyte protoporphyrin (EP elevation). According to the Criteria Document, this phenomenon must, for a number of reasons, be regarded as an indication of an impairment of human health.

* * *

B. *The Proposed Standards*

Simultaneously with the publication of the Lead Criteria Document on December 14, 1977, the Administrator proposed a national primary ambient air quality standard for lead of 1.5 μg Pb/m^3 monthly average. 42 Fed.Reg. 63076. He also proposed that the secondary air quality standard be set at the same level as the primary standard because the welfare effects associated with lead exposure did not warrant imposition of a stricter standard. 42 Fed.Reg. 63081-63082. In the preamble to the proposed standards the Administrator explained the analysis EPA had employed in setting the standards.

The Administrator first pointed out that a number of factors complicate the task of setting air quality standards which will protect the population from the adverse health effects of lead exposure. First, some sub-groups within the population have a greater potential for, or are more susceptible to the effects of, lead exposure. *Id.* at 63077. Second, there are a variety of adverse health effects associated with various levels of lead exposure. *Id.* Third, the variability of individual responses to lead exposure, even within particular sub-groups of the population, would produce a range of blood lead levels at any given air lead level. *Id.* at 63079. Fourth, airborne lead is only one of a number of sources of lead exposure and the relative contribution from each source is difficult to quantify. *Id.* at 63080. Finally, the relationship between air lead exposure and blood lead levels is a complex one. *Id.* at 63079.

In response to the first problem the Administrator began by noting that protection of the most sensitive groups within the population had to be a major consideration in determining the level at which the air quality standards should be set. And he determined that children between the ages of 1 and 5 years are most sensitive to the effects of lead exposure both because the hematologic and neurologic effects associated with lead exposure occur in children at lower threshold levels than in adults, and because the habit of placing hands and other objects in the mouth subjects them to a greater risk of exposure. *Id.* at 63077-63078. Next, the Administrator examined the various health effects of lead exposure and proposed that EP elevation should be considered the first adverse health effect of lead exposure because it indicates an impairment of cellular functions, and should be the pivotal health effect on which the lead standards are based. *Id.* at 63078.

* * *

[T]o address the problem of variable responses to lead exposure, the Administrator selected 15 μg Pb/dl, the lowest reported threshold blood lead level for EP elevation in children, as the target mean population blood lead level. He reasoned that setting the target mean population blood lead level at the lowest reported threshold blood lead level for EP elevation would ensure that most of the target population would be kept below blood lead levels at which adverse health effects occur. *Id.* at 63078.

* * *

Having selected a target mean population blood lead level, the Administrator's next step was to allow for the multiplicity of sources of lead exposure. He thus had to estimate the amount of blood lead that should be attributed to non-air sources. The

Administrator admitted that any amount he selected could be no more than a theoretical national average, and on the basis of the evidence available he proposed that the lead standards should be based on the general assumption that 12 μg Pb/dl of blood lead should be attributed to non-air sources. *Id.* at 63080-63081. Given the target mean population blood lead level of 15 μg Pb/dl and the assumed contribution from non-air sources of 12 μg Pb/dl, the maximum allowable contribution from ambient air is 3 μg Pb/dl. The final step in his analysis was to determine what air lead level would prevent the ambient air contribution to blood lead levels from exceeding 3 μg Pb/dl. This step required determining the relationship between air lead exposure and blood lead levels, i.e., the air lead/blood lead ratio. On the basis of the information in the Criteria Document, the Administrator selected a ratio of 1:2 as appropriate for calculating the effect of air lead exposure on blood lead levels in children. *Id.* at 63079.

Thereafter, calculation of the air quality standard was a mathematical exercise as shown in the following table:

1.	Target mean blood lead level	15 *μg Pb/dl*
2.	Assumed non-air contribution	-12 *μg Pb/dl*
3.	Allowable air contribution	= 3 *μg Pb/dl*
4.	Permissible air lead concentration given assumed air lead/blood lead ratio	

$$3\ \mu g\ Pb/dl \times \frac{1\ \mu g\ Pb/m^3\ air}{2\ \mu g\ Pb/dl\ blood} = 1.5\ \mu g\ Pb/m^3$$

The Administrator concluded, on the basis of available information, that the averaging period for the lead standard should be a calendar month. *Id.* at 63081.

C. *Public Comments*

The public comment period ran from December 14, 1977 to March 17, 1978, and public hearings on the proposed standards were held on February 15 and 16, 1978. 43 Fed.Reg. 46246. The comments on the proposed standards were sharply divided. The comments submitted by the lead industry and its experts uniformly opposed the proposed standards, and many endorsed a standard of 5 μg Pb/m³, the standard proposed in the discredited first draft of the Criteria Document, ... as adequate to protect the public health. 43 Fed.Reg. 46248. On the other hand, environmental groups, medical experts, and state, local, and federal agencies either endorsed the proposed standards or called for even stricter standards. *Id.* None of the comments seriously questioned the selection of children between the ages of 1 and 5 years as the target population group, or the estimate of a contribution from non-air sources of 12 μg Pb/dl. The major areas of controversy were the Administrator's choice of EP elevation as the pivotal adverse health effect and his conclusion that the threshold blood lead level for EP elevation in children is 15 μg Pb/dl, the selection of an appropriate air lead/blood lead ratio, the appropriate allowance for an adequate margin of safety, and the averaging time period for the standards. *Id.*

* * *

D. *The Final Air Quality Standards for Lead*

The Administrator promulgated the final air quality standards on October 5, 1978, prescribing national primary and secondary ambient air quality standards for lead of 1.5 $\mu g\ Pb/m^3$, averaged over a calendar quarter. 43 Fed.Reg. 46246. Although the final standards were the same as the proposed standards (with the exception of the change in the averaging period from 30 to 90 days), the Administrator arrived at the final standards through somewhat different analysis. The preamble to the final standards reveals that the comments on the proposed standards had led the Administrator to reconsider his analysis. In particular, he seemed to feel that legitimate questions had been raised concerning the health significance of the early stages of EP elevation and about the threshold blood lead level for this condition. 43 Fed.Reg. 46248, 46253. The Administrator's reexamination focused on two key questions: (1) What is the maximum safe individual blood lead level for children? and (2) what proportion of the target population should be kept below this blood lead level? *Id.* at 46249, 46252- 46253. Addressing the first issue required a review of the health effects of lead exposure discussed in the Criteria Document. The Administrator concluded that, although EP elevation beginning at blood lead levels of 15-20 μg Pb/dl is potentially adverse to the health of children, only when blood lead concentration reaches a level of 30 μg Pb/dl is this effect significant enough to be considered adverse to health. *Id.* at 46253. Accordingly, he selected 30 μg Pb/dl as the maximum safe individual blood lead level for children. *Id.*

* * *

Having determined the maximum safe individual blood lead level for the target population, the Administrator next focused on the question of what percentage of children between the ages of 1 and 5 years the standard should attempt to keep below this blood lead level. According to the 1970 census, there are approximately 20 million children under the age of 5 years in the United States, 12 million of them in urban areas and 5 million in inner cities where lead exposure may be especially high. The Administrator concluded that in order to provide an adequate margin of safety, and to protect special high risk sub-groups, the standards should aim at keeping 99.5% of the target population below the maximum safe individual blood lead level of 30 μg Pb/dl. *Id.* at 46253, 46255. The next step in the analysis was to determine what target mean population blood lead level would ensure that 99.5% of the children below the age of 5 years would be kept below the maximum safe individual blood lead level of 30 μg Pb/dl. Using the lognormal statistical technique he had alluded to in the proposed standards, he calculated that a target mean population blood lead level of 15 μg Pb/dl (the same number as in the proposed standards, but arrived at through different analysis), would accomplish this task. *Id.* at 46253, 46254. Thereafter, the Administrator used the same estimate of the contribution from non-air sources, 12 μg Pb/dl, and the same air lead/blood lead ratio, 1:2, that he had used in calculating the proposed standards, to compute the final ambient air quality standards for lead. The result was an ambient air quality standard of 1.5 μg Pb/m 3, the same as the proposed standard. *Id.* at 46254. The Administrator did, however, change the averaging period for the standards from one calendar month to one calendar quarter, id. at 46255, because he felt that this change would significantly improve the validity of the data to be used in monitoring the progress toward attainment of the standards without rendering the standards less protective.

* * *

V. STATUTORY AUTHORITY

The petitioners' first claim is that the Administrator exceeded his authority under the statute by promulgating a primary air quality standard for lead which is more stringent than is necessary to protect the public against "sub-clinical" effects which are not harmful to health. According to petitioners, Congress only authorized the Administrator to set primary air quality standards that are aimed at protecting the public against health effects which are known to be clearly harmful. They argue that Congress so limited the Administrator's authority because it was concerned that excessively stringent air quality standards could cause massive economic dislocation.

In developing this argument St. Joe contends that EPA erred by refusing to consider the issues of economic and technological feasibility in setting the air quality standards for lead. St. Joe's claim that the Administrator should have considered these issues is based on the statutory provision directing him to allow an "adequate margin of safety" in setting primary air quality standards. In St. Joe's view, the Administrator must consider the economic impact of the proposed standard on industry and the technological feasibility of compliance by emission sources in determining the appropriate allowance for a margin of safety. St. Joe argues that the Administrator abused his discretion by refusing to consider these factors in determining the appropriate margins of safety for the lead standards, and maintains that the lead air quality standards will have a disastrous economic impact on industrial sources of lead emissions.

This argument is totally without merit. St. Joe is unable to point to anything in either the language of the Act or its legislative history that offers any support for its claim that Congress, by specifying that the Administrator is to allow an "adequate margin of safety" in setting primary air quality standards, thereby required the Administrator to consider economic or technological feasibility. To the contrary, the statute and its legislative history make clear that economic considerations play no part in the promulgation of ambient air quality standards under Section 109.

Where Congress intended the Administrator to be concerned about economic and technological feasibility, it expressly so provided. For example, Section 111 of the Act, 42 U.S.C. § 7411, directs the Administrator to consider economic and technological feasibility in establishing standards of performance for new stationary sources of air pollution based on the best available control technology. *See Nat'l Asphalt Pavement Ass'n v. Train, supra,* 539 F2d 775; S.Rep. No.91-1196, 91st Cong., 2d Sess. 416 (1970). In contrast, Section 109(b) speaks only of protecting the public health and welfare. Nothing in its language suggests that the Administrator is to consider economic or technological feasibility in setting ambient air quality standards.

* * *

VI. HEALTH BASIS FOR THE LEAD STANDARDS

LIA does not question a number of the steps in the Administrator's analysis. It does not disagree with his selection of children between the ages of one and five years as the target population, or the decision to set a standard that would keep 99.5 percent of the children below the maximum safe individual blood lead level. In addition, LIA does not challenge the Administrator's suggestion that the standards should be based on an assumption that non-air sources contribute 12 μg Pb/dl to blood lead levels. LIA does, however, challenge other key elements in the Administrator's analysis.

A. *Maximum Safe Individual Blood Lead Level*

LIA attacks the Administrator's determination that 30 μg Pb/dl should be considered the maximum safe individual blood lead level for children, maintaining that there is no evidence in the record indicating that children suffer any health effects that can be considered adverse at this blood lead level. As previously noted, the Administrator's selection was based on his finding that EP elevation at 30 μg Pb/dl is the first adverse health effect of lead exposure, and his determination that a maximum safe individual blood lead level of 30 μg Pb/dl will allow an adequate margin of safety in protecting children against the more serious effects of lead exposure-anemia, symptoms of which appear at blood lead levels of 40 μg Pb/dl and central nervous system deficits which begin to occur at blood lead levels of 50 μg Pb/dl.

LIA challenges each of these findings. First, it contends that nothing in the record supports the suggestion that EP elevation at 30 μg Pb/dl is harmful to health, arguing that EP elevation is a mere "subclinical effect" — a biological response to lead exposure — which is without health significance, and noting that a number of its experts brought this matter to EPA's attention in their comments on the proposed standards. In LIA's view, the Administrator did not explain precisely how impairment of heme synthesis at blood lead levels of 30 μg Pb/dl adversely affects the health of children. Second, LIA challenges the Administrator's determination that a maximum safe individual blood lead level of 30 μg Pb/dl is justified by the need to allow an adequate margin of safety in protecting children against anemia and central nervous system deficits. It maintains that the evidence in the record does not support the Administrator's conclusion that the blood lead threshold for the symptoms of anemia in children is 40 μg Pb/dl. LIA claims that this error was brought to the Administrator's attention by comments on the proposed standard, but that he failed to respond to these comments, thereby violating the statutory provision requiring him to respond to "significant comments, criticisms, and new data submitted . . . during the comment period." Third, LIA contends that the preamble to the final regulations does not state the basis for the Administrator's finding that central nervous system deficits occur in children at blood lead levels of 50 μg Pb/dl, thereby precluding this court from being able to test the soundness of this determination. Finally, LIA argues that even if it were to concede that EPA's conclusions about the blood lead thresholds for anemia and central nervous system deficits are correct, there is still no explanation of why the Administrator concluded that a maximum individual safe blood level of 30 μg Pb/dl — rather than 35 μg Pb/dl, for example — is necessary to provide an adequate margin of safety against these effects.

Our review of the record persuades us that there is adequate support for each of the Administrator's conclusions about the health effects of lead exposure and, consequently, that LIA's challenges to the evidentiary support for these findings must be rejected. Under the statutory scheme enacted by Congress, the Criteria Document prepared with respect to each pollutant is to provide the scientific basis for promulgation of air quality standards for the pollutant. We have already noted that the Lead Criteria Document was the product of a process that allowed the rigorous scientific and public review that are essential to the preparation of a document "accurately reflect[ing] the latest scientific knowledge useful in indicating the kind and extent of all identifiable effects [of lead exposure] on [the] public health . . . ." In our view, the Criteria Document provides ample support for the Administrator's findings.

The Criteria Document concluded that EP elevation, which begins in children at blood levels of 15-20 μg Pb/dl, is one of the more significant effects of low level lead exposure because it indicates that lead has already begun to affect basic biological functions in the body.

* * *

Relying on the Criteria Document's discussion, as well as other evidence in the record, the Administrator made a judgment that for purposes of setting air quality standards for lead, EP elevation at 30 μg Pb/dl must be considered the first adverse effect on the health of children, and he determined that the maximum safe individual blood lead level should be no higher than 30 μg Pb/dl.

The Administrator's judgment echoes the consensus of a group of clinicians who, in 1975, participated in preparation of a statement issued by the Center For Disease Control and endorsed by the American Academy of Pediatrics. These experts agreed that EP elevation "should be used as an indicator of a significant and worrisome body burden of lead." Moreover, the Center For Disease Control uses EP elevation at 30 μg Pb/dl as the cutoff point for detection of lead poisoning in children in its screening programs, a factor that influenced the Administrator's decision. 43 Fed.Reg. 46253.

* * *

To be sure, the Administrator's conclusions were not unchallenged; both LIA and the Administrator are able to point to an impressive array of experts supporting each of their respective positions. However, disagreement among the experts is inevitable when the issues involved are at the "very frontiers of scientific knowledge," and such disagreement does not preclude us from finding that the Administrator's decisions are adequately supported by the evidence in the record.

* * *

B. *Margin of Safety*

Both LIA and St. Joe argue that the Administrator erred by including multiple allowances for margins of safety in his calculation of the lead standards. Petitioners note that the statute directs the Administrator to allow an "adequate margin of safety" in setting primary air quality standards, and they maintain that as a matter of statutory construction the Administrator may not interpret "margin" of safety to mean "margins" of safety. In petitioners' view, the Administrator in fact did just this insofar as he made allowances for margins of safety at several points in his analysis. They argue that margin of safety allowances were reflected in the choice of the maximum safe individual blood lead level for children, in the decision to place 99.5 percent of the target population group below that blood lead level, in the selection of an air lead/blood lead ratio at 1:2, and in the Administrator's estimate of the contribution to blood lead levels that should be attributed to non-air sources. The net result of these multiple allowances for margins of safety, petitioners contend, was a standard far more stringent than is necessary to protect the public health. St. Joe suggests that EPA should have adopted an approach which required decisions on:

1) The maximum level of lead in air which is protective of health; i.e., a threshold beyond which the public health is not protected; and

2) An adequate margin of safety by which the level which is protective of health must be reduced.

EPA responds by maintaining that allowances for a margin of safety were made only at two points in its analysis: in the selection of a maximum safe individual blood lead level of 30 μg Pb/dl and in the decision to set a standard designed to keep 99.5 percent of the target population below that blood lead level. It argues that the statutory requirement of a margin of safety does not mandate adoption of the method suggested by St. Joe. Rather, EPA suggests, it indicates the precautionary orientation the Administrator is to bring to bear on the task of setting air quality standards. How conservative he must be in making particular judgments must, the Agency maintains, depend on such factors as the amount of uncertainty involved, the size of the population affected, and the severity of the effect. EPA argues that petitioners' claims about multiple allowances for margins of safety indicate that they have failed to recognize the difference between providing for a margin of safety and making a scientific judgment in the face of conflicting evidence.

We agree with the Administrator that nothing in the statutory scheme or the legislative history requires him to adopt the margin of safety approach suggested by St. Joe.

* * *

We also agree with the Administrator's suggestion that petitioners have ignored the distinction between scientific judgments based on the available evidence and allowances for margins of safety. In every instance in which the Administrator's judgment on a particular issue differed from petitioners' they attributed his decision to an allowance for a margin of safety. To be sure, there is no bright line that divides these two types of decisions, but they are nonetheless conceptually distinct.

* * *

IX. THE SECONDARY AIR QUALITY STANDARD

The final challenge to the Administrator's actions that we must consider is LIA's objection to his decision to promulgate a national secondary ambient air quality standard for lead of 1.5 μg Pb/m 3, the same level as the primary standard. The Administrator explained that this decision was based on his conclusion that the evidence on the "welfare effects" of lead exposure did not justify promulgation of a secondary standard more stringent than the primary standard. LIA argues that the Administrator had no authority to adopt the secondary standard without making supporting findings showing that the standard is necessary to protect the public welfare. It contends that this court's decision in *Kennecott Copper Corp. v. EPA*, 462 F.2d 846 (D.C.Cir.1972), mandates remand of the secondary standard. In that case we remanded the national secondary air quality standard for sulphur dioxide because the Administrator had failed to "enlighten the court as to the basis on which he reached the . . . standard from the material in the Criteria [Document]." *Id.* at 850. LIA argues that the Administrator should have considered whether the welfare effects of lead exposure would permit him to set a secondary air quality standard higher than the primary standard. Pointing out that the primary standards are supposed to protect public health and that they are based on a 90-day averaging period, LIA argues that it follows that primary standards need be met only in inhabited areas, whereas the secondary standards must also be met in uninhabited areas.

* * *

LIA's complaint is based on a misconception about the reach of the primary standard. As EPA notes, the primary standard must be met in all parts of the country, whether inhabited or uninhabited. Thus by setting the secondary standard at the same level as the primary standard, the Administrator imposed no additional burdens on the industry, and he properly concentrated his attention on whether the welfare effects of lead exposure justified promulgation of a more stringent secondary standard.

* * *

XI. CONCLUSION

The national ambient air quality standards for lead were the culmination of a process of rigorous scientific and public review which permitted a thorough ventilation of the complex scientific and technical issues presented by this rulemaking proceeding. Interested parties were allowed a number of opportunities to participate in exploration and resolution of the issues raised by the standard-setting exercise. EPA, and ultimately the public whose health these air quality standards protect, have benefitted from their contribution. To be sure, even the experts did not always agree about the answers to the questions that were raised. Indeed, they did not always agree on what the relevant questions were. These disagreements underscore the novelty and complexity of the issues that had to be resolved, and both the EPA and the participants in the rulemaking proceeding deserve to be commended for the diligence with which they approached the task of coming to grips with these difficult issues.

We have accorded these cases the most careful consideration, combining as we must careful scrutiny of the evidence in the record with deference to the Administrator's judgments. We conclude that in this rulemaking proceeding the Administrator complied with the substantive and procedural requirements of the Act, and that his decisions are both adequately explained and amply supported by evidence in the record. Accordingly, we reject petitioners' claims of error. The regulations under review herein are

Affirmed.

NOTES

1. One of the many difficulties facing the Administrator in establishing a NAAQS for lead was the fact that airborne lead is only one of several sources of blood lead levels in humans. The Criteria Document for lead showed that high background levels of lead are common, particularly in industrial areas. 42 Fed. Reg. 63,080 (1977). Nonetheless, in setting the NAAQS for lead, the Administrator used a national average of 12 μg Pb/dl (micrograms of lead/deciliter) as the background blood lead level from non-air sources. What problems do you see with using a national average of background contamination to calculate a NAAQS? Should the Administrator have considered regional or urban/rural standards based on differing levels of background contamination? Are such levels authorized by law? *See American Petroleum Institute v. Costle*, 665 F.2d 1176 (D.C. Cir. 1981), *cert. denied, sub nom. City of Houston v. Gorsuch*, 455 U.S. 1176 ("[T]he agency need not tailor national regulations [setting ambient air quality standards for ozone] to fit each region or locale.")

2. In a portion of the opinion omitted from the excerpt which appears in the text, the court flatly rejected plaintiffs' claim that the economic and technological feasibility of meeting the standards must be considered in establishing the NAAQS for lead. 647 F.2d at 1148-1151. *Compare Union Electric Co. v. EPA*, 427 U.S. 246 (1976) *infra* at Chapter Six.

3. Section 109(b)(1) of the Act provides that national *primary* ambient air quality standards must be established at levels requisite to protect the public health, "allowing an adequate margin of safety." Plaintiffs argued that EPA had violated this provision by including in its lead standards "multiple allowances for margins of safety". Were plaintiffs correct in arguing that multiple allowances for margins of safety were used by EPA? Assuming plaintiffs were correct, have they established a violation of the law?

4. Section 109(b)(2) of the Act provides for the adoption of national *secondary* ambient air quality standards at a level sufficient to protect the public welfare. This is defined to encompass "effects on soils, water, crops, vegetation, man-made materials, animals, wildlife, weather, visibility and climate, damage to and deterioration of property, and hazards to transportation, as well as effects on economic values and on personal comfort and well-being." § 302(b). "Secondary" air standards are generally more stringent than primary standards, *see Kennecott Copper Corp. v. EPA*, 462 F.2d 846,847 (D.C. Cir. 1972), though as the *Lead Industries* case demonstrates, they can be the same as the primary standards. Why does the court reject LIA's argument that secondary standards for lead should be less stringent than the primary standards?

5. What confidence do you have in the ability of our judicial system to grapple successfully with complex technical issues of the utmost importance to public health and safety, such as those raised in *Lead Industries*? In this regard see the concurring opinion of Judge Bazelon in *International Harvester Co. v. Ruckelshaus*, 478 F.2d 615 (D.C. Cir. 1973) which concerned the propriety of EPA's tailpipe emission standards for motor vehicles:

> Socrates said that wisdom is the recognition of how much one does not know. I may be wise if that is wisdom, because I recognize that I do not know enough about dynamometer extrapolations, deterioration factor adjustments, and the like to decide whether or not the government's approach to these matters was statistically valid. Therein lies my disagreement with the majority.
>
> The court's opinion today centers on a substantive evaluation of the Administrator's assumptions and methodology. I do not have the technical know-how to agree or disagree with that evaluation — at least on the basis of the present record. My grounds for remanding the case rest upon the Administrator's failure to employ a reasonable decision-making process for so critical and complex a matter. At this time I cannot say to what extent I could undertake an evaluation of the Administrator's findings if they were based on an adequate decisional process.
>
> I cannot believe that Congress intended this court to delve into the substance of the mechanical, statistical, and technological disputes in this case. Senator Cooper, the author of the judicial review provision, stated repeatedly that this court's role would be to "determine the question of due process." Thus the court's proper role is to see to it that the agency provides "a framework for principled decision-making." Such a framework necessarily includes the right of interested parties to confront the agency's decision and the requirement that the agency set forth with clarity the grounds for its rejection of opposing views.
>
> The majority's interpretation of the present statute and the administrative precedents would give us no right to establish these procedural guidelines. Their opinion maintains that the strict deadlines in the Clean Air Act preclude any right to challenge the Administrator until after the decision had been made. It indicates that, since this hearing was "rule-making" rather than "adjudicatory," cross-examination and confrontation are not required under traditional rules of administrative law.

I understand this viewpoint, but I do not share it. I do not think the authors of the Clean Air Act intended to put such strict limits on our review of the Administrator's decision-making process. Further, the interests at stake in this case are too important to be resolved on the basis of traditional administrative labels. We recognized two years ago that environmental litigation represents a "new era" in administrative law. We are dealing here not with an airline's fares or a broadcaster's wattage, but with all humanity's interest in life, health, and a harmonious relationship with the elements of nature.

This "new era" does not mean that courts will dig deeper into the technical intricacies of an agency's decision. It means instead that courts will go further in requiring the agency to establish a decision-making process adequate to protect the interests of all "consumers" of the natural environment. In some situations, traditional rules of "fairness" — designed only to guard the interests of the specific parties to an agency proceeding — will be inadequate to protect these broader interests. This is such a case. Whether or not traditional administrative rules require it, the critical character of this decision requires at the least a carefully limited right of cross-examination at the hearing and an opportunity to challenge the assumptions and methodology underlying the decision.

* * *

My brethren and I are reaching for the same end — a "reasoned decision" — through different means. They would have us examine the substance of the decision before us. There are some areas of administrative law — involving issues of liberty and individual rights — where judges are on a firm ground in undertaking a substantive review of agency action. But in cases of great technological complexity, the best way for courts to guard against unreasonable or erroneous administrative decisions is not for the judges themselves to scrutinize the technical merits of each decision. Rather, it is to establish a decision-making process which assures a reasoned decision that can be held up to the scrutiny of the scientific community and the public. "[T]he best test of truth is the power of the thought to get itself accepted in the competition of the market." If we were to require procedures in this case that open the administrator's decision to challenge and force him to respond, we could rely on an informed "market" rather than on our own groping in the dark to test the validity of that decision.

* * *

6. Do you agree with Judge Bazelon that the courts should emphasize procedure rather than substance in their review of complex agency rules? In this regard, *see Vermont Yankee Nuclear Power Corp. v. Natural Resources Defense Council*, 435 U.S. 519 (1978) wherein the Supreme Court held that courts may require no more procedure for rulemaking proceedings than are expressly prescribed by law.

7. Should a special "science court" be impaneled to hear cases of a highly technical nature? *See* Kantrowitz, *Controlling Technology Democratically*, 63 AM. SCIENTIST 505 (1975). *See also* Yellin, *Science, Technology, and Administrative Government: Institutional Designs for Environmental Decisionmaking*, 92 YALE L.J. 1300 (1983); Carter, *Separatism and Skepticism*, 92 YALE L.J. 1334 (1983).

8. Under the Clean Air Act, states are given the primary responsibility for achieving the NAAQS promulgated by the Administrator. Consequently, each state is required to submit a plan for implementing the NAAQS for particular pollutants. Prior to the 1990 Amendments, states were given nine months after EPA established a new or revised NAAQS for a particular pollutant, to submit their state implementation plan (SIP) revisions. EPA would either approve or reject these plans within four months. *Natural Resources Defense Council v. Thomas*, 705 F. Supp. 1 (D.D.C. 1988), decided before the 1990 Amendments, highlights the difficulties that states had in achieving the NAAQS, and the need for a different approach to air pollution control. The NAAQS for lead was adopted in 1978. By 1982, however, EPA had failed to approve state plans or create federal implementation plans (FIP) for lead as required by the law. NRDC sued and the court ordered the EPA to either approve or reject SIPs for lead by certain dates. *Id* at 2. By 1986, EPA had met several of these deadlines but had failed to make decisions for four major industrial states. NRDC then brought a second action to enforce the court's earlier order. The district court agreed with NRDC that the EPA had failed to meet the deadlines set out in the earlier court order. Nonetheless, the court refused to impose new 90 day deadlines for these four states as suggested by NRDC, and instead gave the EPA until 1989 to approve or reject the SIPs in question. *Id.* at 3.

9. Instead of the nine months allowed by the earlier law, the 1990 Amendments give the states three years (or such shorter time as EPA may prescribe) to submit a revised SIP after a NAAQS is changed. *See* § 110(a)(1). (EPA may extend the period for submission of a plan to achieve secondary standards for no more than 18 months. § 110(b).) On the surface it may seem that Congress has weakened a key component of the Clean Air Act. In fact, however, the 1990 Amendments may simply recognize a welcome shift away from reliance on ambient air quality standards for cleaning our air, and towards more stringent point source controls. Airborne lead is largely the result of automobile combustion from cars using leaded gasoline. The 1990 Amendments ban the sale of leaded gasoline after 1995. The Acid Deposition Program in Title IV of the 1990 Amendments will substantially reduce the amount of SO_2 in the atmosphere. *See* § 401(b). Further, more stringent tailpipe emission standards and cleaner fuel requirements should help to address ozone, NO_X, and CO pollution. *See* § 202(a)(1)(A); 42 U.S.C. § 7521(a)(1)(A). To be sure, SIP requirements remain substantial. Indeed, as will be discussed in the following chapter, they have become much more onerous for states with ozone, carbon monoxide and particulate nonattainment areas. But no longer does the law rely so heavily on the SIP program to achieve its goal of clean air.

10. *Public Notification of Health Hazards.* Section 127 of the Act requires that the state implementation plans incorporate measures "which will be effective to notify the public" of instances during which the NAAQS are violated, and of the health hazards associated therewith. What form should this notice take?

11. Excessive carbon dioxide (CO_2) emissions are the most significant contributor to the global warming problem. *See The Potential Effect of Global Climate Change on the United States* (EPA-230-05-89-050, 1989) which attributes approximately one half of the global warming force currently occurring to CO_2. *Id. at 13.* Carbon dioxide, of course, occurs naturally in the environment; but its existence in quantities well above natural levels now threatens the ecological balance. Much of the excess CO_2 is created by fossil fuel combustion which is ubiquitous in our society. Should EPA regulate CO_2 as a criteria pollutant? What arguments for and against such regulation can be made?

12. EPA first promulgated NAAQS for sulfur dioxides in 1971. In 1984, EPA issued a revised criteria document for sulfur dioxide but did not revise the sulfur dioxide standards. Should EPA be required to revise the NAAQS following revision of the criteria document? Read § 109(a)(2) of the Act and then review the decision in *Environmental Defense Fund v. EPA*, 27 Env. Rep. Cases 2008 (S.D.N.Y. 1988).

6 STATE IMPLEMENTATION PLANS

Before the 1990 Amendments, the state implementation plan, or "SIP", was the principal mechanism under the Act for achieving and maintaining the national ambient air quality standards. Although SIPs remain important, and will become much more complex as a result of the 1990 Amendments, the onus placed on the SIP for achieving ambient air standards has been diminished largely as a result of a plethora of new standards imposed on motor vehicles and fuels and on new and existing stationary sources of air pollution.

As with most other environmental regulatory statutes enacted by Congress, the Clean Air Act employs a "cooperative federalism" scheme of regulation. States are given the first chance to adopt a SIP that comports with the federal law (§ 110(a)(2)) and EPA's detailed regulations. 40 CFR Part 51 (1991). If a state fails to submit a plan to EPA, or if EPA determines that the plan submitted by the state is inadequate, then EPA must develop a plan for that state. § 110(c). Once a state receives EPA approval for its plan the state becomes the primary regulatory authority responsible for administering and enforcing the plan. EPA, however, retains an oversight role with independent enforcement powers.

The state implementation plan process has spawned much litigation, a sampling of which is set forth for the reader in the pages that follow.

A. Approval and Disapproval of State Implementation Plans

STATE OF TEXAS v. EPA
499 F.2d 289 (5th Cir. 1974)

BELL, Circuit Judge:

This case requires that we resolve a major dispute between the Environmental Protection Agency and the State of Texas, several of that state's political subdivisions, and numerous of its corporate citizens. The difficulties arose after the EPA determined that Texas' own air quality implementation plan for control of photochemical oxidant pollution would not assure the attainment of federal ambient air quality standards by May 31, 1975, as required by Section 110 of the Clean Air Act Amendments of 1970. Pursuant to its statutory authority and duty, the EPA disapproved the Texas plan and issued proposed regulations which would, in its opinion, insure attainment of the air quality standard. These regulations adopted the measures contained in Texas' plan, but also imposed additional controls. After holding public hearings, the EPA promulgated final regulations which in some respects reflected concerns and priorities revealed at the hearings, but which nonetheless imposed on five of the six involved air quality control regions (AQCR's) requirements more severe than those in the Texas Plan. *See* 38 Fed.Reg. 30633-51 (Nov. 6, 1973).

* * *

The principal questions presented are whether it was proper for the EPA first to determine that the state's plan was inadequate, and then to promulgate its own plan incorporating more onerous regulations. While a negative answer to the first question would settle the second question, an affirmative answer to the first issue is not similarly dispositive. It is possible that the EPA could properly determine that Texas' plan would not insure attainment of quality standards, but would be arbitrary, capricious, or beyond its authority, in its determination of the nature and quantity of additional control measures. We hold that the EPA determined in a legal and enforceable manner that the state's plan was inadequate. However, we also hold that certain of the EPA's additional regulations are either invalid or must be deferred for further agency consideration.

* * *

THE DISPUTE IN OUTLINE

Determining the measures required to meet air quality standards for photochemical oxidants involves a multi-step analytical process. Initially, of course, it is necessary to set the standards. These however may not be challenged in this proceeding, and petitioners do not openly do so. The second step, since the control strategy for oxidant pollution relies on control of hydrocarbon emissions, is to determine the relationship between the quantity of those emissions and the resultant maximum level of oxidants. This relationship can be expressed as a 'reduction model' which shows, for each current maximum level of oxidant pollution, the percentage reduction in hydrocarbon emissions that is necessary to achieve the oxidant air quality standard.

* * *

[P]etitioners and the EPA differ as to the model which determines how great a reduction in hydrocarbon emissions is necessary, and also as to how effective in achieving the required reductions particular measures will be. In general, the state's calculations indicate that the ambient air quality standards can be attained in each AQCR through its Regulation V, imposing extensive controls on stationary sources, such as factories and refineries. The EPA's position is that the state not only underestimates the reductions required to meet air quality standards, but also overestimates the reductions to be obtained by its plan. Thus the EPA found it necessary in five of the six regions to impose varying degrees of control on transportation-related emissions, and in one of those regions also to prohibit the construction of additional stationary pollution sources.

Finally, petitioners attack various of the EPA's required control measures on grounds more specific than their general claim that the state's calculations are correct and its plan adequate.

* * *

II. HOW GREAT MUST THE REDUCTIONS BE?

Petitioners first challenge to the EPA's analysis concerns its reduction model. As has been stated, this model determines, for each pre-control level of oxidant pollution, how great must be the reduction in hydrocarbon emissions to attain the ambient air quality standard for oxidants. The implementation plan submitted by the state was based on a reduction model requiring, for a significant range of oxidant pollution, considerably lower emission reductions than does the model used by the agency.

As a general matter, the EPA has required that states use the reduction model contained in Appendix J to 40 C.F.R. § 51.14 (1973). However, in submitting its plan Texas utilized a different model on the grounds that it was employing more sophisticated methodology, based not on total hydrocarbons emitted into the atmosphere, but rather upon hydrocarbon emissions which react with nitrogen oxides to form oxidant pollutants. Since it is only reactive hydrocarbons which contribute to oxidant pollution, the Texas approach is theoretically attractive. However, reactive hydrocarbons have not yet been the subject of extensive pollution control study, and the resulting lack of knowledge restricts the usefulness of reactive hydrocarbon pollution control plans. One important unknown is the configuration of the appropriate reduction model.

The EPA concluded that Texas' reduction curve was not supported by technical data, and was based on impermissible assumptions. However, rather than require that Appendix J be applied to the reactive hydrocarbon approach, it determined that the most reasonable model to use in these circumstances would be the "straight rollback" model.

This model is essentially a method of coping with inadequate information by assuming that reductions in oxidant pollutants will be proportional to reductions in reactive hydrocarbon emissions. The agency does not contend that the model is an accurate representation of reality, but it does contend that there is no information to support divergences from it, either in the direction of higher reduction requirements, as with Appendix J and part of the Texas curve, *see* note 14 *infra*, or in the direction of lower reduction requirements, as in the case of most of the Texas curve. Basically the EPA's position is that in the absence of contrary indications, and given the statutory necessity of accepting some model, the simplistic proportional rollback model is a reasonable resolution.

We will first consider the agency decision to reject the model on which Texas based its plan. We will then consider the agency's use of the straight rollback model.

A.

In rejecting Texas' reduction model the agency pointed out defects which have not adequately been answered on this appeal. Initially, for all practical purposes the state supplied no theoretical or empirical support for its novel model. Upon further inquiry, the EPA learned that the state had modified Appendix J by grasping upon the fact that no reliable data exists connecting hydrocarbon emissions and relatively low maximum levels of oxidant pollution (below .13 ppm but above the national standard of .08 ppm). Faced with this same information gap, the EPA had determined, by a method which is not disclosed in the record, that a maximum oxidant level of .08 would be associated with a nonmethane hydrocarbon concentration of .17 ppm. By contrast, the Texas model assumed the appropriate figure to be in the neighborhood of .20 or .21 — the level of hydrocarbons which Appendix J associates with an oxidant pollution level of slightly below .10 ppm. The effect of this assumption, for the four regions below .15 oxidant concentration, was to significantly lower the necessary reduction in hydrocarbon emissions.

* * *

We can summarize the situation confronting the agency when it chose to reject Texas' reduction model. The model was novel, yet unsupported by data, theory, or even meaningful explanations. It purported to be appropriate for nonreactive hydrocarbons, yet was explicitly based on data for nonmethane hydrocarbons. Finally, it was significantly different from the model the EPA derived from the same data, and even if the EPA model was not known to be accurate, it was part of a promulgated regulation which had been subjected to prior public scrutiny and comment. In these circumstances we cannot conclude that the agency's rejection of Texas' model was arbitrary or capricious.

B.

We must now consider the EPA's use of a straight rollback model, which model it acknowledges to be based upon a simplistic assumption rather than experimental data or proven theory. While we are uneasy that such an unreliable construct should be the basis of wide-ranging government action, we do not consider the use of the straight rollback model to be arbitrary and capricious.

The statute requires implementation plans which will insure attainment of the national air quality standards. To design such plans it is necessary to utilize some model relating reductions in antecedent emissions to resulting reductions in pollutant concentrations. In the absence of sophisticated information, the EPA has been forced to rely on crude assumptions. We cannot object, for it is not our role to judge whether the EPA's projections are accurate, but only whether they represent arbitrary or capricious exercises of its authority. Necessity, which has mothered the EPA's invention of this model, also protects it from a judicial insistence on greater reliability.

Further, we think it significant that the straight rollback model is, in an important sense, neutral, in that it establishes as a starting point the commonsensical proposition that pollutants will be reduced proportionally to reductions in their chemical precursors.

III. REDUCTIONS TO BE OBTAINED

The second broad source of controversy between the state and EPA concerns the reduction in hydrocarbon emissions expected from the state's control of stationary sources.

As with the case of the appropriate reduction model, this controversy has its roots in Texas' reactive hydrocarbon approach. The problem arises in determining the reactive component of total hydrocarbon emissions from each emission category. In general, the agency has determined that reactive hydrocarbons constitute a smaller percentage of total stationary source emissions than has the state, and thus that stationary sources are responsible for a smaller percentage of overall reactive emissions. For example, in Region 7 the EPA calculates that 294,000 tons per year of reactive hydrocarbons are emitted from stationary sources, and 106,000 tons per year from mobile sources. This compares with the state's calculations of 481,000 and 99,000, respectively. Translated into percentages, the EPA attributes 73 per cent of total reactive emissions to stationary sources, while the state attributes 83 per cent. The result of the EPA's calculations is that the state's highly effective Regulation V, unaided by transportation-related controls, does not affect a sufficiently large proportion of the total to achieve the 75 per cent overall reduction.

As we did in the case of the reduction model controversy, we will approach the question in two stages. We will first consider the agency's rejection of Texas' calculations, and then consider petitioners' challenges to the calculations actually used by the EPA.

A.

The state's plan, as originally submitted, was quite summary in nature. It simply stated existing and projected reactive hydrocarbon emissions. The only explanation was by way of reference to a study entitled 'Hydrocarbon Control Strategies for the State of Texas,' Document 4 of the record.

* * *

We conclude that the EPA was not arbitrary or capricious when it rejected Texas' chemical processing reactive hydrocarbon inventory. The figures submitted by Texas were not only apparently quite different from those expected by the EPA, but they were unsupported by intelligible explanations or source material.

* * *

We turn now to the issue whether the EPA, having reasonably rejected Texas' inventory calculations, was arbitrary or capricious in its own calculations of the inventories on which it based the promulgated regulations.

B.

Since no studies have inventoried the actual reactive content of specific emission sources in Texas, the EPA determined the reactive component by applying a 'reactivity factor' to total hydrocarbons. The reactivity factor is a number, running from 0 to 1.0, which indicates the degree of reactivity of a source's hydrocarbon emissions. . . .[T]he factors vary widely, both between different types of emission sources and between the EPA's and state's estimates for identical sources. In obtaining its reactivity factors, the EPA looked to "the relationship between reactive and non-reactive components for identical processes and sources in other areas of the country." 38 Fed.Reg. 30634 (Nov. 6, 1973).

* * *

1. The Chemical Processing Reactive Inventory

. . . [T]he EPA applied a reactivity factor of 0.6 to chemical processing emissions. This figure was derived from empirical studies of chemical industries in Los Angeles and Louisiana, studies which yielded factors of .52 and .47 respectively. The EPA used a 20 per cent higher figure, which in this context benefits Texas, to give the state 'every benefit of the doubt' and to account for having eliminated two minor sources of methane from its Region 7 total hydrocarbon inventory.

Petitioners' only specific criticism of the 0.6 figure is that because the emissions from individual chemical plants vary considerably in reactivity, 'it is unjustified to characterize an entire industry by a single reactivity factor.' Even granting that the reactivity factor for particular plants may be quite different from 0.6, we think it not unreasonable for the EPA to adopt that figure on an industry-wide basis. The figure 0.6 represents an average, and accounts for the fact that the individual figures which go into that average may be higher or lower. So long as 0.6 is applied to the sum of total hydrocarbon emissions from a representative array of chemical plants, its use is proper. Noting that petitioners present no empirical or theoretical material which suggests that typical emissions from the Texas chemical industry are substantially more reactive than those in Los Angeles and Louisiana, we conclude that the agency's use of 0.6 was not arbitrary or capricious.

* * *

CLARK, Circuit Judge, with whom BOYLE, District Judge, joins, specially concurring.

I concur without reservation in the entirety of Judge Bell's thoroughgoing, able opinion. The sole purpose of this addendum is to highlight the adverse effects flowing from the legislative mandate that judicial review proceedings be injected into the court system at the appellate level.

No formal hearing has ever been held in this highly technical, factually complex matter. The administrative "record" upon which we had to base our review was comprised of only the sparest of documentation, for it essentially evolved from an act of agency rule-making. To accentuate the problem the agency contracted the services of a private firm for the formulation of most of the rule requirements it ultimately adopted here, so that not even intra-agency background for these actions was available. The writing judge was required to hold both pre and post-argument conferences with counsel for the parties to enable the three of us as a court to comprehend the substance of the issues and conduct a minimally meaningful review.

The subject matter of this action involves the health and welfare of millions of citizens, the continued business vitality of tens of thousands of firms and compliance expenditures costing billions of dollars.

These extensive rights deserve a more orderly process of judicial reflection.

NOTES

1. As the court intimates, the EPA decision-making process on state implementation plans under the Clean Air Act, like the process for adopting NAAQS, is a rulemaking proceeding. The same procedures applicable to the promulgation of NAAQS apply to the promulgation of SIPs (§ 307(d)), although as with the *NRDC* case, these procedures were not adopted until after the decision in *Texas v. EPA*. *See also Buckeye Power, Inc. v. EPA*, 481 F.2d 162 (6th Cir. 1973).

2. Judicial review of EPA's action is governed by the "arbitrary and capricious" standard of review. *Compare* 5 U.S.C. § 706(2) (A)-(D), which applied to pre-1977 cases, *with* § 307(d) (9) adopted in the 1977 Amendments to the Act. Thus, the question before the court was not whether Texas' proposed plan was arbitrary and capricious. Rather, the Court had to ascertain whether it was arbitrary and capricious for EPA to have disapproved of the plan. On the other hand, the adequacy of EPA's plan for Texas was judged against the arbitrary and capricious standard of review. Compare the court's decision in the *Texas* case with the 6th Circuit's decision in *Cincinnati Gas & Electric v. EPA*, 578 F.2d 660 (6th Cir. 1978), *cert. denied*, 439 U.S. 1114 (1979).

3. EPA used a "straight rollback model" to determine the impact of hydrocarbon reductions on photochemical oxidant levels. Texas employed a more sophisticated model although EPA rejected the use of that model on the grounds that its reliability had not been adequately demonstrated. Generally, EPA must allow states to use "equivalent modeling, emission inventory, and planning procedures" unless it determines that the proposed techniques are less effective than those specified by the EPA. § 172(c)(8).

4. The *Texas* case illustrates the complexity and uncertainty involved in designing a program to meet the national ambient air quality standards. How long should EPA wait to determine whether or not a plan is working, and what should it do if it determines that additional controls are necessary? Section 110(a)(2)(H)(ii) requires revision of the SIP whenever EPA determines that the current plan is "substantially inadequate" to achieve the national ambient air quality standards. Does this mean that EPA cannot require revision of a SIP if regular violations of the health-based primary standards are not substantial?

5. In estimating the amount of photochemical oxidants produced by the hydrocarbon emissions from chemical processing facilities, EPA used a 0.6 reactivity factor. This is about 20 percent higher than the reactivity factor found to exist for similar emissions in Los Angeles and Louisiana. How does this higher reactivity factor "benefit" Texas? Consider that Texas had proposed to reduce photochemical oxidants solely through control of stationary sources.

6. EPA's reason for using the higher reactivity factor was to give Texas "every benefit of the doubt". Is it appropriate for EPA to give states the benefit of the doubt when considering a plan that is to keep air pollution below levels necessary to protect the public health? Compare this policy with § 109(b)(1) of the Act which requires EPA to establish primary air quality standards after allowing for an adequate margin of safety.

7. EPA has recently adopted rules defining volatile organic compounds (VOC). 57 Fed. Reg. 3941 (1992). This is the term most commonly used today to describe hydrocarbons which may contribute to ozone pollution. EPA's rules expressly exclude from the definition of VOCs certain organic compounds which have "negligible photochemical reactivity." *Id.* The policy supported by these rules has taken on new significance with the growing concern regarding stratospheric ozone depletion. *See Chapter 11.* Some negligibly reactive VOCs are being considered for use as chlorofluorocarbon substitutes. If these substitutes are regulated through the SIP process, their use might be unnecessarily discouraged.

8. In his concurring opinion, Judge Clark suggests that the procedure used for reaching a decision on the Texas SIP was inadequate. Do you agree? What authority does the court have to require more stringent procedures? *See Vermont Yankee Nuclear Power Corp. v. Natural Resources Defense Council*, 435 U.S. 519 (1978).

9. The concurring opinion also notes that pre- and post-argument conferences were held in this case "to enable [the Court] to comprehend the substance of the issues and conduct a minimally meaningful review". Should review of the agency's action have been limited to the administrative record? *See* § 307(d)(6)(C). Do the judicial conferences in this case invite "post-hoc rationalizations" which were not subject to public review and comment? *Compare Citizens to Preserve Overton Park v. Volpe*, 401 U.S. 402 (1971).

10. Is the Administrator's decision to approve or disapprove a state implementation plan a major federal action significantly affecting the quality of the human environment for which an environmental impact statement is required? *See Buckeye Power Inc. v. EPA*, 481 F.2d 162 (6th Cir. 1973):

> The petitioners contend that the Administrator's approval of the state plans should be held in abeyance until such time as the Administrator files an Environmental Impact Statement pursuant to the National Environmental Policy Act. 42 U.S.C. §§ 4321-4347 (1973 Supp.).

> Essentially, acceptance of this argument would mean that an agency whose sole purpose is the improvement of the environment, would have to file an Environment Impact Statement with itself. *See* Reorganization Plan No. 3 of 1970, 84 Stat. 2086. We are in accord with the Third, Fourth and D.C. Circuit holding that such action on the part of the Administrator is unnecessary.

Id. at 173-74. In 1974, Congress adopted legislation expressly exempting Clean Air Act activities from NEPA. Energy Supply and Environmental Coordination Act, 15 U.S.C. § 793(c)(l).

11. Do federal facilities, such as those operated by the Tennessee Valley Authority, have to comply with state implementation plans? In *Hancock v. Train*, 426 U.S. 167 (1976), the Supreme Court held that the Act's requirement that federal facilities abate air pollution "to the same extent" as any non-governmental entity made such facilities subject to the SIP's emission standards and compliance schedule, but did not authorize the states to impose on federal facilities administrative and enforcement mechanisms such as permits. The Act was amended in 1977 to provide the states with the authority over federal facilities that had been denied them in *Hancock*. § 118.

KENNECOTT COPPER CORPORATION V. TRAIN

526 F.2d 1149 (9th Cir. 1975), *cert. denied*, 425 U.S. 935 (1976)

BROWNING, Circuit Judge:

Kennecott Copper Corporation petitions for review of an order of the Environmental Protection Agency (EPA) rejecting a portion of the State of Nevada's implementation plan under the Clean Air Act relating to control of sulfur dioxide (SO_2), and substituting provisions formulated by EPA. The problem arises from a single source of SO_2 emissions in Nevada-Kennecott's copper smelter at McGill in White Pine County.

EPA based its order upon an interpretation of the Clean Air Act which requires that national air quality standards be met by continuous emission limitations to the maximum extent possible, and that intermittent controls and dispersion systems be used only when continuous emission controls are not economically feasible. This court denied Kennecott's request for a temporary injunction against enforcement of the substitute plan promulgated by EPA but expedited Kennecott's appeal. We affirm EPA's order.

* * *

I.

Section 109 of the Clean Air Act requires EPA to promulgate national primary and secondary air quality standards. Section 110 of the Act, applicable to existing sources of pollutants such as Kennecott's McGill smelter, provides that the states must devise plans to implement, maintain, and enforce these national standards. EPA must approve state implementation plans if they are adopted after reasonable notice and hearing, and meet other specified requirements. EPA must disapprove any state plan that does not comply with the statute, and propose and adopt a plan of its own.

EPA approved the provisions of Nevada's implementation plan relating to control strategy except those involving control of SO_2 at Kennecott's McGill smelter, the sole stationary source of this pollutant in the Nevada Intrastate Air Quality Control Region. Nevada submitted an amended plan. EPA rejected the state's amendments, and proposed, and eventually adopted, a plan of its own.

The amended Nevada plan provided for a 60 percent reduction of SO_2 emissions from the McGill smelter by installation of a plant to convert SO_2 to sulfuric acid. When weather conditions are so adverse that the 60 percent reduction in emissions resulting from operation of the acid plant would not be sufficient to maintain national air quality standards, the Nevada plan provided for reducing the level of production at the smelter.

EPA rejected the Nevada plan on the ground that an 86 percent reduction of SO_2 emissions from the McGill smelter was required to achieve air quality standards. EPA recognized that it was not presently economically feasible to install an acid plant or other constant emission control that would reduce SO_2 emission from the McGill smelter more than the 60 percent contemplated by the Nevada plan. The EPA plan therefore provided that, as an interim measure, Kennecott might use continuous emission reduction technology capable of reducing emissions by 60 percent, together with such other controls (including reducing production and use of a tall stack) as might be needed to maintain national air standards. However, EPA's plan also provided that, until full compliance with national air quality standards is achieved entirely by means of continuous emission reduction, Kennecott must undertake a research program to improve continuous emission control technology, and must adopt such improved technology as it becomes available for use at the McGill smelter on an economically feasible basis.

Kennecott's basic position is that EPA is not authorized to require continuous emission reduction techniques in preference to intermittent controls or other methods for dispersion, or dilution, of pollutants. Kennecott contends that EPA must approve a state implementation plan that provides for any combination of continuous emission controls and alternative control systems devised by the state, so long as the state plan will attain and maintain national air quality standards within the statutory time periods.

This view of the statute underlies Kennecott's opposition to EPA's requirement that Kennecott engage in research to develop and apply constant emission control technology. It is also the principal source of Kennecott's objection to EPA's determination that an 86 percent reduction in SO_2 emissions from the McGill smelter is required to meet national air quality standards. EPA's calculation rests upon measurements made prior to the installation of a new 750-foot tall smokestack at McGill. Kennecott submitted data to EPA indicating that the new tall stack resulted in a 92 percent decrease in ground level SO_2 concentrations. EPA refused permanent credit for this reduction because, in EPA's view, the statute requires use of continuous emission reduction technology, as opposed to dispersion techniques, whenever economically feasible.

* * *

II.

EPA bases the requirement of constant emission controls upon section 110(a)(2)(B) of the Clean Air Act. This subsection provides that EPA shall approve a state implementation plan if "it includes emission limitations, schedules, and timetables for compliance with such limitations, and such other measures *as may be necessary* to insure attainment and maintenance of such primary or secondary standard, including, but not limited to, land-use and transportation controls; . . . " (emphasis added).

EPA reads the phrase "as may be necessary" as modifying only "such other measures," and not "emission limitations." In EPA's view, measures other than emission limitations are therefore permissible only if "necessary" to achieve applicable air quality standards; such "other measures" are not "necessary" if economically feasible emission limitation technology is available.

* * *

In *Natural Resources Defense Council*, the Fifth Circuit held that EPA may approve tall stack dispersion techniques in a state implementation plan "only (1) if it is demonstrated that emission limitation regulations included in the plan are sufficient *standing alone*, without the dispersion strategy, to attain the standards; or (2) if it is demonstrated that emission limitation sufficient to meet the standard is unachievable or infeasible, and that the state has adopted regulations which will attain the maximum degree of emission limitation achievable." 489 F.2d at 410 (emphasis in original). We agree, in general, with the Fifth Circuit's analysis (489 F.2d at 403-09) of the history and contents of the Clean Air Act Amendments of 1970 leading to this conclusion.

In *Big Rivers Electric Corp.*, the Sixth Circuit extended the Fifth Circuit's decision to intermittent emission control systems, holding that section [110(a)(2)(B)] authorizes EPA to reject state plans providing for the use of intermittent emission control systems without a showing that constant emission controls are unavailable. The Sixth Circuit based its conclusion upon the Fifth Circuit's analysis of the Clean Air Act Amendments of 1970, and upon the Supreme Court's discussion of section [110(a)(2)(B)] in *Train v. Natural Resources Defense Council*. *Train* parses section [110(a)(2)(B)] as EPA's interpretation suggests (421 U.S. at 67), and adopts the position that a state plan must include provisions regulating the composition of substances emitted from a given source. 421 U.S. at 78. The Sixth Circuit noted that since composition means "kind and amount," *Train* recognizes that a state plan must limit the amount of a pollutant. 523 F.2d at 21-22.

We agree with the Sixth Circuit that *Train* adds significant support to EPA's interpretation of section [110(a)(2)(B)] as expressing a preference for emission limitations. Intermittent control systems (such as those restricting production, or utilizing less polluting fuels, during periods of adverse weather) do limit the amount of pollutant emitted while such controls are being applied. However, the reliability and enforceability of such controls is questionable; they may not be implemented when they are in fact needed. Moreover, there is no assurance that temporary reductions in emissions resulting from such controls will not be balanced, or even exceeded, by an increase in the amount of pollutant emitted when weather conditions improve and production is increased to make up for prior losses, or more polluting fuels are again used. Thus, intermittent controls, like tall stacks, may only disperse the pollutant rather than reduce it. Tall smokestacks disperse a pollutant through greater quantities of air; intermittent control systems disperse pollutant peaks through longer periods of time. Neither assures a reduction in the quantity of the pollutant eventually emitted. Under section [110(a)(2)(B)], EPA may require that assurance. We therefore agree with the Sixth Circuit that EPA acted within its authority in refusing to accept intermittent controls as adequate compliance with the statute.

* * *

Kennecott spent $4,000,000 to implement the Nevada plan, but suspended further construction on the $30,000,000 project pending completion of this review proceeding. Kennecott states that the McGill smelter will only support the expenditures required by the Nevada plan, and that the smelter must close if Kennecott is required, in addition, to conduct research to devise new constant control technology which would be economically feasible at McGill.

EPA's plan requires the same immediate capital outlay as the Nevada plan with which Kennecott has said it can comply. Contrary to Kennecott's contention, EPA's plan would not expose Kennecott to the risk that it would be required to make further capital investments for the installation of uneconomic continuous emission control systems in the future. As EPA has undertaken to assure Kennecott, under EPA's interpretation of section [110(a)(2)(B)], EPA could not compel Kennecott to install additional emission reduction systems at McGill unless it were economically feasible for Kennecott to do so.

The order of the Environmental Protection Agency is sustained.

NOTES

1. Nevada proposed to require a 60 percent reduction of Kennecott's McGill smelter SO_2 emissions. On those days when a 60 percent reduction would not be sufficient to meet the ambient air quality standards the McGill smelter would be required to reduce production. Why shouldn't a state allow a company to reduce pollution through production cut-backs rather than emission limits? One response offered by the court without explanation is that the "reliability and enforcement ability of such controls is questionable." Why so?

2. Following the old shibboleth "the solution to pollution is dilution," Kennecott built a 750 foot tall smokestack at the McGill smelter. By releasing emissions through its tall stack, Kennecott was able to disperse its pollutants over a wider area and thus more easily avoid violation of the ambient air quality standards. EPA, however, refused Kennecott any credit for the reduction, again arguing that the statute required continuous emissions reductions rather than dispersion techniques. If ambient air quality standards can be achieved through dispersion techniques why shouldn't EPA approve them? One response might be that such dispersion techniques promote acid deposition in areas far from the pollution sources. A study by the Environmental Defense Fund, a national environmental organization, suggests that acid rain in the Wind River Mountains of Western Wyoming may be caused, in substantial part, by two large copper smelters in southern Arizona. *See* 16 ENV. REP. (Current Developments) 742 (Aug. 30, 1985). Indeed, the acid deposition control program established under Title IV of the Act is premised on the theory that SO_2 emissions are a more or less fungible quantity capable of being traded nationwide. *See*, Chapter 9, *infra*. *See also Alabama Power Company v. Costle* discussed at note 7, *infra*.

3. The 1990 Amendments substantially revised § 110(a)(2) to reflect the many significant changes brought about by those amendments. Section 110(a)(2)(B), at issue in the *Kennecott* case, now appears in revised form at § 110(a)(2)(A). The new provision expands the scope of a state's responsibility under a SIP to include various provisions "as may be necessary or appropriate to meet the applicable requirements of this Act." § 110 (a)(2)(A).

4. In 1977, Congress amended the Clean Air Act to address the "tall stack" phenomenon. Section 123 of the Act provides in relevant part as follows:

> (a) The degree of emission limitation required for control of any air pollutant under an applicable implementation plan under this subchapter shall not be affected in any manner by —

> (1) so much of the stack height of any source as exceeds good engineering practice (as determined under regulations promulgated by the Administrator), or
>
> (2) any other dispersion technique. . . .
>
> (b) For the purpose of this section, good engineering practice means, with respect to stack heights, the height necessary to insure that emissions from the stack do not result in excessive concentration of any air pollutant in the immediate vicinity of the source as a result of atmospheric downwash, eddies and wakes which may be created by the source itself, nearby structures or nearby terrain obstacles (as determined by the Administrator). For purposes of this section such height shall not exceed two and a half times the height of such source unless the owner or operator of the source demonstrates, after notice and opportunity for public hearing, to the satisfaction of the Administrator, that a greater height is necessary as provided under the preceding sentence. In no event may the Administrator prohibit any increase in any stack height or restrict in any manner the stack height of any source.

The Act exempts from this section dispersion techniques implemented prior to 1971. Note that "dispersion technique" is defined broadly to encompass "any intermittent or supplemental control of air pollutants varying with atmospheric conditions." § 123(b). In 1982, the Court of Appeals for the District of Columbia Circuit struck down in part the regulations promulgated by EPA to implement this section. *Sierra Club v. EPA*, F.2d 436 (D.C. Cir. 1983). New rules were promulgated in 1985 and again challenged in federal court. For the most part these rules were upheld. *Natural Resources Defense Council v. EPA*, 838 F.2d 1224 (D.C. Cir. 1988), *cert. denied*, 488 U.S. 888 (1988).

5. In *Dow Chemical Co. v. EPA*, 635 F.2d 559 (6th Cir. 1980), *cert. denied*, 452 U.S. 939 (1981), Dow had devised a scheme to use low sulfur coal at its old power plants during those periods when its normal emissions from high sulfur coal would cause violations of the ambient air quality standards. Since Dow adopted this scheme, no recorded instance of a violation had occurred in Midland County, Michigan, where Dow's facilities are located. Nonetheless, EPA refused to approve a revision of the Michigan SIP to allow Midland County to be redesignated an attainment area for SO_2. EPA claimed that to do so would violate § 123. How should the court rule?

6. The *Sierra Club* decision referenced in note 4 provides an informative discussion of the purpose and intent behind § 123:

> In introducing the bill on the Senate floor, Senator Muskie criticized the 1976 guidelines for allowing any use of tall stacks whatsoever in meeting ambient standards: "Far from prohibiting the construction of tall stacks or the use of intermittent controls, the guidelines proved that once minimal emission control requirements are met, polluters are encouraged to substitute unlimited stack height for any further control of emissions." 123 CONG. REC. 18,027 (1977). The mood in the House was the same, *id.* at 16,203 (remarks of Rep. Waxman, a sponsor of the House bill) ("The committee has unequivocally rejected the use of tall stacks and intermittent controls as a final means of compliance with the Clean Air Act's requirements."), and in section 123 of the amended Act Congress banned virtually all reliance on tall stacks or "any other dispersion technique" in achieving compliance with ambient air quality standards, 42 U.S.C. § 7423(a) (Supp. V 1981).

> Congress did not, however, actually prohibit tall stacks or limit their height; in fact section 123 specifically enjoins the EPA Administrator ("the Administrator") from prohibiting any increase in stack height or restricting the height of any stack in any manner. *Id.* § 7423(c). Rather, the law limits the credit that may be obtained for such stack height in determining whether the plant will cause ambient air standards to be violated or increase pollution by too large an increment. The credit system is based on techniques of modeling whereby, via mathematical or small-scale physical demonstrations, a plant's emissions can be assumed to emerge from a certain stack height and then mapped as they fall to earth in order to see their effect on ambient pollution. Thus, section 123 is intended to eliminate any credit a plan might receive for the dispersive effects of a tall stack in the calculation of its emissions limitations, although the stack itself remains in place.
>
> There were essentially three reasons for Congress's refusal to allow reliance on tall stacks and intermittent control measures. First, dispersion techniques do not reduce the amount of pollution in the air, but merely spread it around, exporting it to other areas where it is too late to control the problem, and exposing previously pristine areas to contamination. *See, e.g.,* HOUSE REPORT, *supra* p. 440, at 84-85. Second, the long-range transport of certain pollutants was also linked to the formation of "acid rain," which is precipitation containing acidic derivations of sulfur oxide and nitrogen oxide emissions. Acid rain was thought responsible for reduced soil and water productivity in certain areas, particularly the Northeast and Canada. *See, e.g., id.* at 83-84, 85-86; 123 CONG. REC. 18,026 (1977) (remarks of Sen. Muskie). Third, intermittent control systems, which are dependent on synchronizing plant operation with weather conditions, were thought to be unreliable and virtually impossible to enforce. *See, e.g. id.;* HOUSE REPORT, *supra* p. 440, at 82-83, 87.

719 F.2d 436, 440-441 (D.C. Cir. 1983).

7. When considering whether a source will violate ambient air quality standards should the agency base its estimate of ambient air quality on the assumption that no pre-existing sources constructed after 1970 use stacks in excess of § 123 height limits? In *Alabama Power Company v. Costle*, 636 F.2d 323 (D.C. Cir. 1979) the court answered in the affirmative:

> Industry petitioners read Section 123 as a ban only on administrative consideration of stacks taller than warranted by good engineering practice (GEP) as an alternative to emission limitations. So, industry concedes, when a facility with a tall stack — a term that really covers a too-tall stack — seeks a permit and it must be determined whether that facility's emissions will threaten a violation of a national ambient standard or an increment exceedance, the calculation must be predicated on the false assumption that the stack has only GEP height. EPA interprets the mandate of Section 123 more broadly, declaring that it further requires emissions from *all* preexisting sources with tall stacks that were built after the effective date of the 1970 Act, and hence were not grandfathered, to be modeled as though the emissions proceeded from GEP-height stacks when ascertaining the emission limitations to be imposed on new facilities.

* * *

> The language of Section 123(a), though not necessarily reflective of a conscious resolution of the point in dispute, is certainly more amenable to EPA's construction. The section specifies that the degree of emission limitation required for control of any air pollutant "shall not be affected in *any manner* by . . . so much of the stack height of *any source* as exceeds good engineering practice . . ." The term "emission limitation" includes any requirement imposed on a source by EPA or a state which restricts the quantity, rate, or concentration or air pollutants on a continuous basis. The interpretation urged by industry petitioners contravenes the natural import of these words, as it would have the degree of emission limitation required for a source reduced by the fact that neighboring, preexisting sources with tall stacks disperse their emissions over a broader region, thus resulting in lower concentrations in the immediate vicinity.
>
> The policy of Section 123, as gleaned from examination of its genesis and progress in Congress, is as supportive of EPA's interpretation. This provision originated in the House, and the 1977 House Report dealt extensively with the problem of dispersion techniques. In addition to disapproving tall stacks and other dispersion-dependent techniques in lieu of constant controls, the House Report detailed some independently deleterious effects of tall stacks. Among other things, the report noted that tall stacks, by increasing the transportation of pollutants, may lead to production of derivative pollutants, such as suspended sulfates and nitrates, which pose a greater health hazard that the parent compounds. Tall stacks also transport pollution problems to distant areas and states "where it is too late to control pollution."

Id. at 389-391.

8. The court notes, with approval, that EPA has assured Kennecott that it would not require Kennecott to install additional emission reduction systems at the McGill smelter "unless it were economically feasible . . . to do so." Is EPA's position consistent with the Supreme Court's holding one year later in *Union Electric Co. v. Train*, 427 U.S. 246 (1976), the case that follows?

9. The subsequent history of the McGill smelter controversy is described in *Kennecott Copper Corp. v. Costle*, 572 F.2d 1349 (9th Cir. 1978), *infra* at Chapter 6, section G.

B. Economic and Technological Feasibility

UNION ELECTRIC COMPANY V. EPA
427 U.S. 246 (1976)

Mr. Justice MARSHALL delivered the opinion of the Court.

After the Administrator of the Environmental Protection Agency (EPA) approves a state implementation plan under the Clean Air Act, the plan may be challenged in a court of appeals within 30 days, or after 30 days have run if newly discovered or available information justifies subsequent review. We must decide whether the operator of a regulated emission source, in a petition for review of an EPA-approved state plan filed after the original 30-day appeal period, can raise the claim that it is economically or technologically infeasible to comply with the plan.

* * *

On April 30, 1971, the Administrator promulgated national primary and secondary standards for six air pollutants he found to have an adverse effect on the public health and welfare. 40 CFR pt. 50 (1975). *See* § 108(a). Included among them was sulfur dioxide, at issue here. 40 CFR §§ 50.4-50.5 (1975). After the promulgation of the national standards, the State of Missouri formulated its implementation plan and submitted it for approval. Since sulfur dioxide levels exceeded national primary standards in only one of the State's five air quality regions — the Metropolitan St. Louis Interstate region, 40 CFR § 52.1321 (1975) — the Missouri plan concentrated on a control strategy and regulations to lower emissions in that area. The plan's emission limitations were effective at once, but the State retained authority to grant variances to particular sources that could not immediately comply. Mo.Rev.Stat. § 203.110 (1972). The Administrator approved the plan on May 31, 1972. *See* 40 CFR § 52.1320 *et seq.* (1975).

Petitioner is an electric utility company servicing the St. Louis metropolitan area, large portions of Missouri, and parts of Illinois and Iowa. Its three coal-fired generating plants in the metropolitan St. Louis area are subject to the sulfur dioxide restrictions in the Missouri implementation plan. Petitioner did not seek review of the Administrator's approval of the plan within 30 days, as it was entitled to do under § 307(b)(1) of the Act, but rather applied to the appropriate state and county agencies for variances from the emission limitations affecting its three plants. Petitioner received one-year variances, which could be extended upon reapplication. The variances on two of petitioner's three plants had expired and petitioner was applying for extensions when, on May 31, 1974, the Administrator notified petitioner that sulfur dioxide emissions from its plants violated the emission limitations contained in the Missouri plan. *See* 40 Fed.Reg. 3566 (1975). Shortly thereafter petitioner filed a petition in the Court of Appeals for the Eighth Circuit for review of the Administrator's 1972 approval of the Missouri implementation plan.

Section 307(b)(1) allows petitions for review to be filed in an appropriate court of appeals more than 30 days after the Administrator's approval of an implementation plan only if the petition is "based solely on grounds arising after such 30th day." Petitioner claimed to meet this requirement by asserting, *inter alia*, that various economic and technological difficulties had arisen more than 30 days after the Administrator's approval and that these difficulties made compliance with the emission limitations impossible. The Court of Appeals ordered briefing on the question of its subject-matter jurisdiction to hear the case and, after argument, granted the motions of the EPA and intervenor-respondents, the Attorney General of Missouri and the Missouri Air Conservation Commission, to dismiss the petition for review of lack of jurisdiction.

The court held that "only matters which, if known to the Administrator at the time of his action [in approving a state implementation plan], would justify setting aside that action are properly reviewable after the initial 30 day review period." 8 Cir., 515 F.2d 206, 216 (1975). Since, in the court's view, claims of economic and technological infeasibility could not properly provide a basis for the Administrator's rejecting a plan, such claims could not serve at any time as the basis for a court's overturning an approved plan. Accordingly, insofar as petitioner's claim of newly discovered or available information was grounded on an assertion of economic and technological infeasibility, the court held itself to be without jurisdiction to consider the petition for review, and so dismissed the petition. In so holding the Court of Appeals considered and rejected the contrary or partially contrary holdings of three other Circuits. *Buckeye Power, Inc. v. EPA*, 481 F.2d 162, 168-169 (CA6 1973) (but *see Id.*, at 173); *Appalachian Power Co. v. EPA*, 477 F.2d 495, 505-507 (CA4 1973); *Duquesne Light Co. v. EPA*, 481 F.2d 1 (CA3 1973); *Getty Oil Co. v. Ruckelshaus*, 467 F.2d 349 (CA3 1972), *cert. denied*, 409 U.S. 1125 (1973). [Citations omitted.] On the other hand, the Eighth Circuit found support for its position in the decisions of several other Circuits. *South Terminal Corp. v. EPA*, 504 F.2d 646, 675-676 (CA1 1974); *Texas v. EPA*, 499 F.2d 289, 317 (CA5 1974); *Natural Resources Defense Council v. EPA*, 507 F.2d 905, 914 (CA9 1974). *See also Indiana & Michigan Electric Co. v. EPA*, 509 F.2d 839, 843-845 (CA7 1975). Cf. *Buckeye Power, Inc. v. EPA*, 525 F.2d 80 (CA6 1975). We granted certiorari to resolve the conflict among the Circuits, 423 U.S. 821 (1975), and we now affirm.

II

A.

We reject at the outset petitioner's suggestion that a claim of economic or technological infeasibility may be considered upon a petition for a review based on new information and filed more than 30 days after approval of an implementation plan even if such a claim could not be considered by the Administrator in approving a plan or by a court in reviewing a plan challenged within the original 30-day appeal period. In pertinent part § 307(b)(1) provides:

> A petition for review of the Administrator's action in approving or promulgating any implementation plan under section 110 . . . may be filed only in the United States Court of Appeals for the appropriate circuit. Any such petition shall be filed within 30 days from the date of such promulgation; approval, or action, or after such date if such petition is based solely on grounds arising after such 30th day.

Regardless of when a petition for review is filed under § 307(b)(1), the court is limited to reviewing "the Administrator's action in approving . . . [the] implementation plan . . . ." Accordingly, if new "grounds" are alleged, they must be such that, had they been known at the time the plan was presented to the Administrator for approval, it would have been an abuse of discretion for the Administrator to approve the plan. To hold otherwise would be to transfer a substantial responsibility in administering the Clean Air Act from the Administrator and the state agencies to the federal courts.

B.

Since a reviewing court — regardless of when the petition for review is filed — may consider claims of economic and technological infeasibility only if the Administrator may consider such claims in approving or rejecting a state implementation plan, we must address ourselves to the scope of the Administrator's responsibility. The Administrator's position is that he has no power whatsoever to reject a state implementation plan on the ground that it is economically or technologically infeasible, and we have previously accorded great deference to the Administrator's construction of the Clean Air Act. *See Train v. NRDC*, 421 U.S., at 75. After surveying the relevant provisions of the Clean Air Amendments of 1970 and their legislative history, we agree that Congress intended claims of economic and technological infeasibility to be wholly foreign to the Administrator's consideration of a state implementation plan.

As we have previously recognized, the 1970 Amendments to the Clean Air Act were a drastic remedy to what was perceived as a serious and otherwise uncheckable problem of air pollution. The Amendments place the primary responsibility for formulating pollution control strategies on the States, but nonetheless subject the States to strict minimum compliance requirements. These requirements are of a "technology-forcing character," *Train v. NRDC, supra*, at 91, and are expressly designed to force regulated sources to develop pollution control devices that might at the time appear to be economically or technologically infeasible.

This approach is apparent on the face of § 110(a)(2). The provision sets out eight criteria that an implementation plan must satisfy, and provides that if these criteria are met and if the plan was adopted after reasonable notice and hearing, the Administrator "shall approve" the proposed state plan. The mandatory "shall" makes it quite clear that the Administrator is not to be concerned with factors other than those specified, *Train v. NRDC, supra*, at 71 n. 11, 79, and none of the eight factors appears to permit consideration of technological or economic infeasibility. Nonetheless, if a basis is to be found for allowing the Administrator to consider such claims, it must be among the eight criteria, and so it is here that the argument is focused.

It is suggested that consideration of claims of technological and economic infeasibility is required by the first criterion that the primary air quality standards be met"as expeditiously as practicable but . . . in no case later than three years . . ." and that the secondary air quality standards be met within a "reasonable time." § 110(a)(2)(A). The argument is that what is "practicable" or "reasonable" cannot be determined without assessing whether what is proposed is possible. This argument does not survive analysis.

Section 110(a)(2)(A)'s three-year deadline for achieving primary air quality standards is central to the Amendments' regulatory scheme and, as both the language and the legislative history of the requirement make clear, it leaves no room for claims of technological or economic infeasibility. The 1970 congressional debate on the Amendments centered on whether technology forcing was necessary and desirable in framing and attaining air quality standards sufficient to protect the public health, standards later termed primary standards. The House version of the Amendments was quite moderate in approach, requiring only that health-related standards be met "within a reasonable time." H.R. 17255, 91st Cong., 2d Sess., § 108(c)(1)(C)(i) (1970). The Senate bill, on the other hand, flatly required that, possible or not, health-related standards be met "within three years." S. 4358, 91st Cong., 2d Sess., § 111(a)(2)(A) (1970).

The Senate's stiff requirement was intended to foreclose the claims of emission sources that it would be economically or technologically infeasible for them to achieve emission limitations sufficient to protect the public health within the specified time. As Senator Muskie, manager of the Senate bill, explained to his chamber:

> The first responsibility of Congress is not the making of technological or economic judgments or even to be limited by what is or appears to be technologically or economically feasible. Our responsibility is to establish what the public interest requires to protect the health of persons. This may mean that people and industries will be asked to do what seems to be impossible at the present time. 116 Cong. Rec. 32901-32902 (1970).

See also id., at 32919 (remarks of Sen. Cooper); 33115 (remarks of Sen. Prouty). This position reflected that of the Senate committee:

> In the Committee discussions, considerable concern was expressed regarding the use of the concept of technical feasibility as the basis of

> ambient air standards. The Committee determined that 1) the health of people is more important than the question of whether the early achievement of ambient air quality standards protective of health is technically feasible; and 2) the growth of pollution load in many areas, even with application of available technology, would still be deleterious to public health.
>
> Therefore, the Committee determined that existing sources of pollutants either should meet the standard of the law or be closed down. . . . S.Rep. No. 91-1196, pp. 2-3 (1970).

The Conference Committee and, ultimately, the entire Congress accepted the Senate's three-year mandate for the achievement of primary air quality standards, and the clear import of that decision is that the Administrator must approve a plan that provides for attainment of the primary standards in three years even if attainment does not appear feasible. In rejecting the House's version of reasonableness, however, the conferees strengthened the Senate version. The Conference Committee made clear that the States could not procrastinate until the deadline approached. Rather, the primary standards had to be met in less than three years if possible; they had to be met "as expeditiously as practicable." § 110(a)(2)(A). Whatever room there is for considering claims of infeasibility in the attainment of primary standards must lie in this phrase, which is, of course, relevant only in evaluating those implementation plans that attempt to achieve the primary standard in less than three years.

It is argued that when such a state plan calls for proceeding more rapidly than economics and the available technology appear to allow, the plan must be rejected as not "practicable." Whether this is a correct reading of § 110(a)(2)(A) depends on how that section's "as expeditiously as practicable" phrase is characterized. The Administrator's position is that § 110(a)(2)(A) sets only a minimum standard that the States may exceed in their discretion, so that he has no power to reject an infeasible state plan that surpasses the minimum federal requirements — a plan that reflects a state decision to engage in technology forcing on its own and to proceed more expeditiously than is practicable. On the other hand, petitioner and Amici supporting its position argue that § 110(a)(2)(A) sets a mandatory standard that the States must meet precisely and conclude that the Administrator may reject a plan for being too strict as well as for being too lax. Since the arguments supporting this theory are also made to show that the Administrator must reject a state plan that provides for achieving more than the secondary air quality standards require, we defer consideration of this question in order to outline the development and content of the secondary standards provision of § 110(a)(2)(A).

Secondary air quality standards, those necessary to protect the public welfare, were subject to far less legislative debate than the primary standards. The House version of the Amendments treated welfare-related standards together with health-related standards, and required both to be met "within a reasonable time." H.R. 17255, 91st Cong., 2d Sess., §§ 107(e)(1), 108(c)(1)(C)(i)(1970). The Senate bill, on the other hand, treated health- and welfare-related standards separately and did not require that welfare-related standards be met in any particular time at all, S. 4358, 91st Cong.,2d Sess. §§ 110(a)(3), 110(b), 111(a)(2)(A) (1970), although the Committee Report expressed the desire that they be met "as rapidly as possible." S.Rep. No. 91-1196, p. 11 (1970). The final Amendments also separated welfare-related standards from health-related standards, labeled them secondary air quality standards, and adopted the House's requirement that they be met within a "reasonable time." §§ 109(b),

110(a)(2)(A). Thus, technology forcing is not expressly required in achieving standards to protect the public welfare.

It does not necessarily follow, however, that the Administrator may consider claims of impossibility in assessing a state plan for achieving secondary standards. As with plans designed to achieve primary standards in less than three years, the scope of the Administrator's power to reject a plan depends on whether the State itself may decide to engage in technology forcing and adopt a plan more stringent than federal law demands.[7]

* * *

Section 116 of the Clean Air Act, as added, 84 Stat. 1689, 42 U.S.C. § 1857d-1 (1970 ed., Supp. IV), provides that the States may adopt emission standards stricter than the national standards. *Amici* argue that such standards must be adopted and enforced independently of the EPA-approved state implementation plan. This construction of §§ 110 and 116, however, would not only require the Administrator to expend considerable time and energy determining whether a state plan was precisely tailored to meet the federal standards, but would simultaneously require States desiring stricter standards to enact and enforce two sets of emission standards, one federally approved plan and one stricter state plan. We find no basis in the Amendments for visiting such wasteful burdens upon the States and the Administrator, and so we reject the argument of *Amici*.

We read the "as may be necessary" requirement of § 110(a)(2)(B) to demand only that the implementation plan submitted by the State meet the "minimum conditions" of the Amendments. *Train v. NRDC*, 421 U.S. at 71 n. 11. Beyond that, if a State makes the legislative determination that it desires a particular air quality by a certain date and that it is willing to force technology to attain it or lose a certain industry if attainment is not possible such a determination is fully consistent with the structure and purpose of the Amendments, and § 110(a)(2)(B) provides no basis for the EPA Administrator to object to the determination on the ground of infeasibility. *See Train v. NRDC*, *supra*, at 79.

In sum, we have concluded that claims of economic or technological infeasibility may not be considered by the Administrator in evaluating a state requirement that primary ambient air quality standards be met in the mandatory three years. And, since we further conclude that the States may submit implementation plans more stringent than federal law requires and that the Administrator must approve such plans if they meet the minimum requirements of § 110(a)(2), it follows that the language of § 110(a)(2)(B) provides no basis for the Administrator ever to reject a state implementation plan on the ground that it is economically or technologically infeasible. Accordingly, a court of appeals reviewing an approved plan under § 307(b)(1) cannot set it aside on those grounds, no matter when they are raised.

* * *

Perhaps the most important forum for consideration of claims of economic and technological infeasibility is before the state agency formulating the implementation plan. So long as the national standards are met, the State may select whatever mix of control devices it desires, *Train v. NRDC*, *supra*, at 79, and industries with particular economic

[7] A different question would be presented if the Administrator drafted the plan himself pursuant to § 110(c). *Cf. District of Columbia v. Train*, 521 F.2d 971 (1975); *South Terminal Corp. v. EPA*, 504 F.2d. 646 (CA1 1974). Whether claims of economic or technical infeasibility must be considered by the Administrator in drafting an implementation plan is a question we do not reach.

or technological problems may seek special treatment in the plan itself. Cf. 40 CFR §§ 51.2(b), (d) (1975); S.Rep. No. 91-1196, p. 36 (1970). Moreover, if the industry is not exempted from, or accommodated by, the original plan, it may obtain a variance, as petitioner did in this case; and the variance, if granted after notice and a hearing, may be submitted to the EPA as a revision of the plan. § 110(a)(3)(A). Lastly, an industry denied an exemption from the implementation plan, or denied a subsequent variance, may be able to take its claims of economic or technological infeasibility to the state courts. *See, e.g.*, Mo. Rev. Stat. § 203.130 (1972); Cal. Health & Safety Code § 39506 (West 1973); Pa. Stat. Ann., Tit. 71, § 1710.41 (1962).

While the State has virtually absolute power in allocating emission limitations so long as the national standards are met, if the state plan cannot meet the national standards, the EPA is implicated in any postponement procedure. There are two ways that a State can secure relief from the EPA for individual emission sources, or classes of sources, that cannot meet the national standards. First, if the Governor of the State so requests at the time the original implementation plan is submitted, and if the State provides reasonable interim controls, the Administrator may allow a two-year extension of the three-year deadline for attainment of primary air quality standards if he finds, *inter alia*, that it is technologically infeasible for the source to comply. § 110(e). Second, again upon application of the Governor of the State, the Administrator may allow a one-year postponement of any compliance date in an implementation plan if he finds, *inter alia*, that compliance is technologically infeasible and that "the continued operation of (the emission source) is essential to national security or to the public health or welfare . . . ." § 110(f). *See Train v. NRDC*, 421 U.S., at 81.

Even if the State does not intervene on behalf of an emission source, technological and economic factors may be considered in at least one other circumstance. When a source is found to be in violation of the state implementation plan, the Administrator may, after a conference with the operator, issue a compliance order rather than seek civil or criminal enforcement. Such an order must specify a "reasonable" time for compliance with the relevant standard, taking into account the seriousness of the violation and "any good faith efforts to comply with applicable requirements." § 113(a)(4) of the Clean Air Act. Claims of technological or economic infeasibility, the Administrator agrees, are relevant to fashioning an appropriate compliance order under § 113(a)(4). Brief for Respondent EPA 36 n. 34.

In short, the Amendments offer ample opportunity for consideration of claims of technological and economic infeasibility. Always, however, care is taken that consideration of such claims will not interfere substantially with the primary goal of prompt attainment of the national standards. Allowing such claims to be raised by appealing the Administrator's approval of an implementation plan, as petitioner suggests, would frustrate congressional intent. It would permit a proposed plan to be struck down as infeasible before it is given a chance to work, even though Congress clearly contemplated that some plans would be infeasible when proposed. And it would permit the Administrator or a federal court to reject a State's legislative choices in regulating air pollution, even though Congress plainly left with the States, so long as the national standards were met, the power to determine which sources would be burdened by regulation and to what extent. Technology forcing is a concept somewhat new to our national experience and it necessarily entails certain risks. But Congress considered those risks in passing the 1970 Amendments and decided that the dangers posed by uncontrolled air pollution made them worth taking. Petitioner's theory would render that considered legislative judgment a nullity, and that is a result we refuse to reach.

Affirmed.

Mr. Justice POWELL, with whom THE CHIEF JUSTICE joins, concurring.

I join the opinion of the Court because the statutory scheme and the legislative history, thoroughly described in the Court's opinion, demonstrate irrefutably that Congress did not intend to permit the Administrator of the Environmental Protection Agency to reject a proposed state implementation plan on the grounds of economic or technological infeasibility. Congress adopted this position despite its apparent awareness that in some cases existing sources that cannot meet the standard of the law must be closed down.

The desire to impose strong incentives on industry to encourage the rapid development and adoption of pollution control devices is understandable. But it is difficult to believe that Congress would adhere to its absolute position if faced with the potentially devastating consequences to the public that this case vividly demonstrates.

Petitioner is an electric utility supplying power demands in the St. Louis metropolitan area, a large part of Missouri, and parts of Illinois and Iowa. It alleges that it cannot continue to operate if forced to comply with the sulfur dioxide restrictions contained in the Missouri implementation plan approved by the Administrator. Specifically, petitioner alleges that since the Administrator's approval of the plan, low-sulfur coal has become too scarce and expensive to obtain; reliable and satisfactory sulfur dioxide removal equipment that would enable it to comply with the plan's requirements simply has not been devised; the installation of the unsatisfactory equipment that is available would cost over $500 million, a sum impossible to obtain by bonds that are contingent on approval by regulatory bodies and public acceptance; and, even if the financing could be obtained, the carrying, operating, and maintenance costs of over $120 million a year would be prohibitive. Petitioner further alleges that recent evidence has disclosed that sulfur dioxide in the ambient air is not the hazard to public health that it was once thought to be, and that compliance with the sulfur regulation in the Missouri plan is not necessary to the attainment of national primary and secondary ambient air standards in the St. Louis area.

At the risk of civil and criminal penalties enforceable by both the State and Federal Governments, as well as possible citizens' suits, [§§ 113, 304], petitioner is being required either to embark upon the task of installing allegedly unreliable and prohibitively expensive equipment or to shut down. Yet the present Act permits neither the Administrator, in approving the state plan, nor the courts, in reviewing that approval under § 307 of the Act, even to consider petitioner's allegations of infeasibility.

Environmental concerns, long neglected, merit high priority, and Congress properly has made protection of the public health its paramount consideration. *See* S.Rep. No. 91-1196, pp. 2-3 (1970). But the shutdown of an urban area's electrical service could have an even more serious impact on the health of the public than that created by a decline in ambient air quality. The result apparently required by this legislation in its present form could sacrifice the well-being of a large metropolitan area through the imposition of inflexible demands that may be technologically impossible to meet and indeed may no longer even be necessary to the attainment of the goal of clean air.

I believe that Congress, if fully aware of this Draconian possibility, would strike a different balance.

NOTES

1. Under § 307(b)(1) of the Act, challenges to state implementation plans may be filed within 60 days from the date of EPA approval or after 60 days only if the challenge is "based solely on grounds arising after such 60th day." (At the time of the *Union Electric* case only 30 days were allowed for such actions.) Union Electric's challenge was filed nearly three years after EPA's approval of the Missouri SIP. Moreover, the Court finds that a claim of economic and technological infeasibility is not a sufficient basis for challenging a SIP whether before or after the 30th day. Why then does the Court proceed to consider the merits of Union Electric's claim?

2. In *Union Electric*, the Court holds that economic and technological feasibility *may* be considered by a state in developing its plan for achieving both primary and secondary standards. What are the limits on the agency's consideration of these factors?

3. If a state fails to submit an acceptable plan to the EPA within the statutory time frame then EPA must promulgate a plan for the state. § 110(c). To what extent must the Administrator consider claims of economic and technological feasibility in promulgating a plan for a state? You represent a utility which claims it cannot feasibly meet the terms of a plan promulgated by EPA for the state. Alternative strategies are available to achieve the ambient air standards without imposing standards on any person that are not feasible. On what basis, if any, can you challenge EPA's plan?

4. Before the 1990 Amendments, the state implementation plan was the principal mechanism for controlling "existing" sources of air pollution. New sources have long been required to meet new source performance standards (NSPS) if the construction or modification of the source commenced after the promulgation of the applicable NSPS rules. The 1990 Amendments greatly expanded the number of "existing" sources that are covered by one or more point-source programs. Two particular programs will force many existing sources to meet federal emission standards for the first time. First, many existing electrical utilities will be covered by the Acid Deposition Program of Title IV. Second, while existing sources of hazardous air pollutants were technically covered under the pre-1990 law, few such sources were actually subject to regulation. The 1990 Amendments will impose point-source requirements on many thousands of existing sources of hazardous air pollutants. Although additional controls on existing sources may be imposed through the SIP, the salutary impacts from the acid deposition control program and the hazardous air pollution program should control much of the air pollution from existing sources.

5. Compare the *Union Electric* holding with the holding of the Court of Appeals for the Ninth Circuit in *Bunker Hill Co. v. EPA*, 572 F.2d 1286 (9th Cir. 1977). That case involved the degree of emission controls that could be imposed under the Idaho SIP on Bunker Hill's zinc and lead smelters near Kellogg, Idaho. The court stated: "The Clean Air Act . . . requires pollution sources to achieve the highest emission control level that is technologically and economically feasible . . . Conversely, the EPA cannot require a level that is technologically and economically infeasible." Although decided more than one year after *Union Electric* the court never cites the *Union Electric* decision. *See also Cleveland Elec. Illuminating Co. v. EPA*, 572 F.2d 1150, 1164 (6th Cir. 1978), where the court rejected the claims of utility companies that the SO_2 controls imposed by EPA in a federal SIP designed for Ohio were too costly. Citing *Union Electric*, the court stated: "We have genuine doubt that this court has the power to review what we regard as petitioner's slightly disguised economic and technological feasibility arguments."

6. Does economic and technological feasibility ever have a role in SIP review? Consider *National Steel Corp. v. Gorsuch*, 700 F.2d 314, 324 (6th Cir. 1983). That case concerns the State of Michigan's implementation of the RACT ("reasonably available control technology") requirement for existing sources in nonattainment areas. § 172(c)(i). At the time of this decision, RACT was defined by EPA as "the lowest emission limitation that a particular source is capable of meeting by the application of control technology that is reasonably available considering technological and economic feasibility." 45 Fed. Reg. 59,331(1980). EPA had determined that the RACT requirements in the Michigan SIP were not adequate and had imposed its own standards on the state. The plaintiff steel companies argued that the RACT requirement imposed on Michigan by the EPA was not technologically and economically feasible. Citing *Union Electric* the court held that it need not consider the steel companies' claims of infeasibility. Do you agree? *See* footnote 7 of the *Union Electric* decision.

7. "Technology forcing" mechanisms are commonplace in environmental statutes. The basic approach is for Congress to impose a standard that must be met several years in the future. At the time the standard is set forth in the law the technology does not exist to achieve it. Facing the prospect of having to shut down if they cannot achieve the standard by the statutory deadline, the industry is "forced" to search for a technological solution that will allow it to continue to operate. Does technology forcing work? *See* La Pierre, *Technology Forcing and Federal Environmental Protection Statutes*, 62 IOWA L. REV. 771 (1976).

8. Despite the Court's ruling in *Union Electric*, the company neither ceased its operations nor met the emission standards in the Missouri SIP. The subsequent history of Union Electric's struggle to avoid compliance with the emissions standards of the Missouri SIP is described in BONINE & MCGARITY, THE LAW OF ENVIRONMENTAL PROTECTION, at 430-31 (West 2d ed. 1992).

9. EPA is required to "assemble and publish a comprehensive document for each state setting forth all requirements of the applicable implementation plan." § 110(h). The 1977 Amendments had required an annual publication for each state. The 1990 Amendments require an initial publication within five years, and every three years thereafter. The required materials relating to each state implementation plan appear at 40 CFR part 52.

C. Nonattainment Areas

The Clean Air Act has succeeded in reducing the ambient pollution levels for all of the six criteria pollutants. The chart below describes the extent of that reduction between 1975 and 1987. In the case of ozone, NO_X, and TSP, however, the improvement has been relatively modest. Indeed, the national ambient levels of ozone currently exceed the primary standard for ozone (0.12 ppm).

NATIONAL AMBIENT CONCENTRATIONS OF CRITERIA AIR POLLUTANTS, 1975-1987

Year	Sulfur dioxide (ppm)	Carbon monoxide (ppm)	Ozone (ppm)	Nitrogen dioxide (ppm)	TSP ($\mu g/m^3$)	Lead (mg/m^3)
1975	0.0154	11.96	0.153	0.029	61.9	1.04
1976	0.0156	11.32	0.153	0.029	62.8	1.05
1977	0.0138	10.66	0.155	0.029	62.9	1.16
1978	0.0129	10.17	0.156	0.029	62.4	1.04
1979	0.0122	9.80	0.142	0.029	63.4	0.79
1980	0.0108	9.08	0.145	0.028	64.8	0.55
1981	0.0104	8.82	0.131	0.027	60.2	0.44
1982	0.0098	8.13	0.128	0.026	50.2	0.47
1983	0.0094	8.02	0.145	0.025	49.7	0.39
1984	0.0095	8.00	0.130	0.026	50.9	0.35
1985	0.0089	7.19	0.127	0.025	48.5	0.23
1986	0.0086	7.21	0.123	0.025	48.4	0.15
1987	0.0084	6.88	0.129	0.025	49.4	0.12

Source: U.S. Environmental Protection Agency, Office of Air Quality Planning and Standards, 1989. National air quality and emissions trends report, 1987. EPA-450/4-09-001. Research Triangle Park, NC.

Notes: ppm = parts per million. $\mu g/m^3$ = micrograms per cubic meter. mg/m^3 = milligrams per cubic meter. TSP = total suspended particulates. Sulfur dioxide and nitrogen dioxide records are arithmetic means. Carbon monoxide and ozone records are second maximum readings over 8- and 24-hour periods, respectively. TSP records are geometric means. Lead records are maximum quarterly recordings.

Over the years, the Clean Air Act has employed a variety of measures aimed at ensuring that all areas of the country achieve primary standards expeditiously. The initial goal of the 1970 law was to bring about compliance by 1975. When that deadline passed without significant improvements in air quality Congress adopted more burdensome standards that provided strong incentives for attainment. Under the 1977 Amendments, nonattainment areas were required to make "reasonable further progress" (RFP) (originally defined to mean annual incremental reductions) toward achieving the NAAQS. §§ 171(1); 172(c)(2). In addition, states were required to implement all "reasonably available control measures" (RACM) and to mandate "reasonably available control technology" (RACT) on existing sources. § 172(c)(1). Major new sources were required to offset the new pollution with reductions from other sources. These measures, among others, were supposed to insure that the NAAQS were achieved no later than 1982, or in the case of CO and O_3, 1987. Failure to achieve the Act's mandate was supposed to lead to a construction moratorium on major new sources. *See* 48 Fed. Reg. 3382 (1983) (*citing* former § 110(a)(2)(I)). In addition, federal highway grants in the offending region were to be suspended. § 176(a).

As the 1987 deadline approached it became clear that many areas would not achieve the Act's mandate. Congress initially responded by extending the deadline for the imposition of sanctions to August 31, 1988. 101 Stat. 1329-199. This date also passed without compliance.

The 1990 Amendments further extend the deadlines for compliance with the NAAQS. The new provisions appear to set more realistic goals for attaining compliance while at the same time imposing strict new standards for nonattainment areas. Special new provisions for nonattainment areas are established under the law. Of these, the ozone provisions are the most detailed and complex, although significant new requirements for CO and PM-10 nonattainment areas are established as well. Section 181 of the Act divides ozone nonattainment areas into five categories depending on the severity of noncompliance. These areas are subjected to increasingly stringent standards to achieve compliance.

The special attention accorded ozone nonattainment areas is a direct reflection of the severity of the ozone problem. When the 1990 Amendments were enacted, it was estimated that nearly one half of all Americans lived in ozone nonattainment areas. As noted above, ozone is the only criteria pollutant for which the national average ambient air concentrations exceed federal standards. *See* ENVIRONMENTAL QUALITY: 20TH ANNUAL REPORT OF THE COUNCIL ON ENVIRONMENTAL QUALITY, Table 41 (1990). Set forth below is a description of the ozone pollution problem from the Senate Report on the 1990 Amendments. Following this description is a chart which describes the Act's new requirements for ozone nonattainment areas. §§ 181-185B. The special requirements which apply to other nonattainment areas are not described separately, and while those relating to CO and PM-10 follow the same general pattern as the O_3 provisions, they are much less detailed than the ozone provisions. §§ 186-192.

> *Health effects of ozone.* The adverse health effects of exposure to ozone are well documented. Ozone is a strong oxidant formed by the interaction of hydrocarbons (also called Volatile Organic Compounds, or VOCs), nitrogen oxides (NO_x), and sunlight. Ozone enters the body by way of the respiratory tract. Ninety percent of the ozone inhaled into the lung is never exhaled. Instead the ozone molecules react rapidly with the cells, fluids, and tissues that line the respiratory tract, irritating and inflaming the lungs.
>
> Ozone is fatal at high concentrations. At lower concentrations found in many urban areas in the United States, extensive research has shown that healthy adults and children begin to exhibit adverse health effects. These include chest pains, shortness of breath, coughing, nausea, throat irritation, and increased susceptibility to respiratory infections.
>
> Potentially more troubling and less well understood are the effects of long-term chronic exposure to summertime ozone concentrations found in many cities. Regular out-of-doors work or play during the hot, sunny summer months in the more polluted cities may cause biochemical and structural changes in the lung, paving the way for chronic respiratory diseases. A growing body of scientific evidence indicates that over the long term, chronic exposure to ozone may produce an accelerated aging of the lung analogous to that produced by cigarette smoke exposure. Ultimately, emphysema may result.
>
> New evidence is also accumulating that the current ozone standard may not be sufficiently protective of public health. In one important test recently performed at EPA's research laboratory, 22 healthy individuals were exposed to 0.08 parts per million ozone for 6.6 hours, including five hours of moderate exercise. Respiratory function decreased with each succeeding hour of exposure. At the end of the exposure, it decreased by an average of seven percent, with one individual having a 26 percent reduction.

> The Environmental Protection Agency has proposed and its Clean Air Scientific Advisory Committee has agreed, that the decreases in respiratory functions become adverse when the magnitude of the change exceeds ten percent. In EPA's study, seven of the 22 individuals crossed this threshold. EPA's results may indicate that the current air quality standard for ozone does not protect public health with the adequate margin of safety required by the Act.
>
> EPA is currently in the process of revising the criteria documents for ozone based on this and other existing data. The adequacy of the one-hour standard and the need for a longer-term standard (six- to eight-hour time average) has been called into question. EPA anticipates it will take approximately two more years to resolve this issue.
>
> The people most likely to be injured from exposure to ozone include the elderly, people with preexisting respiratory problems, children (who have a faster respiration rate and are thus more exposed), and approximately 20 percent of the population, called "responders," that have a markedly strong and unpredictable adverse reaction to ozone. The American Lung Association estimated that over 28 million pre-adolescent children, 17 million elderly, 6 million asthmatics, and 7 million persons with chronic obstructive pulmonary disease live in ozone nonattainment areas.

S. Rep. No. 228, 101st Cong., 1st Sess. 6-7 (1989).

In 1991, the American Lung Association and others filed a lawsuit challenging EPA's failure to review the ozone standard as required by § 109(d). *American Lung Association v. EPA*, No. 91-4114 (E.D. N.Y.). As noted in Chapter 5, this case was settled on February 28, 1992. In that settlement, EPA agreed to commence a rulemaking proceeding to decide whether to retain or revise the ozone standard. Final rules are due March 1, 1993. Assuming that the information contained in the House Report is accurate, is it sufficient to require EPA to revise the current ozone standards?

1990 AMENDMENTS: OZONE NONATTAINMENT AREAS

Current NAAQS (primary and secondary) for ozone: 0.12 ppm (hourly average/day). National NAAQS (1987): 0.129 ppm

MARGINAL AREAS (O_3: 0.121-0.138 ppm)

- Achieve offsets of 1.1 to 1 for all new sources of VOCs (§182(A)(4)).
- Immediately after November 15, 1991, revise SIP to include a vehicle inspection and maintenance plan no less stringent than the plan outlined in H.R. Rep. No. 95-294. (§182(a)(2)(B)(i).
- Inventory all NO_x and VOC sources and their emissions (§182(a)(1)).
- Revise SIP to meet EPA's RACT requirements (§182(a)(2)(A)) and comply with the Act permit standards for locating major new sources in ozone nonattainment areas (§182(a)(2)(C)).
- Attain primary standards by November 15, 1993.

MODERATE AREAS (O_3: 0.138-0.160 ppm)

- Meet all requirements for marginal areas (§182(b)).
- Define reasonable further progress to require VOC reductions of at least 15% by November 15, 1996 (beyond the 15% in first six years) (§182(b)(1)). Smaller reduction allowed if conditions met.
- Revise SIP to achieve RACT for all VOC sources in accordance with any control technology guidance (CTG) document issued by EPA (§182(b)(2)).
- Revise SIP to require most gas stations to install system for vapor recovery during fueling (§ 182(b)(3)).
- Achieve offsets of 1.15 to 1 for all new sources of VOCs (§182(b)(5)).
- Attain the primary standards by November 15, 1996.

SERIOUS AREAS (O_3: 0.160-0.180 ppm)

- Meet all requirements for moderate areas (§182(c)).
- Adopt and implement a program (following EPA's adoption of rules) to improve monitoring of ambient concentrations of ozone, VOCs and NO_x (§182(c)(1)).
- Redefine major stationary source for these areas to include sources which emit at least 50 tons per year of VOCs (§182(c)).
- Define reasonable further progress to require an average annual reduction of 3% per year (beyond the 15% in first six years) of VOC emissions beginning on November 15, 1996.
- Revise SIP to include an enhanced vehicle inspection and maintenance program by November 15, 1992 which meets the requirements of §182(c)(3).
- Revise SIP to include a clean-fuel program (or other measures, if approved by EPA) by May 15, 1994 as required by §182(c)(4).[4]
- Beginning November 15, 1996, and every 3 years thereafter, demonstrate that the existing transportation parameters (mileage, emissions, congestion, etc.) are consistent with projections. (If not, revise SIP to achieve emissions as previously planned.)
- Existing sources emitting between 50 and 100 tons of VOCs which increase VOC emissions can avoid being treated as a modified source if the operator achieves an internal offset of VOC emissions of at least 1.3 to 1. If such sources elect not to achieve the 1.3 to 1 offset they are treated as modifications but they need only meet BACT instead of LAER (§182(c)(7)).
- Modifications of existing sources emitting more than 100 tons of VOCs can avoid LAER (but not the other provisions for major stationary sources in nonattainment areas) by achieving an internal offset of VOC emissions of at

least 1.3 to 1 (§187(c)(10)).
• The standard offset for any new or modified source in serious areas is 1.2 to 1 (§187(c)(10)).
• Attain primary standards by November 15, 1996.

SEVERE AREAS (O_3: 0.180-0.280 ppm)
• Meet all requirements for serious areas (§182(d)).
• Redefine major stationary source in these areas to include sources of VOC emissions of 25 tons or more.
• Revise SIP by November 15, 1992 to include transportation control strategies and measures to offset any growth in emissions from growth in vehicle miles traveled and achieve the required reductions to show reasonable further progress.
• Revise SIP by November 15, 1992 to require employers to adopt programs to reduce employee travel. At a minimum, employers of 100 or more persons must increase the average passenger occupancy for peak period travel between home and work by at least 25% above the pre-existing average.
• The standard offset for any new or modified sources is 1.3 to 1 unless all existing major VOC sources are required to use BACT, in which case the offset is 1.2 to 1 (§182(a)(2)).
• Achieve the primary ozone standards by November 15, 2005.

EXTREME AREAS (O_3 above 0.280 ppm) Los Angeles
• Redefine major stationary sources in these areas to include sources of VOC or NO_x emissions exceeding 10 tons per year (§182(e)).
• Extreme areas may not avail themselves of many of the substitute provisions available to less polluted areas (§182(e)).
• The standard offset for any new or modified source is 1.5 to 1 unless the SIP requires all existing major sources in the areas to use BACT, in which case it is 1.2 to 1.
• Internal offsets of 1.3 to 1 at existing major sources will allow the source to avoid the permit requirements of §173(a)(1) (major sources in NAAs) unless the offsets would have been achieved by compliance with other requirements of the SIP or Act.
• Revise SIP to require existing utilities and industrial and commercial boiler to (1) burn natural gas, ethanol or methanol; or (2) use advanced control technology to reduce NO_x emissions by November 15, 1998.

OZONE REDUCTION MILESTONES
§182(g)
• By November 15, 1996, and every three years thereafter, each state with a serious, severe or extreme ozone NAA must determine whether the percentage reduction milestones have been met. If not, states with serious or severe areas must elect one of 3 remedies. Extreme areas must adopt an economic incentive program in accordance with §182(g)(4). Moreover, if severe and extreme areas fail to meet their milestones, each major stationary source of VOCs must pay a penalty to the state for such failure. (§185(a)).

Note: The House Report referenced under "marginal areas" is the report on the 1977 Amendments to the Clean Air Act. It requires, at a minimum, a vehicle inspection and maintenance program for most light duty vehicles at least as effective as a program that was operating in the State of New Jersey at the time of the 1977 Amendments. This would include an annual emissions test for all regulated vehicles and a prohibition on state licensing and registration for any nonconforming vehicle. H.R. Rep. No. 95-294, 95th Cong. 1st Sess. 289-291 (1977).

CITIZENS AGAINST REFINERY'S EFFECTS V. EPA

643 F.2d 183 (4th Cir. 1981)

K. K. HALL, Circuit Judge.

Citizens Against the Refinery's Effects (CARE) appeals from a final ruling by the Administrator of the Environmental Protection Agency (EPA) approving the Virginia State Implementation Plan (SIP) for reducing hydrocarbon pollutants. The plan requires the Virginia Highway Department to decrease usage of a certain type of asphalt, thereby reducing hydrocarbon pollution by more than enough to offset expected pollution from the Hampton Roads Energy Company's (HREC) proposed refinery. We affirm the action of the administrator in approving the state plan.

The Act

The Clean Air Act establishes National Ambient Air Quality Standards (NAAQS) for five major air pollutants. 42 U.S.C. § 7409; 40 CFR § 50 (1976). The EPA has divided each state into Air Quality Control Regions (AQCR) and monitors each region to assure that the national standard for each pollutant is met. 42 U.S.C. § 7407. Where the standard has not been attained for a certain pollutant, the state must develop a State Implementation Plan designed to bring the area into attainment within a certain period. 42 U.S.C. § 7410. In addition, no new source of that pollutant may be constructed until the standard is attained. 40 CFR § 51.18 (1973).

The Clean Air Act created a no-growth environment in areas where the clean air requirements had not been attained. EPA recognized the need to develop a program that encouraged attainment of clean air standards without discouraging economic growth. Thus the agency proposed an Interpretive Ruling in 1976 which allowed the states to develop an "offset program" within the State Implementation Plans. 41 Fed.Reg. 55524 (1976). The offset program, later codified by Congress in the 1977 Amendments to the Clean Air Act, permits the states to develop plans which allow construction of new pollution sources where accompanied by a corresponding reduction in an existing pollution source. 42 U.S.C. § 7502(b)(6) and § 7503. In effect, a new emitting facility can be built if an existing pollution source decreases its emissions or ceases operations as long as a positive net air quality benefit occurs.

If the proposed factory will emit carbon monoxide, sulfur dioxide, or particulates, the EPA requires that the offsetting pollution source be within the immediate vicinity of the new plant. The other two pollutants, hydrocarbons and nitrogen oxide, are less "site-specific," and thus the ruling permits the offsetting source to locate anywhere within a broad vicinity of the new source.

The offset program has two other important requirements. First, a base time period must be determined in which to calculate how much reduction is needed in existing pollutants to offset the new source. This base period is defined as the first year of the SIP or, where the state has not yet developed a SIP, as the year in which a construction permit application is filed. 41 Fed.Reg. 55529 (1976). Second, the offset program requires that the new source adopt the Lowest Achievable Emissions Rate (LAER) using the most modern technology available in the industry. 41 Fed.Reg. 55528-9 (1976).

The Refinery

HREC proposes to build a petroleum refinery and offloading facility in Portsmouth, Virginia. Portsmouth has been unable to reduce air pollution enough to attain the national standard for one pollutant, photochemical oxidants, which is created when hydrocarbons are released into the atmosphere and react with other substances. Since a refinery is a major source of hydrocarbons, the Clean Air Act prevents construction of the HREC plant until the area attains the national standard.

In 1975, HREC applied to the Virginia State Air Pollution Control Board (VSAPCB) for a refinery construction permit. The permit was issued by the VSAPCB on October 8, 1975, extended and reissued on October 5, 1977 after a full public hearing, modified on August 8, 1978, and extended again on September 27, 1979. The VSAPCB, in an effort to help HREC meet the clean air requirements, proposed to use the offset ruling to comply with the Clean Air Act.

On November 28, 1977, the VSAPCB submitted a State Implementation Plan to EPA which included the HREC permit. The Virginia Board proposed to offset the new HREC hydrocarbon pollution by reducing the amount of cutback asphalt[8] used for road paving operations in three highway districts by the Virginia Department of Highways. By switching from "cutback" to "emulsified" asphalt, the state can reduce hydrocarbon pollutants by the amount necessary to offset the pollutants from the proposed refinery.

EPA requested some changes in the state plan, including certain monitoring changes and verification from the Virginia Attorney General that the offset program was legally enforceable. The plan was transmitted by the EPA Region III director to EPA headquarters on September 9, 1978. Notices of the proposed plan were published on October 10, 1978 and again on May 1, 1979. 43 Fed.Reg. 46554 (1978). 44 Fed.Reg. 25471 (1979). Numerous comments were received, including several from CARE. The EPA administrator carefully considered the comments and approved the Virginia offset plan on January 31, 1980.

CARE raises four issues regarding the state plan. First, they argue that the geographic area used as the base for the offset was arbitrarily determined and that the area as defined violates the regulations. Second, CARE contends that EPA should have used 1975 instead of 1977 as the base year to compare usage of cutback asphalt. Third, CARE insists that the offset plan should have been disapproved since the state is voluntarily reducing usage of cutback asphalt anyway. Fourth, CARE questions the approval of the plan without definite Lowest Achievable Emissions Rates (LAER) as required by the statute. We reject the CARE challenges to the state plan.

* * *

The Geographic Area

CARE contends that the state plan should not have been approved by EPA since the three highway-district area where cutback usage will be reduced to offset refinery emissions was artificially developed by the state. The ruling permits a broad area (usually within one AQCR) to be used as the offset basis. 41 Fed.Reg. 55529 (1976).

---

[8] "Cutback" asphalt has a petroleum base which gives off great amounts of hydrocarbons. "Emulsified" asphalt uses a water base which evaporates, giving off no hydrocarbons.

The ruling does not specify how to determine the area, nor provide a standard procedure for defining the geographic area. 41 Fed.Reg. 55529 (1976). Here the Virginia Board originally proposed to use four highway districts comprising one-half the state as the offset area. When this was found to be much more than necessary to offset pollution expected from the refinery, the state changed it to one highway district plus nine additional counties. Later the proposed plan was again revised to include a geographic area of three highway districts.

The agency action in approving the use of three highway districts was neither arbitrary, capricious, nor outside the statute. First, Congress intended that the states and the EPA be given flexibility in designing and implementing SIPs. *See* H.R.Rep.No. 95-294, 95th Cong., 1st Sess., *reprinted in* (1977) U.S.Code Cong. & Ad.News 1077, 1290-92. Such flexibility allows the states to make reasoned choices as to which areas may be used to offset new pollution and how the plan is to be implemented. Second, the offset program was initiated to encourage economic growth in the state. 41 Fed.Reg. 55525 (1976). Thus a state plan designed to reduce highway department pollution in order to attract another industry is a reasonable contribution to economic growth without a corresponding increase in pollution. Third, to be sensibly administered the offset plan had to be divided into districts which could be monitored by the highway department. Use of any areas other than highway districts would be unwieldy and difficult to administer. Fourth, the scientific understanding of ozone pollution is not advanced to the point where exact air transport may be predicted. Designation of the broad area in which hydrocarbons may be transported is well within the discretion and expertise of the agency.

The Base Year

Asphalt consumption varies greatly from year to year, depending upon weather and road conditions. Yet EPA must accurately determine the volume of hydrocarbon emissions from cutback asphalt. Only then can the agency determine whether the reduction in cutback usage will result in an offset great enough to account for the new refinery pollution. To calculate consumption of a material where it constantly varies, a base year must be selected. In this case, EPA's Interpretive Ruling establishes the base year as the year in which the permit application is made. 41 Fed.Reg. 55529 (1976). EPA decided that 1977 was an acceptable base year. CARE argues that EPA illegally chose 1977 instead of 1975.

Considering all of the circumstances, including the unusually high asphalt consumption in 1977, the selection by EPA of that as the base year was within the discretion of the agency. Since the EPA Interpretive Ruling allowing the offset was not issued until 1976, 1977 was the first year after the offset ruling and the logical base year in which to calculate the offset. Also, the permit issued by the VSAPCB was reissued in 1977 with extensive additions and revisions after a full hearing. Under these circumstances, 1977 appears to be a logical choice of a base year.

The Legally Binding Plan

For several years, Virginia has pursued a policy of shifting from cutback asphalt to the less expensive emulsified asphalt in road-paving operations. The policy was initiated in an effort to save money, and was totally unrelated to a State Implementation Plan. Because of this policy, CARE argues that hydrocarbon emissions were decreasing independent of this SIP and therefore are not a proper offset against the refinery. They argue that there is not, in effect, an actual reduction in pollution.

The Virginia voluntary plan is not enforceable and therefore is not in compliance with the 1976 Interpretive Ruling which requires that the offset program be enforceable. 41 Fed.Reg. 55526 (1976). The EPA, in approving the state plan, obtained a letter from the Deputy Attorney General of Virginia in which he stated that the requisites had been satisfied for establishing and enforcing the plan with the Department of Highways. Without such authority, no decrease in asphalt-produced pollution is guaranteed. In contrast to the voluntary plan, the offset plan guarantees a reduction in pollution resulting from road-paving operations.

The Lowest Achievable Emissions Rate

Finally, CARE argues that the Offset Plan does not provide adequate Lowest Achievable Emission Rates (LAER) as required by the 1976 Interpretive Ruling because the plan contains only a 90% vapor recovery requirement, places an excessive 176.5 ton limitation on hydrocarbon emissions, and does not require specific removal techniques at the terminal. EPA takes the position that the best technique available for marine terminals provides only a 90% recovery and that the 176.5 ton limit may be reduced by the agency after the final product mix at the terminal is determined.

Since the record shows no evidence of arbitrary or capricious action in approving the HREC emissions equipment, the agency determination of these technical matters must be upheld. *Udall v. Tallman*, 380 U.S. 1 (1965).

Conclusion

In approving the state plan, EPA thoroughly examined the data, requested changes in the plan, and approved the plan only after the changes were made. There is no indication that the agency acted in an arbitrary or capricious manner or that it stepped beyond the bounds of the Clean Air Act. We affirm the decision of the administrator in approving the state plan.

NOTES

1. Recall that nonattainment plans are required to "provide for the implementation of reasonably available control measures as expeditiously as practicable", and that existing sources in nonattainment areas are required to use reasonably available control technology (RACT) to control their emissions. § 172(c)(1). Under these provisions should the highway department have been *required* to switch to emulsified asphalt, independent of any offset plan? Note that under EPA's current policy only emission reductions not required by law qualify for the offset program. 51 Fed. Reg 43,814 (1986) *infra*.

2. In order to obtain approval of the offset proposal for the Hampton Roads refinery, Virginia had to submit a request for a SIP revision to the EPA. Under EPA's current procedures, however, states may promulgate "generic" rules for approving offsets so long as they involve "tightly drawn mechanical procedures . . . which ensure that the use of the rules *cannot* interfere with attainment and maintenance of ambient air quality standards." 46 Fed. Reg. 20,551, 20,552 (1981); *see also* 51 Fed. Reg. 43,835 (1986). In 1982, EPA adopted an interim Emissions Trading Policy to further implement, among other things, the offset program. Final rules implementing the policy were promulgated in 1986. 51 Fed. Reg. 43,814 (1986). The policy establishes "emission reduction credits" (ERCs) as "the common currency of all trading activity." *Id.* at 43,831. "[O]nly reductions which are *surplus, enforceable, permanent,* and *quantifiable* can qualify as emission reduction credits and be banked or traded." *Id.* (Emphasis in original.) In order to obtain EPA approval to implement the policy, states must adopt detailed rules to register ERCs and to track their ownership, use, and transfer. *Id.* at 43,835. States without the required rules may continue to use the SIP revision process. *Id.* at 43,836. The Emissions Trading Policy is reproduced in part at Chapter 9, *infra*.

3. As described in *CARE*, the emissions offset policy is essentially a 1 to 1+ policy; *i.e.*, the Act required that major new sources achieve reductions such that "total allowable emissions from existing sources in the region, from new or modified sources which are not major emitting facilities, and from the proposed source will be *sufficiently less than* total emissions from existing sources. . . ." (Emphasis added). The 1990 Amendments specify particular offset ratios for major new sources in ozone nonattainment areas. For example, the standard offset for major new sources in severe ozone nonattainment areas is 1.3 to 1, unless the state requires BACT for all existing sources in which case the offset is 1.2 to 1. § 182(d).

4. The 1990 Amendments now allow the owner or operator of a new or modified major stationary source to obtain their offsets from other nonattainment areas if two conditions are met: (1) the other nonattainment area has an equal or higher nonattainment classification; and (2) the emissions that will be reduced in the other area are the kind of emissions which contribute to the NAAQS violation. § 173(c). Oddly though, the reduction required must only be "equal or greater" than the new emissions; whereas reductions in the *same* nonattainment area must be such that the new emissions "will be sufficiently less than [prior emissions] . . . so as to represent reasonable further progress . . . ." *Compare* § 173 (c)(1) *with* § 173 (a)(1)(A).

5. The "emission offset" policy applies solely to nonattainment areas. It has the advantage of allowing new growth in many industrial areas which have, in recent years, experienced high unemployment. It also assures that air quality in these areas is not further degraded. As applied in the *CARE* decision, does the policy serve or hinder the goal of achieving the NAAQS?

6. The related emission trading policies of "bubbles" and "netting" are addressed in greater detail in Chapter 9, *infra*.

7. The requirement that new sources in nonattainment areas achieve LAER is substantial. Section 171(3) defines LAER as either the most stringent emission limit for that type of source contained in any SIP, unless the new source operator shows that such limits cannot be achieved, or the most stringent limit achieved in practice for such source, *whichever is more stringent*.

D. Nonattainment Area Plans

Section 172 of the Act establishes special standards for nonattainment area plans. When an area is designated nonattainment, EPA is required to establish a schedule that may not extend beyond three years for submitting a plan to achieve the NAAQS. § 172(b). Among other things, nonattainment area plans must provide for the implementation of all "reasonably available control measures" (RACM) and must require existing sources in the area to adopt "reasonably available control technology" (RACT). The plan must also insure "reasonable further progress" (RFP) toward achieving the NAAQS. RFP is defined by law for ozone nonattainment areas as previously described. For other areas the EPA is required to define RFP for a particular plan "as may reasonably be required . . . for the purpose of ensuring attainment . . . by the applicable date." § 171(1). In addition, O_3, CO and PM-10 nonattainment areas must meet certain "milestones" and where a state fails to meet a milestone, EPA may require, among other things, the imposition of contingency measures which each nonattainment area plan is required to adopt. *See e.g.*, §§ 172(c)(9), 182(g), 187(d), 189(c).

Primary standard attainment dates for O_3, CO and PM-10 areas are set out in the statute. §§ 181(a)(1), 186(a)(1), 188(c). For other areas, attainment "shall be the date by which attainment can be achieved as expeditiously as practicable, but no later than five years from the date the area was designated nonattainment . . ." § 172(c)(2)(A). EPA, however, has discretion to allow as much as ten years from the date of designation "considering the severity of nonattainment and feasibility of pollution control measures." *Id.* Moreover, in limited cases, EPA may approve up to two, one-year extensions of the attainment date. §§ 172(c)(2)(C); 181(a)(5); 186(a)(4); 188(d). (In serious PM-10 nonattainment areas, a five-year extension is available.)

NOTES

1. The 1990 Amendments establish many new requirements for SIPs to help insure compliance with the NAAQS by the deadlines set in the statute. What happens, however, if a state ultimately fails to meet these deadlines? In *Delaney v. EPA*, 898 F.2d 687 (9th Cir. 1991), the court reviewed a decision by EPA allowing the State of Arizona three years from the date of a plan approval to meet the NAAQS, notwithstanding the fact that the compliance date set out in the statute had long since expired. The court rejected EPA's decision and found that in such a case, "the national ambient air quality standards must be attained as soon as possible with every available control measure . . . ." *Id.* at 691.

2. A list of all PM-10, carbon monoxide, and ozone nonattainment areas at the time the 1990 Amendments were enacted appears in the House Report, broken down by categories (*i.e.*, extreme, severe, etc.). H.R. Rep. No. 490, 101st Cong., 2nd Sess. 197-98, 204-05, 208-09, 230-31, 258-59 (1990).

NATIONAL STEEL CORPORATION V. GORSUCH

700 F.2d 314 (6th Cir. 1983)

NATHANIEL R. JONES, Circuit Judge.

The Environmental Protection Agency (EPA), in a final agency action pursuant to the Clean Air Act, as amended, 42 U.S.C. § 7401, et seq., has approved, conditionally approved, and disapproved various provisions of the State Implementation Plan adopted by the State of Michigan in an effort to comport with nationally-required air quality standards. Petitioner National Steel Corporation, Great Lakes Steel Division, is seeking review of that action. For the reasons detailed below, we find that the EPA administrator neither overstepped the bounds of her authority nor made decisions which were "arbitrary and capricious, an abuse of discretion, or otherwise not in accordance with law." 5 U.S.C. § 706(2)(A) (1970). Accordingly, we affirm the EPA final action.

I

A combined state and federal program to control air pollution was formulated in 1970 through various amendments to the Clean Air Act, 42 U.S.C. § 7401, *et seq.* (the Act). Pursuant to the mandates of §§ 108 and 109 of the Act, the EPA promulgated national ambient air quality standards (NAAQS) for a variety of pollutants. The standards relevant to the case before us are those governing total suspended particulates in the air. The limitations on particulate matter were set at levels deemed necessary to protect the public health and welfare.

The states were given the primary responsibility for achieving these air quality levels and, absent special circumstances, were required to do so by 1975. In keeping with this responsibility, the states were required, under § 110 of the Act to develop state implementation plans (SIPs) providing for the attainment and maintenance of the federal standards. The administrator was required to approve any state plan satisfying the criteria detailed in § 110(a)(2)(A)-(H).

* * *

As of 1975, portions of many states had failed to achieve the national standards, despite the existence of previously approved SIPs. The Act was amended in 1977 in order to deal with these "nonattainment areas". Under the amendment (now Part D of Title I of the Act), states are required to submit revisions to their SIPS demonstrating that the NAAQS will be attained "as expeditiously as practicable," though no later than the end of the 1982 calendar year.

These Part D plans must meet the requirements of § 172(b) of the Act. In pertinent part, § 172(b) provides that the SIP shall, *inter alia*:

> (2) provide for the implementation of all reasonably available control measures as expeditiously as practicable;
> (3) require, in the interim, reasonable further progress (as defined in Section 171(11)) including such reduction in emissions from existing sources in the area as may be obtained through the adoption, at a minimum, of reasonably available control technology (RACT).

42 U.S.C. § 7502(b).

In an effort to, at minimum, prevent the exacerbation of existing nonattainment problems, Congress required all SIPs to provide for a moratorium on the construction of new sources of pollutants, or on the modification of existing ones, unless the state had an approved Part D plan by July 1, 1979. Michigan did not have an approved plan by the deadline and the EPA imposed the required moratorium.

In determining the requirements for an acceptable Part D plan, the EPA addressed a number of practical concerns. Most relevant to this case was the stance the EPA took with regard to fugitive emissions--*i.e.*, matter having a negative impact on air quality which does not originate from a stack or vent, including, but not limited to, dust from ore storage piles, road dust and dust from nonindustrial urban sources. Since these emissions could easily play a significant role in nonattainment, and are so difficult to measure or control, it was clear that attainment would be difficult to demonstrate. The EPA recognized the possibility that a state might require RACT and still be unable to demonstrate attainment because of these immeasurables.

To avoid this problem, the EPA established alternative criteria for determining whether a state's plan was acceptable. First, the EPA decided to approve state plans where the state mandated RACT on all major stationary sources, met the other requirements of § 172, and agreed to submit a schedule of measures to control fugitive sources of matter. Alternatively, the EPA decided to approve state plans which could demonstrate attainment "as expeditiously as practicable" *without* requiring RACT.

In order to assess whether a particular Part D SIP revision reflected RACT, EPA amassed data indicating levels of performance achieved by application of control technology at particulate sources. A particularly large amount of data was compiled with regard to iron and steel sources. On September 8, 1980, the EPA announced that it had compiled a "guidance" document summarizing that data. The EPA indicated that it would combine this data with that presented by the state and then approve, disapprove or conditionally approve all elements of the SIPs submitted.

Applying this statutory and regulatory scheme, the EPA approved Michigan's original SIP in 1972. In 1978, however, the administrator designated certain areas of Michigan, including Detroit, "nonattainment areas" for particulate matter and various chemicals. On April 25, 1979, Michigan submitted its required Part D revisions for these areas.

On May 22, 1981, the EPA published a notice of final rulemaking with regard to Michigan's Part D revisions for those nonattainment areas containing iron and steel sources. The *overall* strategy for emission and particulate matter control in these source areas was conditionally approved upon the state's commitment to adopt regulations which the EPA felt reflected RACT.

* * *

It is this final rulemaking with regard to iron and steel sources which Great Lakes Steel contests.

III

The petitioner's first argument has several elements, all urging the conclusion that the EPA has overstepped its authority *and* acted arbitrarily in making its RACT determinations in this case.

A

First, petitioner claims that, since fugitive dust significantly contributes to nonattainment, the EPA should not require stationary sources to install RACT before Michigan completes its own studies concerning the relationship between fugitive dust and nonattainment and the possible methods for controlling that particular pollutant. Great Lakes Steel contends that it is unreasonable to interpret the statute as requiring mandatory RACT absent proof that the imposition of the installation cost will in any way contribute to attainment.

The EPA interprets the Act to unambiguously require installation of RACT *at a minimum* on existing sources in the nonattainment areas. While the EPA does not deny that it has itself adopted an administrative exemption to this otherwise "mandatory" requirement, it views that exemption as being narrowly tailored to fit within, and further, the spirit and goals of the Act. On the contrary, the EPA feels that the exemption suggested by Great Lakes Steel, *i.e.*, to wait and see what the state studies show before requiring RACT, would altogether vitiate the mandates of § 172, thereby *undercutting* the purposes of the Act.

* * *

The point is well taken that an action which will *clearly* not further attainment should not be required. However, as noted previously, it is unclear to what extent each source of pollutants contributes to the nonattainment problem. All admit that the nature of the problem is too complex to allow for specific determinations of whether particular actions will or will not best further the attainment goal. It cannot be debated that RACT on existing stationary sources will ensure that *those* sources are not contributing to or exacerbating nonattainment. It does not appear unreasonable for Congress to have granted the EPA the power to act with regard to known, identifiable sources of particulate matter, even though they remain unable to quantify the precise degree to which those sources are preventing the attainment of the NAAQS.

Section 172(b)(3) of the Act specifically states that a SIP "*shall . . . require*" RACT in the circumstances it defines. There is nothing in the statute which indicates that these terms are not to be given their plain meaning. In addition, we could find nothing in the legislative history of these provisions which in any way contradicts the mandatory character of the language employed.

* * *

B

Second, Great Lakes Steel asserts that the EPA has essentially created its own uniform set of RACT standards, bearing no relation to the nonattainment problem in Michigan. They claim that the imposition of the EPA's own standards has improperly usurped the statutory role of the state. This, petitioner argues, is both arbitrary and, by analogy, "ultra vires". EPA counters that it has not adopted "uniform" RACT standards and that the information it has compiled has not been "imposed" upon the states. Instead, EPA argues that its data is merely a starting point for the states to develop RACT requirements and a guideline for EPA's general evaluation of a state's RACT proposals, *given* the economic and technical circumstances surrounding the particular sources being regulated.

* * *

There is no doubt that the EPA is empowered to evaluate proposed RACT standards to *some* extent. While the state does have the primary responsibility for establishing RACT guidelines, the EPA's statutory obligation before approving a SIP is to ensure that RACT is actually provided for. *See* § 110(a)(2)(I) of the Act in conjunction with § 172(b)(3). The EPA claims that it only uses its RACT data as a guide in fulfilling this obligation. It cites a variety of EPA notices and regulations for the proposition that the EPA has not adopted inflexible standards. The EPA defines RACT as:

> the lowest emission limitation that a particular source is capable of meeting by the application of control technology that is reasonably available considering technological and economic feasibility. Therefore, depending on *site-specific considerations*, such as geographic constraints, RACT *can differ* for similar sourccs.

45 Fed. Reg. 59331 (September 9, 1980) (emphasis added). The EPA claims that it will review and evaluate proposed standards on the basis of the *state analysis*, "taking into account all the available data as well as public comment on the state's analysis and the EPA's evaluation thereof." 45 Fed.Reg. 59199 (September 8, 1980).

This picture of flexibility is drawn into question, however, when one considers the practical application of these standards. While the EPA indicates that it only requires a state to make a threshold offering of information on which an evaluation can be based, it does seem to establish a presumption, albeit rebuttable, that its own data defines RACT. Consider EPA Statement at 45 Fed.Reg. 59331 (September 9, 1980):

> USEPA believes that the burden of demonstrating that a regulation represents RACT rests on the state. In reviewing a proposed SIP revision to determine its adequacy, USEPA can verify independently that the provisions in the state plan represent RACT. Although USEPA has not specified uniform RACT standards for the iron and steel industry, it has collected data which reflects the emission limitations achieved by various iron and steel sources applying control technology . . . *Where a state proposed regulations which are not technically supported by USEPA's data, the state must submit adequate data supporting its proposal as representing RACT.*

The EPA is not required to accept a state's data without undertaking a critical evaluation of it. The accumulation of an alternative database would seem to be a necessary framework for such an evaluation. The formulation of a presumption *against* the acceptability of state standards appears troublesome, however. By placing such an additional burden on the states, the EPA seems to be removing some of the flexibility that Congress meant to afford the states in formulating their individual implementation plans. This may, indeed, be beyond the bounds of the discretion which the EPA is permitted to exercise in fulfilling its secondary role. We need not, however, nor do we choose to, resolve that issue in the case before us. In the circumstances presented, we consider the EPA's use of its own data for making its RACT determinations to be in keeping with its statutory role. Reason dictates that the EPA must have some basis from which to evaluate proposed SIPs; "approval" absent data to consider would be no more than rubber-stamping. The EPA can only be in a position to fulfill its statutory obligations if it has some degree of expertise, or some way of getting that expertise, regarding RACT in each relevant industry. In the instant case, Michigan did not supply detailed information in support of its RACT determinations. Where a state fails to supply the information necessary for a proper evaluation by the EPA, the EPA must be free to use its own acquired knowledge. In such circumstances, we readily find that the EPA has neither overstepped the bounds of its authority nor acted unreasonably.

* * *

In sum, we find that the EPA's final rulemaking with regard to Michigan's Part D SIP revisions was wholly within the bounds of its statutory authority and was neither arbitrary and capricious, nor otherwise not in accordance with law. Accordingly, we affirm that rulemaking in all respects.

NOTES

1. One alternative deemed acceptable by EPA for state nonattainment plans was a plan which could demonstrate attainment as expeditiously as practicable without requiring RACT. This alternative was not chosen by Michigan and thus is not at issue in the principal case. Is the alternative lawful? See the references to § 172(b)(2),(3) in the *National Steel* case. Note that these provisions were rearranged and in some cases changed by the 1990 Amendments. The basic RACT requirement remains in the statute, although it now appears at § 172(c)(1).

2. The 1990 Amendments also established a new entity—the RACT/BACT/LAER clearinghouse. § 108(h); *See also* § 173(d). This is intended to be a central repository or database encompassing all information received by EPA under State plan provisions concerning emission control technology. The database will be made available to the general public. How is this information likely to affect an EPA or State determination as to what constitutes RACT?

3. EPA's authority to issue guidance on various control technologies appears at § 108(b) of the Act. The 1990 Amendments reference this authority, and adopt yet another acronym — CTG — for control technique guidelines. *See e.g.*, § 183; *see also* § 178 which requires EPA to issue guidance documents solely with respect to LAER. At the time the 1990 Amendments were adopted EPA had prepared 29 CTGs. Twelve additional CTGs were in production. *See* J. QUARLES & W. LEWIS, THE NEW CLEAN AIR ACT,App. B. (1990).

4. As the *National Steel* case indicates, the sanction for failing to have an approved Part D program under the 1977 Amendments was a moratorium on the construction of major new stationary sources in the nonattainment area. *See* former § 110(a)(2)(I). EPA was also required to disapprove any grants under the Act, and the Secretary of Transportation was required to disapprove highway grants to states which failed to submit a Part D plan in a timely fashion. Former § 176(a). The 1990 Amendments keep in place any construction moratoria in effect under the earlier law until a revised SIP which meets the standards of the new law is approved, but otherwise omits the construction ban. In its place, the 1990 Amendments impose alternative sanctions. § 179. For virtually any violation of the Part D planning requirements, EPA must impose one of two sanctions; either a ban on highway money to the affected state or a 2:1 offset requirement for major new sources subject to § 173. If the violation results from a state's lack of good faith, both sanctions apply. In addition to these sanctions, limits on grants for sewage treatment plants, authorized under the Clean Water Act, may be imposed. § 316.

STATE OF OHIO V. RUCKELSHAUS

776 F.2d 1333 (6th Cir. 1985)

LIVELY, Chief Judge.

Ohio seeks review of final action of the United States Environmental Protection Agency (EPA) under the Clean Air Act as amended (the Act). 42 U.S.C. §§ 7401 *et seq.* The particular provisions of the Act in controversy are portions of Part D of Subchapter I, 42 U.S.C. §§ 7501-7508, and section 107(d) and (e), 42 U.S.C. § 7407(d) and (e), all of which were added to the Act by the Clean Air Act Amendments of 1977, Pub.L. 95-95.

The question for decision is whether EPA may refuse a state's request to redesignate a county from "nonattainment" to "attainment" where actual monitoring or modeling data from the county show that air quality within the county meets the required ambient standard. EPA denied Ohio's request to redesignate Lorain County as an attainment area for ozone upon determining that, although the air within the county satisfied the National Ambient Air Quality Standards (NAAQS) for ozone, pollutants originating in Lorain County added significantly to the ozone levels in the Cleveland urban area, of which Lorain County is a part. All of the counties in the Cleveland urban area are part of the Greater Cleveland Intrastate Air Quality Control Region (AQCR). Ohio argued that the boundary of the Cleveland urban nonattainment area should be changed by removing Lorain County and filed a petition for review of the EPA's action.

* * *

Acting pursuant to section 107(d)(1) of the Act, Ohio listed nonattainment areas within the State. It identified the counties comprising the Cleveland urban area, including Lorain, Medina, Lake and Geauga Counties, as nonattainment for ozone. In 1982 Ohio, acting pursuant to section 107(e)(1) of the Act, 42 U.S.C. § 7407(e)(1), requested a revision of the ozone nonattainment designations to remove 46 counties, including Lorain, Medina, Lake and Geauga Counties. There was no request that Cuyahoga County, where the City of Cleveland is located, be redesignated.

EPA published a notice of proposed rulemaking on August 10, 1983 in response to the request. The notice invited public comment and stated that EPA proposed to grant the request as to 36 counties and deny it as to ten, including Lorain and Medina. Following the period of comment, EPA issued its final rulemaking, approving Ohio's redesignation of 37 counties and disapproving the redesignation of nine counties, including Lorain. 49 Fed.Reg. 24124 (June 12, 1984). The county approved for redesignation as "attainment" in the final action that had been refused redesignation in the first EPA proposal was Medina. Following the final action of EPA, the Cleveland urban nonattainment area consisted of Cuyahoga, Lorain, Geauga and Lake Counties.

It is undisputed that monitoring data showed that the air within Lorain County met the NAAQS for ozone. EPA recognized this fact, but refused to redesignate Lorain County on the ground that a significant portion of the ozone pollution in the Cleveland urban nonattainment area derives from emissions in Lorain County, which lies upwind from the other three counties in the nonattainment area. The geographical relationship of the four counties in the designated nonattainment area, plus Medina County, is shown in the portion of the Ohio map of counties reproduced here:

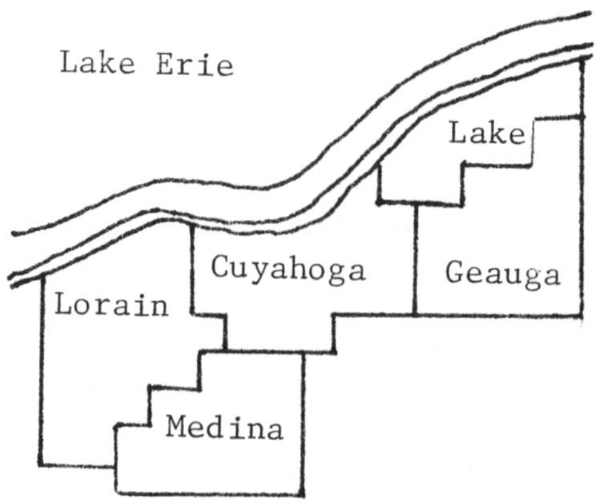

In its comments on proposed rulemaking Ohio conceded that "[e]missions from Lorain County contribute to the ozone concentrations in the Cleveland area and should be included in the design of any control program." (Letter from Ohio EPA to U.S. EPA, August 12, 1983). However, Ohio took the position that Lorain County was not in air quality violation for ozone and should not be listed as nonattainment.

II.

Though Ohio makes a number of subsidiary arguments, its basic position is that the Act does not authorize EPA to disapprove a reasonable state designation of an area as "attainment" on the ground that emissions from the area may potentially add to the pollution of a nonattainment area. Underlying this argument is the contention that the state may treat a county as an "area" for purposes of § 7407(d)(1) and require EPA to so treat it, despite the fact that EPA has designated the county as part of a larger area. Ohio relies on the definition of "nonattainment area" in section 171(2) of the Act, 42 U.S.C. § 7501(2) (1982), "an area which is shown by monitored data or which is calculated by air quality modeling (or other methods determined by the Administrator to be reliable) to exceed any national ambient air quality standard for such pollutant." Since Lorain County has shown by monitored data that its air does not contain ozone in excess of the NAAQS, it cannot be brought within this definition and, thus, may not be designated "nonattainment."

Ohio recognizes that Lorain County is in the Cleveland urban area but insists that it may subdivide that area by counties on the basis of air quality information. Ohio argues that the states have the primary role in making such decisions, and EPA should accord deference to state determinations regarding the size of areas designated. Given the measured air quality data on which the request for redesignation of Lorain County was based, EPA acted arbitrarily and capriciously in continuing to designate Lorain County "nonattainment," according to Ohio.

Ohio also argues that EPA had an alternative and preferable means at its disposal for dealing with the Cleveland ozone problem. EPA should have approved the redesignation of Lorain County to attainment, but required Ohio to amend its State Implementation Plan (SIP) to insure that pollutants from Lorain County, though an attainment area, did not add significantly to the ozone problems of the downwind Cleveland area. Ohio contends that SIPs are at the heart of the entire scheme for improving the quality of the Nation's air, and that EPA should be required to follow this path to achieve NAAQS within Ohio, including the Cleveland area. Ohio's preference for this alternative means of enforcing compliance with the NAAQS arises from the fact that Part D of the Act, which applies only to nonattainment areas, contains significant enforcement tools not available to EPA under other provisions. For example, EPA can impose a ban on new construction, require a new source review program that may require greater emissions reduction than other sections of the Act would require, require a motor vehicle inspection and maintenance program with a cutoff of federal funds for noncompliance and require ozone sources to meet emissions limitations at least reflective of reasonably available control technology. The possibility of a ban on new construction and the loss of federal funds for failure to implement a vehicle inspection and maintenance program are matters of serious concern to a local governmental unit.

Finally, Ohio contends that the record does not support EPA's disapproval of the request for redesignation of Lorain County. Instead of relying on modeling or monitoring in the Cleveland area, EPA based its conclusions about Lorain County's contributions to Cleveland's ozone levels on findings made with respect to other major urban centers such as Chicago, St. Louis, Los Angeles and Detroit. In addition, Ohio charges that EPA was totally inconsistent in approving redesignation of Medina County, which also has a direct association with the Cleveland area, while disapproving the request for Lorain County.

III.

EPA maintains that it acted reasonably and within its clear authority under § 7407 in disapproving Ohio's request with respect to Lorain County. It is not required to designate nonattainment areas by reference to county boundaries. Thus, the fact that a county within a nonattainment area is not in violation of NAAQS for a pollutant is irrelevant. As EPA interprets § 7407(d), it is permitted to designate nonattainment areas by boundaries which include important sources of pollution that contribute to the pollution levels of the area, without making a separate determination for each political subdivision within the area. EPA asserts that its interpretation of the statute is reasonable since it serves the underlying goal of the Act by requiring steps to be taken that will move an area toward attainment. EPA finds nothing in the language or legislative history of the Act or the 1977 Amendments that would require it to make Lorain County a "section 107(d) area" separate from the general Cleveland urban area of which it is a part.

EPA argues that keeping Lorain County within the nonattainment area serves the purpose behind the enactment of Part D. That purpose was to bring about incremental air quality improvement and timely attainment of national standards in those areas that failed to attain the NAAQS by the deadlines originally set out in the Act. The fact that EPA might have proceeded by the alternate route of requiring Ohio to revise its SIP does not deprive it of authority to proceed under § 7407(d) and Part D, which were designed specifically to deal with the nonattainment problem to which the 1977 Amendments were directed.

EPA responds to Ohio's charge that its denial of redesignation was not supported by the record with several contentions. In the first place, it points to Ohio's admission that pollutants from Lorain County contribute to Cleveland's ozone problem. It also argues that the record contains meteorological data which indicate that the prevailing winds during the peak ozone season do flow from Lorain County to Cuyahoga and Lake Counties. Further, monitoring results in the Cleveland urban area showed ozone violations. These are included in the record. In addition, the record contains documentation that significant quantities of ozone precursors are emitted from sources in Lorain County. Lorain County's emissions constitute 18.7% of the total organic pollutant emissions originating in the four county Cleveland urban nonattainment area.

With respect to the use of data from other urban areas, EPA makes two responses. In the first place, it notes that Ohio did not object to the use of these data during the administrative proceedings, and argues that it may not object at this stage. In addition, EPA maintains that the causes of ozone buildups in major urban centers are well known and the testing done in the area of other large cities provides valid data for determining the effect of Lorain County's emissions on Cleveland.

IV.

A.

In considering an agency's construction of a statute which it administers a court applies a narrow standard of review. If Congress has spoken directly to the precise question in issue, and its intent is clear, that ends the inquiry because both the agency and the court "must give effect to the unambiguously expressed intent of Congress." *Chevron, U.S.A., Inc. v. National Resources Defense Council, Inc.*, 467 U.S. 837 (1984). If the court determines that Congress has not addressed the precise question directly, the duty of the court is to determine whether the agency has based its answer to the question "on a permissible construction of the statute." *Id.* The Supreme Court has long recognized the principle of deference which requires courts to accord "considerable weight" to the construction by an executive department of a statute that it administers. *Id.*

B.

With these firmly established principles in mind, we turn to the issues in this case. The statutory provision in question, § 7407(d)(1), does not speak directly to the precise question of whether EPA may include in a nonattainment area a county whose air quality meets national standards. The statute requires each state to identify "those air quality regions, or portions thereof" which do not meet the NAAQS for any air pollutant. Counties are not mentioned, but both Lorain and Medina Counties had previously been included in the Greater Cleveland AQCR. Part D of the Act defines "nonattainment area" as "an area which is shown by monitored data or which is calculated by air quality modeling (or other methods determined by the Administrator to be reliable) to exceed any national ambient air quality standard" for a particular pollutant. § 7501(1). Again, Congress has not directly dealt with the question posed by this appeal. This definition addressed "nonattainment" without prescribing any criteria for determining the proper components of an "area." In addition, § 7407(e)(1) provides no standard which is to be followed by the administrator of EPA in approving or disapproving a request for redesignation. Thus under the Chevron formulation we seek to determine whether EPA's answer to the question is "based on a permissible construction of the statute." *Id.*

We conclude that EPA acted reasonably in determining that Lorain County should be included in the Cleveland urban nonattainment area even though actual monitoring disclosed an acceptable level of ozone within the county. The purpose of the Clean Air Act Amendments of 1977 was to ensure additional efforts to bring those areas of the country which had not met the time requirements of the Act into compliance. Congress adopted the scheme of dividing states into attainment, nonattainment and unclassified areas. For nonattainment areas it provided new stringent sanctions which could be applied by EPA to encourage compliance. *United States Steel Corp. v. United States Environmental Protection Agency*, 605 F.2d 283, 284-85 (7th Cir. 1979), *cert. denied*, 444 U.S. 1035 (1980). Once a state has designated an area "nonattainment," that area may be redesignated only with the approval of EPA. It appears a permissible exercise of this authority for EPA to deny redesignation with respect to a component of a nonattainment area which produces a substantial portion of the area's pollution even though the air within that component tests at an acceptable level. If it were otherwise, the fortuitous circumstance that pollutants and precursors emitted within a county are moved by prevailing winds to a neighboring county would deprive EPA of the tools Congress provided for attacking pollution in the area of which the county is logically a part. The Cleveland urban area fits the definition of a nonattainment area because the ozone levels in and around Cleveland exceed the NAAQS.

C.

Having concluded that EPA acted within the scope of its authority, we must now consider whether it acted arbitrarily and capriciously in this case, as claimed by Ohio.

Ohio admitted on the record that emissions from Lorain County contribute to the ozone concentrations in the Cleveland area. Given this concession, it is difficult to conceive how EPA could be found to have acted arbitrarily or capriciously by including Lorain County in the Cleveland urban nonattainment area. The technical materials in the record support the conclusion that the contribution of Lorain County's emissions to the Cleveland ozone problem is significant. We do not believe the fact that EPA did not conduct measurements of the wind-factor effect in the Cleveland area is important. The tests in other major urban areas demonstrated satisfactorily that ozone precursors are carried long distances in the atmosphere and combine with other substances to form ozone in such areas. The results of tests in a number of urban areas were sufficiently similar to form a reliable basis for concluding that the same condition would occur in Cleveland. Even if these data were not sufficient to support EPA's conclusion, Ohio cannot escape its own concession of the effect of Lorain County's emissions on the ozone concentrations in the Cleveland area.

Ohio also argues that EPA acted arbitrarily in redesignating Medina County while refusing to remove the "nonattainment" designation from Lorain County. Both counties lie upwind from both Cleveland and Lake County which have ozone levels in excess of the NAAQS. However, compared with the emissions from Lorain County, those from Medina County are insignificant. Lorain County is heavily industrialized while Medina is largely rural with only scattered sources of pollution. EPA acted in the exercise of its discretion in removing Medina County from the nonattainment area while refusing to redesignate Lorain County. We find no abuse of discretion.

The petition for review is denied.

NOTES

1. Does the court correctly apply the *Chevron* test to construe the language of the statute at issue in this case? *See Chevron, USA, Inc. v. Natural Resources Defense Council*, 467 U.S. 837 (1984).

2. The problem raised by the *Ohio v. Ruckelshaus* case was addressed, in part, by the 1990 Amendments. In particular, the Amendments provide that for ozone or carbon monoxide nonattainment areas classified as serious, severe or extreme, the entire metropolitan statistical area, as established by the Bureau of the Census, must be included in the nonattainment area. § 107(d)(4)(A)(iv). This designation can be avoided, however, if the Governor of the affected State is able to satisfy EPA that sources in a certain portion of the metropolitan statistical area do not contribute significantly to the ambient air quality standard violation.

3. The 1990 Amendments also changed the definition of a nonattainment area. Under the prior law, nonattainment area was defined as ". . . an area which is shown by monitored data or which is calculated by air quality modeling . . . to exceed any national ambient air quality standard . . . ." The 1990 Amendments define a "nonattainment area" as simply ". . . an area which is designated "nonattainment". . . within the meaning of § 107(d)."

4. Section 107(d) operates by temporarily freezing the designation of all areas, subject to the possible expansion of serious, severe, or extreme ozone or carbon monoxide nonattainment areas as described in note 2. § 107(d)(1)(C). By March 15, 1991, however, states were required to submit to EPA a list of all air quality control regions within the state specifying whether they are attainment areas, nonattainment areas, or unclassifiable for ozone and carbon monoxide. The process works in only one direction — it may be used to designate what had previously been an attainment area as nonattainment, but it cannot be used to redesignate a nonattainment area as attainment. § 107(d)(4)(iii).

5. The general provisions regarding redesignation are at § 107(d)(3). Under these provisions, a redesignation may be made at the instigation of either EPA or a State. Areas may not be redesignated as attainment areas unless EPA finds, among other things, that "the improvement in air quality is due to permanent and enforceable reductions. . ." and that a maintenance plan for the area has been approved in accordance with § 175A. § 107(d)(3)(E). This maintenance plan must provide for maintenance of the ambient air quality standard for at least ten years after redesignation.

PROBLEM #1: STATE IMPLEMENTATION PLANS AND NONATTAINMENT AREAS

The Mohave Air Quality Control Region in the State of Stagnation encompasses a three-county area that includes the City of Mohave and its suburbs. The Mohave metropolitan area has a population of approximately six million people and is one of the fastest growing regions in the country with an annual growth rate of 3%.

As of November 15, 1990, the Mohave Air Quality Control Region was a nonattainment area for ozone, carbon monoxide, and particulate matter. The average ambient concentrations for these pollutants in the region are as follows:

Ozone - 0.21 ppm (hourly average/day)
Carbon Monoxide - 17.5 ppm (8-hour average)
PM-10 - 100 $\mu g/m^3$ (annual geometric mean)

You are responsible for revising and implementing the Stagnation state implementation plan. What action is Stagnation required to take to comply with the Clean Air Act? What additional information, if any, will you need to ascertain the State's obligations? Given the expected increase in population, what additional options should be considered by the City and the State to help ensure that compliance with the law will be achieved? What sanctions are imposed if the State fails to achieve its pollution reduction milestones?

NOTE: The primary NAAQS for O_3 is 0.12 (hourly average/day (can be exceeded once)); for CO, 9 ppm (8-hour average (can be exceeded once)); and for PM-10, 50 $\mu g/m^3$ (annual geometric mean). *See* 40 CFR part 50 (1991).

E. Transboundary Disputes

STATE OF CONNECTICUT V. EPA
696 F.2d 147 (2d Cir. 1982)

IRVING R. KAUFMAN, Circuit Judge:

These challenges to a final ruling of the Environmental Protection Agency ("EPA" or "Agency") call upon us to steer a course through the labyrinth that is the Clean Air Act. Few statutes present more complex problems for the nation's courts than this 120-page treatise designed to safeguard our precious air resources. And, fewer are more important. Indeed, in reaching the proper construction of the Act's requirements we must never forget Congress's aim, universally shared, for a cleaner, healthier environment. At the same time, we remain guided by the fundamental principles of law which give the EPA broad discretion as the guardian of Congress's goal. Our task is not to determine whether the EPA has been the wisest steward but only whether the Agency has violated its legislative mandate, losing sight of the chartered path to the promised land of clean air.

* * *

No aspect of this novel attempt to establish joint state and federal responsibility is more crucial than the provisions which guarantee that air pollution generated in one state does not disrupt another state's plans for complying with the national standards. Indeed, one purpose of the Clean Air Act Amendments of 1977, which further refined the statutory scheme, is to strengthen and clarify EPA's obligation to consider carefully the interstate impact of any revision of a state implementation plan ("SIP"). The 1977 Amendments also outline the type of interstate impacts that are permissible. Petitioners, the State of Connecticut and Connecticut Fund for the Environment ("CFE"), today ask us to determine whether the EPA complied with the stringent requirements of the 1977 Amendments when it approved a revision of New York's state implementation plan allowing five plants owned by the Long Island Lighting Company ("LILCO") to continue burning fuel of 2.8% sulfur content in Suffolk County, New York.

Our careful analysis of petitioners' challenges to EPA's action leads us to conclude that the Agency has indeed satisfied these rigorous conditions.

I

This case reaches us after a somewhat intricate procedural and factual history. Its roots stretch at least as far back as July 20, 1976 when the EPA approved a one-year temporary special limitation in New York's state implementation plan permitting the use of 2.8% sulfur content fuel at LILCO's Port Jefferson Generating Facility units 3 and 4 and 2.5% at Northport Generating Facility units 1-3. 40 C.F.R. § 52.1670(c)(30)(31) (1981). New York's overall environmental regulatory scheme generally authorizes the burning of only 1% sulfur content fuel in Suffolk County, but it also explicitly provides for such special limitations when granted by New York's Commissioner of Environmental Conservation and approved by the EPA. N.Y.Admin.Code Tit. 6, §§ 225.1-225.2 (1979). In 1977 EPA approved a three-year extension of LILCO's special limitation which permitted the burning of 2.8% fuel at all five plants. 40 C.F.R. § 52.1670(c)(33) (1981). This extension expired on May 31, 1980.

Limits on the sulfur content in fuel are designed chiefly to minimize levels of sulfur dioxide ("SO_2") in the surrounding air. *See Connecticut Fund for the Environment v. EPA*, 696 F.2d 169 (2d Cir.1982) (*"Connecticut Fund II "*). . . [H]owever, percentage requirements for sulfur in fuel also help place a ceiling on the amount of total suspended particulates ("TSP") which a fuel burning source, such as a power plant, emits into the atmosphere. The State of Connecticut's and CFE's challenge to EPA's approval of New York's decision to continue permitting LILCO to burn higher sulfur content fuel centers on possible increased concentrations of these two pollutants in Connecticut's air. We note at the outset, however, that because this case involves a continuation of existing practice rather than permission to increase the sulfur content of fuel, no new or additional pollution will result from the challenged Agency action.

New York's Department of Environmental Conservation ("DEC") first made clear its intention to extend LILCO's special limitation beyond the May 31, 1980 deadline in a report dated January 14, 1980. The DEC evaluation, produced following LILCO's November 1979 request for an extension and its submission of data, indicated that continued burning of 2.8% sulfur fuel at Port Jefferson and Northport would not cause a violation of the national ambient air quality standards ("NAAQSs") for sulfur dioxide in New York. This original report did not consider the effect of LILCO's emissions on Connecticut or the impact of those emissions on either state's efforts to comply with the NAAQSs for total suspended particulates.

* * *

On July 3, 1980 EPA published its proposed approval of DEC's request to extend LILCO's special limitation, and invited public comments on whether the extension should be approved. 45 Fed.Reg. 50,832 (1980). The notice directed the public to the rules, set forth in 42 U.S.C. § 7410(a)(2)(A)-(K) (Supp. IV 1980), governing the EPA's decision to approve or disapprove revisions of state implementation plans. These rules apply in this case since New York's approval of LILCO's special limitation is a revision of New York's EPA approved SIP.

In direct response, the State of Connecticut filed comments on August 29, 1980 alleging that Agency approval of New York's proposal would violate 42 U.S.C. § 7410(a)(2)(E) (Supp. IV 1980). This provision establishes guidelines EPA must use in assessing the interstate impact of any state's proposed revision of its state implementation plan. In sum, Connecticut argued that New York's proposal to allow LILCO to continue burning high sulfur fuel would sufficiently harm Connecticut's air so as to violate the Clean Air Act. We will discuss this argument in detail in Part II of our opinion.

In a separate proceeding, Connecticut also petitioned the EPA on August 28, 1980, pursuant to 42 U.S.C. § 7426 (Supp. IV 1980), asking the Agency to find that under New York's proposal, LILCO's emissions would contravene 42 U.S.C. § 7410(a)(2)(E)(i) (Supp. IV 1980) by "preventing the attainment and maintenance" of the NAAQSs in Connecticut. 42 U.S.C. § 7426, added to the Clean Air Act by the 1977 Amendments, extends to states the right to bring such petitions and requires the EPA to find a violation or deny the petition within 60 days. The EPA held hearings on Connecticut's petition on December 3 and 4, 1980. It has yet to act upon them.

The Agency did, however, investigate Connecticut's allegations. It received additional technical analysis from LILCO and the State of New York concerning the effect of the proposed revision on Connecticut's air. This analysis demonstrated that LILCO's emissions would not cause a violation of the EPA's primary or secondary standards for sulfur dioxide in Connecticut. *See* Analyses of Total SO_2 Concentrations

At Selected Sensitive Connecticut Locations, Long Island Lighting Company, April 14, 1981. EPA's evaluation also indicated that burning of 2.8% sulfur fuel at LILCO's plants would create an insignificant impact on concentration levels of total suspended particulates in Connecticut. Technical Support Document to New York State Implementation Plan Revisions Effecting [sic] the Long Island Lighting Company, EPA--Region II, August 12, 1981, ("EPA Technical Support Document"). EPA then extended the comment period until June 19, 1981, to allow the public to respond to this new technical material. 46 Fed.Reg. 27,501 (1981). Connecticut submitted supplemental comments on June 17, 1981, again challenging New York's and EPA's conclusions. In its own technical report EPA responded to the various contentions raised by Connecticut and found that LILCO's emissions under New York's proposal would not violate the Clean Air Act. EPA Technical Support Document, supra, Memorandum, "Review of Comments Received on New York State Supplemental Air Quality Modeling Analysis of the Long Island Lighting Company," from Robert Predale to Raymond Werner. Accordingly, the EPA, on September 24, 1981, issued a final rule approving LILCO's special limitation which expires on Sept. 24, 1984. 46 Fed.Reg. 47,069 (1981).

On November 12, 1981, the State of Connecticut petitioned this Court for review of the Agency's action pursuant to 42 U.S.C. § 7607(b)(1) (Supp. IV 1980). Connecticut Fund for the Environment filed its petition 11 days later. Both petitions raise various challenges to the propriety of the EPA's decision, many of which were presented by Connecticut in its comments submitted to the EPA. We now turn to these challenges.

* * *

II

A

42 U.S.C. § 7410(a)(2)(E)(i)(I) (Supp. IV 1980) prohibits the EPA from approving a revision of a state implementation plan unless the plan as revised contains provisions which ensure that no fuel burning source will "prevent attainment or maintenance of any. . . national primary or secondary ambient air quality standard in any other state." Nowhere, however, does the statute define the word "prevent." Such a definition is required for two distinct situations. When the affected state has attained the national ambient air quality standards ("NAAQSs") for a pollutant, it must be determined when pollution generated in another state will "prevent the maintenance" of that standard. And, when the affected state has not attained a standard, we must decide under what circumstances interstate pollution will "prevent the attainment" of that standard. Both situations are relevant here. Connecticut and CFE allege that LILCO's continued burning of 2.8% sulfur fuel will "prevent the attainment and maintenance" of the NAAQSs in Connecticut for both sulfur dioxide and total suspended particulates. Connecticut has attained the NAAQSs for sulfur dioxide. 40 C.F.R. § 81.307 (1981). It has not attained the secondary standard for total suspended particulates. 40 C.F.R. § 81.307 (1981)

1. Sulfur Dioxide

A literal reading of the word "prevent" in § 7410(a)(2)(E)(i)(I) would require the EPA to approve New York's proposed revision unless petitioners could show that LILCO's emissions would make it impossible for Connecticut to maintain the standards for sulfur dioxide even by imposing stricter control measures upon its own pollution sources. The EPA properly rejected this literal interpretation of the statute.

The legislative history makes clear that the Clean Air Act Amendments of 1977 were designed to ensure that one state would not be able to foist its pollution on another state and accordingly require that state to tighten its regulations to keep its air clean. *See* H.R.Rep. No. 294, 95th Cong., 1st Sess. 329-331, *reprinted in* 1977 U.S.Code Cong.Ad.News 1077, 1408-1410; S.Rep. No. 127, 95th Cong., 1st Sess. 41-42 (1977). Indeed, the 1977 Amendments replaced the earlier provisions of the Clean Air Act of 1970 which only required each state's implementation plan to provide measures for "intergovernmental cooperation." Congress determined that the earlier statute had proved ineffective in solving the difficult problem of interstate air pollution. S.Rep. No. 127, 95th Cong., 1st Sess. 41-42 (1977). It would be inconsistent with congressional purpose, therefore, for EPA to allow a state to increase its emissions if those emissions would cause a violation of the NAAQSs in another state. Accordingly, EPA concluded that regardless of what further regulations Connecticut might adopt, New York's proposed revision could be approved only if it would not cause a violation of the primary or secondary standards for sulfur dioxide in Connecticut given Connecticut's then prevailing emission limitations on its own sources of pollution. We accept this conclusion as reasonable and consistent with the purposes of the Clean Air Act. *See Connecticut Fund for the Environment v. EPA*, 672 F.2d 998, 1006 (2d Cir.1982).

Petitioners would apparently have us go farther and interpret § 7410(a)(2)(E)(i)(I) as requiring the EPA to disapprove New York's proposed revision even if no violation of the standards would result from LILCO's emissions. They ask us to read the words "prevent the maintenance of any . . . national ambient air quality standard" to mean "have a substantial impact on pollution" in the affected state. We decline to do so. Initially, we have every reason to believe that Congress meant what it said. Absent strong indications to the contrary, the plain language of a statute is the best index of its meaning. *Manchester Environmental Coalition v. EPA*, 612 F.2d 56, 60 (2d Cir.1979). Moreover, the question of one state's "substantial impact" on air pollution in another state is covered by other sections of the Clean Air Act. Part C of the Clean Air Act, one of the major additions of the 1977 Amendments, is aimed at preventing the significant deterioration of air quality in areas which have attained the national ambient air quality standards. The Agency correctly points out that § 7410(a)(2)(E)(i)(II) incorporates the provisions of Part C into this section of the statute, designed to achieve interstate pollution abatement. It is therefore entirely reasonable to assume that Congress intended the incorporation of Part C to ensure that pollution from one state would not unfairly contribute to pollution in another state. Accordingly, the EPA reasonably concluded that § 7410(a) (2)(E)(i)(I) was not intended to do more than prohibit the Agency from approving state implementation plan revisions which will cause violations of the NAAQSs in nearby states. The Agency's construction must be upheld where reasonable. *Train v. Natural Resources Defense Council*, 421 U.S. 60, 75 (1975).

Even accepting the EPA's construction, petitioners argue the Agency abused its discretion by concluding that New York's proposed revision would not cause a violation of the NAAQSs for sulfur dioxide in Connecticut. The State of Connecticut and CFE claim the Agency used an improper modeling technique to estimate the effects of LILCO's emissions on Connecticut's air. They further assert that the EPA arbitrarily and capriciously used data obtained at LaGuardia Airport rather than weather readings taken from the closer Bridgeport Airport. Additionally, petitioners contend the Agency abused its discretion by using meteorological data from 1964, by failing to measure the effect of the tall height of LILCO's emissions stacks, and by refusing to take into account a proposed revision in Connecticut's SIP raising from .5% to 1% the permissible percentage of sulfur in fuel burned by pollution sources in Connecticut. *See Connecticut Fund II*. We note initially that EPA carefully considered each of the many technical points raised before approving LILCO's special limitation. Moreover, we stress that while "expertness is not a magic wand which can be indiscriminately waved over the corpus of an agency's findings to preserve them from review," L. Jaffe, Judicial Control of Administrative Action 613 (1965), this kind of technical decision is particularly within the realm of Agency expertise. *See Mision Industrial Inc. v. EPA*, 547 F.2d 123, 129 (1st Cir.1976). With these thoughts in mind, we begin our analysis of the petitioners' technical challenges.

a) Modeling

EPA based its conclusion that LILCO's continued emissions would not cause a violation of the NAAQSs for SO_2 in Connecticut on analyses derived from the CRSTER model. Air quality models, like CRSTER, contain a set of mathematical equations used to calculate pollutant concentrations caused by a pollution source's emissions. Using actual data such as meteorological measurements and stack emission characteristics, the modeling analysis predicts concentrations for an array of points at various distances from the plant. The CRSTER, or single source, model estimates the impact on pollution concentration levels by measuring emission levels at a single source and calculating the likely effect of these emissions at various destinations using meteorological data such as wind velocity and direction. *See* Guideline on Air Quality Models (Office of Air Quality Planning and Standards 1.2-080, EPA, April 1978) incorporated by reference 40 C.F.R. § 51.24(k) (1982), (hereinafter "Guideline on Air Quality Models" or "Guideline"); *see generally Cleveland Electric Illuminating Company v. EPA*, 572 F.2d 1150 (6th Cir.), *cert. denied*, 439 U.S. 910 (1978).

Petitioners challenge the EPA's use of the CRSTER model claiming that it is inadequate to measure the meteorological and terrain complexities created by the flow of air across Long Island Sound from New York to Connecticut. One such problem raised by petitioners is the phenomenon of "fumigation." Fumigation occurs when the stream of air ("plume") carrying emissions from a pollution source comes into contact with a turbulent internal boundary layer of air ("TIBL") created by the temperature differential between warm air over coastal lands and cooler air carried in from the water. The TIBL erodes the plume causing the emissions to disperse over the land mass resulting in higher pollution concentrations at ground level. The Agency itself, however, recognized these problems. In a letter from the EPA's Region II Administrator to the Office of Air Quality Planning and Standards Clearinghouse in North Carolina, the Administrator requested an evaluation to determine the appropriate model to apply to the complexities created by the wind conditions over New York and Connecticut and by Connecticut's high terrain. EPA Technical Support Document, *supra*. The Clearinghouse specifically concluded that the best approach would be to adjust the CRSTER model to account for the complicated terrain. EPA Technical Support Document, supra. It rejected the so-called "Valley Model" suggested by the State of Connecticut as well as other proposed alternatives.[26] Petitioners have failed to

---

[26] The so-called "Valley Model" is designed for situations where emissions arise from low (valley terrain) and impact with rugged terrain such as cliffs and bluffs. It relies on assumed meteorological conditions rather than actual data. EPA Technical Support Document, *supra*.

demonstrate that this carefully considered decision constituted an abuse of the Agency's discretion.

CFE alleges that the Agency contravened its own Guideline on Air Quality Models when it decided to rely on the CRSTER model. Petitioner simply misconstrues this Guideline. The Guideline does recommend the CRSTER model for situations where there are no significant meteorological or terrain complexities. Guideline on Air Quality Models § 4.3.1 at 20, J.A. at 241. It further suggests that where such complexities exist, a model more suitable than the CRSTER model should be applied. Its conclusion, however, is that "*each complex situation be treated on a case by case basis with the assistance of expert advice*" (emphasis added). *Id.* The Guideline further states that "even though specific recommendations are made they should not be considered rigid requirements. The preferred model is that which best simulates atmospheric transport and dispersion in the area of interest." Guideline § 1.0 at 1-2, CFE's Appendix at 1-2.

The EPA adopted exactly this case-by-case approach. It adjusted the CRSTER model to account for the terrain complexities in Connecticut and provided a detailed technical rationale for the inadequacy of other proposed models. Specifically, the Agency rejected the use of the Valley Model because it remains untested for distances as great as those which the LILCO emissions travel to reach Connecticut. While CFE points to problems with the CRSTER model created by breezes blowing pollution toward Connecticut from the air over Long Island Sound, it offers nothing to indicate that another modeling approach would better account for the overall complex situation. Nor is there the slightest indication that the Agency's reliance on the CRSTER model was arbitrary and capricious. To reject the EPA's conclusion under these circumstances would be to substitute our judgment concerning mathematical modeling techniques for that of the Agency. *See Cleveland Electric Illuminating Company v. EPA*, *supra*, 572 F.2d at 1161. This we cannot do. Accordingly, we conclude that CFE's challenge to the Agency's modeling is without merit.

b) Meteorological Data

Petitioners raise two objections to the meteorological data chosen by the Agency in calculating the effect of LILCO's emissions on Connecticut. They assert that the EPA should have used weather readings from Bridgeport rather than those taken from LaGuardia Airport. They further contend the Agency improperly combined meteorological data from 1964 with figures from 1973-1976. Neither of these Agency actions constituted an abuse of discretion.

The EPA's decision to use data from LaGuardia Airport clearly resulted from a considered judgment based on technical factors. The Agency selected LaGuardia weather readings because that airport is located on the same side of Long Island Sound as the LILCO plants. Wind conditions at LaGuardia, therefore, more closely simulate those at Northport and Port Jefferson. Petitioners correctly point out that the Bridgeport Airport is approximately 10 miles closer to the LILCO plants than LaGuardia, and EPA readily admits that proximity is one factor to be considered in determining the appropriate meteorological data to be utilized. Guideline on Air Quality Models § 5.2 at 31, CFE's Appendix at 3. The Agency concluded, however, that the similarity in wind direction was a more significant factor in identifying the proper data than the proximity of the source. It reached that conclusion because the prevailing wind direction at Bridgeport is precisely opposite that at LILCO's plants, thus seriously undermining the usefulness of Bridgeport data regardless of its proximity. Indeed, given the arguments raised by petitioners themselves concerning the importance of the meteorologically complex air patterns over Long Island Sound, the Agency's decision seems quite sound. In any event, there can be no doubt that this considered weighing of competing factors produced a decision which was rationally based, *see Bowman Transportation, Inc. v. Arkansas Best Freight System, Inc.*, 419 U.S. 281, 290 (1974), and well within the Agency's discretion. *See Mision Industrial, Inc. v. EPA*, *supra*, 547 F.2d at 129.

* * *

c) Stack Height

Petitioners further challenge the Agency's assumptions concerning the height of two of LILCO's stacks. EPA performed its calculations by estimating the height of these stacks at 486 feet rather than using the actual height of 600 feet. CFE correctly points out that the use of the smaller figure produced an inaccurately low prediction of LILCO's impact on Connecticut's air. Taller stacks tend to have a greater impact on pollution levels at more distant locations. LILCO's stacks, therefore, create more pollution in Connecticut because of that state's distance from the plants.

CFE fails to recognize, however, that the Agency also conducted a supplemental analysis to assess the differential between the predicted impact using the lower estimated figure and the actual stack height. EPA Technical Support Document, *supra*, Memorandum, "Sensitivity Analysis of LILCO's Impacts on Connecticut Based on GEP versus Actual Stack Height Modeling," from Robert Predale to Raymond Werner, J.A. at 230. The Agency also relied on an analysis submitted by New York's Department of Environmental Conservation which employed actual stack height precisely to calculate a "worst case" scenario. EPA Technical Support Document, *supra*, Memorandum, "Review of the New York State Air Quality Modeling Analysis of LILCO's Impact on Connecticut," from Robert Predale to Raymond Werner, J.A. at 209. Both these additional studies support the Agency's conclusion that LILCO's emissions would not cause violations of the national ambient air quality standards for sulfur dioxide in Connecticut. Under these circumstances, we conclude that the Agency did not abuse its discretion by partially relying on analysis using estimated stack heights when approving LILCO's special limitation.

* * *

d) Connecticut's Proposed Revision

CFE argues that the Agency abused its discretion by failing to take into account a proposed revision in Connecticut's state implementation plan which would raise the permissible percentage of sulfur in fuel burned in that state from .5% to 1%. EPA proposed that revision for approval, 46 Fed.Reg. 45,738 (Sept. 11, 1981), two weeks before it finally approved LILCO's special limitation, 46 Fed.Reg. 47,096 (Sept. 24, 1981). The short answer to CFE's contention is that no provision in the Clean Air Act requires the EPA to consider the impact of a proposed revision of one state's implementation plan upon a restructuring of the state implementation plan of another state. We do not mean to imply, however, that a situation could never arise where the general scheme of the Clean Air Act would require the Agency to consider the combined effect of two proposed revisions before approving either.

In this case, the Agency did consider the combined effect of both revisions on Connecticut's air before permitting Connecticut to revise its SIP. In our holding in *Connecticut Fund II*, we conclude today that the EPA acted within its discretion when it determined that the combined effects of LILCO's emissions and increased pollution created by the burning of 1% sulfur fuel in Connecticut would cause no violations of the NAAQSs in Connecticut. Accordingly, the Agency's failure to consider Connecticut's revision before approving LILCO's special limitation was at worst harmless error. We hold, therefore, that EPA did not violate § 7410(a)(2)(E) when it concluded that New York's proposed revision of its SIP which allowed LILCO to continue burning 2.8% sulfur fuel at Port Jefferson units 3 and 4 and Northport units 1-3 would not "prevent the maintenance" of the national ambient air quality standards for sulfur dioxide in Connecticut.

2. TOTAL SUSPENDED PARTICULATES

The burning of high sulfur fuel at LILCO's Northport and Port Jefferson Plants affects Connecticut's level of total suspended particulates in two ways. The greater sulfur content in the fuel increases the particulate emissions directly pouring out of LILCO's stacks. In addition, sulfur released into the air will under certain atmospheric conditions combine with other airborne molecules to create particulates known as sulfates. Petitioners allege that each of these effects will impermissibly contribute to the already existing violations of the NAAQSs for TSP in Connecticut. More specifically, they claim that EPA violated § 7410(a)(2)(E)(i)(I) when it approved LILCO's special limitation because New York's SIP, petitioners allege, no longer prohibits LILCO from emitting any air pollutant which will "prevent the attainment" of the NAAQSs for TSP in Connecticut.

EPA claims it need not consider the impact of New York's proposed revision on TSP levels in Connecticut. The Agency argues that because limitations on the sulfur content in fuel are part of New York's state implementation plan to control sulfur dioxide, any changes in sulfur regulations require the Agency to examine only the effect on SO_2 levels. In our companion case, *Connecticut Fund II*, we hold today that where the EPA is considering the effect of a proposed revision of a SIP on pollution levels within one state, it may, within the reasonable exercise of its discretion, permit that state to regulate on a pollutant by pollutant basis. Although mindful of the deference to be given to the Agency's interpretation of the statute, we feel we must exercise the utmost caution before extending that ruling to apply to situations like the one presented here where the revision of New York's SIP affects concentration levels of pollutants in another state, namely Connecticut. Indeed the language of the Clean Air Act points toward the opposite conclusion.

Section 7410(a)(1) requires each state to adopt and submit to the EPA a state implementation plan for each national ambient air quality standard within nine months of the promulgation of such standard. Section 7410(a)(2)(B), a provision involved in our companion case, *Connecticut Fund II*, prohibits the Agency from approving a revision of a state implementation plan unless it contains measures necessary to insure the attainment and maintenance of "such standard" (emphasis added). By contrast, § 7410(a)(2)(E)(i)(I) dealing with interstate impacts, forbids EPA approval of a revision of a SIP unless it contains adequate provisions prohibiting any stationary source [here LILCO's plants] within the state from emitting any air pollutant in amounts which will prevent attainment or maintenance by any other state of *any* such national ambient air quality standard. (emphasis added.) Congress's purpose in enacting § 7410(a)(2)(E) indicates that this difference in language was probably not a product of inadvertent drafting.

One central focus of the Clean Air Act Amendments of 1977 was to ensure that the EPA would monitor and control the impact of pollution from one state on air quality in another. H.R. No. 294, 95th Cong., 1st Sess. 329-331, *reprinted in* 1977 U.S.Code Cong. & Ad.News at 1408-10; S.Rep. No. 127, 95th Cong., 1st Sess. 41-42 (1977). *See also State of Connecticut v. EPA*, 656 F.2d 902 (2d Cir.1981). Unlike the intrastate effects in *Connecticut Fund II*, which resulted only after Connecticut had the opportunity to choose for itself between different approaches to controlling SO_2 and particulates, here LILCO's emissions, were they to significantly contribute to Connecticut's TSP concentrations, would deprive Connecticut of that flexibility. Allowing one state to foreclose another from exercising the many options available for controlling its pollution problem seems contrary to the congressional intent of strengthening each state's protection against interstate pollution. The use of the word "any" in § 7410(a)(2)(E), therefore, seems precisely tailored to require the EPA to consider the effect of a revision of one state's implementation plan upon all NAAQSs in other states. Moreover, the Agency presents no evidence that Congress did not intend these words as written. Accordingly, we have serious difficulty with the EPA's contention that New York is free to revise its SIP for SO_2 without any federal consideration of whether the revision will "prevent the attainment" of the NAAQSs for TSP in Connecticut.

We need not uphold the Agency's argument, however, to conclude that no violation of the Clean Air Act occurred, concerning total suspended particulates, when the EPA approved LILCO's special limitation. The Agency did, in fact, consider the effect of LILCO's emissions on TSP concentrations in Connecticut, at least to the extent these effects could be measured. The Agency decided that the burning of 2.8% sulfur fuel at Northport and Port Jefferson created an insignificant impact on TSP levels in Connecticut. For the reasons discussed below, we find that the Agency acted well within its discretion in reaching that conclusion.

a) Direct Emissions

The EPA's analysis of LILCO's direct particulate emissions revealed their impact on TSP levels in Connecticut would be minimal. The maximum estimated impact was 0.10 $\mu g/m^3$ on an annual basis and 2.06 $\mu g/m^3$ on a 24-hour basis. EPA Technical Support Document, *supra*. This compares to primary NAAQSs of an annual geometric mean concentration of 75 $\mu g/m^3$ and an average 24-hour second-high concentration of 260 $\mu g/m^3$. (The secondary NAAQS is an average second high 24-hour concentration of 150 $\mu g/m^3$) 40 C.F.R. §§ 50.6-50.7 (1982). These low-level impacts are not unexpected. LILCO's stacks are equipped with electrostatic precipitators designed to trap virtually all particulates before they are released. Moreover, LILCO's plants must comply with New York's particulate regulations, which are in fact more stringent than Connecticut's. Although CFE challenges the modeling EPA used to obtain its results, we have previously explained that the Agency acted well within its discretion in rejecting petitioners' reliance on the so-called "Valley Model". Accordingly, we accept the EPA's estimates concerning the direct effect of LILCO's particulate emissions on Connecticut.

In addition, we agree with EPA that these minimal impacts will not "prevent [Connecticut's] attainment" of the NAAQSs for TSP in contravention of § 7410(a)(2)(E)(i)(I). The legislative history is again unclear as to the precise meaning of "prevent the attainment" in situations where the affected state has not yet complied with the NAAQSs. *See* H.R.Conf.Rep. No. 564, 95th Cong., 1st Sess. 145-46, *reprinted in* 1977 U.S.Code Cong. & Ad.News at 1526- 27; H.R.Rep. No. 294, 95th Cong., 1st Sess. 329-31, *reprinted in* 1977 U.S.Code Cong. & Ad.News at 1408-10. The Agency suggests that the words of the statute indicate a congressional desire to prohibit revisions to state implementation plans which will "significantly contribute" to already existing violations in other states. The problem with this interpretation, however, is that the statute contains no guidelines as to what would constitute a "significant contribution." Moreover, the 1977 Clean Air Act Amendments unmistakably indicate a strong congressional policy to strengthen the procedure for bringing each state to compliance with the national standards. *See* H.R.Rep. No. 294, 95th Cong., 1st Sess. 1, *reprinted in* 1977 U.S.Code Cong. & Ad.News at 1079; *see also National Resources Defense Council v. Gorsuch*, 685 F.2d 718 (D.C.Cir.1982). We must tread lightly, therefore, in approving any interpretation of the Clean Air Act which might interfere with the statutory goal of ensuring that each state comply with the NAAQSs as "expeditiously as practicable". *See* § 7502.

On the other hand, nothing in the legislative history indicates that § 7410(a)(2)(E)(i)(I) was intended to prevent even minimal impacts upon another state's pollution concentrations simply because that state has not attained the national standards. To adopt this approach would be to hold one state hostage to another's failure to enact the pollution control strategies necessary to conform to the requirements of the Clean Air Act. Moreover, as intervenor LILCO points out, the language of § 7410(a)(2)(E)(i)(I) seems to contemplate a standard which would prohibit SIP revisions only if the emissions they permit would in and of themselves prevent a nearby state from attaining the NAAQSs. Accordingly, we cannot reject the Agency's interpretation of the statute in favor of a blanket rule forbidding the EPA from approving any SIP revision which permits additional amounts of a specific pollutant to be added to concentrations in a nearby state which has not attained the NAAQSs.

At the same time, the facts of this case do not require us to conclusively adopt the Agency's suggestion that § 7410(a)(2)(E)(i)(I) prohibits only those SIP revisions which will "significantly contribute" to pollution concentrations in the affected state. We hold only that where the impact upon a nearby state of another state's revision of its SIP is shown by the Agency to be so insignificant as to be fairly described as minimal, the EPA may approve that revision even where the affected state is not in compliance with the NAAQSs. *See Alabama Power Co. v. Costle*, 636 F.2d 323, 360-61 (D.C.Cir.1979). Here the estimated maximum impact of 2.06 $\mu g/m^3$ is less than 1.5% of even the secondary NAAQS. Because this impact is truly minimal, we conclude that the EPA did not violate § 7410(a)(2)(E)(i)(I) when it determined that LILCO's direct particulate emissions would not "prevent the attainment" of the NAAQSs for TSP in Connecticut.

b) Sulfate Formation

Connecticut and CFE vigorously contend that even if the direct particulate emissions from LILCO's plants will not prevent the attainment of the NAAQSs for TSP in Connecticut, the indirect formation of sulfates will. The possibility does exist that higher sulfur emissions will react with other elements in the atmosphere to create dangerous particulates called sulfates. The short answer to petitioners' contention, however, is that the EPA, as yet, has no adequate model to predict the likelihood of that possibility. *See* Guideline on Air Quality Models (1978). Because of the severe health dangers associated with high concentrations of suspended sulfates,[41] we can reasonably expect that the Agency will continue to strive towards developing techniques capable of measuring the degree of risk posed by sulfate formation. A time may come, therefore, when the Agency will establish NAAQSs for sulfates and when all SIP revisions will be evaluated for their likely impact on sulfate levels. Alternatively, the Agency may take so long to address, or at least measure, the sulfate problem that any further delay could be found to be an abuse of discretion. Until that time, however, it can hardly be said that the Agency's failure to consider an effect it cannot measure constitutes a violation of the Clean Air Act. *See Mision Industrial, Inc. v. EPA*, *supra*, 547 F.2d at 131.

Connecticut and CFE argue that the Agency's inability to measure sulfate formation is insufficient to justify its refusal to at least approximate likely sulfate impacts. Two additional technical factors, however, support EPA's unwillingness to guess at the indirect impact of LILCO's emissions on Connecticut. Initially, the Agency was aware that during the winter periods when sulfate levels in Connecticut posed the greater threat, the wind direction was least likely to blow LILCO's emissions toward Connecticut. In addition, the Connecticut Department of Environmental Protection measured sulfate levels in Connecticut and found them to be relatively homogeneous thus indicating that sulfates in Connecticut's atmosphere probably travelled from points farther away than LILCO's plants. Particularly when faced with these two indications that sulfate levels in Connecticut were not a product of LILCO's emissions, the EPA reasonably concluded that it need not consider the possibility of sulfate formation which the Agency itself could not satisfactorily measure. *See Mision Industrial Inc. v. EPA*, *supra*, 547 F.2d at 131. Accordingly, the Agency did not violate § 7410(a)(2) (E)(i)(I) when it made no specific estimate of the impact of LILCO's emissions on sulfate formation in Connecticut.

Our analysis of each of petitioners' challenges, therefore, reveals that the Agency did not abuse its discretion by concluding that LILCO's burning of 2.8% fuel at Northport and Port Jefferson will not prevent the attainment or maintenance of the NAAQSs in Connecticut.

* * *

The petitions for review are denied.

NOTES

1. In the 1990 Amendments, § 110(a)(2)(E) was moved to § 110(a)(2)(D) and altered slightly. Instead of "prevent[ing] the attainment or maintenance" of the NAAQS, the law now prohibits a State from "contribut[ing] significantly to nonattainment in, or interfer[ing] with maintenance by any other State" with respect to NAAQS. How might this change have altered the analysis in the *Connecticut* case?

2. Although not at issue in the principle case, the court notes that Connecticut, in a separate *administrative* proceeding, had petitioned EPA under § 126(b) of the Act for a finding similar to that which it sought in the judicial proceedings; that is, that the LILCO plants were preventing Connecticut from maintaining compliance with the NAAQS for SO_2. The court's decision effectively resolved this petition against

---

[41] These dangers include higher mortality rates, aggravation of heart and lung disease in the elderly, aggravation of asthma, excess risk of acute lower respiratory disease in children and excess risk of bronchitis.

Connecticut. Note, however, that § 126(b) requires the Administrator to act within 60 days after receipt of the petition. In this case, the petition was filed on August 28, 1980 and had not been decided at the time for the court's decision in 1982. *Compare Air Pollution Control District v. EPA*, 739 F.2d 1200 (6th Cir. 1984),*infra*. (An inordinate delay of 22 months in acting on a § 126 petition did not justify granting the petition unless the delay was arbitrary and capricious.)

3. Shortly after the Second Circuit had decided the *Connecticut* case, New York found itself on the other side of a similar controversy. In *New York v. EPA*, 710 F.2d 1200 (6th Cir. 1983), the State of New York challenged, among other things, Tennessee's application for a revision to its SIP to allow an increase in SO_2 emissions from its Kingston power plant. New York made two principal arguments in its challenge to EPA's approval of the Tennessee SIP revision: (1) that EPA had failed to assess the cumulative impacts of the emissions allowed by the Tennessee SIP on the SIPs of other states; and (2) that EPA had failed to determine the impact of the plant emissions on the formation of suspended sulfate particulates in other states. Both issues, of course, had been decided in New York's favor by the Second Circuit, but in a manner contrary to New York's position before the Sixth Circuit. The Sixth Circuit followed the Second Circuit's lead in dismissing New York's claims. *Id.* One significant distinction between the two cases, however, should be noted. In the *New York* case the state had, like Connecticut, filed a petition under § 126(b) of the Act. The New York petition, however, was considerably broader than its challenge to the Tennessee SIP revision. Indeed, it encompassed proposed revisions to seven other SIPs involving 17 large midwestern power plants. The court found that while EPA need not consider the cumulative impacts of the various plants prior to its approval of the Tennessee SIP revision, it should consider those impacts in its review of New York's § 126(b) petition. Can a state circumvent the restrictions imposed by the courts on cumulative analysis merely by filing a comprehensive petition under § 126(b)?

4. At one point in its opinion, the court states that "no provision in the Clean Air Act requires the EPA to consider the impact of a proposed revision of one state's implementation plan upon a restructuring of the state implementation plan of another." Read § 110(a)(2)(D). Do you agree that it does not require an analysis of the cumulative effects of revisions to state SIPs?

5. The Supreme Court has ruled that mutually exclusive permit applications for radio broadcast licenses must be considered together in order to ensure that granting one license will not deprive the other applicant of a fair hearing. *Ashbaker Radio Corp. v. FCC*, 326 U.S. 327 (1945). The *Ashbaker* doctrine has been applied to a host of other situations involving mutually exclusive permits or licenses. *See* SCHWARTZ, ADMINISTRATIVE LAW, § 6.2 (2d ed. 1984). Should the doctrine have been applied to the New York and Connecticut SIP revision proposals?

6. Despite the acknowledged health dangers associated with suspended sulfates the court refused to require EPA to consider the sulfate particulates contributed from LILCO's emissions to Connecticut's air. The basis for the court's action was the lack of an adequate model to predict their occurrence. 696 F.2d at 147. Does the lack of an adequate model justify EPA's refusal to regulate? Is it consistent with EPA's obligation to set the primary health-based standards "allowing an adequate margin of safety"? § 109 (b)(1).

7. Consider the problem of interstate competition for pollution rights in the context of the *Connecticut* case. The New York SIP had a standard requirement allowing facilities in Suffolk County to burn fuel with one percent or less sulfur content.

Exemptions, however, were granted for two units at LILCO's Port Jefferson facility and for three units at LILCO's Northport Generating facility which allowed fuel with a 2.8 percent sulfur content. By contrast, Connecticut's SIP had required its facilities to burn fuel with 0.5 percent sulfur content or less. Eventually, however, Connecticut succumbed to the competitive pressure, and in November, 1981, after LILCO's special limitation was extended, Connecticut amended its SIP to allow 1.0 percent sulfur content fuel. *Connecticut Fund for the Environment v. EPA,* 696 F.2d 169 (2d Cir. 1982).

8. Competition among the states to attract new industry must surely discourage states like Connecticut from maintaining higher regulatory standards than their neighbors. As one might expect, high sulfur fuel is less expensive than low sulfur fuel. Moreover, EPA policy, approved by the court in the *Connecticut* case, appears to give priority to the first polluting state: "EPA concluded that regardless of what further regulations Connecticut might adopt, New York's proposed revision could be approved only if it would not cause a violation of the primary or secondary standards for sulfur dioxide in Connecticut *given Connecticut's then prevailing emission limitations* on its own sources of pollution." (Emphasis added.) 696 F.2d at 156. What arguments can you make against such a policy?

9. Recall the Supreme Court's declaration in *Illinois v. City of Milwaukee*, 406 U.S. 91 (1972) "A state...may well ask that its strict standards be honored and that it not be compelled to lower itself to the more degrading standard of a neighbor." To what extent does the *Connecticut* decision undermine this pronouncement?

10. Should the courts (or the Congress) devise a system of equitable apportionment of pollution rights in a manner similar to the way in which the Supreme Court has apportioned water rights in various states? *See e.g., Nebraska v. Wyoming,* 325 U.S. 589 (1945). Consider this notion in the context of the following case.

AIR POLLUTION CONTROL DISTRICT V. EPA

739 F.2d 1071 (6th Cir. 1984)

ENGEL, Circuit Judge.

The Air Pollution Control District of Jefferson County, Kentucky, seeks review of an order of the Environmental Protection Agency ("EPA"), reported at 47 Fed.Reg. 6624 (Feb. 16, 1982). That order denied Jefferson County's petition for interstate pollution abatement, filed pursuant to section 126 of the Clean Air Act, 42 U.S.C. § 7426(b) (Supp. V 1981). Jefferson County sought relief upon its claim that the Gallagher Power Station ("Gallagher") in southern Indiana emits air pollutants in violation of section 110 of the Act, 42 U.S.C. § 7410(a)(2)(E)(i) (Supp. V 1981). In that connection, Jefferson County sought a reduction of sulfur dioxide ("SO_2") emissions from the Gallagher generator. The County claimed that Gallagher's SO_2 emissions violated the provisions of the Clean Air Act which prohibit emissions in one state that prevent the attainment or maintenance of national ambient air quality standards ("NAAQSs") in another state. *Id.* Jefferson County also maintained that Gallagher's emissions interfered with the margin for future industrial growth that the County had sought to create by placing strict controls on the emission of SO_2 by Kentucky sources.

The EPA denied Jefferson County's section 126 petition for interstate pollution abatement because it found that Gallagher did not "substantially contribute" to the violation of NAAQSs in Jefferson County.

* * *

II. Regulatory Background and Proceedings Before the EPA.

Jefferson County, Kentucky, and Floyd County, Indiana, share a common boundary on the Ohio River. The City of Louisville is located in the northwest portion of populous Jefferson County. In contrast, Floyd County is relatively undeveloped. However, since Jefferson County and Floyd County draw on the same air resources, they, along with Clark County, Indiana, were designated by the EPA as the Louisville Interstate Air Quality Control Region. 40 C.F.R. § 81.35 (1982).

Because the structure of the Clean Air Act is state-oriented, each state is charged with implementing national clean air standards within its own political boundaries. Thus, although Floyd County and Jefferson County are in the same air quality control region, each county is subject to the implementation plan adopted by its respective state. Initially this was not a problem, since Indiana and Kentucky had adopted identical emission limitations for the pollutant at issue in this case, SO_2.

On May 14, 1973, EPA approved Indiana's SIP for Floyd County. This regulatory scheme set an emission limitation for the Gallagher Power Station of 1.2 pounds of SO_2 per million British Thermal Units ("lbs/MBTU") of heat input. Gallagher is situated less than a mile from the Indiana-Kentucky border and is the largest producer of SO_2 in Floyd County. In 1972, the EPA had approved Kentucky's SIP which set emission limitations of 1.2 lbs/MBTU of SO_2 for the major sources in Jefferson County: three power plants owned by Louisville Gas and Electric.

This uniformity of emission limitations in Floyd County and Jefferson County did not last long. In 1974, Indiana adopted new SO_2 regulations for Floyd County that completely exempted Gallagher from the 1.2 lbs/MBTU emission limitation, though the plant was required to keep on hand a two week supply of low-sulfur fuel should atmospheric conditions require lower SO_2 emissions. At first the EPA proposed to disapprove Indiana's regulation. However, when Indiana submitted technical data which showed that exempting Gallagher from limitations on the emission of SO_2 would not interfere with the attainment and maintenance of SO_2 standards in either Indiana or Kentucky, the EPA approved the regulation. 41 Red.Reg. 35,676 (Aug. 24, 1976). In 1979, Indiana submitted a revision of the SO_2 portion of its SIP to the Agency. The new plan established an emission limitation for SO_2 of 6 lbs/MBTU heat input for most Indiana power plants, including Gallagher. This 6 lbs/MBTU limitation represents the amount of SO_2 currently emitted by the Gallagher plant without any controls; thus, the new "limitation" effectively maintains the status quo of uncontrolled SO_2 emission at Gallagher. On May 26, 1982, EPA proposed to approve the 6 lbs/MBTU limit with respect to the primary NAAQSs in Floyd County, but to disapprove it as to the secondary NAAQS. 47 Fed.Reg. 22,976.

Meanwhile, in Jefferson County the 1.2 lbs/MBTU emission limitation was generally enforced. In 1975 Louisville Gas and Electric negotiated consent orders whereby final compliance with the 1.2 lbs/MBTU limitation would be delayed until 1985. However, even with strict emission limitations, Jefferson County has yet to attain the NAAQSs for SO_2, and on February 23, 1978, Jefferson County was designated a Part D non-attainment area for both primary and secondary standards. 43 Fed.Reg. 8964 (Mar. 3, 1978); 40 C.F.R. § 81.318 (1983).

It can therefore be seen that a significant disparity exists between the permissible emission limits of power plants in Jefferson County, Kentucky, and the Gallagher plant in Floyd County, Indiana. Louisville Gas and Electric, the primary producer of SO_2 in Jefferson County, spent approximately $138 million installing scrubbers to remove SO_2 from its emissions, while across the river, Gallagher's SO_2 emissions were completely uncontrolled.

On May 14, 1979, the Air Pollution Control District of Jefferson County filed a petition for interstate pollution abatement under section 126 of the Clean Air Act, 42 U.S.C. § 7426. The petition requested that EPA find (1) that SO_2 emissions from Gallagher are preventing attainment and maintenance of the NAAQSs for SO_2 in Jefferson County and (2) that once Jefferson County attains the NAAQSs for SO_2, Gallagher's emissions will interfere with Jefferson County's efforts to prevent significant deterioration of air quality under Part C of the Act. The petition sought tighter controls on Gallagher's SO_2 emissions.

* * *

EPA calculated that only about three percent of the SO_2 concentration at any location in Jefferson County where the NAAQSs are violated is attributable to Gallagher. However, an EPA modeling study also stated that:

> The highest second-highest predicted impact on a 24-hour average in Kentucky from Gallagher is 126 $\mu g/m^3$ [micrograms per cubic meter], which is about 34.5% of the primary NAAQS. This is a substantial portion of the NAAQS and has the potential to limit the increment available to new sources in Louisville. The highest second-highest predicted 3-hour concentration in Kentucky resulting from the plant is 608 $\mu g/m^3$. This represents 47% of the secondary NAAQS, and has a far more serious potential for limiting growth in Kentucky.

In fact, the EPA's study concluded that by 1985 Gallagher's emissions "will be the predominate [sic] influence upon air quality in Louisville, Kentucky."

Notwithstanding these determinations, the EPA, on February 16, 1982, finally denied Jefferson County's section 126 petition for interstate pollution abatement. 47 Fed.Reg. 6624. The EPA concluded that "the Gallagher plant does not cause or substantially contribute to a violation of the SO_2 NAAQS." *Id.* at 6628. It is from this decision that the Air Pollution Control District of Jefferson County appeals.

* * *

IV. Substantive Issues.

* * *

B. Fairness and Uniformity in Criteria: Section 7601(a)(2)(A).

Jefferson County argues that the EPA denied the section 126 petition without considering the "interstate inequities" that the interstate pollution provisions were designated to eliminate. One aspect of this argument concerns 42 U.S.C. § 7601(a)(2)(A) which states:

> (2) Not later than one year after August 7, 1977, the Administrator shall promulgate regulations establishing general applicable procedures and policies for regional officers and employees (including the Regional Administrator) to follow

> in carrying out a delegation under paragraph (1), if any such regulations shall be designed —
>
> (A) to assure fairness and uniformity in the criteria, procedures, and policies applied by the various regions in implementing and enforcing the chapter. . . .

Although its argument is rather vague, the County apparently reads section 7601(a)(2)(A) as providing specific protections against "interstate inequities." In the County's view, inequities arise in the present case because the EPA has approved SO_2 emission limitations for Gallagher that are very different from the limitations set for Kentucky sources.

* * *

[W]e are unable to agree that section 7601(a)(2)(A) can be so applied. Section 7601 generally relates to administration and the procedures to be followed by EPA employees in carrying out a delegation of authority from the Administrator. There is simply no indication in the statute that section 7601(a)(2)(A) establishes a substantive standard which requires similar or uniform emission limitations for all sources within a particular area as part of a section 126 determination.

* * *

C. The "Margin For Growth" Argument.

Jefferson County asserts that Kentucky's SIP was designed to create a margin of clean air in Jefferson County by setting stringent emission standards that would leave the air cleaner than the NAAQSs require. Creation of this margin of clean air would allow further industrial growth in Jefferson County without the NAAQSs being violated. Since the operation of Gallagher without controls could in certain parts of Jefferson County contribute 47% of the secondary NAAQS for SO_2, the County contends that the margin for growth contemplated by the Kentucky SIP has been stolen by Gallagher to the economic disadvantage of Jefferson County. The County also seems to contend that once it attains the secondary NAAQS for SO_2, Gallagher's emissions will interfere with future measures to prevent significant deterioration of air quality in Jefferson County. Presently, no such measures are in place, since the County has not achieved the NAAQSs for SO_2.

The EPA's response to this "margin for growth" argument was seemingly inconsistent. Initially, in its notice of the proceedings on Jefferson County's section 126 petition, the EPA interpreted the interstate pollution abatement provisions as prohibiting interference with another state's margin for growth:

> The Agency considers that the degree of protection afforded by the interstate pollution provisions includes not only protection against NAAQS violations, but also protection against unreasonable interference with a maintenance program or margin for growth in the SIP. In reaching this conclusion, the Agency has reviewed the interstate pollution provisions of the Act, including Sections 101, 110, 126 and 301, their legislative history and pertinent case law. The Agency is of the opinion that these provisions evidence Congressional intent to protect against unreasonable interstate interference with State programs to maintain the NAAQS and create margins of growth, as well as efforts to attain the standards, prevent significant deterioration of air quality and protect visibility. Such efforts may include State adoption of emission limitations that are more stringent than needed to attain Federal

> standards. In addition, the Agency believes that the provisions are designed to protect against interstate interference with State or local ambient air standards or other measures more stringent than necessary to attain Federal standards. *See*, H.R.Rep. No. 93-294, 95th Cong., 1st Sess., May 12, 1977, 331, n. 14, U.S.Code Cong. & Admin.News 1977, p. 1077.

45 Fed.Reg. 17,048, 17,049 (Mar. 17, 1980). The EPA also solicited comments from interested parties on whether Gallagher has "a substantial adverse impact on Kentucky's or Jefferson County's efforts to develop a State Implementation Plan which will attain and maintain standards or *create a margin for future growth* for NAAQS or PSD purposes." *Id.* (emphasis added). Thus, at the outset, the EPA suggested that the Clean Air Act permits states to reserve to themselves a margin for growth.

However, when the EPA rendered its final determination on Jefferson County's section 126 petition, the "margin for growth" argument was rejected. In referring to the problem of Gallagher consuming Jefferson County's future PSD increment, the EPA stated:

> *Comment.* One commentator objected to EPA's proposed finding that emissions from Gallagher do not interfere with PSD provisions and urged the Administrator to make a finding on the plant's potential impact on future PSD requirements in Jefferson County.
>
> *Response.* Jefferson County is a nonattainment area for SO_2, and the PSD regulations are not applicable. Consequently the Gallagher plant cannot interfere at this time with PSD requirements in Jefferson County. Section 126 only prohibits interference with PSD measures required by the Clean Air Act, and therefore EPA need not review possible future impacts on regulations not yet in place. "See State of Connecticut v. EPA," 656 F.2d 902 [2d Cir.1981]. Furthermore, Gallagher's emissions will not consume any future PSD increment since its emissions at the time the baseline date is set will be included in the baseline air quality in Jefferson County.

47 Fed.Reg. 6624, 6627 (Feb. 16, 1982).

* * *

Clearly, the EPA's final position on the "margin for growth" issue was markedly different from that first taken in the notice of hearing. However, for several reasons, we are disinclined to hold that it was improper for the EPA to reconsider and revise its initial assessment of the protections which the Clean Air Act affords to state efforts to maintain a margin for growth.

In our view a notice of hearing simply is not, and should not be treated as, a vehicle for final agency pronouncements on sophisticated matters of statutory interpretation.

* * *

Unlike a final agency determination, which is the product of careful consideration of all the evidence, a notice of hearing is necessarily issued without input, and consequently it would be inappropriate to treat it as though it were an irrevocable pronouncement or rule. There is great value in encouraging candor in the framing of notices, inasmuch as this assists the parties in preparing for the hearing.

* * *

The EPA contends that it is irrelevant to the petition brought by Jefferson County under section 126 whether Gallagher infringes on the margin for growth which the County asserts it needs for future industrial development. By utilizing section 126 to prevent upwind states from contributing SO_2 to air that is cleaner than the NAAQSs require, the County is in effect attempting to establish a local air quality standard that is more stringent than the national standard. The EPA argues that the literal language of sections 126(b) and 110(a)(2)(E), 42 U.S.C. §§ 7426(b), 7410(a)(2)(E), indicates that interstate pollution is prohibited only insofar as it prevents another state from attaining or maintaining "any such national primary or secondary ambient air quality standard." 42 U.S.C. § 7410(a)(2)(E)(i) (emphasis added).

Upon consideration of the statute and the relevant case law, we cannot say that the EPA's determination that the Act does not protect future margins for growth is unreasonable. Since Jefferson County has yet to achieve the NAAQSs for SO_2, any "interference" by Gallagher with the asserted margin for growth is necessarily conjectural. Also, the literal language of 42 U.S.C. § 7410(a)(2)(E) supports the EPA's interpretation.

* * *

D. The "Substantial Contribution" Test.

A major objective of the Clean Air Act Amendments of 1977 was to deal with the problem of interstate air pollution, which Congress believed had been inadequately addressed by the 1970 Act. Congress amended section 110 of the 1970 Act to require the Administrator, before approving any SIP or portion thereof, to determine that it contains

> adequate provisions (i) prohibiting any stationary source within the State from emitting any air pollutant in amounts which will (I) prevent attainment or maintenance by any other State of any such national primary or secondary ambient air quality standard, or (II) interfere with measures required to be included in the applicable implementation plan for any other State under part C to prevent significant deterioration of air quality or to protect visibility . . .

42 U.S.C. § 7410(a)(2)(E). Section 126, 42 U.S.C. § 7426, also added by the 1977 amendments, requires states in developing implementation plans to identify existing and proposed sources of pollution that may significantly affect the air quality of neighboring states and to provide notice of this information to the states. Section 126 further provides that neighboring states may petition the Administrator for a finding that a major source emits or would emit any air pollutant in violation of the prohibition of section 7410(a)(2)(E)(i). The question which has plagued the EPA and reviewing courts since that time is, assuming that no upwind state can transmit utterly pure air to its neighbor, how much pollution is too much under the Act?

If the 1977 amendments to the Act have in fact added to the interstate pollution abatement authority of the EPA, and to the ability of states to seek relief from interstate air pollution, the Act has done little to provide guidelines for the equitable allocation of the burden of reducing interstate pollution. The problem is far more complex than it may at first seem and does not consist solely, or perhaps even primarily, of limiting the emissions of upwind stationary sources. The intractable nature of the problem is well described in a law review comment:

> Interstate equity requires that the burden of reducing interstate pollution be allocated fairly among the states involved. Some of the factors that must be considered in defining interstate equity are whether existing or new sources are involved, whether the source state's SIP contains stringent or lax emission standards, whether emission standards are being violated in the source state, the extent to which sources in the receiving state contribute to NAAQS non-attainment there, and whether the contributions by sources in the receiving

> states are due to violations of emissions standards or to lax standards. The number of factors to be considered and their complex interactions demonstrate that no simple definition of interstate equity is likely to be satisfactory.
>
> If interstate pollution would arise with respect to a proposed new source, EPA can simply prevent construction of that source. Recently EPA issued an interim policy for new sources that allows each state to consume only half of the increment that exists at the state line. This interim policy is an initial step toward defining interstate equity, but it involves only the relatively easy case of sources that have not yet been constructed.
>
> Achieving interstate equity when interstate pollution is emitted by existing sources presents a greater problem. Usually non-attainment in the receiving state will be due to emissions from sources inside that state, in addition to the interstate pollution. If both states have SIP's adequate to attain the NAAQS's, and the non-attainment is because of SIP violations in the source state or both states, then SIP enforcement is all that is necessary. But if all sources in the interstate areas are in compliance with their states' emission standards, the issue becomes more complex especially if one state's emission standards are more lenient than the other's.
>
> Perhaps interstate equity requires each state's emission standards to be identical for like sources. However, such a definition would not necessarily apportion the abatement burden equitably in an interstate region if one state has larger, more numerous, or different types of contributing sources than the others. Alternatively, interstate equity may require that economic impacts for each state be the same. If so, further problems arise in measuring the economic impact in each state, and in allocating that impact within each state.

Silverstein, *Interstate Air Pollution: Unresolved Issues*, 3 Harv.Envtl.L.Rev. 292-93 (1979) (citations omitted).

Perhaps the most hotly debated issue in these proceedings is the standard to be applied by the Administrator in interpreting 42 U.S.C. § 7410(a)(2)(E)(i). This section establishes the circumstances under which the interstate pollution abatement provisions of the Clean Air Act are triggered: interstate pollution is forbidden if it will "prevent attainment or maintenance" of the NAAQSs. Under the broad interpretation of section 7410 urged by Jefferson County, the Act would prohibit nearly all interstate pollution. On the other hand, a narrow reading of the same section would allow only the most extreme instances of interstate pollution to come under scrutiny.

When it denied Jefferson County's petition, EPA interpreted the "prevent attainment or maintenance" language of section 7410 to mean that an interstate polluter, here Gallagher, must "cause or substantially contribute" to a violation of a NAAQS in another state before the pollution abatement provisions are triggered. 47 Fed.Reg. 6624, 6628 (Feb. 18, 1982). According to this interpretation, a section 126 petition may not be granted unless there is (a) a violation of the NAAQSs in one state and (b) pollution emissions in another state which substantially contribute to the violation. Jefferson County particularly objects to the use of the term "substantial contribution," describing it as "an unduly restrictive approach" which fails to consider the equitable elements of the Clean Air Act.

Essentially, Jefferson County's objection concerns the meaning of the word "prevent" in section 7410(a)(2)(E)(i). Since the Clean Air Act itself offers no guidance as to what levels of pollution "prevent attainment and maintenance" of the NAAQSs, this language is open to differing interpretations. The County disagrees with the EPA's conclusion that, since only about three percent of the pollutants in areas which violate the SO_2 NAAQSs in Kentucky are attributable to Gallagher, the plant does not "prevent attainment or maintenance" of the NAAQSs in Jefferson County. The County asserts that in effect the EPA has amended section 126 of the Act by adding a requirement that there be a showing that a polluting state "substantially contributes" to a violation of the NAAQSs in the downwind state before a section 126 petition can be granted. The County urges an approach whereby any contribution by a polluting state to a NAAQS violation in a receiving state would be forbidden under section 126: "If the sending state contributes 100% to a problem, then it will be required to contribute 100% of the solution. If the contribution is 1%, then the solution is 1% and any amounts in between."

* * *

Upon examining the language of the Clean Air Act, we believe that the test probably intended by Congress is whether one state "significantly contributes" to NAAQS violations in another state. Although this test is not specifically incorporated into the statute, we do find reference to the phrase in section 126(a), 42 U.S.C. § 7426(a), of the Act, which requires written notice to nearby states of interstate pollution. This new section of the Act provides that all nearby states are entitled to notice of any proposed new or modified source of pollution "which *may significantly contribute* to levels of air pollution in excess of the national ambient air quality standards in any air quality control region outside the state in which such source intends to locate (or makes such modifications)." *Id.* (emphasis added). Since the purpose of written notice is to enable affected states to take action, it seems logical to infer that in enacting section 126, Congress intended to prohibit interstate pollution which does or will "significantly contribute to levels of air pollution in excess of the national air quality standards." We do not believe that Congress intended to prohibit even *de minimis* contributions by one state to NAAQS violations in another state because such a policy would in effect "hold one state hostage to another's failure to enact the pollution control strategies necessary to conform to the requirements of the Clean Air Act." *Connecticut v. EPA*, 696 F.2d 147, 164 (2d Cir.1982).

Having concluded that the proper test to be applied in evaluating the section 126 petition is whether Gallagher's emissions "significantly contribute" to NAAQS violations in Jefferson County, we must ascertain whether the EPA was correct in its determination that Gallagher's emissions are permissible. The EPA performed extensive modeling studies of the effect of Gallagher's emissions and found that Gallagher contributed only about three percent of the pollutants in areas of Jefferson County that violate the NAAQSs. The EPA determined that Gallagher does not "substantially contribute" to NAAQS violations in Jefferson County and that consequently, section 126 does not require pollution abatement. For the purposes of this opinion, we decline to delve into the semantic distinctions between "substantial" and "significant" and choose to treat the terms as having the same meaning. We are convinced that the broad deference which we are statutorily required to accord to the findings of the Agency preclude our disturbing the EPA's determination, at least absent any other criteria established by the EPA, or found elsewhere in the Act, that would require a different result. Jefferson County points to the fact that, although Gallagher may contribute only three percent to actual NAAQS violations, Gallagher contributes a substantially greater percentage of the pollutants present in parts of the County where the NAAQSs are not violated. However, 42 U.S.C. § 7410(a)(2)(E) appears to contemplate interstate pollution abatement actions only where interstate emissions prevent attainment of the NAAQSs, *i.e.*, only where the standards are violated. Thus, we believe that the EPA did not err in denying Jefferson County's section 126 petition.

V. Conclusion

In a most practical sense, Jefferson County's concerns are understandable. There would appear to be a patent unfairness in an Agency policy which would tolerate so much higher a level of SO_2 emissions in one area than in another, especially given the high costs which Jefferson County has already incurred to reduce its own pollution. Nevertheless, we believe that the construction placed upon the statute by the EPA appears to be literally correct, even though arguably at odds with the important policy values represented by the 1977 amendments.

The petition for review of the Agency's final determination to deny Jefferson County's section 126 petition is denied.

NOTES

1. Does the Sixth Circuit agree with the Second Circuit's construction of "prevent attainment or maintenance" as that phrase is used in § 110(a)(2)(D)(i) of the Act (formerly § 110(a)(2)(E)(i))?

2. The Sixth Circuit endorses the Second Circuit's "first in time, first in right" interpretation of §§ 110(a)(2)(D) (formerly 110(a)(2)(E)) and 126 of the Act. Thus, it allows the upwind state, Indiana, to use as much of the remaining SO_2 increment of another as is available. Indeed, it can cause another state to exceed the NAAQS, so long as its contribution is not "substantial", and it can do so with no air pollution controls whatsoever. How does the court respond to Jefferson County's complaint regarding interstate inequities? Under what circumstances would the Sixth Circuit be likely to accept an argument based on interstate inequities? How did Congress respond to these concerns in the 1990 Amendments? *See* §§ 110(a)(2)(D); 176A. What are the responsibilities and powers of an interstate transport commission?

3. Following the decision in the *Air Pollution Control District* case, Jefferson County remained out of compliance with the NAAQS. What measures must the County now take to achieve full compliance as required by the Act? Must it impose additional controls on the Kentucky plants while Gallagher continues to emit pollutants without any controls? Suppose Gallagher increases its emissions so that it now contributes an additional three percent to the nonattainment areas of Jefferson County. Must the Kentucky facilities contribute a corresponding reduction in their emissions?

4. The primary ambient air quality standards for SO_2 must be achieved based on a maximum annual mean of 80 $\mu g/m^3$ and a maximum 24-hour concentration of 365 $\mu g/m^3$. 40 C.F.R. § 50.4 (1990). The secondary standard is a maximum 3-hour concentration of 1300 $\mu g/m^3$. 40 C.F.R. § 50.5. The 24-hour and 3-hour maximum concentrations may be exceeded once annually without violating the rules. *Id.* For this reason, EPA calculated Gallagher's contribution to Jefferson County's pollution problem based on the second highest 24-hour and 3-hour concentrations that were anticipated to occur in Kentucky as a result of the contributions from the Gallagher facility. EPA determined that when emissions from Gallagher were at this level, they would consume 34.5 percent of the maximum 24-hour concentration, and 47 percent of the maximum 3-

hour concentration. EPA further found that by 1985 Gallagher's emissions would be the predominant influence on air quality in Louisville, Kentucky. Nonetheless, EPA determined and the court found that Gallagher's emissions did not contribute substantially to Jefferson County's pollution problem. Why?

5. In 1980, several New England states filed petitions with EPA pursuant to § 126, alleging that SO_2 and NO_x emissions from several midwestern states were causing violations of the NAAQS in these and other states. Underlying the petitioner's allegations regarding NAAQS was an overriding concern that the SO_2 and NO_x emissions from these midwestern states were the principal contributions to New England's acid rain problem — a problem that, until 1990, was not addressed directly by the Clean Air Act. Hearings on the petition were held in 1981 but no action was taken until a lawsuit was filed by several states in 1984 challenging the agency's failure to act within 60 days as required by § 126 of the law. In *New York v. Ruckelshaus*, 21 Env't. Rep. Cas. (BNA) 1721, (D.D.C. 1984) the District Court for the District of Columbia ordered EPA to act on the petition. On December 5, 1984, EPA denied the petition. 49 Fed. Reg. 48,152 (1984). The original lawsuit continued following the decision denying the petition, and evolved to encompass a claim under § 115 of the Act as discussed in the materials that follow. *See Thomas v. New York*, 802 F.2d 1443 (D.C. Cir 1986) *cert. denied*, 482 U.S. 919, (1987), *infra.*

6. Are the *Connecticut* and *Air Pollution Control District* cases consistent with the "prevention of significant deterioration" requirements of the Act? Look closely at § 110(a)(2)(D)(i)(II). *See also* §§ 161-169 and the materials at Chapter 7, *infra.*

7. The new program included in the 1990 Amendments for controlling acid deposition should substantially reduce the likelihood for interstate SO_2 air pollution problems. Clean Air Act, Subchapter IV, *Acid Deposition Control.* As is described in greater detail in Chapter 9, the acid deposition control program is designed to bring all fossil fuel-fired utilities, including Gallagher, to a maximum SO_2 emissions level of 2.5 lbs/mm BTU by 1995 and 1.2 lbs/mm BTU by 2000. The generous emissions trading aspects of the law could conceivably result in continuing problems in localized areas. For example, Gallagher could choose to purchase allowances that would allow it to continue to emit SO_2 at a rate of 6 lbs/mmBtu. Nonetheless, the overall reductions which are supposed to be achieved are so dramatic nationwide (>50%) that interstate conflicts with respect to SO_2 (and perhaps NO_x) should largely be resolved.

HER MAJESTY THE QUEEN IN RIGHT OF ONTARIO V. EPA

912 F.2d 1525 (D.C. Cir. 1990)

BUCKLEY, Circuit Judge:

The question before us is whether the Environmental Protection Agency has any present obligation to take action under section 115 of the Clean Air Act, which establishes a procedure for the prevention of air pollutants in the United States from causing harm in the form of acid deposition to the public health and welfare in Canada. The Province of Ontario and a number of States and environmental groups have petitioned the EPA for a rulemaking that would essentially set in motion section 115's international pollution abatement procedures. We conclude, first, that section 115 does not require the EPA to initiate those procedures until it is able to identify the specific sources in the United States of pollutants that cause harm in Canada; and second, we are satisfied that the EPA is not as yet able to do so.

I. Background

Section 115(a) of the Clean Air Act provides in relevant part as follows:

> Whenever the Administrator, upon receipt of reports, surveys or studies from any duly constituted international agency has reason to believe that any air pollutant or pollutants emitted in the United States cause or contribute to air pollution which may reasonably be anticipated to endanger public health or welfare in a foreign country . . ., the Administrator shall give formal notification thereof to the Governor of the State in which such emissions originate.

42 U.S.C. § 7415(a) (1982). The Administrator's finding that pollution emitted in the United States contributes to such air pollution is referred to as an "endangerment finding."

Under section 115(b), the notice to the Governor of the State in which such emissions originate is deemed to be a finding that its State Implementation Plan ("SIP") under the Clean Air Act is inadequate and must be revised to the extent necessary "to prevent or eliminate the endangerment." *Id.* § 7415(b); *see id.* § 7410(a)(2)(H)(ii). (SIP's impose controls upon individual polluters within each State sufficient to ensure that national ambient air quality standards are met.) This process is referred to as the "SIP revision" procedure.

The remedy provided by section 115 is applicable "only to a foreign country which the Administrator determines has given the United States essentially the same rights with respect to the prevention or control of air pollution occurring in that country as is given that country by this section." *Id.* § 7415(c). This determination is known as a "reciprocity finding."

The dispute in this case is whether the EPA has a present obligation, under section 115, to promulgate endangerment and reciprocity findings as proposed rules with respect to U.S. emissions that allegedly result in harmful levels of acid deposition in Canada. Acid deposition is believed to result primarily from the transportation of sulphur and nitrogen oxide emissions into the atmosphere where they are converted, by chemical processes, into acids that, in combination with water vapors, precipitate in the form of "acid rain," often many hundreds of miles from their source.

Acid rain is alleged to have serious detrimental effects on lakes and streams, soils, crops, building materials, forests, and drinking water. Yet considerable uncertainty and controversy attend the issue, and debate continues over the geographic areas affected by acid rain, the types and extent of damage involved, ambient concentrations and deposition levels, and the ability of scientists to identify the specific sources of the emissions in the United States and Canada that may contribute to each country's and its neighbor's acid rain problem.

The EPA's view of section 115 is that the endangerment finding under section 115(a) is inextricably linked to the requirement that it notify the States whose SIP's must be revised under section 115(b); in other words, the EPA believes that it need not make an endangerment finding until it is able to identify the sources of the pollutants. Otherwise, it will not be able to give the required notification. It then argues that because it currently lacks sufficient information to be able to trace pollutants affecting the Canadian health and welfare to specific sources in the United States, it is not obliged to make endangerment findings at this time. In sum, under the EPA's interpretation, section 115 requires a "unitary proceeding."

Conversely, in petitioners' view the section 115 remedial process may be implemented in stages. They note, first, that the endangerment finding requires only that the Administrator believe that sources within the United States — not in a particular State — are harming Canada, and contend that once the EPA is able to make endangerment and reciprocity findings, it must do so. Petitioners argue that once those findings are made, the statute mandates that the Administrator "shall" proceed with abatement measures even though he may not yet be able to pinpoint the specific sources. They conclude that the EPA has already effectively made endangerment and reciprocity determinations, and therefore it is obliged to publish them as proposed rules; and having made those determinations, the agency may not simply refuse to take *any* corrective action while it continues to study the problem. Petitioners do not base their argument on a belief that the EPA can in fact trace pollutants to their specific sources at the present time.

The case before us has its origins in two letters written in January 1981 by EPA Administrator Douglas M. Costle to Secretary of State Edmund Muskie and Senator George Mitchell. *See New York v. Thomas*, 613 F.Supp. 1472, 1486-93 (D.D.C.1985) (reproducing the two letters), *rev'd*, 802 F.2d 1443 (D.C.Cir.1986), *cert. denied*, 482 U.S. 919 (1987). In the letter to Secretary Muskie, Administrator Costle concluded that "acid deposition is endangering public welfare in the U.S. and Canada and . . . U.S. and Canadian sources contribute to the problem not only in the country where they are located but also in the neighboring country." *Id.* at 1488. Administrator Costle's finding was based on the Seventh Annual Report on Great Lakes Water Quality issued by the International Joint Commission, *id.*, an organization established by the United States and Canada. The IJC is concededly a "duly constituted international agency" for purposes of section 115(a).

In his letter, the Administrator also concluded that Canadian legislation regarding transboundary air pollution "provides the Government of Canada with authority to give the United States essentially the same rights as Section 115 of the Clean Air Act gives to Canada." *Id.* at 1487. Administrator Costle cautioned, however, that whether Canada in fact exercises or interprets that authority in a manner that provides essentially the same rights to the U.S. is a "dynamic" determination "which will continue to be influenced by Canadian action now and in the future." *Id.*

The Administrator's letter to Senator Mitchell contained the same assessments in somewhat greater detail, *id.* at 1488-93, with the additional statements that his conclusions on endangerment and reciprocity were "adequate to warrant the initiation of a Section 115 based plan revision process in appropriate States" and that he had instructed his staff "to develop recommendations regarding the States which should receive formal notification." *Id.* at 1492. Administrator Costle also issued his findings in a press release dated January 16, 1981.

Because the EPA failed to take any further action under section 115, in 1984 several States, environmental groups, and private citizens filed suit under section 304(a)(2) of the Clean Air Act, 42 U.S.C. § 7604(a)(2) (1982), in the U.S. District Court for the District of Columbia. The plaintiffs alleged that the Costle letters imposed upon the EPA a duty to identify and issue SIP revision notices to those States contributing to acid rain in Canada, as provided in section 115. *New York v. Thomas*, 613 F.Supp. at 1476, 1481-86.

In July 1985, the district court granted summary judgment for plaintiffs, holding that the letters constituted both endangerment and reciprocity findings under section 115 and ordering the EPA to issue SIP revision notices to the appropriate States within 180 days. *Id.* at 1481-86; *see Thomas v. New York*, 802 F.2d 1443, 1446 (D.C.Cir.1986), *cert. denied*, 482 U.S. 919 (1987). The court was concerned about the passage of time since the reciprocity determination had been made, however, and allowed the EPA an opportunity to determine whether that conclusion remained valid. 613 F.Supp. at 1484. In October 1985, EPA Administrator Lee M. Thomas found that reciprocity continued to exist. *See Thomas v. New York*, 802 F.2d at 1446.

On appeal, this court reversed, reasoning that Administrator Costle's endangerment and reciprocity findings were rules under section 551(4) of the Administrative Procedure Act, 5 U.S.C. § 551(4) (1988), and therefore could not be promulgated without notice and comment procedures. *Thomas v. New York*, 802 F.2d at 1446-48. As the Costle findings had not been subjected to these procedures, they could not serve as the basis for judicial relief. *Id.* at 1448. The court did not address the issue of whether the EPA was obliged to promulgate such findings, nor did it address their validity.

On April 7, 1988, the Province of Ontario ("Ontario") and a number of States and environmental groups (collectively, "New York") filed petitions for rulemaking with the EPA under section 553(e) of the APA, 5 U.S.C. § 553(e) (1988), requesting the EPA to promulgate endangerment and reciprocity findings pursuant to section 115 of the Clean Air Act. The petitions assert that four reports of duly constituted international agencies support an endangerment finding, that the reciprocity requirements of section 115(c) have been satisfied, and that Administrator Costle has specifically made both endangerment and reciprocity findings which have never been revoked by the EPA. The petitions do not request the EPA to identify the responsible sources or States or to prescribe emissions reductions or other remedial actions, as petitioners view those actions as part of the separate notification and SIP revision processes.

After the lapse of several months without a response, petitioners requested a meeting with EPA officials. The EPA agreed, and a meeting was held on September 9, 1988, with Mr. Don R. Clay, Acting Assistant Administrator for Air and Radiation. At the meeting, petitioners inquired into the status of their petitions and requested that the EPA provide a timetable for addressing them. Mr. Clay refused, but agreed to respond to their concerns in writing.

On October 14, 1988, Mr. Clay sent letters to counsel for the Ontario and New York petitioners. Letter from Don R. Clay to James M. Hecker (Oct. 14, 1988) ("Ontario Letter"); Letter from Don R. Clay to David Wooley (Oct. 14, 1988) ("New York Letter"). The letter to Ontario's counsel explained that it was written in response to counsel's request "for a report on the status of our consideration of those section 115 petitions." Ontario Letter at 1. The first paragraph of the letter contains the following disclaimer: "As discussed in our September 9 meeting, this letter represents only my thoughts on this issue, and does not necessarily reflect the position of the Administrator." *Id.* Mr. Clay also stated: "I do not believe that EPA presently has a sufficient information base to undertake the regulatory program required by section 115. . . . For that reason . . ., I believe it would be premature to rule on your petition at this time." *Id.* at 2.

Then, after describing the EPA's ongoing efforts directed at the acid rain problem, Mr. Clay addressed the interpretation of section 115, declaring that "we continue to hold the view that section 115 is a unitary proceeding which can not be segmented, since the prescribed findings and notification are inextricably interrelated," and that "our present understanding of the acid rain problem is not sufficient to make a judgment regarding the state by state, or even the aggregate reductions necessary to eliminate observed effects." *Id.* at 3. Mr. Clay then stated that "in the absence of that understanding, I do not believe it would be prudent to initiate a regulatory program." *Id.*

The letter concludes as follows:

> In closing, I would like to assure you that we will continue to assess our ability to take action on your petition as we precede [sic] with our ongoing acid rain work. However, at least for the near future, I can not recommend that the Administrator take the discretionary act of making the findings required to trigger the section 115 requirements.

Id. at 4. The New York letter is substantially the same.

Petitioners now seek review of the Clay letters as final agency action denying their petitions for rulemaking.

II. Discussion

Petitioners argue that the EPA has denied their rulemaking petitions, and that its denial was arbitrary, capricious, and not in accordance with law because once the EPA is able to make endangerment and reciprocity findings, it *must* publish them for notice and comment and thereby initiate the remedial process established by section 115. The EPA asserts that we lack jurisdiction over this matter because there has been no final agency action, and that the matter is not ripe for review. The EPA also defends its interpretation of section 115 as reasonable. We address the justiciability issues first, then turn to the merits.

A. Final Agency Action

Section 307(b)(1) of the Clean Air Act, the jurisdictional provision invoked in these petitions, provides for judicial review of final action by the Administrator. 42 U.S.C. § 7607(b)(1) (1982). Accordingly, the threshold question presented is whether we have jurisdiction to review the Clay letters as final action by the Administrator denying petitioners' rulemaking petitions. The EPA claims that the letters simply respond to petitioners' request to be apprised of the status of their petitions and contain nothing more than one subordinate agency official's views with respect to them. The agency maintains that as the letters neither deny nor grant the petitions, they have no direct or immediate effect on the rights of petitioners.

To determine finality, courts must decide "whether the agency's position is definitive and whether it has a direct and immediate . . . effect on the day-to-day business of the parties challenging the action." *Ciba-Geigy Corp. v. EPA*, 801 F.2d 430, 435-36 (D.C.Cir.1986) (internal quotes omitted); *see also FTC v. Standard Oil Co. of California*, 449 U.S. 232, 239 (1980) ("*SOCAL*"). The inquiry seeks to distinguish a tentative agency position from the situation where "the agency views its deliberative process as sufficiently final to demand compliance with its announced position." *Ciba-Geigy*, 801 F.2d at 436. When an agency position is merely tentative, judicial intervention may "den[y] the agency an opportunity to correct its own mistakes and to apply its expertise" and "leads to piecemeal review which at the least is inefficient and upon completion of the agency process might prove to have been unnecessary." *SOCAL*, 449 U.S. at 242, *see also Ciba-Geigy*, 801 F.2d at 436.

Although the EPA emphasizes that it has taken no final action with respect to the petitions, "agency inaction may represent effectively final agency action that the agency has not frankly acknowledged." *Sierra Club v. Thomas*, 828 F.2d 783, 793 (D.C.Cir.1987). When administrative inaction has the same impact on the rights of the parties as an express denial of relief, judicial review is not precluded. *Id.* Similarly, the absence of a formal statement of the agency's position, as here, is not dispositive: An agency may not, for example, avoid judicial review "merely by choosing the form of a letter to express its definitive position on a general question of statutory interpretation." *Ciba-Geigy*, 801 F.2d at 438 n. 9. These principles are consistent with the "flexible and pragmatic way" in which we apply the finality requirement. *Id.* at 435 (internal quotes omitted); *accord NRDC, Inc. v. Thomas*, 845 F.2d 1088, 1094 (D.C.Cir.1988).

On applying the foregoing principles, we conclude that the Clay letters represent final agency action as to the EPA's interpretation of section 115. In other words, although (as we discuss below in part II-C) the EPA concededly made no final decision on petitioners' request that the section 115 remedial process be initiated, it clearly and unequivocally rejected, on the basis of its construction of section 115, petitioners' requests for a separate proceeding limited to the endangerment and reciprocity findings. This is demonstrated by the following language from Mr. Clay's letter to the Ontario petitioners:

> Contrary to your view on the divisibility of the process under Section 115, we continue to hold the view that section 115 is a unitary proceeding which can not be segmented, since the prescribed findings and notification are inextricably interrelated. Making the findings in the manner in which you request would trigger a vast regulatory mechanism which we currently do not believe we can undertake in an informed manner.... [O]ur present understanding of the acid rain problem is not sufficient to make a judgment regarding the state by state, or even the aggregate reductions necessary to eliminate observed effects.

Ontario Letter at 3 (emphasis added).

The EPA contends that this statement merely represents the views of a subordinate agency official and thus cannot be considered final action by the EPA Administrator that is subject to judicial review under section 307(b)(1) of the Clean Air Act. *See* 42 U.S.C. § 7607(b)(1). While it is true, as the EPA emphasizes, that Clay explicitly cautioned that his letters represented his own views and not necessarily those of his agency, there can be little doubt that in this instance, he was speaking for the EPA. This is underscored by his shift from the first person singular consistently used elsewhere in the letter to the collective "we" when asserting the unitary construction of section 115. In so doing, he was clearly speaking in an official rather than a personal capacity. Moreover, in his capacity as Acting Assistant Administrator for Air and Radiation, Mr. Clay was the "principal advisor to the Administrator in matters pertaining to air and radiation programs," 40 C.F.R. § 1.41 (1989), and we have no reason to question his authority to speak for the EPA. *See Ciba-Geigy*, 801 F.2d at 437; *NRDC, Inc. v. Thomas*, 845 F.2d at 1094.

Finally, there is nothing tentative about the EPA's interpretation of section 115; it is unambiguous and devoid of any suggestion that it might be subject to subsequent revision. *See Ciba-Geigy*, 801 F.2d at 437. Furthermore, the interpretation is hardly new: The EPA has adhered to it at least since 1984, when the first lawsuit was filed to compel the issuance of SIP revision notices, and Mr. Clay's pronouncement that "we continue to hold [that] view" can hardly be described as equivocal. *See* Ontario Letter at 3 (emphasis added); *New York v. Thomas*, 613 F.Supp. at 1482-86.

Thus, by adhering to the position that section 115's procedures are not divisible, the Clay letters serve to confirm a definitive position that has a direct and immediate impact on the parties; namely, the denial of their requests that the EPA promulgate endangerment and reciprocity findings even though it is not prepared to proceed with the SIP notification and revision process. The agency's failure to issue a more formal interpretation is irrelevant, as Mr. Clay's statement represents "effectively final agency action [construing section 115] that the agency has not frankly acknowledged." *Sierra Club v. Thomas*, 828 F.2d at 793.

* * *

C. The Merits

In reviewing an agency's interpretation of a statute it administers, we first determine, using traditional tools of statutory construction, "whether Congress has directly spoken to the precise question at issue." *Chevron U.S.A. Inc. v. NRDC, Inc.*, 467 U.S. 837, 842-43 & n. 9 (1984). If the intent of Congress is clear and unambiguous, "that intention is the law and must be given effect." *Id.* at 843 n. 9. If, on the other hand, the statute is silent or ambiguous with respect to a specific issue, then we "must defer to the agency's interpretation ... so long as it is reasonable and consistent with the statutory purpose." *Ohio v. United States Dep't of the Interior*, 880 F.2d 432, 441 (D.C.Cir.1989); *see also Chevron*, 467 U.S. at 843.

We are unable to draw any "unmistakable conclusion" as to whether Congress intended proceedings under section 115 to be unitary or divisible. *See Ohio*, 880 F.2d at 441. The statutory language can be read either way, and the legislative history is meager and unilluminating. And although, as we explain below, the structure of the statute tends to support the EPA's view, we believe it falls short of expressing a clear and unambiguous congressional intent. Under the second step of the Chevron analysis, however, we comfortably conclude that the EPA's view of section 115 is permissible, as it is both entirely reasonable and consistent with the statutory plan.

Section 115(a) provides that "[w]henever" the Administrator, based on certain reports or studies, has "reason to believe" that an air pollutant emitted in the United States causes or contributes to air pollution that may reasonably be anticipated to endanger health or welfare in a foreign country, he "shall give formal notification thereof to the Governor of the State in which such emissions originate." 42 U.S.C. § 7415(a) (emphasis added). The words "whenever" the Administrator "has reason to believe" imply a degree of discretion underlying the endangerment finding. Once that finding is made, however, the remedial action that follows is both specific and mandatory — the Administrator "shall" notify the Governor of the specific State emitting the pollution and require it to revise its SIP.

The statute thus creates a specific linkage between the endangerment finding and the remedial procedures: Once the endangerment finding is made, the SIP revision process must follow. As a result, if there is insufficient information to enable the Administrator to implement those remedies, the promulgation of an endangerment finding alone would largely be pointless. For this reason, the EPA's view that the Administrator must have sufficient evidence correlating the endangerment to sources of pollution within a particular State before he can exercise his discretion to make endangerment findings is both reasonable and consistent with the statute.

Our view of the EPA's interpretation is further supported by section 115(b), which mandates a revision of the polluting State's SIP. Under subsection (b), the

Administrator's notice to the Governor represents a finding that the State's SIP must be revised "with respect to so much of the ... plan as is inadequate to prevent or eliminate the endangerment referred to in subsection (a) of this section." 42 U.S.C. § 7415(b) (emphasis added). This provision reinforces the linkage between the endangerment finding and the remedy that Congress has prescribed. If the EPA does not have a sufficient base of knowledge to trace endangering pollutants to sources within specific States, then a simple endangerment finding would leave subsection (b) without effect. The unitary approach adopted by the EPA avoids that result.

Having decided that the EPA's interpretation of section 115 is permissible, we must next address whether, under that interpretation, the agency's refusal to initiate rulemaking proceedings was arbitrary, capricious, an abuse of discretion, or otherwise not in accordance with law. *See American Horse Protection Ass'n v. Lyng*, 812 F.2d 1, 4 (D.C.Cir.1987). On this issue, we hold that the Clay letters do not represent final agency action, and we are therefore precluded from reviewing the EPA's present refusal to commence proceedings under section 115.

As the letters indicate, the agency has not made any final decision on whether endangerment and reciprocity findings can be made, nor has it conclusively determined whether it can adequately trace pollutants to specific sources in order to issue SIP revision notices. To the contrary, Mr. Clay explained that the EPA is actively working to develop the kind of information that would enable it to initiate section 115 abatement procedures upon making an endangerment finding. Given the complexity of the technical and factual issues that the agency is required to address in this case, we see little basis for questioning its own assessment of its current capabilities.

* * *

We are, of course, fully aware that more than nine years have elapsed since Administrator Costle advised Secretary of State Muskie and Senator Mitchell of his conclusion that pollutants from sources in the United States were endangering the public welfare in Canada. But we are also aware of the unusual complexity of the factors facing the agency in determining the effects of acid rain and in tracing the pollutants from the point of deposition back to their sources. In fact, it was for the purpose, among others, of developing a better understanding of the acid rain phenomenon that Congress enacted the Acid Precipitation Act of 1980, 42 U.S.C. §§ 8901-8912 (1982).

This statute initiated a ten-year program, commonly known as the National Acid Precipitation Assessment Program ("NAPAP"), that is designed to identify the causes and sources of acid rain, to evaluate its environmental, social, and economic effects, and to assess potential methods of control. *See* 42 U.S.C. § 8903. We note that the final NAPAP report is due in December 1990. At oral argument the EPA pointed to this study as evidence of specific research being conducted that could enable the agency to take action under section 115; the EPA also asserted that the report should provide it with a sufficient basis to make a reasoned decision on the petitioners' rulemaking petitions.

It is in part on the basis of this information that we conclude that the EPA's delay in acting on the petitions has been neither arbitrary, nor capricious, nor contrary to law.

III. Conclusion

We find that the Clay letters are final agency action and ripe for review on the specific issue of whether section 115 provides for a unitary or divisible proceeding. We also hold that the EPA's interpretation of section 115 as unitary is reasonable. Finally, we hold that the EPA, in applying its view of section 115, has not taken final action on petitioners' requests for rulemaking, which if granted would set in motion the whole of section 115's pollution abatement procedures. The petitions for review are therefore

Denied.

NOTES

1. Read § 115(a) of the statute. Do you agree with Judge Buckley's conclusion that EPA's interpretation is reasonable? Is EPA required to identify particular sources of pollution under § 115?

2. In some states, it is difficult to determine with certainty the sources of air pollution that are contributing to a nonattainment problem. Recall, for example, the disagreements between Texas and EPA over the source of hydrocarbon emissions (also Michigan & EPA — *Nat'l Steel* case) *State of Texas v. EPA*, 499 F.2d 289 (5th Cir. 1974) *infra*. Why shouldn't the state be permitted to make the same argument that EPA made in the *Ontario* case about the need to ascertain the source of air pollution before it amends its plan to address a nonattainment problem?

3. The limitations of the various models available to predict impacts from long-range transport of air pollution leads to considerable scientific uncertainty about the specific contribution of individual sources to the acid deposition problem. Does the decision in *Ontario* open up the door for EPA to claim insufficient information to act under § 115 in virtually any case that might be presented to the agency?

4. The Acid Deposition Program included in the Clean Air Act Amendments of 1990 should ultimately render the issue raised in the *Ontario* case moot. Interestingly, however, the program ultimately adopted by Congress made no effort to identify particular sources which might be contributing to unacceptable pollution levels in Canada or the United States. All fossil-fuel fired utilities will eventually be subjected to the program. Moreover, the liberal trading policy authorized by the 1990 Amendments suggests that the location of the pollution source is not a significant concern in addressing the acid deposition problem. What does this tell you about EPA's claim that it lacked sufficient information to make the state-by-state reductions that were necessary to address the problem?

F. Enforcement of State Implementation Plans

This section is limited to the enforcement or enforceability of the SIP itself. Enforcement actions against individual stationary sources for other violations of the law are considered in Chapter 10.

GENERAL MOTORS CORPORATION V. UNITED STATES.
_U.S._, 110 S.Ct. 2528 (1990)

Justice BLACKMUN delivered the opinion of the Court.

This case concerns a Clean Air Act enforcement action by the Environmental Protection Agency (EPA) against petitioner General Motors Corporation (GMC). We are asked to decide whether the 4-month time limit on EPA review of an original state implementation plan (SIP) also applies to its review of a SIP revision, and whether, if EPA fails to complete its review of a SIP revision in a timely manner, EPA is prevented from enforcing an existing SIP.

I

What is known as the Clean Air Act, 77 Stat. 392, became law on December 17, 1963. Twenty years ago, Congress enacted the Clean Air Act Amendments of 1970, 84 Stat. 1676, a comprehensive national program that made the States and the Federal Government partners in the struggle against air pollution. The threats to human health were regarded as urgent, and the 1970 Amendments were designed to result in the expeditious establishment of programs to deal with the problem. The Amendments specified a detailed timetable for Federal and State action to accomplish this objective. They required the EPA Administrator, within 30 days of the passage of the Amendments, to promulgate national ambient air quality standards (NAAQS). § 109(a)(1), 42 U.S.C. § 7409(a)(1). Within nine months thereafter, each State was to submit a state implementation plan (SIP) to implement, maintain, and enforce the NAAQS. § 110(a)(1), 42 U.S.C. § 7410(a)(1). As the final step in this start-up phase of the program, EPA was to act on a proposed SIP within four months: "The Administrator shall, within four months after the date required for submission of a plan under paragraph (1), approve or disapprove such plan or any portion thereof." § 110(a)(2), as amended, 42 U.S.C. § 7410(a)(2). The Administrator was directed to approve the SIP if he determined that it was adopted after reasonable notice and hearing and that it met various substantive requirements, including emissions limitations, devices for monitoring air-quality data, and enforcement mechanisms.

* * *

II

A

The entire Commonwealth of Massachusetts is a nonattainment area for NAAQS with respect to ozone. *See* 40 CFR § 81.322, p. 126 (1989). Petitioner GMC owns and operates an automobile assembly plant in Framingham, Mass. The plant's painting operation is a source of volatile organic compounds that contribute to ozone. In 1980, EPA approved Massachusetts' proposed nonattainment area SIP governing volatile organic compound emissions from automobile-painting operations. The SIP permitted GMC to meet emissions limits in stages, but required full compliance by December 31, 1985. In 1981, EPA published a policy statement suggesting that new technology in automobile-painting operations might justify deferral of industry compliance until 1986 or 1987. 46 Fed.Reg. 51386. Three years later, in November 1984, GMC sought an extension from the December 31, 1985, compliance date imposed by the existing SIP, not for the new technology, but rather for additional time to install emission controls on its existing lines. In June 1985, GMC proposed converting to the new technology and requested a summer 1987 deadline. The Commonwealth approved the revision and submitted the proposal to EPA on December 30, 1985, one day before the existing SIP compliance deadline.

GMC began construction of a new painting facility but continued to operate its existing plant. On August 14, 1986, EPA sent GMC a Notice of Violation informing GMC that it was in violation of the applicable SIP. Approximately one year later, on August 17, 1987, respondent filed an enforcement action under § 113(b) of the Act, 42 U.S.C. § 7413(b), alleging violations of the existing SIP's 1985 deadline. On September 4, 1988, the agency made its final decision to reject the revision. 53 Fed.Reg. 36011.

B

The District Court construed § 110(a)(3) as imposing a 4-month time limit on EPA review of a SIP revision and concluded that when EPA failed to complete its review within four months, it was barred from enforcing the existing SIP during the interval between the end of the 4-month period and the time EPA finally acted on the revision. Because EPA had not issued a Notice of Noncompliance until well after the 4-month period had elapsed and, at the time of the court's ruling, had yet to make a final decision on the Commonwealth's SIP revision, summary judgment was entered for GMC.

The Court of Appeals for the First Circuit reversed that judgment and remanded the case for further proceedings. 876 F.2d 1060 (1989). The Court of Appeals agreed with the District Court that the Act imposed a 4-month deadline on EPA review of a SIP revision, but concluded that the failure to meet that deadline did not preclude EPA from enforcing the existing SIP.

Reasoning that an enforcement bar was too drastic a remedy for agency delay, the court concluded that the appropriate remedies for agency inaction were those provided by the Act itself: a suit to compel agency action under § 304(a)(2), 42 U.S.C. § 7604(a)(2), or a request pursuant to § 113(b), 42 U.S.C. § 7413(b), for reduction or elimination of penalties during the period in which unreasonable agency delay resulted in prejudice. 876 F.2d, at 1067-1068. We granted certiorari because of a disagreement among the Circuits as to whether EPA is barred from enforcing an existing SIP if the agency fails to take action on a proposed SIP revision within four months.[42] — U.S. —, 110 S.Ct. 537 (1989).

III

To assure that some form of pollution-control requirements were put in place quickly, the 1970 Amendments established a series of deadlines. One of these was the requirement that EPA act on a proposed SIP within four months after the State submits its plan. § 110(a)(2), 42 U.S.C. § 7410(a)(2). Specifically, the provision requires EPA to act within "four months after the date required for submission of a plan." This seems to us to refer only to the action required on the original SIP. Section 110(a)(2), by its terms, therefore does not impose such a time restraint on EPA review of a SIP revision.

Petitioner nevertheless claims that § 110(a)(3) requires EPA to act on a proposed SIP revision within four months. That provision requires the Administrator to approve "any revision of an implementation plan . . . if he determines that it meets the

---

[42] *See e.g., American Cyanamid Co. v. U.S. Environmental Protection Agency*, 810 F.2d 493 (CA5 1987); *Duquesne Light Co. v. EPA*, 698 F.2d 456 (D.C. Cir. 1983).

requirements of paragraph (2) [§ 110(a)(2)] and has been adopted by the State after reasonable notice and public hearings." Petitioner contends that the reference to § 110(a)(2) was intended to incorporate both the substantive and the procedural requirements of that provision.

We are not persuaded. The Administrator is to approve the proposed revision if he determines that "it" — that is, the revision — meets the substantive requirements imposed on a SIP by § 110(a)(2). There is no requirement that "he" — that is, the Administrator — meet the deadline of that section. Petitioner's reading, moreover, makes nonsense of the further requirement in § 110(a)(3) that the Administrator find that the proposed revision "has been adopted by the State after reasonable notice and public hearings." If, as petitioner contends, § 110(a)(3) incorporates the procedural provisions of § 110(a)(2), it surely incorporates § 110(a)(2)'s requirement that the Administrator find that the SIP was adopted after reasonable notice and hearing. The separate mention in § 110(a)(3) of the notice and hearing requirement demonstrates that it does not simply incorporate every direction of § 110(a)(2); and since § 110(a)(3) does not separately require the Administrator to process a proposed revision within four months, we are not free to read that limitation into the statute.

This suffices to dispose of petitioner's contention, but if additional support is needed, it is available. The statute elsewhere explicitly imposes upon the Administrator deadlines of the kind that petitioner would insert into § 110(a)(3). Indeed, the very next provision of the Act contains just such an express time restraint on EPA approval of a SIP revision. *See* § 110(a)(3)(B) (with respect to certain SIP revisions for fuel-burning stationary sources, "[t]he Administrator shall approve or disapprove any revision no later than three months after its submission").

Petitioner's final contention is that § 110(g) imposes a 4-month limitation on EPA's action on a proposed SIP revision. That section provides: "(1) In the case of any State which has adopted and submitted to the Administrator a proposed plan revision which the State determines - "(A) meets the requirements of this section, and "(B) is necessary (i) to prevent the closing for one year or more of any source of air pollution, and (ii) to prevent substantial increases in unemployment which would result from such closing, and which the Administrator has not approved or disapproved under this section within the required four month period, the Governor may issue a temporary emergency suspension of the part of the applicable implementation plan for such State which is proposed to be revised with respect to such source. . . . "(2) A temporary emergency suspension issued by a Governor under this subsection shall remain in effect for a maximum period of four months. . . ." (Emphasis added.) According to petitioner, § 110(g) on its own terms "require[s]" the Administrator to process a proposed revision within a "four month period." This is petitioner's strongest claim, but we are constrained to reject it. Section 110(g) does not, by its terms, require the Administrator to take any action. It merely authorizes the Governor to suspend the existing SIP if certain action has occurred. True, it presupposes that some "four month period" is "required," but the incorporation of that mistaken presupposition does not, of itself, create a general requirement that the Administrator process all proposed revisions within four months. Whatever may be the correct interpretation of § 110(g)'s "required four month period," we do not think this passing mention can be inflated into a requirement that the Administrator process each and every proposed revision within four months.

IV

Although the 4-month deadline does not apply, EPA remains subject to the Administrative Procedure Act's (APA's) statutory requirements of timeliness. The APA requires agencies to conclude matters "within a reasonable time," 5 U.S.C. § 555(b), and provides a remedy for agency action "unreasonably delayed." 5 U.S.C. § 706(1). Respondent concedes, as we think it must, that its action on a proposed SIP revision is subject to that mandate.

Petitioner's main claim is that any delay over four months is categorically unreasonable because it violates EPA's statutory duty to process a revision within that period. We have rejected that claim above, but we nevertheless must consider petitioner's alternative contention that EPA may not bring an action to enforce an existing SIP if it unreasonably delays in acting on the proposed revision. Without deciding whether the delay in this case was unreasonable, we now address this claim. Because the statute does not reveal any congressional intent to bar enforcement of an existing SIP if EPA delays unreasonably in acting on a proposed SIP revision, we agree with the Court of Appeals that such an enforcement action is not barred.

The language of the Clean Air Act plainly states that EPA may bring an action for penalties or injunctive relief whenever a person is in violation of any requirement of an "applicable implementation plan." § 113(b)(2), 42 U.S.C. § 7413(b)(2). There can be little or no doubt that the existing SIP remains the "applicable implementation plan" even after the State has submitted a proposed revision. The statute states: "For purposes of this chapter, an applicable implementation plan is the implementation plan, or most recent revision thereof, which has been approved under [§ 110(a), 42 U.S.C. § 7410(a)] or promulgated under [110(c), 42 U.S.C. § 7410(c)] and which implements the requirements of this section." § 110(d), 42 U.S.C. § 7410(d). Both this Court and the Courts of Appeals have recognized that the approved SIP is the applicable implementation plan during the time a SIP revision proposal is pending. *See, e.g., Train v. Natural Resources Defense Council, Inc.*, 421 U.S. 60, 92 (1975); *United States v. Alcan Foil Products Division*, 889 F.2d 1513, 1519 (CA6 1989), cert. pending, No. 89-1104; *United States v. Wheeling-Pittsburgh Steel Corp.*, 818 F.2d 1077, 1084 (CA3 1987); *Duquesne Light v. EPA*, 698 F.2d 456, 471 (D.C. Cir. 1983). The commentators agree with this conclusion. *See* D. CURRIE, AIR POLLUTION § 8.07, n. 14 (Supp.1990); 1 W. RODGERS, JR., ENVIRONMENTAL LAW: AIR AND WATER § 3.39(c) (1986 and Supp.1988).

There is nothing in the statute that limits EPA's authority to enforce the "applicable implementation plan" solely to those cases where EPA has not unreasonably delayed action on a proposed SIP revision. Moreover, we find it significant that Congress expressly enacted an enforcement bar elsewhere in the statute. *See* § 113(d)(10); 42 U.S.C. § 7413(d)(10) ("During the period of the order . . . no Federal enforcement action pursuant to this section and no action under section 304 of this Act shall be pursued against such owner . . . ."). The fact that Congress explicitly enacted an enforcement bar similar to the one proposed by petitioner in one section of the statute, but failed to do so in the section at issue in this case reinforces our refusal to import such a bar here. *See Russello v. United States*, 464 U.S. 16, 23 (1983).[3]

---

[3] Our conclusion is further supported by the language of § 110(g), 42 U.S.C. § 7410(g), discussed above. Section 110(g) grants certain authority to a State's governor to suspend the existing SIP after four months. As the Court of Appeals discerned, 876 F.2d, at 1069, n. 6, there would have been no reason for Congress

We note that other statutory remedies are available when EPA delays action on a SIP revision. Although these statutory remedies may not appear to be so strong a deterrent to EPA delay as would an enforcement bar, these are the remedies that Congress has provided in the statute. *Cf. Brock v. Pierce County*, 476 U.S. 253, 260 (1986) ("We would be most reluctant to conclude that every failure of an agency to observe a procedural requirement voids subsequent agency action, especially when important public rights are at stake. When, as here, there are less drastic remedies available for failure to meet a statutory deadline, courts should not assume that Congress intended the agency to lose its power to act" (footnote omitted)). In the absence of a specific provision suggesting that Congress intended to create an enforcement bar, we decline to infer one.

The judgment of the Court of Appeals is affirmed.

It is so ordered.

NOTES

1. The 1990 Amendments wholly revised the submission and approval process for SIPs. Under § 110(k), EPA was required by August, 1991 to promulgate rules establishing numerous criteria which plans must meet before EPA is required to act on them. Within six months following submission, EPA must advise the State whether a SIP or revision meets their minimum criteria. If EPA fails to so advise the state, the plan or revision is deemed to meet the minimum criteria. (The statute actually appears to contemplate a decision by EPA within 60 days in at least some instances. But the language of § 110(k)(1)(B) is unclear, and since the sanctions are not imposed until six months have expired, this appears to be the operative deadline.) Within 12 months thereafter, EPA must act on the plan or revision. Existing SIPs, however, remain in effect until a revision is approved, and the law does not impose any sanctions should EPA fail to meet the 12 month deadline. § 110(k)(2). In light of the *GMC* decision, what is the likely result if EPA fails to meet the new 12 month deadline?

2. The temporary emergency suspension provisions at § 110(g), outlined in the *GMC* case, were not revised in 1990 except to recognize the 12 month (rather than four month) period that EPA is given to act on a SIP.

---

to add that section if the existing SIP automatically became unenforceable after some period of EPA delay. The existence of this explicit exception indicates that in all other circumstances the existing SIP remains in effect.

PROBLEM #2: THE SCOPE OF FEDERAL AUTHORITY UNDER STATE IMPLEMENTATION PLANS

The State of Confusion was required by the 1990 Amendments to submit a revised SIP to address nonattainment problems in the Bedlam Air Quality Control Region. The Bedlam AQCR is a moderate ozone nonattainment area. Bedlam is a large metropolitan area, and the ozone nonattainment problem has been attributed to inadequate controls on motor vehicles. Confusion proposed to adopt only those requirements specifically delineated at § 182(b) for moderate ozone nonattainment areas. EPA determined that these changes would not be sufficient to achieve the primary ozone standards by November 15, 1996. Accordingly, EPA rejected the Confusion revision and adopted a federal plan for the State. Among other things, EPA's plan requires Confusion to — (1) provide for the construction and maintenance of a light rail system for the Bedlam AQCR by the end of 1996; (2) create a network of at least 100 miles of bike lanes within the Bedlam AQCR by the end of 1996; (3) require the retrofit of pre-1980 vehicles registered in the Bedlam AQCR with certain pollution control devices; (4) adopt, implement and enforce a vehicle inspection and maintenance program for the Bedlam AQCR.

Does EPA have the authority (or the responsibility) to impose such requirements on the State of Confusion? *See* § 110(c). What constitutional problems, if any, might be raised by Confusion in a challenge to EPA's action? Assuming that the four requirements noted are found to be necessary to achieve the NAAQS for ozone, what alternative means, if any, does EPA have to achieve these requirements? What problems will the EPA have employing alternative means assuming they are available? *See District of Columbia v. Train*, 521 F.2d 971 (D.C. Cir. 1975), *vacated and remanded for consideration of mootness, sub nom., EPA v. Brown*, 431 U.S. 99 (1977).

G. Judicial Review of State Implementation Plans

Section 307(b) of the Clean Air Act provides in relevant part:

> A petition for review of the Administrator's action in approving or promulgating any implementation plan under Section 110 [of this title] . . . may be filed only in the United States Court of Appeals for the appropriate circuit.

In *Anaconda Co. v. Ruckleshaus*, 482 F.2d 1301 (10th Cir. 1973), the court held that "where, as [under Section 307(b)], Congress has specifically designated a forum for judicial review of administrative action and does so in unmistakable terms, except under extraordinary circumstances, that forum is exclusive." *Id.* at 1304-05. Note the "extraordinary" machinations that Kennecott Copper Corporation employed in an unsuccessful effort to circumvent this holding as described in the following case.

KENNECOTT COPPER CORP. V. COSTLE

572 F.2d 1349 (9th Cir. 1978)

SNEED, Circuit Judge:

I.
Procedural History

This action, which we designate as *Kennecott II*, is merely the latest stage in a continuing battle between Kennecott Copper Company and the EPA as to the appropriate methods of pollution control to be employed at Kennecott's smelter in McGill, Nevada. A brief review of the procedural history of this controversy at this point will be helpful.

The SIP proposed by Nevada pursuant to § 110 of the Clean Air Amendments of 1970 (42 U.S.C. § 7410) was approved by the EPA except for, *inter alia*, the provisions pertaining to control of sulfur dioxide. Following the statutory mandate, the EPA promulgated SO_2 emission limitations for Nevada. As applied to Kennecott's McGill smelter, these regulations required an acid plant capable of reducing SO_2 emissions by 60%, an intermittent control system (a tall stack and production curtailments) to assure maintenance of national ambient air quality standards, and a research program aimed at creating improved constant control technology capable of reducing SO_2 emissions by 86%.

Kennecott sought judicial review of this regulation pursuant to § 307(b)(1) of the Clean Air Amendments of 1970 (42 U.S.C. § 7607(b)(1)), which provides for direct review in the applicable Court of Appeals. This court, in what we designate as *Kennecott I*, upheld the EPA regulations, holding that "air quality standards must be met by continuous emission reduction controls so far as possible." *Kennecott Copper Corp. v. Train*, 526 F.2d 1149, 1159-60 (9th Cir. 1975), *cert. denied*, 425 U.S. 935 (1976). Kennecott, in objecting to the research program requirement, took the position that the EPA was "not authorized to require continuous emission reduction techniques in preference to intermittent controls or other methods for dispersion, or dilution, of pollutants" when the combination of such techniques and other controls devised by the state in its SIP would "attain and maintain national air quality standards within the statutory time periods." *Id.* at 1152. Under such circumstances the EPA must approve the state's SIP, argued Kennecott.

We rejected this contention and sustained the EPA's research program requirement. In doing so, we held that national ambient air quality standards must be met to the extent feasible by constant emission controls. A state plan which meets these standards by not utilizing feasible constant emission controls must be rejected under the authority of section 110(a)(2)(B) of the Clean Air Amendments of 1970. In so holding we took special note of the fact that, because EPA has undertaken to assure Kennecott that under its interpretation of the statute economically infeasible constant emission controls would not be required, "EPA could not compel Kennecott to install additional emission reduction systems at McGill unless it were economically feasible for Kennecott to do so." *Id.* at 1160. Inasmuch as Kennecott in *Kennecott I* did not object to the SIP requirement of an acid plant capable of reducing emissions by 60%, we assumed that the requirement was considered by both Kennecott and EPA as economically feasible. *Id.* at 1151.

Subsequent to the decision in *Kennecott I*, the company decided that construction of any acid plant was economically infeasible. This conclusion was based on an asserted multimillion dollar rise in the cost of constructing the acid plant and a decline in the price of copper. Since the EPA was planning to enforce the regulations which had been approved in *Kennecott I* the company chose to shut down completely in July 1976, rather than to risk sanctions for noncompliance.

Kennecott's next step was to petition the State of Nevada to revise its SIP. The revision requested by Kennecott required only a 40% reduction in SO_2 emissions and allowed achievement of this reduction through production curtailments rather than by use of an acid plant. In addition, dispersion through a tall stack was recognized as an acceptable method by which the State would achieve compliance with national ambient air quality standards. Kennecott also sought a variance for one year which would exempt it from meeting any requirements other than those which, by one means or another, would enable the State to achieve the national standards. On October 1, 1976 the State Environmental Commission approved both the revision of the SIP and the variance. On October 7 both were submitted to the EPA for action pursuant to § 110(a)(3). *See Train v. Natural Resources Defense Council*, 421 U.S. 60 (1975).

Before the EPA had a chance to act on these submissions, however, Kennecott filed suit on October 12, 1976 against the Administrator of the EPA in the U.S. District Court for the District of Nevada. This action sought a declaratory judgment that the revision complied with the requirements of the Clean Air Amendments, a mandatory injunction or mandamus requiring the Administrator to approve the variance and the revision, and an injunction prohibiting the Administrator from enforcing the originally approved SIP or taking any other action to impede the operation of the McGill smelter. On November 24, 1976, the district court granted all the requested relief. 424 F.Supp. 1217 (D.Nev.1976). On April 25, 1977, this court granted the EPA's motion for a stay of the district court's order pending the determination of this appeal.

II.
The Issues.

The EPA attacks the jurisdiction of the district court to entertain this action. It first argues that § 307(b)(1) of the Clean Air Amendments of 1970 (42 U.S.C. § 7607(b)(1)) provides for exclusive jurisdiction in the appropriate Court of Appeals to review revisions of SIPs, thereby foreclosing this action at the district court level. The EPA further argues that § 304 of the Clean Air Amendments of 1970 (42 U.S.C. § 7604), the citizen's suit jurisdictional grant relied on by the district court, is inapplicable because the Administrator has discretionary responsibility in reviewing the state promulgated changes and because Kennecott failed to comply with the notice requirements of that section.

Kennecott responds by asserting that it is uncertain whether § 307 review is applicable to EPA denial of a revision of a SIP and that § 304 jurisdiction is appropriate because the Administrator has a mandatory duty to approve revisions of the SIP approved by the state which meet the requirements of § 110. Kennecott in support of § 304 jurisdiction argues that the Clean Air Amendments, as interpreted by the Supreme Court, give the states final authority in passing on the economic feasibility of such constant emission control systems as might be suggested by EPA. Kennecott makes the final argument that even if jurisdiction in the district court was technically improper, this court should consider the action as an original petition for review and hold that constant emission control systems are only required to the extent economically feasible and that a state's determination of economic infeasibility is binding on the EPA.

The district court, to establish its jurisdiction, relied primarily on section 304(a)(2) of the Clean Air Amendments of 1970 and secondarily on the Administrative Procedure Act, 5 U.S.C. § 701 *et seq.*, federal question jurisdiction, 28 U.S.C. § 1331, and the Mandamus Act, 28 U.S.C. § 1361. Under the circumstances of this case we believe this reliance in its entirety was misplaced. Section 304(a)(2) does not afford jurisdiction because the duty of the EPA to review the variance Nevada granted is one which is discretionary. With respect to the other jurisdictional grounds relied on by the district court we believe judicial intervention at this point in the administrative process to be either invalid or inappropriate. Therefore, we must set aside the district court's preliminary injunction and remand this proceeding to the district court with directions to enter an order dismissing this cause of action.

III.
Citizen Suit Provision - § 304.

Section 304(a)(2) of the Clean Air Amendments of 1970 (42 U.S.C. 7604(a)(2)) provides that "any person may commence a civil action on his own behalf . . . against the Administrator where there is alleged a failure of the Administrator to perform any act or duty under the Act which is *not discretionary* with the Administrator." (Italics added). Its legislative history reveals that Congress recognized the potential for disruption of the administrative process inherent in a broad grant of jurisdiction to hear all cases involving the alleged failure of the Administrator to take actions authorized by the Act. Senate Comm. on Public Works, 93d Cong., 2d Sess., A Legislative History of the Clean Air Amendments of 1970, Serial No. 93-18, Vol. 1 at 278 (1970) (hereinafter cited as Legislative History). Therefore, in the Conference Committee action on the bill, the words "which is not discretionary with the Administrator" were added to the end of § 304(a)(2). Explaining this change, it was stated that "citizen suits against the Administrator will be limited to those duties which are mandatory under the legislation and the suits will not extend to those areas of enforcement with regard to which the Administrator has discretion." Legislative History at 112. Thus, the non-discretionary duty requirement imposed by § 304 must be read in light of the Congressional intent to use this phrase to limit the number of citizen suits which could be brought against the Administrator and to lessen the disruption of the Act's complex administrative process.

Under the circumstances of this case, we are convinced that the Administrator does not have a *mandatory* duty to approve either the revision or the variance. The Supreme Court has clearly established that state promulgated variances and revisions are each to be dealt with by the Administrator under the procedures set out in § 110(a)(3). *Train v. Natural Resources Defense Council, supra* at 80. That section provides that "[t]he Administrator shall approve any revision of an implementation plan applicable to an air quality control region if he determines that it meets the requirements of paragraph (2) and has been adopted by the State after reasonable notice and public hearings." In *Train v. Natural Resources Defense Council* the Court observed, "Under § 110(a)(2), the Agency is required to approve a state plan which provides for the timely attainment and subsequent maintenance of ambient air standards, *and which also satisfies that section's other general requirements*." (Immediately preceding italics added). 421 U.S. at 79.

* * *

In the case before us Kennecott would have us permit the state to dictate to the Administrator how he should perform his discretionary duties and, following this usurpation, have the district court enforce the state's will. Our refusal to adopt this construction permits the Administrator to exercise his discretion in the manner the Administrator did in *Natural Resources Defense Council v. Train* when he determined that lead resulting from mobile and stationary sources was injurious to health and welfare. Once the Administrator, in the case before us, has determined that the revised SIP either does or does not meet all the requirements of § 110(a)(2) there is a nondiscretionary duty to act in accordance with his determination. Moreover, his determination, as will be pointed out, is not beyond the reach of proper judicial review. Thus, we need not adopt the characterization of "not discretionary" in order to avoid what would otherwise be unlimited, unreviewable discretion.

IV.
Other Bases for Jurisdiction.

Two additional bases of jurisdiction relied on secondarily by the district court can be disposed of quickly. *Califano v. Sanders*, 430 U.S. 99. L.Ed.2d 192 (1977) established that the Administrative Procedure Act, 5 U.S.C. § 701 *et seq.*, is not an independent source of jurisdiction. In addition, the Mandamus Act, 28 U.S.C. 1361, is not applicable for the same reason § 304 fails to provide jurisdiction. That is, to invoke § 1361 the act to be compelled must be mandatory or ministerial and not discretionary. *Short v. Murphy*, 512 F.2d 374 (6th Cir. 1975); *United States v. Walker*, 409 F.2d 477, 481 (9th Cir. 1969). Moreover, the existence of alternate remedies, which we believe exist in this case, precludes reliance on § 1361. *Cartier v. Secretary of State*, 506 F.2d 191 (1974), *cert. denied*, 421 U.S. 947 (1975).

Federal question jurisdiction under 28 U.S.C. § 1331, also relied on by the district court, presents a more difficult issue. *Califano v. Sanders*, in foreclosing the Administrative Procedure Act as an independent source of jurisdiction, relied on the 1976 amendment to § 1331 which removed the amount in controversy requirement for suits brought against the United States. This strongly suggests that § 1331 provides a jurisdictional basis for the action of the district court in this case.

We decline, however, to decide whether § 1331 so provides because, even if it does, first, the district court relied on incorrect legal principles in granting the preliminary injunction, and, second, the relief granted interferes with the exercise of administrative discretion. These two reasons provide ample grounds for our setting aside the preliminary injunction of the district court.

* * *

Our second reason for concluding that, even if § 1331 jurisdiction exists, intervention by the district court was improper rests on the view that until the EPA acts on the proposed revision of Nevada's SIP and variance it is improper to intervene judicially. While the doctrine of primary jurisdiction has not, to our knowledge, been applied to the EPA, its use with respect to the Interstate Commerce Commission, Railway Labor Board, and the National Labor Relations Board reflects a general concern with premature interference with the administrative process which we believe applicable to this case in its present posture. Although it is likely the Administrator will act in due course to reject the proposed revision and variance on the ground that constant emission controls are not being employed to the "maximum extent possible," we believe it unwise presently to proceed on that assumption. We cannot close our eyes to the fact that this opinion is being written in the year 1978 and that in 1977 the Clean Air Act was significantly amended. Circumstances have changed; we should not assume that both Kennecott and the EPA are unchanged. In any event, at this point we are convinced the judiciary should stand aside. *Cf. Sampson v. Murray*, 415 U.S. 61, 68 (1974); *Far Eastern Conference v. United States*, 342 U.S. 570, 574 (1952); *Wilderness Society v. Morton*, 479 F.2d 842, 886, *cert. denied*, 411 U.S. 917 (1973).

This conviction also precludes us from deciding whether the proceeding can be treated as an original petition for review under § 307 of the Clean Air Amendments of 1970. Prior to the 1977 Amendments considerable uncertainty existed with respect to whether the availability of § 307 review was to be broadly or narrowly construed. *Compare Oljato Chapter of Navajo Tribe v. Train*, 515 F.2d 654 (1975) with *Utah Power & Light Co. v. EPA*, 553 F.2d 215 (1977) and *District of Columbia v. Train*, 533 F.2d 1250 (1976). The 1977 Amendments to the Clean Air Act (§ 305(c)(2), Pub.Law No. 95-95) amended § 307(b)(1) of the Act to provide for exclusive court of appeals review of "any other final action of the Administrator under this Act which is locally or regionally applicable." This enables us to stand aside, as we believe it proper to do, reasonably confident that in due course either the concern with the revision and variance will become moot or that final action with respect thereto by the Administrator will be subject to judicial review.

We reverse and remand with directions to dismiss the cause of action.

Reversed and remanded.

* * *

[The opinion of Judge HAUK, concurring in part and dissenting in part, is omitted.]

NOTES

1. "[C]ourts traditionally have been reluctant to apply [injunctive and declaratory remedies] to administrative proceedings unless they arise in the context of controversy "ripe" for judicial resolution . . . [T]he basic rationale is to prevent courts, through the avoidance of premature adjudication, from entangling themselves in abstract disagreements over administrative policies . . . and also to protect the agencies from judicial review until an administrative decision has been formalized and its effects felt in a concrete way by the challenging parties. The problem is best seen in a two fold aspect, requiring us to evaluate both the fitness of the issues for judicial decision and the hardship to the parties of withholding court action." *Abbott Laboratories v. Gardner,* 387 U.S. 136 (1967).

2. Was the *Kennecott* case "ripe" for judicial review? How does the "ripeness" doctrine differ from the doctrine of primary jurisdiction described by the court in the second part of its opinion? *See United States v. Western Pacific Railroad,* 352 U.S. 59 (1956): "Primary jurisdiction . . . applies where a claim is originally cognizable in the courts and comes into play whenever enforcement of a claim requires the resolution of issues which, under a regulatory scheme, has been placed within the special competence of an administrative body." *Id.* at 63-64.

3. Primary nonferrous smelters that were in operation before the enactment of the 1977 Amendments, such as Kennecott's McGill smelter, were eligible for a nonferrous smelter order (NSO). § 119. NSOs were allowed only for SO_2 emissions where the facility was "unable to comply with such [SO_2 emissions] requirement by the applicable date for compliance because no means of emission limitation applicable to such smelter which will enable it to achieve compliance with such requirement has been adequately demonstrated to be reasonably available . . . ." § 119(b)(3). Any eligible source could obtain two NSOs. The first extended compliance to January 1, 1983; the second to January 1, 1988. The NSO provisions finally afforded Kennecott a temporary solution for the compliance problems at its McGill smelter.

H. The Right to be Heard

ANACONDA CO. V. RUCKELSHAUS
482 F.2d 1301 (10 Cir. 1973)

WILLIAM E. DOYLE, Circuit Judge:

This is an action instituted in the United States District Court for Colorado by Anaconda Copper Company of Butte, Montana, seeking injunctive relief against various officials of the Environmental Protection Agency. Plaintiff sought relief against the promulgation of a proposed rule controlling emissions of sulfur oxide in Deer Lodge County, Montana unless and until defendants-appellants conduct an adjudicatory hearing.

* * *

The district court granted the requested relief in an extensive opinion which is reported at 352 F.Supp. 697 (D.Colo.1972).

* * *

The questions presented to this court on appeal are whether the Environmental Protection Agency is obligated to grant to Anaconda an adjudicatory hearing with the right to subpoena and cross-examine witnesses before promulgating or indeed holding further hearings on its proposed regulation under § 110(c) of the Clean Air Act Amendments. The crucial aspect of the case is then the validity of the *proposed* EPA regulation for the control of sulfur oxide emissions in Deer Lodge County, Montana where Anaconda operates its smelter. The company is the only significant source of sulfur oxide pollution in the county and so concededly the proposed regulation, although general in form, would apply to Anaconda alone.

Preliminary to the issuance by EPA of the proposed regulation, efforts were made to persuade state officials to issue a plan as required by the Clean Air Act Amendments of 1970. The Montana State Board of Health held a public hearing on Montana's proposed implementation plan. Anaconda was present and presented its views on the state's proposed regulation for restricting sulfur oxide emissions. Following this hearing, Montana submitted to the EPA an implementation plan, but the provision for control of sulfur oxide emissions was omitted. The state plan then was disapproved by the EPA on May 31, 1972, insofar as it excluded the sulfur oxide emissions provisions. Following this action the administrator of the EPA, on July 27, 1972, proposed a regulation to control the emission of sulfur oxide within the County. This proposal would have limited emissions to a discharge of 7,040 pounds of sulfur oxides per hour. At the same time, EPA gave notice of intent to hold public hearings on its proposal on a date 30 days after the issuance. This provision of the regulation is said to have been patterned after the sulfur oxide emissions limitation which had been in the state's proposal which was deleted.

Anaconda immediately demanded an adjudicatory hearing on EPA's proposed regulation, but EPA's reply was that the public hearings were to be legislative or informational and not adjudicatory. Subsequently, it was further explained that the hearing would not be conducted in the nature of the trial. Instead, any interested persons or corporations could make a statement and all relevant testimony would be received. Also, the hearing record would remain open until October 7, 1972, for written statements or other submissions. After that there would be a further hearing to allow further public statements.

Anaconda's position expressed at the hearing was that it was spending large sums of money on its own initiative in an effort to control sulfur oxide emissions; that it was preparing to restrict them from the current rate of 64,000 pounds per hour to 50,000 pounds per hour. Its position was further expressed that the 7,040 pounds per hour would be technologically and economically unfeasible and would create a significant water pollution problem.

Soon after this the present suit was filed (on September 26, 1972). An extensive evidentiary hearing was conducted. The district court then rendered its decision on December 19, 1972.

* * *

[The court held that the case was not ripe for review, that there was no justification for intervention by the district court, and moreover, that EPA was not required to prepare an environmental impact statement prior to promulgating a SIP revision under the Act. The court then proceeded to the following procedural question.]

III.

Our final question is whether there was sufficient substance to Anaconda's contention so that it would appear that it has been deprived of procedural due process by the EPA's refusal to grant a trial type adjudicatory hearing. Assuming that a showing of real deprivation would justify a threshold injunctive hearing, we must determine that the showing here was grossly insufficient to justify the action taken. The trial court saw as a result of denial of an adjudicatory hearing a violation of procedural due process together with a violation of the Clean Air Act and the Administrative Procedure Act. We must disagree. The Administrative Procedure Act requires that there be an adjudicatory hearing only if the agency statute specifies that the particular rule-making hearings be "on the record after opportunity for an agency hearing." No such requirement is set forth in the Clean Air Act. Notwithstanding that these words are used in other sections of the Act, omission of them in § 110(c) is therefore significant. *See Allegheny-Ludlum Steel Co.,* 406 U.S. 742, 757 (1972); 2 K.DAVIS, ADMINISTRATIVE LAW TREATISE § 13.08, at 225 (1958).

By requiring that the hearing under § 110(c) be public Congress sought to bring about broad and flexible participation from all interested groups subject always to a review by the court of appeals. The fact that the proceedings are transcribed does not, of course, mean that the hearing is "on the record."

The fact that Anaconda alone is involved is not conclusive on the question as to whether the hearing should be adjudicatory, for there are many other interested parties and groups who are affected and are entitled to be heard. So the guidelines enunciated by Mr. Justice Holmes in *Bi-Metallic Investment Co. v. State Board of Equalization*, 239 U.S. 441 (1915) are not applicable.

We have also examined the early decision in *Londoner v. Denver*, 210 U.S. 373, 386 (1908), and nothing therein imposes the adjudicatory requirement.

* * *

From our examination of the Act and the related case law and statutes, it would appear that the congressional requirement of a public hearing has been satisfied. Notice has been given and the proposed regulation has been issued. Anaconda appeared at that hearing and submitted material and was given an opportunity to submit more material and information for a period of 75 days following the public hearing. We perceive no violation of Anaconda's right to procedural due process. *See Myers v. Bethlehem Shipbuilding Corp.*, [303 U.S. 41]; *NLRB v. Jones & Laughlin Steel Corp.*, [301 U.S. 1]; *Anniston Mfg. Co. v. Davis*, [301 U.S. 337]; *Buckeye Power, Inc. v. EPA*, [481 F.2d 162 (6th Cir. 1973)]; *Pax Co. of Utah v. United States*, [454 F.2d 93 (10th Cir. 1972)].

Unending procedure could be produced by an adjudicatory hearing. This could bring about unending delay which would not only impede but completely stifle congressional policy. We do not, of course, condemn the trial court's concern for the rights of Anaconda. Those rights are important and the court should be sensitive to them, but those rights are not of such magnitude as to overcome congressional policy and the rights of the remainder of the community.

The judgment of the district court is reversed and the cause is remanded with directions to vacate its judgment herein and to dismiss the action.

NOTES

1. State implementation plans and revisions may be adopted by a state and submitted to EPA only after "reasonable notice and public hearings." § 110(a)(1)(l). What kind of hearings did Congress contemplate in imposing this requirement on the states?

2. Compare the Tenth Circuit's analysis with that of the District Court:

> [O]rdinarily the typical requirements of due process of law form no part of a rulemaking hearing, and I agree emphatically that ordinarily a person is not entitled to any adjudicatory hearing when the purpose of the hearing is one of rulemaking. Citation of authority in support of this hornbook principle is not necessary. However, there are certain well delineated exceptions to this general principle, and I think that this case falls squarely and undeniably within those exceptions. To determine whether or not an adjudicatory hearing is or is not required cannot be decided upon the basis of any single test. Generally two tests are said to be of primary importance. First, one must answer the question: Is this action aimed at a single individual or company? Secondly, one must determine whether adjudicative facts form the basis for the proposed action. Emphatically both of those tests are met here. The so-called rule which is under consideration has to do with emissions of sulphur dioxide in Deer Lodge County, Montana, in a quantity of 7,040 pounds per hour. There is one and only one company at which this so-called rule is directed and that is the only company it can be directed at within the foreseeable future. This is a special rule. It is a single shot attack, aimcd at the plaintiff and only at the

> plaintiff, and plaintiff's rights cannot be destroyed without due process of law under the guise of rule making.
>
> Passing now to the second test, the record made in this case demonstrates that the proposed rule is dependent almost in its entirety on bitterly contested factual issues applicable to the only smelter in Deer Lodge County, Montana. The very cross-examination which was not permitted in the administrative hearing would have established (as it did at time of trial) that the proposed rule is dependent upon a determination of contested facts. Good faith consideration of the information which was brought out on cross-examination in this court might well change the provisions of the proposed rule, but the vital cross-examination was not permitted.

Anaconda Co. v. Ruckelshaus, 352 F.Supp. 697, 792-793 (D.Col. 1972). Which court is right? Consider that all SIPs specify emission requirements and schedules for individual sources. If the District Court's decision is correct, what "adjudicative" facts likely formed the basis for EPA's decision?

3. In *Londoner v. Denver,* 210 U.S. 373 (1903) the Supreme Court addressed the validity of a statute that authorized the paving of a street upon petition of a majority of owners of property fronting on the street. Costs were to be apportioned among all property owners abutting the street in proportion to the benefits received. The landowners were given notice and the right to submit written objections, but had no right to an oral hearing. The court held that the landowners were denied due process of law. Subsequently, in *Bi-Metallic Investment Co. v. Colorado*, 239 U.S. 441 (1915) the Court sustained an order of the Colorado Tax Commission which increased the valuation of all taxable property in the city of Denver by 40 percent without providing the landowners the opportunity to be heard. *Londoner v. Denver* was distinguished on the grounds that it involved "[a] relatively small number of persons . . . who were exceptionally affected, in each case upon individual grounds . . ." Where does the *Anaconda* case fall in this continuum?

4. Suppose that rather than a single source of SO_2, three sources of SO_2 contributed the entire SO_2 load for a region. Suppose further that the state decided to impose the burden of reducing SO_2 emissions entirely on one source, even though each source contributed approximately the same amount of SO_2 emissions, and each source used essentially the same pollution control technology. Does due process require an adjudicatory hearing in this situation?

7 PREVENTION OF SIGNIFICANT DETERIORATION

The Prevention of Significant Deterioration (PSD) provisions found at SubPart C of the Act are among the few that escaped relatively unscathed by the 1990 Amendments. Set forth below is a substantial excerpt from an important case involving the PSD program.

ALABAMA POWER COMPANY V. COSTLE

636 F.2d 323 (D.C. Cir. 1979)

LEVENTHAL, Circuit Judge:

This is one of three opinions issued today considering challenges to the validity of final regulations promulgated by the Environmental Protection Agency (EPA) on June 19, 1978 generally embracing the prevention of significant deterioration of air quality in the nation's "clean air areas." These "PSD" regulations interpreted and began the implementation of various provisions of the Clean Air Act Amendments of 1977. Pertinent provisions are gathered in title I, part C of the Clean Air Act as amended (hereafter sometimes referred to as the "PSD part" or the "PSD provisions").

* * *

I. BACKGROUND OF PSD PROGRAM AND REGULATIONS UNDER REVIEW

* * *

B. The PSD Program Prior to the 1977 Amendments

1) *Genesis of PSD Program.* Section 110 of the Act contained no explicit provision addressing potential deterioration of ambient air quality in those areas where ambient pollutant levels were lower than those mandated by primary and secondary NAAQS. EPA did not impose on the states any requirement to control new sources of pollution that posed no threat to ambient standards.

In 1972, the Sierra Club brought suit alleging that the Act required state plans to include measures to prevent the "significant deterioration" of air quality in those parts of the country where the ambient standards were being met. The District Court for the District of Columbia held that the Act's statement of purpose, contained in section 101(b)(1), imposed such an obligation. On June 12, 1972, it issued a preliminary injunction directing the Administrator to disapprove state plans and to promulgate regulations where the plan failed to take the measures necessary to prevent such deterioration. This court affirmed. On June 11, 1973, the Supreme Court affirmed by an equally divided court. In response to the injunction, EPA disapproved all state plans in November, 1972, and in 1973, following the Supreme Court's action, the agency initiated rulemaking to incorporate PSD requirements into each state plan.

2) *1974 PSD Regulations*. In December, 1974, the Administrator promulgated final regulations amending each state plan to include a PSD requirement. The new PSD program implemented through preconstruction reviews of new or modified sources of sulfur dioxide and particulate matter. "Significant deterioration" was defined in terms of allowable numerical increases in the concentration of sulfur dioxide and particulate matter in areas where ambient pollution levels were presumed by the regulations to be lower than those mandated by primary and secondary NAAQS. These regulated areas came to be referred to as "clean air areas," although, as will become clear from our subsequent discussion, the term encompasses areas that in fact need not possess air quality better than the applicable NAAQS. These allowable increases, or "increments," determined whether air quality deterioration associated with a new facility was permissible. Increment consumption, or "use," was calculated by reference to a "baseline" level of air quality. Under the 1974 regulations this baseline was defined as the representative air quality during 1974 *plus* the projected emissions from sources that had received permits to construct before January 1, 1975, but were not in operation by that date.

The 1974 regulations established a program under which the amount of new growth allowed — the size of increment — would depend upon the amount of growth desired for the area. Areas subject to PSD regulations were divided into three groups. Initially, all such areas were designated Class II, for which increments were set permitting moderate growth. Areas could be redesignated Class I, for which much smaller increments applied, allowing virtually no growth, or Class III, for which increases in pollution were allowed up to the national ambient standards. Procedures were established for redesignations by the state (or, with respect to areas within their jurisdiction, by Federal Land Managers and Indian Governing Bodies).

* * *

C. Clean Air Act Amendments of 1977

The 1977 Amendments maintain the basic structure of regulation of stationary sources through state plans, but made substantial changes in the requirements governing those plans. The Amendments provide for additional controls on existing sources to ensure protection of the ambient standards and visibility. Further, they establish strict requirements for major new sources to be located in areas where the national standards have not yet been attained ("non-attainment areas").

The central focus of this case is Part C of title I (sections 160-169) added to the Clean Air Act by the 1977 Amendments. Section 161 of the Act now provides an express directive that state plans include measures to prevent the significant deterioration of air quality in areas designated by the states under section 107(d)(1)(D) & (E) of the Act as having ambient air quality better than the applicable national primary or secondary ambient air quality standard, or for which there is insufficient data to make a determination of the air quality. An area so designated has commonly been referred to in the legislative history and in the literature that has developed as a "clean air area," a description often contrasted with the term "non-attainment area," which is defined by section 171(2) of the Act as an area that has been demonstrated to exceed an NAAQS for a given pollutant. We wish to alert the reader that the phrase "clean air areas" is a generalization that may be confusing when employed in technical usages. A so-called clean air area for a given air pollutant may include an area that for the same pollutant would be classified as a non-attainment area if sufficient data existed. Further, since classification of areas is pollutant-specific, the same area may be a clean air area due to the air quality with respect to one pollutant, yet be a non-attainment area with respect to another pollutant. Finally, the areas of the country subject to regulation under the PSD provisions of the Act include areas other than those commonly referred to as clean air areas. With these caveats, which will be explained in greater detail as they become pertinent to our discussion, we will continue to use the term "clean air areas" as a shorthand expression where we do not feel the context calls for a more technical usage.

Under the provisions of the 1977 Amendments, areas subject to PSD regulation are divided into three classes; increments are set for each class; new major facilities to be located in such areas must meet technology-based emission limitations reflecting BACT; these facilities cannot commence construction if their emissions would cause or contribute to a violation of the applicable increments in a Class I, II or III area; and demonstrations that new facility emissions would not violate the applicable increments are to be based on both monitoring and diffusion modeling. The list of 19 major sources which emit, or have the potential to emit, 100 tons per year or more of any pollutant are subject to PSD review. In addition, any other source having the potential to emit 250 tons per year or more of any pollutant is also covered. As in the 1974 regulations, "modifications" of such major sources are also subject to PSD review. Section 165 of the Act tightens the requirement that must be included in state plans for the PSD preconstruction review and permitting of major new sources to be located in clean air areas. These stricter requirements include: (1) case-by-case determination of BACT rather than automatic application of NSPS; (2) requirements of air quality impact analyses performed in accordance with EPA regulations; (3) requirements for the protection of visibility in Class I areas even though Class I increments are met; and (4) provisions requiring public hearings in all cases instead of mere opportunity for written comment. Other changes in the 1974 regulations effected by the 1977 Amendments include provision for "variances" from Class I increments if stringent criteria are satisfied, and modification of the definition of "baseline." Congress also structured the program to minimize disruption, by exempting existing sources from the permit requirement of section 165 until "modifications" of those facilities increased emissions, and by phasing sources under construction into the program. In addition, section 166 directs EPA to develop within two years PSD programs for pollutants other than particulates and sulfur dioxide. EPA is not required to follow the "area classification" approach for these other pollutants, but implementation through a permit program is contemplated.

D. PSD Regulations Under the 1977 Amendments

* * *

The regulations require that each major stationary source and each modification covered by the regulations undergo a detailed preconstruction review and obtain a permit prior to the commencement of construction. The PSD review process contains a number of steps:

1) *Control Technology Review.* Each new major source must meet all applicable new source performance standards promulgated under section 111 of the Act, all emission standards for hazardous pollutants under section 112 of the Act, and all applicable state implementation plan requirements. In addition, each such source must apply best available control technology (BACT) for sulfur dioxide and particulates unless emissions of that pollutant will be less than 50 tons per year, 1,000 pounds per day and 100 pounds per hour, whichever is most restrictive.

2) *Air Quality Review*. At the time an application for a PSD permit is submitted, the owner or operator of the proposed source must demonstrate that allowable emissions from the source will not cause or contribute to a violation of any NAAQS or the applicable increments. Estimates of ambient concentrations that must be provided in order to determine compliance with these requirements must "be based on the applicable air quality models, data bases, and other requirements" specified in EPA's modeling guidelines. The models described in these guidelines may be modified, or other models substituted, only after notice and opportunity for comment by the public, and written approval by the Administrator.

3) *Monitoring Requirements*. Two types of monitoring requirements are imposed on sources submitting PSD applications after August 7, 1978. An application must include a full year of continuous monitoring data for any pollutant emitted by the source for which there is an ambient standard. This monitoring data, along with the required modeling results, will form the basis for the permitting authority's determination of whether the proposed source would cause or contribute to a violation of a primary or secondary NAAQS. The second requirement is for post-construction monitoring, to be used as the state or EPA feels necessary to determine actual impact of the source on primary or secondary ambient standards.

4) *Source Information*. The PSD permit application must include, at a minimum, information on the location, design, and planned operating schedule of the proposed facility, a detailed construction schedule, and a description of the control technology that is proposed as BACT. In addition, the applicant must provide an "analysis of impairment to visibility, soils, and vegetation" in the area, and an analysis of the air quality impacts of the expected growth associated with the proposed source. Meteorological and topographical information on the air quality impacts and nature and extent of any growth in the locale of the proposed facility since August 7, 1977, must also be provided if requested by EPA or the state.

5) *Processing Applications*. The regulations establish a complex process for handling the permit application. Within 30 days of receipt of the application, EPA must inform the applicant of any additional information required. EPA or the state must make a final determination on the application within one year after the application is complete. During that time, EPA or the state must: (a) make a preliminary determination whether the proposed source will be approved, disapproved, or approved with conditions; (b) give public notice of the preliminary determination, provide opportunity for comment and public hearing and the applicant's responses, and give the applicant and the public notice of the final determination.

The regulations also require that, even after the PSD review process is completed and permit issued, the state plan must be revised and individual source emissions reduced if the state or EPA determines that an applicable increment or maximum permissible concentration is being violated.

II. Potential To Emit

At the heart of the PSD provisions lies a definition that is jurisdictional in nature. We refer to the section 169(1) definition of "major emitting facility," which identifies sources of air pollution that are subject to the preconstruction review and permit requirements of section 165. The definition is not pollutant-specific, but rather identifies sources that emit more than a threshold quantity of *any* air pollutant. Once a source has been so identified, it may become subject to section 165's substantial administrative burdens and stringent technological control requirements for each pollutant regulated under the Act, even though the air pollutant, emissions of which caused the source to be classified as a "major emitting facility," may not be a pollutant for which NAAQS have been promulgated or even one that is otherwise regulated under the Act. As will become apparent from consideration of the ramifications of this definition, Congress's intention was to identify facilities which, due to their size, are financially able to bear the substantial regulatory costs imposed by the PSD provisions and which, as a group, are primarily responsible for emission of the deleterious pollutants that befoul our nation's air. Such facilities are defined in section 169(1) as those stationary sources of air pollutants from among 28 listed categories which "emit, or have the potential to emit" 100 tons per year or more of any air pollutant plus any other stationary source with the "potential to emit" 250 tons per year or more of any air pollutant.

EPA has interpreted the phrase "potential to emit" as referring to the measure of a source's "uncontrolled emissions" — *i. e.*, the projected emissions of a source when operating at full capacity, with the projection increased by hypothesizing the absence of air pollution control equipment designed into the source. Yet, the language and comprehensive scheme of the statute reveal that an emitting facility is "major" within the meaning of section 169(1), only if it either (1) actually emits the specified annual tonnage of any air pollutant, or (2) has the potential, when operating at full design capacity, to emit the statutory amount.

* * *

Looking at language, we see that the first sentence provides that a major emitting facility (in enumerated categories) must "emit, or have the potential to emit" 100 tons per year of any air pollutant. Plainly, the pollutants that sources "emit" is a reference to some measure of actual emissions. However, under EPA's interpretation of "potential to emit," the actual emissions calculation called for by the verb "emit" would lose all significance. When potential emissions are calculated, as EPA provided, by assuming operation at full capacity, without any reduction to take into account the operation of the facility's air pollution control equipment, then potential emissions will always and inherently exceed actual emissions. Under our construction a meaning is given to the use of "emit" and "or," as applicable in those instances when for any reason, whether or not there is fault or accident, the "cleansing" equipment has not been operated, or has been operated at variance from design.

* * *

Congress was presumably also aware of the high rate of effectiveness with which control equipment eliminates pollutants from unprocessed industrial emissions. For example, at the time of the enactment of the PSD provisions, technology in operation was capable of eliminating over 99% of the particulate matter from emissions. Thus, a source with the potential — according to EPA's "uncontrolled emissions" standard — to emit 100 tons per annum of particulate matter would emit in actuality less than one ton per year. The record illustrates that the heating plant operating in a large high school or in a small community college would become "major" sources under such a test. We have no reason to believe that Congress intended to define such obviously minor sources as "major" for the purposes of the PSD provision.

* * *

IV. PROTECTION OF THE INCREMENTS

The regulations provide that once it is determined that a state implementation plan "is substantially inadequate to prevent significant deterioration or that an applicable increment is being violated," then the SIP must "be revised to correct the inadequacy or the violation." We rule that EPA has authority under the statute to prevent or to correct a violation of the increments, but the agency is without authority to dictate to the States their policy for management of the consumption of allowable increments.

The PSD part of the statute, by its title and by its terms, is designed to prevent significant deterioration of air quality in the nation's "clean air areas" in general, those areas that have or are presumed to have air quality better than that specified in the applicable primary and secondary national ambient air quality standards (NAAQS). The fundamentals of the statutory approach include differentiation within the clean air areas of Class I, II, and III areas, and specification for each class of areas of maximum allowable increases ("increments") in pollution concentrations for particulate matter and sulfur dioxide, with provision for the Administrator to promulgate allowable increments or similar limitations for other pollutants governed by NAAQS. These provisions set as the threshold of "significant deterioration" for each pollutant in each area the lower of the allowable increment of the applicable NAAQS, and the emphatic goal of the PSD provisions is to prevent those thresholds from being exceeded. It is evident that the principal mechanism for monitoring the consumption of allowable increments and for preventing significant deterioration is the preconstruction review and permit process required for new or modified major emitting facilities by the provisions of section 165. However, we cannot agree with industry's contention that section 165 provides the exclusive mechanism for protection of the increments. The Administrator has authority beyond the provisions of section 165 to prevent or to remedy a violation of the thresholds specified in the Act.

The statutory provisions central to our conclusion are sections 161 and 163(a). Section 161 provides in pertinent part:

> each applicable implementation plan shall contain emission limitations and such other measures as may be necessary, as determined under regulations promulgated under this part, to prevent significant deterioration of air quality in each (clean air area).

Section 163 provides in part:

> each applicable implementation plan shall contain measures assuring that maximum allowable increases over baseline concentrations of, and maximum allowable concentrations of (sulfur oxides and particulates) shall not be exceeded.

On their face, these provisions establish the thresholds as limitations that are not to be exceeded and contemplate that state implementation plans shall include such measures "as may be necessary" to ensure the observance of this command. The section 165 permit process alone does not ensure that maximum concentrations or allowable increments will not be exceeded. Significant deterioration may occur due to increased emissions from unregulated minor sources and major emitting facilities grandfathered out of the permit process, due to the use of different models to calculate increment consumption, due to the discovery through monitoring that limitations inadvertently have been exceeded, due to redesignation of an area to a more restrictive class, or due to allocation through administrative error of too many permits. Nothing in the plain language of the statute limits the measures in the state implementation plan to the preconstruction permit process.

* * *

The environmental groups have petitioned us to require EPA to promulgate guidelines detailing the manner in which States may permit consumption of the available increments. They also seek to have EPA set aside some portion of the available increments to ensure that current development does not inadvertently cause a violation of the maximum thresholds. EPA has evidenced an intention to promulgate guidelines to help the states manage the allocation of available increments. This is an appropriate step. But this is not to say that the agency may prescribe the manner in which states will manage their allowed internal growth. In the allocation of responsibilities made by Congress, maximum limitations have been set. These must be observed by the states, but assuming such compliance, growth-management decisions were left by Congress for resolution by the states.

V. Sources Located in Non-attainment Areas

Section 165(a) provides that a PSD permit is required before a major emitting facility "may be constructed in any area to which this part applies." Industry petitioners contend that this language limits the application of the PSD review requirements to sources constructed in certain locations, and that those locations are the statutorily defined "clean air areas." On this premise, industry petitioners argue that section 165 does not apply to sources located in the so-called "non-attainment" areas. EPA, on the other hand, takes the position that the identification of "clean air" and "non- attainment" areas in section 107(d) of the Act are only a starting point for the planning process that will lead to revised state implementation plans, that these identifications do not shape the "area" to which the PSD review requirements apply, and that preconstruction review must precede the construction anywhere of a major emitting facility which will adversely affect the air quality of an area to which this part applies. EPA's regulations extend the permit requirements of section 165 to all sources, wherever located, if the emissions from the source have an *impact* on any clean air area. The issue, then, is whether a source becomes subject to the PSD review process because of its *location* within an area to which this part applies, or because of its *impact* upon the air quality of one.

EPA discovers in the purposes of the Clean Air Act and the 1977 Amendments an authority sufficient to justify its regulation applying section 165 according to impact. It asserts that such a reading is necessary to prevent the significant deterioration of air quality in fact. Section 160(4) sets forth as a purpose of Part C (PSD) "to assure that emissions from any source in any State" (regardless of whether the location of the source is designated an attainment area) "will not interfere with" any portion of the PSD plan for any other State. Clearly, EPA argues, the concern is with the air quality in clean air areas, not with the location of the source affecting that air quality. Finally, the agency contends, Section 161 incorporates the purpose set out in Section 101(b)(1), — to *protect* and enhance the quality of the nation's air resources — which prompted this Court's holding in *Sierra Club v. Ruckelshaus*.

* * *

After careful consideration of the statute and the legislative history, we must accept the contention of the industry petitioners that the phrase "constructed in any area to which this part applies" limits the application of Section 165 to major emitting facilities to be constructed in certain *locations*. But, we reject the proposition that the only statutory means available to fulfill the purposes of Part C are the permit provisions of § 165.

The plain meaning of the inclusion in section 165 of the words "any area to which this part applies" is that Congress intended location to be the key determinant of the applicability of the PSD review requirements. That this is the correct interpretation is underscored by the inclusion of the same words in section 165(a)(3)(A), and by the precise language employed by Congress in those provisions where its concern was more source (rather than area) specific.

The legislative history supports our interpretation. The language of the pertinent provision, section 165(a), derives from the original bill reported to the Senate in 1976 by the Public Works Committee. That bill stated in pertinent part that "[no] major emitting facility . . . may be constructed in any area designated under this subsection." That plainly means location in a designated (clear air) area. In 1977, when Senator Muskie introduced the bill, he said, with respect to its PSD provisions, that it was "in every significant detail identical to last year's bill." When the Senate provision limited the PSD permit process to sources in areas "designated under this subsection," it was expressly limiting that process to sources located in the areas subject to PSD protection. The Conference bill maintained the principle of the Senate version in that regard, but substituted for the Senate provisions the House provisions which designated the areas subject to PSD protection. Because of this combined approach, the conferees could not refer to areas "designated under this subsection" (or even "section") because, unlike the Senate bill, the PSD provisions of the Conference bill comprised several sections (§§ 160-169 of Part C). Accordingly, in order to make the intended reference, the language was changed to area "to which this part applies." This change in language preserved location as a determinant of the applicability of section 165. Therefore, we conclude, as noted above, that the phrase "constructed in any area to which this part applies" limits the application of section 165 to major emitting facilities to be constructed in certain locations.

* * *

Our review of the petitions for reconsideration submitted by both the industry petitioners and EPA has led us to conclude that sections other than section 165 are available to fulfill that congressional objective of need to cope with the problem of interstate pollution.

Section 110(a)(2)(E)(i) provides a vehicle for implementing the congressional objective of abating substantial interstate air pollution. That provision requires that an SIP shall contain "adequate provisions . . . prohibiting any stationary source within the State from emitting any air pollutant in amounts which will . . . interfere with *measures required to be included in the applicable implementation plan for any other state* under [the PSD part]." The phrase "measures required to be included" in an SIP clearly incorporates at least (1) the absolute emissions limitation for each pollutant for which increment limitations have been set under section 163 or 166, (2) the monitoring and modeling requirements of section 165(e), and (3) "such other measures as may be necessary, as determined under regulations promulgated under [part C]," as provided in section 161. EPA's authority, under § 110(a)(2)(E)(i), to prevent interstate inference with these measures — to prevent, in other words, the industry of one state from interfering with the PSD program of another — is clear. And, it does not depend upon the permit process of section 165 for its effectiveness.

So also, section 126 of the Act is a vehicle for abating substantial interstate air pollution independent of permitting. That provision allows that, upon petition by a state or political subdivision, the EPA may determine that a source in a neighboring state "emits or would emit any air pollutant in violation of the prohibition of section 110(a)(2)(E)(i)." If such a violation is found, the remedy provided by section 126(c) — which remedy is applicable "[n]otwithstanding any permit which may have been granted by the State" is not denial or revocation of a permit, but a prohibition against construction or operation for a new source and a prohibition against continued operation for an existing source, unless EPA authorizes continued operation for up to three years while the source is being brought into compliance with § 110(a)(2)(E)(i).

* * *

Section 161 provides still another vehicle for implementing the congressional objective of abating substantial interstate air pollution. We realize that, at oral argument, EPA disclaimed invocation of section 161 rulemaking authority to address this problem. However, that disclaimer came at a time when, in the agency's view, section 165, by its own terms, applied PSD review to sources of interstate air pollution impacting on clean air areas. Given such a view of section 165, the agency's disclaimer of authority under section 161 was reasonable. We have now held that section 165 does not, by its own terms, apply to sources located outside of clean air areas. In this light, and in view of the legislative desire to prevent interstate impacts, the authority granted to the EPA by the plain language of section 161 — "each [SIP] shall contain emission limitations *and such other measures as may be necessary, as determined under regulations promulgated under this part*, to prevent significant deterioration of air quality [in clean air areas]" grants to the Administrator the power to promulgate rules requiring that SIPs adequately address the problem. We hold that the Administrator may promulgate rules to require the inclusion of such provisions in the SIP of the state whose clean air area is affected, of the state which is the source of the adverse impact, or of both.

* * *

ROBINSON, Circuit Judge:

I. Baseline Date

A central feature of the statutory program for the prevention of significant deterioration of air quality in attainment areas, with respect to sulfur dioxide and particulate matter at least, is the establishment of maximum allowable increases, known as increments, in concentrations of pollutants. The increment concept incorporates the idea of a baseline from which deterioration is calculated, by models or monitors, to determine whether it is permissible. Congress has defined with specificity the time and manner in which the baseline for an attainment area is to be determined. The first sentence of Section 169(4), the part now relevant, provides:

> The term "baseline concentration" means, with respect to a pollutant, the ambient concentration levels which exist at the time of the first application for a permit in an area subject to [Part C], based on air quality data available in the Environmental Protection Agency or a State air pollution control agency and on such monitoring data as the permit applicant is required to submit.

EPA has acknowledged that the literal purport of the statutory definition is that the starting point for determining the baseline in a particular clean air region is the existing ambient pollution level in that area at the time of the first application for a permit by a major emitting facility. Yet, in a remarkable assertion of administrative power to revise what Congress has wrought, EPA's final regulations define baseline concentration in terms of actual air quality as of August 7, 1977. The Administrator explained this decision as follows:

> [T]he regulations promulgated today recognize the severe technical and administrative problems with implementing a definition of baseline concentration that relates to the date of first permit application in an area. The administrator believes that a strict interpretation of the Act's language would create thousands of different areas each with different baseline starting points. Moreover, these areas would eventually overlap as more and more sources applied for PSD permits. The final regulations . . . resolve those problems by establishing a uniform starting date for determining the baseline concentration in all areas.

Without disavowing that rationale, EPA's counsel has offered, as a second justification for the selection of a single date for calculation of the baseline, the following "anomaly":

> There is no apparent reason why in one clean air area five "minor" sources constructed at the same time as five "minor" sources in another clean air area should be counted against the increment simply because the first application by a major facility for a PSD permit came at an earlier date in the first area than in the second.

Industry petitioners, the State of Texas and the District of Columbia urge that EPA's uniform baseline date be set aside and the statutory baseline date reinstated. We agree. EPA has no authority to overrule a clear, consistent congressional directive: "the sound principle of according deference to administrative practice normally applies only where the relevant statutory language is unclear or susceptible of differing interpretations."

The statutory definition of baseline concentration was in no sense a product of legislative inadvertence. Congress focused on how to define the baseline and fully understood the consequences of its chosen resolution. The Conference Committee explicitly acknowledged its adoption of the Senate definition of baseline, and the Senate report had explicitly rejected EPA's uniform date approach. Indeed, it purposely embraced the situation EPA's counsel considers anomalous: "Under this definition [of baseline] it is possible for nonmajor emitting sources to be constructed in the area after the date of enactment without having their emissions affect the ability of major emitters to use the increment available."

This differential treatment of clean air areas, keyed to when the first major emitting facility applies for a permit, is based on a sound, practical consideration. As the Senate explained,

> [t]he purpose is to use actual air quality data to establish the baseline. Where sufficient actual data are not available, the State may require the applicant to perform whatever monitoring the State believes is necessary to provide that information. This may involve monitoring for 12 months or more to establish an annual average.

In other words, the task of monitoring existing ambient pollution levels in attainment areas is assigned to the first permit applicant, who will provide the information essential to calculation of the baseline.

The Administrator's recitation of the administrative and technical burdens obviated by a uniform date for the setting of the baseline simply blinks reality. A uniform date for calculating the baseline does not result in establishment of a uniform baseline. Ambient concentration levels of regulated pollutants varied considerably in different clean air areas on August 7, 1977, or any date for that matter, and thus baselines inevitably must differ. EPA's regulations requiring baseline concentration to be figured as of August 7, 1977, must be set aside in favor of the statutory directive to ascertain the baseline in each region as of the date of the first permit application.

* * *

WILKEY, Circuit Judge:

II. "MAJOR MODIFICATION" AND "BUBBLE"

* * *

A. EPA's Regulatory Definition of "Modification"

Standards for PSD review of construction of facilities apply also to the "modification" of any source or facility, as defined by section 111(a) (4). That section of the Act defines "modification" as "any physical change in, or change in the method of operation of, a stationary source which increases the amount of any air pollutant emitted by such source or which results in the emission of any air pollutant not previously emitted."

By regulation EPA has limited PSD review to only those modifications deemed "major" within the following definition:

> "Major modification" means any physical change in, change in the method of operation of, or addition to a stationary source which increases the potential emission rate of any air pollutant regulated under the act . . . by either 100 tons per year or more for any source category identified in [the first sentence of Clean Air Act § 169(1)], or by 250 tons per year or more for any stationary source.

This definition incorporates the same 100 or 250-ton per year threshold that Congress established for the term "major emitting facility." The regulation differs from the statute by exempting from PSD review any modification that does not exceed this threshold.

For this departure in regulation language, no reasonable basis can be found in the statute. The Act requires PSD review for any construction of a major emitting facility; the same PSD review requirement applies for any modification of a major emitting facility; and the term "modification" is nowhere limited to physical changes exceeding a certain magnitude. . . We are constrained here to follow the clear language.

EPA does have discretion, in administering the statute's "modification" provision, to exempt from PSD review some emission increases on grounds of *de minimis* or administrative necessity. The exemption in question, however, has not been so justified, and thus cannot stand.

* * *

B. EPA's Qualified Application of the "Bubble" Concept of PSD

An important issue under the Act arises from the problem of determining what types of industrial changes will be construed as "modifications" subject to PSD review requirements. Under the Act, the PSD permit and review process applies to construction and modification of major emitting facilities. As discussed in the previous section, the Act defines "modification" as any physical or operational change in a stationary source which "increases the amount of any air pollutant emitted by such source." There are two possible ways to construe the term "increases." First, one can look at any change proposed for a plant, and decide whether the net effect of all the steps involved in that change is to increase the emission of any air pollutant — this is commonly termed the "bubble" concept. Second, one can inspect the individual units of a plant, which are affected by an operational change, and determine whether any of the units will consequently emit more of a pollutant. In its regulations, EPA has adopted a qualified form of the "bubble" concept for defining modifications subject to PSD review.

Congress did not, in any pertinent part of legislative history, specify which of these two constructions was to be controlling; but an analysis of the implications of the two possible interpretations shows the second to be unreasonable and contrary to the expressed purposes of the PSD provisions of the Act. It is important first to recognize that alterations of almost any plant occur continuously; whether to replace depreciated capital goods, to keep pace with technological advances, or to respond to changing consumer demands. This dynamic aspect of American industry was not disputed by the parties. To apply the second construction of "increases," however, would require PSD review for many such routine alterations of a plant; a new unit would contribute additional pollutants, these increases could not be set off against the decrease resulting from abandonment of the old unit, and thus the change would become a "modification" subject to PSD review. Not only would this result be extremely burdensome, it was never intended by Congress in enacting the Clean Air Act Amendments.

The intent of the relevant portion, Part C, of the Clean Air Act as amended in 1977, is succinctly stated by the title of that part: "Prevention of Significant Deterioration of Air Quality" — in areas that currently attain air quality standards. According to their stated purposes, the PSD provisions seek "to assure that any decision to permit *increased* air pollution *in any area* to which this section applies is made only after careful evaluation of all the consequences of such a decision and after adequate procedural opportunities for informed public participation in the decision-making process."

Congress wished to apply the permit process, then, only where industrial changes might increase pollution in an area, not where an existing plant changed its operations in ways that produced no pollution increase. It is true that Congress intended to generate technological improvement in pollution control, but this approach focused upon "rapid adoption of improvements in technology as new sources are built," not as old ones were changed without pollution increase. The interpretation of "modification" as requiring a net increase is thus consistent with the purpose of the Act; while the other interpretation is not. The EPA has properly exempted from best available control technology (BACT) and ambient air quality review those "modifications" of a source that do not produce a net increase in any pollutant. Within the terminology of the Act, of course, industrial changes meeting this standard are not "modifications" at all.

* * *

The Agency retains substantial discretion in applying the bubble concept. First, any offset changes claimed by industry must be substantially contemporaneous. The agency has discretion, within reason, to define which changes are substantially contemporaneous. Second, the offsetting changes must be within the same source, as defined by EPA. In light of the statutory intent to treat modification the same as construction, EPA's definition of "statutory source" for the PSD provisions will govern both the definition of "modification" and the coverage of section 169(1).

The Agency's regulations, however, impose on the use of the bubble concept an additional limitation, which is challenged in this case. The regulations define "major modification" by means of accumulated increases in potential emissions after 7 August 1977, with no offset allowed for contemporaneous emission decreases. The effect of this definition is to subject major changes to PSD review, even when they are offset by contemporaneous reductions. The only effect of the EPA's bubble concept then is to exempt the facility from certain substantive review standards when there are such offsetting changes, leaving the facility subject to all procedural PSD requirements. The most important procedural requirement is that a permit be issued, under section 165 of the Act, before construction begins. Under the Act, however, PSD procedural requirements, just like substantive ones, apply only to construction and modification of sources. We must therefore resolve the question whether EPA has authority to impose procedural requirements where there is no net increase of any pollutant from contemporaneous changes.

The Agency concedes that a literal reading of the Act would allow exemption from all PSD review requirements for offsetting changes. But it argues that a total exemption from section 165 requirements would contravene the basic purpose of the 1977 Amendments. We disagree.

There is no basis in the Act for establishing two different definitions of "modification," one that looks only at net increases for substantive requirements, and a second that looks at all increases, without allowing offsets, for procedural requirements. If a particular set of industrial alterations is not a "modification" within the terms of the Act, then it is subject to neither procedural nor substantive PSD requirements.

The Act gives the EPA Administrator authority "to prescribe such regulations as are necessary to carry out his functions" under the Act. The Agency argues that the permit process is necessary to ensure that it receives information about industrial plans, so that it can decide whether proposed emission increases are in fact offset. But the PSD provisions set several thresholds, below which Agency review authority does not extend. The 100 and 250-ton per year limit for "major emitting facilities" is one such threshold. The logic of the Agency's argument would justify permit requirements for any industrial action that falls below any of the thresholds. Rather than allow such an extension of Agency review authority, Congress has set clear limits outside which PSD review does not apply. If industries falsely claim to be below the thresholds for PSD applicability, there exist means to uncover and penalize such abuses. An extension of PSD permit requirements beyond the wording of the Act is therefore neither necessary nor appropriate to carry out EPA's functions under the Act. Such extension would seriously delay and impede industrial changes that Congress did not intend to regulate. Where there is no net increase from contemporaneous changes within a source, we hold that PSD review, whether procedural or substantive, cannot apply.

* * *

NOTES

1. The *Alabama Power* decision consumes 88 pages in the Federal Reporter. The problems it raises are so numerous and complex that portions of the opinion are written by each of the three judges who heard the case.

2. The court finds that the permit requirements of § 165 apply only to those major emitting facilities located in "clean air" areas. EPA had argued, on the basis of § 161 of the Act, that the requirements should extend to all major emitting facilities that adversely impact clean air areas. In the same part of the opinion, however, the court held that EPA may impose virtually any requirements, including those at § 165, on

maximum allowable increases or the maximum allowable concentrations permitted . . ." EPA had promulgated rules requiring monitoring only to determine whether an applicable NAAQS has been exceeded. The court found these rules inadequate. 636 F.2d at 372. What more was required?

(3) *Post-Construction Review.* Section 165(a)(7) provides as a condition of permit approval that the applicant "conduct such monitoring as may be necessary . . ." Pursuant to this provision EPA had imposed no general requirement for post-construction monitoring. The court upheld EPA's decisions against a challenge from several environmental plaintiffs on the grounds that the monitoring requirement of § 165(a)(7) (unlike the requirements of § 165(e)(1) and(d)) is discretionary. 636 F.2d at 373.

c. Applications of PSD Requirements to All Pollutants Emitted By a Major Facility. EPA promulgated rules which limited the applicability of PSD requirements to those pollutants for which the proposed construction would be a major source or a major modification. Thus, for example, under the EPA rules, a proposed primary copper smelter that would emit 150 tons/year of sulfur dioxide and 50 tons/year of particulates would only have to meet PSD requirements, including BACT, for sulfur dioxide and not for particulates. The court held the rule invalid. "Section 165 states that no major emitting facility may be constructed [in a clean air area] unless it is subject to BACT 'for each pollutant subject to regulation under this Act emitted from . . . such facility.'" 636 F.2d at 405.

5. *Bubbles.* One of the more controversial policy decisions made by EPA in recent years was its provision for treating emissions from one large facility as one source for purposes of regulation under the Clean Air Act. All emission points within the facility are considered as if they are under a bubble, with one source emanating from the bubble. As described in the *Alabama Power* decision, this policy cuts two ways. First, by encompassing within the meaning of a single "source" all units on contiguous or adjacent properties which are commonly owned or controlled, EPA broadened the scope of new facilities that fall within the 100/250 ton/year jurisdictional requirement for PSD review. On the other hand, by treating all sources under the "bubble" as a single source, a facility can avoid PSD review for modifications of the facility if it can offset emissions from one or more points sufficiently to keep the increase in pollutants below the 100/250 ton/year threshold. Both of EPA's bubble policies as applied to the PSD program were sustained by the court. 636 F.2d at 396-397, 400-402. The Supreme Court has addressed the bubble concept in a different context in *Chevron, U.S.A., Inc. v. Natural Resources Defense Council,* 467 U.S. 837 (1984), *infra* at Chapter 9.

6. Section 165 of the Act provides that "[n]o major emitting facility on which construction is commenced after August 7, 1977, may be constructed in any area which . . . [Part C (PSD)] applies unless . . . [a PSD permit that meets the Act's standards is obtained.]" Section 168 of the Act provides, however, that "[u]ntil such time as an applicable [state] implementation plan is in effect for any area . . . applicable regulations under this Act prior to enactment of this part shall remain in effect . . ." You represent a company that wants to site a major industrial facility in a PSD area in a state without an approved PSD plan. Do the requirements of the 1977 statutory amendments, or the pre-1977 Act regulations apply? *See Citizens to Save Spencer County v. EPA*, 600 F.2d 844 (D.C. Cir. 1979).

7. The definition of "major emitting facility" at § 169(1) of the Act authorizes the state to exempt new or modified facilities operated by nonprofit or educational institutions from the PSD requirements of the Act. The Court of Appeals for the First

Circuit upheld such an exemption obtained by Harvard College from the State of Massachusetts against a challenge by a local community and several of its residents. *See Town of Brookline v. Gorsuch*, 667 F.2d 215 (1st Cir. 1981).

8. In states without an approved PSD permit program (§ 110(a)(2)(C)), EPA may nonetheless delegate PSD permitting authority to the state. *See In the Matter of Pennsauken County, New Jersey Resource Recover Facility*, PSD Appeal No. 88-8, 1988 PSD LEXIS 8 (1988). All such permits, however, are considered to be EPA-issued under federal law, and federal administrative review procedures apply. The regulations at 43 CFR Part 124 govern the issuance, public comment, and review of PSD permits. These rules are part of EPA's consolidated permit program which allow the consolidation of several different kinds of EPA permits from different programs into a single process. 40 CFR § 124.4 (1991). Under EPA's rules, the public must be afforded a minimum of 30 days following public notice to comment on an application. *Id.* at § 124.10(b). A public hearing may also be held. Within 30 days from a permit decision a person who filed comments or participated in a public hearing on the application may petition the Administrator to review the decision. A person who did not participate in the comment process may also petition for review, but may only raise issues relating to changes from the draft to the final permit. *Id.* at § 124.19. The Administrator has the discretion to grant or deny a petition. Decisions involving the review of PSD permits are available on LEXIS in the ENVIRN library and EPAPSD file.

9. Unlike LAER, which applies only to those pollutants for which an area is out of attainment, sources subject to § 165 have generally been required to meet BACT "for each pollutant subject to regulation under this chapter." § 165(a)(4). The 1990 Amendments, however, provide that pollutants listed under § 112 as hazardous air pollutants are not subject to the PSD program. Presumably then, the MACT standards which apply to hazardous air pollutants will override the BACT standards. Suppose, however, that MACT standards have not yet been promulgated for a particular hazardous air pollutant. Can a major emitting facility avoid both BACT and MACT for such pollutants until MACT standards are adopted? *See In the Matter of Robbins Resource Recovery Company*, PSD Appeal No. 90-8A, 1991 PSD LEXIS 2 (1991).

10. EPA has traditionally followed a "top down" approach to determine the appropriate technology for a source subject to BACT. EPA has explained this approach as follows:

> The first step in this approach is to determine, for the emission source in question, the most stringent control available for a similar or identical source or source category. If it can be shown that this level of control is technically or economically infeasible for the source in question, then the next most stringent level of control is determined and similarly evaluated. This process continues until the BACT level under consideration cannot be eliminated by any substantial or unique technical, environmental or economic objections. Thus, the "top-down" approach shifts the burden of proof to the applicant to justify why the proposed source is unable to apply the best technology available. It also differs from other processes in that it requires the applicant to analyze a control technology only if the applicant opposes that level of control; the other processes required a full analysis of all possible types and levels of control above the baseline case.

In the Matter of Pennsauken County, New Jersey Resource Recover Facility, PSD Appeal No. 88-8 at 5-6, 1988 PSD LEXIS 8 (1988). The American Paper Institute filed a lawsuit against the EPA alleging that the "top-down" policy was inconsistent with the law. On

July 28, 1991, EPA announced that it had reached a proposed settlement in the case and opened the proposal to public comment. 56 Fed. Reg. 34202 (1991). Under the terms of the settlement, EPA agreed to propose new rules to revise or clarify the regulations defining BACT (50 CFR §§ 51.166(j), 52.21(j)) and the manner in which BACT determinations should be made. Although the agreement called for proposed rules by January 10, 1992, no proposal had been published by June, 1992.

KERR-MCGEE CHEMICAL CORP. V. U.S. DEPARTMENT OF THE INTERIOR

709 F.2d 597 (9th Cir. 1983)

EUGENE A. WRIGHT, Circuit Judge:

This case presents the question whether, under section 164(d) of the Clean Air Act Amendments of 1977, a recommendation by the Department of Interior has caused injury to Kerr-McGee sufficient to give it standing and create a case ripe for decision. The district court decided that Kerr-McGee had been injured and granted its motion for summary judgment. We reverse and remand with instructions to dismiss because Kerr-McGee has not demonstrated that legally cognizable injury results from Interior's recommendation.

FACTS

Under section 164 of the Clean Air Act Amendments of 1977, the states alone have the power to change the air quality designations of federal lands within their boundaries. 42 U.S.C. § 7474(a) (Supp.1982). Certain federal lands, such as national monuments, may be redesignated only from Class II to Class I, the strictest pollution control category. *Id.*

Section 164(d) of the amendments requires the federal land manager to review specified federal lands to determine whether redesignation is appropriate. 42 U.S.C. § 7474(d). In 1980, the Department of the Interior, the land manager for Death Valley National Monument, recommended that California redesignate Death Valley from class II to class I. 45 Fed.Reg. 43,002 (1980).

Following Interior's recommendation, Kerr-McGee brought this declaratory judgment action against Interior and the State of California. It has pending a permit application to expand its chemical processing plant in California's Searles Valley, about 18 miles from the boundary of Death Valley. In theory, at least, the Searles facility and expansion may be subjected to increased pollution controls if California follows Interior's recommendation and redesignates Death Valley.

Kerr-McGee alleged that Interior had not complied with the requirements of section 164(d) because it had considered only whether "air quality related values" were an important attribute of Death Valley. It argued that section 164(d) required Interior to assess in addition the health, environmental, economic, social, and energy effects of redesignation before making a recommendation to California.

Kerr-McGee asserted that the statute precluded action by California until Interior made a "lawful" analysis. It contended also that the recommendation under section 164(d) acted as a "trigger" to state action on redesignation, setting in motion a chain of events that would affect drastically its Searles operations. These effects included delay in processing the permit application, the skewing of proceedings in favor of redesignation, and the likelihood that the plant would face stricter emission standards.

Finally, Kerr-McGee contended that Interior violated the National Environmental Policy Act of 1969 (NEPA), 42 U.S.C. §§ 4321-4347; §§ 4361-4370, by not preparing an Environmental Impact Statement (EIS) for the recommendation. It argued that the recommendation, which was forwarded to Congress, was a proposal for legislation that required an EIS. *See* 42 U.S.C. § 4332(C).

California and Interior moved to dismiss. Among other arguments, they contended that the claims were barred by the standing and ripeness doctrines. They argued that the federal recommendation caused Kerr-McGee no injury because section 164 allowed California to act without any recommendation, and allowed it to ignore the recommendation once made.

The court concluded that Kerr-McGee had alleged injuries sufficient to confer standing. It noted that Kerr-McGee alleged that California had delayed action on the permit application because of the federal recommendation. It concluded that ripeness did not bar the suit because the federal action was "final agency action" within the meaning of the Administrative Procedure Act, and because California apparently planned to initiate redesignation proceedings.

On the merits, the court granted summary judgment to Kerr-McGee and ruled that Interior had not considered the relevant factors in making its recommendation. Although it did not rule that the recommendation "triggered" action by California, it held that a lawful recommendation was a prerequisite to redesignation.

* * *

Standing and Ripeness

On appeal, California and Interior have renewed their contentions that the standing and ripeness doctrines bar Kerr-McGee's claims. Because standing and ripeness are jurisdictional issues, we must consider them first.

* * *

Both standing and ripeness require some demonstration of injury. Standing requires that the plaintiff show that the challenged action has caused it threatened or actual injury. *See Gladstone, Realtors v. Village of Bellwood*, 441 U.S. 91, 99 (1979).

To determine ripeness, the court assesses the appropriateness of the issue for judicial resolution and the hardship that will result from the denial of relief at this stage. *Toilet Goods Association v. Gardner*, 387 U.S. 158, 1627 (1967). Even when the agency action challenged is "final" and the issues raised are purely legal, a case is not ripe for adjudication absent the threat of significant and immediate impact on the plaintiff. *Id.* at 162-64, 87 S.Ct. at 1523-25.

In effect, the issues of standing and ripeness here merge into a determination whether the federal recommendation has injured Kerr-McGee. *See* 4 K. Davis, *Administrative Law Treatise* 350 (1983). If not, we have no jurisdiction.

A. Source of Kerr-McGee's Injury

Kerr-McGee has alleged no direct injury resulting from the federal recommendation. It admits that California retains ultimate control over the decision to redesignate Death Valley and that the direct source of its injury will be action or inaction by the state.

Instead, Kerr-McGee argues that the statute establishes a causal relationship between the recommendation and injurious action by California. It asserts that under section 164, the federal recommendation triggers state action on redesignation and makes redesignation's "harmful" effects inevitable.

It argues also that the recommendation is a statutory prerequisite to action by California, an interpretation accepted by the district court. If this is correct, the recommendation has harmed Kerr-McGee because it allows California to act when otherwise it could not.

* * *

The question whether Kerr-McGee has been injured depends on the effect upon state proceedings of a federal recommendation under section 164(d). We must examine the statute and make a partial determination on the merits to decide whether we have jurisdiction.

* * *

B. The Recommendation as a Prerequisite

Section 164(d) provides that the "Federal Land Manager shall review all national monuments. . . and shall recommend any appropriate areas for redesignation as class I where air quality related values are important attributes of the area." 42 U.S.C. § 7474(d). Although the section requires that the land manager consult with the appropriate states before making a recommendation, its language does not suggest that the recommendation acts as a prerequisite.

* * *

Examination of the statute and its background convinces us that the district court erred in deciding that federal recommendation was a prerequisite to redesignation by California. In enacting the 1977 Clean Air Act Amendments, Congress stated specifically that it was removing the federal land manager's power to control classification of federal lands. H.R.Rep. No. 294, 95th Cong., 1st Sess. 7-8, *reprinted in* 1977 U.S.Code Cong. & Ad.News 1077, 1085.

* * *

The statute leaves the state free to act without a recommendation if the federal government does not respond within 60 days. Even if the land manager responds with a recommendation, the state may redesignate against the federal recommendation if it lists and explains the inconsistencies between the state and federal positions. 42 U.S.C. § 7474(b)(1)(B). Because California can act independently of and inconsistently with the recommendation, we conclude that the court erred in holding that the recommendation was a prerequisite to redesignation.

We disagree also with the conclusion that the federal recommendation is surplusage merely because the state may reject it. The structure of the statute reveals that Congress intended redesignation to be a cooperative effort between the state and the federal government, with final authority in the state.

The mandatory review of federal lands required by section 164(d) places the federal government on record regarding redesignation. When and if the state decides to redesignate, the recorded federal recommendation allows the state to fulfill quickly its duty under section 164(b)(1)(B) to consult with the federal government. The recommendation does play a role in facilitating the redesignation process without restricting state action.

C. The Recommendation as a Trigger

We consider next Kerr-McGee's contention that the recommendation "triggers" state action on redesignation. Kerr-McGee alleges that the triggering effect injures it because California will not act on permit applications until the conclusion of redesignation proceedings.

There is no basis in the statute for a "trigger" interpretation. The statute allows states to initiate redesignation proceedings. 42 U.S.C. § 7474(a). It does not suggest that federal land managers may initiate redesignation or that the states must act once a federal recommendation has been made.

* * *

California may or may not plan to redesignate Death Valley and "injure" Kerr-McGee in the manner alleged. The federal recommendation, however, is purely advisory and is neither a trigger nor a prerequisite to California's action. It subjects Kerr-McGee to no federal control or regulation, and has caused the company no injury. Without an injury, Kerr-McGee has no standing and its claim is not ripe for decision.

We reverse and remand to the district court with instructions to dismiss for lack of jurisdiction.

NOTES

1. Section 162 of the Act designates as Class I areas all international parks, national wilderness areas and national memorial parks in excess of 5,000 acres, and national parks in excess of 6,000 acres, so long as those areas were in existence on August 7, 1977. These Class I areas may not be redesignated. All such areas that are created after August 7, 1977 are subject to redesignation by the states under § 164 of the Act. However, certain protected federal lands (such as national monuments and post-1977 national parks) in excess of 10,000 acres may only be redesignated as Class I or Class II.

2. Indian reservations may only be redesignated by the appropriate Indian governing body. § 164(c). In *Nance v. EPA*, 645 F.2d 701 (9th Cir. 1981) the court sustained the authority of the Cheyenne Tribe to redesignate the Northern Cheyenne Reservation in Montana from Class II to Class I. Westmoreland Resources and other companies with coal interests in the region had protested the redesignation on the grounds that it might unduly interfere with their plans to conduct strip mining operations in the area. The court held: (1) that neither the Tribe's decision nor EPA's approval of the decision was arbitrary and capricious; (2) that neither EPA nor the Secretary of the Interior had breached its fiduciary duty owed to the neighboring Crow Tribe in approving the redesignation; (3) that the delegation of authority to Indian tribes to redesignate their reservation lands was not unlawful under either the Clean Air Act or the federal Constitution; and (4) that the question of whether the property rights of the plaintiffs had been "taken" in violation of the Fifth Amendment was not ripe for review.

3. Redesignation of an area to Class III is permitted only where "such redesignation will not cause, or contribute to, concentration of any air pollutant which exceeds any maximum allowable increase or maximum allowable concentration permitted under the classification of any other area." § 164(a)(2)(B). Consider how states might use this provision to limit redesignation and development in bordering states. For facilities in one state that adversely affect a clean air area of another state. The court finds support for this holding in the language of § 110(a)(2)(E) (now § 110(a)(2)(D)) which authorizes EPA to require measures necessary to prevent the significant deterioration of air quality in another state. 636 F.2d at 366-367. Compare the language of § 110(a)(2)(D) with the language of § 161. Is there any rational basis for the court's holding that EPA may impose PSD requirements on facilities in nonattainment areas only if it adversely affects a clean air area in another state?

3. Despite his disagreement with the court's interpretation of this aspect of EPA's rules, Professor Currie notes that the ruling should have little practical effect. "[Because] virtually every area of the country shows attainment for at least one pollutant, the PSD review will be a requisite virtually everywhere." 43 Fed. Reg. 8963 (1978), CURRIE, AIR POLLUTION, FEDERAL LAW AND ANALYSIS § 7.03 (Callaghan & Co. 1981).

4. Several issues addressed in the *Alabama Power* opinion which are not reproduced in the text are nonetheless worthy of note.

a. Fugitive Emissions. Fugitive emissions are emissions that escape from a facility from other than a point source. Resource development activities such as mining and forestry typically contribute substantial fugitive emissions to the ambient air. The PSD requirements of the statute are limited to "major emitting facilities." These are defined at § 169(1) of the Act to encompass any of 28 specified categories of sources "which emit, or have the potential to emit 100 tons per year or more of any air pollutant . . ." The definition also encompasses "any other source with the potential to emit 250 tons per year or more of any air pollutant . . ." No mention is made of sources of fugitive emissions in § 169(1). In the general definition section of the statute, however, "major emitting facility" is defined "except as otherwise expressly provided" to include any "source of air pollutants which . . . emits, or has the potential to emit 100 tons per year of any air pollutant (including any . . . source of fugitive emissions, . . . as determined by rule by the Administrator)." § 302(j). EPA promulgated rules which required major sources of fugitive emissions in PSD areas to meet the BACT requirement, but required no showing that emissions from the source would not result in a violation of the NAAQS or the allowable increments. The court held that § 169(1) did not "expressly" modify § 302(j). Thus, major sources of fugitive emissions fell within the jurisdictional limits of § 302(j), subject to that sections "rule" requirement for fugitive emissions, 636 F.2d at 370. Following the court's decision in this case, the EPA promulgated rules setting fugitive emission standards for 27 categories of facilities. The EPA's failure to include strip mines among these 27 categories was unsuccessfully challenged in *Natural Resources Defense Council v. EPA*, 937 F.2d 641 (D.C. Cir. 1991), the second case that follows in the text.

b. Monitoring.

(1) *Preconstruction Review: For What Pollutants?* Section 165(e)(1) of the Act requires that preconstruction review of a facility "shall be preceded by an analysis . . . for each pollutant subject to regulation under this Act which will be emitted" from the facility. EPA's rules required monitoring only for those pollutants for which NAAQS have been established. The court held that the Act required some form of preconstruction analysis (presumably monitoring or modeling) for all pollutants regulated under the Act, subject to certain express monitoring requirements in § 165(e)(2). 636 F.2d at 371.

(2) *Preconstruction Review: For What Purpose?* Section 165(e)(2) of the Act provides that the analysis required by § 165(e)(1) "shall include continuous air quality monitoring . . . for purposes of determining whether emissions . . . will exceed the

example, could Nebraska designate its western border as a Class I area and thereby limit industrial development in eastern Wyoming? *See* § 165(d)(2)(C)(i).

4. Where disputes arise between states and Indian tribes over classification of lands, the governor of the affected state or the ruling body of the affected Indian tribe may request that the EPA Administrator resolve the dispute. The Administrator's resolution is binding on the affected governments. § 164(e).

5. As suggested by *Kerr-McGee*, the Act imposes on federal land managers "an affirmative responsibility to protect the air quality related values (including visibility) of any . . . lands within a Class I Area . . . " § 165(d)(2)(B). To implement this requirement, the Act requires EPA to notify the federal land manager of any permit applications for major emitting facilities which might affect a Class I area over which the manager has responsibility. § 165(d)(2)(A). "Where the Federal Land Manager demonstrates *to the satisfaction of the state* that the emissions from such facility will have an adverse impact on the air quality-related values (including visibility) of such lands . . . a permit shall not be issued." § 165(d)(2)(C)(ii)) (Emphasis added). Note that this prohibition applies even where the new facility would not cause violations of the PSD increments. Conversely, however, "where the owner or operator of a facility demonstrates to the satisfaction of the Federal Land Manager . . . that the emissions from such facility will have no adverse impact on air quality-related values . . . the state may issue the permit," even though the emissions may result in pollution that exceeds the Class I increments. § 165(d)(2)(C)(iii). In this case, however, the emissions from such a facility may not result in pollution that exceeds other increments established under the law which are roughly equivalent to Class II increments. § 165(d)(2)(C)(iv).

PROBLEM #3: AIR QUALITY RELATED VALUES

The High Plains Power Company has filed a permit application for a new coal-fired power plant in the State of Buffalo in accordance with Buffalo's EPA approval SIP. The proposed power plant would be located in an attainment area for all criteria pollutants, approximately 100 miles west (upwind) of the Grand Mesa National Park, a mandatory Federal Class I area. Each year, the 500 MW plant will emit approximately 300 tons of particulate matter, 3,000 tons of SO_2, and 5,000 tons of NO_x. The Superintendent of the Grand Mesa National Park is strongly opposed to the proposed plant. She believes that the emissions from the proposed plant may degrade the air quality in the park, but will certainly degrade the vistas that may be seen to the west from the park. The Governor of Buffalo is an ardent supporter of the project and has vowed to let nothing stand in its way. Consider and discuss the Clean Air Act hurdles that will have to be overcome if this plant is to be built. What additional information would you need to fully analyze this problem?

NATURAL RESOURCES DEFENSE COUNCIL v. EPA
937 F.2d 641 (D.C. Cir. 1991)

STEPHEN F. WILLIAMS, Circuit Judge:

Surface coal mining operations throw up dust. This "fugitive dust"[1] comes primarily from traffic on unpaved "haul roads" and from wind erosion, *see "Requirements for Implementation Plans: Surface Coal Mines and Fugitive Emissions"*, 54 Fed.Reg. 48,870, 48,879/2 (1989), and it accounts for virtually all of the air pollution generated at surface coal mines, *id.* at 48,875/2. We deal here with a decision of the Environmental Protection Agency concluding that such fugitive emissions should not count in identifying facilities that are so "major" as to trigger application of the Clean Air Act's provisions on "prevention of significant deterioration" ("PSD"), §§ 160 *et seq.*, 42 U.S.C. §§ 7470 *et seq.* (1988).

The PSD provisions impose stringent permit requirements on construction of any new "major emitting facility" in an area that has attained compliance with national ambient air quality standards. § 165, 42 U.S.C. § 7475 (1988); *see also* § 169(2)(C), 42 U.S.C. § 7479(2)(C) (1988) (defining "construction" to include modification of an existing source). The Act defines such facilities as plants of certain listed types that produce 100 tons or more of any air pollutant per year, together with "any other source with the potential to emit two hundred and fifty tons per year or more of any air pollutant." § 169(1), 42 U.S.C. § 7479(1) (1988). Most surface coal mines of economically viable size have the potential to emit more than 250 tons of dust. *See "Requirements for Preparation, Adoption and Submittal of Implementation Plans"*, 49 Fed.Reg. 43,211, 43,212/1 (1984).

In *Alabama Power Co. v. Costle,* 636 F.2d 323, 369-70 (D.C.Cir.1979), however, we held that § 169(1)'s definition of "major emitting facility" was limited by the Clean Air Act's generic definition, § 302(j), 42 U.S.C. § 7602(j) (1988), which reads as follows:

> Except as otherwise expressly provided, the terms "major stationary source" and "major emitting facility" mean any stationary facility or source of air pollutants which directly emits, or has the potential to emit, one hundred tons per year or more of any air pollutant (including any major emitting facility or source of fugitive emissions of any such pollutant, *as determined by rule by the Administrator* [of the EPA]).

Id. (emphasis added). The result, we held in *Alabama Power,* is that calculation of § 169(1)'s 250-ton threshold "may include fugitive emissions only as determined by rule by the Administrator." 636 F.2d at 370. The primary issue before us is the scope of the Administrator's authority in making that determination.

In 1984 EPA promulgated a list of 27 categories of industrial stationary sources for which fugitive emissions are to be included in determining whether a source is "major". *See "Requirements for Preparation, Adoption and Submittal of Implementation Plans"*, 49 Fed.Reg. 43,202, 43,208-10 (1984). It simultaneously issued a companion notice proposing to add surface coal mines to the list. *See id.* at 43,211. In the end, it declined to add them, *see* 54 Fed.Reg. at 48,870, relying primarily on a finding that the socioeconomic costs of regulating the mines would outweigh any environmental benefits,

---

[1] "Fugitive emissions" are air pollution which is emitted to the atmosphere without passing through a smokestack or other centralized emission point. 40 CFR § 52.21(b) (1990).

id. at 48,879/3. The petitioners argue that cost-benefit is not the right standard, and that in any event, it would, if correctly applied, require EPA to count coal mines' fugitive emissions when identifying major emitting facilities, at least in some circumstances.

We find EPA's construction of the relevant statutory language permissible, and we uphold its application of cost-benefit analysis.

* * *

The petitioners claim that Congress clearly expressed an intent in § 302(j) to impose a nondiscretionary duty on EPA to subject *all* sources of fugitive emissions to the full panoply of PSD and nonattainment requirements. In their view, the provision's "by rule" requirement contemplates nothing more than the simple ministerial task of determining which sources have the potential to emit more than the threshold limit. *See* 49 Fed.Reg. at 43,206/1. As surface coal mines concededly fall within this category, they claim that EPA *must* subject them to the permit requirements of the PSD rules.

Not surprisingly, petitioners do not stress the language of § 302(j). It appears to constrain the Administrator's discretion only by requiring that he act "by rule". Petitioners instead point to four passages from a House committee report (accompanying its version of the bill that led to the 1977 amendments), which in their view expressed Congress's "intention on the precise question at issue", *Chevron U.S.A. v. NRDC,* 467 U.S. 837, 843 n. 9, (1984). We find nothing remotely approaching such an expression of intent.

1. In summarizing the changes to be wrought by the proposed amendments, the House Committee observed that

> the "major stationary source" definition is clarified to indicate the inclusion of major sources of fugitive emissions (last year's bill was unclear in this respect).

H.Rep. No. 294, 95th Cong., 1st Sess. 4 (1977) [citations omitted]. Of course, no one disputes that the new definition of "major stationary source" included language on fugitive emissions. The question is what it meant — whether the EPA Administrator was authorized to "determine" under what circumstances such emissions should be included, or only to perform some technical task; the cited passage provides not a clue.

2. The House report made reference to § 169(1)'s explicit authority for *states* to exempt nonprofit educational and health institutions that would otherwise qualify as "major" emitting facilities. *See* House Report at 144-45 [citations omitted]. Petitioners argue that this "enumeration of specific regulatory exemptions" precludes the implication of others. But the issue is EPA's authority, not the states', and EPA is applying § 302(j), as construed in *Alabama Power,* not § 169(1). Further, EPA claims not that Congress exempted coal mines, but only that Congress gave EPA discretion whether to include them (and other sources of fugitive emissions).

3. The House bill contained a provision authorizing a state's governor to exclude "naturally occurring particulate matter" from the computation of an area's compliance with the emission ceilings permitted by the PSD that come into play once a major emitting facility is licensed.[3] *See* House Report at 402-03, *reprinted in* 4 Leg. Hist. at 2869-70. Of course, this provision does not relate to the distinct problem of inclusion of

[3] In order to obtain a PSD permit an applicant proposing a new or modified "major" source must demonstrate that the proposed source will not cause ambient pollution concentrations to rise above the statutorily specified "increment". Once the PSD baseline date is triggered by the first PSD permit application in the area, all increases in actual emissions consume the permissible amount regardless of their source. See Alabama Power, 636 F.2d at 361-64.

fugitive emissions for purposes of the definition of a major emitting facility. Moreover, it did not survive. While in existence, however, it served as grist for the committee's defense to claims that the amendments would limit the size or operation of large surface coal mines:

> "Naturally occurring particulate matter" includes dust resulting from wind erosion of fields, farms, or open strip mines prior to or during reclamation. (Of course, the committee does not intend to exempt particulate emissions resulting from the mining process itself, dust created by moving vehicles, or from other coal-processing related activities.)

House Report at 165.

* * *

Petitioners grasp at the parenthetical as evidence that the Administrator's § 302(j) authority is not as broad as it appears. But the committee's recognition that this aborted gubernatorial authority did not itself *exempt* surface coal mines is quite consistent with the Administrator's understanding of his authority to define the circumstances when fugitive emissions are to be included in the definition of a major emitting facility.

4. Finally, the House committee stated that

> the ultimate decision on whether to classify the lands or to grant a permit to a proposed strip mine will rest with the State, just as it does with other proposed sources.

House Report at 166 [citations omitted]. The petitioners read this passage as grouping surface coal mines with the categories of industrial sources expressly made subject to PSD requirements by § 169(1). Again, they ignore context. Responding to concerns over the effects of the proposed bill on energy resources, the committee was discussing the availability of various sources of state flexibility. It noted the ill-fated gubernatorial authority to exclude naturally occurring particulate matter and the states' authority to reclassify affected lands to allow a higher increment. The passage contains no discussion of the conditions under which surface coal mines (or other fugitive emission sources) would in fact be subject to PSD requirements. It simply argues that even if mines are listed, they will still be feasible by virtue of authorities granted the states.

Thus, while the statutory language and legislative history do not bar petitioners' construction, they provide little support and no necessity for it. In fact, if petitioners are correct that the only prerequisite to PSD regulation is a determination that an industry's plants might pollute more than the threshold limit, one wonders why Congress thought it necessary to force EPA through burdensome rulemaking hoops — what issues did it expect to be illuminated by public participation?

We must next determine whether the agency's construction is a permissible one. *Chevron,* 467 U.S. at 845. EPA concluded that Congress intended it to make two findings before requiring inclusion of fugitive emissions in the threshold applicability determinations for sources in a particular category: "(1) That the sources have the potential to degrade air quality significantly and (2) that no unreasonable socioeconomic impacts relative to the benefits would result from subjecting the sources to [PSD requirements]." 49 Fed.Reg. at 43,208/1.

As we noted above, Congress placed no explicit constraints on the rulemaking discretion of the EPA Administrator; he is to act "as [he] determine[s]". Nor is the issue addressed in the legislative history. So long as the agency construction represents a reasonable accommodation of conflicting congressional policies, see *Chevron,* 467 U.S. at 845, we must defer. That standard is easily met here.

The purposes of the PSD provisions of the Clean Air Act include:

> (3) to insure that economic growth will occur in a manner consistent with the preservation of existing clean air resources ... [and]
> (5) to assure that any decision to permit increased air pollution in any area to which this section applies is made only after careful evaluation of all the consequences of such a decision....

Section 160, 42 U.S.C. § 7470 (1988) (emphasis added). Nothing in the legislative history undermines the inference that Congress believed that its PSD provisions should balance the values of clean air, on the one hand, and economic development and productivity, on the other, and much confirms it. *See, e.g.,* House Report at 163 * * * ; S.Rep. No. 127, 95th Cong., 1st Sess. 29 (1977) * * * . In *Alabama Power* we said, "[Section 302(j)] may be welcomed as serendipitous, for it gives EPA flexibility to provide industry-by-industry consideration and the appropriate tailoring of coverage." 636 F.2d at 369. The EPA construction of § 302(j) thus fits the statutory language, the overall congressional purposes, and our prior understanding of § 302(j)'s role.

EPA's approach seems especially appropriate for extractive industries. The idea of special rules for prevention of significant deterioration was born from a fear that polluters might avoid air quality regulations by relocating their plants to pristine areas where ambient pollution levels were well below statutory ceilings. *See* House Report at 151 [citations omitted] ("there is a strong national interest in not encouraging industries to go forum shopping, seeking to locate new plants in areas which allow the greatest pollution"). The extractive industries pose such a fear only indirectly, as one may extract a mineral deposit only where one finds it. Compare 49 Fed.Reg. at 43,212/2. While air-related controls over surface coal mines will at the margin tend to increase underground mines' share of total coal production, thus in a sense shifting the locale of coal production, the impact of exclusion from PSD treatment is less direct than for more mobile industries.

Finally, EPA's decision not to list surface coal mines under § 302(j) hardly means that their operators are free to pollute at will. As EPA noted, they remain subject to other Clean Air Act limitations (e.g., national ambient air quality standards and, in areas in which the PSD baseline has been triggered, PSD increment limitations) and, more importantly, to the authority of the Department of Interior under the Surface Mining Control and Reclamation Act and other provisions, see 54 Fed.Reg. at 48,875/2, a matter discussed more fully below. The agency construction of § 302(j) is reasonable.

* * *

The petitioners urge that even if cost/benefit analysis is appropriate under § 302(j), EPA's application of its chosen methodology was flawed. EPA posited four basic alternatives:

Alternative I: The status quo; no listing.

Alternative II: Listing for surface coal mines, but with a proviso that emissions from existing mines would not count toward consumption of the permitted increments, i.e., a kind of grandfathering of existing mines.

Alternative III: Listing of surface coal mines, with no exclusion of emissions from existing mines.

Alternative IV: Listing of surface coal mines only to the extent that they have an impact on air quality in the most highly protected of the various classes into which regions are sorted for PSD purposes, Class I areas and "mandatory" Class II areas (which, unlike other class II areas, states may not reclassify into Class III areas).

See 54 Fed.Reg. at 48,872-73. In its Regulatory Impact Analysis, EPA assessed the costs and benefits of the three regulatory alternatives against the baseline of no regulation. It concluded that the costs of Alternatives II and III greatly outweighed their benefits. *See* 54 Fed.Reg. at 48,873/2. On this score it pointed to the relatively low background ambient pollution levels in the remote areas where surface coal mines are generally located, the limited distance from the mine that ambient impacts occur, and the general absence of population centers exposed to surface coal mine particulate matter. Petitioners appear not to contest these conclusions.

The Regulatory Impact Analysis found the evaluation of Alternative IV inconclusive, estimating that it might have anywhere from a $300,000 net advantage to a $300,000 net detriment for the two sample areas considered. This did not include certain hard-to-value benefits that the extra regulation might afford. *Id.* EPA noted, however, that the study failed to consider the effects of Department of Interior regulation of surface coal mining, and concluded that Alternative IV was not cost justified, noting that regulation by Interior would achieve "many if not all of the visibility and other benefits" of inclusion. 54 Fed.Reg. at 48,873/3.

* * *

There are two branches to petitioners' attack on EPA's theory that regulation by the Department of Interior (under the Surface Mining Control and Reclamation Act and other authorities) made many of the benefits of listing coal mines redundant, leaving the net cost-benefit evaluation of Alternative IV negative. First, they note that EPA's Clean Air Act authority trumps Interior's as to general control of air quality hazards of mining, unless there is a " 'regulatory gap' in the coverage of [the Clean Air Act]". *National Wildlife Federation v. Hodel,* 839 F.2d 694, 765 (D.C.Cir.1988); *see also* SMCRA § 702(a)(4), 30 U.S.C. § 1292(a)(4) (1988). As our conclusion in *Hodel* that no such regulatory gap existed rested on EPA's being in the process of considering listing surface coal mines, 839 F.2d at 765, and as it has now resolved that in the negative, the premise for any limit on Interior's jurisdiction no longer applies. Moreover, *Hodel's* finding of preemption was extremely limited, and did not encompass the Interior regulations on which EPA now relies. *Id.* EPA's action is simply a recognition that many of the benefits of listing can be achieved by Interior under SMCRA, not, as petitioners see it, a "deferral in favor of SMCRA contraven[ing] congressional intent." Petitioners' Brief at 29.

Second, petitioners argue that Interior's authority to regulate fugitive emissions from surface coal mines is an imperfect substitute for PSD regulation by EPA. But EPA never claimed that Interior's SMCRA regulation was a clone of listing for PSD purposes. It merely found that Interior's programs would "provide benefits equivalent to Alternative IV through the mitigation or prevention of adverse effects on air quality related values in national parks and other areas of special concern, ... assuming a roughly similar mix of pollution control measures, reductions in SCM size, and SCM relocations as was assumed would accompany Alternative IV." 54 Fed.Reg. at 48,879/3 (emphasis added). Thus, EPA reasoned, a significant portion of the benefits that the Regulatory Impact Analysis attributed to Alternative IV were phantom benefits. With them removed, the cost-benefit analysis of Alternative IV (which came out inconclusively balanced) would come out decidedly negative. *Id.* at 48,878/3.

That conclusion hardly seems arbitrary or capricious. By virtue of SMRCA, surface coal mining is forbidden in some areas, subject to Interior's veto in others, and everywhere subject to Interior regulation for air quality purposes, restrictions that EPA reviewed in considerable detail. 54 Fed.Reg. at 48,674/1-75/2.

Prohibition. Section 522(e)(1), 30 U.S.C. § 1272(e)(1) (1988), prohibits surface coal mining within the boundaries of mandatory Class I and Class II areas.[6] Further, § 522(e)(3) prohibits, subject to valid existing rights, surface coal mining that will "adversely affect" these areas, unless the mining is approved jointly by Interior and the federal, state or local agency with jurisdiction over the park.

Veto authority. Section 522(c) allows any person whose interests may be adversely affected by surface coal mining to petition the regulatory authority to have any area designated as unsuitable for mining, and the grounds on which the petition may be granted include a showing that the operations will "affect fragile or historic lands in which such operations could result in significant damage to important historic, cultural, scientific, and aesthetic values and natural systems", see § 522(a)(3)(B), 30 U.S.C. § 1272(a)(3)(B) (1988), which Interior interprets to include areas of recreational value due to high environmental quality, critical habitats for threatened species and uncommon geologic formations, 30 CFR § 762.5 (1990).

Controls. SMCRA provides Interior authority to require mine operators to "stabilize and protect all surface areas ... to effectively control erosion and attendant air and water pollution." § 515(b)(4), 30 U.S.C. § 1265(b)(4) (1988); see also § 515(b)(17), 30 U.S.C. § 1265(b)(17) (1988). Under this authority, Interior has promulgated extensive regulations, requiring, for example, that all surface coal mining permit applications include a plan for fugitive dust control and an air quality monitoring program to evaluate its effectiveness. 30 CFR § 780.15 (1990). In addition, haul roads must be located, designed, constructed, used, maintained, and reclaimed so as to "[c]ontrol or prevent erosion ..., including road dust as well as dust occurring on other exposed surfaces, by measures such as vegetating, watering, using chemicals or other dust suppressants." *Id.* § 816.150(b)(1).

Finally, EPA relied on the Bureau of Land Management's authority over coal mining on federal lands (exercised primarily through lease requirements), noting that 80% of western coal reserves are located on federal lands. See 54 Fed.Reg. at 48,675/1. Areas of outstanding scenic quality are considered unsuitable for leasing unless the BLM determines that "mining operations will not significantly diminish or adversely affect the scenic quality of the designated area". 43 CFR § 3461.5(e)(2) (1990).

Thus we find that EPA was not arbitrary or capricious in its decision not to list surface coal mines on the basis of its projection of the effects of the prohibitions and regulations that Interior will enforce. EPA recognized, however, that its projection might prove incorrect, and committed itself to reconsider listing surface coal mines on evidence that Interior "will not protect visibility and other air quality values" in "national parks, wilderness areas, national memorial parks, and international parks that are Class I PSD areas." 54 Fed.Reg. at 48,870/3. Presumably it will do so on such a showing by petitioners.

* * *

The petitions for review are *denied.*

---

[6] Subject to valid rights existing on August 3, 1977, § 522(e)(1) prohibits mining in National Park Systems, the National Wildlife Refuge System, the National System of Trails, the National Wilderness Preservation System, the Wild and Scenic Rivers System, and National Recreation Areas. This overlaps completely with PSD mandatory Class I areas and appears to cover all mandatory Class II areas except national lakeshores and seashores.

NOTES

1. Section 702 of the Surface Mining Control and Reclamation Act provides that nothing in that law should be construed as "superseding, amending, modifying or repealing" various federal laws including the Clean Air Act. As the court notes in *NRDC*, the D.C. Circuit had previously construed this language to allow the Secretary of the Interior to fill in "regulatory gaps" in the coverage of another statute. *In re Surface Mining Regulation Litigation*, 627 F.2d 1346, 1367 (D.C. Cir. 1980). Regarding fugitive emissions from coal mines, the court had determined that no regulatory gap existed because, at that time, the EPA was still considering whether or not it would regulate fugitive emissions from coal mines. *National Wildlife Federation v. Hodel*, 839 F.2d 694, 765 (D.C. Cir. 1988). How does the *NRDC* court reconcile the earlier holding in *National Wildlife Federation*?

2. In an earlier case the court had rejected EPA's proposal to delay its decision as to whether to list coal mines as sources of fugitive emissions subject to regulation. *Sierra Club v. Gorsuch*, 715 F.2d 653 (D.C. Cir. 1983). EPA had asserted the need for delay because it lacked "quantification techniques for applying PSD regulations to individual mines." With respect to other sources of fugitive emissions, however, EPA had concluded that "quantification was necessary only to determine whether a *particular source* was subject to review, not to determine whether a *category* of sources should be regulated." Furthermore, EPA had decided that all sources meeting a 250 ton threshold requirement should be regulated but had ignored a report which found that most surface coal mines exceed that 250 ton threshold. EPA insisted that its distinction between coal mines and other sources was justified, but failed to explain its reasons. Judge Bazelon was not impressed:

> If there is reasoned decisionmaking lurking behind such agency behavior it has yet to be articulated. For agency action to be upheld, it must not only be explainable; it must be explained. Without such explanation, we cannot properly exercise review.

Id. at 660-661. The court remanded EPA's decision so that it could either justify its decision not to regulate surface coal mines or decide that they should be regulated.

3. The PSD provision of the Act establishes standards only for SO_2 and particulates. Section 166(a) of the Act, however, requires EPA to study HC, CO, NO_x and photochemical oxidants and to promulgate regulations by August 7, 1979 "to prevent the significant deterioration of air quality which would result from the emission of such pollutants." Criteria pollutants designated after the 1977 Amendments (lead is currently the only one) must be addressed in the same manner within two years from the date that NAAQS are promulgated for such pollutants. The Act sets out standards to which EPA must adhere in promulgating these rules, including the requirement that they contain specific numerical measures against which permit applications may be evaluated. *Id.* at § 166(d). In 1980 EPA took initial steps to comply with § 166(a) by announcing its intention to promulgate PSD rules for lead, O_3, CO and NO_x. In 1981, however, EPA canceled the rulemaking proceedings without explanation. In *Sierra Club v. Thomas*, 658 F. Supp. 165 (N.D. Cal 1987), EPA was ordered to promulgate final PSD rules for NO_x by October, 1988. The court rejected EPA's claim that it would need a minimum of 50 months to complete such a rulemaking. EPA missed the court's deadline by approximately one year. Final rules were promulgated on October 17, 1989. 53 Fed.

Reg. 40,656 (1989). In *Environmental Defense Fund v. EPA,* 898 F.2d 183 (D.C. Cir. 1990), those rules were remanded to the EPA to take new evidence and consider whether modifications might be appropriate.

VISIBILITY PROTECTION

STATE OF VERMONT V. THOMAS

850 F.2d 99 (2nd Cir. 1988)

ALTIMARI, Circuit Judge:

Petitioners, the State of Vermont, Conservation Law Foundation of New England, Inc., and Vermont Natural Resources Council, seek review, pursuant to 42 U.S.C. § 7607(b)(1), of a final ruling of respondent, the Environmental Protection Agency ("EPA"), taking "no action" on those portions of Vermont's state implementation plan ("state implementation plan" or "SIP") addressing "regional haze" submitted under section 169A of the Clean Air Act of 1970, as amended (the "Clean Air Act" or the "Act"), 42 U.S.C. § 7491 (1982). Because we agree with respondent Lee Thomas, Administrator of the EPA (the "Administrator"), that current regulations do not encompass federally enforceable measures to alleviate "regional haze," we deny the petition for review.

BACKGROUND

Congress enacted the Clean Air Act to address the increasingly grave threat of air pollution to the environment, public health and the general welfare of the nation. 42 U.S.C. § 7401 (1982). The Act directs EPA to prescribe national "ambient air quality standards" and requires states to ensure that the national standards are complied with by adopting implementation plans. *Id.* §§ 7409-10. The statutory scheme establishes shared state and federal responsibility for achieving a cleaner and safer environment by providing for federal coordination of regional air pollution control measures implemented by the states. *Id.* § 7401(a)(3), (4). To ensure that the various state implementation plans meet the requirements of the Act and EPA regulations, EPA is empowered to approve or disapprove SIPs and any subsequent revisions thereto. *Id.* § 7410.

At issue in this case are the 1977 amendments to the Act which directed EPA, in pertinent part, to adopt regulations protecting visibility in certain national parklands and wilderness areas, designated as "class I Federal areas." Clean Air Act § 169A, 42 U.S.C. § 7491; *see id.* § 162(a), 42 U.S.C. § 7472(a) (defining class I areas to include international parks, national wilderness areas exceeding 5,000 acres, national memorial parks exceeding 5,000 acres, and national parks exceeding 6,000 acres). Class I areas were singled out by Congress as requiring special protection in view of the aesthetic importance of visibility to the continued enjoyment and preservation of the country's scenic vistas. Accordingly, Congress set as a "national goal the prevention of any future, and the remedying of any existing, impairment of visibility . . . result[ing] from man-made air pollution" in class I areas, *id.* § 7491(a)(1), and directed EPA to provide guidelines for the states in order "to assure . . . reasonable progress toward meeting the national goal" of visibility enhancement in those areas. *Id.* § 7491(a)(4), (b).

Pursuant to its authority under section 169A of the Act, EPA promulgated regulations in 1980 designed to "establish long-range goals, a planning process, and implementation procedures" toward achieving the national visibility goal. 45 Fed.Reg. 80,084 (codified at 40 C.F.R. § 51.300 et seq.). Specifically, EPA determined that visibility impairment is of two types: 1) "plume blight," i.e., traceable streams of smoke, dust or colored gas emanating from single sources or small groups of sources; and 2) "regional haze," i.e., widespread, homogeneous haze from a multitude of sources which impairs visibility in large areas, often for hundreds of miles from the sources of the pollution. Of the two types of air pollution, EPA recognized that plume blight obviously was more susceptible to identification, measurement and thus control. The more vexing problem of how to alleviate regional haze was, in EPA's view, subject to certain scientific and technical limitations. Consequently, the 1980 regulations adopted a "phased approach to visibility protection." *Id.* at 80,085. Under "Phase I" of the program, EPA regulations targeted plume blight while deferring for "future phases" the complexities of regional haze and urban plumes. *Id.* at 80,085-86. "Phase II" would address regional haze once monitoring and other scientific techniques progressed to a point that EPA could develop a regulatory program for that type of impairment. *Id.* at 80,087.

The effect of the 1980 regulations was to require the 36 states containing class I areas to revise their SIPs to implement a visibility protection program, consistent with the new regulations, to assure reasonable progress toward section 169A's national visibility goal. The regulations mandated that each of the affected states' SIPs contain, *inter alia*, a "long-term (10-15 years) strategy" to combat visibility impairment in each class I area. 40 C.F.R. § 51.306(a) (1987).

In April 1986, Vermont submitted to EPA its proposed plan addressing visibility impairment at the Lye Brook National Wilderness Area, a 12,000 acre mountain plateau in the southern portion of the Green Mountain National Forest and the state's only class I area. As indicated in Vermont's 300-page SIP, the Lye Brook area is afflicted with summertime haze that has drastically reduced visibility by as much as 40 percent since the mid 1950s. The Vermont plan contained extensive technical analysis demonstrating that Lye Brook's visibility impairment is due primarily to sulfur dioxide pollution originating from out-of-state sources, e.g., power plants and coal and oil company factories. Vermont found that sulfate particle emissions from a multitude of sources located in 8 upwind states — Ohio, Pennsylvania, West Virginia, Kentucky, Tennessee, Illinois, Indiana, and Michigan — were principally responsible for the haze blanketing Lye Brook during the summer months.

Vermont's SIP concluded that while adequate in-state measures to prevent plume blight were already in place, a reduction program aimed at out-of-state sulfate emissions would be necessary to assure reasonable progress toward the national visibility goal. Consequently, Vermont proposed a federally enforceable "long-term strategy" to combat the effects of regional haze at Lye Brook. The long-term strategy included a summertime ambient sulfate standard and a 48-state emissions reduction plan in order to meet the air quality standard by 1995. In addition, Vermont asked EPA to disapprove and revise the SIPs of the eight upwind states which were the major contributors to visibility impairment at Lye Brook, *see* Clean Air Act § 110(c)(1)(B), 42 U.S.C. § 7410(c)(1)(B) ("[t]he Administrator shall . . . set[ ] forth an implementation plan . . . for a State if . . . the plan . . . submitted for such State is determined by the Administrator not to be in accordance with the requirements of this section"), and also asked that four of these states not containing class I areas (Ohio, Illinois, Indiana, and Pennsylvania) be added to the list of 36 states required to submit visibility plans.

In December 1986, EPA issued a proposed ruling on Vermont's SIP. 51 Fed.Reg. 43,389. EPA agreed with Vermont's assessment that visibility impairment at Lye Brook is due predominantly to regional haze caused by out-of-state sulfur dioxide emissions. *Id.* at 43,391. Nevertheless, EPA proposed taking "no action" on those portions of Vermont's SIP addressing regional haze "because EPA has yet to establish requirements for strategies relating to regional haze." *Id.* at 43,392. EPA objected to Vermont's program as dictating a single solution to a national problem without the benefit of EPA regulations implementing a Phase II regional haze program.

In July 1987, EPA issued its final ruling on Vermont's proposal. 52 Fed.Reg. 26,973. While EPA approved limited portions of Vermont's SIP complying with existing plume blight regulations under section 169A of the Act, EPA decided to take "no action" on those parts of the SIP aimed at controlling regional haze. EPA also denied Vermont's request to disapprove the SIPs of the eight upwind states as well as its request to add four states to the list of states required to submit visibility protection plans for class I areas. In explaining its "no action" ruling, EPA concluded that Vermont's proposal establishing an ambient sulfate standard and its long-term strategy for emissions reduction throughout the continental United States were outside the scope of EPA's existing regulations. EPA viewed as federally enforceable only those portions of a state implementation plan submitted in response to regulations promulgated by the agency. According to EPA, Vermont's regional haze measures could not become federal rules "until such time as EPA decides to promulgate a national regional haze program." *Id.* at 26,974.

Petitioners thereupon filed a petition for review of EPA's "final rule" pursuant to 42 U.S.C. § 7607(b)(1). We permitted the Alabama Power Company, et al. to intervene as respondents.

Discussion

Petitioners argue that EPA's refusal to approve Vermont's SIP in its entirety violates both EPA's own regulations and the Clean Air Act, and accordingly seek reversal of EPA's ruling as an administrative action "not in accordance with law." 42 U.S.C. § 7607(d)(9)(A); 5 U.S.C. § 706(2)(A); *see Connecticut v. EPA*, 696 F.2d 147, 155 (2d Cir.1982); *Friends of the Earth v. EPA*, 499 F.2d 1118, 1123 (2d Cir.1974). Specifically, petitioners contend that the 1980 regulations encompass measures to alleviate regional haze and that EPA's contrary interpretation of its regulations is inconsistent with the terms and the underlying purposes of the Clean Air Act. For the reasons that follow, we disagree.

* * *

Our inquiry into determining whether the Administrator's action in this case was "in accordance with law" is a limited one. *See Kennecott Corp. v. EPA*, 684 F.2d 1007, 1013 (D.C.Cir.1982). "Although this inquiry . . . is to be searching and careful, . . . [a] court is not empowered to substitute its judgment for that of the agency." *Friends of the Earth*, 499 F.2d at 1123 (*quoting Citizens to Preserve Overton Park, Inc. v. Volpe*, 401 U.S. 402, 416 (1971)). Indeed, in view of the EPA's responsibility to administer the Clean Air Act, we must give great deference to the Administrator's interpretation of the statute. *EPA v. National Crushed Stone Ass'n*, 449 U.S. 64, 83 (1980); *Udall v. Tallman*, 380 U.S. 1, 16 (1965). And, when the Administrator's interpretation of his own regulations is at issue, "deference is even more clearly in order." *Udall*, 380 U.S. at 16. Consequently, certainly true that the actual implementation of visibility protection measures is the responsibility of the states, the statute and its legislative history make clear that Congress charged EPA with the responsibility through its rulemaking power to ensure attainment of the national goal. *Id.* § 169A(a)(4), § 7491(a)(4); H.R.Rep. No. 294, 95th Cong., 1st Sess. 206, reprinted in 1977 U.S.Code Cong. & Admin.News 1077, 1285. Without EPA rulemaking on regional haze, therefore, Vermont's proposed interstate measures are outside the scope of the regulations and thus are not subject to federal enforcement under the Act.

Since Vermont's regional haze measures were not required to be included in its SIP, we believe that EPA's "no action" response was appropriate. Petitioners maintain, however, that EPA's "no action" ruling deprives Vermont of a definitive decision on the merits of its proposal and violates section 110 of the Act. *See* 42 U.S.C. § 7410(a)(2) (Administrator "shall . . . approve or disapprove" proposed SIP). We have held previously that the Clean Air Act should not be read to permit only outright approval or disapproval of state plans so long as EPA's action was reasonable. *Connecticut Fund for the Environment, Inc. v. EPA*, 672 F.2d 998, 1006-07 (2d Cir.), *cert. denied*, 459 U.S. 1035 (1982). In this case, the effect of EPA's ruling was to "keep [Vermont's] measures out of the Federally enforceable SIP." 52 Fed.Reg. 26,976 (1987). EPA explained its action in this regard as an attempt to "avoid the appearance of a premature judgment as to [the measures'] ultimate approvability, and [to] prevent confusion regarding their present enforceability as a matter of state law." *Id.* Given that Vermont was free to adopt within its borders air quality standards more stringent than federal law requires, 42 U.S.C. § 7416, it is evident that EPA's "no action" ruling — as opposed to outright rejection of Vermont's regional haze measures — was more than reasonable.

We recognize, of course, that without federal enforcement of Vermont's plan, little, if any, progress will be made on regional haze at Lye Brook. While this is indeed lamentable, until such time as a federal regional haze program is in place, Vermont may not impose its standards on upwind states. *See Air Pollution Control Dist. v. EPA*, 739 F.2d 1071, 1087-88 (6th Cir.1984) (downwind state's air quality standards that are more stringent than national standards do not require upwind state to alter its otherwise valid SIP); *Connecticut v. EPA*, 656 F.2d 902, 909 (2d Cir.1981) (same); *see also* Clean Air Act § 110(a)(2)(E)(i), 42 U.S.C. § 7410(a)(2)(E)(i). Consequently, we find that EPA's denial of Vermont's request to disapprove the SIPs of the eight upwind states contributing to visibility impairment at Lye Brook was in accordance with federal law, *see* Clean Air Act § 110(c)(1)(B), 42 U.S.C. § 7410(c)(1)(B) (providing that EPA may revise SIP if it is not in compliance with requirements of the Act), and likewise that EPA's refusal to add four regional haze producing states to those now required to develop class I visibility protection programs was reasonable in view of the limited scope of the 1980 regulations.

Finally, we note that, more than ten years after the enactment of section 169A, there still is no national program addressing regional haze. We are sympathetic to petitioners' argument that something must be done soon. EPA's assurances of future action on regional haze are little comfort to Vermont and visitors to Lye Brook. We can only hope that EPA will act quickly in furtherance of the national visibility goal. In the meantime, Vermont can pursue an alternative remedy, namely, the filing with EPA of a petition for rulemaking under the Administrative Procedure Act, 5 U.S.C. § 553(e), with eventual judicial review in the D.C. Circuit. 42 U.S.C. § 7607(b)(1). In any event, we are convinced that the issues raised by the petition in the instant case are best left to the national rulemaking process rather than to an SIP approval proceeding.

CONCLUSION

For all of the foregoing reasons, the petition for review is denied.

NOTES

1. The court suggests that Vermont can petition the EPA for a rulemaking to address the regional haze problem. How likely is it that such a petition would be successful? Can Vermont avail itself of any other remedy? *See* §§ 110(a)(2)(D)(i)(II); 126(b).

2. Following the designation of federal Class I areas for visibility protection (*see* 40 CFR § 81.400 *et seq.* (1991)), the states are required to alter their SIPs as necessary to make reasonable progress toward the national goal of protecting these areas from visibility impairment. § 169A(b)(2). To help achieve this goal, the Act requires major stationary sources, which began operating before August 7, 1977 and after August 7, 1962, and which may reasonably be anticipated to cause or contribute to any impairment of visibility in a Class I area designated for visibility protection, to install, as expeditiously as practicable, the best available retrofit technology (BART). § 169A(b)(2)(A). BART is to be determined by the state, taking into account costs of compliance, the remaining useful life of the source, and other factors. §§ 169A(b)(2)(A); 169A(g)(2). For fossil fuel-fired power plants, with a capacity in excess of 750 megawatts, BART standards must be established by the state according to EPA guidelines. Should BART apply to new facilities? Why or why not?

3. To help prevent visibility degradation, the EPA has adopted rules to protect "integral vistas". An integral vista is "a view from within a mandatory Federal Class I area of a specific landmark or panorama located outside the boundary of the mandatory Class I federal area." 40 CFR § 51.301(n) (1990). (Emphasis added.) States are required to list in their SIPs integral vistas that have been identified by the responsible federal land managers. 40 CFR § 51.304(c).

4. Section 169A(a)(1) establishes a goal of protecting visibility values "*in* mandatory Class I federal areas . . . ." (Emphasis added.) Are the integral vista rules consistent with this requirement?

5. The most highly publicized issue surrounding visibility protection involves the Grand Canyon National Park. For many years, the Navajo Generating Station at Page, Arizona has been criticized for contributing to the haze that afflicts the Park. In 1991, an agreement was reached among the principal parties to the controversy that many hope will abate the problem. Set forth below is the EPA decision adopting the parties' memorandum of understanding.

GRAND CANYON NATIONAL PARK VISIBILITY IMPAIRMENT

EPA Final Rule, 56 Fed. Reg. 50172-01 (1991)
(to be codified at 40 CFR Part 52)

SUMMARY: This notice revises the Federal implementation plan (FIP) for the State of Arizona to include a sulfur dioxide ($S0_2$) emission limit of 42 nanograms per Joule (ng/J) [0.10 pound per million British thermal units (lb/MMBtu)], heat input for the Navajo

Generating Station (NGS) to remedy visibility impairment in the Grand Canyon National Park (GCNP). Compliance with this emission limit will be phased-in by unit in 1997, 1998, and 1999 and determined on a plant-wide annual rolling average basis. In addition, NGS will be required to reschedule its maintenance such that 6 unit-weeks of maintenance will be performed during the winter months.

* * *

SUPPLEMENTARY INFORMATION:

I. Background

A. Regulatory Requirements

Section 169A of the Act, 42 U.S.C. 7491, sets as a national goal "the prevention of any future, and the remedying of any existing, impairment of visibility in mandatory Class I Federal areas which impairment results from manmade air pollution." Mandatory Class I Federal areas are certain national parks, wildernesses, and international parks as described in section 162(a) of the Act, 42 U.S.C. 7472(a). Section 169A requires that EPA promulgate regulations to assure reasonable progress toward meeting the national goal for mandatory Class I Federal areas where EPA has determined that visibility is an important value. On November 30, 1979, EPA identified 156 such areas, including the GCNP in Arizona, where visibility is an important air quality-related value (44 FR 69122). Section 169A specifically requires EPA to promulgate regulations requiring States to amend their State implementation plans (SIP's) to provide reasonable progress toward meeting the national goal for the 156 areas. On December 2, 1980, EPA promulgated the required visibility regulations (45 FR 80084, codified at 40 CFR 51.300 et seq.). The visibility regulations require the 36 States listed in section 51.300(b), including Arizona, to:

1. Coordinate SIP development with the appropriate Federal land managers (FLM's).
2. Develop programs to assess and remedy Phase I visibility impairment from existing sources and to prevent visibility impairment from new sources.
3. Develop a long-term (10 to 15 years) strategy to address, among other things, Phase I visibility impairment to assure reasonable progress toward the national goal.
4. Develop a visibility monitoring strategy to collect information on visibility conditions.
5. Consider in all aspects of visibility protection any "integral vistas" (important views of landmarks or panoramas that extend outside of the boundaries of the Class I area) identified by the FLM's as critical to the visitors' enjoyment of the Class I areas. The affected States were required to submit revised SIP's satisfying these provisions by September 2, 1981 (see 45 FR 80091, codified at 40 CFR 51.302(a)(1)).[1]

[1] The EPA's 1980 regulations implementing the statutory requirements of section 169A address visibility impairment that is reasonably attributable to a single source or small group of sources ("Phase I" impairment) (see generally 45 FR 80084 (December 2, 1980)). Recognizing certain scientific and technical limitations, EPA, in promulgating the 1980 regulations, deferred regulatory action on more "complex problems such as regional haze and urban plumes." Id. at 80086. Today, in accordance with the 1980 regulations, EPA is taking

The second and third requirements listed above are of particular relevance to today's action. Pursuant to 40 CFR 51.302(c)(2), each affected State is required to include in its SIP such emission limitations, schedules of compliance, and other measures as may be necessary to make reasonable progress toward the national visibility goal. Under 40 CFR 51.302(c)(1), an FLM may certify to a State that there exists impairment of visibility in any mandatory Class I Federal area. Such impairment must be addressed in accordance with 40 CFR 51.302(c) which sets forth measures for achieving reasonable progress, including best available retrofit technology (BART) and a long-term strategy (see 40 CFR 51.302(c) (1) and (2), section 169A(b)(2) (A) and (B)). Pursuant to 40 CFR 51.302(c)(4)(i), where impairment is certified at least 6 months prior to plan submission, an affected State must identify each existing stationary facility which may "reasonably be anticipated to cause or contribute" to any such impairment which is "reasonably attributable to that existing stationary facility," and analyze for BART any facility so identified. "Reasonably attributable" impairment is impairment "attributable by visual observation or any other technique the State deems appropriate" (40 CFR 51.301(s)). Where a State defaults on its obligations under the visibility regulations, EPA may act in place of the State pursuant to a FIP under section 110(c) of the Act, 42 U.S.C. 7410(c), and promulgate such limitation and measures as are required to achieve reasonable progress. In such cases, all of the rights and duties that would otherwise fall to the State accrue instead to EPA.

The visibility regulations promulgated at 40 CFR 51.302(c)(4)(i) require that once a Phase I impairment has been certified, a State (or EPA if the State's visibility protection program addressing BART has not been approved, and EPA is acting in its place) must analyze for BART any specific existing stationary facility it identifies as a "reasonably attributable" source of the impairment. Pursuant to section 169A(b) of the Act (42 U.S.C. 7491(b)) and 40 CFR 51.302(c)(4)(iii), the emission limitation representing BART for fossil fuel-fired power plants with a generating capacity in excess of 750 megawatts (MW) must be determined pursuant to guidelines promulgated by the Administrator. This statutorily-required procedure for conducting a BART analysis is found in "Guidelines for Determining Best Available Retrofit Technology Analysis for Coal-Fired Power Plants and Other Stationary Facilities" (EPA-450/3-80-009b BART Guidelines). A copy of this document may be found in Docket A-89-02A.

In December 1982, environmental groups, including EDF, filed a citizen's suit in the United States District Court for the Northern District of California alleging that EPA had failed to perform a nondiscretionary duty under section 110(c) of the Act, 42 U.S.C. 7410(c), to promulgate visibility FIPs for the 35 States[3] that, at that time, had failed to submit SIPs to EPA as called for by the 1980 visibility regulations, *EDF v. Reilly*, No. C82-6850 RPA (N.D. Cal.). The State of Arizona was one of the 35 States that failed to submit a revised SIP to EPA.

The EPA and the plaintiffs negotiated a settlement agreement for the remaining States which the court approved by order on April 20, 1984. For more information on

---

regulatory action to remedy visibility impairment that is caused by NGS. The EPA is in the process of establishing the Grand Canyon Visibility Transport Commission as required by section 169B of the Act. The duties of that commission include making recommendations on "promulgation of regulations under section 169A to address long-range strategies for addressing regional haze which impairs visibility in * * * the GCNP" (section 169B(d)(2)(C)).

[3] The State of Alaska had submitted a SIP which was approved on July 5, 1983 at 48 FR 30623.

details of the provisions of the original settlement, including a schedule of actions by EPA, see EPA's announcement of the agreement at 49 FR 20647 (May 16, 1984).

B. Settlement Agreement

To remedy the States' failure to submit the necessary SIP revisions during the time specified by the regulations, the settlement agreement replaced the original regulatory deadlines for visibility SIP provisions with a rulemaking schedule agreed to by the parties and approved by the court. This schedule required EPA to review the existing SIP's to determine any deficiencies, allow the States to cure those deficiencies, and to promulgate FIPs on a specified schedule for those States that still did not submit visibility SIP revisions to EPA. Specifically, the first part of the agreement required EPA to promulgate FIP's which cover the monitoring and NSR provisions of 40 CFR 51.305 and 51.307. The EPA promulgated its monitoring strategy for 23 States and its NSR provisions for 21 States, including Arizona, at 50 FR 28544 (July 12, 1985), 51 FR 5504 (February 1, 1986), and 51 FR 22937 (June 24, 1986). In separate notices, EPA approved the SIPs of the other States with respect to monitoring and NSR.

The second part of the settlement agreement required EPA to determine the adequacy of the SIPs to meet the remaining provisions of the visibility regulations and gave the States until December 1986 to submit additional measures that would avoid the need for a FIP. These provisions are the general plan provisions for achieving reasonable progress toward the national visibility goal including BART and other implementation control strategies (§ 51.302), integral vista protection (§ 51.302-307), and long-term strategies (§ 51.306). The settlement agreement required EPA to promulgate FIP's to remedy any deficiencies on a specified schedule.

Pursuant to 40 CFR 51.302(c)(1), on November 14, 1985, the Department of the Interior (DOI) certified the existence of visibility impairment in all Class I areas within its jurisdiction in the lower 48 States.

On January 23, 1986, EPA determined that the SIPs of 32 States (including Arizona) were deficient with respect to the remaining visibility provisions (51 FR 3046) and offered the States an opportunity to submit corrective SIP revisions. Thereafter, EPA and the plaintiffs negotiated revisions to the settlement agreement which extended the deadlines for State action or, if the States failed to respond, Federal action proposing FIPs to remedy these deficiencies. The court approved these revisions by its order of September 9, 1986.

* * *

Thirty-two affected States failed to submit visibility SIP revisions in response to the notice of deficiency. Consequently, in accordance with the revised settlement agreement, on March 12, 1987 (52 FR 7802), EPA proposed to disapprove the SIPs of 32 States, including Arizona, for failing to meet the remaining provisions of the visibility regulations, including general plan requirements to achieve reasonable progress toward the national visibility goal (which in turn includes BART, long-term strategies, and other control strategies). Also in accordance with the agreement, on November 24, 1987 (52 FR 45132), EPA took final action disapproving the affected SIPs, again including Arizona. In that action, EPA also promulgated, as FIP measures under section 110(c), general plan requirements for these States. The EPA also determined that BART was unnecessary in 28 States because it could not reasonably attribute the visibility impairment of mandatory Class I Federal areas in these States to specific sources or small groups of sources. In addition, under the revised agreement, EPA deferred until August 31, 1988 a decision regarding the need for BART or other control measures in the FIPs for the States of Arizona, Maine, Minnesota, and Utah to address certified visibility impairments in seven Class I areas in these States which potentially could be reasonably attributed to a specific source pending acquisition and evaluation of additional technical information regarding the potential sources of impairment.

Because all of the additional information needed by EPA was forthcoming but still not available by August 1988, the Agency sought and received a second extension, until August 31, 1989, of the deadline for issuing a rulemaking proposal regarding the need for BART or other control measures to remedy visibility impairments in three of the remaining Class I areas (Moosehorn Wilderness, GCNP, and Canyonlands National Park). With regard to the impairment in the GCNP, EPA delayed action in order to allow the National Park Service (NPS) time to analyze the data from a 1987 winter visibility attribution study, termed the Winter Haze Intensive Tracer Experiment (WHITEX), conducted in the Colorado Plateau where the GCNP is located. In the meantime, on May 19, 1989 (54 FR 21904), in accordance with the second revision to the settlement agreement, EPA promulgated final decisions concerning certified visibility impairments in four of the seven Class I areas. Based on monitoring conducted in these areas, EPA found that the visibility impairments were not reasonably attributable to any specific source. Therefore, EPA determined that it was not necessary to revise the FIPs for the States of Maine, Minnesota, and Arizona to include BART or other control strategies to remedy impairments in Roosevelt Campobello International Park (Canada), Voyageurs National Park (Minnesota), Saguaro Wilderness (Arizona), and Petrified Forest National Park (Arizona).

In April 1989, EPA received a draft report on WHITEX from the NPS. Because of the delay in receiving this report, EPA believed that it lacked sufficient time to complete its analyses and issue a proposed rule by the August 31, 1989 deadline. Accordingly, EPA and EDF filed a joint motion to revise the settlement agreement for a third time, which was approved by order of the court dated July 6, 1989. Under this revision, there was no change in the deadlines for proposed action regarding Canyonlands National Park or Moosehorn Wilderness. As to GCNP, the third revision to the settlement agreement divided EPA's duty into two parts. The EPA would proceed, on a preliminary basis, to issue a finding on reasonably attributable impairment by the August 31, 1989 deadline. However, if EPA did provisionally identify a specific source of impairment, it would solicit comments on that finding and would have additional time to conduct a BART analysis. The EPA was to issue a rulemaking proposal on the need for BART by February 1, 1990 unless, in response to comments, EPA rejected its proposed identification and instead determined that BART was unnecessary.

In accordance with the third revision to the settlement agreement, EPA published a notice of proposed rulemaking on September 5, 1989 (54 FR 36948). Regarding Moosehorn Wilderness, EPA identified a source of the certified impairment but proposed that BART was unnecessary because the impairment would be adequately remedied by the retirement of certain existing emission units and the addition of pollution controls on other units pursuant to a permit issued under the Act's prevention of significant deterioration provisions. As to Canyonlands National Park, EPA could not reasonably attribute the certified impairment to a specific source at that time and so proposed that BART was unnecessary. On June 13, 1990 (55 FR 24060), EPA issued final decisions that BART was not necessary to address impairment in either the Moosehorn Wilderness or the Canyonlands National Park.

unless petitioners can demonstrate that EPA's action was plainly unreasonable, we cannot disturb its ruling. *See Connecticut v. EPA*, 696 F.2d at 155.

We begin with the statute itself. Section 169A of the Clean Air Act directs EPA to promulgate regulations requiring states containing class I areas to adopt through their SIPs long-term strategies assuring reasonable progress toward meeting the national visibility goal. 42 U.S.C. § 7491(b). Pursuant to this legislative mandate, in 1980 EPA issued regulations providing that each SIP include a long-term strategy designed to remedy any existing, and prevent any future, impairment of visibility in class I areas. 40 C.F.R. § 51.306(a) (1987).

Vermont claims that its long-term strategy addressing regional haze fits within the purview of the 1980 regulations and must be approved by EPA. *See* Clean Air Act § 110(a)(2)(J), 42 U.S.C. § 7410(a)(2)(J) ("Administrator shall approve [the SIP] . . . if he determines that . . . it meets the requirements" of, inter alia, section 169A). The Administrator responds by arguing that the 1980 regulations do not cover regional haze impairment and that measures addressing that type of impairment are not required by section 169A and therefore cannot be part of a federally enforceable SIP. *See id.* § 110(d), § 7410(d) (federally enforceable SIP is one which "implements the requirements " of the statute) (emphasis added).

In support of its interpretation of the 1980 regulations, EPA cites the preamble to the final regulations in which EPA explained its adoption of a "phased approach" to visibility protection in class I areas. The preamble indicates that "Phase I" of the program "[r]equire[s] control of impairment that can be traced to a single existing stationary facility or small group of . . . facilities" while "[f]uture phases will . . . address[] more complex problems such as regional haze and urban plumes." 45 Fed.Reg. 80,085-86. Although petitioners concede that action on regional haze was deferred for future phases of the visibility program, they nonetheless argue that the 1980 regulations were intended to allow, as technologies improved, for the evolution of long-term strategies combating regional haze. We disagree.

It is one thing to recognize that the regulatory mechanism put into place by the 1980 regulations anticipated long-term strategies designed to alleviate regional haze, *see* 45 Fed.Reg. 34,764 ("[e]ven though we are calling these . . . regulations 'Phase I of the visibility protection program,' the basic structure . . . will remain constant for all phases"); it is quite another to suggest that the 1980 regulations actually authorized states containing class I areas to implement regional haze measures through federally enforceable SIPs. Petitioners would have us ignore the preamble language in favor of the "plain meaning" of the regulations. But *see New York State Comm'n on Cable Tel. v. FCC*, 571 F.2d 95, 98 (2d Cir.), *cert. denied*, 439 U.S. 820 (1978) ("[m]ere incantation of the plain meaning rule, without placing the language to be construed in its proper framework, cannot substitute for a meaningful analysis"). Respondents correctly note, however, that no "plain meaning" to regulate regional haze can be discerned from the face of the regulations. Consequently, having looked to the preamble to determine the scope of the 1980 regulations, *see Wiggins Bros., Inc. v. Dep't of Energy*, 667 F.2d 77, 88 (Temp.Emer.Ct.App.1981), *cert. denied*, 456 U.S. 905 (1982) ("preamble to a regulation . . . should be considered in construing . . . and determining the meaning of the regulation"), we find that EPA intended to limit the regulations to plume blight.

Petitioners also contend that even in the absence of EPA regulatory "guidelines" addressing regional haze, Clean Air Act § 169A(b)(1), 42 U.S.C. § 7491(b)(1), the Act imposes upon states an independent duty to develop visibility protection standards to assure "reasonable progress" toward achieving the national visibility goal. While it is

Regarding the GCNP, in the September 5, 1989 notice, EPA preliminarily attributed several episodes of wintertime visibility impairment to emissions from the NGS. In that regard, EPA reviewed the draft NPS report on WHITEX and concurred with the findings of the NPS. The EPA solicited comments on the merits of its preliminary attribution finding.

On November 28, 1989, the Salt River Project Agricultural Improvement and Power District (SRP), et al., and Alabama Power Company, et al., intervenors in *EDF v. Reilly*, filed a motion requesting a 1-year delay in the rulemaking schedule so that, among other things, the intervenors could conduct their own studies of the visibility impairment in the GCNP. By order dated January 9, 1990, the court granted the intervenors' motion to extend the deadlines. This order set February 1, 1991, as the new deadline for EPA to propose whether or not to require BART emission limits for the NGS to remedy winter visibility impairment. The order also extended the deadline for final action on any proposal regarding BART until October 1991 (6 months after the close of the comment period).

C. Navajo Generating Station

The NGS is a 2250 MW coal-fired power plant located near Page, Arizona, approximately 20 kilometers from the northern boundary of the GCNP. The NGS is a baseload generating station consisting of three 750 MW units which became operational between 1974 and 1976. The SRP is the operating agent for NGS which is jointly owned by the SRP,[7] the Los Angeles Department of Water and Power, the Arizona Public Service Company, the Nevada Power Company, and the Tucson Electric Power Company. Existing pollution control equipment at NGS includes electrostatic precipitators for particulate matter (PM) removal and specific burner design for nitrogen oxides (NOx) control.

D. February 8, 1991 Proposal

On February 8, 1991, EPA proposed to revise the FIP for Arizona to include emission limits to address the visibility impairment observed in GCNP. The following is a summary of the main issues discussed in the proposal notice.

1. Emission Limitation

The EPA proposed to adopt a continuous SO_2 emission limitation of 0.30 lb/MMBtu. Compliance would be determined on a 30-day rolling average and would be phased in between 1995 and 1999. Because of the uncertainty in determining the improvement in visibility expected as a result of reducing emissions at the NGS, EPA solicited comments on three alternative control strategies for NGS:

a. A continuous SO_2 emission limitation of 0.50 lb/MMBtu. Compliance would be determined on a 30-day rolling average and would be phased in between 1995 and 1999.

---

[7] The SRP owns 21.7 percent of the NGS project for its own use and benefit, and 24.3 percent for the use and benefit of the United States in accordance with the NGS project agreements. The term "NGS participants" is used in this notice to refer to the parties which have rights and responsibilities associated with the operation of NGS and includes the owners, the operators, and the U.S. Bureau of Reclamation (for the United States).

b. A continuous SO_2 emission limitation of 0.10 lb/MMBtu. Compliance would be determined on a 30-day rolling average and would be phased in between 1995 and 1999.

c. A January 10, 1991 proposal submitted by SRP under which it would test alternative control technologies, and if one of the technologies met a minimum removal efficiency at a set cost, the NGS would install that technology and operate it in the wintertime. If none of the technologies met the test criteria, NGS would reduce its emissions by 70 percent (0.30 lb/MMBtu emission limit) measured on an annual basis by the year 2000.

In addition, EPA requested comment on whether another emission limitation or a different averaging period may be more appropriate.

2. Attribution

As part of the February 8, 1991 proposal, EPA reopened the comment period on its September 5, 1989 preliminary finding that several episodes of wintertime impairment in the GCNP was reasonably attributable to NGS.

3. BART Analysis

In light of its attribution finding, EPA conducted an analysis in accordance with the BART Guidelines (EPA-450/3-80-009b) and 40 CFR 51.301(c)(4)(iii). That analysis included consideration of the following: the costs of compliance, the energy and non-air quality environmental impacts, any existing pollution control technology in use at the facility, the remaining useful life of the source, and the degree of improvement in visibility anticipated to result from application of controls.

Considering the requirements found in the BART Guidelines, EPA divided its analysis into two major parts. In the first part, EPA identified the SO_2 emission controls that are readily available to the source, the costs of such controls, and other impacts of installing and operating the controls. In the second part of the analysis, EPA attempted to define the source-impairment relationship which was then used to predict the improvements in visual air quality that can reasonably be expected to occur as a result of installing and operating the controls defined in the control technology analysis. Because EPA was faced with some uncertainties in each of the parts of the analysis, EPA bounded its results by giving low and high estimates. A detailed discussion of this analysis for NGS was provided in EPA's February 8, 1991 proposal.

To estimate the cost of controlling the SO_2 emissions at NGS, EPA used the Integrated Air Pollution Control System (IAPCS) cost model to predict the capital and operating cost estimates for 0.10, 0.30, and 0.50 lb/MMBtu control levels. The results from the IAPCS indicated that wet flue gas desulfurization (FGD) achieving a 0.30 lb/MMBtu emission limit for all three units, the control level that was proposed by EPA, was estimated to have total capital cost requirements of between \$245.9 million and \$402 million with total levelized annual costs (including amortized capital, interest, operating, and maintenance costs) estimated to be between \$91.9 million and \$128.3 million.

In its February 8, 1991 proposal, EPA also estimated the potential costs to residential electricity customers serviced by the NGS participants as well as the potential costs to Central Arizona Project (CAP) customers.

One of the more complicated tasks in the BART analysis was defining the relationship between the SO_2 emissions at NGS and the visibility impairing sulfate in the GCNP. This relationship had to be addressed in order to estimate the degree of improvement in visibility that could be anticipated to result from the use of the alternative SO_2 control systems. Because of the complex terrain in and around the GCNP, EPA defined the source/impairment relationship using the ratio of SO_2 emissions at NGS to sulfate in the GCNP attributable to NGS as found in the final WHITEX report. Using this ratio, EPA then applied a linear rollback model. However, in light of the uncertainties surrounding these analyses EPA considered a broad range of source-impairment relationships. In addition, EPA developed and applied a nonlinearity factor to the rollback model to estimate the improvements in visibility that would result from reductions in SO_2.

Because no single standard method exists for measuring improvements in visibility, the EPA employed two of the most widely used techniques to define the improvements in visibility expected to occur in the GCNP. One of the methods used to estimate the visibility improvements in the GCNP was analyzing the changes in contrast expected to occur as a result of reducing SO_2 emissions at NGS. The EPA stated in the proposal that this method is particularly relevant because human observers use contrast to make judgments of how atmospheric clarity changes with pollutant concentration. The contrast is defined as the percent difference between the brightness of a scenic element and its background. The second technique was to analyze the seasonal average visual range change (see 56 FR 5182 Table 1).

Although not specifically addressed in the BART analysis, the proposal noted that EPA suspected that NGS emissions may contribute to visibility impairment in the GCNP during other seasons of the year and in other Class I areas in the region. Thus, EPA sought comment on any other potential visibility impairments caused by NGS.

The EPA also noted in the proposal that it was not required as a part of its analysis to estimate monetary benefits associated with improving visibility in the GCNP. However, EPA evaluated the monetary benefits in developing a part of the preliminary Regulatory Impact Analysis (RIA) (as required by Executive Order 12291) for the proposed rule.

* * *

E. New Information After the Close of the Initial Comment Period

After the comment period closed on April 19, 1991, at the recommendation of EPA, representatives of SRP, Grand Canyon Trust (GCT), and EDF met to discuss alternative approaches to EPA's February 8, 1991 proposal. In August 1991, the outside parties reached agreement and together recommended that EPA adopt an alternative control for NGS consisting of a 0.10 lb/MMBtu SO_2 emission limitation (approximate to a 90 percent control level) based on a rolling annual average and phased in by unit in November 1997, November 1998, and August 1999. In addition, under the agreement, NGS would shift its maintenance schedule such that 6 unit-weeks of planned maintenance would occur between November 1 and March 15 each year. Under specific conditions, the Administrator of EPA may allow NGS to shift the maintenance schedule outside of that period or not to conduct scheduled maintenance in a given year.

Representatives of EPA participated in many of the meetings with the parties and provided technical assistance. Representatives of the State of Arizona also attended several of the meetings and provided additional technical support. New technical materials and cost information, including adjustments of the potential control costs, were exchanged between the parties and EPA. Summaries of the meetings and significant conversations in which EPA was involved and copies of the new material and information which were submitted to or developed by EPA have been included in Docket A-89-02A.

The outside parties memorialized their agreement in an MOU which they submitted to EPA along with recommended regulatory requirements for EPA's final rulemaking action. The SRP estimated (in 1992 dollars) a capital cost of $430 million and a total levelized annual cost of $89.6 million for the parties' recommended alternative. In comparison, SRP estimated a capital cost of $510 million and a total levelized annual cost of $106 million to meet the alternative EPA proposed in February 1991.

Noting that the alternative incorporated in the MOU would provide more visibility protection for the GCNP at a lower cost for NGS and its customers, EPA, on August 8, 1991, reopened the comment period on its February 8, 1991 proposed action (56 FR 38399, August 13, 1991). In the notice, EPA stated that it was giving serious consideration to the control option recommended by the outside parties and incorporated in an appendix to the notice a memorandum from EPA's Office of General Counsel concluding that the outside parties' legal rationale in support of their recommended control option was meritorious.

* * *

II. Today's Action

After reviewing the option recommended by SRP, EDF, and GCT in their MOU, EPA has determined that such a control strategy will provide a substantially greater degree of emissions reduction, and a correspondingly greater degree of visibility improvement at a substantially lower cost than the alternative proposed in February 1991. For these reasons, EPA also concludes that this option will make additional reasonable progress towards attainment of the national visibility goal in comparison to the February 1991 proposal. Thus, in today's action EPA is promulgating an SO_2 emission limitation of 42 ng/J (0.10 lb/MMBtu) heat input to be phased in by unit in November 1997, November 1998, and August 1999, with compliance determined on a rolling annual average basis.

* * *

NOTES

1. How does the plan approved in this decision differ from that which EPA had originally proposed? Why were these negotiations successful?

2. Where the interstate transport of air pollutants from one or more states contributes significantly to visibility impairment of Class I areas, the EPA may establish a "visibility transport region." § 169B(c)(1). Upon establishing the region, EPA must establish a "visibility transport commission." § 169B(c)(2). The commission is responsible for — (1) assessing data relevant to the impact of air pollution on visibility; and (2) issuing a report recommending measures to remedy adverse visibility impacts. § 169B(d). EPA was required to establish a visibility transport commission for the region affecting the Grand Canyon National Park by November, 1991. § 169B(f).

3. Congress appropriated 40 million dollars over five years for research on visibility. EPA is required to assess and evaluate this research, as well as other data and information, to identify the sources or source regions of visibility impairment. Interim findings are due in November, 1993. § 169B(a).

PROBLEM #4: VISIBILITY

A copper smelter in the State of Crow is adversely affecting the visibility in the Frosty Buttes National Park, a federal Class I area designated for visibility protection. The State of Crow has an approved visibility program, and has decided that BART for the smelter requires no further pollution controls because the useful life of the facility is less than ten years. What authority, if any, does the EPA have to override the State's decision? *See* §§ 169A(b)(2)(A); 169A(g)(2).

8 MONITORING AND MODELING

As we have seen, the Clean Air Act requires the EPA to establish ambient air quality standards and to set emission limitations for point sources as necessary to insure that those standards are actually being met throughout a region. How does it predict the impact that will result from a new source? The answer lies in the sciences of monitoring and modeling.

Monitoring informs the agency about emissions from a point source, or the ambient air quality at the monitoring site. Computer models are generally used to determine ambient air quality beyond the monitor site, and to predict ambient air quality changes that will result from the construction of new sources of air pollution. How accurate are these models?

The 1990 Clean Air Act Amendments have imposed new monitoring requirements on various sources. In particular, sources subject to the acid deposition provisions of the law must install a "continuous emission monitoring system" (CEMS) or its equivalent. § 412(a). These computer-driven monitors provide a constant record of the emissions from a source. *See also* § 402(7). Other sources subject to regulation under the Act may be required to install new monitoring devices, including CEMS, unless "alternative methods are available that provide sufficiently reliable and timely information for determining compliance." § 504(b).

Because of the importance of monitoring and modeling to the clean air effort, the courts have frequently been asked to grapple with these issues. But the highly technical nature of the problem and the difficulty that the courts have had understanding the science seems inevitably to result in deference to agency choices. Below is a sampling of cases which wrestle with monitoring and modeling problems.

PPG INDUSTRIES V. COSTLE

659 F.2d 1239 (D.C. Cir. 1981)

BAZELON, Senior Circuit Judge:

In 1971, pursuant to the Clean Air Amendments of 1970, Pub.L.No. 91-604, 84 Stat. 1679, the Administrator of the Environmental Protection Agency (EPA) promulgated a series of national ambient air quality standards, known as the NAAQS, for sulfur oxides. The standards established maximum acceptable average concentrations for one-year periods, 24-hour periods, and 3-hour periods. Under the Act and the EPA regulations, if the outdoor air of a locality exceeds either the 24-hour or 3-hour standard more than once during a year, construction of new pollution sources would be restricted and existing sources could be restricted in the technology they may employ.

Prior to 1979, compliance with the 24-hour NAAQS for sulfur oxides, 40 C.F.R. § 50.4(b), was generally determined by analyzing daily average concentrations based on air samples collected during midnight-to-midnight periods. In 1979, however, pursuant to section 110 of the Clean Air Act, as amended, 42 U.S.C. § 7410(a)(2)(C) (Supp. III 1979), the Administrator promulgated a new rule which implemented a national air quality monitoring system. In promulgating the rule, EPA purported to require the new monitoring system to measure sulfur oxide concentrations continuously and to calculate hourly running averages for 24-hour periods, rather than only midnight-to-midnight averages. The use of running averages would reveal whether concentrations of sulfur oxides exceed the NAAQS level for any 24-hour period during the year, whereas midnight-to-midnight measurement would only reveal exceedances for 365 specific 24-hour periods. Depending on the times of the day at which sulfur oxide concentrations reach their high and low points, a locality with concentrations that exceed the level set by the standard for many 24-hour periods would be detected by the running average technique but would escape detection under the midnight-to-midnight sampling method.

These appeals challenge the 1979 rule that requires the running average technique for measuring sulfur oxide concentrations. Petitioners operate major stationary sources of sulfur dioxide. They would face significant economic burdens if the air monitoring statistics showed their localities to be in violation of the NAAQS for sulfur oxides. Petitioners charge that the challenged rule, in effect, revises the 24-hour NAAQS for sulfur oxides, and that it therefore should have been promulgated according to the exacting procedures set forth in section 307(d) of the Clean Air Act, 42 U.S.C. § 7607(d) (Supp. III 1979). Respondent argues that the rule does not constitute a revision of the NAAQS, but merely establishes closer and more uniform air quality monitoring, as mandated by section 319, 42 U.S.C. § 7619 (Supp. III 1979). Therefore, respondent contends, the agency properly proceeded by informal rulemaking, 5 U.S.C. § 553 (1976).

The scope of review, as well as the lawfulness of EPA procedures, depends upon the characterization of the agency's action. If the rule effects a revision of the NAAQS, then its adoption would require the procedures set out in § 7607(d), which are more demanding than those of the Administrative Procedure Act (APA). At the same time, however, § 7607(d) would preclude our invalidation of the rule on procedural grounds without a much stronger showing of prejudicial error than is required in cases under the APA. If, on the other hand, the rule does not effect a revision of the NAAQS, then it would have to be adopted only according to the APA procedures.

To decide whether the agency's action amounts to a revision of the 24-hour NAAQS for sulfur oxides, this court must resolve a fundamental ambiguity in the meaning of the NAAQS itself. The question, explained more fully below, is whether an exceedance of the standard's "[m]aximum 24-hour concentration" can be computed on the basis of *all* periods of twenty-four consecutive hours ("running averages"), or whether it must be computed on the basis of midnight- to-midnight periods only. Unfortunately, EPA has complied no administrative record directed toward that issue. Petitioners were apparently caught off-guard because of the obscurity of the notice given. They claim they were unaware that this issue was presented in the challenged rulemaking, and so offered no comments at all. We thus find ourselves in a "catch-22": the agency's procedures have produced no visible basis upon which to review its interpretation of the 24-hour NAAQS; yet, without reviewing that interpretation, we cannot determine the adequacy of its procedures. We, therefore, must examine the 24-hour sulfur oxide NAAQS directly, but only to the extent necessary to determine whether EPA's interpretation was not wholly unreasonable.

We conclude that the 24-hour NAAQS does not require a midnight-to-midnight sampling period, and that the new rule, therefore, does not revise that standard.

Therefore, EPA's rulemaking proceeding under the APA, rather than the Clean Air Act, was not facially unlawful. We also find, however, that EPA failed to publish a critical provision of the new rule in the Federal Register and thereby violated the publication requirement of the APA. Belated publication cannot cure this omission. Because the proposed rule did not notify the public that the use of running averages was being proposed and because that proposal was an important aspect of the rule, EPA failed to comply with the notice requirement of the APA in its attempt to mandate the use of running averages. We therefore remand the record to the EPA to consider that part of the rule, after proper notice, by whatever procedures are adequate to develop a proper record for decision. Further, we admonish the parties that an important interpretation of an agency standard must, in the first instance and in clear fashion, be carried out by the agency itself, with review by the court following only upon an adequate record.

* * *

The Administrator of EPA promulgated primary and secondary sulfur oxides NAAQS on April 30, 1971, 36 Fed.Reg. 8186.

* * *

The primary NAAQS set maximum average concentrations for long- term (one year) and short-term (24-hour) periods; the secondary NAAQS sets a maximum 3-hour average concentration. The 24-hour and 3-hour concentrations are "not to be exceeded more than once per year." All concentrations are to be measured by "the reference method," described in Appendix A to 40 C.F.R. Part 50 [hereinafter Appendix A], or by an "equivalent method." A separate set of procedures is set out in 40 C.F.R. 53.30-53.32 to test a "candidate method" against the reference method in order to certify it as "equivalent."

The reference method is not automated: air is sampled through a "gas bubbler" for a given length of time, then removed and chemically analyzed. The average concentration of sulfur dioxide for that period is determined from the contents of the bubbler. Appendix A provides for several sampling periods in order to accommodate a variety of data-gathering tasks.[7] Until about 1977, compliance with the 24-hour NAAQS was determined by analyzing daily average concentrations, based on 24-hour samples. The reference method specifies that 24-hour samples be collected "from midnight to midnight." Thus, from a given monitoring station, not more than 365 24-hour samples could be tested by the reference method each year. If the "second highest" concentration among these samples exceeded the prescribed level for the 24-hour NAAQS, a non-attainment designation would be made.

It is possible, however, for a locality to experience 24-hour concentrations of sulfur dioxide that are above the NAAQS concentration levels and yet go undetected by a monitoring station using the 24-hour sampling technique of the reference method. Not only does the use of 24-hour samples under the reference method allow sampling for

---

[7] The reference method is used not only for designating nonattainment areas, but also for making the various other determinations required of monitoring stations under the state plans. Air quality control regions, for example, are to be given priority classifications based upon measured or estimated concentrations for various pollutants. *See* 40 C.F.R. § 51.3(a). Steps taken to prevent "significant deterioration of air quality," *id.* § 51.24, require the measurement of "baseline concentrations" and "ambient air increments" for sulfur dioxide. *See id.* § 51.24(b)(11) and § 51.24(c). Air pollution emergency episodes are triggered when the 24-hour average sulfur dioxide concentration reaches 2,260 micrograms/cubic meter, twice as high as the highest NAAQS concentration. *See id.* § 51.16. To make these determinations, the state plans require that significant amounts of data be gathered, generally by reference or equivalent methods. *See id.* § 51.13(g).

only 365 out of the infinite number of twenty-four hour periods during the year, it requires that each sampling period begin and end at the same times every day. As a result, sulfur dioxide concentrations that exceed the NAAQS level during a period other than midnight to midnight noon to noon, for example would not be detected unless the average concentration also exceeds the standard during a contiguous midnight-to-midnight period. The graph below illustrates the importance of the sampling period in identifying periods of concentration above the standard:

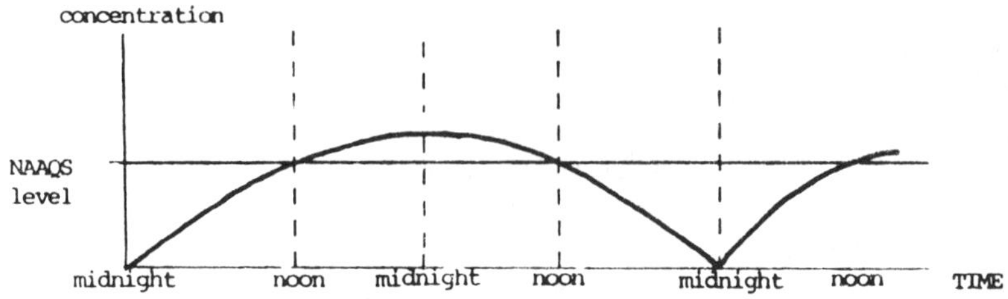

If the average concentration of sulfur dioxide in a locality follows the path charted either at discrete times during the year or regularly the 24-hour sampling technique of the reference method would not detect concentrations higher than the NAAQS levels. In this example, continuous monitoring and calculation of running averages, in contrast, would indicate an exceedance of that level for the 24-hour periods beginning close to noon and ending at the same time the next day.

Over the years, a number of newer methods have been certified as "equivalent," and have gradually replaced the reference method at many air-monitoring facilities. These newer methods permit instantaneous and continuous monitoring of sulfur dioxide concentrations. Running averages of concentrations can be calculated for continuous 24-hour periods. Using such methods, it becomes easier to detect exceedances of the NAAQS level for any period of 24 consecutive hours, whether it runs from midnight to midnight or not.

In February, 1977, EPA prepared and distributed to the state monitoring offices a revised "Guidelines for the Interpretation of Air Quality Standards" [hereinafter *Guidelines*]. The *Guidelines* took advantage of the newer techniques to request data based on running averages. EPA recommended that, wherever continuous monitors were available, running 24-hour average concentrations should be calculated, with each hour beginning a new 24-hour period. *Id.* The Guidelines also provided a methodology for computing the statistics used in determining compliance with the 24-hour NAAQS, *Id.* Any 24-hour period with an average concentration greater than the standard would be deemed an exceedance. If a locality experienced two such periods that did not overlap in one year, the locality would be deemed out of compliance. The *Guidelines* were not published in the Federal Register.

II. THE CHALLENGED RULEMAKING

In August, 1977, Congress again amended the Clean Air Act. It added section 307(d), 42 U.S.C. § 7607(d), which made the promulgation or revision of any NAAQS subject to demanding procedures. It also added a new section 319, directing the EPA Administrator to "promulgate regulations establishing an air quality monitoring system throughout the United States which . . . utilizes uniform air quality monitoring criteria and methodology." 42 U.S.C. § 7619. The section 319 regulations were not subject to the requirements of section 307(d), but were to follow "notice and opportunity for public hearing."

One year later, EPA proposed rules to implement section 319. 43 Fed.Reg. 34892 (1978). The notice expressly stated that the APA's informal rulemaking procedures would be followed. *Id.* at 34896. The proposed rules required each state to maintain a network of "state and local air monitoring stations" (SLAMS), some of which would be designated "national air monitoring stations" (NAMS). The NAMS were to be equipped with certified monitoring devices capable of continuous measurement. *Id.* at 34918. The proposed rules also contained about 30 pages of technical appendices designed to assure the quality and uniformity of data collected by these networks. One of these appendices Appendix F required each station in the SLAMS network to calculate and report annually, among other statistics, the "[h]ighest and second highest 24-hour averages" for sulfur dioxide, presumably to determine compliance with the 24-hour NAAQS. *Id.*, at 34928. A footnote to that requirement [hereinafter Footnote 3] specified that the averages should be "[b]ased on nonoverlapping values computed according to procedures described in reference (1)." "Reference (1)" was identified at the end of the appendix as the Revised *Guidelines* document, discussed *supra*. Thus, the proposed rule attempted to adopt the use of running averages as a means of determining compliance with the 24-hour NAAQS for sulfur oxides. Previously, EPA had only recommended that method.

The proposed rules were adopted with little change in May, 1979. None of the comments indicated a contradiction between the proposed monitoring and reporting method and the 24-hour NAAQS. *See* 44 Fed.Reg. 27567 (1979). The only discussion of reporting methods came from state environmental agencies, which had earlier received the *Guidelines*. We are informed by counsel that petitioners did not comment because they were unaware that the rule would affect the stringency with which the NAAQS was applied. Although running averages were apparently being reported by some monitoring stations at that time, petitioners did not learn of this until the county in which they do business was designated a nonattainment area. That occurred in October, 1978, at the very end of the comment period for the challenged rulemaking.

* * *

Petitioners argue that a running average requirement creates a significantly more stringent 24-hour NAAQS. This was done, they assert, without substantive support and in violation of the procedures provided for such changes by the Clean Air Act, 42 U.S.C. § 7607(d)(1)(A). In addition, because EPA adopted a portion of the rule by means of an obscure reference, never incorporated into the Federal Register — cited in a footnote to an appendix to a 46-page rule on air quality reporting — petitioners argue that the agency violated the publication and notice requirements of the APA.

III. DISCUSSION

* * *

A. *The 24-Hour Standard*

To perform our reviewing function, we must reach at least a preliminary interpretation of the 24-hour NAAQS. Whether any procedural errors were sufficiently prejudicial to warrant further notice and comment, for example, may depend on whether the APA or the more demanding test of the Clean Air Act, 42 U.S.C. § 7607(d), is applied. In any event, our opinion should inform EPA as to the procedures that are statutorily required on remand. On the basis of our own review of the record before us, we believe that the reference method of Appendix A does not confine the 24-hour sulfur dioxide NAAQS to midnight-to- midnight sampling periods. Accordingly, we believe EPA acted within its authority when it attempted to change the reporting requirements so as to mandate running averages through informal APA rulemaking. Our conclusion, however, is not meant to prevent the agency from reaching a different interpretation of the NAAQS on remand.

Ordinarily, we would accord the greatest deference to EPA's construction of its own standard, as well as to its choice of procedures. In this case, however, the agency's construction can only be inferred from its actions; we have no direct and contemporaneous statement of its views on the meaning of the NAAQS. We therefore look principally to the language and structure of the regulatory scheme, and to the policies that underlie it. Our interpretation is based on three grounds. First, the reference method itself does not clearly mandate midnight-to-midnight samples. Second, a change in method does not necessarily entail a change in the NAAQS. Third, running averages are consistent with the apparent purpose of the 24-hour NAAQS.

* * *

B. *Notice*

A central policy issue raised by the new rule is whether the 24-hour NAAQS for sulfur oxides *should* only apply to midnight-to-midnight periods. The most obvious reason for EPA's silence on that issue is that no apposite comments were offered at the rulemaking. While an absence of comments in no way implies inadequate notice, it does alert us to that possibility. Petitioners charge that essential provisions in both the proposed and final rules cannot be understood without the *Guidelines* document, which was neither published nor properly incorporated in the Federal Register. We agree.

In most respects, the agency's notice met the APA's notice requirement. It included "the terms . . . of the proposed rule," 5 U.S.C. § 553(b)(3) (1976), and was fully adequate to apprise the public "of the 'subjects and issues involved' so that (interested parties) may offer informed criticism and comments." *Ethyl Corp. v. EPA*, 541 F.2d 1, 48 (D.C.Cir.), *cert. denied*, 426 U.S. 941 (1976). The notice, however, did not fully meet the APA's notice requirement. In one particular, the rule itself, without the *Guidelines*, is extremely unclear. By basing certain critical compliance data on "nonoverlapping values," Footnote 3 appears simply to demand that reported exceedances not overlap. 40 C.F.R. Part 58, App. F at 2.1.2 & fn.3. The provision does not in itself effect a change in the longstanding practice of accepting midnight-to-midnight measurements. Unless the *Guidelines'* definition of "nonoverlapping values" is read into the rule, in other words, we cannot say that Footnote 3 *requires* running averages to be reported. Nor can we find that the same language in the proposed rule notified the public that such a requirement was being considered.

* * *

IV. CONCLUSION

For the reasons set forth, the record is remanded so that respondent may consider the issues raised by petitioners in a properly noticed rulemaking. The agency is free to conduct that rulemaking pursuant to the APA, and to continue using its *Guidelines* to encourage but not to require, the reporting of running averages. Certain materials lodged with this court belong, if anywhere, in the administrative record; petitioners' motion to supplement the record on this appeal is accordingly denied. As stated above, this court is prepared to reconsider its interpretation of the 24-hour sulfur oxides standard if and when EPA has first addressed that issue.

So ordered.

NOTES

1. Why did PPG Industries object to EPA's monitoring program? What effect did the court's decision have on PPG's objectives?

2. Following the court's decision, EPA declined the invitation to engage in a new rulemaking proceeding. What effect do you think this has had on the monitoring program?

3. As described in *PPG Industries,* the monitoring program required by § 319 of the Act is carried out through a network of state and local air monitoring stations (SLAMS). 40 CFR 58.20 (1991). A separate network of SLAMS sites from around the country make up the national air monitoring stations (NAMS). 40 CFR 58.30 (1991). The design of each network and the location of monitoring stations is the subject of detailed design standards. 40 CFR Part 58, Appendix D (1991). The regulations also establish a computer system (SAROAD - Storage and Retrieval of Aerometric Data) for storing and reporting information relating to ambient air quality. 40 CFR 58.1(p)(1991).

4. As Judge Bazelon notes in *PPG Industries*, monitoring data is used not only to ascertain nonattainment areas, but for other purposes such as establishing the baseline concentrations in PSD areas. 659 F.2d at 1243, n.7. Can modeling be used to determine whether an area should be classified as nonattainment? What possible problems do you see with allowing its use in this situation?

CLEVELAND ELECTRIC ILLUMINATING CO. V. EPA

572 F.2d 1150 (6th Cir. 1978), *cert. denied*, 439 US 910 (1978)

EDWARDS, Circuit Judge.

This court now has before it 23 petitions involving 32 companies filed against the United States Environmental Protection Agency which levy a variety of complaints against the federal agency's imposition of a sulfur dioxide (SO_2) pollution control plan for industrial discharges into Ohio's ambient air. The issues, which have been extensively briefed and argued, divide into general legal and procedural complaints which might be applicable to any one of the petitioners and a wider variety of specific complaints about the application of the EPA controls to particular power-generating or industrial plants. The cases dealt with in this opinion present the major general issues. Other individual cases, in addition to presenting one or more of the general issues, also present specific issues of fact. These are reserved pending a review of and reports on the factual disputes between the United States EPA and the individual petitioners.

The major issues dealt with in this opinion are:

* * *

3) petitioners claim that the major model employed by the United States Environmental Protection Agency in establishing specific emission limitations for particular plans is invalid both intrinsically and as applied. This model is termed the "Real-Time Air-Quality-Simulator Model" (hereinafter RAM).

* * *

3. The RAM Model

The petitioners in these cases center most of their criticisms upon the United States EPA's use of the Real-Time Air-Quality-Simulation Model ("RAM") which was employed by the agency in preparation of the Ohio sulfur dioxide control plan. RAM is a dispersion model which evaluates the interaction of a variety of facts in order to make predictions concerning the contribution to the pollution of the ambient air by specific plants. Its formula takes into account the capacity of each plant on a stack-by-stack basis and adds thereto smokestack height, surrounding terrain, and weather conditions. The model is operated on the assumption that the plants concerned operate 24 hours a day at full capacity and predictions are made for every day of the year. The ultimate standards are set according to the predicted second-worst day in terms of pollution results shown.

In comparison to all other prior methods of controlling pollution, RAM starts with a solid, ascertainable data base. This is the established design capacity of the power plants in question related to the sulfur content of the fuel used by each. From these factors the "emissions data" for each plant are developed.

When stack height, wind, weather, terrain, land use, etc., are figured in, the RAM model has the additional value of allowing its user to predict with considerable accuracy the relative contributions of specific power plant stacks to the points of maximum concentration of pollution of the ambient air.

The RAM model was actually developed as a result of United States EPA's public hearings on the proposed plan for Ohio after five days of hearings on said proposed plan in Columbus, Cleveland, Cincinnati, and Steubenville at which petitioners involved in this current litigation were given an opportunity (which most accepted) to appear, testify, or submit comments. At those hearings the major source of criticism from industries, including some of the present petitioners, was that the plan then under consideration did not determine limitations by individual stacks to a sufficient degree. EPA in its brief in this case compares the "rollback" model employed in the preparation of the first Ohio plan to dispersion models like RAM, which is now the source of present controversy:

> Unlike the rollback model, the dispersion models used in developing the promulgated plan allow a determination of the cause-effect relationship between the SO_2 emissions of the pollution sources in an area and the resulting ambient air quality. Therefore, it is possible to determine the proportion by which each source must reduce emissions to meet ambient standards. With the use of the rollback model, in contrast, each source's emissions in the region, whether or not they contributed to a pollution problem, were required to be reduced. Through dispersion modeling, emission limitations can now be set with increased precision. Overcontrol is minimized, so that the plan will still insure attainment and maintenance of the air quality standards, but at a much reduced cost to the sources. This is most clearly demonstrated by comparing emission limitations for

power plants under the various plans. Power plants account for approximately 80% of the sulfur dioxide emissions in the State.

However, achievement of this added precision requires a massive analytical task. Tremendous amounts of data are required for each source analyzed. In addition to the emissions data for each source, dispersion modeling requires detailed information on all the factors that affect the dispersion of emissions. These include the height of the source's stack (or usually stacks), the spatial orientation of the sources to each other, the topography of the area and the effects it will have on dispersion, and, of crucial importance, detailed weather data for the area.

All this information is needed so that the computer analysis reflects actual conditions. For example, a gaseous pollutant emitted over a grassy field will disperse much differently than if the pollutant is emitted over a large urban area. There the dispersion will be affected not only by the local weather conditions but also by the greater turbulence caused by the different types of surface areas and heat sources throughout a city.

EPA goes on to point out that there are more than 1,000 point sources in the State of Ohio and more than 2,000 area sources, and that in relation to emission data, United States EPA utilized (among other sources) the data base on sulfur dioxide required to be reported to the State of Ohio under Ohio Rev.Code Ann. §§ 3704.03(I), 3704.05(C) (Page 1971 & 1976 Supp.).

It is, of course, no part of the responsibility of this court to determine whether the RAM model represents the best possible approach to determining standards for the control of sulfur dioxide emissions. Our standard of review of the actions of United States EPA is whether or not the action of the agency is "arbitrary, capricious, an abuse of discretion, or otherwise not in accordance with law." Clean Air Act Amendments of 1977, Pub.L. No. 95-95, § 305(a), 91 Stat. 775 (to be codified as 42 U.S.C. § 7607(d)(9)(A)). Thus, we are required to affirm if there is a rational basis for the agency action and we are not "empowered to substitute [our] judgment for that of the agency." *Citizens to Preserve Overton Park v. Volpe*, 401 U.S. 402, 416 (1971).

Our review of this record convinces us that we cannot properly hold that United States EPA's adoption of the RAM model for predicting sulfur dioxide emissions and for fixing maximum levels of sulfur dioxide emissions by specific sources was arbitrary and capricious or beyond the agency's authority under the Clean Air Act. The factors cited below support EPA's argument that the RAM model is supported by sufficient evidence so that EPA's adoption cannot be held arbitrary and capricious:

1) United States EPA's use of the "rollback" model — the principal basis of its first plan on which five days of public hearings were conducted in Ohio — was strenuously objected to by representatives of many of the present petitioners because it was not source-specific and, as a consequence, tended to require more stringent sulfur dioxide controls than would be required if plant capacity, fuel, population, smokestack height, wind and climate were all taken into account. Thus John R. Martin, of Smith & Singer Meterologists, Inc., commented on behalf of Ohio utilities on the first United States EPA plan as follows:

> More sophisticated modeling is necessary in all seven of the urban counties that use the proportional rollback. In this way, the Federal air quality standards can be attained without unnecessary SO_2 emission restrictions being imposed upon sources that do not contribute to an SO_2

problem. We recommend that new strategies be tested which will more fairly identify and control SO_2 sources that create SO_2 problems.

* * *

2) EPA responded to these arguments favorably by devising and adopting the RAM model which did employ all of these source-specific factors.

3) Further, as shown on the following charts, the United States EPA 1976-1977 SO_2 control plan (principally based upon the RAM and MAX-24 models) shows less stringent regulation on a county-by-county basis when compared to the Ohio SO_2 control plans originally promulgated in 1972 and 1974. In addition, when the comparison is limited to petitioners involved in this litigation, but including all of their facilities which were subjected to RAM modeling (and which are identified in this record), we find the plan slightly less strict on a facility comparison basis than the Ohio 1972 plan by a count of 24 to 17, and slightly more strict than the Ohio 1974 plan by a count of 23 to 20.

These comparisons do not, of course, necessarily demonstrate RAM's accuracy. Rather, the comparison with Ohio's previous plans (based upon the earlier rollback model which was used and accepted nationwide) tends simply to show that the choice of RAM modeling lay within administrative discretion.

4) While this court has currently before it some 32 petitioners protesting the United States EPA's plan for SO_2 emission control for Ohio, it must be remembered that Ohio is estimated to have over 1,000 point sources and over 2,000 area sources of SO_2 pollution.

5) The RAM model is a general formula which can be applied to many individual sources of pollution to derive specific estimates of SO_2 emission rates for each. It employs a wider, more complete and more accurate data base than any prior model yet employed in devising a sulfur dioxide control strategy for a state or county. The crucial data with which the RAM model starts are the design capacity figure, plus the fuel sulfur content, from which is computed the SO_2 emission rate for each of the heating or power plants sought to be controlled. Thus at the outset the RAM model starts with ascertainable specific figures for each source where disputes can be resolved by inspection of the equipment or fuel concerned. Many of the additional components such as stack height, wind direction, physical relationship of sources to each other, and topography of the area are similarly ascertainable as matters of fact. With the enormous financial stakes involved in this litigation, every effort to avoid disputes about the accuracy of the data base should be made. This record shows that United States EPA's design of the RAM model was brought about at least in large part by Ohio industry's requests for greater specificity and hence lower costs of compliance with National Air Quality Standards.

6) While there may yet be developed (and hopefully will be) a better method of establishing a control strategy for sulfur dioxide emissions than the RAM model, no one has yet come forward with such. Nor do petitioners point to any such.

This is not to ignore that petitioners do cite Enviroplan's claims of a superior model termed Air Pollution Evaluation System. This record shows, however, that United States EPA asked for the Enviroplan model and was refused, and is now refused the operative details of that model on the grounds of proprietary interest. While such withholding may be both defensible as a matter of law and understandable as a matter of economics, this court cannot consider Enviroplan's model as available technology until and unless it is fully disclosed and evaluated by United States EPA — the agency charged by Congress with making these decisions.

7) We recognize that this record does not present positive proofs of the accuracy of RAM's predictions. Thus far technology has not developed foolproof methods for validating predictions concerning pollution of the ambient air absent years of collection of monitoring data with far more monitors and far more personnel than have thus far been available. Obviously, also, the monitor locations and the receptor sites for the RAM predictions must correspond.

* * *

8) Finally, as we pointed out at the beginning of this opinion, SO_2 emissions have a direct impact upon the health and the lives of the population of Ohio—particularly its young people, its sick people, and its old people. If the RAM model did overpredict emission rates, such a conservative approach in protection of health and life was apparently contemplated by Congress in requiring that EPA plans contain "emission limitations . . . necessary to insure attainment and maintenance" of national ambient air standards. 42 U.S.C. § 1857c-5(a)(2)(B) (1970). (Emphasis added.)

In summary, we hold that United States EPA's adoption and employment of the RAM model as its general working tool was based upon informal rulemaking which satisfied the requirements of both the Clean Air Act and the Administrative Procedure Act, and the due process requirements of the United States Constitution. Further, the record indicates that the Administrator's action in promulgating the sulfur dioxide control regulations for Ohio through use of the RAM model was a rational choice which was well within the discretion committed to him and his agency. We decline petitioners' requests to set the disputed orders aside on the ground that they are arbitrary and capricious.

NOTES

1. Why are the standards set according to the predicted second-worst day in terms of pollution results shown? *See* 40 CFR 50.4: "That national primary ambient air quality standards for sulfur oxides . . . are . . . (b) 365 micrograms per cubic meter (0.14 ppm) — Maximum 24-hour concentration not to be exceeded more than once per year."

2. In a related case, the Sixth Circuit upheld the MAXT-24 model which is designed for use in predicting SO_2 pollution from single sources in rural areas. *Cincinnati Gas & Elec. Co. v. EPA*, 578 F.2d 660 (6th Cir. 1978), *cert. denied*, 439 U.S. 1114 (1978). Unlike the RAM model, which was designed for use in urban areas, MAXT-24 does not estimate comparative contributions of SO_2 pollution from a number of point sources. Rather it treats each source as an isolated problem. *Id.* at 661. In other respects, the MAXT-24 model closely resembles RAM. Notwithstanding the complaints by industry that RAM overestimates pollution potential, one recent study has found that RAM generally underestimates SO_2 concentrations by about 25 percent. STERN, BOUBEL, ET AL., FUNDAMENTALS OF AIR POLLUTION, 316 (Academic Press, 2d ed. 1984).

3. Shortly after the Court of Appeals sustained the RAM model, and the Supreme Court denied industry's petition for certiorari, EPA stayed enforcement of the emission limits required by RAM. It then proposed changing the emission limits to levels equal to the plants' uncontrolled emissions. Finally, it adopted a new model, CRSTER, which set new SO_2 standards, but for only two plants. (Recall that the CRSTER model was described in *Connecticut v. EPA, supra* at Chapter 6.) EPA again found itself in litigation, this time in a suit brought by several neighboring states and the Northern Ohio Lung Association. An excerpt from that case follows.

STATE OF OHIO v. EPA

784 F.2d 224 *aff'd on rehearing*, 798 F.2d 880 (6th Cir. 1986)

MERRITT, Circuit Judge.

This case seeks review of air pollution emissions limitations established by the Environmental Protection Agency for the smokestacks of two electric utility plants in the Cleveland area. Petitioners' principal argument is that the computer model, called CRSTER, used by EPA to forecast pollution from these plants and to set emissions limits allows too much pollution. They assert that this model should not be used in its present form to set emissions standards at the plant. We conclude that EPA acted arbitrarily in using the CRSTER model to set emissions limits without adequately validating, monitoring, or testing its reliability or its trustworthiness in forecasting pollution in the vicinity of these plants, and we order further action to test and validate the model as an adequate forecasting technique for these plants.

* * *

The Cleveland, Ohio region is a nonattainment area for sulfur dioxide; the region includes areas where the concentration of sulfur dioxide in the ambient air exceeds the national standard. *See* 40 C.F.R. § 52.1871 (1985); *Ohio v. Ruckelshaus*, 776 F.2d 1333 (6th Cir.1985). The two major sources whose sulfur dioxide levels are in question in this case, the Eastlake and Avon Lake plants, are electric utility plants owned by the Cleveland Electric Illuminating Company.

In the early 1970s, the state of Ohio developed a state plan setting emissions limits for producers of sulfur dioxide in Ohio. In 1973, EPA's approval of this plan was set aside by the Sixth Circuit because of procedural irregularities, *Buckeye Power Co. v. EPA*, 481 F.2d 162 (6th Cir.1973), and Ohio subsequently withdrew key portions of its plan including the sulfur dioxide emissions limits at the two plants involved in this case. In 1976, because Ohio failed to develop a new plan, EPA promulgated a plan for the state of Ohio as required by 42 U.S.C. § 7410(c). In developing this plan, EPA used a computer model called the "Urban RAM model" to predict how sulfur dioxide emitted from the two power plants would be dispersed and would contribute to the pollution level in the atmosphere in the vicinity of the plants. The plan limited the amount of sulfur dioxide that the plants could emit to 1.43 pounds per million BTUs generated by fuel combustion at the Eastlake plant and 1.15 pounds per million BTUs for the Avon Lake plant.

In 1978, the utility company requested that EPA relax the emissions standard on the Eastlake and Avon Lake plants. In support of its request the company submitted studies showing that the Urban RAM model's predictions of sulfur dioxide concentrations in the air were significantly higher than actual empirically tested or monitored concentrations. These "validation studies" convinced EPA that the Urban RAM model overpredicted sulfur dioxide concentrations and that that model was not an appropriate tool for setting emissions limits at the plants. EPA tentatively concluded that the uncontrolled emissions of the plants would not result in a violation of national standards for sulfur dioxide. Consequently, on June 12, 1979 (before the date when the plants were required to comply with the 1976 emissions limits), EPA stayed enforcement of the limits, then proposed under § 7410(c) to change the emissions limits to levels equalling the plants' uncontrolled emissions, and asked for public comment.

The responses EPA received cast doubt on EPA's tentative conclusion that the proposed emissions limits would ensure that the region would come into compliance with the national standard. After the comment period had closed on the proposed change, EPA conducted additional modeling on the two plants. This time it used a model known as "CRSTER." On June 24, 1980, based on sulfur dioxide concentration predictions generated by the CRSTER model, EPA set the sulfur dioxide emissions limits at 5.65 pounds per million BTUs for the Eastlake plant and 4.1 or 4.65 pounds—depending on the sulfur content of the oil burned—per million BTUs for the Avon Lake plant.

* * *

B. THE CRSTER MODEL

In "nonattainment areas" the Clean Air Act provides for measuring the amount and the spread of dirty air from a source by actual testing or by "air quality modeling," 42 U.S.C. § 7501(2). In such areas, the Act emphasizes the need for "a comprehensive, accurate, current inventory of actual emissions from all sources" in order "to assess the need" for more "reduction" to meet national standards, and presumably as a check on modeling techniques. 42 U.S.C. § 7502(b)(4).

An "air quality model" or "computer model" is a forecasting technique. It is a mathematical equation or algorithm expressing a theory and a set of predictions about the content and circulation of air in a limited area, usually less than 50 kilometers in radius. After plugging data in numerical form into the variables of the algorithm, the model uses the mathematical theory to forecast the physical and chemical behavior of pollutants in the air and to describe the way the pollutants will spread out in space and time. Models can be used to predict pollution from a single source, after factoring in an assumption about the amount of background pollution, or they can be used to predict the spread of pollution from each of a number of sources. The model must be supplied with a "data base" consisting of information about variables such as the capacity of the power plants, the sulfur content of the fuel used, the height and diameter of the smoke stacks, the geographical characteristics of the surrounding terrain, and at least one year's monitored weather conditions. *See* Case, *Problems in Judicial Review Arising from the Use of Computer Models and Other Quantitative Methodologies in Environmental Decision Making*, 10 B.C.Env.Aff.L.Rev. 251, 317, 324-25 (1982). In order to be useful, a model must accurately predict the "behavior" of the air system being modeled.

Most of the controversy in the instant case arises from EPA's use of one such model, known as CRSTER, in setting emissions limits for the two power plants. The CRSTER model is a single source model designed for application to hot, buoyant, stack effluents of the kind commonly produced by power plant and furnace chimneys. After factoring in background pollution, the CRSTER model is actually capable of modeling up to 19 sources, but only if they are in close proximity to one another — multiple stacks at a single plant, for example. It treats all sources being modeled as occupying the same location. *See* U.S. EPA 450/2-77-013, User's Manual for Single-Source (CRSTER) Model, at 2-24, 2-25 (1977) (hereinafter referred to as the "CRSTER Manual"). The CRSTER model is a "gaussian plume dispersion" model, which means that it describes how a plume of dirty air emerging from a smoke stack will spread upward and outward according to the principles of fluid dynamics.

The model consists of a "preprocessor subroutine," which translates input data such as meteorological conditions and source characteristics into a format suitable for the model, and a set of subroutines that perform the actual modeling. These subroutines use data translated by the preprocessor to calculate how pollution from the source will spread out in light of the conditions (*e.g.*, wind speed and direction) embodied in that data. In so doing, the model makes a number of simplifying assumptions about such factors as the constancy of wind speed and direction, the uniformity of emission, the inability of the plume to cross a low atmospheric layer called the "mixing level," the absence of vertical wind shear, the nonreactivity of the effluent, and the degree of diffusion of the plume.

The model's predictions are presented in the form of readings at a hypothetical network of sensors or monitors surrounding the source. The model provides for five rings of such sensors along 36 compass azimuths evenly spaced every ten degrees. In addition, the model produces outputs of highest and second-highest concentrations at each receptor, a ranking of the 50 highest concentrations for the year, and various other useful data, some of which are suitable for use as input data for other analytic programs.

C. VALIDATION

The user's manual for the CRSTER model indicates that EPA subjected CRSTER to four validation studies at locations not involved in this case. CRSTER Manual at App. D-F. In an effort to determine the validity and overall accuracy of CRSTER, EPA attempted to validate the model at the Canal power plant, along Cape Code Bay in Massachusetts, and at the Philo, Stuart, and Muskingum plants in southern Ohio.

Based on empirical testing, EPA concluded that CRSTER generally tends during any given year to underestimate the highest and second-highest 24-hour estimated average and the 3-hour estimated average concentrations of sulfur dioxide. With respect to the 1-hour average, the CRSTER model overpredicted as often as it underpredicted. The amount of over- or underprediction varied from plant to plant, but the model is, according to the user's manual, "generally accurate within a factor of 2," a 200% deviation from actual fact. The user's manual states that this "accuracy is widely accepted for such point [i.e., 'single'] source models." *Id.*, at D-4.

Several conclusions may be drawn about the CRSTER model on the basis of these four validation studies. First, CRSTER predicted the second-highest 1-hour sulfur dioxide estimated concentrations within a factor of two at two-thirds of the sampling sites. EPA believes that this is an acceptable range of accuracy. Second, CRSTER consistently underpredicted the second-highest 24-hour sulfur dioxide concentrations. Third, plant-specific factors appear to affect the degree to which CRSTER over- or underpredicts sulfur dioxide concentrations. Finally, CRSTER tends to underpredict at greater distances from the pollution source. The four validation tests described here make clear that EPA can validate the CRSTER at a particular site. It appears that on-site validation of CRSTER requires at least one full year of data gathering by EPA.

II. ACCURACY OF THE CRSTER MODEL

Petitioners' primary argument is that EPA has not shown that the new emissions limits, based on predictions generated by the CRSTER model, will ensure attainment of the national air quality standard for sulfur dioxide as required by the Clean Air Act.

42 U.S.C. § 7410(a)(2)(B). The main thrust of their argument is an attack on the CRSTER model. They assert that the model's predictions are not accurate reflections of actual pollution concentrations.

The first issue presented is whether EPA has demonstrated the CRSTER model to be sufficiently accurate to be used in setting emissions limits for the plants. In other words, is the CRSTER model accurate enough that EPA's reliance on this model was reasonable rather than arbitrary? 42 U.S.C. § 7607(d)(9)(A). We are asked to assess the model's accuracy even though we are limited by a lack of information in the record demonstrating how reliably the model predicts the diffusion of sulfur dioxide in the region around the plants. No on-site study has been performed on the CRSTER model, as was done on the Urban RAM model, comparing the model's predictions of sulfur dioxide concentration for the areas surrounding the plants with actual monitored concentrations in these areas. No one has empirically tested the model or cross-checked its predictions against reality at the locations of the company's power plants.

* * *

EPA's reliance on the CRSTER model without testing the model against any monitored emissions from the plants and ambient air quality data from the area around the plants is arbitrary under these circumstances. The CRSTER model's unimpressive showing in the validation studies conducted at other sites in Ohio and Massachusetts suggests that the model's accuracy is suspect. Moreover, these studies emphasize that site-specific factors, such as local geography and weather conditions, affect the model's accuracy. We have no information in the record about what effect Lake Erie has on the diffusion of sulfur dioxide from these plants built along the shoreline, although all sides appear to agree that this factor is significant. In the absence of reliable data of some type, the trustworthiness of CRSTER predictions cannot be assessed.

In so holding, we recognize that other courts, in some cases, have not required EPA to test model predictions against monitored air quality data. *See, e.g., South Terminal Corp. v. EPA*, 504 F.2d 646 (1st Cir.1974); *Mision Industrial, Inc. v. EPA*, 547 F.2d 123 (1st Cir.1976). However, in *South Terminal*, the First Circuit required EPA to demonstrate that its regulation was supported by adequate technical evidence. 504 F.2d at 663-67; *see also Citizens to Preserve Overton Park v. Volpe*, 401 U.S. 402, 416 (1971); *Appalachian Power Co. v. EPA*, 477 F.2d 495, 507 (4th Cir.1973) (agency has discretion in rulemaking, but must "explicate fully" its course of inquiry, analysis and reasoning so that reviewing court can conduct meaningful review). This circuit has favored requirements that EPA back up its regulations with checks against real world data. *See, e.g., Northern Ohio Lung Association*, 572 F.2d at 1182 (requiring emissions monitoring and correlation of emissions data with air quality data as provided for under 42 U.S.C. § 7410(a)(2)(F)).

The problems that complex technical cases such as this one pose for reviewing courts have been widely discussed. *See, e.g.*, Case, *supra*; Yellin, *High Technology and the Courts*, 94 Harv.L.Rev. 489 (1981); Merges, *Apple v. Franklin: An Essay on Technology and Judicial Competence*, 2 Yale L. & Pol'y Rev. 62 (1983). No matter how sophisticated or involved the methods employed by EPA in reaching its decisions, in order to uphold those decisions under the Clean Air Act we must be able to see that the agency's actions were not arbitrary. In the absence of a record supporting the trustworthiness of agency decision-making tools as they were applied, we cannot uphold those tools' application. EPA has failed to provide such a record.

Furthermore, EPA's own guidelines explicitly recognize the importance of validation using monitored data.

> It must be noted that [we] ha[ve] never encouraged the use of air quality models in place of measured data. In fact, EPA encourages the use of measured data in evaluating the effectiveness of control strategies and in determining emission limits. The two should be used in a complementary manner whenever possible. The air quality data can be especially useful in validating air quality models and thus have a direct impact on the air quality assessment.

U.S. EPA, Guideline on Air Quality Models 6 (1978).

Given the CRSTER model's demonstrated sensitivity to site-specific characteristics, EPA's failure to validate CRSTER at the Eastlake and Avon Lake plants in accordance with its own guidelines was arbitrary and capricious.

9 PERMITS AND PERFORMANCE STANDARDS FOR STATIONARY SOURCES

The materials in this chapter are the most difficult in the course. They are nonetheless critical to understanding how the pieces of the enormously complex puzzle, called the Clean Air Act, fit together. The Clean Air Act Amendments of 1990 have radically altered both the permitting requirements and performance standards that apply to stationary sources of air pollution. When fully implemented, these changes will have a profound impact on the way that air pollution from stationary sources is regulated in the United States.

This chapter is divided into five parts. Part one addresses new source performance standards which are established under § 111 of the Act. Part two describes the new permitting requirements contained in Title V of the 1990 Amendments. Thousands of previously unpermitted sources of air pollution will now have to meet stringent permit requirements. Part three concerns the vastly expanded program for regulating hazardous air pollutants under § 112 of the Act. EPA's bubble policy is the subject of Part four. Finally, the new Acid Precipitation Program from Title IV of the 1990 Amendments is considered.

A. New Source Performance Standards

NATIONAL ASPHALT PAVEMENT ASSOCIATION V. TRAIN
539 F.2d 775 (D.C. Cir. 1976)

McGOWAN, Circuit Judge:

Section 111 of the Clean Air Act directs the Administrator of the Environmental Protection Agency (EPA) to maintain a list of stationary sources which "may contribute significantly to air pollution which causes or contributes to the endangerment of public health or welfare." *Id.* Within 120 days after the Administrator designates a particular source category as a "significant contributor," he must publish proposed standards of performance for sources within that category. The statute defines a standard of performance as:

> [A] standard for emissions of air pollutants which reflects the degree of emission limitation achievable through the application of the best system of emission reduction which (taking into account the cost of achieving such reduction) the Administrator determines has been adequately demonstrated.

Id. [§ 111 (a)(1).] The Administrator must afford interested parties an opportunity to comment on the proposed standards, and, after considering such comments and making appropriate modifications, he must promulgate final standards within 90 days after publication of the proposed standards. *Id.* [§ 111 (b)(1)(B).]

On June 11, 1973 the Administrator published a notice in the Federal Register indicating that he had amended his list of "significant contributors" to include asphalt concrete plants. 38 Fed.Reg. 15380. On that same day he also published proposed standards of performance for new or modified asphalt concrete plants. *Id.* at 15406. After considering written comments on the proposed standards, the Administrator published final standards of performance on March 8, 1974. 39 Fed.Reg. 9307.

The National Asphalt Pavement Association (NAPA) and various asphalt concrete plants then invoked our exclusive review jurisdiction, 42 U.S.C. § [7607], filing a petition in this court challenging the action of the Administrator on the following grounds: (1) the Administrator failed to provide interested parties with a meaningful opportunity to comment on the designation of the asphalt concrete industry as a "significant contributor"; (2) the Administrator erred in determining that asphalt concrete plants are "significant contributors" within the meaning of the Act; and (3) there is insufficient evidence in the record (a) to support the Administrator's conclusion that the standards of performance are achievable through the best systems of emission reduction and (b) to show that the Administrator took attendant costs into account. For the reasons set forth below, we affirm the action of the Administrator.

* * *

Petitioners argue that, in determining whether the asphalt cement industry is a "significant contributor", the Administrator relied on a study conducted in 1967 which estimated that in 1967 total particulate emissions from the asphalt concrete industry amounted to 243,000 tons, and that the amount would increase to 403,000 tons in 1977 if the 1967 control level of ninety-five percent were maintained. By the time the Administrator made the designation and promulgated proposed standards, however, a large number of asphalt concrete plants had installed various control devices, especially in response to state and local regulations; according to NAPA, by 1973 virtually every asphalt concrete plant in the United States was equipped with a two stage collection system. NAPA estimates suggest that in 1972 total industry particulate emissions amounted to 40,000 tons, a figure nowhere near as high as the Administrator's estimate based on the 1967 study. Petitioners suggest that the Administrator failed to explain his reliance on the 1967 data, and that his "significant contributor" designation is therefore "arbitrary and capricious."

We see no merit in petitioners' argument. First, the Administrator never relied on the disputed study to estimate the level of *controlled* emissions; to the contrary, the Administrator specifically noted that *one* of the factors he considered was the rate of *uncontrolled* emissions. Moreover, the Administrator also stated that he was aware of and took into account the stringency of existing local and state limitations on emissions from asphalt concrete plants. The Administrator has thus determined that given the number of existing plants, the expected rate of growth in the number of plants, the rate of uncontrolled emissions, and the level of emissions currently tolerated, *potential emissions* from new asphalt concrete plants would contribute "significantly" enough to warrant additional regulation to prevent deterioration of clean air. Petitioners have pointed to nothing in the record that indicates that the Administrator was arbitrary and capricious in reaching that determination.

We also find a fundamental flaw in the contention that once an industry complies with regulations designed to *reduce* air pollution to the level established by national primary and secondary air quality standards, it is no longer a "significant contributor" subject to new source regulation. Compliance with existing regulations may well enable the states to achieve the national standards, but it does not mean that the Administrator is precluded from exercising regulatory authority to *prevent* deterioration of clean areas. Given the Administrator's statement that he examined current state and local emission limitations, we take his decision to be that construction of new plants subject only to current emission limitations would "significantly contribute" to future air pollution problems. For that reason he promulgated standards of performance that are more stringent than typical state and local regulations, and we can find no basis to upset that determination.

III

We turn next to petitioners' contention that the Administrator acted in an arbitrary and capricious manner in promulgating the following standards of performance for new or modified asphalt concrete plants:

Standard for particulate matter

> (a) On and after the date on which the performance test required to be conducted by § 60.8 is completed, no owner or operator subject to the provisions of this subpart shall discharge or cause the discharge into the atmosphere from any affected facility any gases which: (1) Contain particulate matter in excess of 90 mg/dscm (0.04 gr/dscf). (2) Exhibit 20 percent opacity, or greater. Where the presence of uncombined water is the only reason for failure to meet the requirements of this paragraph, such failure shall not be a violation of this section.

40 C.F.R. § 60.92.

Those standards were promulgated pursuant to section 111(a)(1) of the Act, which defines a standard of performance as "a standard for emissions of air pollutants which reflects the degree of emission limitation achievable through the application of the best system of emission reduction which (taking into account the cost of achieving such reduction) the Administrator determines has been adequately demonstrated." The components of that definition have been clarified in prior cases in this circuit reviewing standards of performance for other new source categories. We have indicated that "[i]t is the system which must be adequately demonstrated and the standard which must be achievable." *Essex Chemical Corporation v. Ruckelshaus*, 486 F.2d 427, 433 (1973), *cert. denied*, 416 U.S. 969 (1974). "Adequately demonstrated" does not mean that existing asphalt concrete plants must be capable of meeting the standard; to the contrary, "[s]ection 111 looks toward what may fairly be projected for the regulated future, rather than the state of the art at present. . . ." *Portland Cement Association v. Ruckelshaus, supra*, at 391. And an "achievable standard" is one "within the realm of the adequately demonstrated system's efficiency and which, while not at a level that is purely theoretical or experimental, need not necessarily be routinely achieved within the industry prior to its adoption." *Essex Chemical Corporation v. Ruckelshaus, supra*, at 433-34. Moreover, the system must be one "which can reasonably be expected to serve the interests of pollution control without becoming exorbitantly costly in an economic or environmental way." *Id.* at 433.

The standard of review of actions of the Administrator in setting standards of performance is an appropriately deferential one, *see Ethyl Corporation v. EPA, supra*, and we are to affirm the action of the Administrator unless it is "arbitrary, capricious, an abuse of discretion, or otherwise not in accordance with law," 5 U.S.C. § 706(2)(A) (1970). Since this is one of those "highly technical areas, where our understanding of the import of the evidence is attenuated, our readiness to review evidentiary support for decisions must be correspondingly restrained." *Ethyl Corporation v. EPA, supra*, at —, 541 F.2d at 67 (Bazelon, C. J., concurring). "Our 'expertise' is not in setting standards for emission control, but in determining if the standards as set are the result of reasoned decision-making." *Essex Chemical Corporation v. Ruckelshaus, supra*, at 434.

The Administrator concluded, and petitioners concede, that the best system of emission reduction that has been adequately demonstrated for the asphalt concrete industry is represented by a venturi-scrubber with a twenty-inch pressure drop or a baghouse with an air-to-cloth ratio of six-to-one. Indeed, petitioner Warren Brothers informs us that those control technologies can be installed and operated at reasonable cost, and that various asphalt concrete companies are prepared to install those devices on plants that become subject to the final standards of performance.

Petitioners do not accept, however, the finding of the Secretary that a well-maintained venturi-scrubber with a twenty-inch pressure drop or a well-maintained baghouse with an air-to-cloth ratio of six-to-one will keep emissions at or below 90 mg/dscm (.04 gr/dscf). According to petitioners, the EPA performed tests on only a handful of asphalt concrete plants; that in performing those tests the EPA departed substantially from its prescribed testing procedures; that the Administrator relied on various tests conducted by states and localities which also failed to conform to proper testing procedures; that the Administrator refused to consider the results of tests conducted by NAPA which indicated that the standard could not be achieved on a regular basis; that in interpreting the various test results the Administrator completely overlooked or ignored a number of variables which should have been taken into account (including variations in the size, shape, and smoothness of particles in the feed aggregate, type of fuel, atmospheric conditions, and startup/shut down plant operations); and that the Administrator failed to show that guarantees issued by manufacturers of the relevant control devices supported the established mass emissions limitation.

We have considered these and other objections to the .04 gr/dscf standard promulgated by the Administrator, and, recognizing "the tempered review we exercise in these matters of non-judicial expertise," *Portland Cement Association v. Train*, 513 F.2d 506, 508 (after remand), *cert. denied*, 423 U.S. 1025 (1975), we cannot say that the Administrator's actions are either arbitrary or capricious. On the basis of our evaluation of the record evidence on these issues and the Administrator's responses thereto, we are unable to say that he did not engage in reasoned decision-making when he set the final performance standard at .04 gr/dscf rather than the originally proposed level of .031 gr/dscf.

We recognize that, for a variety of reasons, the Administrator conducted tests on only four plants. But we think that the record evidence with respect to those tests, and tests conducted by others, including NAPA, preclude us from overturning the action of the Administrator. The four tests conducted by the Administrator had average emission levels of .007, .008, .018, and .031 gr/dscf, all below the final standard of .04 gr/dscf. Two of the tests conducted by NAPA also fell below the final standard; and EPA considered the results of the other two NAPA tests which showed average emission levels of .043 and .108 but concluded that the plants were not well-controlled and should therefore not be used as a basis for determining standards for well- maintained new plants. In addition, the Administrator considered test results submitted by various local and state authorities, which ranged from .010 to . 025 gr/dscf, as well as fifty-six other sets of test results submitted after publication of the proposed standards.

Some of these tests admittedly failed to comply strictly with prescribed testing procedures, but we do not think that the departures were substantial enough to warrant reversal. Moreover, we think the record undercuts petitioners' claim that the Administrator "ignored" or "completely overlooked" relevant factors such as particle size and shape; we think the Administrator's statements indicate an awareness of and a willingness to adjust for such factors. Given the record before us, we are simply unable to say that the Administrator acted in an arbitrary and capricious manner in promulgating the less stringent performance standard of .04 gr/dscf (rather than the proposed . 031 gr/dscf) after the completion of the rulemaking proceeding. We therefore uphold the .04 gr/dscf mass emissions limitation.

* * *

For all these reasons, the decision of the Administrator is affirmed.

It is so ordered.

NOTES

1. As discussed in the *NAPA* opinion, the EPA Administrator is required to promulgate standards of performance for any category of stationary sources "if, in his judgment, it causes or contributes significantly to air pollution which may reasonably be anticipated to endanger public health or welfare." § 111(b)(1)(A). Note that the language of § 111 was changed somewhat in the 1977 and 1990 Amendments, after the *NAPA* case was decided, though the basic thrust of the section remains the same. As of 1991, EPA had promulgated NSPS for 70 separate categories of stationary sources. 40 CFR Part 60 (1991).

2. As a general rule, the NSPS are *emission limitations*, although as with asphalt concrete plants they may also contain opacity standards. Further, if the Administrator determines it is not feasible to do otherwise he may impose design, equipment, work practice or operational standards. § 111(h)(1). Consider the comparative advantages and disadvantages of design standards and emissions limitations. Emission limitations afford greater flexibility and encourage innovation but pose for the government greater enforcement problems. Why?

3. NSPS also prescribe monitoring, testing and reporting requirements. 40 CFR Part 60 (1991). They may not prescribe any particular technological system unless it is not feasible to do otherwise. § 111(b)(5). The standards must reflect "the degree of emission reduction achievable through the application of the best system of continuous emission reduction which (taking into consideration the cost of achieving such emissions reduction, any nonair quality health and environmental impact and energy requirements) the Administrator determines has been adequately demonstrated [for that category of sources]." § 111(a)(1). To what does the phrase "nonair quality health and environmental impact and energy requirements" refer?

4. Frequently, the NSPS for a particular category are established only for the criteria pollutants; *i.e.*, those to which the NAAQS apply. The statute, however, requires that NSPS be set for any air pollutants which might endanger the public health and welfare. Thus, for example, fluoride, which is not a criteria pollutant, is regulated under the NSPS for primary aluminum reduction plants. 40 CFR 60.192 (1991). Air pollutants which are neither criteria pollutants nor hazardous pollutants, but which are regulated from categories of stationary sources, are sometimes referred to as "designated" pollutants.

EPA is required to prescribe performance standards for existing sources of such "designated" pollutants as well as for new sources. *See* §§ 111(a)(1)(C); 111(d)(1).

5. New source performance standards apply to any stationary sources "the construction or modification of which is commenced after the publication of regulations (or, if earlier, proposed regulations) prescribing a standard of performance . . . applicable to that source." § 111(a)(2). Several cases have addressed the question of when construction or modification has "commenced" for purposes of this provision. *See e.g., Sierra Pacific Power Co. v. EPA*, 647 F.2d 60 (9th Cir. 1981); *Northern Plains Resources Council v. EPA,* 645 F.2d 1349 (9th Cir. 1981); *United States v. City of Painesville*, 644 F.2d 1186 (6th Cir. 1981). In each of these cases, the agency's determination that construction had not commenced prior to promulgation of the rules was sustained.

6. A "modification" for purposes of the NSPS program is defined as "any physical change in, or change in the method of operation of, a stationary source which increased the amount of any air pollutant emitted by such source or which results in the emission of any air pollutants not previously emitted." § 111(a)(4) *see also*, 40 CFR §§ 60.2, 60.14 (1991). By regulation, however, EPA has provided that replacement of a substantial portion of an existing facility's components constitutes "reconstruction" and not "modification." 40 CFR § 60.15 (1990). A reconstructed facility is subject to the same standards as a new source "irrespective of a change in emission rate." *Id.* In *United States v. Narragansett Improvement Co.*, 571 F. Supp. 688 (D.R.I. 1983), the court held that EPA's reconstruction rules could not be applied retroactively.

7. One problem with setting uniform NSPS is that they are virtually impossible to meet during "upset" conditions — periods of start-up, shut down, and malfunction. Under EPA's rules, these periods are not considered as representative conditions, and emissions in excess of applicable emission limits during such periods are not treated as violations of the NSPS unless otherwise specified in the applicable standards. 40 CFR § 60.8(c)(1991). Nonetheless, operators are required to maintain and operate their facilities "in a manner consistent with good air pollution control practice for minimizing emissions," during such periods. *Id.* at § 60.11 (d). In *Essex Chemical Corporation v. Ruckelshaus,* 486 F.2d 427, 433 (D.C. Cir. 1973), the Court of Appeals for the D.C. Circuit held that some provision for "upset" conditions was necessary "to preserve the reasonableness of the standards as a whole." *But see National Lime Association v. EPA*, 627 F.2d 416, 434 n. 54 (D.C. Cir. 1980) wherein the court suggests that the 1977 Amendments, which require that NSPS be achieved under systems of *continuous* emission control, "[may] have effectively repealed the regulations permitting flexibility to account for startups, shutdowns and malfunctions. . . ."

8. States are permitted to adopt more stringent new source performance standards than are required by the EPA. They may not adopt less stringent standards. § 116.

9. Fossil fuel fired stationary sources present a special problem under the Clean Air Act. Eastern and midwestern coal producers were concerned that the Act's SO_2 standards might cause many of their buyers to shift to lower sulfur western coal. In 1977, they convinced Congress to enact a provision that required the NSPS for fossil fuel fired stationary sources to include a "percentage reduction" in the emissions from such sources. Thus, a fossil fuel fired source which used low sulfur coal would still be required to reduce its SO_2 emissions by a certain percentage, no matter how low the sulfur content (and thus, SO_2 emissions) of the coal. This provision was criticized for encouraging the production of high sulfur coal to the environmental and economic detriment of the nation. ACKERMAN & HASSLER, CLEAN COAL/DIRTY AIR: OR HOW THE CLEAN AIR ACT BECAME A MULTI-BILLION DOLLAR BAIL OUT FOR HIGH SULFUR COAL

PRODUCERS AND WHAT SHOULD BE DONE ABOUT IT. (Yale Univ. Press 1981). The 1990 Amendments repealed the percentage reduction although new NSPS regulations for these sources are not expected to be promulgated until 1993. *See* Clean Air Act Amendments of 1990, § 403.

10. Under § 307(b)(1) of the Act, judicial review of new source performance standards may be obtained only in the Court of Appeals for the District of Columbia Circuit. The scope of review is narrow. Agency action may be turned aside only if found to be arbitrary and capricious, an abuse of discretion or otherwise not in accord with the law. § 307(d)(9). Even under this standard, the decision in the *NAPA* case seems highly deferential. The court does not engage in any detailed discussion of the record before the Agency in upholding the rules. Contrast this approach with two later opinions by Judge Wald of the same court. In *National Lime Association v. EPA*, *supra*, the court struck down EPA's NSPS regulations for lime manufacturing plants, essentially on the grounds that the agency had not demonstrated that the standards were "achievable" within the meaning of § 111. In a 33-page opinion, Judge Wald examines in detail the NLA's arguments before striking down the EPA rules.

11. Even more striking is the court's opinion in *Sierra Club v. Costle*, 657 F.2d 298 (D.C. Cir. 1981). That decision, which concerns the NSPS for fossil fuel fired generators, consumes 132 pages in the Federal Reporter before closing with this telling remark:

> We reach our decision after interminable record searching (and considerable soul searching). We have read the record with as hard a look as mortal judges can probably give its thousands of pages. We have adopted a simple and straight-forward standard of review, probed the agency's rationale, studied its references (and those of appellants), endeavored to understand them where they were intelligible (parts were simply impenetrable), and on close questions given the agency the benefit of the doubt out of deference for the terrible complexity of its job. We are not engineers, computer modelers, economists or statisticians, although many of the documents in this record require such expertise — and more.
>
> Cases like this highlight the critical responsibilities Congress has entrusted to the courts in proceedings of such length, complexity and disorder. Conflicting interests play fiercely for enormous stakes, advocates are prolific and agile, obfuscation runs high, common sense correspondingly low, the public interest is often obscured.
>
> We cannot redo the agency's job; Congress has told us, at least in proceedings under this Act, that it will not brook reversal for small procedural errors; *Vermont Yankee* reinforces the admonition. So, in the end, we can only make our best effort to understand, to see if the result makes sense, and to assure that nothing unlawful or irrational has taken place. In this case, we have taken a long while to come to a short conclusion: the rule is reasonable.
>
> *Affirmed.*

Id. at 410.

12. The *National Lime Association* decision, referred to above, offers a refreshingly intelligible description of particulate control technology, which is also at issue in the *NAPA* case:

> *Baghouses*
>
> The baghouse method employs fabric filters ("bags"), situated within an enclosed area (a "house"), to remove particulate from the kiln exhaust gas which is channeled through the house.

As the exhaust gas passes through, a dust cake forms on the filters. The cake itself improves filtration efficiency, but from time to time filters must be cleaned. This is done by forcing a reverse gas flow through the fabric, thus releasing the cake for disposal.

EPA acknowledges that fabric filter effectiveness is primarily a function of kiln exhaust particle size distribution, fabric type, fabric age and maintenance history.

Electrostatic Precipitators

Under this method, "dust particles are charged [by discharge electrodes] and pass through an electrical field [collector plates] of the opposite charge, thus causing the dust to be precipitated out of the exhaust gas . . ." *Portland Cement I*, 486 F.2d at 390. Two basic criteria must be met before an ESP can be utilized: (1) the suspended particle must be able to accept an electric charge; and (2) the particle must then pass through an electric field of sufficient strength to ensure removal of the particulate from the gas stream at the desired efficiency.

Precipitability is a function of the chemical composition of the dust particles, and will vary with the different kinds of material that make up the kiln exhaust dust (limestone, quicklime, fly ash, calcium sulfate, etc.). Assuming precipitability, the two main factors influencing the efficiency of a precipitator are the gas velocity and treatment time. The ESP method experiences a relatively low collection efficiency on submicron particles.

Although most particles collected by an ESP fall by gravity into waiting hoppers, programmed rapping of the electrodes is also required to keep the collector plates and discharge electrodes clean. As with the baghouse method, the dust collected is dry and may be disposed of in a variety of ways. A high level of maintenance skill is needed to keep an ESP in operation at design conditions.

Scrubbers

Scrubbers operate on the principle that wet particles are easier to control than dry. High pressure (or high energy) scrubbers of the type EPA considers capable of meeting the promulgated standards are those which because of their design increase the likelihood of contact between particle and water.

The most common high pressure drop scrubber used for controlling emissions from rotary lime kilns is the venturi scrubber. This scrubber operates by accelerating the velocity of the exhaust gas through a narrow venturi-shaped throat, where it is then brought into contact at great force with a spray of water. The particles thus dampened coalesce to form a slurry that can be then collected by a comparatively simple water gas separation device. The separated gas is then released into the atmosphere.

The efficiency of particulate removal is a direct function of energy input, measured by pressure drop across the venturi throat. Gaswater contact in the venturi scrubber is so thorough that even submicron particles are removed. Although low pressure drop scrubbers use less energy than high pressure drop scrubbers, even a low efficiency scrubber requires more energy than either the baghouse or the ESP. The slurry which is the byproduct of scrubber use is deposited in ponds, where the collected particulates settles out from the scrubbing water. The "clean" scrubbing water is then reused. Under present law settling ponds must be located so that they do not receive excessive rainwater runoff, causing overflow into local navigable waters.

627 F.2d at 424-25.

B. New Source Review

New source review (NSR) generally refers to the preconstruction review requirements of parts C and D (PSD and nonattainment) for major stationary sources and major emitting facilities. QUARLES & LEWIS, THE NEW CLEAN AIR ACT, 13 (Morgan, Lewis, & Bockius, 1990). These subjects have been addressed previously in Chapters Six and Seven. One recurring issue which has not yet been discussed, however, is the problem of modifications of existing sources. The *WEPCO* case, excerpted below, has generated much controversy, and is currently the subject of an EPA proposed rulemaking. *See* 56 Fed. Reg. 27,630 (1991).

WISCONSIN ELECTRIC POWER COMPANY V. REILLY

893 F.2d 901 (7th Cir. 1990)

CUDAHY, Circuit Judge.

The Petitioner, Wisconsin Electric Power Company ("WEPCO"), challenges two final determinations issued by the Environmental Protection Agency (the "EPA"). In these determinations, the EPA concluded that WEPCO's proposed renovations to its Port Washington power plant would subject the plant to certain pollution control provisions of the Clean Air Act, as amended, 42 U.S.C. §§ 7401 et seq. (1982). We affirm in part, vacate in part and remand to the EPA.

I. The Underlying Dispute

A. Relevant Provisions of the Clean Air Act

* * *

In section 111 of the 1970 Amendments, Congress required the EPA to promulgate New Source Performance Standards ("NSPS") in order to regulate the emission of air pollutants from new sources. These standards addressed hourly rates of emission and, in addition to new sources, applied to modifications of existing facilities that created new or increased pollution. Indeed, section 111(a)(2) of the Act stated that NSPS would apply to any stationary source, the construction or modification of which is commenced after the publication of regulations (or, if earlier, proposed regulations) prescribing a standard of performance under this section which will be applicable to such source. 42 U.S.C. § 7411(a)(2) (emphasis supplied). Congress then defined "modification" as any physical change in, or change in the method of operation of, a stationary source which increases the amount of any air pollutant emitted by such source or which results in the emission of any air pollutant not previously emitted. 42 U.S.C. § 7411(a)(4) (emphasis supplied).

Subsequently, faced with only varying degrees of success in controlling pollution in different parts of the country, Congress enacted the Clean Air Act Amendments of 1977, Pub.L. No. 95-95, 91 Stat. 685 (codified at 42 U.S.C. §§ 7401-7642 (1982)). Congress revised the NSPS so that regulated sources of pollution would have to use "the best system of continuous emission reduction which (taking into consideration the costs of achieving such emission reduction, and any nonair quality health and environmental impact and energy requirements) the Administrator determines has been adequately demonstrated...." 42 U.S.C. § 7411(a)(1)(C). In addition, Congress added a program for the Prevention of Significant Deterioration ("PSD"), concerned with increases in total annual emissions, to ensure that operators of regulated sources in relatively unpolluted areas would not allow a decline of air quality to the minimum level permitted by NAAQS. Air quality is preserved in this program by requiring sources to limit their emissions to a "baseline rate"; regulated owners or operators in areas that have attained NAAQS must obtain a permit before constructing or modifying facilities. 42 U.S.C. § 7475(a)(1). Congress also essentially adopted its NSPS definition of "modification" for the PSD program. 42 U.S.C. § 7479(2)(C).

From this statutory framework, the EPA promulgated regulations for both the NSPS and PSD programs. In this case, its regulations concerning modifications are central. The EPA defines "modification" in substantially the same terms used by Congress:

> [A]ny physical or operational change to an existing facility which results in an increase in the emission rate to the atmosphere of any pollutant to which a standard applies shall be considered a modification within the meaning of section 111 [42 U.S.C. § 7411] of the Act.

40 C.F.R. § 60.14(a) (1988). To determine whether a physical change constitutes a modification for purposes of NSPS, the EPA must determine whether the change increases the facility's hourly rate of emission. 40 C.F.R. § 60.14 (1988). For PSD purposes, current EPA regulations provide that an increase in the total amount of emissions activates the modification provisions of the regulations. 40 C.F.R. § 52.21(b)(3) (1988).

Even at first blush, the potential reach of these modification provisions is apparent: the most trivial activities — the replacement of leaky pipes, for example — may trigger the modification provisions if the change results in an increase in the emissions of a facility. As a result, the EPA promulgated specific exceptions to the modification provisions:

> The following shall not, by themselves, be considered modifications under this part: (1) Maintenance, repair, and replacement which the Administrator determines to be routine for a source category ... (2) An increase in production rate of an existing facility, if that increase can be accomplished without a capital expenditure on that facility. (3) An increase in the hours of operation....

40 C.F.R. § 60.14(e) (1988) (NSPS program); *see* 40 C.F.R. § 52.21(b)(2)(iii) (1988) (PSD program). These regulations (and the statutes from which they derive) are the focal point of this case.

B. WEPCO's Proposed Life-Extension Project

WEPCO's Port Washington electric power plant is located on Lake Michigan north of Milwaukee, Wisconsin. The plant consists of five coal-fired steam generating units that were placed in operation between 1935 and 1950. Each generating unit has a design capacity of 80 megawatts, but the recent performance of some of the units has declined due to age-related deterioration of the physical plant.

WEPCO and its consultant, Bechtel Eastern Power Corporation, conducted a Plant Availability Study in 1983 to examine and assess the condition of the power plant. As a result of the Study, WEPCO concluded "that *extensive renovation* of the five units and the plant common facilities is needed if operation of the plant is to be continued." [Citation omitted.] (Emphasis supplied). The Study noted that the air heaters on the first four units had deteriorated severely, while the rear steam drums in units 2 through 5 had experienced serious cracking. Air heater deterioration prevented units 1 and 4 from operating at full capacity, while the potential for steam drum blowout required a reduction in pressure (and output) in units 2 and 3. The possibility of catastrophic failure (steam drum blowout) in unit 5 was so great that WEPCO shut down the unit completely.

As a result of this Study, WEPCO submitted a proposed replacement program (which it termed a "life extension" project) to the Wisconsin Public Service Commission for its approval, as required by state law. Wis.Stat. § 196.49 (1987). WEPCO explained in its proposal that "[r]enovation is necessary to allow the Port Washington units to operate beyond their currently planned retirement dates of 1992 (units 1 and 2) and 1999 (units 3, 4 and 5) ... [and that renovation would render the plant] capable of generating at its designed capability until year 2010...." [Citation omitted.] Among the renovations required were repair and replacement of the turbine-generators, boilers, mechanical and electrical auxiliaries and the common plant support facilities. After preliminary review of the program, the Public Service Commission consulted the Wisconsin Department of Natural Resources (which then consulted EPA Region V) to determine whether WEPCO needed to obtain a PSD permit before commencing the repair and replacement program. David Kee, the Director of EPA Region V's Air and Radiation Division, then referred the matter to EPA Headquarters. *See, e.g.*, 40 C.F.R. § 60.5 (1988) (discussing the EPA's procedures regarding determinations of construction or modification).

EPA staff members conferred with WEPCO representatives between March and September 1988 to gain additional information regarding the proposed repair and replacement project. On September 9, 1988, EPA Acting Assistant Administrator Don R. Clay issued a memorandum in which he preliminarily concluded that the project would subject the plant to both NSPS and PSD requirements. Memorandum from Don R. Clay, Acting Assistant Administrator for Air and Radiation of the EPA, to David A. Kee, Director of Air and Radiation Division, Region V (Sept. 9, 1988) [Clay Memorandum]. The Clay Memorandum pointed out that the project would constitute a "physical change" resulting in an increase of production and emissions, which would therefore subject the plant to the relevant strictures of the Clean Air Act. Id. at 3-4. Further, the Clay Memorandum dismissed WEPCO's contention that the program was routine and was therefore exempt from the requirements of NSPS and PSD. This conclusion was adopted in toto by EPA Administrator Lee M. Thomas. Letter from Lee M. Thomas, Administrator of the EPA, to John Boston, Vice President of WEPCO (Oct. 14, 1988) [Thomas Letter].

Following the Thomas Letter, WEPCO continued to conduct capacity tests on the units. Based upon these tests, Assistant Administrator Clay issued a "revised final determination" that generally affirmed the EPA's earlier findings, but modified the baseline figures used by the EPA for units 2 and 3. Letter from Don R. Clay, Acting Assistant Administrator for Air and Radiation of the EPA, to John W. Boston, Vice President of WEPCO (Feb. 15, 1989) [Supplemental Determination].

Alleging that the EPA has misconstrued both the Clean Air Act and its own regulations, WEPCO appeals the EPA's final determination. We have jurisdiction to hear this appeal pursuant to 42 U.S.C. § 7607(b) (1982).

III. Like-Kind Replacement and Modification under the Act

A. The Underlying Statutory Framework

* * *

1. Physical Change

Certainly, under the plain terms of the Act, WEPCO's replacement program constitutes a "physical change." WEPCO proposes to replace rear steam drums on units 2, 3, 4 and 5; each of these steam drums measures 60 feet in length, 50.5 inches in diameter and 5.25 inches in thickness. Clay Memorandum at 4. In addition, WEPCO plans to replace another major component, the air heaters, in units 1-4. To implement this four-year program, WEPCO will need to make the replacements by taking the units successively out of service for nine- month periods. *Id.* These steps clearly amount to a "physical change" in the Port Washington plant.

* * *

WEPCO does not dispute that its steam drum and air heater replacements will result in an altered plant. But WEPCO does assert that Congress did not intend for simple equipment replacement to constitute a physical change for purposes of the Clean Air Act's modification provisions: The plain meaning of "modify" is "to change or alter" [Webster's New World Dictionary] or "to make basic or fundamental changes in" [Webster's Ninth New Collegiate Dictionary.] Reflecting the plain meaning of this term, Congress provided that a facility (1) must undergo a physical or operational "change" before it is evaluated under the modification provision.... Thus, under the plain meaning of the Act, a unit should not be deemed "modified" as a result of replacement of equipment with equipment similar to that replaced. As in the case of Port Washington, such like-kind replacement does not "change or alter" the design or nature of the facility. Rather, it merely allows the facility to operate again as it had before the specific equipment deteriorated.

Chevron instructs us to rely more on congressional direction and on agency construction (pursuant to congressional delegation) than on glosses found in the dictionary. What WEPCO calls "plain" is anything but plain and takes the definition far beyond the words enacted by Congress. *Chevron,* 467 U.S. at 843-45. [Citation omitted.] Thus, whether the replacement of air heaters and steam drums is a "basic or fundamental change" in the Port Washington plant is irrelevant for our purposes, given Congress's directions on the subject: "The term 'modification' means *any* physical change...." 42 U.S.C. § 7411(a)(4) (emphasis supplied). We follow Congress's definition of "modification" — not Webster's — when interpreting this term within the context of the Clean Air Act.

* * *

2. Increase in Emissions

The controversy involving WEPCO's alleged increase in emissions primarily concerns the regulations, not the statute: WEPCO argues that the EPA's *regulatory* method of measuring emissions is arbitrary and capricious. From a statutory standpoint, however, the modification provisions of the Clean Air Act Amendments are activated once a physical change is coupled with an "increase [in] the amount of any air pollutant emitted." 42 U.S.C. § 7411(a)(4). *See, e.g., United States v. Narragansett Improvement Co.,* 571 F.Supp. at 694. In the case before us, WEPCO does not dispute that its replacement program — intended to enable its deteriorated generators to operate at full capacity — will cause its emissions to increase from their current operating levels. The question for resolution, however, is whether the EPA properly construed its regulations by comparing actual emission rates with so-called "baseline" rates to determine the increase in emissions for NSPS and PSD purposes. We will discuss this subject later; but for purposes of the statutory requirement, we simply observe that the rejuvenated Port Washington plant will produce more emissions after the completion of the renovation project than the operating deteriorated plant produced shortly before the project was undertaken.

B. The EPA's Regulations

Although we have determined that WEPCO's repair and replacement program satisfies the modification provisions of the Clean Air Act Amendments, this is not the end of our inquiry. WEPCO's attack focuses primarily on EPA regulations, which in a number of respects are narrower than the statute. WEPCO argues that the EPA applied its regulations arbitrarily and capriciously to the Port Washington project.

1. Physical Change and the "Routine" Exception

EPA regulations define "modification" as "any physical or operational change to an existing facility which results in an increase in the emission rate to the atmosphere of any pollutant to which a standard applies." 40 C.F.R. § 60.14(a) (1988). To a major degree, this definition parallels 42 U.S.C. section 7411(a)(2), and it is unnecessary to repeat the analysis already applied to the statute. *See supra* III(A)(1). However, the EPA has, in addition, used its regulations to exempt a number of activities from the broader definition. The exemption that may be relevant here is accomplished by the following language:

> The following shall not, by themselves, be considered modifications under this part:
> (1) Maintenance, repair, and replacement which the Administrator determines to be routine for a source category....

40 C.F.R. § 60.14(e) (1988). See 40 C.F.R. § 52.21(b)(2)(iii). WEPCO relies on this language to argue that, even if its repair and replacement program amounts to a physical change, it was specifically exempted by the regulations.

Again, we accord substantial deference to an agency's interpretation of its own regulations, especially with respect to technical and complex matters. *Lyng v. Payne,* 476 U.S. 926, 939 (1986); *Aluminum Co. of Am. v. Central Lincoln Peoples' Util. Dist.,* 467 U.S. 380, 390 (1984). In this connection, to determine whether proposed work at a facility is routine, "EPA makes a case-by-case determination by weighing the nature, extent, purpose, frequency, and cost of the work, as well as other relevant factors, to arrive at a common-sense finding." Clay Memorandum at 3. The EPA considered all these factors in determining that the Port Washington project was not routine; first, the EPA observed that the nature and extent of the project was substantial: WEPCO proposed to replace sixty-foot steam drums (in units 2, 3, 4 and 5) and air heaters (in units 1, 2, 3 and 4) during successive nine-month outages at each unit. *Id.* at 4. Certainly, the magnitude of the project (as well as the down-time required to implement it) suggests that it is more than routine.

* * *

2. Increase in Emissions

Thus far, we have not had to address the important differences between the PSD and NSPS programs. At this point, however, the differences become crucial, because each program measures emissions in a fundamentally distinct manner.

a. NSPS Measurements

As previously noted, the EPA's NSPS program is concerned primarily with increases in emission rates, expressed in kilograms per hour of discharged pollutants. 40 C.F.R. § 60.14 (1988). The EPA compares the hourly emissions of the unit at its current maximum capacity to its potential emissions at maximum capacity after the change. Clay Memorandum at 9; *see* 40 C.F.R. § 60 App. C (1988) (providing complex formulae for determining emission rate change). In this calculation, the agency disregards the unit's maximum *design* capacity; this factor often sheds little light on the unit's *actual current* capacity to produce emissions.

The EPA applied these procedures in examining the generating units at Port Washington. The EPA asked WEPCO to submit figures for the actual operations and emissions of each unit at the Port Washington plant for the years 1978 to 1987; the EPA then relied upon the 1987 figures to calculate the emissions baseline against which post-replacement emissions could be compared. WEPCO, however, challenged the EPA's acceptance of these preliminary baseline figures, arguing that units 1, 2, 3 and 4 were capable of operating at higher rates of production than those calculated by the EPA based upon the 1987 figures. WEPCO conducted five ten-hour tests at each unit to determine its maximum capacity. Upon reviewing the test results, the EPA agreed that units 2 and 3 could be operated at their design capacities, and it revised the baseline levels for these units. The agency concluded that because there would be no increase in production or emissions, NSPS would not apply to these units following the renovation project. Nonetheless, the EPA refused to alter the baseline levels for units 1 and 4, noting that WEPCO's tests had not been conducted pursuant to the test protocol as required by the regulations and the Wisconsin State Implementation Plan (units 1 and 4 exceeded certain maximum allowable emission limits). Supplemental Determination at 8-9. Comparing these 1987 baseline levels to the maximum capacity of the plant after renovation, the EPA concluded that the renovation project would be subject to the provisions of NSPS.

WEPCO asks us to overturn the EPA's final ruling that the Port Washington project triggers NSPS. Specifically, WEPCO argues that, by using 1987 figures in determining the emissions baseline, the EPA failed to apply its own regulations: WEPCO asserts that these figures "reflected voluntary decisions by WEPC[O] regarding safety considerations (e.g., the 'zero' rate for Unit 5) and an electricity demand which did not require operation of the units at higher capacities." Petitioner's Brief at 15-16. WEPCO also posits that the EPA's refusal to compare representative pre-renovation emissions with actual post-renovation emissions is contrary to EPA regulations and amounts to an abuse of agency discretion. [The court finds that EPA properly applied its rules regarding modifications for purposes of the NSPS program, to WEPCO's facility.]

b. PSD Measurements

Unlike NSPS, PSD is concerned with changes in total annual emissions, expressed in tons per year. The PSD regulations require preconstruction review of the construction or modification of major emitting facilities. These regulations define their key term — "major modification" — as "any physical change in or change in the method of operation of a major stationary source that would result in a significant[10] net emissions increase of any pollutant subject to regulation under the Act." 40 C.F.R. § 52.21(b)(2)(i) (1988).

Here the question is whether WEPCO's renovation project will result in "a significant net emissions increase" so as to trigger the "major modification" provision of the regulations and, as a result, PSD. To determine whether the project would result in an emissions increase, the EPA compared actual pre-renovation emissions with potential post-renovation emissions at the Port Washington plant. Specifically, the EPA first examined the two-year period of 1983 through 1984 as the pre-renovation baseline period, pursuant to 40 C.F.R. section 52.21(b)(21)(ii):

> In general, actual emissions as of a particular date shall equal the average rate, in tons per year, at which the unit actually emitted the pollutant *during a two-year period which precedes the particular date and which is representative of normal source operation. The Administrator shall allow the use of a different time period upon a determination that it is more representative of normal source operation.* Actual emissions shall be calculated using the unit's actual operating hours, production rates, and types of materials processed, stored, or combusted during the selected time period.

40 C.F.R. § 52.21(b)(21)(ii) (1988) (emphasis supplied). Because Administrator Thomas determined that the discovery of cracks in the rear steam drums led to a more recent "source curtailment," he relied upon the data from earlier years, 1983 and 1984, as the baseline to determine whether the renovation would cause an increase in emissions. Thomas Letter at 5. WEPCO does not challenge this component of the EPA's calculation.

Second, the EPA calculated the actual emissions of the plant *following* completion of the project. Generally, in order to apply PSD, the regulations require the EPA to find an "increase in *actual emissions* from a particular physical change or change in method of operation." 40 C.F.R. § 52.21(b)(3)(i)(a) (1988) (emphasis supplied). The EPA reasoned, however, that because the source "ha[d] not yet begun operations following the renovation, 'actual emissions' following the renovation [were] deemed to be the source's 'potential to emit.' " Clay Memorandum at 7. In support of its reliance on WEPCO's potential to emit, the EPA pointed to the regulations: "For any emissions unit which has not begun normal operations on the particular date, actual emissions shall equal the potential to emit of the unit on that date." 40 C.F.R. § 52.21(b)(21)(iv) (1988).

WEPCO objects strenuously, and with good reason. In calculating the plant's post-renovation potential to emit, the EPA bases its figures on round-the-clock operations (24 hours per day, 365 days per year) because WEPCO *could potentially* operate its facility continuously, despite the fact that WEPCO has never done so in the past. And the EPA has admitted that it "assumed that emissions increases at Port Washington would come not from an increase in emission rate, but rather from increases in production rate or hours of operation." Supplemental Determination at 9; *see* Clay Memorandum at 7-8. The EPA responds that WEPCO can avoid these maximum calculations simply by consenting to federally enforceable restrictions on production rates and hours of operation, but WEPCO declines to do so. Clay Memorandum at 8; *see* 40

---

[10] The regulations define "significant" in terms of threshold emissions increases of individual pollutants: for example, an increase of 40 tons per year of nitrogen oxides is a "significant" net emissions increase. *See* 40 C.F.R. § 52.21(b)(23) (1988).

C.F.R. §§ 52.21(b)(4), 52.21(b)(16) (1988). Thus, argues the EPA, it has no choice but to assume that the plant will be operated continuously.

The first issue to be addressed is whether the EPA properly invoked the "potential to emit" concept in calculating the emissions increase. As explained above, the PSD regulations state that the EPA may rely upon a facility's potential to emit if the unit "has not *begun normal operations* on the particular date." 40 C.F.R. § 52.21(b)(21)(iv) (1988) (emphasis supplied). WEPCO argues that this phrase should be interpreted to include only those units that have never been in operation, while the EPA urges that the phrase can be applied to both new and modified units.

The regulatory history of this phrase sheds little light on its proper interpretation. The EPA argues that it has always interpreted this phrase to include modified units; it asserts that its formulae for determining emissions increases have consistently assumed that "new or *modified units* " would be deemed to operate at maximum physical or federally enforceable levels. 45 Fed.Reg. 52676, 52718 (1980) (emphasis supplied). But the EPA's analysis here seems circular: in order to demonstrate that the Port Washington like-kind replacement project constitutes a modification, the EPA applies the potential to emit concept (to show an increase in emissions). And in order to apply the potential to emit concept to like-kind replacement, the EPA assumes that the plant is a "modified" unit. Although we accord great deference to an agency construing the statute it administers, *Chevron,* 467 U.S. at 844, and even more deference to an agency interpreting its own complex regulations, *Aluminum Co. of Am. v. Central Lincoln Peoples' Util. Dist.,* 467 U.S. at 390, we cannot defer to agency interpretations that, as applied here, appear to assume what they seek to prove.

We are also troubled by the EPA's assumption of continuous operations in calculating potential to emit at the Port Washington plant. Although we agree that the EPA cannot reasonably rely on a utility's own unenforceable estimates of its annual emissions, we find no support in the regulations for the EPA's decision wholly to disregard past operating conditions at the plant. Indeed, *Alabama Power Co. v. Costle,* 636 F.2d 323 (D.C.Cir.1979), which contributes importantly to the EPA's current PSD program, suggests otherwise. There, the D.C. Circuit held, in part, that the EPA must "take[ ] into account the anticipated functioning of the air pollution control equipment designed into the facility" when calculating the facility's potential to emit. *Id.* at 353. More important for our purposes, however, was the court's discussion of a unit's potential to emit:

> If the source has no actual emissions because it has yet to commence operating, its hypothetical, projected emissions are included in the baseline. *If, however, the source is an established operation, a more realistic assessment of its impact on ambient air quality levels is possible, and thus is directed.*

Id. at 379 (emphasis supplied). The district court in *United States v. Louisiana-Pacific Corp.,* 682 F.Supp. 1141 (D.Colo.1988), relying on *Alabama Power,* recently reached the same conclusion:

> The broad holding of *Alabama Power* is that potential to emit does not refer to the maximum emissions that can be generated by a source hypothesizing the worst conceivable operation. Rather, the concept contemplates the maximum emissions that can be generated while operating the source as it is intended to be operated and as it is normally operated. Of course, it is possible that a source could be operated without the control equipment designed into it or that a Konus heater could be operated so badly that the fire would go out. Yet, *Alabama Power* stands for the proposition that hypothesizing the worst possible

emissions from the worst possible operation is the wrong way to calculate potential to emit.

Id. at 1158.

In sum, we certainly do not suggest that the EPA may never subject replaced units to the potential to emit concept under its regulations. The EPA may, if it wishes, undertake notice and comment procedures to apply the potential to emit concept to like-kind replacement. See 42 U.S.C. § 7607(d). But existing regulations do not seem to us to support such an application. We therefore believe that the EPA's reliance on an assumed continuous operation as a basis for finding an emissions increase is not properly supported. The EPA's determination that there has been a major modification for PSD purposes must be set aside.

* * *

V. CONCLUSION

In an era of increasing environmental concern, Congress enacted the Clean Air Act to "speed up, expand, and intensify the war against air pollution in the United States with a view to assuring that the air we breathe throughout the Nation is wholesome once again." H.R.Rep. No. 1146, 91st Cong., 2d Sess. 1, 1, 1970 U.S.Code Cong. & Admin.News 5356, 5356. The EPA is entitled to substantial deference in interpreting the technical provisions of the Act and its own regulations. We cannot grant deference, however, where the EPA has attempted to implement the Act's lofty goals in contravention of its own statutory regime. We therefore affirm in part and vacate in part, remanding the cause to the EPA for further proceedings not inconsistent with this opinion.

NOTES

1. The NSPS program and the NSR program use different approaches in determining what constitutes a modification. How do these approaches differ as explained in the *WEPCO* case? *See also*, 56 Fed. Reg. 2760 (1991). *Compare* § 111(a)(4) *with* § 171(4). Are these different approaches justified under the language of the Act? Note that Part C of the Act, relating to the PSD program, does not contain a separate definition of modification. In the 1990 Amendments, however, Congress amended § 167 to provide for enforcement against the construction *or modification* of any major emitting facility which does not conform to the requirements of this part . . . ."

2. In *Puerto Rican Cement Co. v. EPA*, 889 F.2d 292 (1st Cir.1989), the owner of a cement plant sought to convert one of its "wet" kilns to a "dry" kiln, and to combine that kiln with another kiln. The old kilns operated at only 60% of their capacity. In deciding whether this change should be treated as a modification for purposes of the PSD program, EPA compared the annual emissions from the two kilns operating at 60% capacity, with the single new kiln operated at full capacity. While the new kiln was cleaner and more efficient it nonetheless was capable of emitting significantly more pollutants. In light of the WEPCO decision, how should the court rule? Can the cases be distinguished?

C. The Permit Program for Stationary Sources

PERMITTING AND ENFORCEMENT UNDER THE CLEAN AIR ACT AMENDMENTS OF 1990

Stephen E. Roady, 21 ELR 10178 (News & Analysis)(April, 1991)

To understand why the Clean Air Act Amendments of 1990 contain a permits title, it is necessary to begin with the rationale advanced when the Administration bill was presented to the Congress in July 1989. Most fundamentally, the drafters of the permits title at EPA had concluded after a number of years of experience under the Clean Air Act that air pollution would be more efficiently regulated if sources were required to comply with permits as a condition of operations. They believed that it would be easier for sources to understand their obligations under the Act if those obligations were collected in one document — a permit. They also were convinced that it would be easier for the government to enforce the requirements of the Act if the government could rely on permit conditions as a benchmark against which to judge performance. In addition, they believed that the existing mechanism for regulating air pollution, the state implementation plan (SIP) process, was too cumbersome. Although the SIP process was perceived as a useful planning device, permits were viewed as the better way to enforce Clean Air Act requirements against specific sources. Finally, some believed that permits could serve other useful functions, such as acting as a convenient reference point in calculating allowable emissions for trading purposes under the acid rain title of the Amendments.

* * *

Although there were key differences between the Senate and the House versions of the permit title, both bills contained the same basic program outline — an outline that remains unchanged in the Amendments as signed into law.

The permits title establishes the generic permit program that will prove essential to the proper functioning of the permit system under the Act. Significantly, however, specific kinds of sources must also look to other portions of the Amendments to find additional permit requirements applicable to their operations. Thus, separate permit requirements relevant to construction of new sources remain in the Act at §§ 165, 172, and 173. In addition, new permit requirements relevant to hazardous air pollutants appear in new § 112(j). Finally, separate permit requirements relevant to sources regulated under the acid rain title are set out in § 408 of the new Act. Those framing the final language in each case endeavored to coordinate the various permit requirements and timetables, and the results of those efforts will be noted in this Article. A snapshot of the permit title as enacted is provided below. Important details of the title are addressed in succeeding sections of this Article.

□*Section 501: Definitions.* Section 501 defines certain key terms. The term "affected source" is defined by reference to title IV of the new law, which states that all sources regulated under that title (the acid rain title) shall be deemed "affected sources."

Section 501 defines "major source" by reference to § 112 of the Act, and also by reference to § 302 and to part D of title I (the nonattainment part). In addition, § 501 defines "schedule of compliance" (an important term that resurfaces in § 503 as an item that must be submitted along with the permit application) as a schedule of remedial measures leading to compliance with the Act. Finally, § 501 defines "permitting authority" as either the Administrator of EPA "or the air pollution control agency authorized by the Administrator to carry out a permit program under this title."

□*Section 502: Permit Programs.* Section 502(a) states the basic premises of the title: that after the effective date of any approved permit program, it shall be unlawful for a source subject to the title to operate without a permit, or to violate any requirement of permit. Sources subject to the title are listed in this section. In addition to major sources, these include "affected sources" as provided in title IV, any source "subject to standards or regulations under section 111 or 112," and any source required to have a permit under parts C or D of title I. The Administrator is granted authority to expand the number of sources covered, and also to exempt sources (other than major source) from the requirement to obtain a permit.

Section 502(b) requires the Administrator to promulgate regulations establishing the minimum elements of permitting programs to be administered by permitting authorities, and to do so within 12 months following enactment of the Amendments. In addition, this section enumerates in some detail what it is that the Administrator must include in these minimum elements. The list includes provisions for the collection of fees, ensuring compliance with permits, public notice and expeditious processing of permit applications, public availability of certain permit documents, permit revisions if new requirements become applicable to a permitted source, and operational flexibility without the need for permit modifications under certain conditions.

The balance of § 502 provides, *inter alia*, that: (1) "a single permit may be issued for a facility with multiple sources"; (2) states must submit approvable permit programs to EPA within three years following enactment of the Amendments (the states were given three years because of a concern that many states might need to obtain legislative authority to be able to satisfy all the "minimum elements" necessary for EPA approval); (3) EPA must approve state programs within one year after they are submitted (or, assuming the states consume their full three years, sometime in 1994); (4) if EPA does not initially approve a state program, the state is allowed six months to revise and resubmit the program; (5) EPA will finally approve or disapprove the state program — or will establish, administer, and enforce a federal program for that state — by the end of 1995; (6) EPA may impose sanctions on states for failing to submit approvable programs and for failing to administer and enforce programs adequately; and (7) EPA may, by rule, grant "interim approval" to a state program on a one-time basis for a two-year term when the program "substantially meets the requirements of this title, but is not fully approvable."

□*Section 503: Permit Applications.* Section 503 requires sources to file their applications for an operating permit within one year after they become subject to a permit program. This section also provides that, "[e]xcept for sources required to have a permit before construction or modification under the applicable requirements of this Act," the filing of a complete application in a timely fashion will protect the source from any allegation that it is operating without the required permit during the time the application is pending. Permitting authorities are allowed up to three years to act on applications that are submitted within the first year after a program becomes effective. Otherwise, they are required to take final action to approve or disapprove — and issue or deny — permits within 18 months after receipt of the permit application.

□*Section 504: Permit Requirements and Conditions.* Section 504 sets out the required contents of each permit. These include: enforceable emission limitations and standards, a "schedule of compliance," a requirement to report the results of required monitoring no less often than every six months, and "such other conditions as are necessary to assure compliance with applicable requirements of this Act, including the requirements of the applicable implementation plan." This section also authorizes the Administrator to require monitoring and analysis of pollutants; requires permits to include monitoring, inspection, and reporting requirements; and allows issuance of "general" permits (covering "numerous similar sources"), as well as permits covering "temporary sources." In addition, this section establishes a permit "shield" that protects sources that are in compliance with their permits against allegations that they are in violation of the requirements of § 502, and that allows permitting authorities some discretion to expand the shield under certain conditions.

□*Section 505: Notification to Administrator and Contiguous States.* Section 505 requires each permitting authority to provide to EPA copies of each permit application as well as a copy of each permit the authority proposes to issue. In addition, permitting authorities are required to notify all states whose air quality may be affected and that are contiguous to the state in which the source is located, or that are within 50 miles of the source, of each permit application or proposed permit, and to allow those states to comment on the permit.

This section also grants EPA the authority to object to permits proposed to be issued by the permitting authorities, and requires the Administrator to issue such an objection upon receipt of a petition demonstrating that the permit would violate the Act. It provides that interested persons may seek judicial review if the Administrator fails to object to a permit that would violate the Act. Permitting authorities are allowed 90 days to revise permits to resolve an EPA objection. If no such revision is accomplished, EPA is required to take final action to issue or deny the permit. The Administrator may waive the requirements for review and objection for sources other than major sources.

□*Section 506: Other Authorities.* Section 506 preserves the ability of states and interstate permitting authorities to establish "additional permitting requirements not inconsistent with this title." In addition, this section makes clear that the provisions of this title shall apply to permits implementing the requirements of title IV (the acid rain title) "except as modified by that title."

□*Section 507: Small Business Stationary Source Technical and Environmental Compliance Assistance Program.* Section 507 requires states to establish programs to assist "small business stationary sources" with permit compliance. Such programs are to work with eligible sources to ensure that the requirements of the permit program are understandable and to assist the sources in their compliance efforts.

□*Permits for Sources of Hazardous Air Pollutants.* Title III of the Amendments (which revises Clean Air Act § 112) establishes certain separate requirements for permitting with respect to sources of hazardous air pollutants. These requirements are designed to be coordinated with the timetable and the requirements set out in the permits title, but they also address permitting for such sources in two situations where standards for regulating hazardous air pollutants are not yet established.

In the first situation, where the Administrator has failed to promulgate a "maximum achievable control technology" (MACT) standard by the date required for that standard,

§ 112(j) provides that a source must apply for a permit and that the Administrator and the state must establish an emission limitation in the permit that is equivalent to the standard that would have been promulgated had the deadline not been missed. In the second situation, where the administrator promulgates a MACT standard applicable to a source that has already received a permit, the standard shall be included in the permit when the permit is renewed, and the source shall be allowed a reasonable time to comply (no longer than eight years after the standard is promulgated, or eight years after compliance was required under the "equivalent emission limitation" described in § 112(j)(5)).

□*Permits Under the Acid Rain Title.* Permits for sources regulated under title IV of the Act are designed to be coordinated with the requirements of the permit title. However, title IV establishes a somewhat different timetable than that created in the permits title for the submission of permits and separates the permit process into two distinct phases. Section 408(c) addresses permits required of sources participating in "Phase I" reductions of sulfur dioxide emissions. It requires sources classified as "affected sources" under §§ 404 and 407 of title IV to submit a permit application within 27 months of enactment of the Amendments (by February 1993). This deadline falls well before the deadline for permit applications established in §§ 502 and 503, which contemplates that the first wave of applications for permits from sources that are not affected by title IV or by the new provisions of § 112 might not occur until sometime in 1995 or 1996. Accordingly, title IV provides that EPA (not the states) shall administer the permits issued to these Phase I sources.

Title IV also provides for "Phase II" emission reductions. Sources required to have permits for Phase II must submit their permit applications on or before January 1, 1996. Phase II permits are to be implemented by the states consistent with the requirements of title V.

* * *

NOTES

1. The permit provisions of the 1990 Amendments are modeled after the NPDES permit system contained at § 402 of the Clean Air Act. Like the NPDES program, Title V requires "each source of air pollution covered by the permitting requirements...to obtain a permit that set[s] out an enforceable list of all conditions, emission standards, and limitations applicable to that source, and...to comply with each condition, standard and limitation in that permit as a condition of operations." Roady, *Permitting and Enforcement Under the Clean Air Act Amendments of 1990*, 21 ELR 10178, 10182 (1991).

2. *Permit Fees.* One of the most remarkable provisions of the Clean Air Act Amendments of 1990 is the requirement that permitted sources pay an annual fee that is "sufficient to cover all reasonable (direct and indirect) costs required to develop and administer the permit program . . . ." § 502(b)(3)(A). These include the costs of — (i) reviewing and acting on permit applications; (ii) implementing and enforcing the permit; (iii) monitoring ambient air quality as well as emissions from the source; (iv) preparing rules and other guidance; (v) modeling, analyses and demonstrations; and (vi) preparing inventories and tracking emissions. *Id.* The *minimum* fee is $25/ton of regulated pollutant emitted by the source (unless EPA determines that some lower amount will allow full recovery of the "reasonable costs" noted above) § 502(b)(3)(B). Aside from the costs to permittees, what makes this provision so remarkable?

3. *Exemptions.* EPA may exempt categories of sources from the permit requirements if it finds that such requirements are "impracticable, infeasible or unnecessarily burdensome on such categories. Exemptions are not allowed, however, for "major sources." § 502(a). What is a "major source" within the meaning of this section? *See* § 501(2).

4. *Permit Shield.* Section 504(f) of the Act makes clear that compliance with the terms of a permit "shall be deemed compliance with" the permit requirements of § 502 of the Act. Moreover, EPA may, under certain circumstances, provide by rule that compliance with a permit shall be deemed compliance with other applicable provisions of the Act.

5. *EPA Veto Authority.* Section 505(b) of the Act gives the EPA authority to veto permits that are not in compliance with the law. The Act requires EPA to object to the issuance of a permit within 45 days from receipt of the application. EPA's objection must be accompanied by a statement of reasons. If EPA fails to object within 45 days, "any person" may petition the EPA within 60 days thereafter to file such an objection. § 505(b)(2). A petitioner may only raise objections, however, that were raised during the public comment period on the application. EPA has 60 days to grant or deny the petition. The permitting authority may not issue a permit to which EPA objects until it is revised as necessary to meet EPA's objections. If the permitting authority fails to revise the permit as required by EPA within 90 days following the objection, EPA must issue or deny the permit in accordance with the Act. Judicial review is not available until a permit has been finally issued or denied. §505(c).

6. *Monitoring and Reporting.* The Act establishes a comprehensive system for self-monitoring of air pollution emissions and of self-reporting of compliance. *See e.g.*, §§ 114(a)(3); 502(b)(2); 504(b), (c). Stiff criminal penalties may be imposed for falsifying data (§ 113(c)(2)), and substantial civil penalties are allowed for any violation of the permitting requirements. § 113(d)(1)(B). Furthermore, "bounties" are allowed to persons who furnish information which leads to the imposition of criminal or civil sanctions. § 113(f). Taken together, these provisions should help insure that the public will play an aggressive watchdog role in monitoring compliance with the law.

7. *Operational Flexibility.* In response to operator's concerns about the need for minor permit revisions without a cumbersome regulatory process, § 502(b)(10) allows changes to a permitted facility without obtaining a permit revision if the changes are not "modifications" within the meaning of any of the various definitions of that term found in Title I of the Act (*see e.g.*, §§ 111(a)(4); 112(a)(5); 171(4); 182(c)(7)(8); 182(e)(2)), and the emissions do not exceed that allowed under the permit. Both EPA and the state must generally be afforded seven days' notice before such changes may take effect.

8. The new permitting provisions contained in Title V of the Act are significant but they are not the only permitting standards contained in the law. Permitting standards are also established for sources subject to the Acid Precipitation Program contained in Title IV of the Act (§ 408), sources of hazardous air pollution (§ 112(j)), new or modified major stationary sources in nonattainment areas (§ 173), and, as the following case illustrates, new or modified major emitting facilities in attainment or "PSD" areas. § 165.

HAWAIIAN ELECTRIC CO. V. EPA
723 F.2d 1440 (9th Cir. 1984)

GOODWIN, Circuit Judge.

Hawaiian Electric Company, Inc. (HECO) seeks review of an EPA determination not to proceed with consideration of modifying PSD permit HI 78-02 until HECO complies with the procedure for permit revision applying to major modifications. HECO's appeal is timely under 42 U.S.C. § 7607(b) (Clean Air Act). We affirm EPA's determination and hold that all other issues raised are not ripe for review.

HECO's Kahe power plant is Oahu's greatest source of sulfur dioxide emissions. In 1978 it consisted of five oil-fired units, all built before 1975, with a total capacity of about 500 megawatts. In 1978 HECO burned 2% sulfur oil. Unit 6, a new 146 megawatt oil-fired unit, began operation in November 1980.

EPA issued Prevention of Significant Deterioration (PSD) Permit HI 78-02 to HECO on January 26, 1979. EPA issues PSD permits in Hawaii because the state does not have an EPA approved PSD permit program as part of its State Implementation Plan (SIP), 42 U.S.C. § 7410; 40 C.F.R. § 51.18. To allow operation of Unit 6, the PSD permit required that the existing units reduce emissions by shifting to 0.5% sulfur oil. When Unit 6 began operation, all six units began burning the 0.5% oil.

A PSD permit was required because in 1978 EPA designated the surrounding area as not able to be classified for compliance with National Ambient Air Quality Standards (NAAQS) for sulfur dioxide (40 C.F.R. 81.312 (1978)).[11] The use of 0.5% sulfur oil was required because a wind tunnel dispersion model indicated that higher sulfur content would not meet NAAQS. After the use of 0.5% oil began, HECO determined by a mathematical model that the wind tunnel analysis was inadequate. EPA refused to accept HECO's conclusions, but as a result of further discussions, HECO established a seven-station monitoring network. Based on results at the end of one year of monitoring (completed on March 15, 1983), HECO concluded that Units 1-5 could burn higher sulfur fuel without violating NAAQS.[12] On March 18, 1983, HECO submitted the information to EPA and petitioned for reconsideration of the PSD permit requirement that Units 1-5 use 0.5% sulfur fuel.

In its March 25, 1983, response EPA stated:

> Our preliminary review of the new information submitted by HECO confirms that HECO would be able to increase the fuel sulfur content at Units 1-5 without adversely affecting air quality.

However, EPA went on to state that under 40 C.F.R. § 52.21(b)(2)(iii)(e)(1) of its PSD regulations, the change in fuel would be a "major modification" requiring a new PSD permit for Units 1-5.

To obtain a PSD permit for Units 1-5, additional data would have to be submitted. 42 U.S.C. § 7475; 40 C.F.R. § 52.21(j)-(p). In the March 25, 1983, letter EPA specified that the additional data required were an analysis of Best Available Control Technology (BACT) and an "additional impacts analysis" (dealing with potential impairment to visibility, soils, and vegetation). Additionally, BACT would have to be employed on Units

---

[11] In 1979 the area was reclassified as nonattainment for sulfur dioxide (40 C.F.R. § 81.312 (1982)).

[12] HECO apparently argues that respect of PSD increments is not a relevant consideration.

1-5. 42 U.S.C. § 7475(a)(4); 40 C.F.R. § 52.21(j)(2). There is a strong possibility that BACT for Units 1-5 would be identical to that already required for Unit 6, i.e., 0.5% sulfur oil. As part of BACT, control of other pollutants such as particulate matter could also be required. 40 C.F.R. § 52.21(j)(3).

I. Final Action

A. Application of major modification definition

EPA has determined that HECO's proposed change to higher sulfur fuel is a major modification, and has refused to consider HECO's petition until further information is submitted.

* * *

Intervenors American Lung Association, et al., argue that there is insufficiently immediate impact on an interest of HECO because the Kahe plant is within an area designated as nonattainment for sulfur dioxide. If the Kahe area continues to be subject to the requirements of Part D of the Clean Air Act, dealing with nonattainment, rather than Part C, dealing with PSD, a different kind of permit will be required to allow a fuel switch. It appears very unlikely that such a permit could be obtained. EPA indicated to HECO in 1981 that as long as the Kahe area remains nonattainment, Part D of the Act would apply. EPA further indicated that since the State of Hawaii does not have an acceptable new source review procedure, the Kahe area is covered by the construction moratorium implemented by 40 C.F.R. § 52.24. *See* 42 U.S.C. § 7410(a)(2)(I); *Connecticut Fund for Environment v. E.P.A.*, 672 F.2d 998 (2d Cir.1982), *cert. denied*, 459 U.S. 1035 (1982). Until the State of Hawaii establishes a new source review procedure, it is unlikely that the construction moratorium will be lifted. *Id. Cf. e.g.*, 48 *Fed.Reg.* 50,686 (1983).

It thus appears that for any change to be foreseeable in the air pollution controls required at the Kahe plant, the Kahe area must be redesignated attainment and HECO's request for a change in its PSD permit must be granted. Indeed, the State of Hawaii has requested EPA to redesignate the area as attainment. And, EPA may be able to do so after complying with the Administrative Procedure Act. *Western Oil & Gas v. EPA*, 633 F.2d 803 (9th Cir.1980). That the two decisions are intimately connected is emphasized by the fact that the nonattainment designation applies only to the area immediately surrounding the Kahe plant. *See* 40 C.F.R. § 81.312 (1982).

* * *

B. The PSD permit

* * *

b. Modeling

HECO's petition for reconsideration essentially depends on its assertion that the modeling which justified the original imposition of the permit was flawed.

Congress' concern about modeling science led it to require EPA to establish uniform modeling techniques for use in PSD permitting and to review and update those models periodically as modeling science developed. *See* 42 U.S.C. §§ 7475(e)(3)(D) and 7620. EPA did develop modeling guidelines, 40 C.F.R. 52.21(1), and they were subsequently upheld on judicial review. *Alabama Power Co. v. Costle*, 636 F.2d 323, (D.C.Cir.1979). The courts have recognized the need for agency discretion in applying the results of modeling. *Wisconsin Electric Power Co. v. Costle*, 715 F.2d 323 at 330-31 (7th Cir.1983)

* * *

Nothing in the Clean Air Act or its legislative history indicates that Congress intended that EPA should have to reconsider each and every PSD permit if modeling predictions were subsequently drawn into question. In fact, Congress attempted to avoid excessive bureaucratic contention by requiring EPA to make a decision on all PSD permit applications within one year. 42 U.S.C. § 7475(c). This effort would be frustrated if PSD permits could routinely be challenged de novo.

In addition, we have held that post-decision studies may not be used to challenge an agency decision absent a showing that such a decision was based on assumptions that "were entirely fictional or utterly without scientific support." *Ass'n of Pac. Fisheries v. EPA*, 615 F.2d 794, 812 (9th Cir.1980); *accord, Wisconsin Electric Power Co. v. Costle*, 715 F.2d 323 (7th Cir.1983). In this case, HECO concedes that the permit was reasonable when issued.

c. Policy challenge to PSD

HECO maintains that the 0.5% sulfur oil requirement was included in the original permit solely to achieve NAAQS. It argues that its request for reconsideration of the permit should therefore not involve PSD review. It argues that the Clean Air Act gives EPA no authority to require reductions in emissions from existing sources which are not being modified except if necessary to attain and maintain NAAQS. HECO, however, overlooks the point that the requirement was imposed on existing generators as a condition of approval to operate a new generator which would add to pollution emissions. Had the limitation not been imposed, both HECO and EPA agree that available information indicated NAAQS might have been violated for sulfur dioxide.

* * *

HECO also attempts to maintain that EPA may not impose emission restrictions that are more stringent than necessary to protect NAAQS. But HECO itself admits in its brief that the ultimate purpose of the PSD program is to maintain air quality better than NAAQS. Indeed, Congress repeatedly emphasized that NAAQS alone were insufficient to protect public health and welfare.

* * *

In sum, Congress found that it was important to reduce pollution levels below those mandated by the standards and that the best means of doing so was to require the installation of BACT on all sources which would otherwise increase pollution. Therefore, it is absurd for HECO to maintain that EPA may not, through a PSD permit, require pollution controls which yield air quality better than NAAQS.

II. Major Modification

* * *

Title 40 C.F.R. 52.21(b)(2) provides:

> (2)(i) "Major modification" means any physical change in or change in the method of operation of a major stationary source that would result in a significant net emissions increase of any pollutant subject to regulation under the Act.
>
> * * *
>
> (iii) A physical change or change in the method of operation shall not include:
>
> * * *
>
> (e) Use of an alternative fuel or raw material by a stationary source which: (1) The source was capable of accommodating before January 6, 1975, unless such change would be prohibited under any federally enforceable permit condition

> which was established after January 6, 1975 pursuant to 40 C.F.R. 52.21 or under regulations approved pursuant to 40 C.F.R. 51.18 or 40 C.F.R. 51.24[.]

An increase in sulfur content of fuel constitutes a "major modification" under this definition if the increase (1) results in a significant net emissions increase and (2) amounts to a physical or operational change. HECO does not dispute that the increase it proposes would result in a significant net emissions increase. Rather, HECO argues that the increase would not be a physical or operational change. HECO is wrong.

The market recognizes 0.5% and 2% sulfur oil as different fuels with distinct prices. Also, EPA in the past has clearly distinguished the two fuels when, as in this case, there is a permit condition specifying the sulfur content of fuel. Although Units 1-5 were able to use 2% sulfur fuel before January 6, 1975, the sulfur content increase is prohibited by an enforceable permit condition established after January 6, 1975, pursuant to 40 C.F.R. 52.21. As a result, the proposed fuel switch does not fit within the fuel switching exemption from the definition of major modification contained in 40 C.F.R. § 52.21(b)(2)(iii)(e)(1).

In one past instance, EPA explained the requirements of 40 C.F.R. 52.21(b)(2)(iii)(e)(1) as follows:

> Concerning PSD applicability, a change in sulfur content of a fuel burned at a source (e.g. 1% sulfur oil to 2.2% sulfur oil) is not considered a modification and, therefore not subject to PSD permit procedures *unless the content of the fuel is limited by an enforceable permit condition* and/or the source is not physically capable of burning the higher sulfur fuel. Normally a source is physically capable of using a particular fuel without regard to the fuel's sulfur content and therefore, *enforceable permit condition [sic] tend to be the more important concern when determining PSD applicability.* (Emphasis added.) Internal EPA memo concerning Delmarva Edge Moor Station.

* * *

HECO and amici argue that the environmental benefit of using 0.5% sulfur oil is not worth the economic expense. This argument is untimely. Economic considerations are not relevant in determining whether a PSD permit is required. Economic considerations are only evaluated in determining the control level (BACT) required under PSD. *See* 40 C.F.R. 52.21(b)(12) (1982) and 42 U.S.C. § 7479(3). Thus the economic issues are not yet ripe for review.

A policy reason for requiring PSD review, in addition to those discussed in preceding sections, is that subsequent PSD permits to other sources are premised on stability of the level of emissions from existing sources. 42 U.S.C. §§ 7470-7479. The preamble to the 1980 PSD regulations stated that "[i]n EPA's view, any switch to another fuel or raw material that would distort a prior assessment of a source's air quality impact should have to undergo [PSD] scrutiny." 45 *Fed.Reg.* 52,676, 52,704 (1980). Such distortion is exactly the effect HECO's proposed fuel switch would have. EPA notes that other projects have in fact relied upon HECO's PSD permit in calculating their air quality impact for PSD purposes. The Hawaiian Independent Refinery, Inc., located on Oahu, received a PSD permit for several preheaters on June 25, 1980, and submitted an application for a permit for a hydrogen plant on January 25, 1981. The applications for both of these projects calculated available PSD increment in the Kahe area based upon use of no greater than 0.5% sulfur fuel at Kahe Units 1-5. Any emissions increase HECO makes will consume this available PSD increment.

Thus, based on a literal reading of the applicable regulation and on policy considerations, we affirm EPA's application of the "major modification" definition to HECO's proposed fuel switch. We decline to review all other issues.

Remanded to the Environmental Protection Agency for any further proceedings.

NOTES

1. HECO seeks reconsideration of the 0.5 percent sulfur oil condition in its permit on the theory that the model used to predict the level of pollution caused by various sulfur content oils was inaccurate. Suppose HECO is correct and that 2.0 percent sulfur oil could be used by HECO without violating the PSD increments. Under the Ninth Circuit's decision, what, if anything, can HECO do to obtain a permit change that reflects a more accurate model?

2. The HECO plant was located in an area designated as nonattainment for sulfur dioxide. 723 F.2d at 1441, n.1. Why then was a PSD permit for SO_2 emissions required?

3. The court notes that if the area continues to be subject to the nonattainment requirements of the Act, a different kind of permit will be required. How will this permit differ from the PSD permit? Which will be more difficult to obtain? When should such a permit be required?

4. In 1979, HECO received a PSD permit only for Unit 6. Note, however, that the permit required as a condition that the existing Units 1-5 shift from 2.0 percent to 0.5 percent sulfur oil. When HECO tried to change Units 1-5 back to 2.0 percent sulfur oil, EPA informed HECO that such a shift would constitute a major modification and require HECO to obtain PSD permits for Units 1-5. What problems does this create for HECO? Why wasn't the original shift from 2.0 percent to 0.5 percent deemed a major modification? *See* §§ 111(a)(2), (3), (4); 169(a); 40 CFR 52.21(b)(2).

5. In seeking to change the fuel in Units 1-5 back to 2% sulfur oil, HECO argues that the NAAQS will not be violated, and that respect of PSD increments is not a relevant consideration. 723 F.2d at 1441, n. 2. Is HECO right? When was the baseline set for this PSD area under the law?

PROBLEM #5: PERMITS FOR STATIONARY SOURCES

The City of Magnolia in the State of Potomac proposes to construct a municipal incinerator capable of burning 250 tons of refuse per day. The uncontrolled emissions from the plant are estimated at 150 tons of particulates/year. (No other criteria pollutants will be emitted.) Magnolia is located in the Flower Pot Intrastate Air Quality Control Region, approximately 100 miles due east of the Tecumseh National Park, a Class I area. The Flower Pot AQCR has been designated a nonattainment area for carbon monoxide and ozone. It is an attainment area for all other criteria pollutants.

You are the Magnolia City Attorney. The City Council has asked you to explain the process for review, approval and operation of the incinerator under the federal Clean Air Act and the Potomac SIP. (Review §§ 111, 112, 129, 169(1); 169A(g)(7); 172(b)(6); 302(j), and Title V.)

In addressing this problem consider the following:

(a) whether a permit is required by Subchapter V;

(b) whether a permit is required by subchapters C and/or D of Title I of the Act;

(c) whether the facility is subject to visibility protection requirements;

(d) whether there are applicable NSPSs (*see* 40 CFR Part 60).

(e) whether the facility is (or may be) subject to the hazardous air pollutant provisions of § 112 (*See also* § 129(h)(31)

D. *Hazardous Air Pollutants*

The Clean Air Act Amendments of 1990 dramatically changed the program for regulation of hazardous air pollutants. The following case was decided under prior law and thus cannot be read to understand the current standards. Nonetheless, the case offers a useful background to the difficulties associated with regulating hazardous air pollutants and the reasons for the changes adopted in 1990.

NATURAL RESOURCES DEFENSE COUNCIL V. EPA

824 F.2d 1146, *en banc*, (D.C. Cir. 1987)

BORK, Circuit Judge:

Current scientific knowledge does not permit a finding that there is a completely safe level of human exposure to carcinogenic agents. The Administrator of the Environmental Protection Agency, however, is charged with regulating hazardous pollutants, including carcinogens, under section 112 of the Clean Air Act by setting emission standards "at the level which in his judgment provides an ample margin of safety to protect the public health." 42 U.S.C. § 7412(b)(1)(B) (1982). We address here the question of the extent of the Administrator's authority under this delegation in setting emission standards for carcinogenic pollutants.

Petitioner Natural Resources Defense Council ("NRDC") contends that the Administrator must base a decision under section 112 exclusively on health-related factors and, therefore, that the uncertainty about the effects of carcinogenic agents requires the Administrator to prohibit all emissions. The Administrator argues that in the face of this uncertainty he is authorized to set standards that require emission reduction to the lowest level attainable by best available control technology whenever that level is below that at which harm to humans has been demonstrated. We find no support for either position in the language or legislative history of the Clean Air Act. We therefore grant the petition for review and remand to the Administrator for reconsideration in light of this opinion.

I.

Section 112 of the Clean Air Act provides for regulation of hazardous air pollutants, which the statute defines as "air pollutant[s] to which no ambient air quality standard is applicable and which in the judgment of the Administrator cause[ ], or contribute[ ] to, air pollution which may reasonably be anticipated to result in an increase in mortality or an increase in serious irreversible, or incapacitating reversible, illness." 42 U.S.C. § 7412(a)(1) (1982). The statute requires the Administrator to publish a list containing each hazardous pollutant for which he intends to adopt an emission standard, to publish proposed regulations and a notice of public hearing for each such pollutant, and then, within a specified period, either to promulgate an emission standard or to make a finding that the particular agent is not a hazardous air pollutant. *See id.* § 7412(b)(1)(B). The statute directs the Administrator to set an emission standard promulgated under section 112 "at the level which in his judgment provides an ample margin of safety to protect the public health." *Id.*

This case concerns vinyl chloride regulations. Vinyl chloride is a gaseous synthetic chemical used in the manufacture of plastics and is a strong carcinogen. In late 1975, the Administrator issued a notice of proposed rulemaking to establish an emission standard for vinyl chloride. 40 Fed.Reg. 59,532 (1975). In the notice, the EPA asserted that available data linked vinyl chloride to carcinogenic, as well as some noncarcinogenic, disorders and that "[r]easonable extrapolations" from this data suggested "that present ambient levels of vinyl chloride may cause or contribute to ... [such] disorders." *Id.* at 59,533. The EPA also noted that vinyl chloride is "an apparent nonthreshold pollutant," which means that it appears to create a risk to health at all non-zero levels of emission. Scientific uncertainty, due to the unavailability of dose-response data and the twenty-year latency period between initial exposure to vinyl chloride and the occurrence of disease, makes it impossible to establish any definite threshold level below which there are no adverse effects to human health. *Id.* at 59,533-34. The notice also stated the "EPA's position that for a carcinogen it should be assumed, in the absence of strong evidence to the contrary, that there is no atmospheric concentration that poses absolutely no public health risk." *Id.* at 59,534.

Because of this assumption, the EPA concluded that it was faced with two alternative interpretations of its duty under section 112. First, the EPA determined that section 112 might require a complete prohibition of emissions of non-threshold pollutants because a "zero emission limitation would be the only emission standard which would offer absolute safety from ambient exposure." 40 Fed.Reg. at 59,534. The EPA found this alternative "neither desirable nor necessary" because "[c]omplete prohibition of all emissions could require closure of an entire industry," a cost the EPA found "extremely high for elimination of a risk to health that is of unknown dimensions." *Id.*

The EPA stated the second alternative as follows:

> An alternative interpretation of section 112 is that it authorizes setting emission standards that require emission reduction to the lowest level achievable by use of the best available control technology in cases involving apparent non-threshold pollutants, where complete emission prohibition would result in widespread industry closure and EPA has determined that the cost of such closure would be grossly disproportionate to the benefits of removing the risk that would remain after imposition of the best available control technology.

Id. The EPA adopted this alternative on the belief that it would "produce the most stringent regulation of hazardous air pollutants short of requiring a complete prohibition in all cases." *Id.*

On October 21, 1976, the EPA promulgated final emission standards for vinyl chloride which were based solely on the level attainable by the best available control technology. 41 Fed.Reg. 46,560 (1976). The EPA determined that this standard would reduce unregulated emissions by 95 percent. *Id.* With respect to the effect of the standard on health, the EPA stated that it had assessed the risk to health at ambient levels of exposure by extrapolating from dose- response data at higher levels of exposure and then made the following findings:

> EPA found that the rate of initiation of liver angiosarcoma among [the 4.6 million] people living around uncontrolled plants is expected to range from less than one to ten cases of liver angiosarcoma per year of exposure to vinyl chloride. . . . Vinyl chloride is also estimated to produce an equal number of primary cancers at other sites, for a total of somewhere between less than one and twenty cases of cancer per year of exposure among residents around plants. The number of these effects is expected to be reduced at least in proportion to the reduction in the ambient annual average vinyl chloride concentration, which is expected to be 5 percent of the uncontrolled levels after the standard is implemented.

Id. The EPA did not state whether this risk to health is significant or not. Nor did the EPA explain the relationship between this risk to health and its duty to set an emission standard which will provide an "ample margin of safety."

The Environmental Defense Fund ("EDF") filed suit challenging the standard on the ground that section 112 requires the Administrator to rely exclusively on health and prohibits consideration of cost and technology. The EDF and the EPA settled the suit, however, upon the EPA's agreement to propose new and more stringent standards for vinyl chloride and to establish an ultimate goal of zero emissions.

The EPA satisfied its obligations under the settlement agreement by proposing new regulations on June 2, 1977. While the proposal sought to impose more strict regulation by requiring sources subject to a 10 parts per million ("ppm") limit to reduce emissions to 5 ppm, and by establishing an aspirational goal of zero emissions, the EPA made it clear that it considered its previous regulations valid and reemphasized its view that the inability scientifically to identify a threshold of adverse effects did not require prohibition of all emissions, but rather permitted regulation at the level of best available technology. 42 Fed.Reg. 28,154 (1977). The EPA received comments on the proposal, but took no final action for more than seven years. On January 9, 1985, the EPA withdrew the proposal. Noting that certain aspects of the proposed regulations imposed "unreasonable" costs and that no control technology "has been demonstrated to significantly and consistently reduce emissions to a level below that required by the current standard," 50 Fed.Reg. 1182, 1184 (1985), the EPA concluded that it should abandon the 1977 proposal and propose in its place only minor revisions to the 1976 regulations.

This petition for review followed.

* * *

III.

The NRDC's challenge to the EPA's withdrawal of the 1977 amendments is simple: because the statute adopts an exclusive focus on considerations of health, the Administrator must set a zero level of emissions when he cannot determine that there is a level below which no harm will occur.

We must determine whether the EPA's actions are arbitrary, capricious, an abuse of discretion, or otherwise not in accordance with law. 42 U.S.C. § 7607(d)(9)(A) (1982). Review begins with the question of whether "Congress has directly spoken to the precise question at issue" and has expressed a clear intent as to its resolution. *Chevron, U.S.A., Inc. v. NRDC*, 467 U.S. 837, 842-43 (1984). If so, "that intention is the law and must be given effect." *Id.* at 843 n. 9. "[I]f the statute is silent or ambiguous with respect to the specific issue," we must accept an agency interpretation if it is reasonable in light of the language, legislative history, and underlying policies of the statute. *Id.* at 843; *NRDC v. Thomas*, 805 F.2d 410, 420 (D.C.Cir.1986). We find no support in the text or legislative history for the proposition that Congress intended to require a complete prohibition of emissions whenever the EPA cannot determine a threshold level for a hazardous pollutant. Instead, there is strong evidence that Congress considered such a requirement and rejected it.

Section 112 commands the Administrator to set an "emission standard" for a particular "hazardous air pollutant" which in his "judgment" will provide an "ample margin of safety." Congress' use of the term "ample margin of safety" is inconsistent with the NRDC's position that the Administrator has no discretion in the face of uncertainty. The statute nowhere defines "ample margin of safety." The Senate Report, however, in discussing a similar requirement in the context of setting ambient air standards under section 109 of the Act, explained the purpose of the "margin of safety" standard as one of affording "a reasonable degree of protection . . . against hazards which research has not yet identified." S.Rep. No. 1196, 91st Cong., 2d Sess. 10 (1970) (Emphasis added). This view comports with the historical use of the term in engineering as "a safety factor . . . meant to compensate for uncertainties and variabilities." *See* Hall, *The Control of Toxic Pollutants Under the Federal Water Pollution Control Act Amendments of 1972*, 63

Iowa L.Rev. 609, 629 (1978). Furthermore, in a discussion of the use of identical language in the Federal Water Pollution Control Act, this court has recognized that, in discharging the responsibility to assure "an ample margin of safety," the Administrator faces "a difficult task, indeed, a veritable paradox — calling as it does for knowledge of that which is unknown — [but] . . . the term 'margin of safety' is Congress's directive that means be found to carry out the task and to reconcile the paradox." Environmental Defense Fund v. EPA, 598 F.2d 62, 81 (D.C.Cir.1978). And while Congress used the modifier "ample" to exhort the Administrator not to allow "the public [or] the environment . . . to be exposed to anything resembling the maximum risk" and, therefore, to set a margin "greater than 'normal' or 'adequate,' " Congress still left the EPA "great latitude in meeting its responsibility." *See id.*

Congress' use of the word "safety," moreover, is significant evidence that it did not intend to require the Administrator to prohibit all emissions of non-threshold pollutants. As the Supreme Court has recently held, "safe" does not mean "risk-free." *Industrial Union Dep't, AFL-CIO v. American Petroleum Inst.*, 448 U.S. 607, 642 (1980). Instead, something is "unsafe" only when it threatens humans with "a significant risk of harm." *Id.*

Thus, the terms of section 112 provide little support for the NRDC's position. The uncertainty about the effects of a particular carcinogenic pollutant invokes the Administrator's discretion under section 112. In contrast, the NRDC's position would eliminate any discretion and would render the standard "ample margin of safety" meaningless as applied to carcinogenic pollutants. Whenever any scientific uncertainty existed about the ill effects of a nonzero level of hazardous air pollutants — and we think it unlikely that science will ever yield absolute certainty of safety in an area so complicated and rife with problems of measurement, modeling, long latency, and the like — the Administrator would have no discretion but would be required to prohibit all emissions. Had Congress intended that result, it could very easily have said so by writing a statute that states that no level of emissions shall be allowed as to which there is any uncertainty. But Congress chose instead to deal with the pervasive nature of scientific uncertainty and the inherent limitations of scientific knowledge by vesting in the Administrator the discretion to deal with uncertainty in each case.

* * *

IV.

We turn now to the question whether the Administrator's chosen method for setting emission levels above zero is consistent with congressional intent. The Administrator's position is that he may set an emission level for non-threshold pollutants at the lowest level achievable by best available control technology when that level is anywhere below the level of demonstrated harm and the cost of setting a lower level is grossly disproportionate to the benefits of removing the remaining risk. The NRDC argues that this standard is arbitrary and capricious because the EPA is never permitted to consider cost and technological feasibility under section 112 but instead is limited to consideration of health-based factors. Thus, before addressing the Administrator's method of using cost and technological feasibility in this case, we must determine whether he may consider cost and technological feasibility at all. *See Chemical Mfrs. Ass'n v. NRDC*, 470 U.S. 116, 134 (1985) . . .

A.

On its face, section 112 does not indicate that Congress intended to preclude consideration of any factor. Though the phrase "to protect the public health" evinces an intent to make health the primary consideration, there is no indication of the factors the Administrator may or may not consider in determining, in his "judgment," what level of emissions will provide "an ample margin of safety." Instead, the language used, and the absence of any specific limitation, gives the clear impression that the Administrator has some discretion in determining what, if any, additional factors he will consider in setting an emission standard.

B.

The petitioner argues that the legislative history makes clear Congress' intent to foreclose reliance on non-health-based considerations in setting standards under section 112. We find, however, that the legislative history can be characterized only as ambiguous.

* * *

C.

The petitioner argues next that a finding that section 112 does not preclude consideration of cost and technological feasibility would render the Clean Air Act structurally incoherent and would be inconsistent with the Supreme Court's interpretation of section 110 of the Act, *see Union Electric Co. v. EPA*, 427 U.S. 246 (1976), and this court's interpretation of section 109 of the Act, *see Lead Indus. Ass'n v. EPA*, 647 F.2d 1130 (D.C.Cir.), *cert. denied*, 449 U.S. 1042 (1980), as precluding consideration of these factors. We do not believe that our decision here is inconsistent with either the holding or the statutory interpretation in either case.

First, as discussed below, the court in each case rejected an argument that the EPA must consider cost and technological feasibility as factors equal in importance to health. We reject the same argument here. *See infra* pp. 1163-1166. In this case, however, we must also address the question of whether the Administrator may consider these factors if necessary to further protect the public health. This issue was not addressed in either *Union Electric* or *Lead Industries.*

Second, these decisions do not provide precedential support for the petitioner's position that, as a matter of statutory interpretation, cost and technological feasibility may never be considered under the Clean Air Act unless Congress expressly so provides. In each case there was some indication in the language, structure, or legislative history of the specific provision at issue that Congress intended to preclude consideration of cost and technological feasibility. As discussed above, we find no such indication with respect to section 112.

In *Union Electric*, the Court addressed the issue of whether the Administrator could reject a state implementation plan submitted for approval under section 110 of the Clean Air Act on the ground that the plan was not economically or technologically feasible. The Court noted that section 110 sets out eight criteria that a state plan must meet and further provides that if these criteria are met, and if the state adopted the plan after notice and a hearing, the Administrator "shall" approve the plan. 427 U.S. at 257. The Court then held that "[t]he mandatory 'shall' makes it quite clear that the Administrator is not to be concerned with factors other than those specified, ... and none of the eight factors appears to permit consideration of technological or economic infeasibility." *Id.* (Citation omitted). In a footnote to this statement, the Court found its position bolstered by a "[c]omparison of the eight criteria of § 110(a)(2)" with other provisions of the Act which expressly permit consideration of cost and technological feasibility. *Id.* at 257 n. 5, 96 S.Ct. at 2525 n. 5. The Court concluded that "[w]here Congress intended the

Administrator to be concerned about economic and technological infeasibility, it expressly so provided." *Id.* We simply do not, as the NRDC does, read these statements as announcing the broad rule that an agency may never consider cost and technological feasibility, under any delegation of authority, and for any purpose, unless Congress specifically provides that the agency is authorized to consider these factors. At most, we believe that these statements stand for the proposition that when Congress has specifically directed an agency to consider certain factors, the agency may not consider unspecified factors. Because Congress chose not to limit specifically the factors the Administrator may consider in section 112, this discussion in *Union Electric* is not in point here. The factors that the Administrator may consider under section 112 could conceivably include all of the specific factors listed in other parts of the Act if necessary "to protect the public health."

A similar analysis distinguishes this court's reasoning in *Lead Industries*. In *Lead Industries*, we held that the Administrator is not required to consider cost and technology under the mandate in section 109 of the Clean Air Act to promulgate primary air quality standards which "allow[ ] an adequate margin of safety . . . to protect the public health." 42 U.S.C. § 7409(b)(1) (1982). The NRDC argues that the decision in *Lead Industries*, which involved the more permissive language "adequate," rather than "ample," "margin of safety," compels the conclusion that section 112 precludes consideration of economic and technological feasibility. We think not.

The *Lead Industries* court did note that the statute on its face does not allow consideration of technological or economic feasibility, but the court based its decision that section 109 does not allow consideration of these factors in part on structural aspects of the ambient air pollution provisions that are not present here. First, besides "allowing an adequate margin of safety," ambient air standards set under section 109(b) must be based on "air quality criteria," which section 108 defines as comprising several elements, all related to health. *See* 42 U.S.C. § 7408(a)(2)(A), (B)(C)(1982). The court reasoned that the exclusion of economic and technological feasibility considerations from air quality criteria also foreclosed reliance on such factors in setting the ambient air quality standards based on those criteria. 647 F.2d at 1149 n. 37. The court also relied on the fact that state implementation plans, the means of enforcement of ambient air standards, could not take into account economic and technological feasibility if such consideration interfered with the timely attainment of ambient air standards, and that the Administrator could not consider such feasibility factors in deciding whether to approve the state plans. *Id.*; *see* 42 U.S.C. § 7410 (1982). This provided further grounds for the court to believe that Congress simply did not intend the economics of pollution control to be considered in the scheme of ambient air regulations. *See* 647 F.2d at 1149 n. 37.

In *Lead Industries*, moreover, the relevant Senate Report stated flatly that "existing sources of pollutants either should meet the standard of the law or be closed down." 647 F.2d at 1149. This is a far clearer statement than anything in the present case that Congress considered the alternatives and chose to close down sources or even industries rather than to allow risks to health.

The substantive standard imposed under the hazardous air pollutants provisions of section 112, by contrast with sections 109 and 110, is not based on criteria that enumerate specific factors to consider and pointedly exclude feasibility. Section 112(b)(1)'s command "to provide an ample margin of safety to protect the public health" is self-contained, and the absence of enumerated criteria may well evince a congressional intent for the Administrator to supply reasonable ones. . . .

* * *

V.

Since we cannot discern clear congressional intent to preclude consideration of cost and technological feasibility in setting emission standards under section 112, we necessarily find that the Administrator may consider these factors. We must next determine whether the Administrator's use of these factors in this case is "based on a permissible construction of the statute." *Chevron*, 467 U.S. at 843. We must uphold the Administrator's construction if it represents "a reasonable policy choice for the agency to make." *Id.* We cannot, however, affirm an agency interpretation found to be "arbitrary, capricious, or manifestly contrary to the statute." *Id.* at 844, 104 S.Ct. at 2782. Nor can we affirm if "it appears from the statute or its legislative history that the accommodation [chosen] is not one that Congress would have sanctioned." *United States v. Shimer*, 367 U.S. 374, 383 (1961).

Our role on review of an action taken pursuant to section 112 is generally a limited one. Because the regulation of carcinogenic agents raises questions "on the frontiers of scientific knowledge," *Industrial Union Dep't, AFL-CIO v. Hodgson*, 499 F.2d 467, 474 (D.C.Cir.1974), we have recognized that the Administrator's decision in this area "will depend to a greater extent upon policy judgments" to which we must accord considerable deference. [Citations omitted We have also acknowledged that "EPA, not the court, has the technical expertise to decide what inferences may be drawn from the characteristics of . . . substances and to formulate policy with respect to what risks are acceptable," *Environmental Defense Fund*, 598 F.2d at 83-84, and we will not second-guess a determination based on that expertise. Despite this deferential standard, we find that the Administrator has ventured into a zone of impermissible action. The Administrator has not exercised his expertise to determine an acceptable risk to health. To the contrary, in the face of uncertainty about risks to health, he has simply substituted technological feasibility for health as the primary consideration under Section 112. Because this action is contrary to clearly discernible congressional intent, we grant the petition for review.

Given the foregoing analysis of the language and legislative history of section 112, it seems to us beyond dispute that Congress was primarily concerned with health in promulgating section 112. Every action by the Administrator in setting an emission standard is to be taken "to protect the public health." In setting an emission standard for vinyl chloride, however, the Administrator has made no finding with respect to the effect of the chosen level of emissions on health. Nor has the Administrator stated that a certain level of emissions is "safe" or that the chosen level will provide an "ample margin of safety." Instead, the Administrator has substituted "best available technology" for a finding of the risk to health.

In the decision withdrawing the proposed 1977 amendments, the Administrator mentioned the risks to health, *see* 50 Fed.Reg. 1182 (1985), but based his decision solely on the finding that "there is no improved or new control technology that has been demonstrated to significantly and consistently reduce emissions to a level below that required by the current standard." *Id.* at 1184. Nowhere in the decision did the Administrator state that the 1976 emission standards provide an "ample margin of safety" such that revisions to those standards are not necessary.

In the 1977 proposal to decrease the level of emissions, the Administrator did not determine the risk to health under the then existing standard or under the proposed new standard. Nor did the Administrator explain why one standard was "safe" and the other was not. *See* 42 Fed.Reg. 28, 154-157 (1977).

The absence of any finding regarding the relationship between the risk to health at a certain level of emissions and the "ample margin of safety" standard is also evident in the Administrator's decision adopting the 1976 standards. Again, the Administrator mentioned the risks to health before and after regulation, *see* 41 Fed.Reg. 46,560 (1976), but did not provide any explanation as to whether the risk was significant, or whether the chosen standard provided an "ample margin of safety."

In the three decisions regarding emission standards for vinyl chloride, the Administrator has made one finding regarding the duty to set emission standards that will provide an "ample margin of safety." The Administrator has determined that he is not required to determine on a case-by-case basis the risk to health at a particular level of emissions or to determine the relationship between that risk and "safety." Instead, the Administrator has adopted a generic rule, which when met, will always result in an "ample margin of safety." The Administrator has determined that this standard is met whenever he sets "emission standards that require emission reduction to the lowest level achievable by use of the best available control technology in cases involving apparent non-threshold pollutants where complete emission prohibition would result in widespread industry closure and EPA has determined that the cost of such closure would be grossly disproportionate to the benefits of removing the risk that would remain after imposition of the best available control technology." 40 Fed.Reg. 59,532, 59,534 (1975).

Thus, in setting emission standards for carcinogenic pollutants, the Administrator has decided to determine first the level of emissions attainable by best available control technology. He will then determine the costs of setting the standard below that level and balance those costs against the risk to health below the level of feasibility. If the costs are greater than the reduction in risk, then he will set the standard at the level of feasibility. This exercise, in the Administrator's view, will always produce an "ample margin of safety."

If there was any doubt that the Administrator has substituted technological feasibility for health as the primary consideration in setting emission standards under section 112, that doubt was dispelled by counsel for the EPA at oral argument. In response to a question from the court regarding a carcinogenic pollutant known to cause certain harm at 100 ppm, counsel stated that the Administrator could set an emission level at 99 ppm if that was the lowest feasible level and the costs of reducing the level below 99 ppm would be grossly disproportionate to the reduction in risk to health. Given the strong inference that harm would also certainly result at 99 ppm, the Administrator appears to have concluded that the "ample margin of safety" standard does not require any finding that a level of emissions is "safe." Instead, the Administrator need only find that the costs of control are greater than the reduction in risk to health. We disagree.

We find that the congressional mandate to provide "an ample margin of safety" "to protect the public health" requires the Administrator to make an initial determination of what is "safe." This determination must be based exclusively upon the Administrator's determination of the risk to health at a particular emission level. Because the Administrator in this case did not make any finding of the risk to health, the question of how that determination is to be made is not before us. We do wish to note, however, that the Administrator's decision does not require a finding that "safe" means "risk-free," *see Industrial Union Dep't*, 448 U.S. at 642, or a finding that the determination is free from uncertainty. Instead, we find only that the Administrator's decision must be based upon an expert judgment with regard to the level of emission that will result in an "acceptable" risk to health. Environmental Defense Fund, 598 F.2d at 83-84. In this regard, the Administrator must determine what inferences should be drawn from available scientific data and decide what risks are acceptable in the world in which we live. *See Industrial Union Dep't*, 448 U.S. at 642 ("There are many activities that we engage in every day — such as driving a car or even breathing city air — that entail some risk of accident or material health impairment; nevertheless, few people would consider those activities 'unsafe.' "); *Alabama Power Co. v. Costle*, 636 F.2d 323, 360-61 (D.C.Cir.1979). This determination must be based solely upon the risk to health. The Administrator cannot under any circumstances consider cost and technological feasibility at this stage of the analysis. The latter factors have no relevance to the preliminary determination of what is safe. Of course, if the Administrator cannot find that there is an acceptable risk at any level, then the Administrator must set the level at zero.

Congress, however, recognized in section 112 that the determination of what is "safe" will always be marked by scientific uncertainty and thus exhorted the Administrator to set emission standards that will provide an "ample margin" of safety. This language permits the Administrator to take into account scientific uncertainty and to use expert discretion to determine what action should be taken in light of that uncertainty. [Citations omitted.] In determining what is an "ample margin" the Administrator may, and perhaps must, take into account the inherent limitations of risk assessment and the limited scientific knowledge of the effects of exposure to carcinogens at various levels, and may therefore decide to set the level below that previously determined to be "safe." This is especially true when a straight line extrapolation from known risks is used to estimate risks to health at levels of exposure for which no data is available. This method, which is based upon the results of exposure at fairly high levels of the hazardous pollutants, will show some risk at every level because of the rules of arithmetic rather than because of any knowledge. In fact the risk at a certain point on the extrapolated line may have no relationship to reality; there is no particular reason to think that the actual line of the incidence of harm is represented by a straight line. Thus, by its nature the finding of risk is uncertain and the Administrator must use his discretion to meet the statutory mandate. It is only at this point of the regulatory process that the Administrator may set the emission standard at the lowest level that is technologically feasible. In fact, this is, we believe, precisely the type of policy choice that Congress envisioned when it directed the Administrator to provide an "ample margin of safety." Once "safety" is assured, the Administrator should be free to diminish as much of the statistically determined risk as possible by setting the standard at the lowest feasible level. Because consideration of these factors at this stage is clearly intended "to protect the public health," it is fully consistent with the Administrator's mandate under section 112.

We wish to reiterate the limited nature of our holding in this case because it is not the court's intention to bind the Administrator to any specific method of determining what is "safe" or what constitutes an "ample margin." We hold only that the Administrator cannot consider cost and technological feasibility in determining what is "safe." This determination must be based solely upon the risk to health. The issues of whether the Administrator can proceed on a case-by-case basis, what support the Administrator must provide for the determination of what is "safe," or what other factors may be considered, are issues that must be resolved after the Administrator has reached a decision upon reconsideration of the decision withdrawing the proposed 1977 amendments.

For the foregoing reasons, the petition for review is granted, the decision withdrawing the 1977 proposed rule is vacated, and this case is hereby remanded for timely reconsideration of the 1977 proposed rule consistent with this opinion.

It is so ordered.

NOTES

1. The unanimous *en banc* opinion of Judge Bork overturns his own earlier opinion before a three-judge panel. *Natural Resources Defense Council v. EPA*, 804 F.2d 710 (D.C. Cir. 1986). In that opinion, Judge Bork distinguished between "non-threshold pollutants" which pose a certain health risk at all non-zero emission levels, and "*apparent* non-threshold pollutants", such as vinyl chloride, which *appear* to pose a risk at all non-zero emission levels. EPA discretion to set standards based on costs was deemed appropriate only in the latter case. How far does Judge Bork stray from that position in his *en banc* opinion?

2. In the *en banc* opinion, Judge Bork argues that Congress' use of the term "ample margin of safety" in describing the level at which to set emission standards, was intended to afford EPA discretion in deciding what levels of emissions were safe. How persuasive is his argument?

3. A dissenting opinion by Judge Wright in the earlier decision goes much farther in rejecting EPA's action than does the unanimous *en banc* opinion. *Id.* at 1120. Judge Wright specifically found that § 112 precluded any consideration of technological and economic feasibility. He cites an impressive array of authority to support that position. *Id.* at 1124. In particular, he notes that § 112 contains two exemptions from the emission standards established under that section which expressly allow consideration of technological and economic factors. Section 112(c)(2) authorizes the President to exempt any stationary source from compliance with the emission standards for up to two years if the technology necessary to meet the standard is unavailable, and the operation of the facility is need for national security reasons. Section 112(e)(1) authorizes EPA to promulgate a design, equipment, operational, or work standard if it is not feasible to prescribe an emission standard. Judge Wright argued that Congress would not have created exemptions for technological and feasibility reasons if such factors could be considered in setting the emission standards in the first instance. Is he right?

4. The *en banc* opinion in the *NRDC* case holds that "the Administrator cannot consider cost and technological feasibility in determining what is 'safe'." How then does EPA consider these factors in setting an emission limit "at a level which . . . provides an ample margin of safety to protect the public health?" § 112(b)(1)(B). Why does the court strike down the standards set by EPA? Does Judge Bork successfully distinguish the *Union Electric* and *Lead Industries* opinions?

5. Under the standard articulated by Judge Bork, does EPA have the discretion to decide that a risk to 100 lives per year is acceptable and that emission levels that may lead to 100 deaths per year are "safe"?

THE 1990 AMENDMENTS TO SECTION 112

Under the law in effect at the time of the *NRDC* decision, a hazardous air pollutant (HAP) was defined as "an air pollutant to which no ambient air quality standard is applicable and which . . . causes or contributes to air pollution which may reasonably be anticipated to result in an increase in mortality or an increase in serious irreversible, or incapacitating reversible illness." The 1990 Amendments dramatically lower the threshold for finding an air pollutant to be hazardous. Under § 112(b)(3)(B), a substance must be listed as a HAP if it is "known to cause, or may reasonably be anticipated to cause adverse effects to human health or adverse environmental effects." Adverse effects on the environment, however, may not be the sole basis for listing a HAP. §112(b)(2).

The 1990 Amendments have also radically altered the manner for regulating HAPs. Initially at least, regulation will be based upon technological rather than health standards. The new program has five significant parts as described below.

1. Listing HAPs. First is a list of hazardous air pollutants. Congress established a list of 189 such pollutants but the list can be modified by the EPA, on its own motion, or by petition. § 112(b)(2), (3). A petition must include supporting documentation and EPA must grant or deny a petition within 18 months. § 112 (b)(3)(A). EPA may not deny a petition solely on the grounds that it has inadequate resources or time for review, but it is not clear what remedy is available to a petitioner if EPA simply fails to act on a petition within the prescribed time.

2. Listing Categories and Classes of HAPs. By November 15, 1991, EPA was required to publish a list of categories and subcategories of sources of all listed HAPs. A proposed list containing more than 700 categories of sources was promulgated in June 1991 (56 Fed. Reg. 28548 (1991)) but a final list had not been published at the time of this writing in June, 1992. EPA is expected to consolidate categories on the final list so that it will contain fewer than 200 separate categories.

3. Phase I Emission Standards. Following publication of the list of categories of sources, EPA is required to establish emission standards for coke ovens and 40 other sources. These standards must be established by the end of 1992. § 112(e)(1)(A), (B). For 25% of the remaining sources, standards must be established by November, 1994; for 25% more sources, by November 1997; and for all sources by November 15, 2000. If EPA fails to meet its deadlines, a standard, determined *ad hoc*, will nonetheless be imposed on major sources of HAPs "equivalent to the limitation that would have applied to such source if an emission standard had been promulgated in a timely manner . . . ." § 112(j)(5). This provision does not take effect, however, until 18 months after the deadline, and then only where a Title V permit program is in effect. § 112(j)(2).

Unlike the standards imposed under prior law, Phase I emission standards are technology-based. Both new and existing sources of HAPs are required to meet the "maximum achievable control technology (MACT)." EPA is required to promulgate MACT standards for those categories and classes of facilities included on its list. This program should work much like the current NSPS program.

MACT for existing sources must be no less stringent than "the average emission limitation achieved by the best performing 12 percent" in that category. § 112(d)(3)(A). (If fewer than 30 sources exist in a category the MACT is to be based upon the best five. § 112(d)(3)(B).) Note that these are *minimum* standards, and EPA has discretion to impose more stringent standards for individual categories. For new sources, MACT may be no less stringent than "the emission control that is achieved in practice by the best controlled similar source." § 112(d)(3).

Generally, MACT standards apply to all sources of HAPs, but EPA may limit their applicability to "major sources" which are defined to include sources which emit 10 tons or more of a single HAP each year or 25 tons or more of any combination of HAPs each year. § 112(a)(1). EPA may impose separate standards for smaller "area sources." § 112(a)(2). At a minimum, such standards must reflect generally available control technology (GACT) or management practices. § 112(d)(5).

To encourage early emissions control, § 112(i)(5) allows sources to obtain a six year extension on meeting MACT if they can achieve a 90% reduction of gaseous HAPs, or a 95% reduction of particualte HAPs before applicable standards are proposed.

4. Report to Congress. By November 15, 1996, EPA is required to report to Congress on — (a) the methods of calculating the risk to public health that remains after applying MACT; (b) the public health significance of such estimated remaining risk and the technology and commercially available methods and costs of reducing such risks; (c) the actual health effects to persons living in the vicinity of HAP sources; and (d) recommendations for legislation regarding the residual risk from HAPs. The purpose of this report is to help Congress to decide whether it should enact new legislation before Phase II of the HAP program takes effect. *See* H.R. REP. NO. 490, 101st Cong., 1st Sess. 330 (1990).

5. Residual Risk — Phase II Emission Standards. Assuming that Congress does not enact new legislation, EPA is obliged to promulgate additional emission standards eight years after the promulgation of standards for particular categories or classes of sources. These Phase II standards are intended to be more like the standards required under the pre-1990 law. In particular, they must assure an ample margin of safety to protect public health, unless a more stringent standard is necessary, taking into account costs, energy, safety and other relevant factors, to prevent an adverse environmental effect. For known or suspected carcinogens, the standards must be sufficient to reduce the lifetime excess cancer risk of the most exposed person to less than one in one million.

6. Accidental Releases. In addition to the HAP regulatory program, a separate program is established under § 112 to address the accidental release of substances that are "known to cause or may reasonably be anticipated to cause death, injury or serious adverse effects to human health or the environment." § 112(r)(3). The initial list, which must be promulgated by November 15, 1992, must contain at least 100 substances which pose the greatest risk. Sixteen of these substances are listed in the statutes. *Id.*

In conjunction with this program, a five person Chemical and Safety Hazard Investigation Board is established. § 112(r)(6). The Board is responsible for, among other things, investigating accidents, issuing periodic reports with recommendations to reduce the likelihood or consequences of accidents, and issuing binding regulations regarding reporting of accidents. § 112(r)(6)(C).

NOTES

1. The hazardous air pollution program alone will add an estimated 34,000 additional sources to the new permit program. ENV. REP. (Current Developments), 1936 (Dec. 6, 1991).

2. Consider the manner in which the 1990 Amendments address the issue of risk in Phase II of the regulatory program. Assuming Congress does not amend the law, the agency must reduce the lifetime excess cancer risk to the most exposed individual to less than one in one million. If the most exposed person has less than a one in one million risk of contracting cancer, what is the likely risk to the average person? Are the Phase II standards good policy? Consider this question as you read the following article.

DISCERNIBLE RISK — A PROPOSED STANDARD FOR SIGNIFICANT RISK IN CARCINOGEN REGULATION

Cross, Byrd & Lave, 43 Admin. L. Rev. 61 (1991)

I. INTRODUCTION

Society's concerns about carcinogenic chemicals have led to the creation of several federal regulatory agencies and many statutes. Yet two decades of regulatory attempts to manage known or suspect carcinogens have led only to a morass of standards, goals and procedures. These standards and goals lack consistency across agencies and often even within a single agency. As a result, the regulatory fate of any substance, or even an industry, depends on the unpredictable vagaries of circumstances and individual decisionmakers.

The current morass accrues advantages only to lobbyists and power brokers. It delays innovation, increases the costs of doing business, and leaves workers and consumers with less protection than could easily be made available. In our judgment, improving the management of carcinogens and potential carcinogens requires articulation of a clear definition of what constitutes a "significant risk worth regulating." We will explore the need for defining significant risk, examine some proposed approaches, and present our own suggested standard.

II. THE NEED FOR SIGNIFICANT RISK THRESHOLDS IN REGULATION

Traditionally, government regulation of certain threats to public health employed standards of "unreasonable risk" or "reasonable probability of harm." Congress and the regulators understood that regulation needed to strike a balance between purity and economics—weighing, for example, the riskiness of food due to natural contaminants such as insect parts, rodent feces, or aflatoxin against the consequences of extra cost and reduced quantities or variety of food. Public health would not be improved by regulations that ensured that food was pure if that meant that little food was available at a very high price. While Food and Drug Administration (FDA) decisions provoked an occasional controversy, the system largely worked.

In contrast, people were so concerned about contracting cancer that Congress rushed to adopt Representative Delaney's infamous amendment in 1958. This amendment prohibited any food additive that had been shown to induce cancer in humans or laboratory animals. In that era, when only a dozen or so carcinogens were seen in only a few products or places, the Delaney Amendment made some sense. However, today there are more than six hundred substances shown to be carcinogenic in rodents, and these substances can be detected (in minute concentrations) nearly anywhere one looks. Under these circumstances, adherence to the Delaney Clause zero-risk approach now constitutes "a pernicious guide to regulators confronted with complicated problems."

The government faces particularly intractable problems in regulating today's hazardous pollutants, especially the putative carcinogens. Continued scientific uncertainty about the mechanisms of cancer development and cancer's long latency period make it difficult to discover causes of cancer in humans. Consequently, scientists and regulators generally rely on animal tests, which create a host of additional questions about test protocols and extrapolation to humans.

The greatest difficulty facing regulators, however, might be referred to as the "carcinogen dilemma." The first prong of the dilemma arises from the no-threshold hypothesis for carcinogens. Science has been unable to demonstrate the existence of a safe threshold of exposure for carcinogens. Regulators presume that *any* exposure to a carcinogen presents at least some risk of cancer, even though that risk may be minuscule, such as one-in-one million or less. Courts have endorsed this no-threshold assumption, observing that "[c]urrent scientific knowledge does not permit a finding that there is a completely safe level of human exposure to carcinogenic agents." The Delaney Clause, zero-risk approach to carcinogens in the environment would ban entirely discharges of all carcinogens.

This Delaney Clause approach is unrealistic, however, due to the second prong of the dilemma — at least some carcinogenic substances are essential to modern society. Literal application of the zero-risk paradigm would require the government "to shut down every manufacturing operation in the nation," which, of course, neither the Environmental Protection Agency (EPA) nor Congress would ever attempt to do, even in the name of cancer prevention. Many federal agency scientists tend to ignore the zero-risk paradigm for carcinogens. Unfortunately, elected officials find the rhetoric of zero risk appealing. When statutory or regulatory language mouths such a commitment to zero risk, it creates more insidious risks to public health. Devotion to the unrealistic zero risk paradigm deters the issuance of necessary public heath regulations and distracts regulators from pressing health concerns, with little countervailing benefit.

* * *

III. THE LEGAL CONTEXT OF SIGNIFICANT RISK THRESHOLDS

* * *

The seminal decision in carcinogen regulation is the Supreme Court's holding in *Industrial Union Department, AFL-CIO v. American Petroleum Institute*, which is commonly known as the *Benzene* decision. While this decision did not invent the concept of significant risk, it thrust the concept of a significant risk threshold into the forefront of regulatory attention. Moreover, the *Benzene* decision established a potentially broad foundation for using a significant risk test throughout federal regulation of carcinogens and other hazardous substances.

In *Benzene*, the Court reviewed OSHA's decision to reduce the occupational exposure to benzene from ten ppm (parts per million) to one ppm, a level selected as the lowest feasible in the workplace. The case presented squarely the carcinogen dilemma — benzene was an economically important petroleum product that rather clearly caused cancer at high exposure levels. Relying on the no-threshold hypothesis, OSHA declared that no level benzene exposure was safe and presented no risk assessment to justify the standard. In Justice Steven's words:

> OSHA's rationale for lowering the permissible exposure limit to 1 ppm was based, not on any finding that leukemia has ever been caused by exposure to 10 ppm of benzene and that it will not be caused by exposure to 1 ppm, but rather on a series of assumptions indicating that some leukemias might result from exposure to 10 ppm and that the number of cases might be reduced by reducing that exposure level to 1 ppm.

The American Petroleum Institute and other industry representatives challenged OSHA's standard as unnecessary and as having social costs that exceeded its social benefits.

After carefully analyzing the language of the Occupational Safety and Health Act, the Court emphasized that words such as "safe" did not necessarily mean "absolutely risk free," notwithstanding common dictionary definitions. Rather, the Act was intended "to require the elimination, as far as feasible, of *significant risks* of harm."

* * *

After establishing the requirement of a significant risk standard for OSHA, the Court implicitly recognized that the phrase "significant risk" can be as vague and undefined as any existing regulatory test. Consequently, the Court sketched out the meaning of a significant risk, for OSHA at a minimum. First, the Court ruled that the agency has the burden of proof to demonstrate the significance of a risk. Second, the Court emphasized that this burden was not a terribly onerous one. The agency need not prove significant risk "with anything approaching scientific certainty." Rather, "so long as they are supported by a body of reputable scientific thought, the Agency is free to use conservative assumptions in interpreting the data with respect to carcinogens, risking error on the side of overprotection rather than under protection." In essence, the Court's decision enabled agencies to conduct a plausible scientific risk assessment that may err on the side of conservatism.

Once the magnitude of carcinogenic risk is assessed, the Court granted the agency considerable discretion in determining whether that risk is "significant," emphasizing that any such determination would be "based largely on policy considerations." The Court provided little substantive guidance on its own view of risk significance, but it did state that a one in one thousand risk of cancer from air pollution might reasonably be considered significant, whereas a one in one billion risk of cancer from drinking chlorinated water "clearly could not be considered significant."

C. The *Vinyl Chloride* Decision

The second most prominent decision involving significant risk thresholds in carcinogen regulation is that of the United States Court of Appeals for the District of Columbia Circuit in *Natural Resources Defense Council v. EPA*, often referred to as the *Vinyl Chloride* decision. The *Vinyl Chloride* decision pointedly extended the holdings of the *Benzene* decision beyond the Occupational Safety and Health Act to the Clean Air Act and carved out a major role for significant risk analysis in the regulation of hazardous air pollutants.

In *Vinyl Chloride*, EPA had rejected the zero-risk paradigm and had based its vinyl chloride air emissions regulation on the feasibility and relative costs and benefits of controls. The court overturned this standard and held that the language of the Clean Air Act required a health-based standard and that cost or feasibility considerations were irrelevant in defining the necessary level of health production. In addition, the court elaborated on the permissible considerations and appropriate procedures for setting hazardous air pollutant standards under section 112 of the Clean Air Act.

The court rejected a zero-risk interpretation of the Act, finding it contrary to congressional intent. Citing *Benzene*, the court wrote:

> Congress' use of the word "safety," moreover, is significant evidence that it did not intend to require the Administrator to prohibit all emissions of non-threshold pollutants. As the Supreme Court has recently held, "safe" does not mean "risk-free." Instead, something is "unsafe" only when it threatens humans with "a significant risk of harm."

Thus, the EPA Administrator must make "an expert judgment with regard to the level of emission that will result in an 'acceptable' risk to health." As in *Benzene*, the court recognized the agency's broad discretion in making such a determination and emphasized that "it is not the court's intention to bind the Administrator to any specific method of determining what is 'safe' or what constitutes an 'ample margin.'" The court gave virtually no substantive guidance regarding risk significance but observed that many activities involving a risk of death are considered "acceptable in the world in which we live."

D. Other Significant Risk Decisions

While *Benzene* and *Vinyl Chloride* are landmark decisions mandating a significant risk test for carcinogen regulation, a number of other cases have grappled with the issue of what risks are legally significant. Courts have reviewed a number of OSHA standards under the Supreme Court's significant risk requirement. In reviewing OSHA's asbestos standard, a court affirmed that a risk of forty-four extra cancer deaths per thousand could be significant. Upon review of OSHA's standard for ethylene oxide, the court accepted that twelve to twenty-three excess deaths per ten thousand would be significant. Review of OSHA's arsenic standard observed that 2.2 excess deaths per thousand "easily exceeds the excess risk of one per thousand that the Supreme Court stated 'a reasonable person might well consider . . . significant.'" Although none of the courts elaborated on standards for risk significance, an overriding theme in their decisions is judicial recognition of the broad discretion accorded OSHA in deciding what risks should be considered significant.

Perhaps the most extensive judicial analysis of significant risk is found in dicta in the D.C. Circuit's analysis of the Delaney Clause. Describing risks below one-in-one million, the court found it "altogether correct to characterize these risks as trivial." As the court elaborated:

> [A] consumer would run a one-in-a-million lifetime risk of cancer if he or she ate *one* peanut with the FDA-permitted level of aflatoxins once every *250* days (liver cancer). Another activity posing a one-in-a-million lifetime risk is spending 1,000 minutes (less than 17 hours) every year in the city of Denver—with its high elevation and cosmic radiation levels—rather than in the District of Columbia. Most of us would not regard these as high-risk activities. Those who indulge in them can hardly be thought of as living dangerously. Indeed, they are risks taken without a second thought by persons whose economic position allows them a broad range of choice . . . .
>
> . . . [A] person would have to be exposed to more than 2,000 chemicals bearing the one-in-a-million lifetime risk, at the rates assumed in the risk assessment, in order to reach 100th the risk involved in smoking.

* * *

At best, the decisions may suggest that a significant risk lies somewhere between one in one million and one in one thousand. This leaves quite a broad range, and courts have made it clear that the significant risk determination is within agency discretion. Moreover, the courts have not considered other important issues, such as whether agencies should rely on average or maximum individual risk. As a result, regulators still have a relatively clean slate upon which to determine risk significance.

IV. IDENTIFYING THE CHARACTERISTICS OF RISK SIGNIFICANCE

Before determining the magnitude of cancer risk that should be considered significant, we must identify the characteristics by which risk significance is to be measured. The first task is to settle upon a "currency" of risk—some internally consistent measure of risk quantity. Second, we must consider external factors, beyond the simple quantity of risk, that may influence the decision on risk significance.

In selecting a currency of risk, we can choose from among at least four alternatives:

1. *average lifetime (or perhaps annual) risk* (a measure of the probability of incurring cancer for the average member of the exposed population, usually expressed in probablistic terms, such as 1 x 10^{-5});
2. *maximum lifetime (or perhaps annual) risk* (a measure of the probability of incurring cancer for the maximally exposed member or subgroup of the exposed population, usually expressed in probablistic terms, such as 1 x 10^{-4});
3. *annual expected cancers* (a measure of the additional number of cancers to be expected each year in the exposed population, expressed in numeric terms, such as twelve cancers); or
4. *reduced life expectancy* (a measure of the average life expectancy lost due to cancer in the exposed population, expressed in terms of time, such as thirty-five hundred hours).

Each of these potential currencies for risk has its benefits and drawbacks. Initially, we may dismiss reduced life expectancy as a comparative test for regulating carcinogens. Because the delay between first exposure to a carcinogen and the onset of cancer usually is measured in decades, death from cancer is arguably less of a concern than death from an auto crash, which often kills early in life. A notable exception occurs with children exposed to a leukemogen, since the latency period for leukemia is relatively short. While the life expectancy measure is able to compare different types of hazards, such as carcinogen exposures and household accidents, reduced life expectancy contributes little to comparisons between types of carcinogens.

The remaining three currencies each possess some merit. Average lifetime risk reflects the average hazard that most individuals face; this measure is most frequently referenced in court decisions on significant risk. Maximum lifetime risk reflects the hazard that might be posed to a highly exposed individual; this measure recognizes our traditional concern for the welfare of each individual. Total population risk reflects the magnitude of the risk to the entire exposed population and is most relevant if our concern is the absolute reduction of deaths due to cancer. Fortunately, we need not make a definitive choice among these currencies but can define risk significance so as to encompass consideration of each measure.

The selection of risk currency does not permit regulators to establish an inviolable level of significant risk. Other features should play some role in significant risk determinations. First, the degree of confidence in the underlying scientific finding of carcinogenicity should be considered. While risk assessments of two different substances may present the same estimate of risk, one may be based upon unfounded human epidemiological evidence of carcinogenicity, while the other may be based upon cautious and debatable extrapolations from a limited animal bioassay. The threat presented by the first substance is more certain.

Second, the exposure estimates (part of the risk calculation) can vary greatly in accuracy. Some exposure estimates are based on actual measurements, in contrast to the maximally exposed individual whose exposure is hypothetical and often unrealistic. Under the Clean Air Act, the maximally exposed individual has been defined as an implausible imaginary person who lives twenty-four hours a day for seventy years at the downwind fence line of a plant.

Third, the context of a risk bears upon its significance. For example, higher risks may be acceptable for occupational exposures to carcinogens than for public environmental exposures. Other types of risks, such as large-scale, catastrophic risks, may be particularly feared by the American public, and a significant risk test might consider such public preferences.

Fourth, the level of risk deemed significant may depend on the type of regulatory restriction under contemplation. When reviewing a standard requiring medical surveillance of workers exposed to cotton dust, a federal appellate court ruled that "*Benzene* dictates a significant risk analysis for monitoring requirements considerably laxer than for other workplace standards." Perhaps the significant risk threshold should be lower for less burdensome and costly types of regulation. A similar interpretation in *Vinyl Chloride* led to the conclusion that consideration of cost and feasibility may be incorporated when selecting the size of the margin of safety required under the Clean Air Act once an exclusively health-based standard has been met.

* * *

VI. THE DISCERNIBLE RISK STANDARD

Identifying any risk, especially a significant risk, has its basis in the physical concept of a manifest, observable, or detectable event. Interpreting the meaning of some observed events, however, is extremely difficult. For example, suppose that one worker in a particular plant or one person in a community contracts cancer. Do these occurrences mean that the workers or residents are being exposed to a chemical carcinogen?

Unfortunately, many workers and consumers contract cancer daily, and the vast majority of these unfortunate events are unrelated to environmental carcinogens in the workplace or community. The popular notion is that some workplaces are so dangerous that the cancer would be endemic, as occurred, for example, with men working on top of coke ovens for longer than a decade or asbestos insulation workers. In these cases, there is no question that something must be done as promptly as possible.

Once these obvious cases have been resolved, what remains are cases where the effects are more subtle. The United States has tens of thousands of plants that employ fifty or more workers. In which of these plants are workers exposed to significant amounts of carcinogens? Current data allow, with some difficulty, a compilation of the incidence of cancer among present and past workers. With a bit of work, the expected incidence of cancer can be calculated. The incidence of cancer is related to genetic inheritance, diet, tobacco use, sexual behavior, and occupational exposure, among other factors. The workers in one plant might have less healthy diets, or more of them might smoke or otherwise increase the incidence of cancer in a way unrelated to occupational exposures. Epidemiologists attempt to control for these other factors when examining the incidence of cancer in a workplace. In addition, the incidence of cancer seems to have a large random component, which suggests that scientists do not understand all the causes of cancer.

If all workplaces in the United States were surveyed, just under half would have cancer incidences greater than the median. If the survey were repeated in the following year, again just under half of the workplaces would have more cancer than the median, but the set of plants would be somewhat different. A plant whose number of cancer incidences was high in one year and low in the next probably would not have exposed workers to high levels of carcinogens. It follows that, if OSHA tried to regulate all plants that had a higher than median incidence of cancer in one year, it would squander its resources and the nation's resources. Since many of these plants would be found to have a lower than median incidence in the following year even absent increased regulation, arguably there would be little reason to be alarmed.

Epidemiologists use the criterion of "statistical significance" to decide when the elevated incidence of cancer is unlikely to have occurred by chance. While there is the possibility that a plant exposing workers to low levels of carcinogens might not lead to a statistically significant increase in cancer, that plant's cancer increase would be relatively small. The level of statistical significance is an attempt to balance the number of cases where the plant was indicted for exposing its workers to carcinogens (although this was not true) against the number of cases where the plant was missed, even though it did expose workers to carcinogens.

The ability to detect a "significant" increase in some cancer rate is related to the total incidence of disease and the size of the population. For example, the cancer death rate in the United States population is about 20 percent. Among a population of one hundred people, twenty of them would be expected to die of cancer, but it would not be surprising if the observed number of cancer deaths were anywhere between twelve and twenty-eight, due to chance. Only if the number of cancer deaths were twenty-nine or greater would it be unlikely (less than one chance in twenty) that the population was not uniquely exposed to any carcinogen. Similarly, if the population in question were ten thousand people, the number of cases of cancer would have to be greater than 2,080 before the numbers indicated that it was unlikely that this number of cancers came from an ordinary group that was not exposed to a carcinogen. In a small population, the observed number of cancers would have to be at least 45 percent greater than the expected number (20 percent) before it would be taken seriously by biostatisticians. In a larger population, the increase need only be slightly greater than 4 percent over the expected percentage to be taken seriously.

If the type of cancer were extremely unusual, observation of even a single case would be likely to raise suspicions and observation of two cases would be likely to be sufficient to indicate the presence of a carcinogen. For example, when several cases of angiosarcoma of the liver, an extremely rare cancer, were found among the workers at a B.F. Goodrich plant that made vinyl plastic, epidemiologists knew immediately that there was a problem.

* * *

The two examples above suggest that the intrinsic ability to discern a risk to the individual varies with the size of the population (among other factors). If we expect twenty cases in a population of one hundred and statisticians would attribute any increase less than twenty-eight cases to chance, the lowest discernible individual risk is approximately 8/100 or 8×10^{-2}. In a population of ten thousand people, however, the lowest discernible cancer risk from the same exposure would be 80/10,000 or 8×10^{-3}. Risks lower than these could not be detected from a lifetime study of the population.

All other things being equal, the ability to discern the difference between an increase in individual risk and chance fluctuation in background incidence will increase as population size increases. This scientific barrier to the detection of smaller increases in individual risk means neither that small risks are absent nor that small risk increases cannot be an appropriate subject of social concern. It does mean, however, that the smaller risks cannot be said to be *significant* in a statistical sense.

* * *

[The authors conclude that federal agencies should regulate only those cases where the agency detects a statistically significant risk.]

PROBLEM #6: TECHNOLOGY-BASED STANDARDS

Match the technology-based standard that applies to the source. (More than one standard may apply to any given source.)

SOURCE

a. A new petroleum refinery in a PSD area that will emit 200 tons of SO_2, 150 tons of particulate matter, and 150 tons of CO each year. This facility will also emit currently unknown amounts of toluene, reylenes, and benzene each year.

b. A new magnetic tape coating facility in a PSD area that will emit 200 tons of VOCs per year.

c. A new magnetic tape coating facility in a severe ozone nonattainment area which will emit 50 tons of VOCs each year.

d. An existing coal-fired power plant (built in 1965) which emits 25,000 tons of SO_2, 10,000 tons of NO_x and 20,000 tons of particulate matter each year and is located in a PSD area. This facility will emit currently unknown amounts of arsenic and lead.

e. An existing coal-fired power plant (as described at (d) above) in a SO_2 nonattainment area.

STANDARD

BACT

BART

GACT

LAER

MACT

NSPS

RACT

E. The Emissions Trading Program

CHEVRON U.S.A., INC. v. NATURAL RESOURCES DEFENSE COUNCIL

467 U.S. 837 (1984)

Justice STEVENS delivered the opinion of the Court.

In the Clean Air Act Amendments of 1977, Pub.L. 95-95, 91 Stat. 685, Congress enacted certain requirements applicable to States that had not achieved the national air quality standards established by the Environmental Protection Agency (EPA) pursuant to earlier legislation. The amended Clean Air Act required these "nonattainment" States to establish a permit program regulating "new or modified major stationary sources" of air pollution. Generally, a permit may not be issued for a new or modified major stationary source unless several stringent conditions are met. The EPA regulation promulgated to implement this permit requirement allows a State to adopt a plant-wide definition of the term "stationary source." Under this definition, an existing plant that contains several pollution-emitting devices may install or modify one piece of equipment without meeting the permit conditions if the alteration will not increase the total emissions from the plant. The question presented by this case is whether EPA's decision to allow States to treat all of the pollution-emitting devices within the same industrial grouping as though they were encased within a single "bubble" is based on a reasonable construction of the statutory term "stationary source."

I

The EPA regulations containing the plant-wide definition of the term stationary source were promulgated on October 14, 1981. 46 Fed.Reg. 50766. Respondents filed a timely petition for review in the United States Court of Appeals for the District of Columbia Circuit pursuant to 42 U.S.C. § 7607(b)(1). The Court of Appeals set aside the regulations. *National Resources Defense Council, Inc. v. Gorsuch*, 685 F.2d 718 (1982).

The court observed that the relevant part of the amended Clean Air Act "does not explicitly define what Congress envisioned as a 'stationary source', to which the permit program . . . should apply," and further stated that the precise issue was not "squarely addressed in the legislative history." 685 F.2d at 723. In light of its conclusion that the legislative history bearing on the question was "at best contradictory," it reasoned that "the purposes of the nonattainment program should guide our decision here." 685 F.2d at 726, n. 39. Based on two of its precedents concerning the applicability of the bubble concept to certain Clean Air Act programs, the court stated that the bubble concept was "mandatory" in programs designed merely to maintain existing air quality, but held that it was "inappropriate" in programs enacted to improve air quality. 685 F.2d at 726. Since the purpose of the permit program — its "*raison d'etre*," in the court's view — was to improve air quality, the court held that the bubble concept was inapplicable in this case under its prior precedents. *Ibid.* It therefore set aside the regulations embodying the bubble concept as contrary to law. We granted certiorari to review that judgment, 461 U.S. 956 (1983), and we now reverse.

The basic legal error of the Court of Appeals was to adopt a static judicial definition of the term stationary source when it had decided that Congress itself had not commanded that definition. Respondents do not defend the legal reasoning of the Court of Appeals.[7] Nevertheless, since this Court reviews judgments, not opinions, we must determine whether the Court of Appeals' legal error resulted in an erroneous judgment on the validity of the regulations.

---

[7] Respondents argued below that EPA's plant-wide definition of stationary source is contrary to the terms, legislative history, and the purposes of the amended Clean Air Act. The court below rejected respondents argument based on the language and legislative history of the Act. It did agree with respondents contention that the regulations were inconsistent with the purposes of the Act, but did not adopt the construction of the statute advanced by the respondents here. Respondents rely on the arguments rejected by the Court of Appeals in support of the judgment, and may rely on any ground that finds support in the record. *See Ryerson v. United States*, 312 U.S. 405, 408 (1941); *LeTulle v. Scofield*, 308 U.S. 415, 421 (1940); *Langnes v. Green*, 282 U.S. 531, 533-539 (1931).

II

When a court reviews an agency's construction of the statute which it administers, it is confronted with two questions. First, always, is the question whether Congress has directly spoken to the precise question at issue. If the intent of Congress is clear, that is the end of the matter; for the court, as well as the agency, must give effect to the unambiguously expressed intent of Congress. If, however, the court determines Congress has not directly addressed the precise question at issue, the court does not simply impose its own construction on the statute, as would be necessary in the absence of an administrative interpretation. Rather, if the statute is silent or ambiguous with respect to the specific issue, the question for the court is whether the agency's answer is based on a permissible construction of the statute.

"The power of an administrative agency to administer a congressionally created . . . program necessarily requires the formulation of policy and the making of rules to fill any gap left, implicitly or explicitly, by Congress." *Morton v. Ruiz*, 415 U.S. 199, 231 (1974). If Congress has explicitly left a gap for the agency to fill, there is an express delegation of authority to the agency to elucidate a specific provision of the statute by regulation. Such legislative regulations are given controlling weight unless they are arbitrary, capricious, or manifestly contrary to the statute. Sometimes the legislative delegation to an agency on a particular question is implicit rather than explicit. In such a case, a court may not substitute its own construction of a statutory provision for a reasonable interpretation made by the administrator of an agency.

* * *

IV

The Clean Air Act Amendments of 1977 are a lengthy, detailed, technical, complex, and comprehensive response to a major social issue. A small portion of the statute — 91 Stat. 745-751 (Part D of Title I of the amended Act, 42 U.S.C. § 7501-7508) — expressly deals with nonattainment areas. The focal point of this controversy is one phrase in that portion of the Amendments.

Basically, the statute required each State in a nonattainment area to prepare and obtain approval of a new SIP by July 1, 1979. In the interim those States were required to comply with the EPA's interpretative ruling of December 21, 1976. 91 Stat. 745. The deadline for attainment of the primary NAAQS's was extended until December 31, 1982, and in some cases until December 31, 1987, but the SIP's were required to contain a number of provisions designed to achieve the goals as expeditiously as possible.

Most significantly for our purposes, the statute provided that each plan shall:

> (6) require permits for the construction and operation of new or modified major stationary sources in accordance with section 173 . . . . 91 Stat. 747.

Before issuing a permit, § 173 requires the state agency to determine that (1) there will be sufficient emissions reductions in the region to offset the emissions from the new source and also to allow for reasonable further progress toward attainment, or that the increased emissions will not exceed an allowance for growth established pursuant to § 172(b)(5); (2) the applicant must certify that his other sources in the State are in compliance with the SIP, (3) the agency must determine that the applicable SIP is otherwise being implemented, and (4) the proposed source complies with the lowest achievable emission rate (LAER).

The 1977 Amendments contain no specific reference to the "bubble concept." Nor do they contain a specific definition of the term "stationary source," though they did not disturb the definition of "stationary source" contained in § 111(a)(3), applicable by the terms of the Act to the NSPS program. Section 302(j), however, defines the term "major stationary source" as follows:

> (j) Except as otherwise expressly provided, the terms "major stationary source" and "major emitting facility" mean any stationary facility or source of air pollutants which directly emits, or has the potential to emit, one hundred tons per year or more of any air pollutant (including any major emitting facility or source of fugitive emissions of any such pollutant, as determined by rule by the Administrator). 91 Stat. 770.

V

The legislative history of the portion of the 1977 Amendments dealing with nonattainment areas does not contain any specific comment on the "bubble concept" or the question whether a plant-wide definition of a stationary source is permissible under the permit program. It does, however, plainly disclose that in the permit program Congress sought to accommodate the conflict between the economic interest in permitting capital improvements to continue and the environmental interest in improving air quality. Indeed, the House Committee Report identified the economic interest as one of the "two main purposes" of this section of the bill. It stated:

> Section 117 of the bill, adopted during full committee markup establishes a new section 127 of the Clean Air Act. The section has two main purposes: (1) to allow reasonable economic growth to continue in an area while making reasonable further progress to assure attainment of the standards by a fixed date; and (2) to allow States greater flexibility for the former purpose than EPA's present interpretative regulations afford.
>
> The new provision allows States with nonattainment areas to pursue one of two options. First, the State may proceed under EPA's present 'tradeoff' or 'offset' ruling. The Administrator is authorized, moreover, to modify or amend that ruling in accordance with the intent and purposes of this section.
>
> The State's second option would be to revise its implementation plan in accordance with this new provision. H.R.Rep. No. 95-294, p. 211 (1977), U.S.Code Cong. & Admin.News 1977, pp. 1077, 1290.

* * *

VI

As previously noted, prior to the 1977 Amendments, the EPA had adhered to a plant-wide definition of the term "source" under a NSPS program. After adoption of the 1977 Amendments, proposals for a plant-wide definition were considered in at least three formal proceedings.

In January 1979, the EPA considered the question whether the same restriction on new construction in nonattainment areas that had been included in its December 1976 ruling should be required in the revised SIP's that were scheduled to go into effect in July 1979. After noting that the 1976 ruling was ambiguous on the question "whether a plant with a number of different processes and emission points would be considered a single source," 44 Fed.Reg. 3276 (1979), the EPA, in effect, provided a bifurcated answer to that question. In those areas that did not have a revised SIP in effect by July 1979, the EPA rejected the plant-wide definition; on the other hand, it expressly concluded that the plant-wide approach would be permissible in certain circumstances if authorized by an approved SIP. It stated:

> Where a state implementation plan is revised and implemented to satisfy the requirements of Part D, including the reasonable further progress requirement, the plan requirements for major modifications may exempt modifications of existing facilities that are accompanied by intrasource offsets so that there is no net increase in emissions. The agency endorses such exemptions, which would provide greater flexibility to sources to effectively manage their air emissions at least cost. *Ibid.*

In April, and again in September 1979, the EPA published additional comments in which it indicated that revised SIP's could adopt the plant-wide definition of source in nonattainment areas in certain circumstances. *See id.*, at 20372, 20379, 51951, 51924, 51958. On the latter occasion, the EPA made a formal rulemaking proposal that would have permitted the use of the "bubble concept" for new installations within a plant as well as for modifications of existing units. It explained:

> "Bubble" Exemption: The use of offsets inside the same source is called the "bubble." EPA proposes use of the definition of "source" (*see above*) to limit the use of the bubble under nonattainment requirements in the following respects:
>
> i. Part D SIPs that include all requirements needed to assure reasonable further progress and attainment by the deadline under section 172 and that are being carried out need not restrict the use of a plant-wide bubble, the same as under the PSD proposal.
>
> ii. Part D SIPs that do not meet the requirements specified must limit use of the bubble by including a definition of "installation" as an identifiable piece of process equipment.

Significantly, the EPA expressly noted that the word "source" might be given a plant-wide definition for some purposes and a narrower definition for other purposes. It wrote:

> Source means any building structure, facility, or installation which emits or may emit any regulated pollutant. "Building, structure, facility or installation" means plant in PSD areas and in nonattainment areas except where the growth prohibitions would apply or where no adequate SIP exists or is being carried out. *Id.*, at 51925.

The EPA's summary of its proposed ruling discloses a flexible rather than rigid definition of the term "source" to implement various policies and programs:

> In summary, EPA is proposing two different ways to define source for different kinds of NSR programs:
>
> (1) For PSD and complete Part D SIPs, review would apply only to plants, with an unrestricted plant-wide bubble.
>
> (2) For the offset ruling, restrictions on construction, and incomplete Part D SIPs, review would apply to both plants and individual pieces of process equipment, causing the plant-wide bubble not to apply for new and modified major pieces of equipment.
>
> In addition, for the restrictions on construction, EPA is proposing to define "major modification" so as to prohibit the bubble entirely. Finally, an alternative discussed but not favored is to have only pieces of process equipment reviewed, resulting in no plant-wide bubble and allowing minor pieces of equipment to escape NSR regardless of whether they are within a major plant. *Id.*, at 51934.

In August 1980, however, the EPA adopted a regulation that, in essence, applied the basic reasoning of the Court of Appeals in this case. The EPA took particular note of the two then — recent Court of Appeals decisions, which had created the bright-line rule that the bubble concept should be employed in a program designed to maintain air quality but not in one designed to enhance air quality. Relying heavily on those cases,

EPA adopted a dual definition of "source" for nonattainment areas that required a permit whenever a change in either the entire plant, or one of its components, would result in a significant increase in emissions even if the increase was completely offset by reductions elsewhere in the plant. The EPA expressed the opinion that this interpretation was "more consistent with congressional intent" than the plant-wide definition because it "would bring in more sources or modifications for review" 45 Fed.Reg. 52697 (1980), but its primary legal analysis was predicated on the two Court of Appeals decisions.

In 1981 a new administration took office and initiated a "Government-wide reexamination of regulatory burdens and complexities." 46 Fed.Reg. 16281. In the context of that review, the EPA reevaluated the various arguments that had been advanced in connection with the proper definition of the term "source" and concluded that the term should be given the same definition in both nonattainment areas and PSD areas.

In explaining its conclusion, the EPA first noted that the definitional issue was not squarely addressed in either the statute or its legislative history and therefore that the issue involved an agency "judgment as how to best carry out the Act." *Ibid.* It then set forth several reasons for concluding that the plant-wide definition was more appropriate. It pointed out that the dual definition "can act as a disincentive to new investment and modernization by discouraging modifications to existing facilities" and "can actually retard progress in air pollution control by discouraging replacement of older, dirtier processes or pieces of equipment with new, cleaner ones." *Ibid.* Moreover, the new definition "would simplify EPA's rules by using the same definition of 'source' for PSD, nonattainment new source review and the construction moratorium. This reduces confusion and inconsistency." *Ibid.* Finally, the agency explained that additional requirements that remained in place would accomplish the fundamental purposes of achieving attainment with NAAQ's as expeditiously as possible. These conclusions were expressed in a proposed rulemaking in August 1981 that was formally promulgated in October. *See id.*, at 50766.

VII

In this Court respondents expressly reject the basic rationale of the Court of Appeals' decision. That court viewed the statutory definition of the term "source" as sufficiently flexible to cover either a plant-wide definition, a narrower definition covering each unit within a plant, or a dual definition that could apply to both the entire "bubble" and its components. It interpreted the policies of the statute, however, to mandate the plantwide definition in programs designed to maintain clean air and to forbid it in programs designed to improve air quality. Respondents place a fundamentally different construction on the statute. They contend that the text of the Act requires the EPA to use a dual definition—if either a component of a plant, or the plant as a whole, emits over 100 tons of pollutant, it is a major stationary source. They thus contend that the EPA rules adopted in 1980, insofar as they apply to the maintenance of the quality of clean air, as well as the 1981 rules which apply to nonattainment areas, violate the statute.

Statutory Language

The definition of the term stationary source in § 111(a)(3) refers to "any building, structure, facility, or installation" which emits air pollution. *See supra*, at 2784. This definition is applicable only to the NSPS program by the express terms of the statute;

the text of the statute does not make this definition applicable to the permit program. Petitioners therefore maintain that there is no statutory language even relevant to ascertaining the meaning of stationary source in the permit program aside from § 302(j), which defines the term major stationary source. *See supra*, at 2786. We disagree with petitioners on this point.

The definition in § 302(j) tells us what the word "major" means — a source must emit at least 100 tons of pollution to qualify — but it sheds virtually no light on the meaning of the term "stationary source." It does equate a source with a facility — a "major emitting facility" and a "major stationary source" are synonymous under § 302(j). The ordinary meaning of the term facility is some collection of integrated elements which has been designed and constructed to achieve some purpose. Moreover, it is certainly no affront to common English usage to take a reference to a major facility or a major source to connote an entire plant as opposed to its constituent parts. Basically, however, the language of § 302(j) simply does not compel any given interpretation of the term source.

Respondents recognize that, and hence point to § 111(a)(3). Although the definition in that section is not literally applicable to the permit program, it sheds as much light on the meaning of the word source as anything in the statute. As respondents point out, use of the words "building, structure, facility, or installation," as the definition of source, could be read to impose the permit conditions on an individual building that is a part of a plant. A "word may have a character of its own not to be submerged by its association." *Russell Motor Car Co. v. United States*, 261 U.S. 514, 519 (1923). On the other hand, the meaning of a word must be ascertained in the context of achieving particular objectives, and the words associated with it may indicate that the true meaning of the series is to convey a common idea. The language may reasonably be interpreted to impose the requirement on any discrete, but integrated, operation which pollutes. This gives meaning to all of the terms — a single building, not part of a larger operation, would be covered if it emits more than 100 tons of pollution, as would any facility, structure, or installation. Indeed, the language itself implies a bubble concept of sorts: each enumerated item would seem to be treated as if it were encased in a bubble. While respondents insist that each of these terms must be given a discrete meaning, they also argue that § 111(a)(3) defines "source" as that term is used in § 302(j). The latter section, however, equates a source with a facility, whereas the former defines source as a facility, among other items.

We are not persuaded that parsing of general terms in the text of the statute will reveal an actual intent of Congress. We know full well that this language is not dispositive; the terms are overlapping and the language is not precisely directed to the question of the applicability of a given term in the context of a larger operation. To the extent any congressional "intent" can be discerned from this language, it would appear that the listing of overlapping, illustrative terms was intended to enlarge, rather than to confine, the scope of the agency's power to regulate particular sources in order to effectuate the policies of the Act.

* * *

The fact that the agency has from time to time changed its interpretation of the term source does not, as respondents argue, lead us to conclude that no deference should be accorded the agency's interpretation of the statute. An initial agency interpretation is not instantly carved in stone. On the contrary, the agency, to engage in informed rulemaking, must consider varying interpretations and the wisdom of its policy on a continuing basis. Moreover, the fact that the agency has adopted different definitions in different contexts adds force to the argument that the definition itself is flexible, particularly since Congress has never indicated any disapproval of a flexible reading of the statute.

Significantly, it was not the agency in 1980, but rather the Court of Appeals that read the statute inflexibly to command a plantwide definition for programs designed to maintain clean air and to forbid such a definition for programs designed to improve air quality. The distinction the court drew may well be a sensible one, but our labored review of the problem has surely disclosed that it is not a distinction that Congress ever articulated itself, or one that the EPA found in the statute before the courts began to review the legislative work product. We conclude that it was the Court of Appeals, rather than Congress or any of the decisionmakers who are authorized by Congress to administer this legislation, that was primarily responsible for the 1980 position taken by the agency.

Policy

The arguments over policy that are advanced in the parties' briefs create the impression that respondents are now waging in a judicial forum a specific policy battle which they ultimately lost in the agency and in the 32 jurisdictions opting for the bubble concept, but one which was never waged in the Congress. Such policy arguments are more properly addressed to legislators or administrators, not to judges. [38]

In this case, the Administrator's interpretation represents a reasonable accommodation of manifestly competing interests and is entitled to deference: the regulatory scheme is technical and complex, the agency considered the matter in a detailed and reasoned fashion, and the decision involves reconciling conflicting policies. Congress intended to accommodate both interests, but did not do so itself on the level of specificity presented by this case. Perhaps that body consciously desired the Administrator to strike the balance at this level, thinking that those with great expertise and charged with responsibility for administering the provision would be in a better position to do so; perhaps it simply did not consider the question at this level; and perhaps Congress was unable to forge a coalition on either side of the question, and those on each side decided to take their chances with the scheme devised by the agency. For judicial purposes, it matters not which of these things occurred.

Judges are not experts in the field, and are not part of either political branch of the Government. Courts must, in some cases, reconcile competing political interests, but not on the basis of the judges' personal policy preferences. In contrast, an agency to which Congress has delegated policy-making responsibilities may, within the limits of that delegation, properly rely upon the incumbent administration's views of wise policy to inform its judgments. While agencies are not directly accountable to the people, the Chief Executive is, and it is entirely appropriate for this political branch of the Government to make such policy choices — resolving the competing interests which

---

[38] Respondents point out if a brand new factory that will emit over 100 tons of pollutants is constructed in a nonattainment area, that plant must obtain a permit pursuant to § 172(b)(6) and in order to do so, it must satisfy the § 173 conditions, including the LAER requirement. Respondents argue if an old plant containing several large emitting units is to be modernized by the replacement of one or more units emitting over 100 tons of pollutant with a new unit emitting less — but still more than 100 tons — the result should be no different simply because "it happens to be built not at a new site, but within a pre-existing plant." Brief for Respondents 4.

Congress itself either inadvertently did not resolve, or intentionally left to be resolved by the agency charged with the administration of the statute in light of everyday realities.

When a challenge to an agency construction of a statutory provision, fairly conceptualized, really centers on the wisdom of the agency's policy, rather than whether it is a reasonable choice within a gap left open by Congress, the challenge must fail. In such a case, federal judges — who have no constituency — have a duty to respect legitimate policy choices made by those who do. The responsibilities for assessing the wisdom of such policy choices and resolving the struggle between competing views of the public interest are not judicial ones: "Our Constitution vests such responsibilities in the political branches." *TVA v. Hill*, 437 U.S. 153, 195 (1978).

We hold that the EPA's definition of the term "source" is a permissible construction of the statute which seeks to accommodate progress in reducing air pollution with economic growth. "The Regulations which the Administrator has adopted provide what the agency could allowably view as . . . [an] effective reconciliation of these twofold ends . . . ." *United States v. Shimer*, 367 U.S. at 383.

The judgment of the Court of Appeals is reversed.

[Justice MARSHALL and Justice REHNQUIST did not participate in the consideration or decision of these cases. Justice O'CONNOR did not participate in the decision of these cases.]

NOTES

1. The Natural Resources Defense Council did not even attempt to defend the reasoning of the Court of Appeals in the proceedings before the Supreme Court. Why? What was the argument put forth by NRDC?

2. Before the *Chevron* decision, the Court of Appeals for the District of Columbia Circuit had approved the use of "bubbles," but only in PSD areas. *Compare Alabama Power Co. v. Costle,* 636 F.2d 323 (D.C. Cir. 1979) *with ASARCO, Inc. v. EPA*, 578 F.2d 319 (D.C. Cir. 1978). What was the basis for the court's distinction? *See Alabama Power*, 636 F.2d at 392.

3. Consider the problem with "bubbles" posed by the NRDC at note 38 of the opinion. The Court responds by describing the problem as a "policy argument." Is the bubble concept good policy? In this context, compare the permit requirements for major stationary sources in nonattainment areas at § 173 with the requirements established under the bubble program, *infra* at 252.

4. The Court finds that "[t]he fact the agency has from time to time changed its interpretation of the term source does not, as respondents argue, lead us to conclude that no deference should be accorded the agency's interpretation of the statute." On the other hand, the Court has suggested in several other recent cases, that "[a]n agency interpretation of a relevant provision which conflicts with the agency's earlier interpretation is 'entitled to considerably less deference' than a consistently held agency view. *I.N.S. v. Cardoza Fonseca*, 480 U.S. 421, n. 30, *citing Watt v. Alaska*, 451 U.S. 125, 143 (1981). *See also Motor Vehicle Manufacturers Ass'n v. State Farm Insurance*, 463 U.S. 29 (1983).

5. *Chevron* is one of the most commonly cited cases in the field of administrative law. Nonetheless, many commentators are critical of its basic holding. Consider, for example, the following comments of Timothy Dyk:

> [S]urely one of the most important developments in administrative law in the last several decades has been the Supreme Court's *Chevron* decision, under which the Supreme Court will defer to the agency's interpretation of its own governing statute where the statute is ambiguous and the agency's construction is reasonable. This reflects a conscious refusal on the part of the Supreme Court to play its traditional role in interpreting federal statutes. It represents, as Professor Sunstein has noted, a kind of "counter-*Marbury*." Judge Starr has described *Chevron* as "a case which all appellate judges these days bear firmly in mind in reading statutes," and they do. *Chevron* has had an enormous impact upon judicial review of administrative action in both the Courts of Appeals and in the Supreme Court. Two Terms after *Chevron*, Judge Starr commented that in the Supreme Court "*Chevron* has been employed with regularity, and in all cases save one the agency won the case." While the agency record in the past two Terms is more mixed, the centrality of *Chevron* to review of administrative agencies continues.
>
> * * *
>
> In recognition of its importance, *Chevron* receives attention not only from law professors and the courts. On April 19, 1990, Congress held hearings to consider whether the *Chevron* interpretive principles should be altered. Even the public pays attention to *Chevron*. On July 18, 1990, Walter Dellinger condemned *Chevron* before a cheering throng of several hundred. That might have had something to do with the Court's use of *Chevron* in *Rust v. Sullivan* to find the regulation authorized by the statute, and the fact that those assembled were about to lobby on the Hill for a change in that legislation. I like to think, however, that the opposition was more broadly based.
>
> More specifically, I agree with those who suggest that *Chevron* went too far in deferring to agency interpretations and that the *Chevron* approach is an abdication of the function of judicial review conferred by the Constitution and the Administrative Procedure Act. Many who practice both before the Supreme Court and in the area of administrative law believe that there are special reasons to question the wisdom of reposing trust in administrative agencies with respect to issues of statutory construction. This mistrust arises from several different sources.
>
> (1) The political agenda of the Executive Branch is largely controlling at administrative agencies. . . This influence stems in part from the ability of the incumbent administration to appoint the agency chair and the large role of the chair in setting the agency agenda, appointing staff, and formulating policy.
>
> * * *
>
> (2) Many agency members, even if they have no ambition for higher political office, often conduct themselves at their agencies with a view to later employment opportunities in the private sector.
>
> (3) To the extent that agencies pay attention to the legislative branch, and they do, they are likely to be far more interested in the views of the current congressional appropriations and oversight committees than they are likely to care about the views of some past Congress.
>
> * * *

* * *

> (4) One of the justifications for *Chevron* is that members of the administrative agencies are supposedly expert in construing their organic statute. In fact, the agency members often have no real claim to expertise. . . Because of conflict problems, some come to the agency with little or no background in the area of the agency's authority. And, again, the short tenure discourages the intellectual commitment that would be necessary to understand the complex issues of statutory construction. The expertise of the agency usually resides in the agency bureaucracy rather than in the members who formulate policy. This seems to belie the claim that the appointed agency members, who are ultimately responsible for policy formulation, have a special claim to expertise. Just as criticism has been directed at congressional staff for usurping the authority of the members, so too it can suggested that the agency bureaucracy in this area of interpretation has usurped the policymaking function of the agency members.

Dyk, *The Supreme Court's Role in Not Shaping Administrative Law,* 44 ADMIN. L. REV. 429 (1992). Mr. Dyk goes on to suggest that the *Chevron* decision may be a product of the "lack of competence" of our federal courts in dealing with complex regulatory matters. He offers four suggestions for addressing this problem. First, establishing an independent research office within the Supreme Court. Second, allowing divided arguments by private parties. Third, requiring that *amicus* briefs be consolidated. And finally, selecting more experienced law clerks. Do you agree with his criticism and suggested solutions?

EMISSIONS TRADING POLICY STATEMENT; GENERAL PRINCIPLES FOR CREATION, BANKING, AND USE OF EMISSION REDUCTION CREDITS

EPA, 51 Fed. Reg. 43,814 (1986)

* * *

I. INTRODUCTION: BASIC ELEMENTS OF EMISSIONS TRADING

This statement details EPA policy on emissions trading. It sets out conditions EPA considers necessary for emissions trades to satisfy the Clean Air Act. It also clarifies and otherwise makes final the Interim Policy proposed on April 7, 1982 (47 FR 15076). It is accompanied by a Technical Issues Document which elaborates and provides greater detail on principles set forth below. Finally, it addresses new issues, and incorporates certain additional safeguards as a result of past trading experience, to better assure the environmental integrity of future trades.

A. What is Emissions Trading

Emissions trading consists of bubbles, netting, emission offsets, and emission reduction banking. These steps involve creation of surplus emission reductions at certain stacks, vents or similar sources of emissions and use of these emission reductions to meet or redefine pollution control requirements applicable to other emission sources. Such emissions trades can provide more flexibility to meet environmental requirements, and may therefore be used to reduce control costs and encourage faster compliance. Moreover, by developing "generic" trading rules (see Section III below) states may be able to expedite bubble approvals by eliminating the need for case-by-case SIP revisions and by providing more predictable approval criteria.

B. The Bubble

EPA's bubble lets *existing* plants (or groups of plants) increase emissions at one or more emission sources in exchange for compensating extra decreases in emissions at other emission sources. Approved bubbles give plant managers the ability to implement less costly ways of meeting air quality requirements. To be approvable, each bubble must produce results which are equivalent to or better than the baseline emission levels in terms of ambient impact and enforceability. Thus, bubbles should jeopardize neither ambient standards nor applicable PSD increments and visibility requirements. Under EPA's bubble, emission reductions from existing sources can not be used to meet technology-based requirements applicable to new or modified stationary sources.

C. Netting

Netting may exempt "modifications" of existing major sources from certain preconstruction permit requirements under New Source Review (NSR), so long as there is no net emissions increase within the major source or any such increase falls below significance levels. By "netting out," the modification is not considered "major" and is therefore not subject to associated preconstruction permit requirements for major modifications under 40 CFR 51.18, 51.24, 52.21, 52.24, 52.27, or 52.28. The modification must nevertheless meet applicable new source performance standards (NSPS), national emissions standards for hazardous air pollutants (NESHAPs), preconstruction applicability review requirements under 40 CFR 51.18(a)-(h) and (l), and SIP requirements.

Netting's scope is determined by the definition of "source" for review of major modifications. In general, PSD areas use a single, plantwide definition, allowing actual emission reductions anywhere in a contiguous plant to compensate for potential emission increases at individual emitting units within the plant. Nonattainment areas can choose either this single, plantwide definition or a dual definition, so long as the definition selected does not interfere with attainment and maintenance of NAAQS and is consistent with progress towards attainment. Under the plantwide definition, significant net actual increases at the plant as a whole will trigger new source review. Under the dual definition, significant increases at either the plant as a whole or individual emitting units will trigger new source review.

In addition to these federal definitions for major new sources and modifications, state preconstruction permits for major or minor new sources and modifications may be required under 40 CFR 51.18(a), and some states preclude netting.

D. Emission Offsets

In *nonattainment areas*, major new stationary sources and major modifications are subject to a preconstruction permit requirement that they secure sufficient surplus emission reductions to more than "offset" their emissions. This requirement is designed to allow industrial growth in nonattainment areas without interfering with attainment and maintenance of ambient air quality standards. It is currently implemented through SIP regulations adopted by states to meet the requirements of 40 CFR 51.18(j).

In *attainment areas*, some new sources and modifications might not otherwise be able to be constructed because their emissions would result in an exceedance of the applicable PSD increment or ambient air quality standard, would significantly contribute to a violation of an ambient air quality standard in a designated primary nonattainment area, or would significantly contribute to visibility impairment in a Federal Class I area. These sources may use emissions offsets to allow desired growth while protecting that increment, standard, or visibility.

E. Emission Reduction Banking

Firms may store qualified emission reduction credits (ERCs) in EPA-approvable banks for later use in bubble, offset or netting transactions. Depending on the bank's rules, banked ERCs may also be sold or transferred to other firms which seek to meet certain regulatory requirements by use of emissions trades.

EPA's revised Offset Ruling (40 CFR Part 51, Appendix S) allows states to establish banking rules as part of their SIPs. This Policy Statement and accompanying Technical Issues Document detail the necessary components of a complete state banking rule approvable under the Clean Air Act. While many areas also allow banking of emission reductions for various purposes through various formal or informal banking mechanisms, banks which do not meet today's criteria (*e.g.*, by not making banked emission reductions enforceable by the state by the time the reductions are actually banked, or by not assuring that deposits are taken explicitly into account for SIP planning purposes) cannot qualify emission reductions as ERCs, and may offer substantially less protection in the event of future SIP corrections or changes in ambient attainment status.

F. Generic Trading Rules

Generic rules adopted as part of the SIP can authorize states to approve certain types of individual transactions without the need for case-by-case SIP revisions or associated federal review prior to approval. The first state generic bubble rule was approved by EPA April 6, 1981 (46 FR 20551). For the current scope of permissible rules, see Section III below.

G. Effect of this Policy Statement

Emissions trading is largely voluntary: no source is required to trade, and no state is required by EPA to approve a particular trade or to adopt a generic rule. Trading merely offers states and stationary sources alternative ways to meet regulatory requirements. For example, states are free to adopt generic rules or continue to implement trades as individual SIP revisions. They may adopt rules which incorporate all or any combination of the above trading approaches.

* * *

This policy requires that substantial additional reductions (at least 20%) in emissions remaining beyond applicable baselines be produced by future bubbles in primary nonattainment areas which require but lack approved demonstrations of attainment. However, applications for bubbles in such areas which are still pending at EPA without formal action under the 1982 policy, or which were previously submitted to EPA Regions under the 1982 policy but not accepted for evaluation, will be reexamined and processed for approval if they meet the requirements of the 1982 policy and contribute to progress towards attainment. "Progress towards attainment" means some extra reduction beyond equivalence to a lowest-of-actual-SIP-allowable-or-RACT-allowable emissions baseline, with this baseline applied as of the time applicants originally sought credit. Pending bubbles in attainment areas and nonattainment areas with approved demonstrations of attainment will be processed for approval if they meet the requirements of the 1982 policy and show that ambient standards, PSD increments and visibility will not be jeopardized.

* * *

II. REQUIREMENTS FOR CREATING, USING, OR BANKING EMISSION REDUCTION CREDITS

A. Creating Emission Reduction Credits

Emission reduction credits (ERC's) are the common currency of all trading activity. ERCs may be created by reductions from either stationary, area, or mobile sources. To assure that emissions trades do not contravene relevant requirements of the Clean Air Act, only reductions which are *surplus, enforceable, permanent*, and *quantifiable* can qualify as ERCs and be banked or used in an emissions trade.

1. Surplus. At minimum, only emission reductions not required by current regulations in the SIP, not already relied on for SIP planning purposes, and not used by the source to meet any other regulatory requirement, can be considered surplus. To determine the quantity of emission reductions that are surplus, the state must first establish an appropriate emissions baseline from which surplus reductions can be calculated. Baseline emissions for any source are the product of three factors — emission rate, capacity utilization, and hours of operation.

In attainment areas, the lower of actual or allowable values must generally be used for each of these baseline factors. However, allowable values for one or more of these factors, when higher than actual values, may be used in calculating the baseline emissions, provided those values are shown to be used or reflected in an approved demonstration. The burden of meeting this test by written evidence rests with the state or applicant which seeks to use an allowable value.

When allowable values for one or more baseline factors are not used or reflected in an approved demonstration, such values may still be used in calculating baseline emissions. However, in such cases applicants must perform appropriate modeling to demonstrate that allowable values which are higher than actual values will not delay or jeopardize attainment and maintenance of ambient standards.

In attainment areas where the PSD baseline has been triggered, credit may be granted consistent with the PSD baseline concentration as specified in 40 CFR 51.24(b)(13) and 52.21(b)(13). This will generally require use of actual values for each of the baseline factors. However, states may use allowable values if they show through appropriate modeling that attainment and maintenance of neither the ambient standards nor applicable PSD increments will be jeopardized, and quantify the amount of increment consumed.

In nonattainment areas with approved demonstrations of attainment, the baseline must be consistent with assumptions used to develop the area's demonstration. This generally means that actual values must be used for each baseline factor where actual values were used for such demonstrations, and that higher allowable values for these factors may be used where allowable values were used for such demonstrations. The burden of showing that an allowable value was used or reflected in the approved demonstration rests with the state or applicant which seeks to use an allowable value. In the absence of written evidence to that effect, full Level III modeling would be required to make use of an allowable value in baseline calculations.

In primary nonattainment areas which need but lack approved demonstrations of attainment, states must show that bubbles meet special "progress" requirements designed to produce a net air quality benefit. This must be demonstrated by (1) using the lowest-of-actual-SIP-allowable-or-RACT-allowable emissions baseline for each source involved in the trade; (2) meeting the ambient equivalence tests outlined in sections II.B.2 of this policy and I.B.1.b. of the Technical Issues Document; and then (3) producing a substantial net reduction in actual emissions (i.e., a reduction of at least 20% in the emissions remaining after application of the baseline specified above). The state must also provide assurances that the bubble is consistent with ambient progress and future air quality planning goals.

2. *Enforceable*. To assure that Clean Air Act requirements are met, each transaction which revises any emission limit upward must be approved by the state and be federally enforceable. Means of making emission limits federally enforceable include SIP revisions (see section IV below), EPA-approved generic bubble rules (see Section III below), and new source preconstruction permits issued by states under EPA-approved SIP regulations pursuant to provisions of 40 CFR 51.18, 51.24, or 51.307, as well as construction permits issued by EPA or delegated states under 52.21. Bubbles should be incorporated in an enforceable compliance instrument which requires recordkeeping based on the averaging period over which the bubble is operating, so it may easily be determined over any single averaging period that bubble limits are being met.

3. *Permanent*. Only permanent reductions in emissions can qualify for credit. Permanence may generally be assured by requiring federally enforceable changes in source permits or applicable state regulations to reflect a reduced level of allowable emissions.

4. *Quantifiable*. Emission reductions must be quantifiable both in terms of *estimating* the amount of the reduction and *characterizing* that reduction for future use. Quantification may be based on emission factors, stack tests, monitored values, operating rates and averaging times, process or production inputs, modeling, or other reasonable measurement practices. The same method of calculating emissions should generally be used to quantify emission levels both before and after the reduction.

B. *Using Emission Reduction Credits*

ERCs may be used by sources in bubble, offset or netting transactions. The general principles below will assure that all uses of ERCs are consistent with ambient attainment and maintenance considerations under the Clean Air Act. They are further articulated in the accompanying Technical Issues Document.

1. *Emissions trades must involve the same criteria pollutant*. An emission reduction may only be traded against an increase in the same criteria pollutant. For example, only reductions of SO_2 can be substituted for increases of SO_2 .

2. *All uses of ERCs must satisfy applicable ambient tests*. The Clean Air Act requires that all areas throughout the country attain and maintain national ambient air quality standards and meet applicable ambient requirements relating to PSD increments and Class I protection, including visibility. The ambient effect of a trade depends on the dispersion characteristics of the pollutant involved. With the exception of visibility for

NO_x, dispersion considerations will generally not affect trades involving VOC or NO_x, whose impacts occur across broad geographic areas. For these pollutants "pound for pound" trades may be treated as equal in ambient effect where all sources involved in the trade are located in the same control strategy demonstration area, or where the state otherwise shows such sources to be sufficiently close that a "pound for pound" trade can be justified. However, dispersion characteristics are important for bubble and offset trades of SO_2, particulates, CO, or lead, whose ambient impact may vary with where the emission increases and decreases occur. To assure ambient equivalence, such trades of these pollutants must satisfy ambient tests under the modeling screen discussed in the Technical Issues Document or under a similar, equally effective approach.

3. Bubbles must not increase hazardous pollutants. Bubbles may not be used to meet applicable requirements of National Emissions Standards for Hazardous Air Pollutants (NESHAPs) promulgated under section 112 of the Clean Air Act, to increase emissions at any source beyond the levels applicable NESHAPs prescribe, or to create any net increase in baseline emissions of a pollutant regulated under section 112. The applicable baseline for regulated sources is the lower of actual or NESHAPs-allowable emissions of the hazardous pollutant.

Where a NESHAP has been proposed but not yet promulgated for a source category which emits a pollutant listed under section 112, the proposal will serve as an interim guideline for evaluating the effects of any proposed emissions trade involving a source that would be subject to the proposed standard. In general, such trades will be approvable with respect to the emissions component of the trade subject to the proposal, so long as they result in emission limits at each source emitting the relevant pollutant which are equivalent to or lower than those the proposed NESHAP would have required if already promulgated.

Where a pollutant has been *listed* under section 112 or where EPA has published a Notice-of-Intent-to-List, but no regulations for the source category involved in the trade have yet been proposed or promulgated, the trade will generally be acceptable with respect to the emissions component of the trade subject to notice or listing, if there is no net increase in actual emissions of that pollutant as a result of the trade.

* * *

4. ERCs from existing sources cannot be used to meet technology-based requirements applicable to new sources. Under Clean Air Act section 111 and EPA implementing regulations, new affected facilities must satisfy technology-based New Source Performance Standards (NSPS), regardless of the attainment status of the area in which they are located. Under sections 165 and 173 and EPA implementing regulations, new or modified major stationary sources must also satisfy technology-based control obligations associated with pre-construction permits. These requirements prohibit use of credits from existing sources to meet or avoid applicable NSPS, and bar use of such credits to meet applicable new source review requirements for best available control technology (BACT) in PSD areas, or lowest achievable emission rate control technology (LAER) in nonattainment areas.

5. States may approve bubbles in primary nonattainment areas which require but lack approved demonstrations of attainment, provided such trades meet requirements designed to produce a net air quality benefit and the state provides certain assurances. See section II.A.1. above and the Technical Issues Document, section I.A.1.b. Bubbles which meet these objective requirements will be processed for approval by EPA.

6. Sources need not be subject to binding compliance schedules based on current SIP requirements before they can apply for a bubble which would supersede those requirements. Sources that are already subject to binding compliance schedules should be aware, however, that such schedules remain fully enforceable until a bubble affecting the schedule has been approved by EPA or under a state generic rule and the schedule has been modified accordingly. Sources subject to compliance schedules in administrative orders or judicial decrees must obtain prior approval from EPA or the relevant court, as appropriate, to be relieved from the schedule contained in the order or decree. Sources that are subject to SIP requirements remain responsible for meeting those requirements unless and until a bubble has become effective under Federal law. See section II.B.12 below.

7. States may extend certain compliance schedules. States may no longer grant compliance extensions under new or revised generic rules in *nonattainment areas*, whether or not such areas have demonstrations. However, states may continue to grant compliance date extensions under generic rules in *attainment areas*, provided EPA has approved the extension provisions of the generic rule as being adequate to comply with the Clean Air Act, including requirements for attainment and maintenance of ambient air quality standards.

* * *

8. States may approve bubbles involving open dust sources of particulate emissions, based on modeling demonstrations. Open dust trades may be approved through individual SIP revisions based on acceptable modeling and/or monitoring demonstrations, provided sources agree to post-approval monitoring to determine if predicted air quality results have been realized and make an enforceable commitment to achieve necessary additional reductions if predicted results do not materialize.

9. Trade involving lead. Unlike other criteria pollutants, EPA does not designate nonattainment areas for lead. However, the Regional Administrator will review lead trades, as all other trades, to assure that they do not interfere with attainment and maintenance of NAAQS.

10. Trades involving ERCs from mobile source measures. ERCs from mobile source measures may be used to meet SIP requirements applicable to existing stationary sources, so long as such reductions are surplus, permanent, quantifiable, and enforceable. Reductions from certain types of mobile-source measures (*e.g.*, mechanical conversion of existing vehicle fleets to cleaner fuels such as methanol) may satisfy these criteria more readily than those from other transport-related measures. However, due to possible difficulties in determining whether specific mobile-source reductions fully meet these criteria, all such trades must be implemented as case-by-case SIP revisions.

11. Interstate trades. Trades involving sources located in neighboring states may be approved, provided they meet all other requirements of today's notice. However, in order to avoid complex SIP accounting issues, where state trading requirements differ EPA will require that such trades meet the substantive requirements of the more stringent state. In general, EPA will deem ERCs created in one state to contribute to progress in the state where used to the extent of that use, provided that applicable ambient tests (section II.B.2 above) are met. Interstate trades must be implemented through case-by-case SIP revisions.

12. Bubbles must not impede enforcement. In general, bubbles are a form of SIP revision which should be treated neither more nor less stringently than other SIP revisions. Bubbles should not become a shield against enforcement actions for sources which have failed to take necessary steps to meet required control obligations on time.

Sources seeking trades should note that they remain subject to enforcement of existing (pre-trade) SIP limits until the bubble is approved. EPA will use the same principles and procedures for deciding whether to initiate enforcement actions in these circumstances as the Agency applies to any other source which is subject to a proposed or final SIP revision.

* * *

C. Banking Emission Reduction Credits

Only emission reductions that are surplus, permanent, quantifiable, and enforceable can qualify as ERCs and be deposited in EPA-approvable banks. Such banks offer sources legal recognition that qualifying reductions meet these ERC requirements. However, the fact that an ERC has been banked does not relieve it from the need to meet all criteria of the specific regulatory program under which it is to be used. Because some trades have special limitations (*e.g.*, only reductions occurring at the same major stationary source can be used for netting), banks do not guarantee the validity or specific amount of particular banked ERCs for all potential uses or for all time. To provide maximum protection for the environment and sources and to avoid potential legal problems, state banking rules may specify the types of sources eligible to bank ERCs and any additional conditions placed on certifying, holding or using banked ERCs.

* * *

III. STATE GENERIC TRADING RULES

Use of emission reduction credits under state regulations approved by EPA as generic for identified classes of trades will not require individual SIP revisions for those trades. The Technical Issues Document explains acceptable generic procedures which states may adopt to reduce the need for individual SIP revisions.

Emissions trades can be approved without case-by-case SIP revisions if evaluated by the state under EPA-approved procedures which assure that no trade which meets their terms will interfere with timely attainment and maintenance of ambient standards, protection of applicable PSD increments, or visibility provisions. State generic rules are approvable only if their procedures are sufficiently replicable in operation to meet this test. By approving the generic rule, EPA approves in advance an array of SIP-compatible emission limits, and no further case-by-case Federal review or approval is required for individual trades which meet the terms of the rule.

* * *

Any trade under a generic rule will involve emission increases at some sources and extra emission decreases at others. For trades to be approvable under a generic rule, the sum of these increases and decreases (beyond applicable net baseline emissions) must be zero or less.

* * *

In primary nonattainment areas which need but lack approved demonstrations, new generic rules must require, and existing generic rules must, as requested by EPA, be revised to require bubbles to use lowest-of-actual-SIP-allowable-or- RACT-allowable emissions baselines, and produce a net air quality benefit. New or revised generic rules in these nonattainment areas must be accompanied by certain assurances of consistency with air quality planning goals as well as a commitment to make certain additional assurances when the state approves individual bubbles under the rule. Bubbles approved under existing generic bubble rules before the effective date of this policy will not be affected by these requirements. Because EPA-approved state regulations have independent legal force, future bubbles submitted under existing generic rules may also be approved by states in accord with those rules, until such rules are modified to meet the criteria below.

* * *

IV. Bubbles Which Require Case-By-Case SIP Revisions

States and sources must use the case-by-case SIP revision process to implement bubbles which are not covered by a generic rule. Because the case-by-case SIP revision process can take account of many more individual variations, numerous trades which could not be accomplished through generic rules or similar means may still be approvable as case-by-case SIP revisions.

EPA will take action on generic rules and individual trades submitted as SIP revisions as quickly as circumstances permit after a state has adopted a SIP revision and submitted the action to EPA. EPA encourages "parallel processing" of such SIP revisions, with EPA and the state conducting concurrent review so that both agencies can propose and take final action at roughly the same time. EPA will also publish noncontroversial SIP revisions as immediate final actions, converting them to proposals only if requests to submit adverse comments are received within 30 days (see 46 FR 44477, September 4, 1981). In all bubble actions EPA will clearly identify (or require states to identify, as appropriate) both pre- and post-trade actual and allowable emissions for each source involved in the trade, so that the ambient effects of each bubble may be known.

V. Conclusion

This Policy Statement sets out basic principles for approving individual trades and generic trading rules. It tightens many requirements in order to better ensure SIP integrity and environmental progress, while offering ample opportunities for use of approvable, environmentally-sound trades. EPA encourages states and sources to use these principles as a framework and refer to the accompanying Technical Issues Document for further discussion and examples. EPA also encourages states to develop other approaches which satisfy these principles while meeting their specific needs.

As a policy statement, this notice does not establish conclusively how EPA will resolve issues in individual cases. EPA will accept public comment on specific SIP changes submitted under it, and will review individually each generic rule and those emissions trades submitted as SIP revisions to determine their acceptability under the Clean Air Act. Interested parties will have full opportunity to scrutinize application of these principles in specific cases, and to seek subsequent judicial review of such cases after EPA has taken final action on particular trades or generic rules.

Dated: November 18, 1986.

Lee M. Thomas, *Administrator.*

NOTES

1. The preamble to the Emissions Trading Policy Statement states that the policy "does not constitute final action of the Agency within the meaning of § 307(b) of the Clean Air Act, and therefore is not reviewable. Rather it establishes general guidance on approvable voluntary trades. EPA will implement this guidance in later rulemaking actions that will be judicially reviewable." 51 Fed. Reg. 43,814 (1986). Do you agree with EPA's assessment of the policy statement? Is the policy statement a rule within the meaning of the Administrative Procedure Act? *See* 5 U.S.C. §§ 551(4), 704.

2. The Policy Statement makes frequent reference to "nonattainment areas with approved demonstrations of attainment." This language may seem unclear but it simply refers to nonattainment areas with EPA approved plans for attaining the NAAQS under § 172. (Likewise, nonattainment areas which lack approved demonstrations of attainment lack such EPA approved plans.)

3. In accordance with the Clean Air Act, EPA set many different kinds of standards of performance based on the category of the facility and its size. New sources must meet new source performance standards (NSPS) which are set at the emission levels achievable through application of the best system of continuous emission reduction, taking into consideration cost and other values, which has been adequately demonstrated. § 111(a)(1). Major new stationary sources in nonattainment areas must also comply with the lowest achievable emission rate (LAER). § 173(2). This is defined as the more stringent of either the most stringent emission limit in any state SIP, or the most stringent emission limitation achieved in practice for the category of source. § 171(3). Major new emitting facilities in attainment or "PSD" areas are subject to the best available control technology (BACT). Like the NSPS and LAER, BACT is also an emission limitation. BACT is based on "the maximum degree of reduction of each pollutant subject to regulation" and emitted from the facility, which the permitting authority determines is achievable taking into account energy, environmental and economic impacts and other costs. § 169(3). Under EPA's Policy, emission trades, including the bubble, cannot be used to meet these technology-based emission limitations. How then can the bubble be used? *See* the discussion of "netting" at § I.C. of the Policy Statement. *See also* 47 Fed. Reg. 15083 (1982). What is the reason for this restriction? How does one "net out" of new source review? Why is "reasonably available control technology" (RACT), which must be achieved by all existing, major stationary sources in nonattainment areas, omitted from this list? *See* 40 CFR § 51.100(o) (1990).

4. In the 1986 policy statement, EPA changed its previous policy and now allows the bubble to be used to meet NSPS. *See* Levin, *Statutes and Stopping Points: Building a Better Bubble at EPA*, REGULATION (March/April, 1985). This policy change, however, is not as broad as it may seem. EPA has not changed its fundamental position that you cannot net out of NSPS. It has, however, decided to allow a new source in Illinois to meet NSPS on a plant-wide basis rather than at each stack. *See* 52 Fed. Reg. 27,849 (1987). How does this complicate the bubble policy?

5. EPA's bubble policy allows firms to "bank" emission reduction credits (ERCs) for later use in bubble, netting or offset transactions. Further, ERCs are freely transferable. What ramification does the banking program have for nonattainment areas? How does the policy seek to assure that the banking program will not interfere with attainment of the NAAQS?

6. Recall the practical pollution problem identified in the *Air Pollution Control District* case, *supra*, Chapter Six. The Gallagher Plant in Indiana contributed substantial quantities of SO_2 to portions of a nonattainment area in Jefferson County, Kentucky, that were actually in compliance with NAAQSs. A smaller percentage of SO_2 was contributed to those portions of the nonattainment area actually out of compliance. What relevance does this problem have for emissions trading?

7. For a comprehensive analysis of EPA's emissions trading policy, its history and implementation, *see* LIROFF, REFORMING AIR POLLUTION REGULATION: THE TOIL AND TROUBLE OF EPA'S BUBBLE (Conservation Foundation, 1986). *See also*, Dudek & Palmisano, *Emissions Trading: Why is This Thoroughbred Hobbled?*, 13 COLUM. J. of ENV. L. 217 (1988).

PROBLEM #7: PERMITS, BUBBLES, AND VISIBILITY

The Zion Corporation proposed to increase the capacity of its existing copper smelter located just outside of Sage Brush City in the State of Deseret. The facility is located in the Central Deseret Air Quality Control Region, which is a nonattainment area for SO_2 and an attainment area for all other criteria pollutants. The proposed modification will result in a net increase in SO_2 and particulate emissions from the smelter. Current SO_2 emissions are 20,000 tons/year. Particulate emissions are currently 25,000 tons/year. Projected emissions following the changes are 24,000 tons of SO_2/year and 30,000 tons of particulates/year. No change is proposed at the adjacent 50 megawatt power plant which services the smelter. The power plant, which along with the original smelter was constructed in 1965, burns high sulfur coal and employs no emission controls.

You are the General Counsel for the Zion Corporation. The President of the Corporation has asked you to chair a committee that will insure that all necessary permits and approvals are obtained in a timely fashion. How should you proceed? (Begin by reviewing §§ 172 and 173 of the Act.) What standards of performance will apply to Zion's smelter? Will Zion have to obtain a PSD permit as well as a nonattainment permit? What emission trading options might be available to Zion?

Prior to Zion's proposed modification, the State of Deseret had required Zion to install the best available retrofit technology (BART) to control its emissions insofar as they were impairing visibility at a national park located in a neighboring state (and another AQCR) more than 500 miles from Zion's smelter. Was Deseret's action lawful? *See* § 169A. *Compare Alabama Power Co. v. Costle*, 636 F.2d at 364-68 wherein the court held that a new facility located in a nonattainment area did not have to meet the preconstruction review requirements for PSD areas even where the facility would adversely affect the air quality in that area. What authority does the national park manager have to block the proposed modification of the smelter? *See* § 165(d).

F. The Acid Precipitation Program

One of the thorniest air pollution problems confronting the EPA is acid rain. Its difficulty stems, in large measure, from the that fact the northeastern states and Canadian provinces experiencing acid rain are generally not the chief source of the SO_2 and NO_x that creates the problem. Jurisdictions adversely affected are understandably upset at having to accept the costs associated with acid rain, while the benefits of unregulated pollution accrue to the polluting states. Congress responded to this issue in 1977 by enacting international air pollution provisions of § 115, and interstate pollution standards at §§ 110 (a)(2)(D) and 126. As discussed in Chapter Six, however, these provisions were not successful in ameliorating the problem. The 1990 Amendments adopt a massive new program with a fundamental goal of reducing SO_2 emissions by ten million tons and NO_x emissions by two million tons by the year 2000. S. REP. NO. 228, 101st Cong., 1st Sess. 302 (1989). These impressive reductions are to be achieved through an innovative market system. During Phase I of the program, which begins in 1995, 111 of the dirtiest fossil fuel fired power plants in the country receive emission allowances[1] equal to an emissions rate of 2.5 lbs/mmBtu.[2] This rate is approximately one-half of the current emissions rate for many of these facilities. *See* COMPLIANCE STRATEGIES REVIEW, GUIDE TO PHASE I UNITS (Fieldston, 1992).

Phase II of the program begins in the year 2000 and will encompass all fossil fuel fired power plants. Total allowances issued will be 8.9 million. Under Phase II, utilities will receive maximum allowances equivalent to an emissions rate of 1.2 lbs/mmBtu. Sources already below that rate will generally receive allowances based upon their 1985 emissions. Many other exceptions exist, however, to address particular situations.[3]

Utilities subject to Phase I of the program have several options from which to choose. First, they can change their fuel or fuel mixture. For example, a utility might switch from high sulfur coal to low sulfur coal, or from coal to natural gas. *See e.g.,* COMPLIANCE STRATEGIES REV., VOL. 3, No. 6, p. 1 (1992), announcing a decision by the Niagara Mohawk Power Co. to switch its Dunkirk plant to low sulfur coal. *See also,* COMPLIANCE STRATEGIES REV., VOL 3, No. 1, p. 1 (1992). Second, a company can install pollution control technology to limit its emissions. *See e.g.,* COMPLIANCE STRATEGIES REV. VOL. 3, NO. 3, p. 1 (1992)("Scrubber is Keystone of KU Compliance Plan"); COMPLIANCE STRATEGIES REV. VOL. 2, No. 24, p. 1 ("WVPSC Okays Harrison Scrubbers"). Third, it can purchase allowances from other sources with excess allowances. COMPLIANCE STRATEGIES REV., VOL. 3, NO. 11, p. 1 (1992) ("WP&L is the First to Sell Allowances"). Fourth, it can choose some combination of the first three options. COMPLIANCE STRATEGIES REV. VOL. 3, NO. 11, p. 1 (1992) ("PEPCO to Switch And Enter Allowance Market"). Finally, it can retire and/or replace one or more of its units.

---

[1] An "allowance" is equal to one ton of SO_2. § 402(3).

[2] The Act distinguishes between "affected sources" and "affected units". §402(1),(2). Affected sources are the broader category and may contain one or more affected units.

[3] *See* Garrett & Winner, *A Clean Air Act Primer*, CLEAN AIR DESKBOOK 56 (Env. L. Inst. 1992).

Although it is probably too early to know how successful the market strategy will be, the initial indications are that the price of allowances may be much lower than originally anticipated. Early predictions ranged from \$600-\$800/allowance, but a recent study has suggested that the price might be as low as \$80/allowance. 22 ENV. REP. (Current Developments) 2630 (March 27, 1992). Allowances will be traded in 25-ton increments on the Chicago Board of Trade. *Id.* The high level of uncertainty currently surrounding the cost of SO_2 allowances may be hindering the market. *See* COMPLIANCE STRATEGIES REV., *Emission Allowance Trading: Coping With Uncertainty*, (Expert Opinion Supplement, March 2, 1992); *Emission Allowance Prices Lower Than Expected*, (Expert Opinion Supplement, Feb. 17, 1992). Set forth below is an extended excerpt from EPA's proposal for implementing the acid deposition program.

ACID RAIN PROGRAM: PERMITS, ALLOWANCE SYSTEM, CONTINUOUS EMISSIONS MONITORING, AND EXCESS EMISSIONS

56 Fed. Reg. 63,002 (1991)

* * *

ACTION: Proposed Rules

* * *

II. GENERAL BACKGROUND

Acid rain is the accepted term which encompasses a complex set of phenomena that begins with fossil fuel emissions, includes the transport and transformation of those emissions through the atmosphere, and ends with the effects of those emissions and their resulting transformation products on the environment. Specifically, the burning of fossil fuels, particularly coal and oil, releases emissions of sulfur dioxide (SO_2) and nitrogen oxide (NO_x) into the atmosphere. In the atmosphere, SO_2 and NO_x may undergo various chemical reactions, resulting in the transformation of the emissions into chemical products including sulfates, nitrates, sulfuric acid and nitric acid. These compounds can fall to earth near the source or be transported hundreds of miles. They may be deposited during any stage of their transformation, returning to earth as dry deposition in the form of gases, aerosols, and particles as well as wet deposition through precipitation such as rain, fog, or snow. The presence of these emissions and their transformation products in the atmosphere contributes to reduced visibility and is suspected of posing a threat to human health at current levels. The acidic deposition resulting from SO_2 and NO_x emissions and their byproducts damages both ecosystems and man-made materials. Of the approximately 23 million tons of SO_2 and 19 million tons of NO_x emitted annually from all sources in the United States in 1985, about 16 million tons of SO_2 and 7 million tons of NO_x were emitted by electric utilities.

Title IV of the Act authorizes EPA to establish the acid rain program to reduce the adverse effects of acidic deposition. Specifically, the Act mandates a national emissions cap of 8.95 million tons per year on electric utility SO_2 emissions, to be achieved in two phases. In Phase I, which begins in 1995, the 110 largest, highest-emitting utility plants, located in 21 States, must meet an intermediate SO_2 emissions limitation requirement. By 2000, the start of Phase II, virtually all existing utility units with output capacity greater than 25 megawatts and all new utility units will be required to meet emissions limitations. As a result, total annual SO_2 emissions will be reduced by 10 million tons below 1980 levels. In addition, SO_2 sources not explicitly affected by Phase II requirements (e.g. industrial facilities) may elect to participate by "opting-in" to the acid rain program. Title IV also requires that certain coal-fired electric utility boilers reduce their emissions of NO_x through installation of low NO_x burner technologies or their equivalent, at the same time they are required to comply with the SO_2 limitations.

The acid rain program requirements will be codified in six regulations:

Acid rain regulation	40 CFR part No.
Permits	72
Allowance system	73
Opt-in	74
Continuous emissions monitoring	75
Nitrogen oxides control	76
Excess emissions	77

The rules for opt-in and for NO_x control are reserved for future rulemaking actions. In addition, 40 CFR part 78 is reserved for the acid rain program. EPA is soliciting comment on whether to use part 78 to contain the appeals procedures for the acid rain program, which are proposed in today's notice as one subpart of the permits rule (Subpart H, 40 CFR part 72).

Today's notice covers four proposed rulemakings: permits (40 CFR part 72); the allowance system (40 CFR part 73); continuous emissions monitoring (40 CFR part 75); and excess emissions (40 CFR part 77). Following the general discussion of the acid rain program in this preamble, the reader will find specific discussions tailored to each of the four proposed rulemakings, in order.

* * *

III. Acid Rain Regulations Introduction

The centerpiece of the acid rain program is an innovative trading system with a fixed number of fully marketable allowances. An allowance authorizes the emission of one ton of SO_2. Existing utility sources are allocated allowances based on their historic fuel use and the emissions limitations specified in the Act. Utility units must not emit SO_2 in quantities that exceed the number of allowances they hold.

* * *

Today's proposal includes the primary structure of the allowance system (background, tracking, and trading) and the requirements for applying for allowances from the conservation and renewable energy reserve.

Since allowances are fully transferrable, utilities may meet their emissions control requirements in the most cost-effective manner possible. However, because the Act explicitly specifies annual SO_2 emissions tonnage limitations for each affected utility unit, in order to operate and to trade allowances each affected source must apply for a permit which, among other things, certifies that the source will hold a sufficient number of allowances to cover its SO_2 emissions, or specifies the source's alternate planned method of compliance. The permit regulation will be codified in 40 CFR part 72.

In order to ensure that source compliance collectively results in the achievement of the nationally mandated reductions in SO_2 and NO_x emissions, each affected source is required to install a system to continuously monitor the concentration and flow of emissions, in order to collect, record, and report emissions data. The continuous emissions monitoring rule will be codified in 40 CFR part 75.

Finally, if an affected unit exceeds its emissions limitation for either SO_2 or NO_x, the Act requires the affected source to pay penalties and, for SO_2, to meet emissions offset requirements. These requirements are designed to act as a strong incentive for compliance with the mandated emissions reductions of the acid rain program. The excess emissions penalties requirements will be codified in 40 CFR part 77.

Because the acid rain program is designed to allow sources to meet the mandated emissions reductions in the most cost-effective manner possible, SO_2 sources not explicitly affected by the Act's requirements (e.g. industrial sources) may elect to participate in the allowance market by "opting in" to the acid rain program. The opt-in rule will be the subject of a separate future rulemaking (to be codified in 40 CFR part 74).

* * *

The acid rain program addresses the annual average NO_x emissions rate requirements as a separate component of the program. Specifically, certain coal-fired electric utility boilers are required to reduce their emissions of NO_x through installation of low NO_x burner technologies or their equivalent. The NO_x control rule, which will be the subject of a future rulemaking, will be codified in 40 CFR part 76. However, procedures to apply for some of the NO_x compliance options are addressed in the Permits rule proposed at 40 CFR part 72.

In summary, the four rules covering the core acid rain program requirements — the permit, the allowance system, the continuous emissions monitoring system, and the excess emissions program — are proposed in today's Federal Register following this notice.

IV. PERMITS REGULATION

A. Overview of the Acid Rain Permit Program

Section 408(a) of the Clean Air Act, as amended by Public Law 101-549 (the Act) requires that the Acid Rain program, mandated by title IV of the Act, be implemented through operating permits. Acid Rain permits must ensure source accountability for the emissions reductions mandated by title IV of the Act, yet afford sources flexible planning opportunities to help minimize the costs of compliance. In addition, the Acid Rain permit program must integrate smoothly with State operating permits issued under programs approved pursuant to title V of the Act, yet ensure the national consistency necessary to support the allowance trading market.

1. *Flexibility.* The Agency believes that an active allowance trading market, supported by flexible compliance planning opportunities, will help affected sources to minimize compliance costs. EPA's goal is to structure simple, flexible and predictable Acid Rain permit program requirements that will promote these objectives.

* * *

2. *National Consistency.* National consistency in implementation of the Acid Rain program requirements is necessary to ensure the effective functioning of a national allowance trading market. Inconsistent implementation could affect the value and fungibility of allowances across Regions, States, and localities. This, in turn, could impede the economies inherent in a national market. Today's proposal would, therefore, establish nationally standardized permitting. Standardized forms for permit applications,

compliance plans, permits, and compliance certifications are one important mechanism proposed today by which national consistency would be achieved. In addition, to help ensure a nationally consistent body of judicial precedent, today's rule proposes that EPA be given notice of any challenges to Acid Rain permit conditions brought in State court during Phase II of the program, and an opportunity to intervene in the action.

3. *Integration of Titles IV and V.* Title V establishes a regime for State adoption and EPA approval of operating permit programs for implementing all air quality requirements of the Act (*e.g.*, air toxics, State implementation plans, and during Phase II, Acid Rain standards). (*See* regulations proposed at 40 CFR part 70 May 10, 1991 56 FR 21712). The regulations proposed today at 40 CFR part 72 set forth requirements for affected sources to obtain Acid Rain permits, or the Acid Rain portion of permits issued under 40 CFR parts 70 or 71, under three different situations: (1) During Phase I, when EPA is the permitting authority; (2) during Phase II, when the State or local permitting authority issues a 40 CFR part 70 permit which includes a specific Acid Rain Section; and (3) during Phase II, when EPA is the permitting authority under 40 CFR part 71 where the State or local agency is not adequately administering or enforcing a 40 CFR part 70 program.

* * *

4. *Accountability.* The Agency plans to ensure accountability by requiring strict compliance with the stringent excess emissions offset and penalty requirements provided for in section 411 of the Act. The excess emissions requirements are proposed today at 40 CFR part 77. Section 411 of the Act provides that for each ton of SO_2 or NO_x emitted in excess of an affected unit's emissions limitation, the source must pay a statutory base penalty of $2000. This penalty is estimated to be more than twice the expected market value of an allowance. In addition, a unit with excess emissions of SO_2 will be required to expeditiously offset the excess tons emitted. For SO_2 excess emissions, EPA must automatically deduct allowances from the affected unit's account absent an approved alternative offset plan. The Agency believes that the economic implications of these stringent requirements, along with the risk of additional enforcement, will go far to ensure accountability in the program.

* * *

C. Designated Representative

1. *Role and Certification Requirement.* Subpart B of today's proposal governs the process for certifying, and the duties of, the designated representative. As a prerequisite to obtaining a permit, section 408(i) of the Act requires that a designated representative for the owners and operators of each affected unit at the affected source file a certificate of representation with regard to Acid Rain matters. In addition, section 408(c)(1) and (d)(2) require the designated representative for the affected source to submit the source's permit applications. Under subpart B, no more than one designated representative must be certified for each affected source. The designated representative would represent the owners and operators of each affected unit at the affected source, as well as the owners and operators of the affected source as a whole, in matters pertaining to the Acid Rain program including: each affected unit's and source's submission of and compliance with Acid Rain permits, permit applications, and compliance plans; and the holding, transfer and disposition of allowances for each affected unit at the affected source. These duties are consistent with the provisions of title IV, which require that the owners and operators of affected units act through a "designated representative" with respect to such matters.

* * *

2. *Owner/Operator Liability*. As a result of the binding authority of the designated representative, subpart B states that the designated representative and the multiple owners and operators of an affected source or affected unit would share liability for any violation by the source or unit of, or any failure by the source or unit to comply with, the requirements of title IV. In certifying an affected source's permit application, the designated representative and the owners and operators of the affected source and of each affected unit at the source would be bound to comply with its terms, and would be responsible for ensuring the affected source's and unit's compliance with those terms.

* * *

3. *Designated Representative, Multiple Unit Permits, and Multiple Source Compliance Options*.

a. *Multi-unit sources*. Since permits would be issued to each affected source, and affected sources typically will have more than one affected unit, the rule proposes that there be one designated representative certified for each affected source. Thus, even though ownership of multiple units at an affected source might vary, the important programmatic need of dealing with one representative for the affected source would be preserved. The owners and operators of any one affected unit at an affected source would not, however, be liable for violations of the title IV requirements by another affected unit at the same affected source in which they had no ownership or operator interest merely because the two units shared the same designated representative. Multi-unit liability would only be involved to the extent the two units were governed by a multi-unit compliance plan that was violated, or if the violation was of a source requirement (such as the requirement to submit a complete permit application in a timely manner).

* * *

D. Acid Rain Permit Applications and Compliance Plans

Section 408(a) of the Act specifies that the program be implemented through permits issued to affected sources in accordance with titles IV and V, which in turn provide that it is illegal for a source to operate without a permit. Consistent with other environmental permit programs, such as the National Pollutant Discharge Elimination System (NPDES) under the Clean Water Act, the Resource Conservation and Recovery Act (RCRA), and as provided by title V of the Act, this rule would place the burden of ensuring that an affected source is permitted on the responsible official for the source, which in the case of the Acid Rain program is the duly certified designated representative. (See discussion of subpart B, above). The Act makes it clear that affected sources are responsible for ensuring compliance with the requirements of the Act; this responsibility does not rest with EPA. (See further discussion, below, concerning permit application shields.)

Subpart C sets forth the basic requirements for permit applications, including the requirement to accompany the application with a proposed compliance plan for each affected unit at the source. In accordance with section 408 of the Act, subpart C provides that permit applications and proposed compliance plans would be binding on the source until the permit was issued. Today's proposal, therefore, would require that the designated representative certify that the source will comply with certain standard conditions contained on the forms pursuant to the Act.

Another information requirement would be that each unit must specify the most stringent federally enforceable allowable emissions limitation for that unit at the time of application. This limitation would be calculated using the annualization factors included with the National Allowance Data Base proposal (Friday, July 19, 1991, 56 FR 33278).

* * *

2. *Mandatory Use of Forms/Paperwork Reduction Act.* The Agency believes that it is important to minimize the imposition of duplicative or inconsistent information requirements on sources. Today's proposal would do so through the use of standardized forms and by codifying certain critical information concerning existing sources in the Appendices. (See, e.g., appendices A, B and C). It is also important, however, to ensure that all necessary permit information and enforceable requirements be specified in one consolidated format, in order to expedite permit processing, to afford meaningful public review of proposed permit actions, and to ensure compliance. Ensuring that permit applications and proposed compliance plans have complete information is particularly important to the Acid Rain program since, pursuant to sections 408(c)(1)(A) and 408(d)(3) of the Act, an Acid Rain permit application and proposed compliance plan submitted in accordance with title IV is binding on the source until superseded by a permit and approved compliance plan. Today's proposal would, thus, require permit applications to include certain information which EPA could obtain by other methods. In balancing these competing interests, the Agency has determined that the costs to sources of providing certain critical information that might be otherwise available are outweighed by the benefits of having all of the information about a source necessary to write a permit and ensure compliance prior to a permit's effective date provided by the applicant in one document.

* * *

EPA is also developing the Acid Rain permit program with a view toward eventual electronic reporting for permit applications and compliance plans for Phase II. Consistent with current EPA policy, set forth at 55 FR 31030 (July 30, 1990), the forms proposed today have been developed in a way that is compatible with ANSI-X12, a computer-reporting system which is in widespread use throughout the United States for commercial reporting of information.

* * *

3. *Relationship of Acid Rain Permits to Emissions Monitoring Requirements.*

a. *Monitoring plans and certifications.* The permit application for the source would have to indicate how each affected unit at the source would meet its emissions monitoring requirements under section 412 of the Act and 40 CFR part 75. The Agency is, consequently, proposing in the emissions monitoring rules at 40 CFR part 75 that the designated representative for each Phase I affected source submit a proposed monitoring plan to EPA for approval for each affected unit at the source, prior to or concurrent with the source's permit application. * * *

b. *Alternative monitoring applications.* Unless a source had obtained Agency approval under 40 CFR part 75 of an alternative monitoring system by the time a permit application was submitted, the permit would be issued requiring compliance with the CEMS requirements of 40 CFR part 75.

* * *

E. Acid Rain Compliance Options

A fundamental feature of the Acid Rain program is the flexibility provided in the Act for sources to choose cost effective means of complying with the mandated SO_2 and NO_x emissions reductions requirements. Sections 404, 405, 407, 408, 409, and 410 of the Act provide various compliance options by which an affected unit may obtain special relief to assist in its efforts to comply with its emissions limitations under the program. Section 408(b) specifies that the option or options chosen for each affected unit must be articulated in the proposed compliance plan submitted with the permit application for the source. It is important to note, however, that no special compliance planning would be required by the Acid Rain program for sources choosing to fuel switch, or (except for Phase I extension, repowering, and some of the NO_x options) to install control equipment. Rather, Acid Rain program compliance planning is limited to affected units seeking special regulatory treatment as provided in subpart D.

Subpart D describes the proposed requirements for each of the compliance options specifically authorized by the Act. As provided in subpart C each permit application would contain at least a standard permit application form specifying information and applicable standard requirements for each affected unit at an affected source. These would include the standard compliance requirement, i.e., a certification for each affected unit that it will meet the applicable emissions limitation requirements of the program in a timely manner, including a certification that for purposes of SO_2 compliance the affected unit will hold enough allowances in its Allowance Tracking System compliance subaccount to cover its SO_2 emissions for the year. (For NO_x , the emissions limitation would be the applicable limitation specified in 40 CFR part 76, and each permit application would have to identify the type of boiler involved so that the applicable 40 CFR part 76 NO_x limitation would be clear).

If an affected unit planned to comply with the Acid Rain program SO_2 or NO_x standard compliance requirements without any special exceptions, a simple check-box on the permit application would indicate this choice. However, for affected units relying on one or more of the compliance options for SO_2 or NO_x authorized by the Act, a proposed compliance plan using the appropriate form for the option or options chosen would have to be included with the permit application package. Upon approval, the unit-specific compliance plans would be attached to the permit for that source and, depending on the option approved, would modify the program's standard requirements.

* * *

1. *Multi-Unit Requirements*. The rule proposes that the permitting authority can approve multi-unit compliance plans where the units are located at different sources. In such cases, the designated representative of each source would have to certify the compliance plan, a copy of which would have to be included in the permit application for each source. This provision is intended to provide utilities with flexibility in determining least-cost methods of compliance, and to allow compliance plans that are consistent, for example, with pre-existing power pooling arrangements. Restricting compliance plans to one source would greatly interfere with this flexibility.

2. *Phase I Substitution Plans*. Subsections 404 (b) and (c) of the Act authorize any source with a Phase I appendix A affected unit to propose in its Acid Rain compliance plan a reassignment of the affected unit's Phase I sulfur dioxide emissions reduction requirements, in whole or in part, to one or more existing Phase II, appendix B units. The designated substitution unit would, in turn, become a Phase I unit. The intent of this provision is to give any appendix A Phase I unit the flexibility to reassign its Phase I emissions reductions obligations by allowing an appendix B unit to achieve reductions in its place, above and beyond what the Phase II unit would otherwise be required to achieve. It also would provide Phase II appendix B units the opportunity to participate in the Acid Rain program allowance system early, and to benefit from the economies associated with the allocation and banking of allowances.

The following example illustrates how a substitution plan might work: A Phase I unit emits 100,000 tons of SO_2 a year, but is only entitled to receive 50,000 allowances to cover its annual SO_2 emissions. It, therefore, needs 50,000 tons of extra allowances. Under a substitution plan, a utility may meet its allowance obligations by reducing emissions from one or more appendix B units by a total of 50,000 tons from its 1985 level of emissions and transfer the appendix B unit's allowances to the appendix A unit.

a. *Applicable units/exclusions.* Only existing Phase II units (listed in appendix B) would be eligible to participate in substitution plans with Phase I units.

* * *

b. *"Common control" requirement.* The proposed requirement in § 72.41(a) that the substitution unit be under the "common control" of the same designated representative as the appendix A unit for which the proposed plan is submitted is based on the statutory requirement that the units be under the control of the same "owner or operator".

c. *Conditions of plan.* The Act requires that the substitution plan ensure that the same or greater emissions reductions be achieved as would have been required to be achieved without the plan.

3. *Phase I Extension Plans.* Section 72.42 of the rule would implement the authority in section 404(d) of the Act, which provides that Phase I units may apply for a two-year extension of the Phase I compliance deadline of January 1, 1995, provided that the units install 90% sulfur dioxide removal technology or transfer their emissions reduction obligations to a unit or units that install such technology. * * * The Act provides that applications for Phase I extensions be acted upon by the Administrator in the "order of receipt". A limited reserve of up to 3.5 million allowances is authorized in title IV to provide units that apply early enough and are granted Phase I extensions the extra allowances they will need to cover their sulfur dioxide emissions during the extension period.[2] The unit which installs the 90% control technology ("control unit") would also be eligible for additional allowance awards from this reserve for the three years after the extension period (1997-1999). These additional allowances would be provided to the extent the control technology reduces emissions at the unit beyond the standard Phase II emissions limitation of 1.2 lbs/mmBtu. (See, section 404(d)(4)(c)).

Section 404(d) was included in the Act to reduce the impact of the Acid Rain emissions reduction program on employment in high-sulfur coal mining communities, and to defray the compliance costs and consequent electricity rate increases that would otherwise be charged by some of the Phase I utilities currently using high-sulfur coal.

* * *

4. Phase I Reduced Utilization Plans and Under-utilization Accounting Requirements

a. *Background.* Utilities with units subject to emissions limitations in Phase I of the Acid Rain program may choose among a number of compliance strategies. One such strategy is to reduce utilization at higher emitting units, and to replace this generation

[2] A unit granted an "extension" under section 404(d) is not exempted by title IV from the requirement to prevent emissions of sulfur dioxide in excess of the allowances held in the unit's Allowance Tracking System account. Section 404(d) is, thus, better understood as authorizing a higher sulfur dioxide emissions limitation (and more allowances) for a two-year period, rather than an "extension" of the compliance date.

through increased utilization of low-emitting units.[4] In enacting title IV, however, Congress recognized that during Phase I of the Acid Rain program, reductions in emissions attributable to a decrease in utilization of Phase I affected units below their baseline could prevent full achievement of expected emissions reductions if the generation were shifted to non-affected units.[5] This is because such load shifting would result in a decrease in emissions and concomitant creation of excess allowances at the Phase I unit, despite the fact that there was an emissions increase at the non- affected unit providing compensating generation.

At the same time, Congress recognized that in order to ensure electric reliability, it was necessary to accommodate temporary changes in emissions (and shifts in utilization) resulting from decisions related to normal dispatching procedures and responses to emergencies. Because such load shifting between affected and non-affected units, whether planned or unplanned, could cut the actual aggregate emissions reductions expected during Phase I by as much as 50% a year, the Act includes two provisions, section 408(c)(1)(B) and section 403(d), to address these related but distinct situations. Both provisions give EPA the authority to require an allowance accounting for increases in emissions at otherwise non-affected units providing compensating generation.

Throughout the rule and preamble the term "under-utilization" is used to refer to any decrease in utilization at a Phase I unit below its baseline.[6] The term "reduced utilization" is used to refer only to under-utilization subject to the planning requirements of section 408(c)(1)(B) of the Act.

(1) Section 408(c)(1)(B). Under section 408(c)(1)(B), the designated representative, owners, and operators of any Phase I affected unit planning to achieve Phase I emissions limitation requirements by reducing the unit's utilization below its baseline or shutting the unit down, and shifting generation to a unit that is not otherwise affected during Phase I, are required to designate the otherwise unaffected unit as a Phase I compensating unit. The designated compensating unit becomes a Phase I affected unit subject to the Phase I emissions limitation, permitting, monitoring and excess emissions requirements of the Act. In addition, the designated compensating unit is allocated allowances by the Administrator approximately equal to its 1985 emissions, pursuant to a formula set out in section 408(c)(1)(B).[7]

In this way, the Act allows shifts in generation from a Phase I unit to a designated compensating unit, while ensuring that emissions increases at the compensating unit

---

[4] The inherent fungibility of allowances and emissions reflects Congress' intent to enable utilities to utilize least-emissions dispatching procedures, in order to minimize their compliance costs. (See, Sen. Rept. No. 228, 101st Cong., 1st Sess., pp. 316, 319 (1989), House Rept. No. 490, 101st Cong., 2nd Sess. p. 373 (1990).)

[5] *E.g.* Phase II appendix B or new units.

[6] "Baseline" refers to the unit's annual average 1985 through 1987 heat input or utilization measured in mmBtu. With certain specified exceptions, the Acid Rain program allowance allocation scheme established in title IV is based on the unit's baseline utilization. Generally speaking, yearly allowance allocations are calculated by multiplying the baseline for a unit by the presumptive emissions limitation for the Phase. It is important to note that neither the rule nor the statutory provisions are concerned about decreases in utilization at Phase I units that do not cause the unit's total utilization for a Phase I year to be less than its baseline.

[7] New units, having a zero baseline, would not receive any allowance under the formula.

are accounted for in the allowance system. In addition, all allowance savings resulting from the reduced utilization at the Phase I unit can be banked by the source, since these unused allowances will correspond to actual net reductions in SO_2 emissions for the year.

* * *

6. *New Unit Plans.* New units are defined in Section 402(10) of the Act as units which commenced commercial operation on or after November 15, 1990. Such units are generally subject to the Acid Rain program during Phase II. The proposed rule would require new units to begin complying with the Phase II Acid Rain emissions reduction requirements upon "commencement of operation," i.e., when the unit begins emitting SO_2 and NO_x.

Although most new units which commence operation between enactment and 1995 will receive some allowances pursuant to section 405(g) of the Act, new units which commence commercial operation after 1995 will receive no allocations. Rather they are required under title IV to obtain allowances to cover their SO 2 emissions from the market. A detailed discussion of which new units would be allocated allowances can be found in the preamble discussion of 40 CFR Part 73.

Although new units are generally not subject to Acid Rain program emissions reduction requirements until Phase II, a new unit may become an affected unit during Phase I if it shares a common stack with a Phase I affected unit and does not monitor emissions independently (or has not been approved for alternative monitoring pursuant to 40 CFR part 75), or if it is designated as a compensating unit in a reduced utilization plan. Today's proposal specifies that each such new unit would not be allocated allowances during Phase I and would be deemed to have a baseline of zero. Although under section 405(g) the Administrator is authorized to allocate allowances to some new units, beginning on January 1, 2000, the statute does not provide for these units to receive allowances in Phase I.

* * *

7. *Nitrogen Oxides Options—Generally.* Section 407 of the Act requires that the Administrator promulgate nitrogen oxides emissions limitations for boilers[15] that are affected units under the sulfur dioxide requirements of title IV of the Act.

* * *

8. *Phase I or Phase II Nitrogen Oxides Emissions Averaging Plans.* Pursuant to section 407(e), a NO_x emissions averaging plan would allow two or more units subject to the applicable emission limitations established pursuant to section 407 at 40 CFR part 76, to petition the permitting authority for alternative contemporaneous annual emission limitations for such units. Section 72.46 would specify the procedures by which a proposed NO_x emissions averaging plan would have to be submitted for approval, and some of the information requirements of the application.

* * *

[15] Section 402 of the Act defines the term "unit" to mean any "fossil fuel-fired combustion device." This can be a boiler, a turbine, or any other fossil fuel-fired device. The nitrogen oxides requirements of section 407, however, apply only to units that are boilers.

9. *Phase I or Phase II Nitrogen Oxides Alternative Emission Limitations Plans.* Section 72.47 of today's proposal would implement the NO_x alternative emission limitation compliance option authorized by section 407(d) of the Act. Under this section the designated representative for a unit subject to the NO_x emission limitation requirements of title IV of the Act and 40 CFR part 76, could request an alternative, less stringent, limitation, if a demonstration is made that appropriate control equipment, as specified in 40 CFR part 76, cannot meet the applicable limitation at that unit.

* * *

10. *Phase I Nitrogen Oxides Compliance Deadline Extension Plans.* Section 72.48 would implement the provisions under section 407(d) of the Act which allow for an extension of 15 months of the Phase I NO_x compliance deadline. The intent of this provision is to alleviate a potential timing problem that may be faced by some sources during Phase I of the program. Specifically, Congress was concerned about the ability of sources affected in Phase I to comply on time due to the cumulative impacts of the following: (1) The limited number of vendors of low-NO_x burner technology, (2) the statutory schedule for promulgation of the NO_x emission limitations for affected units, and (3) the compliance deadline of January 1, 1995.

The NO_x compliance deadline extension would apply only during Phase I and only to the NO_x emission reduction provisions. Any unit which is an affected unit for NO_x during Phase I would be eligible to apply for the extension.

* * *

F. Acid Rain Permit Contents.

Subpart E describes the content requirements of all Acid Rain permits, including general information, designated representative certifications, prohibitions, the incorporation of Acid Rain program definitions, allowance information, compliance plans, monitoring requirements, and reporting and recordkeeping requirements. These requirements are mandated by the statute or are necessary to ensure that the permit provisions are enforceable and will achieve the emissions reductions required by the Act. Each permit would specify the annual basic and bonus allowance allocation for each unit because if the allowance system were to fail, the annual emissions limit for each unit would be that unit's annual allowance allocation.

The Acid Rain permit content requirements would apply to all Phase I and Phase II Acid Rain permits, whether those permits were issued by EPA or by a State or local permitting authority with a program approved under Title V. The purpose of the Acid Rain permit is to provide a document where all of the Acid Rain requirements that apply to an individual source, and to each unit at the source, are articulated. This would provide certainty to the source, the permitting authority, and the public regarding exactly what requirements the source is subject to under the program.

1. *Permit Shield.* This subpart would also address the "permit application shield" and "permit shield" effects of permit submissions under the Acid Rain program. Section 72.53(a) would, consistent with section 503(d) of the Act, shield any source which has submitted a timely and complete permit application, from any possible liability under section 502(a) of the Act for operating without a permit, where the source's failure to have a permit is the result of inaction on the part of the permitting authority and no fault of the source. The application shield would also apply where an affected source operates

in compliance with an approved permit application and compliance plan binding on the source prior to the permit's effective date.

In addition, consistent with section 504(f) of the Act and § 70.6(h)(1) of the proposed title V regulations, § 72.52(b) of today's proposal would shield any source operated in accordance with a permit properly issued under title IV and 40 CFR part 72, from enforcement. The provision would give certainty to affected sources operated in compliance with the terms of a properly issued permit that they would no longer be subject to other requirements of the program that might otherwise apply. For example, a unit governed by a properly approved repowering extension, would no longer be subject to the January 1, 2000 Phase II compliance deadline.

Section 72.52(b) would, however, limit the shield that is being proposed by the Agency under section 504(f) at § 70.6(h)(1). Specifically, as required by section 408(h)(2) and as authorized by section 504(f), EPA proposes that a source would not be shielded by a provision of a permit that does not clearly comply with the requirements of title IV or the Acid Rain program, including any provision in a title V permit or State decision interpreting a title V permit in a manner that would alter the applicability of a title IV requirement to a source. The Agency interprets the language in section 504(f) authorizing such limitations on the shield and the limiting language in section 408(h)(2) as a protection against permit conditions, including conditions resulting from a State interpretation of a permit provision, that would alter essential Acid Rain program requirements such as the requirements governing designated representatives, emissions monitoring, recordkeeping, and reporting, approval of compliance options, and liability.

* * *

G. Acid Rain Phase I Implementation

1. *Description of Process*. Subpart F describes the proposed implementation of the Phase I Acid Rain permit program. The units covered under Phase I of the program, listed in appendix A, generally include the largest plants with the highest SO_2 emissions in the United States. In addition, certain other units may become affected units in Phase I of the program under one or more of the compliance options provided in subpart D. Title IV of the Act mandates that SO_2 and NO_x emissions reductions for Phase I affected units begin on January 1, 1995 and continue in effect until December 31, 1999. While the Phase I emissions reduction obligations begin on January 1, 1995, some Phase I requirements begin earlier.

Title IV requires that Phase I permitting be implemented by EPA. The Agency will process permit applications, write and issue permits, and process permit revisions. In addition, in cooperation with State and local air quality agencies, EPA will monitor compliance and take appropriate enforcement action as necessary. In contrast, permitting for Phase II of the Acid Rain program, which begins January 1, 2000, will be implemented by States with approved operating permit programs under title V of the Act, and by EPA only for sources in States where an operating permit program has not been approved. This subpart includes the proposed deadlines and procedures for the Phase I permit program only.

Consistent with section 408, the basic permitting process for Phase I would be as follows: The designated representatives for Phase I affected sources would be required to submit Acid Rain permit applications and proposed compliance plans to the Agency on or before February 15, 1993. (Designated representative certifications under subpart B, would have to be filed for each Phase I affected source not later than with the permit application.) The Agency would review and act on these applications, using the procedures set forth in subpart G including an opportunity for public comment, within 6 months of receipt. (For sources applying on February 15, this would be about August 15, 1993; earlier applications would receive earlier attention.) The rule would afford sources and persons who commented on proposed permits an opportunity to appeal permitting decisions (using the procedures set forth in subpart H). The appeals would have to be filed within 60 days of the Agency's decision; thus, ensuring that disputes will be resolved prior to the emissions reduction requirements that begin on January 1, 1995.

2. *Treatment of Effective Date of Permits*. Section 408(a) of the Act specifies that Acid Rain permits have a term of five years, but section 408(c)(2) requires EPA to act on compliance plans by August 15, 1993. EPA believes that the clear intent of Congress was for Phase I Acid Rain permits to remain in effect for the 5-year duration of Phase I. Thus, the Agency is proposing to issue Phase I permits on or about August 15, 1993, and to have those permits take effect on January 1, 1995. This interpretation of the statutory deadlines would ensure that the Phase I permits will not expire in the middle of Phase I.

* * *

I. Appeal Procedures for Acid Rain Permits

* * *

Section 307 of the Act provides an opportunity for judicial review of final Agency action under the Act in Federal circuit court. Such judicial review is available after the petitioner has exhausted all administrative remedies, such as administrative appeals procedures. Use of an administrative appeals procedure is consistent with other environmental permitting programs, including the NPDES, RCRA, and PSD programs. An administrative appeals procedure is, moreover, appropriate since it would allow the Agency to review permitting decisions for correctness before having to defend permitting actions in Federal court. This approach would also provide petitioners with a less resource intensive (and less time-consuming) process for resolving disputes concerning Acid Rain permit conditions, than would be involved in a judicial action.

The administrative appeals procedures proposed in subpart H are guided by two concerns: (a) The need to expedite the appeals process (particularly since an opportunity for public comment would have already been provided before any permitting decision was reached), and (b) the need to provide a forum for resolving factual disputes if necessary in any final review by the Administrator.

The rule would allow appeals of decisions by the Administrator on the basis of factual, legal, or policy issues. The rule would include limited opportunity for an evidentiary hearing to resolve disputes concerning genuine issues of material fact. Specifically in reviewing any appeal involving disputed issues of fact, the Administrator would have the option of referring the case to a Presiding Officer (see definitions) appointed by the Chief Administrative Law Judge to conduct an evidentiary hearing. If permit issuance responsibility is delegated to the Regions (see discussion of subparts F and G), the Agency proposes that such appeals would be heard in the Region in which the affected unit is located.

The rules and procedures proposed today for conducting evidentiary hearings are based on the procedures used for permit appeals in the NPDES program, and on the Federal Rules of Civil Procedure. To ensure expedition, Presiding Officers would be required to: limit evidentiary hearings to genuine issues of material fact, limit evidence to such factual issues, and bar testimony on legal and policy issues. The Presiding Officer would, moreover, be authorized to limit the hearing to a paper evidentiary hearing where direct- and cross-examination of witnesses would not be necessary for a full and true disclosure of the facts. This is appropriate since permitting is an essential rulemaking function and, as previously mentioned, there would already have been an opportunity for public comment.

The rule proposes that the standard of review to be applied by the Administrator and Presiding Officer be as follows. The person seeking a permit would bear the burden of proof that the permit should be issued. Any person challenging the permitting decision would bear the burden of going forward and showing that: (1) with regard to any factual finding or legal conclusion underlying the permitting decision, the standard is "clearly erroneous"; and (2) with regard to an exercise of discretion or a policy determination underlying the permitting decision, the standard would be "arbitrary and capricious". These standards are consistent with the traditional standards for reviewing actions of agencies under the Administrative Procedures Act.

After a petition for review is filed, the Administrator would grant or deny the petition and have the option to refer the petition to a Presiding Officer for evidentiary hearing. If the petition for review is granted and an evidentiary hearing is not granted, the parties may file briefs. The Administrator would, thereafter, issue a final order addressing the appealed issues. The order, supplemented by the record of the appeal and of the decision, would become the final Agency action.

If the case is referred to a Presiding Officer for hearing, the Presiding Officer's review would conclude with a proposed order. The proposed order would become a final Agency action, unless (a) the Administrator issued a notice of intent to review within 30 days, sua sponte; or (b) a party filed a further appeal to the Administrator objecting to the proposed order within 15 days and the Administrator issued a notice of intent to review the proposed order pursuant to the objection. An appeal of a proposed order to the Administrator would have to allege that a finding of fact or conclusion of law was clearly erroneous, or that an exercise of discretion or a policy determination was arbitrary and capricious. In issuing a notice of review, the Administrator would have discretion to allow briefs by the parties.

* * *

J. Acid Rain Phase II Implementation

Subpart I sets forth the permitting requirements for Phase II of the Acid Rain program.[18] Unlike Phase I, section 408 requires that Phase II permitting be implemented by States with operating permit programs approved under 40 CFR part 70 by July 1, 1996. In the event a State's permit program has not been approved in time under 40 CFR part 70, EPA would implement the Acid Rain permit requirements for affected sources in that State in accordance with 40 CFR part 71 and this part. (The process for Federal permitting of Phase II requirements would be the same as for Phase I and for other Federal permit issuance under 40 CFR part 71 in instances of State

[18] Phase II emissions reductions begin on January 1, 2000 following the conclusion of Phase I. Some other Phase II requirements begin earlier (e.g. emissions monitoring, and schedules for sources applying for repowering extensions). In Phase II, the remaining affected units that were not regulated in Phase I, e.g., those listed in appendix B of today's proposal, will be subject to Acid Rain Program emissions reduction requirements. New units and units that "opt in" under the terms of 40 CFR part 74 will be regulated as well.

defaults under 40 CFR part 70.) In some cases, a State may obtain 40 CFR part 70 program approval after July 1, 1996, but before the EPA has issued initial Phase II permits to all of the Acid Rain sources in the State. Some States may have relatively few Phase II Acid Rain sources to begin with. The EPA, thus, proposes to reserve the right to delegate responsibility for permit review and implementation to such a State, potentially including permit issuance for all unpermitted Acid Rain sources, if EPA determines that such a delegation would not result in undue burden for the permitting authority or delay.

Pursuant to the schedules and procedures of title IV, subpart I would require affected sources to submit Phase II permit applications and proposed compliance plans for SO_2 by January 1, 1996, for NO_x by January 1, 1998, and for new units twenty four months before the latter of January 1, 2000 or the date the unit "commences operation". Copies of each application would have to be sent to the State, to EPA Headquarters, and to the Region.

Subpart I provides that the State with an approved program would make a determination of completeness in accordance with 40 CFR 70.5(c), and would notify the Administrator of such determination.[19] The permitting authority then would write a "draft permit" (See, § 72.2 definitions) and allow opportunity for public comment in accordance with section 502(b)(6) and proposed 40 CFR part 70(i). Following the public comment period, the State would submit a "proposed permit" to EPA for review. Following EPA review, and assuming EPA did not veto the proposed permit as provided in proposed Section 70.8, the Acid Rain permit would be issued. Section 408 mandates that Phase II SO_2 permits be issued by States on or before December 31, 1997. As is discussed above regarding subpart E, applications would be binding on sources before the permit is issued.

* * *

1. *Appeals of State Issued Permits.* Consistent with 40 CFR 70.4(b)(3)(x) and section 502(b)(6) of the Act, appeals of Acid Rain provisions in State-issued permits would occur through State administrative and judicial appeals procedures. The Agency believes this requirement is appropriate since the expression of Congressional intent in section 502(b)(6) that States undertake these functions is clear. In addition, with the exception of matters constituting actions of the Administrator (See discussion below), the State will have made the permitting decisions which will be considered on appeal. Furthermore, the Acid Rain requirements will be only one portion of the State-issued operating permit applicable to an affected source, and other operating permit provisions may also be at issue in any appeal.

Decisions of the Administrator that are incorporated into State issued Acid Rain permits would, however, be subject to the administrative appeals procedures set forth at subpart H, and to judicial review in Federal circuit court pursuant to section 307(b)(1) of the Act which provides an opportunity for Federal court review of "final actions of the Administrator". Decisions of the Administrator that must be incorporated into the source's operating permit include: acceptance of a designated representative certification

---

[19] The permit application and proposed compliance plan are binding on the source prior to permit issuance. (See § 408(d)(3).) The Agency is proposing that the application and proposed compliance plan be binding upon submission to the permitting authority. The Agency believes, however, that a disapproved or incomplete application should not be binding because it does not meet the applicable requirements of the Act. The rule proposes that the State inform EPA if any completeness determination in order to know whether the application is binding on the source and enforceable.

and issuance of a designated representative identification number, approval of a monitoring plan, certification of a monitoring system and or of an alternative emissions monitoring system under 40 CFR part 75, approval of an excess emissions offset plan under 40 CFR part 77, and determination of whether a proposed technology meets the criteria for a repowering extension under subpart D. The Agency believes that such decisions of the Administrator should be appealed federally rather than through State procedures because: (1) The State was not involved in making the decision, (2) a Federal review procedure for these decisions will help ensure a nationally consistent body of judicial precedent, and (3) as final Agency action, the decisions will be reviewable in Federal rather than State court. The Agency is, therefore, proposing that decisions of the Administrator that are incorporated into the Acid Rain portion of a State permit be subject to Federal administrative, and (upon becoming final) Federal judicial appeal procedures if challenged. This is consistent with statutory authority, as any final decision of the Administrator is reviewable in Federal court under section 307(b)(1) of the Act, and is therefore not appropriate for State court review. State court actions in such cases is preempted.

* * *

K. Permit Revisions.

Subpart J specifies the procedures that would apply for revising Acid Rain permits. The rule proposes that permit revisions would become effective upon approval in accordance with the procedures specified in subpart J. This is to ensure that no proposed revision could be used to insulate a source from the obligation to comply with a permitted requirement, and to provide clarity regarding what applies to a source at any given point in time.

* * *

L. Compliance Certification.

Compliance certifications are a fundamental element of the Acid Rain program's implementation strategy. The term "compliance certification" is defined in today's proposal as a report signed and verified by the designated representative of the source's or unit's compliance or non-compliance with applicable requirements. The statutory authority for this requirement can be found in section 114(a) of the Act (as amended by section 702 of Act Amendments of 1990), which requires that the Administrator promulgate enhanced monitoring and compliance certification regulations, and in section 504(c) in title V of the Act, which requires that compliance certification requirements be included in each source's operating permit.

The Agency believes that heavy reliance on compliance certifications in the Acid Rain program will greatly increase flexibility, reduce the burden on sources of demonstrating compliance while maintaining the Agency's ability to ensure program accountability. They will also provide a helpful vehicle for resolving misunderstandings concerning applicable requirements before there has been a violation. This feature which should greatly increase program certainty for sources.

The strategy of relying heavily on certifications evidences a dramatic departure from the methods traditionally used to determine compliance, i.e., on-site inspections and source-specific investigatory letters requiring the collection and submission of emissions data and operational reports. The Agency proposes that every Acid Rain program submittal be certified as to its truth and accuracy by the designated representative. As is discussed in Subpart B, only the designated representative can submit compliance certifications.

Compliance certifications are categorized in today's proposal according to frequency of submission, such as quarterly or annual. The proposal specifies the contents and submission dates for these certifications and reports. The submission deadlines are consistent with the Agency's proposal today at 40 CFR part 73, specifying an end of year allowance transfer deadline for sources to consolidate data and conform their allowance accounts, and the emissions data reporting requirements of 40 CFR part 75.

* * *

M. Phase I Extension Early Ranking Procedures.

Subpart L would provide the procedures for early ranking of Phase I Extension plans submitted under § 72.42 of today's proposal. Subpart L addresses two concerns: (1) The statutory mandate in section 404(d)(3) of the Act that submissions for Phase I Extensions be considered by the Administrator "in order of receipt", and (2) the need of the regulated community to know as early as possible whether they will be eligible for Phase I Extension allowances. Because of the economic benefits a source would derive from a Phase I Extension, some estimates indicate that the Phase I Extension allowance reserve of up to 3.5 million tons, mandated by section 404(a)(2) of the Act, may be oversubscribed. Many sources can, therefore, be expected to apply for Phase I Extension allowances in a short period of time, making it difficult to determine the "order of receipt" of a proposed Phase I Extension plan submitted under § 72.42 by relying exclusively on postal delivery services.

The Agency is, thus, proposing an Early Ranking procedure for determining the order in which to act on Phase I Extension applications. The Agency proposes to use a voice-mail telephone queuing procedure followed by a written Phase I Extension Early Ranking application submission mailed not later than midnight of the same business day of the phone queue. The "order of receipt" established by the Early Ranking procedure would be conditional. In particular, it would be conditioned on timely submission by the designated representative for each applicant, in accordance with the procedures proposed in subpart C and § 72.42 of subpart D of today's proposal, of a complete and approvable permit application and proposed compliance plan by the Phase I permit application deadline of February 15, 1993 specified in section 408 of the Act.

* * *

V. Sulfur Dioxide Allowance System Regulation

A. Allowance Rule Background and Summary

* * *

2. *Function of Allowances in the Acid Rain Program.* As discussed in sections II and III of this preamble, the fundamental compliance mechanism for the SO_2 reduction program is an innovative system of marketable allowances. Since allowances are the fundamental instruments of SO_2 compliance, the Act requires EPA to establish a system for tracking allowances. Accordingly, the Allowance Tracking System must be reliable, and it must be designed and must function in a way that does not impair the ability of affected units to use allowance transfers to maximize efficiency in their compliance strategies.

3. *Statutory Authority for the Proposed Allowance System.* Section 403 of the Act creates the primary authority for the regulations proposed today. Excepting certain

provisions in effect only through the year 2009, section 403(a) of the Act mandates that EPA allocate allowances for each affected unit in an amount equal to its statutory SO_2 emissions limitation requirement (expressed in tons), provided that no more than 8.95 million allowances are allocated annually after January 1, 2000.

Section 403(b) of the Act authorizes the transfer of allowances between and among units through the "designated representative" for the owners and operators of each unit, and between and among any other person holding allowances. Section 403(b) also requires EPA to promulgate regulations to "establish the allowance system prescribed under this section, including, but not limited to, requirements for the allocation, transfer, and use of allowances under this title." Pursuant to section 403(b), the regulations are to "prohibit the use of any allowance prior to the calendar year for which the allowance was allocated," while providing for "unused allowances to be carried forward and added to allowances allocated in subsequent years." Section 403(b) further requires "written certification of * * * transfer(s), signed by a responsible official of each party to the transfer * * *." Finally, paragraph (b) of the section states that "recorded pre-allocation transfers shall be deducted by the Administrator from the number of allowances which would otherwise be allocated to the transferor and added to those allowances allocated to the transferee." In addition, section 403(d) of the Act requires EPA to promulgate "a system for issuing, recording, and tracking allowances, which shall specify all necessary procedures and requirements for an orderly and competitive functioning of the allowance system."

* * *

Finally, when a unit's SO_2 emissions exceed the number of allowances held for the unit, section 411(b) of the Act, in addition to imposing a $2,000 penalty for each ton (or fraction of a ton) of exceedance, requires EPA to "deduct allowances equal to the excess tonnage from those allocated for the source for the calendar year, or succeeding years during which offsets are required, following the year in which the excess emissions occurred."

4. *Summary of Today's Proposed Rule.*

a. Regulatory approach to the allowance system. The design of the allowance trading and tracking system proposed today reflects the implicit roles Congress devised for the Agency, other regulatory agencies, and the market participants.

EPA views its role as filling three critical needs of the allowance trading market: (i) Neutral, low-cost rules of exchange; (ii) basic tracking information on allowances; and (iii) certainty in the identification of a person's authority to transfer allowances. EPA therefore approached the trading rules with the view that the system should be simple to understand and should impose minimal burdens on the participants. Under today's proposal EPA would provide the authoritative record of allowance account holdings and transfers, in order to fulfill its implied statutory mandate to assure certainty for the allowance market and its express mandate to ensure compliance with SO_2 emissions requirements. These roles are clearly laid out in section 403 of the Act and are implicit in Congress' direction that EPA establish an orderly and well-functioning market.

* * *

The market participants themselves, which include both affected units and others, are the only parties who can "make the market work" by providing the various private commercial arrangements markets need to function efficiently. Indeed, in previous emission trading programs, the private market has created all necessary contractual and informational functions for the orderly operation of the markets. In view of this record and the ultimate exclusive role of private actors in determining the level of activity and efficiency of the market, it is EPA's belief that the EPA allowance system must provide flexibility to participants and be as unconstrained by regulatory authority as is reasonable while meeting the stated environmental protection objectives of the Act. Therefore, in designing the proposed regulations for part 73, EPA eschewed any option that would cast the Agency in new purportedly "market-making" roles beyond those expressly prescribed by the Act.

b. Overview of proposed rule. As proposed here in part 73, pursuant to section 403(b) and section 403(d) of the Act, EPA will establish a system of allowance accounts for each affected unit and for any other person likely to hold allowances. Allowances initially allocated by EPA for each affected unit pursuant to sections 403(a), 404, 405, 406, 408, 409 and 410 of the Act and proposed parts 72, 73 and 74 will be held in these accounts. Transfers of allowances recorded with EPA will be effected by deducting allowances from the transferor's account and adding them to the transferee's account. To determine whether or not a unit has met its annual emissions control requirements, EPA proposes to deduct, at the end of each year from each unit's account allowances usable in that year in an amount equal to the unit tons of SO_2 emissions for the year, as recorded and reported pursuant to the emissions monitoring regulations proposed today at part 75 and part 72, subpart K. If a unit's allowances exceed its emissions of SO_2 for the year, allowances remaining in the account after each year's deduction will be carried forward and banked in the unit's account for the following year. If the unit's total emissions of SO_2 for the year exceed the number of allowances usable in the year held in the unit's account, then EPA proposes to deduct, at the end of each year from each unit's account, allowances usable in that year for the following year in an amount equal to the unit's excess emissions, pursuant to an excess emissions offset plan submitted for the unit under part 77.

Part 73 of the proposed Acid Rain rules sets forth the procedures for establishing accounts, and the procedures applicable to EPA and account holders in operating the account system.

c. Design of the tracking system. For an affected unit, each allowance account would include a "compliance subaccount" (and for accounts held by others, a "current year subaccount"), for allowances that may be used for compliance purposes in that calendar year, and a subaccount for each future calendar year. For example, in Phase I each unit would have a separate subaccount for 1995, 1996, 1997, 1998, and 1999. The latter subaccounts will reflect allowances that may be used for compliance in each subsequent specified year. Each compliance and future subaccount initially would reflect the number of allowances that the Act authorizes EPA to allocate for each year for the unit. Thereafter, each subaccount's allowances would be credited or debited to reflect any allowance transfers. EPA proposes to assign a unique identification number for each allowance, which will reflect the calendar year for which the allowance may first be used for purposes of compliance ("the compliance use date").

EPA proposes to provide for the automatic banking of allowances by retaining in the compliance subaccount any allowances remaining in the subaccount that are not deducted to meet the unit's emissions limitation requirements.

The proposed rule requires EPA to establish an Allowance Tracking System account for every existing affected unit, even if the unit is affected only in Phase II, by no later than January 30, 1993. This proposed action permits EPA to record in the accounting system any allowances Phase II units may acquire, through the allowance auction or from a private seller, during Phase I (i.e., 1995-1999) and allows the Phase II units to trade their Phase II allowances immediately. In addition, EPA would establish accounts for new units, and for SO_2 sources that elect to participate or "opt in" to the allowance system, by becoming affected units for purposes of title IV (under part 74 and section 410 of the Act). Finally, any person may apply to EPA to establish a non-unit account for purposes of holding allowances, after the effective date of the part.

All matters pertaining to the account would be carried out by a person designated and certified as the authorized account representative for the account. In the case of unit accounts, the authorized account representative would be the designated representative for the unit, as established pursuant to the Acid Rain Permits regulations proposed today at part 72, subpart B.

* * *

e. Recordation of Transfers. In the proposed rule, the exchange of allowances between account holders is made by submitting to EPA a request to record the transfer of allowances from one account to another. Until allowance transfers are recorded by EPA in a unit's account, they will not be available for meeting the unit's SO_2 emissions requirements. This is true regardless of what any commercial contractual obligation between two units to transfer allowances may be. Submissions to EPA of requests to record transfers may specify the identification numbers of the allowances to be transferred. As required by the Act, the proposed rule prohibits the transfer of an allowance usable in a specified calendar year to an allowance subaccount for an earlier year. In addition, EPA proposes not to record the transfer of any allowance if the allowance as specifically identified by its serial number in the transfer request does not appear in the transferor's account.

* * *

3. *Non-Unit Accounts.* EPA is also proposing to establish accounts for persons other than affected units because section 403(b) of the Act expressly authorizes "any person," in addition to the designated representatives for affected units, to hold and transfer allowances. These non-unit accounts would provide the vehicle through which persons, such as brokers or utility power pools, seeking to aggregate allowances allocated for individual units could hold and transfer allowances. Non-unit accounts would include a current year subaccount and subaccounts for each of the 30 future years following the current year, beginning with 1996.

EPA is proposing to establish a non-unit account following the receipt of a new account application. The application would be required to include a certification by the authorized account representative. This is intended to protect ownership interests in any allowances held in the account, through disclosure of information and verification that the owners have agreed to the authorized account representative.

Both the legislative history of section 403(b), of the Act and EPA analysis suggest that brokers, investors and other market-makers may play a crucial role in facilitating allowance transfers. (See S. Rep. No. 228, 101st Congress, 1st Sess., p. 320 (1989).) In addition, as suggested by section 403(d)(2) of the Act, groups of units may choose to pool some or all of the allowances allocated for each unit. A non-unit account, created by the owners of such units but separate from the individual unit accounts, may serve as the mechanism for pooling their allowances.

* * *

7. *Compliance*

a. Allowance transfer deadline. The Allowance Tracking System account will be used by EPA to determine compliance by a unit with its SO_2 emissions limitation requirements. Consistent with the requirements in § 403(b) of the Act, EPA is proposing that no allowance can be used for the purposes of compliance with a unit's annual emissions limitation requirements for SO_2 unless, as of the allowance transfer deadline, such allowance is recorded in, or properly submitted for recordation in, the compliance subaccount for the unit. EPA is proposing that the allowance transfer deadline be January 30 of the calendar year following the year for which a unit's compliance is being determined.

* * *

14. *Public Availability.* EPA is proposing to make all information in the Allowance Tracking System accounts available to the public. Initially, EPA will make written records available. EPA is, however, developing a system of electronic access and will prescribe the appropriate methods of such access in the future, following public notice. EPA believes it is important to make account information publicly available for several reasons.

* * *

D. Energy Conservation and Renewable Energy Reserve

1. *Authority.* Section 404(f) of the Act requires the Administrator to establish a Conservation and Renewable Energy Reserve (the "Reserve") of 300,000 allowances for distribution to electric utilities engaging in energy conservation or in renewable energy generation. The Reserve is to be created by deducting from total annual Phase II allocations 30,000 allowances per year in each of the first ten years of Phase II. Utilities may begin applying for allowances from the Reserve in 1993, one year following promulgation of the regulations, and may continue to apply until all 300,000 allowances have been allocated or until the year 2010 if any remain. The allowances will not be restricted by a compliance use date, but will be allocated for emissions avoided through the use of qualified renewable generation or as a result of qualified energy conservation measures initiated after January 1, 1992, and before the earlier of December 31, 2000 or the date on which any unit owned or operated by the electric utility becomes affected under title IV of the Act.

* * *

VI. Continuous Emission Monitoring Regulation

A. Rule Background and Summary

1. *Applicability.* Pursuant to section 412 of the Clean Air Act Amendments of 1990 (the Act), proposed part 75 of the Acid Rain program applies to existing affected units, to each unit that elects to become an affected unit, and to each new utility unit upon commencement of its operation. Emission monitoring equipment required by the proposed rule would be installed, operational, and certified by November 15, 1993, for Phase I affected units; by January 1, 1995, for existing Phase II affected units; and upon commencement of operation for new units. An affected unit that formally commits to retirement before December 31, 1994, would be exempt from the requirements of the proposed rule.

2. *Purpose of the Continuous Emission Monitoring Program.* Continuous emission monitoring systems (CEMS) are indispensable to the successful implementation of the Acid Rain program because of two unique characteristics that distinguish this program from traditional emission limitation programs. First, the compliance flexibility provided

by the allowance trading provisions of the sulfur dioxide (SO_2) control program mandates complete and accurate reporting of emissions data by the affected units. Second, the Act expresses the program's emission goals in terms of absolute tons of SO_2 and nitrogen oxides (NO_x). (Traditionally, such goals have been expressed in terms of pollutant mass emission rates relative to the heat input of the fuel which, for utilities, have been in pounds of pollutant per million British thermal units (lbs/mmBtu).)

The CEMS program proposed in today's rule is essential to the proper functioning of the allowance trading provisions of the Acid Rain program because the Act uses the newly created "commodities" of allowances as proxies for emissions in the trading. As noted previously, allowances may be freely bought and sold, and EPA will compare each unit's allowances held against the unit's SO_2 emissions reported for each year. Therefore, if continuous emission monitoring fails to provide an accurate, timely, impartial, and comprehensive estimate of SO_2 emissions, the value of allowances will be unstable and uncertain, and the confidence of market participants in the trading program will be undermined.

EPA's review of other markets, including environmental emission trading markets, reinforces this conclusion. The U.S. General Accounting Office's 1986 Study of EPA's regulations for Lead Rights Banking noted that the self-reported, but unverified and uncertified, data on lead emissions from refineries produced numerous inaccuracies, which resulted in possible overstatements of both the emission reductions and the number of lead rights that were created. A similar outcome for the Acid Rain program would frustrate the emission reduction goals of the Act and undermine the value of emission control investments.

Numerous other markets reviewed by the Agency, including various stock markets, futures exchanges, and commodity markets, illustrate that there is a fundamental, essential feature to smoothly operating markets: A method for certifying the existence and quantity of the commodity to be traded. Most often, certification of the commodities are made by independent institutions whose integrity and reputation are such that their certification is trusted. The CEMS program proposed today incorporates that feature by requiring the regular reporting of emission data certified to be accurate. Additionally, regular verification and certification of the accuracy of the CEMS data by sources is reinforced by EPA's independent audit authority.

* * *

4. *Summary of Today's Proposed Rule*. Under the proposed rule, the owner(s) and operator(s) of an affected unit (or units) would be required to install and operate a CEMS on each affected unit unless otherwise specified in the regulation. The CEMS is defined as including the following components: (1) An SO_2 pollutant concentration monitor, (2) a NO_x pollutant concentration monitor, (3) a volumetric flow monitor, (4) an opacity monitor, (5) a diluent gas monitor, and (6) a data acquisition and handling system (usually computer-based) for recording and performing calculations with the data.

* * *

G. CO_2 Emissions Monitoring

Section 821 of the Act states that EPA must require each unit subject to title IV of the Act to monitor and report annual emissions of CO_2 . There are no CO_2 emission limits associated with the monitoring requirement. The emissions data are collected as a means of constructing a database that characterizes CO_2 emissions from electric utilities.

The Agency believes CO_2 emission data for affected units that generate such emissions only through fuel combustion can be obtained with sufficient accuracy for the purposes intended by either: (1) Monitoring the CO_2 concentration in the flue gas stream and calculating CO_2 emissions as the product of CO_2 concentration and measured flue gas flow rate, or (2) calculating daily CO_2 emissions based on the measured carbon content of the fuel through fuel sampling and analysis, and the annual amount of fuel combusted. Therefore, today's proposed rule provides the owner(s) and operator(s) of affected units that generate CO_2 emissions only through fuel combustion with the option of either: (1) Monitoring CO_2 emissions directly; or (2) using specified procedures and American Society for Testing and Materials (ASTM) methods to calculate CO_2 emissions based on the measured carbon content of the fuel and the amount of fuel combusted.

* * *

J. Alternative Monitoring Systems

In general, the Act requires affected units to install and operate continuous emission monitoring systems for monitoring SO_2 and NO_x emitted into the atmosphere. However, it also allows units to use an alternative monitoring system for monitoring one or both of these emissions, or a component of such emissions (e.g., SO_2 concentration, flow), provided that EPA can certify that the data produced by the alternative monitoring system is equivalent to that from a CEMS on four criteria: Precision, reliability, accessibility, and timeliness.

* * *

1. *Demonstrations of Equivalency to CEMS*. Under the proposed rule, EPA would use the performance of certified SO_2 pollutant concentration monitors, flow monitors, and NO_x continuous emission monitoring systems, defined in the previous sections, as benchmarks for approving or rejecting proposals for alternative monitoring systems. Thus, to qualify under the precision criterion, the difference between measurements from an alternative monitoring system for measuring SO_2 concentration or flow and a certified SO_2 pollution concentration or flow monitor would be required to fall within defined statistical limits.

* * *

VII. Excess Emissions Regulation

A. Background and Purpose

Part 77 of today's proposal sets forth the requirements for excess emissions offset planning and offset penalties, pursuant to section 411 of the Clean Air Act, as amended (the Act). As a general rule title IV of the Act is intended to provide maximum flexibility for sources to determine the means by which they would comply with the sulfur dioxide and nitrogen oxides emissions limitations of the Acid Rain program. However, Congress deemed the statutory goal of reducing acid deposition precursors as paramount.

Section 411 eliminates any financial benefit owners and operators of affected sources might otherwise derive from exceeding their emissions limitations, by imposing an automatically due and payable statutory penalty for each ton of excess sulfur dioxide or nitrogen oxides emissions emitted by an affected unit in a calendar year. (See, section 411(a) and (c)).

These penalties are in addition to penalty liability any source risks under other enforcement provisions of the Act (Section 411(e)). In addition, the Administrator is required to deduct sulfur dioxide allowances to the extent an affected unit has experienced excess emissions of sulfur dioxide in any calendar year. (See, section 411(b)). (This obligation is in addition to other allowance deductions that would be required for, e.g., violations of Phase I Extension plan's provisions under section 404(d)(7), or the reduced utilization planning provisions.)

Finally, Congress underscored the severity with which it viewed violations of Acid Rain program requirements, including excess emissions, by providing specifically that nothing in section 411 limits or affects the liability that a source might have under the Act's other enforcement authorities, including section 113 which authorizes the imposition of civil and criminal sanctions for violations of the section 411(e)).

Given the degree of flexibility otherwise afforded sources under title IV, the Agency proposes to ensure strict compliance by affected sources with the emissions reduction requirements of the Acid Rain program, and the excess emissions offset and penalty requirements of section 411 of the Act. Consistent with the program generally, however, the proposal does afford flexible excess emissions offset planning opportunities for sources.

* * *

D. Sulfur Dioxide Excess Emissions Offset Planning

Section 77.2 sets forth the requirements related to sulfur dioxide excess emissions offset planning. Section 411(b) provides that for each ton of sulfur dioxide emissions in excess of an affected unit's Acid Rain program sulfur dioxide emissions limitation (i.e., the allowances held for use by the unit for the calendar year in the unit's Allowance Tracking System compliance subaccount), the unit must offset the excess emissions with allowances. Today's proposal requires that the offsets be achieved by a deduction of one allowance from the affected unit's Allowance Tracking System account established pursuant to 40 CFR part 73 for each excess ton of emissions. Section 411(b) also provides that the allowances must be offset in the year following the year when the excess emissions occurred, unless the Administrator approves a longer offset period. Accordingly today's proposal specifies that, unless the designated representative for the unit submits an approvable excess emissions offset plan providing otherwise, allowances would be deducted by the Administrator from the allowances contained in the affected unit's Allowance Tracking System compliance subaccount account for the year in which excess emissions occurred.

NOTES

1. The Acid Deposition Program in the 1990 Amendments is surely the most ambitious marketable pollution rights experiment ever undertaken in the United States. Still, it does not go far enough for some economists. Terry Anderson and Donald Leal, leaders of the "free market environmentalism" movement, have criticized the program as follows:

> [T]radeable permits do not represent a truly free-market approach to reducing acid rain. A government agency still must determine the level of

> permits, and the permits do not force polluters to compensate those harmed by the pollution. In this system, the political process determines the initial or optimal pollution levels, not the polluters bargaining with those who bear the costs of the pollution. The 10-million-ton target established by the Bush administration, for example, "was not based on scientific or economic grounds. It was selected because it was viewed as 'creditable' — that is, it was acceptable to Congress, the environmental community, and our Canadian neighbors." As Robert Hahn observed, "Until people see a direct connection between environmental cleanup and their consumption of other goods and services and seriously question the judgment of their political leaders on these matters, things are unlikely to change."

T. Anderson & D. Leal, FREE MARKET ENVIRONMENTALISM, 158-59 (Pac. Res. Inst. 1991).

2. Related to Anderson's and Leal's criticism of the acid deposition program is the underlying question of whether the ten million ton SO_2 reduction intended to be achieved by the law can be justified on health or welfare grounds. The National Acid Precipitation Assessment Program released a study in the fall of 1990 which concluded that acid rain was a far less serious problem than had previously been believed. The study has been criticized by some scientists. *See e.g.*, Howard Kurtz, *Is Acid Rain a Tempest in a Media Teapot?*, Washington Post, A3, January 14, 1991. Others, however, have questioned whether the new program isn't a "billion dollar solution to a million dollar problem." S. Fred Singer, *The Answers on Acid Rain Fall on Deaf Ears*, Wall Street Journal, March 6, 1990.

3. Congress' justification for this massive new program is set out in great detail in a Senate Report on the law. S. REP. NO. 228, 101st Cong., 1st Sess. 261-282 (1989).

4. The Internal Revenue Service has ruled that EPA's allocation of allowances under the Acid Deposition Program "does not cause a utility to realize gross income . . ." IRS Revenue Ruling 92-16 (1992).

10 INSPECTIONS AND ENFORCEMENT OF STATIONARY SOURCES

A. Inspections and Recordkeeping

Section 114(a) of the Act authorizes the Administrator to require any person who owns or operates an emission source to establish and maintain records, make reports, establish and maintain monitoring equipment, sample emissions or provide such other information as may be reasonably required. Section 114(a)(2) authorizes the Administrator, *or his authorized representative*, to enter the premises of anyone subject to the Act, have access to records and equipment, and conduct inspections as necessary to enforce the law. Perhaps the most litigated issue under this section concerns the meaning of the phrase "authorized representative." The following case describes the controversy.

STAUFFER CHEMICAL CO. V. EPA
647 F.2d 1075 (10th Cir. 1981)

McWILLIAMS, Circuit Judge.

The principal issue here to be resolved is whether, under Section 114(a)(2) of the Clean Air Act, an employee of a private company under contract with the Environmental Protection Agency (EPA) is an "authorized representative" of the EPA Administrator for the purpose of entering and inspecting the premises of an emission source. 42 U.S.C. § 7414(a)(2) (Supp. II 1978 and Supp. III 1979). The District Court held that an employee of such independent contractor is not an "authorized representative" of the Administrator, and EPA appeals.

Stauffer Chemical Company is a chemical manufacturer whose facilities include a phosphate ore processing plant located in Lincoln County, near Sage, Wyoming, which will hereinafter be referred to as the Leefe Plant. Pursuant to the Clean Air Act, EPA has developed an oversight inspection program which is designed to evaluate the effectiveness of the individual states' inspection and regulatory procedures as well as to assess the compliance status of the country's major sources of air pollution. Under this program, state pollution control agencies are responsible for conducting annual inspections at each of the major sources in the state. EPA's regional offices are responsible for conducting annual oversight inspections at ten percent of the major sources within each state.

Region VIII of the EPA has responsibility for a six-state area encompassing Colorado, Montana, North Dakota, South Dakota, Utah, and Wyoming. There are about 1,000 major stationary sources of air pollution in these six states, of which 230 are located in Wyoming. The decision as to which sources will be inspected is based on a neutral administrative scheme that focuses on classes of industry, their geographic location, and the frequency of past inspections. As indicated, to implement its role in the oversight inspection program, Region VIII selected ten percent of its major sources of air pollution for inspection in 1980. Stauffer's Leefe Plant was one of the sources selected for inspection by EPA under the described administrative scheme.

At 10:00 a. m. on April 10, 1980, a team of EPA inspectors arrived unannounced at Stauffer's Leefe Plant. The inspection team consisted of Dr. Charles O'Boyle, an EPA environmental engineer, Lee Gribb, an official of Wyoming's Division of Air Quality, and two employees of GCA Corporation, a North Carolina corporation under contract to EPA to aid in carrying out oversight inspections. It was intended that the GCA employees would make the actual inspection, with supervision from Dr. O'Boyle, who was to be present at all times. Without going into any great detail, Stauffer's employees, upon direction of their supervisors, refused to admit the team of inspectors. Stauffer's employees told the inspection team that it would admit EPA and state officials, but would not admit the two GCA employees unless the latter signed a nondisclosure and hold harmless agreement. The EPA team did not agree to the conditions which Stauffer had imposed, and left the plant premises without making an inspection.

Negotiations then ensued between Stauffer and EPA in an effort to resolve the matter. Although it did impose some additional conditions, Stauffer's basic position was that the two GCA employees would have to sign nondisclosure and hold harmless agreements before being admitted to the plant. Stauffer claimed that it was simply trying to protect its trade secrets.[3]

When the negotiations between Stauffer and EPA came to a standstill, EPA sought an administrative search warrant. On May 8, 1980, the United States Attorney for the District of Wyoming applied to a United States Magistrate in Cheyenne, Wyoming for an administrative search warrant authorizing EPA to conduct an inspection of the Leefe Plant through the use of the two GCA employees. Supporting affidavits set forth the purpose of the inspection, the need for a warrant, and the neutral administrative scheme underlying the selection of the Stauffer facility. In addition, the application specifically provided that though the GCA employees would make the actual inspection, they would be accompanied by EPA employees.

Based on the showing thus made, the Magistrate issued a warrant for the inspection of Stauffer's Leefe Plant. The warrant authorized "any duly designated enforcement officers and employees of the Environmental Protection Agency, and authorized employees of EPA's contractor, GCA Corporation, who have been duly authorized to conduct inspections as EPA representatives," to enter Stauffer's Leefe Plant during normal operating hours for the purpose of conducting a compliance evaluation oversight inspection pursuant to Section 114 of the Clean Air Act, 42 U.S.C. § 7414.

On the morning of May 13, 1980, the inspection team, which still included two GCA employees, attempted to execute the warrant and inspect the Leefe Plant. The inspection team again appeared unannounced. Stauffer, again, refused to admit the inspection team unless the GCA employees signed a nondisclosure and hold harmless agreement. EPA

---

[3] We note that the District Court entered a finding of fact in this regard which stated: "Many of the processes used at the Leefe Plant are highly proprietary and involve the application of trade secrets or confidential 'know-how' and information developed by Stauffer during its years of operation." The District Court went on to find that some of these trade secrets, including Stauffer's method for providing fuel for use in calcining phosphate ore, "could be noted by an inspector merely by visual observation of equipment in the facility."

and the GCA employees refused to agree to Stauffer's conditions, and the team left the plant.

On the afternoon of May 13, 1980, Stauffer went to court. On that date Stauffer filed the following with the United States District Court for the District of Wyoming: (1) an application for a temporary restraining order enjoining EPA and the two GCA employees from executing the warrant, and (2) a motion to quash the warrant. A temporary restraining order issued the same day. Thereafter, on June 20, 1980, after an extended evidentiary hearing, the District Court permanently enjoined EPA from using GCA employees, or employees of other companies under similar contract with EPA, in inspections of any Stauffer plant in Wyoming without the permission of Stauffer Chemical Company. It is from the June 20, 1980, injunctive order that EPA appeals.

The issue as presented on appeal is a very narrow question of statutory interpretation. The starting point in every case involving the construction of a statute is the language of the statute itself. *Greyhound Corp. v. Mt. Hood Stages, Inc.*, 437 U.S. 322, 330 (1978); *Blue Chip Stamps v. Manor Drug Stores*, 421 U.S. 723, 756 (1975) (Powell, J., concurring). Section 114(a)(2) of the Clean Air Act, enacted in 1970, appears as 42 U.S.C. § 7414(a)(2) and provides as follows:

> (2) *the Administrator or his authorized representative*, upon presentation of his credentials
>
> (A) *shall have a right of entry* to, upon, or through any premises of such person or in which any records required to be maintained under paragraph (1) of this section are located, and
>
> (B) may at reasonable times have access to and copy any records, inspect any monitoring equipment or method required under paragraph (1), and sample any emissions which such person is required to sample under paragraph (1). (Emphasis added).

The particular phrase in the foregoing statute with which we are concerned is: "the Administrator or his authorized representative." The question is whether, in the fact setting described above, the two employees of GCA, the North Carolina corporation under contract with EPA, are "authorized representatives" of the EPA Administrator. As indicated, the trial court held that they were not. We agree.

The term "authorized representative" is not defined in the Clean Air Act. The present statute, therefore, does not expressly state whether employees of a company under contract with the EPA may, or may not, be authorized by the Administrator to serve as his representative. Such being the case, it is up to the courts when called upon, as we now are, to define the term. The touchstone in construing statutory language is legislative intent. *Caminetti v. United States*, 242 U.S. 470, 490 (1917). The EPA suggests that legislative intent may best be ascertained in this case by applying the "plain meaning" test and that an "authorized representative" simply means "any person duly authorized to act or speak for another or others." EPA cites in support of its position Webster's New World Dictionary, 2d Coll. Edition 1974. We decline to give such a literal interpretation.

In the belief that the "plain meaning" test does not solve our problem, we turn next to legislative history. Although the relevant legislative history is not entirely clear or consistent, in our view it is nonetheless helpful. As previously stated, Section 114(a)(2) of the Clean Air Act was enacted in 1970. The legislative history of the Clean Air Act, which pertains to that Section, indicates that, upon the disagreeing votes of the two Houses, a committee of conference agreed to a substitute for both the proposed House Bill and Senate Amendment. By way of explanation, the conferees published their discussion of the House Bill, the Senate Amendment and the substitute provision agreed upon, in regard to each section. The conference report stated that in the Senate's proposed amendment, referred to as Section 116 of Senate Bill 4358, "the Senate *authorized entry and inspection by DHEW personnel* of buildings, facilities, and monitoring equipment for purposes of setting standards and enforcing them." The conference report then stated that "[t]he provisions of the conference report with regard to inspections, monitoring and entry follow substantially the provisions of the Senate amendment." (Emphasis added). H.R. (Conf.) Rep.No.91-1783, 91st Cong., 2d Sess., *reprinted in* (1970) U.S.Code Cong. & Ad.News, 5356, 5379-81.

The foregoing would seem to indicate that under Section 116 of the Senate Bill, which later substantially became Section 114(a)(2) of the Clean Air Act, an "authorized representative" of the Administrator was restricted to "DHEW personnel." In this regard we note that the Clean Air Act was administered by the Department of Health, Education and Welfare before EPA was created. The phrase "DHEW personnel" in the legislative history, therefore, must now be read as "EPA personnel." EPA points out that the legislative history referred to above does not, in so many words, limit such authorization to "DHEW personnel." We are not impressed by this particular argument. In our view an affirmative grant of authority to a described group precludes a grant of that same authority, by implication, to a different group. In any event, counsel does not suggest that the employees of GCA are "EPA personnel." They are not, of course. They are GCA personnel.

Furthermore, there is additional legislative history which sheds light on this issue. In 1972 Congress amended the Clean Water Act, to include Section 308, which now appears as 33 U.S.C. § 1318(a)(B). That particular section is virtually identical to Section 114(a)(2) of the Clean Air Act, and provides, in part, as follows:

> (B) the *Administrator or his authorized representative*, upon presentation of his credentials
>
> (i) *shall have a right of entry* to, upon, or through any premises in which an effluent source is located or in which any records required to be maintained under clause (A) of this subsection are located, and
>
> (ii) may at reasonable times have access to and copy any records, inspect any monitoring equipment or method required under clause (A), and sample any effluents which the owner or operator of such source is required to sample under such clause. (Emphasis added).

Because Section 308 of the Clean Water Act uses the identical language of Section 114(a)(2) of the Clean Air Act, *i. e.*, "the Administrator or his authorized representative," we find the legislative history of Section 308 to be relevant to our determination of the present case. The Report of the Senate Public Works Committee, which discusses Section 308 of the Clean Water Act, includes the following commentary:

> It should also be noted that the authority to enter, *as under the Clean Air Act*, is reserved to the Administrator and his authorized representatives *which such representatives must be full time employees of the Environmental Protection Agency*. The authority to enter is not extended to contractors with the EPA in pursuit of research and development. S.Rep.No.92-414, 92d Cong., 2d Sess., *reprinted in* [1972] U.S.Code Cong. & Ad.News 3668, 3729. (Emphasis added).

We recognize that the legislative history of Section 308 of the Clean Water Act was published in 1972, whereas Section 114(a)(2) of the Clean Air Act was enacted in 1970. Post-enactment legislative history is generally not to be accorded the same weight as legislative history occurring in connection with the enactment of the statutory language under immediate consideration. There is, however, only a two-year interval between the enactment of Section 114(a)(2) of the Clean Air Act and Section 308 of the Clean Water Act, and there is of course a close subject-matter relationship between the two acts. In light of such considerations we find the legislative history of Section 308 of the Clean Water Act to be supportive of our holdings. Further, we observe that, if the EPA's position were to be accepted, an employee of a company under contract with the EPA could not be an authorized representative of the Administrator for the purposes of entry and inspection under the Clean Water Act, whereas, such person could be an authorized representative of that same EPA Administrator under the Clean Air Act. Such a result, to us, seems anomalous.

It is on this basis that we conclude that the employees of an independent contractor, such as GCA, are not authorized representatives of the EPA Administrator for the purposes of Section 114(a)(2) of the Clean Air Act. The trial court was correct in so holding and, under the circumstances, properly enjoined the use of the two GCA employees by the EPA in executing the Magistrate's administrative search warrant. Having determined that the warrant was fatally flawed because it authorized GCA employees to go onto Stauffer's Leefe Plant, we need not consider the other objections which Stauffer raised concerning the warrant.

* * *

Judgment affirmed.

NOTES

1. The Court of Appeals for the Ninth Circuit reached the opposite conclusion, on a different reading of the legislative history:

> This interpretation [of the legislative history by the 10th Circuit] is unpersuasive. The Conference Committee was confronted with differing language in the Senate and the House versions of the bill, with the Senate version granting broader inspection authority. Section 115 of the Senate bill, for example, broadened the basis upon which inspections could be made and deleted certain requirements imposed by the House. More particularly, section 116(a)(3) of the Senate bill granted inspection authority to "the Secretary or his authorized representatives," while section 112(f) of the house bill limited the right to enter and inspect to "officers or employees." The Conference Committee adopted the Senate version for inspections of stationary sources, section 114(a)(2), 42 U.S.C.A. § 7414(a)(2), and the House version for inspections of motor vehicle manufacturers, section 206(c). 42 U.S.C.A. § 7525(c). Hence, where Congress meant to limit inspections to officers and employees it did so. Congress must be deemed to have understood its choice of the phrase "authorized representative" in contrast to the limited phrase "officers and employees."

Bunker Hill Co. v. EPA, 658 F.2d 1280 (9th Cir. 1981). *See also* § 114(c) of the Act which refers to "officers, employees *or authorized representatives*." The Ninth Circuit found the use of the disjunctive here to indicate Congressional awareness that authorized representatives were a separate category of individuals. *Id.* 658 F.2d 1283, n.1.

2. In *United States v. Stauffer Chemical Company*, 684 F.2d 1174 (6th Cir. 1982) *aff'd*, 464 U.S. 165 (1984), the Court of Appeals for the Sixth Circuit held that the United States was barred from relitigating the "authorized representative" issue against another facility owned by Stauffer, but in a different jurisdiction, under the doctrine of collateral estoppel. The appellate court nonetheless ruled on the merits, reaching the same conclusion as the Tenth Circuit. The Supreme Court affirmed on the collateral estoppel issue without reaching the merits of the claim.

3. Recall the standard of review for agency interpretation of statutes which they are charged with administering, as announced by the Supreme Court in *Chevron, USA, Inc. v. Natural Resources Defense Council,* 467 U.S. 837 (1984), *supra* at Chapter 9. How should this case be viewed under that standard?

4. The 1990 Amendments significantly enhanced EPA's authority to require additional record-keeping and monitoring of stationary sources. § 114(a)(1),(3). In particular, owners and operators of major stationary sources are subject to new record-keeping and monitoring requirements, and are required to submit compliance certifications. Submission of these certifications will enable both the agencies and the public to ascertain quickly whether the source is complying with its permit. Noncompliance may lead to enforcement by the agency or a citizen suit under § 304 of the Act.

DOW CHEMICAL CO. V. UNITED STATES

476 U.S. 227 (1986)

Chief Justice BURGER delivered the opinion of the Court.

We granted certiorari to review the holding of the Court of Appeals (a) that the Environmental Protection Agency's aerial observation of petitioner's plant complex did not exceed EPA's statutory investigatory authority, and (b) that EPA's aerial photography of petitioner's 2,000-acre plant complex without a warrant was not a search under the Fourth Amendment.

I.

Petitioner Dow Chemical Co. operates a 2,000-acre facility manufacturing chemicals at Midland, Michigan. The facility consists of numerous covered buildings, with manufacturing equipment and piping conduits located between the various buildings exposed to visual observation from the air. At all times, Dow has maintained elaborate security around the perimeter of the complex barring ground-level public views of these areas. It also investigates any low-level flights by aircraft over the facility. Dow has not undertaken, however, to conceal all manufacturing equipment within the complex from aerial views. Dow maintains that the cost of covering its exposed equipment would be prohibitive.

In early 1978, enforcement officials of EPA, with Dow's consent, made an on- site inspection of two powerplants in this complex. A subsequent EPA request for a second inspection, however, was denied, and EPA did not thereafter seek an administrative search warrant. Instead, EPA employed a commercial aerial photographer, using a standard floor-mounted, precision aerial mapping camera, to take photographs of the facility from altitudes of 12,000, 3,000, and 1,200 feet. At all times the aircraft was lawfully within navigable airspace. *See* 49 U.S.C. App. § 1304; 14 CFR § 91.79 (1985).

EPA did not inform Dow of this aerial photography, but when Dow became aware of it, Dow brought suit in the District Court alleging that EPA's action violated the

Fourth Amendment and was beyond EPA's statutory investigative authority. The District Court granted Dow's motion for summary judgment on the ground that EPA had no authority to take aerial photographs and that doing so was a search violating the Fourth Amendment. EPA was permanently enjoined from taking aerial photographs of Dow's premises and from disseminating, releasing or copying the photographs already taken. 536 F.Supp. 1355 (ED Mich.1982).

* * *

The Court of Appeals reversed. 749 F.2d 307 (CA6 1984).

* * *

II.

The photographs at issue in this case are essentially like those commonly used in map-making. Any person with an airplane and an aerial camera could readily duplicate them. In common with much else, the technology of photography has changed in this century. These developments have enhanced industrial processes, and indeed all areas of life; they have also enhanced law enforcement techniques. Whether they may be employed by competitors to penetrate trade secrets is not a question presented in this case. Governments do not generally seek to appropriate trade secrets of the private sector, and the right to be free of appropriation of trade secrets is protected by law.

Dow nevertheless relies heavily on its claim that trade secret laws protect it from any aerial photography of this industrial complex by its competitors, and that this protection is relevant to our analysis of such photography under the Fourth Amendment. That such photography might be barred by state law with regard to competitors, however, is irrelevant to the questions presented here. State tort law governing unfair competition does not define the limits of the Fourth Amendment. *Cf. Oliver v. United States, supra* (trespass law does not necessarily define limits of Fourth Amendment). The Government is seeking these photographs in order to regulate, not to compete with, Dow. If the Government were to use the photographs to compete with Dow, Dow might have a Fifth Amendment "taking" claim. Indeed, Dow alleged such a claim in its complaint, but the District Court dismissed it without prejudice. But even trade secret laws would not bar all forms of photography of this industrial complex; rather, only photography with an intent to use any trade secrets revealed by the photographs may be proscribed. Hence, there is no prohibition of photographs taken by a casual passenger on an airliner, or those taken by a company producing maps for its map-making purposes.

Dow claims first that EPA has no authority to use aerial photography to implement its statutory authority for "site inspection" under § 114(a) of the Clean Air Act, 42 U.S.C. § 7414(a); second, Dow claims EPA's use of aerial photography was a "search" of an area that, notwithstanding the large size of the plant, was within an "industrial curtilage" rather than an "open field," and that it had a reasonable expectation of privacy from such photography protected by the Fourth Amendment.

III.

Congress has vested in EPA certain investigatory and enforcement authority, without spelling out precisely how this authority was to be exercised in all the myriad circumstances that might arise in monitoring matters relating to clean air and water standards. When Congress invests an agency with enforcement and investigatory authority, it is not necessary to identify explicitly each and every technique that may be used in the course of executing the statutory mission. Aerial observation authority, for example, is not usually expressly extended to police for traffic control, but it could hardly be thought necessary for a legislative body to tell police that aerial observation could be employed for traffic control of a metropolitan area, or to expressly authorize police to send messages to ground highway patrols that a particular over-the-road truck was traveling in excess of 55 miles per hour. Common sense and ordinary human experience teaches that traffic violators are apprehended by observation.

Regulatory or enforcement authority generally carries with it all the modes of inquiry and investigation traditionally employed or useful to execute the authority granted. Environmental standards such as clean air and clean water cannot be enforced only in libraries and laboratories, helpful as those institutions may be.

Under § 114(a)(2), the Clean Air Act provides that "upon presentation of . . . credentials," EPA has a "right of entry to, upon, or through any premises." 42 U.S.C. § 7414(a)(2)(A). Dow argues this limited grant of authority to enter does not authorize any aerial observation. In particular, Dow argues that unannounced aerial observation deprives Dow of its right to be informed that an inspection will be made or has occurred, and its right to claim confidentiality of the information contained in the places to be photographed, as provided in § 114(a) and (c), 42 U.S.C. § 7414(a), (c). It is not claimed that EPA has disclosed any of the photographs outside the agency.

Section 114(a), however, appears to expand, not restrict, EPA's general powers to investigate. Nor is there any suggestion in the statute that the powers conferred by this section are intended to be exclusive. There is no claim that EPA is prohibited from taking photographs from a ground-level location accessible to the general public. The EPA, as a regulatory and enforcement agency, needs no explicit statutory provision to employ methods of observation commonly available to the public at large: we hold that the use of aerial observation and photography is within the EPA's statutory authority.

IV.

We turn now to Dow's contention that taking aerial photographs constituted a search without a warrant, thereby violating Dow's rights under the Fourth Amendment. In making this contention, however, Dow concedes that a simple fly-over with naked-eye observation, or the taking of a photograph from a nearby hillside overlooking such a facility, would give rise to no Fourth Amendment problem.

In *California v. Ciraolo*, 476 U.S. 207 (1986), decided today, we hold that naked-eye aerial observation from an altitude of 1,000 feet of a backyard within the curtilage of a home does not constitute a search under the Fourth Amendment.

In the instant case, two additional Fourth Amendment claims are presented: whether the common-law "curtilage" doctrine encompasses a large industrial complex such as Dow's, and whether photography employing an aerial mapping camera is permissible in this context. Dow argues that an industrial plant, even one occupying 2,000 acres, does not fall within the "open fields" doctrine of *Oliver v. United States* but rather is an "industrial curtilage" having constitutional protection equivalent to that of the curtilage of a private home. Dow further contends that any aerial photography of this "industrial curtilage" intrudes upon its reasonable expectations of privacy. Plainly a business establishment or an industrial or commercial facility enjoys certain protections under the Fourth Amendment. *See Marshall v. Barlow's, Inc.*, 436 U.S. 307 (1978); *See v. City of Seattle*, 387 U.S. 541 (1967).

Two lines of cases are relevant to the inquiry: the curtilage doctrine and the "open fields" doctrine. The curtilage area immediately surrounding a private house has long been given protection as a place where the occupants have a reasonable and legitimate expectation of privacy that society is prepared to accept. *See Ciraolo, supra.*

As the curtilage doctrine evolved to protect much the same kind of privacy as that covering the interior of a structure, the contrasting "open fields" doctrine evolved as well. From *Hester v. United States*, 265 U.S. 57 (1924), to *Oliver v. United States*, 466 U.S. 170 (1984), the Court has drawn a line as to what expectations are reasonable in the open areas beyond the curtilage of a dwelling; "open fields do not provide the setting for those intimate activities that the [Fourth] Amendment is intended to shelter from governmental interference or surveillance." *Oliver*, 466 U.S., at 179. In *Oliver*, we held that "an individual may not legitimately demand privacy for activities out of doors in fields, except in the area immediately surrounding the home." *Id.*, at 178. To fall within the open fields doctrine the area "need be neither 'open' nor a 'field' as those terms are used in common speech." *Id.*, at 180, n. 11.

Dow plainly has a reasonable, legitimate, and objective expectation of privacy within the interior of its covered buildings, and it is equally clear that expectation is one society is prepared to observe. *E.g., See v. City of Seattle, supra*. Moreover, it could hardly be expected that Dow would erect a huge cover over a 2,000-acre tract. In contending that its entire enclosed plant complex is an "industrial curtilage," Dow argues that its exposed manufacturing facilities are analogous to the curtilage surrounding a home because it has taken every possible step to bar access from ground level.

The Court of Appeals held that whatever the limits of an "industrial curtilage" barring *ground*-level intrusions into Dow's private areas, the open areas exposed here were more analogous to "open fields" than to a curtilage for purposes of aerial observation. 749 F.2d, at 312-314. In *Oliver*, the Court described the curtilage of a dwelling as "the area to which extends the intimate activity associated with the 'sanctity of a man's home and the privacies of life.' " *Oliver, supra*, 466 U.S., at 180 (quoting *Boyd v. United States*, 116 U.S. 616, 630 (1886)). *See California v. Ciraolo, supra*. The intimate activities associated with family privacy and the home and its curtilage simply do not reach the outdoor areas or spaces between structures and buildings of a manufacturing plant.

Admittedly, Dow's enclosed plant complex, like the area in *Oliver*, does not fall precisely within the "open fields" doctrine. The area at issue here can perhaps be seen as falling somewhere between "open fields" and curtilage, but lacking some of the critical characteristics of both. Dow's inner manufacturing areas are elaborately secured to ensure they are not open or exposed to the public from the ground. Any actual physical entry by EPA into any enclosed area would raise significantly different questions, because "[t]he businessman, like the occupant of a residence, has a constitutional right to go about his business free from unreasonable official entries upon his private commercial property." *See v. City of Seattle, supra*, 387 U.S., at 543. The narrow issue raised by Dow's claim of search and seizure, however, concerns aerial observation of a 2,000-acre outdoor manufacturing facility *without* physical entry.

We pointed out in *Donovan v. Dewey*, 452 U.S. 594, 598-599 (1981), that the Government has "greater latitude to conduct warrantless inspections of commercial property" because "the expectation of privacy that the owner of commercial property enjoys in such property differs significantly from the sanctity accorded an individual's home." We emphasized that unlike a homeowner's interest in his dwelling, "[t]he interest of the owner of commercial property is not one in being free from any inspections." *Id.*, at 599. And with regard to regulatory inspections, we have held that "[w]hat is observable by the public is observable without a warrant, by the Government inspector as well." *Marshall v. Barlow's, Inc.*, 436 U.S., at 315 (footnote omitted).

Oliver recognized that in the open field context, "the public and police lawfully may survey lands from the air." 466 U.S. at 179 (footnote omitted). Here, EPA was not employing some unique sensory device that, for example, could penetrate the walls of buildings and record conversations in Dow's plants, offices or laboratories, but rather a conventional, albeit precise, commercial camera commonly used in map-making. The Government asserts it has not yet enlarged the photographs to any significant degree, but Dow points out that simple magnification permits identification of objects such as wires as small as one-half inch diameter.

It may well be, as the Government concedes, that surveillance of private property by using highly sophisticated surveillance equipment not generally available to the public, such as satellite technology, might be constitutionally proscribed absent a warrant. But the photographs here are not so revealing of intimate details as to raise constitutional concerns. Although they undoubtedly give EPA more detailed information than naked-eye views, they remain limited to an outline of the facility's buildings and equipment. The mere fact that human vision is enhanced somewhat, at least to the degree here, does not give rise to constitutional problems. An electronic device to penetrate walls or windows so as to hear and record confidential discussions of chemical formulae or other trade secrets would raise very different and far more serious questions; other protections such as trade secret laws are available to protect commercial activities from private surveillance by competitors.

We conclude that the open areas of an industrial plant complex with numerous plant structures spread over an area of 2,000 acres are not analogous to the "curtilage" of a dwelling for purposes of aerial surveillance; such an industrial complex is more comparable to an open field and as such it is open to the view and observation of persons in aircraft lawfully in the public airspace immediately above or sufficiently near the area for the reach of cameras.

We hold that the taking of aerial photographs of an industrial plant complex from navigable airspace is not a search prohibited by the Fourth Amendment.

Affirmed.

NOTES

1. In his summary of the facts, Justice Burger notes that EPA had made an initial inspection of the facility with Dow's consent. A subsequent request to Dow for a second inspection was denied, which led to the aerial inspection made without Dow's consent. Why was Dow's consent necessary for the initial inspection? Did Congress intend for EPA to seek the prior consent of a company to be inspected? *See* §§ 114(b),(d)(1). What problems might prior consent raise for the inspection and enforcement program?

2. Congress did not provide in the Clean Air Act for warrantless searches, as it has done in some other regulatory statutes. *See e.g.*, Surface Mining Control and Reclamation Act, § 517, 30 U.S.C. § 1267. Accordingly, absent consent, EPA must obtain a warrant prior to entry on the premises of a regulated source. *Public Service Co. of Indiana v. EPA*, 682 F.2d 626 (7th Cir. 1982), *cert. denied*, 459 U.S. 1127. However, EPA may conduct aerial inspections without a warrant. *See also Air Pollution Variance Board v. Western Alfalfa Corp.*, 416 U.S. 861 (1974) wherein the Court held that violations of the Act observed from an open field may be cited without a warrant.

3. What standards govern issuance of a warrant under statutes such as the Clean Air Act? In *Marshall v. Barlows*, 436 U.S. 307 (1978) the Supreme Court required the Secretary of Labor to obtain a warrant for inspections under the Occupational Safety and Health Act. In its decision, the Court described the showing required for issuance of an administrative warrant as follows:

> Probable cause in the criminal law sense is not required. For purposes of an administrative search such as this, probable cause justifying the issuance of a warrant may be based not only on specific evidence of an existing violation, but also on a "showing that reasonable legislative or administrative standards for conducting. . . .an inspection are satisfied.". . . A warrant showing that a specific business has been chosen for an OSHA search on the basis of a general administrative plan for enforcement of the Act derived from neutral sources... would protect an employer's Fourth Amendment rights.

Id. at 320-321. If, to obtain a warrant, EPA need only show a general plan for choosing a site to inspect, does the warrant requirement afford any substantial protection? As the excerpt from *Marshall* suggests, the Fourth Amendment provides that "no warrant shall issue, but upon probable cause." "Probable cause" for what? Are the standards adopted by the Court in *Marshall* consistent with this requirement for "probable cause"?

4. EPA may obtain administrative search warrants *ex parte*, without a showing of a need for surprise. *Bunker Hill Co. v. EPA*, 658 F.2d 1280 (9th Cir. 1981).

B. Enforcement

With the exception of the emergency authority provided for at § 303 of the Act, and discussed in greater detail below, stationary sources and mobile sources are treated differently under the Clean Air Act for purposes of enforcement. The latter subject is addressed separately in the section on mobile sources. *Infra* at Chapter 12. The principal enforcement tools for stationary sources are set out at §§ 113 and 120 of the Act. The 1990 Amendments to the Act strengthened the general enforcement powers significantly. A brief review of the enforcement provisions is set forth below.

Administrative Remedies. Section 113(a) of the Act prescribes administrative remedies for violations of the Act. Under § 113(a)(1), the Administrator "shall notify" the state and any person in violation of a SIP. If the violation extends for 30 days after the Notice of Violation, the Administrator "may issue" a compliance order. The order must specify a time for compliance, which cannot exceed one year. § 113(a)(4). Further, it cannot take effect until the person to whom it is issued has an opportunity to confer with EPA concerning the alleged violation. *Id.* As an alternative to issuing the compliance order the Administrator may commence a civil action in accordance with § 113(b).

The value of administrative action as an enforcement tool was greatly enhanced by the provision in the 1990 Amendments allowing administrative assessment of civil penalties. § 113(d). Under this provision, which is described in greater detail below, the Administrator may issue civil penalties of up to $200,000 for virtually any violation of the Act or state implementation plan.

Federally Assumed Enforcement of a SIP. Section 113(a)(2) authorizes the EPA to assume enforcement of a SIP or an approved permit program under Title V of the Act where violations of the SIP or the permit program "are so widespread that such violations appear to result from a failure of a State . . . to enforce the plan or permit program effectively." In addition, § 113(a)(5) provides that where a state is not acting in compliance with any requirement relating to construction of new sources or modification of existing sources, the EPA may issue an order prohibiting construction or modification of any major stationary source in the SIP area that is out of compliance. An injunction against such construction or modification may also be obtained.

Direct Federal Enforcement. Section 113(a)(3) authorizes direct federal enforcement by EPA for virtually any violation of Titles I, III, IV, V or VI of the Act. The only substantial limit imposed on EPA is the requirement that it give 30 days' prior notice to the state and affected operator for permit and SIP violations, in those states with approved SIPs.

Civil Actions. Section 113(b) of the Act authorizes the Administrator to commence civil actions for temporary or injunctive relief, or to assess and recover a penalty of not more than $25,000 per day. Such actions "shall, as appropriate" be commenced "against any person that is the owner or operator of an affected source, a major emitting facility, or a major stationary source" and "may" be commenced against any other person, whenever such person — (1) violates a SIP during federally assumed enforcement of the SIP or after 30 days' notice; (2) violates a requirement of Title I, IV, V, VI or § 303 (relating to emergency powers); or (3) attempts to construct or modify any source upon a finding that the source failed to comply with new source requirements.

Civil Penalties. A key provision of the 1990 Amendments extends to EPA the authority to assess civil penalties. Before those amendments, EPA had to convince overworked lawyers from the Justice Department or the local U.S. Attorney's Office to bring a civil action. Civil penalties of up to $25,000 per day of violation may be assessed under an administrative order so long as the total penalty does not exceed $200,000. § 113(d)(1). The category of violations for which penalties may be assessed generally tracks the language of § 113(b) relating to civil actions. The criteria to be used for assessing civil penalties, whether by administrative or court order, are set out at § 113(e), and include the size of the business, the violator's compliance history and good faith efforts at compliance, the duration of the violation, the economic benefit of the violation, and the seriousness of the violation.

Field citation authority is also authorized by the 1990 Amendments. Under § 113(d)(3), EPA may authorize its officers and employees to assess penalties of up to $5,000 for minor violations of law. § 113(d)(3). All administrative penalties are subject to formal adjudicatory hearings in accordance with the Administrative Procedure Act. § 113(d)(2).

The 1990 Amendments also added a unique "bounty" provision. Under § 113(f), EPA may grant awards not to exceed $10,000 to any person who furnishes information or services that lead to a criminal conviction or the issuance of a civil penalty for a wide variety of violations of the law.

Noncompliance Penalties. Penalties assessed under §§ 113(b) and (d) are in addition to any penalties that may be imposed by the EPA or the state under § 120 of the Act. § 120(f). Such "noncompliance penalties" are required to be assessed for certain broad categories of violations in an amount "no less than the economic value" derived from delayed compliance. §§ 120(a)(2)(A); 120(d). It is EPA's policy, however, to offset that amount of a penalty paid under § 113(b), but attributable to the economic value factor of § 120, against a penalty imposed under § 120. *EPA Civil Penalty Policy for Major Source Violators,* 8 ENV. REP. (Current Developments), 2011, 2018 (1978).

EPA employs a computer model called "BEN" to calculate the economic benefit from illegal conduct. Libber, *Penalty Assessment at the Environmental Protection Agency: A view from Inside*, 6 NAT'L. ENV. ENF. J. 3 (April, 1991). One economist has challenged Mr. Libber's assessment that BEN "yields a reliable objective dollar figure." Fuhrman, Comments on Mr. Libber's Article on the EPA Civil Penalty Assessment Model, 6 NAT'L. ENV. ENF. J. 20 (Dec. 1991/Jan. 1992).

Criminal Sanctions. The 1990 Amendments incorporated tough, new criminal sanctions into § 113(c) of the Act. Fines of up to $1,000,000 and prison terms of 15 years may be imposed. Furthermore, penalties may be doubled for second offenses. Although criminal sanctions may be imposed only for "knowing" violations of the law, the detailed compliance certification requirements imposed under § 114(a)(3) of the Act should make it much easier for EPA to support criminal actions against recalcitrant operators.

Citizen Suits. Section 304 of the Act authorizes a private right of action by affected persons directly against any person who is in violation of the law. § 304(a)(1), (3). In addition, private citizens may bring an action against the Administrator for failing to perform any nondiscretionary duty. § 304(a)(2). Such actions must be preceded by a 60 day notice (*see Council of Commuter Organizations v. Metropolitan Transportation Authority*, 683 F.2d 663 (2d Cir. 1982)), and may be filed only in the judicial district where the source is located. § 304(c). Prevailing parties may be awarded the costs of litigation including attorney fees. § 302(d). *See also Ruckelshaus v. Sierra Club*, 463 U.S. 68 (1983). *See infra*, Chapter 13. One significant change to § 304 included in the 1990 Amendments is a provision that allows citizen suits for past as well as present violations of the law "if there is evidence that the alleged violation has been repeated." § 304(a)(1). This effectively overturns the Supreme Court's decision in *Gwaltney of Smithfield, Ltd, v. Chesapeake Bay Foundation,* 484 U.S. 49 (1987), as it applied to the Clean Air Act.

Emergency Powers. One final enforcement tool worthy of note is set forth at § 303. Under this section, which is common to the Clean Water Act and Resource Conservation and Recovery Act, EPA may file suit to abate any air pollution that presents "an imminent and substantial endangerment to the health of persons" whether or not there has been a violation of the law. In the alternative, if it is not practicable to commence a civil action, the Administrator may issue such orders as may be necessary to protect the public health. The order may not be effective for more than 24 hours unless the Administrator commences a civil action in accordance with § 303.

Below are several cases which explore some of the problems raised by the Clean Air Act's enforcement provisions.

CITY OF SEABROOK V. COSTLE
659 F.2d 1371 (5th Cir. 1981)

REAVLEY, Circuit Judge:

Plaintiffs brought this action in federal district court pursuant to § 304(a)(2) of the Clean Air Act, 42 U.S.C. § 7604(a)(2) (Supp. III 1979), to compel the Administrator of the Environmental Protection Agency to perform allegedly nondiscretionary duties imposed by the Act. The district court dismissed the suit for lack of subject matter jurisdiction. Plaintiffs appeal. We affirm.

This suit is a companion to the petitions which we have denied today in *City of Seabrook v. United States Environmental Protection Agency*, 659 F.2d 1349 (5th Cir. 1981). The parties in both cases are the same. The complaint alleges many of the same violations of the Clean Air Act alleged in the petitions.

* * *

II. *Failure to Give Notification Required by Section 113 of the Act*

Section 113 of the Clean Air Act provides in pertinent part:

> (a)(1) Whenever, on the basis of any information available to him, the Administrator *finds* that any person is in violation of any requirement of an applicable implementation plan, the Administrator *shall* notify the person in violation of the plan and the State in which the plan applies of such finding. . . .
>
> (2) Whenever, on the basis of information available to him, the Administrator *finds* that violations of an applicable implementation plan are so widespread that such violations appear to result from a failure of the State in which the plan applies to enforce the plan effectively, he *shall* so notify the State. If the Administrator *finds* such failure extends beyond the 30th day after such notice, he *shall* give public notice of such finding.

42 U.S.C. § 7413 (Emphasis added). Even if the words "shall notify" impose a nondiscretionary duty on the Administrator to give notifications under certain circumstances, plaintiffs did not allege a failure to perform a nondiscretionary duty entitling them to bring a "citizens' suit" under § 304(a)(2).

Plaintiffs do not allege that the Administrator has ever made any finding either that "any person is in violation of any requirement of [the Texas] implementation plan" or that "violations of [the Texas] implementation plan are so widespread that such violations appear to result from a failure of the State . . . to enforce the plan effectively." Nor do plaintiffs ask leave to amend their complaint to make such allegations. Instead, plaintiffs argue that the Administrator had a nondiscretionary duty to make such findings on the basis of information available to him. We cannot agree with this argument.

A district court has jurisdiction under § 304(a)(2) only if the plaintiff has alleged a duty which is not discretionary under the Clean Air Act. 42 U.S.C. § 7604(a)(2). The language of neither § 113 nor any other section of the statute imposes a mandatory duty on the Administrator to make a finding every time some information concerning a possible violation of a SIP is brought to his attention. In the absence of a clear statutory mandate, we decline to impose such a duty on the Administrator.

The branches of government charged with the investigation of violations of the law and with enforcement of the law have traditionally been afforded broad discretion in carrying out these duties. We have held, for example, that the Attorney General's discretion "in choosing whether to prosecute or not to prosecute . . . is absolute." *Smith v. United States*, 375 F.2d 243, 247 (5th Cir.), *cert. denied*, 389 U.S. 841 (1967). The courts have recognized that, at least in the absence of a contrary statutory command, administrative agencies should be afforded similarly broad discretion. *See Rockford Redi-Mix Co. v. Zipp*, 632 F.2d 30, 32 n.5 (7th Cir. 1980) (collecting numerous cases holding NLRB's decision not to issue an unfair labor practice complaint nonreviewable), *cert. denied*, *Countryman v. Zipp*, 450 U.S. 929 (1981); *Kixmiller v. SEC*, 492 F.2d 641, 645 (D.C.Cir.1974) ("An agency's decision to refrain from an investigation or an enforcement action is generally unreviewable . . . ."). This principle of almost absolute discretion in initiating enforcement action should apply with equal force to the decision to take the preliminary investigatory steps that would provide the basis for enforcement action.

Given this tradition of broad prosecutorial discretion, we do not think that § 113(a) should be interpreted to impose a nondiscretionary duty to make findings whenever a violation of a SIP is alleged.

Plaintiffs rely heavily on *Wisconsin's Environmental Decade, Inc. v. Wisconsin Power & Light, Inc.*, 395 F.Supp. 313 (W.D.Wis.1975), in which the court held that the Administrator does indeed have a nondiscretionary duty under § 113(a) to make a finding when information concerning a possible violation is made available to him. *Id.* at 320. The *Wisconsin Environmental* court acknowledged that its interpretation found clear support in neither the statutory language nor its legislative history. *Id.* The court first held that the Administrator had a nondiscretionary duty to issue a notice of violation under § 113(a) whenever he actually did find a violation. *Id.* at 317-20.[3] Having begun with that conclusion, the district judge reasoned,

> I must also conclude that when presented with evidence indicating that a violation may exist, the Administrator must make a finding that a violation does or does not exist. Because I consider that Congress made a deliberate decision that the duty to issue notices of violation should be non- discretionary, I cannot accept an interpretation of the language of § (113(a)) which would make this duty an empty one by permitting the Administrator to make a finding or not make a finding as he or she sees fit. *Contra, New Mexico Citizens v. Train*, 6 ERC 1061 (D.N.M.1974). 395 F.Supp. at 320.

We think that the *Wisconsin Environmental* court's creation of a nondiscretionary duty which is not imposed by the statutory language pays too little heed to the doctrine of prosecutorial discretion. One of the principal bases for the doctrine is judicial recognition that enforcement agencies have only limited resources at their command. The enforcement agencies are duty-bound to allocate those resources in the interest of the general public as they perceive it, not in the causes deemed most important by individual citizens. The *Wisconsin Environmental* court would require the EPA to investigate and make considered findings on every alleged violation, without regard to the significance of the alleged violation, the reliability or credibility of the information received, or the most efficient allocation of the agency's resources in carrying out its many statutory duties.

The *Wisconsin Environmental* court's argument that the duty to issue a notice upon finding a violation would be an "empty one" if the Administrator could avoid the duty by failing to make a finding is based ultimately on the assumption that the EPA will not carry out its investigatory duties in good faith. This is an assumption which, in the absence of clear statutory language or legislative history, we are unwilling to attribute to Congress. We hold that § 113(a) does not impose a nondiscretionary duty to make a finding on every alleged violation of a SIP. Therefore, the district court correctly decided

[3] In reaching this initial conclusion, the *Wisconsin Environmental* court relied on the maxim that the word "shall" is normally interpreted to impose a mandatory duty. *See* 395 F.Supp. at 318. We note that, when duties within the traditional realm of prosecutorial discretion are involved, the courts have not found this maxim controlling. *See, e. g., Sierra Club v. Train*, 557 F.2d 485, 488-91 (5th Cir. 1977) (construing a clause of the Federal Water Pollution Control Act quite similar to § 113(a)); *Inmates of Attica Correctional Facility v. Rockefeller*, 477 F.2d 375, 381 (2d Cir. 1973) (mandatory nature of the statutory term "required" is insufficient to evince congressional intent to bar the exercise of prosecutorial discretion).

that § 304(a)(2) conferred no jurisdiction over plaintiffs' claim. *See Sierra Club v. Train*, 557 F.2d 485, 491 (5th Cir. 1977) (when no mandatory duty is alleged, claim is properly dismissed for lack of subject matter jurisdiction).

The judgment of the district court is AFFIRMED.

NOTES

1. The Court of Appeals for the Second Circuit appears to take a contrary view as to the nondiscretionary nature of the requirement at § 113(a) that EPA issue a notice of violation. *See Council of Commuter Organizations v. Metropolitan Transportation Authority*, 683 F.2d 663, 671-72 (2d Cir. 1982). Which court is correct as a matter of law? Which view is more likely to encourage compliance with the law?

2. The 1990 Amendments expanded the scope of § 113(a)(1) to include permit violations as well as plan violations. As previously noted, they also provided for the issuance of administrative civil penalties so long as the amount does not exceed $25,000 per violation or a $200,000 total penalty.

3. In *City of Seabrook*, the Court of Appeals for the Fifth Circuit relies substantially on notions of prosecutorial discretion to support its conclusion that the notice requirement of § 113(a) is mandatory. At the time that this case was decided, the only consequence of a notice of violation was that it triggered a 30 day period after which a compliance order could be issued or a civil action filed. Given the limited effect of a notice of violation, is the court's analogy sound? What were the consequences for issuance of a notice as compared with a decision to prosecute? How have the 1990 Amendments changed the law in this area?

4. In *City of Seabrook*, the court finds that EPA has discretion to issue the preliminary notice of violation, despite Congress' use of the word "shall" to describe the Administrator's obligation. Compare § 113(b) of the Act:

> The Administrator *shall, as appropriate,* in the case of any person that is the owner or operator of an affected source, a major emitting facility, or a major stationary source, and *may*, in the case of any other person, commence a civil action for a permanent or temporary injunction, or to assess and recover a civil penalty . . . [whenever such person violates any of several enumerated provisions of the law].

If Congress had intended to grant EPA discretion to issue a notice of violation should it not also be deemed to have discretion to commence a civil action which, after all, is more closely akin to prosecutorial discretion? Is this what Congress intended by its use of the word "shall, as appropriate" to describe EPA's obligation toward major sources, and "may" to describe EPA's obligation toward all other sources?

5. The Fifth Circuit states that "the *Wisconsin Environmental* court would require EPA to investigate and make considered findings on every alleged violation, without regard to the significance of the alleged violation, the reliability or credibility of the information received, or the most efficient allocation of the agency's resources. . . ." 659 F.2d at 1375. Is the burden of the *Wisconsin Environmental* decision as onerous as the Fifth Circuit suggests?

6. When should EPA take action against a violator in a state with an approved SIP? In a 1984 memorandum entitled "Guidance on Timely and Appropriate EPA/State Enforcement Response for Significant Air Violators," EPA announced a policy which allows states up to five months to initiate formal enforcement action against significant violators before EPA may issue a Notice of Violation. *See* Mintz, *EPA Enforcement: Critical Assessment Yields Mixed Review*, ENVIRONMENTAL FORUM (ELI), 12, 14 (November, 1984).

UNION ELECTRIC COMPANY V. EPA

593 F.2d 299 (8th Cir. 1979)

HEANEY, Circuit Judge.

The Environmental Protection Agency appeals from a judgment of the United States District Court for the Eastern District of Missouri which enjoined the EPA from instituting an enforcement proceeding under the Clean Air Act, 42 U.S.C. § 7401 *et seq.*, against the Union Electric Company or its officers while that Company is actively and in good faith pursuing a revision or variance of the sulfur dioxide (SO_2 regulations of the Missouri Implementation Plan in the administrative agencies and/or courts of the State of Missouri. We reverse the judgment of the District Court and direct that the complaint of Union Electric be dismissed.

Union Electric serves the metropolitan St. Louis area and parts of Illinois and Iowa. Its three coal-fired generating plants, Labadie, Meramec and Sioux, are subject to the SO_2 and opacity restrictions in the Missouri Implementation Plan as approved by the EPA on May 31, 1972.

Union Electric did not seek review of the approved Missouri Implementation Plan within thirty days as it was entitled to do under § 307(b)(1) of the Act, 42 U.S.C. § [7607(b)(1)]. It did, however, obtain one-year variances from the appropriate state and county agencies which eased the emission limitations affecting its three plants. The variances for two of the three plants had expired and Union Electric was applying for extensions when, on May 31, 1974, the Administrator of the EPA notified the Company that the SO_2 emissions from its plants violated the emission limitations contained in the Missouri Implementation Plan, and advised it of the probability that enforcement proceedings would soon be instituted.

* * *

On January 13, 1978, the EPA notified Union Electric of its alleged violations of the SO_2 and opacity standards of the Missouri Implementation Plan. The EPA stated that Union Electric's Labadie and Sioux power plants were in violation of SO_2 and opacity regulations, and that the Meramec plant was in violation of opacity regulations. The notice invited Union Electric to a conference to discuss the violations, and set forth the statutory responsibilities of the Agency if the matter was not resolved within thirty days.

On February 3, 1978, the EPA held the conference with Union Electric. At this conference, the EPA indicated that it would commence enforcement proceedings without waiting for the decision of the Missouri Commission on the Company's request for variances for its plants. The EPA indicated that it was required to proceed with enforcement by § 113(b) of the Clean Air Act Amendments of 1977, 42 U.S.C. § 7413(b)(2)(B).

On February 8, 1978, Union Electric brought this action in federal District Court for the Eastern District of Missouri, seeking a declaratory judgment and temporary and permanent injunctive relief. It simultaneously sought action by the State of Missouri on its variance requests.

On March 16, 1978, the District Court granted the preliminary injunction requested by Union Electric 450 F.Supp. 805. The court found: (1) that Union Electric was in the unenviable position of having daily penalties for noncompliance with the Missouri Implementation Plan accrue while it sought variances pursuant to the statutorily authorized procedure contained in Mo.Ann.Stat. § 203.110 (Vernon); (2) that the failure of Union Electric to comply with any governmental directive could constitute an act of default under its first mortgage and deed of trust and make its bonds callable, and that a calling of the bonds could force it into bankruptcy; (3) that compliance with the SO_2 regulations is not possible because compliance can be achieved only by installing flue gas desulfurization (FGD) equipment at an initial cost of $713 million and annual operating costs of $137 million, that the FGD equipment could not be relied upon to operate continually or satisfactorily, that the use of low sulfur coal as an alternative was not possible because the annual cost of such coal would be $179 million per year and would require a capital investment of $49 million, resulting in a rate increase of twenty-five percent, assuming that there was no reduction in the use of electricity, and that, in any event, it was impossible to obtain a sufficient supply of low sulfur coal to meet the SO_2 emission regulations; (4) that compliance with SO_2 regulations could be achieved only by a shutdown of the Union Electric plants which would result in a widespread electrical breakdown throughout the Midwest and drastic financial consequences to Union Electric; (5) that the injury to the EPA was not substantial because Union Electric's plants did not violate the National Air Quality Standards for SO_2; and (6) that Union Electric had a substantial likelihood of success on the merits because the Missouri Air Conservation Commission had informally indicated it would approve the variance.

The court concluded that: (1) considerations of procedural due process required that Union Electric be permitted to seek a variance under state procedures for SO_2 emissions prior to suffering a grievous loss which may result from an enforcement proceeding by the EPA; (2) that it had the general equitable power to stay an enforcement proceeding to prevent irreparable harm while Union Electric seeks the variances, in good faith, under state procedures; and (3) that the only fair interpretation of the Clean Air Act is to allow the variance proceeding to proceed to completion prior to the initiation of an enforcement action. This appeal was filed on May 15, 1978.

On July 26, 1978, more than two months after this appeal was filed, the Missouri Air Conservation Commission granted the variance in the SO_2 standards requested by Union Electric for its Sioux and Labadie plants. A petition to review that variance was subsequently filed in the Circuit Court of Cole County, Missouri, by the Coalition for the Environment and by the State of Illinois. That action is still pending.

In *Lloyd A. Fry Roofing Co. v. United States E.P.A.*, 554 F.2d 885 (8th Cir. 1977), we held that pre-enforcement judicial review of an abatement order on grounds of technological or economic infeasibility is inconsistent with the enforcement mechanism established by Congress in the Clean Air Act. Senior Judge M. C. Matthes, writing for the Court, pointed out that a company seeking to have these issues reviewed could do so in state court, or could present its cause as a defense to any enforcement proceedings initiated by the EPA in federal district court. He also noted that if the Agency seeks retroactive civil penalties, a company can protect itself by invoking the equitable doctrine of laches if the Agency failed to promptly seek enforcement. *Id.* at 891 & n.4.

Union Electric would have us distinguish *Fry* on the grounds that the plaintiff in *Fry* sought pre-enforcement review of an EPA compliance order while, here, it seeks only a temporary stay of any enforcement action which may be undertaken by the EPA pursuant to the notice of violation while a state variance from the emission limitations is sought.

Certainly this case cannot be distinguished from *Fry* on the grounds that *Fry* involved a compliance order and this case involves a notice of violation. If an abatement order may not be the subject of an anticipatory lawsuit enjoining its enforcement, then surely a notice of violation, which is a procedural prerequisite to an abatement order, may not be the subject of such a suit.

Nor can it be distinguished from *Fry* on the grounds that *Fry* involved an attempt to obtain a pre-enforcement decision in Federal court on the merits of the Missouri Implementation Plan, while here, the attempt is only to secure a temporary stay of any further enforcement procedures while the Company is actively and in good faith pursuing a revision of the SO_2 emission regulations in state administrative agencies or courts. This distinction, of course, exists. However, it is not one which permits us to reach a result different than that which was reached in *Fry*. Section 7413(b) specifically requires the Administrator to commence a civil action for injunctive relief or for the assessment of civil or criminal penalties thirty days after notice of violation has been given to a major stationary source. One purpose of this section is to require the states to act promptly in granting or denying variance requests. This purpose would be thwarted if federal courts were permitted to remove the pressures that Congress clearly thought necessary to accomplish the objectives of the Clean Air Act. The heart of the decision in *Fry* is that federal courts should not interfere with the pre-enforcement procedures established by the Act to obtain compliance. *Fry* recognized that Congress intended the 1970 Amendments to the Clean Air Act to "expedite the implementation and enforcement of air quality standards" and that the Amendments were " 'a drastic remedy to what was perceived as a serious and otherwise uncheckable problem.' " *Id.* at 889, 891.

No case could better illustrate the need for expeditious enforcement than this one. The Missouri Implementation Plan was approved on May 31, 1972. Now, nearly seven years later, Union Electric is still not in compliance with the plan's SO_2 emissions limitations at its Labadie or Sioux plants, and the State of Missouri has yet to finally approve or disapprove its request for a variance from existing standards.

This statement of fact is not necessarily intended to point the finger at Union Electric, the State of Missouri or the EPA. All have been responsible in one way or another for the delays that have occurred. It is only to emphasize that we can only be faithful to the mandate of Congress if we require strict adherence to the procedural routes which it established for bringing clean air to the nation.

In *Fry*, we did not consider a contention by Union Electric which was deemed important by the District Court, *i.e.*, that Union Electric has a due process right to contest the validity of the emission standard without necessarily having to face ruinous penalties if it loses its action. The District Court relied on *Ex Parte Young*, 209 U.S. 123 (1908), in so holding. In *Young*, the State of Minnesota enacted a number of statutes which established maximum rates which could be charged by railroads within the State and which fixed penalties for the railroads' failure to comply. Railroad officials contended that the statutes were invalid because the penalties imposed were so severe that no company official would run the risk of violating the statutes in order to test their validity. The Supreme Court sustained their contention. It stated:

* * *

> [W]hen the penalties for disobedience are by fines so enormous and imprisonment so severe as to intimidate the company and its officers from resorting to the courts to test the validity of the legislation, the result is the

> same as if the law in terms prohibited the company from seeking judicial construction of laws which deeply affect its rights.
>
> Now, to impose upon a party interested the burden of obtaining a judicial decision of such a question (no prior hearing having ever been given) only upon the condition that, if unsuccessful, he must suffer imprisonment and pay fines, as provided in these acts, is, in effect, to close up all approaches to the courts, and thus prevent any hearing upon the question whether the rates as provided by the acts are not too low, and therefore invalid. The distinction is obvious between a case where the validity of the act depends upon the existence of a fact which can be determined only after investigation of a very complicated and technical character, and the ordinary case of statute upon a subject requiring no such investigation, and over which the jurisdiction of the legislature is complete in any event.

We do not believe *Young* to be applicable here. Union Electric has an opportunity to test the validity of the Missouri Implementation Plan without necessarily incurring confiscatory fines and penalties. *See Brown & Williamson Tobacco Corp. v. Engman*, 527 F.2d 1115 (2d Cir. 1975), *cert. denied*, 426 U.S. 911 (1976). The Administrator of the EPA . . . has two alternatives. He can either seek injunctive relief or can seek to impose civil or criminal penalties. We should not anticipate what the Administrator will seek in advance of his decision. Thus, it cannot be said that confiscatory fines and penalties will *necessarily* be incurred. Indeed, the Administrator apparently feels, in this case, that he has a third alternative — that of staying enforcement until the resolution of Union Electric's variance request.[8]

* * *

We cannot, of course, read more into *Fry* or into the EPA's concession than was intended. We do not now hold that the Clean Air Act will ultimately permit a noncomplying polluter to continue operations without change if such change is not technologically or economically feasible. We do hold, however, that this question can be raised in any future enforcement proceeding, and that Union Electric at that time will be able to argue that Congress did not intend that result or that, if it was intended, the statute is unconstitutional. We reserve our decision on that issue until it is properly presented to us.

We reaffirm our decision in *Lloyd A. Fry Roofing Co. v. United States E.P.A., supra*, and reverse the District Court. Any other course of action would be inconsistent with the enforcement mechanism which Congress has established in the Clean Air Act and would unreasonably delay achieving the objectives of that Act.

---

[8] On September 13, 1978, the EPA notified Union Electric that it will not initiate any enforcement proceedings against that Company with respect to its alleged violations of the existing SO_2 emission limitations until the Regional Administrator of the EPA has informed Union Electric, in writing, of its decision regarding a recommended approval or disapproval of the variance. The Company was further notified that if EPA's Regional Office recommended approval, the enforcement stay would be extended until such time as the Administrator of EPA has taken final action on the variance request. This notification would also appear to eliminate any risk that the Company's bonds would be called for failure to follow a governmental directive. We express no opinion as to whether this stay is authorized by the Act.

NOTES

1. As the court correctly points out in the *Union Electric* case, the notice of violation at issue there is a prerequisite to issuance of any compliance order. Yet both notices of violation (NOVs) and compliance orders (COs) are subject to enforcement through a civil action. Injunctive relief and civil penalties can be obtained for a violation of either an NOV or a CO. The only real distinction is that an NOV cannot be enforced through a civil action unless EPA has assumed enforcement authority in the state or 30 days have elapsed since the notice of violation was issued. § 113(a)(1)(C). In the *Union Electric* case, EPA had not assumed enforcement responsibility over the Missouri SIP. Thus, the 30-day grace period applied. Four days prior to its expiration, Union Electric filed suit. What consequences did Union Electric face if it waited beyond the 30-day period? How compelling is the court's distinction of *Ex Parte Young*, 209 U.S. 123 (1908)? *See also West Penn Power Co. v. Train*, 522 F.2d 302 (3d Cir. 1975). Does the *Union Electric* decision survive the *Harrison v. PPG Industries* decision? *See infra* at Chapter 13. What about *Fry*? Is the action involved here "pre-enforcement review" as characterized by the Court in *Fry*? *See* CURRIE, AIR POLLUTION: LAW AND ANALYSIS, § 9.04 (1981). *Compare Abbott Laboratories v. Gardner*, 387 U.S. 136 (1967): "Where the legal issue presented is fit for judicial resolution, and where a regulation requires an immediate and significant change in the plaintiffs' conduct of their affairs with serious penalties attached to noncompliance, access to the courts. . . .must be permitted, absent a statutory bar or some other unusual circumstance. . . ." *Id.* at 153.

2. Suppose that the government files a civil action against the owner or operator of a major source alleged to be in violation of the Act. The action seeks injunctive relief and civil penalties in accordance with § 113(b) of the Act. Does the owner or operator have a Seventh Amendment right to a jury trial in such a case? In *Tull v. United States*, 481 U.S. 412 (1987), the Court held that a jury trial must be afforded in the context of an analogous Clean Water Act case. The Court determined that the Seventh Amendment had traditionally been applied to civil penalty proceedings. Furthermore, "if a 'legal claim [civil penalties] is joined with an equitable claim [injunction], the right to a jury trial on the legal claim, including all issues common to both claims, remains intact.'" *Id.* at 425 (*quoting Curtis v. Loether*, 415 U.S., at 196, n. 11). The Seventh Amendment does not, however, guarantee a right to have a jury assess a civil penalty. The legislative history of the Clean Water Act demonstrated that Congress intended that the trial judge perform this function and, over the dissent of Justices Scalia and Stevens, the Court found this practice consistent with the Seventh Amendment. *Id.*

3. The Labadie and Sioux plants are Phase I "affected sources" under Title IV of the Clean Air Act. Their 1985 SO_2 emissions were estimated to be 4.45 lbs/mmBtu at Labadie, and 4.71 lbs/mmBtu at Sioux. COMPLIANCE STRATEGIES REVIEW, GUIDE TO PHASE I UNITS, 38 (Fieldston, 1992). Under the Phase I requirements these facilities will receive allowances equivalent to 2.5 lbs/mmBtu beginning in 1995.

ADAMO WRECKING CO. V. UNITED STATES
434 U.S. 275 (1978)

Mr. Justice REHNQUIST delivered the opinion of the Court.

The Clean Air Act authorizes the Administrator of the Environmental Protection Agency to promulgate "emission standards" for hazardous air pollutants "at the level which in his judgment provides an ample margin of safety to protect the public health." § 112(b)(1)(B), 84 Stat. 1685. The emission of an air pollutant in violation of an applicable emission standard is prohibited by § 112(c)(1)(B) of the Act. The knowing violation of the latter section, in turn, subjects the violator to fine and imprisonment under the provisions of § 113(c)(1)(C) of the Act. The final piece in this statutory puzzle is § 307(b) of the Act, which provides in pertinent part:

> "(1) A petition for review of action of the Administrator in promulgating . . . any emission standard under section 112 . . . may be filed only in the United States Court of Appeals for the District of Columbia. . . . Any such petition shall be filed within 30 days from the date of such promulgation, or approval, or after such date if such petition is based solely on grounds arising after such 30th day.
>
> "(2) Action of the Administrator with respect to which review could have been obtained under paragraph (1) shall not be subject to judicial review in civil or criminal proceedings for enforcement."

It is within this legislative matrix that the present criminal prosecution arose.

Petitioner was indicted in the United States District Court for the Eastern District of Michigan for violation of § 112(c)(1)(B). The indictment alleged that petitioner, while engaged in the demolition of a building in Detroit, failed to comply with 40 CFR § 61.22(d)(2)(i) (1975). That regulation, described in its caption as a "National Emission Standard for Asbestos," specifies procedures to be followed in connection with building demolitions, but does not by its terms limit emissions of asbestos which occur during the course of a demolition. The District Court granted petitioner's motion to dismiss the indictment on the ground that no violation of § 112(c)(1)(B), necessary to establish criminal liability under § 113(c)(1)(C), had been alleged, because the cited regulation was not an "emission standard" within the meaning of § 112(c). The United States Court of Appeals for the Sixth Circuit reversed, 545 F.2d 1 (1976), holding that Congress had in § 307(b) precluded petitioner from questioning in a criminal proceeding whether a regulation ostensibly promulgated under § 112(b)(1)(B) was in fact an emission standard. We granted certiorari, 430 U.S. 953 (1977), and we now reverse.

I

We do not intend to make light of a difficult question of statutory interpretation when we say that the basic question in this case may be phrased: "When is an emission standard not an emission standard?" Petitioner contends, and the District Court agreed, that while the preclusion and exclusivity provisions of § 307(b) of the Act prevented his obtaining "judicial review" of an emission standard in this criminal proceeding, he was nonetheless entitled to claim that the administrative regulation cited in the indictment was actually not an emission standard at all. The Court of Appeals took the contrary view. It held that a regulation designated by the Administrator as an "emission standard," however different in content it might be from what Congress had contemplated when it authorized the promulgation of emission standards, was sufficient to support a criminal charge based upon § 112(c), unless it had been set aside in an appropriate proceeding commenced in the United States Court of Appeals for the District of Columbia Circuit pursuant to § 307(b).

The Court of Appeals in its opinion relied heavily on *Yakus v. United States*, 321 U.S. 414 (1944), in which this Court held that Congress in the context of criminal proceedings could require that the validity of regulatory action be challenged in a particular court at a particular time, or not at all. That case, however, does not decide this one. Because § 307(b) expressly applies only to "emission standards," we must still inquire as to the validity of the Government's underlying assumption that the Administrator's mere designation of a regulation as an "emission standard" is sufficient to foreclose any further inquiry in a criminal prosecution under § 113(c)(1)(C) of the Act. For the reasons hereafter stated, we hold that one such as respondent who is charged with a criminal violation under the Act may defend on the ground that the "emission standard" which he is charged with having violated was not an "emission standard" within the contemplation of Congress when it employed that term, even though the "emission standard" in question has not been previously reviewed under the provisions of § 307(b) of the Act.

II

* * *

This relatively simple statutory scheme contrasts with the Clean Air Act's far more complex interrelationship between the imposition of criminal sanctions and judicial review of the Administrator's actions. The statutory basis for imposition of criminal liability under Subchapter I of the Act, under which this indictment was brought, is § 113(c)(1):

"(c)(1) Any person who knowingly —

> "(A) violates any requirement of an applicable implementation plan (i) during any period of Federally assumed enforcement, or (ii) more than 30 days after having been notified by the Administrator under subsection (a)(1) that such person is violating such requirement, or
>
> "(B) violates or fails or refuses to comply with any order issued by the Administrator under subsection (a), or
>
> "(C) violates section 111(e), section 112(c), or section 119(g) "shall be punished by a fine of not more than $25,000 per day of violation, or by imprisonment for not more than one year, or by both. If the conviction is for a violation committed after the first conviction of such person under this paragraph, punishment shall be by a fine of not more than $50,000 per day of violation, or by imprisonment for not more than two years, or by both."

Each of the three separate subsections in the quoted language creates criminal offenses. The first of them, subsection (A), deals with violations of applicable implementation plans after receipt of notice of such violation. Under § 307(b)(1), judicial review of the Administrator's action in approving or promulgating an implementation plan is not restricted to the Court of Appeals for the District of Columbia Circuit, but may be had "in the United States Court of Appeals for the appropriate circuit." But § 307(b)(2) does provide that the validity of such plans may not be reviewed in the criminal proceeding itself.

Subsection (C), which we discuss before turning to subsection (B), provides criminal penalties for violations of three separate sections of the Act: § 111(e), which prohibits operation of new stationary sources in violation of "standards of performance" promulgated by the Administrator; § 112(c), which is the offense charged in this case;

and § 119(g)[9] which requires compliance with an assortment of administrative requirements, set out in more detail below. The Administrator's actions in promulgating "standards of performance" under § 111, or "emission standards" under § 112 are, by the provisions of § 307(b)(1), made reviewable exclusively in the Court of Appeals for the District of Columbia Circuit. However, his actions under subsections (A), (B), and (C) of § 119(c)(2), compliance with which is required by § 119(g)(2), are reviewable "in the United States Court of Appeals for the appropriate circuit." Those subsections define the Administrator's authority to issue compliance date extensions to particular stationary sources with regard to various air pollution requirements. The preclusive provisions of § 307(b)(2) prohibit challenges to all of *these* administrative actions in both civil and criminal enforcement proceedings. But these restrictive review provisions do *not* apply to *other* violations of § 119(g); with regard to those offenses, the invalidity of administrative action may be raised as a defense to the extent allowable in the absence of such restrictions.

Finally, subsection (B) of § 113(c)(1) subjects to criminal penalties "any person who knowingly . . . violates or fails or refuses to comply with any order issued by the Administrator under subsection (a)." Subsection (a), in turn, empowers the Administrator to issue orders requiring compliance, not only with those regulations for which criminal penalties are provided under subsections (A) and (C), but also with the recordkeeping and inspection requirements of § 114, for which only civil penalties are ordinarily available under § 113(b)(4). The restrictive review provisions of § 307(b)(1), again do *not* apply to orders issued under § 113(a) or to the underlying requirements of § 114. Those administrative actions would likely be reviewable under the Administrative Procedure Act, 5 U.S.C. § 701 *et seq.*, and any infirmity in them could be raised as a defense in enforcement proceedings to the same extent as it could be in the absence of a provision such as § 307(b)(2).

III

* * *

The stringency of the penalty imposed by Congress lends substance to petitioner's contention that Congress envisioned a particular type of regulation when it spoke of an "emission standard." The fact that Congress dealt more leniently, either in terms of liability, of notice, or of available defenses, with other infractions of the Administrator's orders suggests that it attached a peculiar importance to compliance with "emission standards." Unlike the situation in *Yakus*, Congress in the Clean Air Act singled out violators of this generic form of regulation, imposed criminal penalties upon them which would not be imposed upon violators of other orders of the Administrator, and precluded them from asserting defenses which might be asserted by violators of other orders of the Administrator. All of this leads us to conclude that Congress intended, within broad limits, that "emission standards" be regulations of a certain type, and that it did not empower the Administrator, after the manner of Humpty Dumpty in Through the Looking-Glass, to make a regulation an "emission standard" by his mere designation.

The statutory scheme supports the conclusion that § 307(b)(2), in precluding judicial review of the validity of emission standards, does not relieve the Government of the duty of proving, in a prosecution under § 113(c)(1)(C), that the regulation allegedly violated

---

[9] Section 119, which was in effect at the inception of this prosecution, has lately been replaced by a new § 113(d). Clean Air Act Amendments of 1977, Pub.L. 95-95, § 112, 91 Stat. 705.

is an emission standard. Here, the District Court properly undertook to resolve that issue. In so doing, the court did not undermine the twin congressional purposes of insuring that the substantive provisions of the standard would be uniformly applied and interpreted and that the circumstances of its adoption would be quickly reviewed by a single court intimately familiar with administrative procedures. The District Court did not presume to judge the wisdom of the regulation or to consider the adequacy of the procedures which led to its promulgation, but merely concluded that it was not an emission standard.

In sum, a survey of the totality of the statutory scheme does not compel agreement with the Government's contention that Congress intended that the Administrator's designation of a regulation as an emission standard should be conclusive in a criminal prosecution. At the very least, it may be said that the issue is subject to some doubt. Under these circumstances, we adhere to the familiar rule that, "where there is ambiguity in a criminal statute, doubts are resolved in favor of the defendant." *United States v. Bass*, 404 U.S. 336, 348 (1971). *Cf. Rewis v. United States*, 401 U.S. 808, 812 (1971).

We conclude, therefore, that a federal court in which a criminal prosecution under § 113(c)(1)(C) of the Clean Air Act is brought may determine whether or not the regulation which the defendant is alleged to have violated is an "emission standard" within the meaning of the Act.

* * *

IV

It remains to be seen whether the District Court reached the correct conclusion with regard to the regulation here in question. In the Act, Congress has given a substantial indication of the intended meaning of the term "emission standard." Section 112 on its face distinguishes between emission standards and the techniques to be utilized in achieving those standards. Under § 112(c)(1)(B)(ii), the Administrator is empowered temporarily to exempt certain facilities from the burden of compliance with an emission standard, "if he finds that such period is necessary for the installation of controls." In specified circumstances, the President, under § 112(c)(2), has the same power, "if he finds that the technology to implement such standards is not available." Section 112(b)(2) authorizes the Administrator to issue information on "pollution control techniques."

Most clearly supportive of petitioner's position that a standard was intended to be a quantitative limit on emissions is this provision of § 112(b)(1)(B): "The Administrator shall establish any such standard *at the level* which in his judgment provides an ample margin of safety to protect the public health from such hazardous air pollutant." (Emphasis added.) All these provisions lend force to the conclusion that a standard is a quantitative "level" to be attained by use of "techniques," "controls," and "technology." This conclusion is fortified by recent amendments to the Act, by which Congress authorized the Administrator to promulgate a "design, equipment, work practice, or operational standard" when "it is not feasible to prescribe or enforce an emission standard." Clean Air Act Amendments of 1977, Pub.L. 95-95, § 110, 91 Stat. 703.

This distinction, now endorsed by Congress, between "work practice standards" and "emission standards" first appears in the Administrator's own account of the development of this regulation. Although the Administrator has contended that a "work practice standard" is just another type of emission standard, the history of this regulation demonstrates that he chose to regulate work practices only when it became clear he could not regulate emissions. The regulation as originally proposed would have prohibited all visible emissions of asbestos during the course of demolitions. 36 Fed.Reg. 23242 (1971). In adopting the final form of the regulation, the Administrator concluded "that the no visible emission requirement would prohibit repair or demolition in many situations, since it would be impracticable, if not impossible, to do such work without creating visible emissions." 38 Fed.Reg. 8821 (1973). Therefore the Administrator chose to "specif[y] certain work practices" instead. *Ibid.*

The Government concedes that, prior to the 1977 Amendments, the statute was ambiguous with regard to whether a work-practice standard was properly classified as an emission standard, but argues that this Court should defer to the Administrator's construction of the Act. Brief for United States 32, and n. 22. While such deference is entirely appropriate under ordinary circumstances, in this case the 1977 Amendments to the Clean Air Act tend to undercut the administrative construction. The Senate Report reiterated its "strong preference for numerical emission limitations," but endorsed the addition of § 112(e) to the Act to allow the use of work-practice standards "in a very few limited cases." S.Rep.No.95-127, p. 44 (1977). Although the Committee agreed that the Amendments would authorize the regulation involved here, it refrained from endorsing the Administrator's view that the regulation had previously been authorized as an emission standard under § 112(c). The clear distinction drawn in § 112(e) between work-practice standards and emission standards practically forecloses any such inference. *Cf. Red Lion Broadcasting Co. v. FCC*, 395 U.S. 367, 380-381 (1969).

* * *

[W]e conclude that the work-practice standard involved here was not an emission standard. The District Court's order dismissing the indictment was therefore proper, and the judgment of the Court of Appeals is

Reversed.

[The concurring opinion of Justice Powell, and the dissenting opinions by Justice Stewart, with whom Justices Brennan and Blackman join, and Justice Stevens are omitted.]

NOTES

1. Following the court's decision in *Adamo Wrecking*, the Act was amended to provide that "any design, equipment, work practice or operational standard, or any combination thereof. . . .shall be treated as an emission standard. . . ." P.L. 95-623, § 13(b). Still, the courts have struggled with the implications of the *Adamo Wrecking* decision. *See e.g., United States v. Ethyl Corporation*, 761 F.2d 1153 (5th Cir. 1985), *cert. denied*, 474 U.S. 1070 (1986).

2. As noted previously, the 1990 Amendments impose significant new criminal sanctions on persons who knowingly violate the law. § 113(c). It also imposes criminal penalties on persons who negligently allow the release of hazardous air pollutants listed under § 112 of the Act, or extremely hazardous air substances listed under § 302(a)(2) of the Superfund Amendments and Reauthorization Act (SARA), where such releases pose an imminent threat of death or serious bodily injury.

DUQUESNE LIGHT COMPANY V. EPA
698 F.2d 456 (D.C. Cir. 1983)

MIKVA, Circuit Judge:

To speed improvement of the nation's air quality, Congress adopted the Clean Air Act Amendments of 1977, Pub.L. No. 95-95, 91 Stat. 685 (Amendments). An innovative feature of the 1977 Amendments was the authorization of penalties to recoup the economic benefits derived by pollution sources that fail to comply with air pollution limitations, 1977 Amendments § 120. Section 120 directed the Administrator of the Environmental Protection Agency (EPA) to promulgate regulations by February 1978 for assessing the noncompliance penalties. *Id.* § 120(a)(1)(A). EPA's final rules implementing section 120 were adopted nearly a year and one half later. 45 Fed.Reg. 50,086 (1980) (codified at 40 C.F.R. §§ 66.1 to 67.43 (1981)).

In these twenty consolidated cases, industry petitioners seek review of a variety of aspects of the final rules. In nearly all respects, we find that EPA complied with the statutory mandate: to recover the economic benefits of continued noncompliance with air quality standards, swiftly but fairly.

* * *

I. THE CLEAN AIR ACT AND SECTION 120

* * *

Section 120 is a unique federal experiment with economic penalties. It is designed to alter economic behavior by changing the costs of emitting pollutants in violation of applicable air quality standards. *See* H.R.Rep. No. 294, 95th Cong., 1st Sess. 72-79 (1977) [hereinafter 1977 House Report], *reprinted in* 4 A LEGISLATIVE HISTORY OF THE CLEAN AIR ACT AMENDMENTS OF 1977 at 2539-46 (1978) [hereinafter 1977 LEGISLATIVE HISTORY]. Congress added section 120 to the Act because it anticipated that even the augmented civil and criminal penalty scheme would not create sufficient incentives for sources to comply with air quality standards. *Id.* at 72. Congress also hoped that the section 120 penalties would increase administrative flexibility in enforcing the Act, by serving as a middle ground between stiff criminal sanctions or shutdown of noncomplying facilities. *Id.* at 5. Equally important, by removing the economic benefits of noncompliance with the Act, Congress hoped to place polluters on the same economic footing as those who had limited their emissions through increased anti-pollution expenditures. *Id.*

Section 120 begins by specifying the sources made subject to noncompliance penalties. Under section 120(a)(2), penalties may be assessed against any major stationary source — defined as any source that emits or has the potential to emit one hundred or more tons of any pollutant per year, Act § 302(j) — not in compliance with any applicable emission limitation. Such penalties also are to be assessed against other stationary sources not in compliance with federal new source performance standards or standards for hazardous pollutants. Finally, sources operating under certain types of delayed compliance orders allowed by the Act are to be assessed penalties if they fail to comply with the terms of such orders.

Sources meeting certain conditions, however, are to be exempted from the noncompliance penalties. For example, sources converting from petroleum to coal pursuant to orders issued under the Act, and complying with the terms of such orders, are exempt from noncompliance penalties. § 120(a)(2)(B)(i). So are sources experimenting with innovative technology under the Act, § 120(a)(2)(B)(iii), and certain sources unable to comply with emission limitations for reasons utterly beyond their control, § 120(a)(2)(B)(iv). These exemptions are mandatory, although the burden of demonstrating entitlement to any of them falls on the source. In addition, EPA may exempt sources from penalties for certain instances of noncompliance that are de minimis in nature and duration. § 120(a)(2)(C).

Penalties are to be assessed against noncomplying sources either by EPA or by the individual states. Section 120 directs EPA to promulgate regulations implementing the penalties after notice and opportunity for public hearing — the regulations we must evaluate here. Individual states may take over responsibility for administering the noncompliance penalty program if they submit plans approved by EPA, § 120(a)(1)(B)(i), in which case the penalties are paid to the states, § 120(d)(1). To date, however, states have shown little interest in taking responsibility for the program. In any event, the statute does not differentiate substantively between the penalty program as administered by EPA and by the states, and the discussion to follow will for convenience refer principally to EPA as administering the program.

Section 120 sets out carefully the procedures to be followed in assessing the noncompliance penalties. Sources not complying with applicable air quality standards are to be given "a brief but reasonably specific notice of noncompliance." § 120(b)(3). Upon receipt of a notice of noncompliance, a source must either calculate the amount of the penalty owed, which begins to accrue with the issuance of the notice of noncompliance, § 120(d)(3)(C)(ii), or submit a petition within forty-five days challenging the notice of noncompliance or asserting entitlement to an exemption. EPA is to provide a hearing on the record and to act on the petition within ninety days. § 120(b)(5). Should a source in receipt of a noncompliance notice fail to respond, EPA may contract for calculation of the penalty. § 120(c).

Penalties are to be calculated to reflect the projected economic value of noncompliance to a source. EPA is to promulgate regulations for calculating the penalty, which must include at least the quarterly equivalents of capital costs, operating costs, and maintenance expenses avoided as a result of noncompliance. § 120(d)(2)(A). The penalty is to be paid on a quarterly basis, in equal installments during the entire period of noncompliance, beginning with issuance of the notice of noncompliance and ending when the source comes into full compliance with applicable air quality standards. § 120(d)(3)(B), (C). Expenditures made during a quarter for the purpose of bringing the source into compliance with air quality standards, and not otherwise reflected in the calculation of the penalty amounts, are to be credited against the penalty assessment for that quarter. § 120(d)(2)(B). Credits not taken into account fully in a given quarter may be carried over and offset against the next quarter's penalty assessment. § 120(d)(2). When a source reaches full compliance with air quality standards, the penalty is to be recalculated to take into account the actual — rather than the projected — expenditures required to bring the source into compliance with air quality standards and the length of the actual period of delay in the expenditures. § 120(d)(4). Sources that have overpaid are entitled to reimbursement, at interest rates set by the United States Treasury (or by the state, if the state is administering the penalty program); sources that have underpaid are to be assessed the deficiency, again with interest. § 120(d)(4)(A), (B).

Initial penalty payments are due six months after issuance of the notice of noncompliance. A source may seek judicial review of a determination by EPA that penalizes the source under section 120, but the penalty is not stayed pending the review process, § 120(e). The penalties are in addition to other civil and criminal penalties under the Act, and do not alter a source's other obligations under the Act. § 120(f).

* * *

II. THE APPLICABILITY OF SECTION 120

Industry petitioners' challenge to EPA's regulations implementing section 120 begin with the threshold question of which sources are subject to noncompliance penalties. EPA interprets the scope of the statute broadly, while industry petitioners argue for a narrow interpretation.

Section 120 provides that noncompliance penalties are to be assessed against "every person who owns or operates" one of three categories of noncomplying sources. The statutory language reads:

> (i) a major stationary source (other than a primary nonferrous smelter which has received a primary nonferrous smelter order under section 119) which is not in compliance with any emission limitation, emission standard or compliance schedule under any applicable implementation plan (whether or not such source is subject to a Federal or State consent decree), or
>
> (ii) a stationary source which is not in compliance with an emission limitation, emission standard, standard of performance, or other requirement established under section 111 or 112 of this Act, or
>
> (iii) any source referred to in clause (i) or (ii) (for which an extension, order, or suspension referred to in subparagraph (B), or Federal or State consent decree is in effect), or a primary nonferrous smelter which has received a primary nonferrous smelter order under section 119 which is not in compliance with any interim emission control requirement or schedule of compliance under such extension, order, suspension, or consent decree.†

§ 120(a)(2)(A). Section 120 penalties thus apply most extensively to major stationary sources, which may be liable to pay penalties for failure to comply with any type of air quality standard, interim or permanent, applicable under the Clean Air Act. Other, smaller stationary sources will be assessed penalties only for failures to meet federal new source performance standards, § 111, federal standards for particularly hazardous pollutants, § 112, or the types of interim standards listed in subpart (iii).

EPA's regulations implementing section 120 specify that a notice of noncompliance—the first step in the penalty assessment process-is to be sent to the owner or operator of any source that is in violation of "applicable legal requirements." 40 C.F.R. § 66.11(a) (1981). The regulations defining the term "applicable legal requirements" track the language of the applicability provisions set out above. *See id.* § 66.3(c)(1)-(4). Industry petitioners challenge this definition, together with two other EPA interpretations of the applicability provisions. The first of these is EPA's definition of "owner or operator" of a source to include both lessees and supervisory companies of sources not in compliance with applicable legal requirements. *Id.* § 66.3(i). The second is EPA's broad definition of "potential to emit," a term of art used in deciding which stationary sources are "major." *Id.* §§ 66.3(g), (j). We now turn to those definitions.

---

† Editor's note: The 1990 Amendments added a fourth category: "a stationary source which is not in compliance with any requirement of Title IV [acid deposition], V [permits], or VI [stratospheric ozone] of the Act . . ." § 120(a)(2)(A)(iii).

A. *"Applicable Legal Requirements"*

EPA's regulations define "applicable legal requirements" for major sources as follows:

> (1) In the case of any major source, any emission limitation, emission standard, or compliance schedule under any EPA-approved State implementation plan (regardless of whether the source is subject to a Federal or State consent decree). . . .

40 C.F.R. § 66.3(c) (1981).

Industry raises two objections to this definition. The first is that it permits the assessment of penalties against sources operating under consent decrees and complying with their terms, but not yet in compliance with applicable legal requirements. The second is that EPA's regulations dictate that penalties are to be assessed against major sources failing to comply with limits stipulated in state SIPs, even though proposed revisions of the SIPs are pending, and even though EPA has not acted on the revisions within the time limits mandated in the Act. With regard to the first objection, we affirm EPA's determination that section 120 penalties are to be applied to sources operating under consent decrees. With regard to the second, we conclude that EPA's application of section 120 penalties pending SIP revisions must be modified in part.

1. Sources in Compliance with Consent Decrees

The regulations require noncompliance penalties to be assessed against major stationary sources operating under consent decrees. They explicitly provide that a major source is liable for failures to comply with emission limitations set for that source in the SIP of the state in which the source is located, 40 C.F.R. § 66.3(c)(1) (1981), even though the source has been sued for violation of the limitations in question, the suit has resulted in a consent decree, and the consent decree sets out a schedule for the source to come into compliance with the limitations in exchange for an agreement by EPA not to pursue the civil or criminal penalties set out in the enforcement section of the Act, § 113(c).

Industry petitioners concede that the statutory parenthetical "(whether or not such source is subject to a Federal or State consent decree)," § 120(a)(2)(A)(i), permits assessment of noncompliance penalties against some major sources operating under consent decrees. They contend, however, that such penalties may be assessed only in two kinds of cases: (1) if the source fails to comply with a different emission limitation that was not the subject of the consent decree and (2) if the source fails to comply with the terms of the consent decree itself. Petitioners argue that by assessing penalties against major sources for failure to comply with emission limitations that were themselves the subject of consent decrees, EPA has misinterpreted the statutory parenthetical. In the alternative, they contend that if EPA's interpretation of the statute is correct, the statute interferes with previous court decrees in an unconstitutional manner.

EPA rested its decision to permit assessment of noncompliance penalties against major stationary sources operating under consent decrees squarely on its reading of the statutory language. 45 Fed.Reg. 50,086-87 (1980). EPA also pointed out that assessing penalties against sources operating under consent decrees would further the purposes of section 120, for sources out of compliance with emissions limitations derive benefits from their noncompliance regardless of whether they have been subject to consent decrees. *Id.* at 50,087.

We think that EPA's interpretation of the statute is sound. Section 120 distinguishes three categories in which noncompliance penalties are to be assessed. *See supra* pp.

465-466. The disputed parenthetical language appears in the first of these--major sources failing to comply with any SIP limitations. Reference to consent decrees also appears in the third category, which provides for the assessment of penalties against sources failing to comply with the terms of consent decrees or other interim orders. Industry petitioners' reading of the parenthetical — that it principally indicates that penalties may be assessed against sources failing to comply with their consent decrees — accounts only for the reference to consent decrees in the third category. It would render the parenthetical superfluous, for the third category makes absolutely plain that sources failing to comply with consent decrees may be subject to penalties for that very failure. Thus the function of the initial parenthetical is to make clear that consent decrees do not bar the imposition of penalties against major sources in violation of any emission limitation.

* * *

Industry petitioners' principal constitutional complaint is that by assessing a noncompliance penalty against a source subject to a consent decree, EPA interferes with the *res judicata* effect of the decree, in violation of the separation of powers. Petitioners' position is that EPA, should it wish to assess a penalty, may do so only by petitioning the issuing court for modification of the decree. Although petitioners are correct that consent decrees, like final judgments, do have a *res judicata* effect, they misconstrue the statutory situation.

Congress always has the power to impose a new penalty on continuing activity. Here, under its power to regulate interstate commerce, Congress has imposed a new penalty. As it specifically noted in passing this section, "[a]ny orders, payments, sanctions, or other requirements under [section 120] shall be in addition to any other permits, orders, payments, sanctions, or other requirements established under this Act." § 120(f). Thus, when EPA promulgated its regulations, it was not seeking to relitigate, revise, or otherwise overturn a validly entered consent decree; rather, it was merely acting in furtherance of the additional, constitutionally proper, mandate Congress gave it in the 1977 Amendments.

* * *

2. Sources Claiming Compliance with Pending SIP Revisions

Industry petitioners' second major objection to the definition of "applicable legal requirements" in EPA's regulations implementing section 120 is that it allows penalties to be assessed against a major source in violation of current SIP requirements, despite the fact that revisions to the requirements have been proposed and are under consideration by EPA, and despite the fact that the source is in compliance with the proposed revisions. 40 C.F.R. § 66.3(c)(1) (1981). Under the regulations, current SIP provisions continue to be the standard by which compliance is measured. If and when a proposed revision to a SIP is approved by EPA, it becomes the standard by which compliance is measured. A source which comes into compliance with SIP requirements by virtue of a SIP revision will thus cease to be liable for penalties as of the time the SIP revision becomes effective. *See* § 120(d)(4).

In defining "applicable legal requirements" in terms of current SIPs, EPA rested on the ground that current SIPs remain in force until EPA grants formal approval to a revision. EPA is clearly correct as to the legal status of proposed revisions: they are proposals and nothing more. Otherwise, as this court has noted, states could circumvent requirements of the Act by proposing revisions to their SIPs. *Metropolitan Washington*

Coalition for Clean Air, 511 F.2d at 813. We therefore reject the interpretation petitioners would impose upon EPA: that SIP provisions under review should be excluded from the definition of applicable legal requirements.

At the same time, however, we are unable to agree with EPA that it may continue to assess section 120 penalties against sources out of compliance with present SIPs, that would be in compliance with a proposed revision, no matter how long EPA takes to act on the proposed revision. Industry petitioners cite examples of delays of over one year by EPA in acting on proposed revisions. Supplemental Brief of Duquesne Light Company and Pennsylvania Power Company on Issues Regarding Revised "SIP" Provisions at 12. We are not sanguine about the possibility that EPA will act expeditiously on all proposed SIP revisions; for example, we note that although EPA was directed to promulgate the regulations implementing section 120 within six months, § 120(a)(1)(A), it did not do so for nearly three years. *See* 45 Fed.Reg. 50,086 (1980).

Although EPA is correct that a proposed SIP has no legal weight until it is finally approved, the fact that EPA often exceeds the statutory time limit for considering a revision, enabling EPA to collect noncompliance penalties which may be unwarranted, violates congressional intent. Such an inequitable use of the penalty powers is neither called for nor authorized. Nor does the fact that sources can petition under section 304(a) to compel EPA to perform its duties act as a full safeguard. *See* § 307(g). If the SIP is ultimately approved, the penalty assessed during the period between the end of the statutory time limit and the final approval is the result not of the source's failure to comply but of EPA's failure to act on time. We do not hold, however, as petitioners ask, that the penalty should be tolled once the statutory deadline for acting on revisions has expired. Otherwise, if the SIP were ultimately not approved, the source in noncompliance would benefit undeservedly.

We therefore remand EPA regulation 40 C.F.R. § 66.3(c)(1) (1981) to the agency and direct that it develop a new regulation so that once the statutory deadline for acting on a SIP revision passes, the noncompliance penalty is held in abeyance pending final action on the SIP by EPA. Should EPA ultimately reject the SIP, the penalty should be calculated back to the deadline, with interest. Such a regulation will protect a source in compliance with air quality standards from the time EPA should have approved an eventually approved SIP revision and will remove any economic benefit accruing to a source not in compliance with the law if the SIP revision is not approved.

B. *"Owner or Operator" of a Source*

Section 120 provides for the assessment of noncompliance penalties against any person who "owns or operates" a noncomplying source. EPA's regulations implementing section 120 define "owner or operator" to include:

> any person who owns, leases, operates or supervises a facility, building, structure or installation which emits or has the potential to emit any air pollutant regulated by EPA under the Act.

40 C.F.R. § 66.3(i) (1981). Industry petitioners object to the inclusion of lessees and supervisors in EPA's definition.

The term "owner or operator" is not defined in section 120 or in the general definitional section of the Clean Air Act. The legislative history of the 1977 Amendments to the Act is silent both as to Congress' failure to define the terms and as to their intended meaning. "Owner or operator" is, however, defined in two specific sections of the Act, the sections dealing with the standards of performance for new stationary sources and the standards for hazardous air pollutants. In both cases, the definition includes lessees and individuals with supervisory power. *See* § 111(a)(5). Industry petitioners would have us infer a negative: that because "owner or operator" is not defined to include lessees and supervisors in section 120, Congress chose to exclude them from the definition.

Such an inference is inconsistent with the purpose of section 120. Congress gave broad application to the statute and stated that any exemptions should be narrowly construed. Within such a statutory scheme, we cannot read legislative silence to mean creation of a unique usage. EPA's interpretation is sensible, and we affirm it here. The ordinary meaning of "operator" surely includes one who runs a facility as a lessee and one who supervises its operation. Were either of these categories omitted from the definition, EPA might be unable to assess penalties against the party that benefits from noncompliance. EPA would therefore be unable to achieve two central goals of section 120: ending the profits derived from failure to comply with the Act and equalizing the position of sources that have made the expenditures necessary to bring themselves into compliance with the Act with the position of sources that have not. The inclusion of lessees and supervisors enables EPA to target section 120 penalties as the statute intended, against those who benefit from violating the Act.

C. *"Potential to Emit"*

Because section 120 imposes more extensive liability on major stationary sources than on other sources, subjecting them to penalties for violations of any applicable SIP standard, the definition of "major stationary source" is a crucial factor in determining liability. Section 120 does not define "major stationary source," but the general definitional section of the Act stipulates that a stationary source is major if it "directly emits, or has the potential to emit, one hundred tons per year or more of any air pollutant (including any major emitting facility or source of fugitive emissions of any such pollutant, as determined by rule by the Administrator)." § 302(j). The regulations implementing section 120 track this definition. *See* 40 C.F.R. § 66.3(g) (1981). The term "potential to emit" is not defined in either section 120 or in the general definitional section of the Act. EPA's regulations implementing section 120 define the term as follows:

> "Potential to emit" means the capability at maximum design capacity to emit a pollutant after the application of air pollution control equipment. Annual potential shall be based on the larger of the maximum annual rated capacity of the stationary source assuming continuous operation, or on a projection of actual annual emissions. Enforceable permit conditions on the type of materials combusted or processed may be used in determining the annual potential. Fugitive emissions, to the extent quantifiable, will be considered in determining annual potential for those stationary sources whose fugitive emissions are regulated by the applicable state implementation plan.

40 C.F.R. § 66.3(j) (1981). Petitioners object, first, that this definition measures emission potential on the assumption that a source is in continuous operation. Second, they contend that EPA improperly included so-called "fugitive" emissions — emissions that come from a source, but not from an identifiable "point" within it, such as a smokestack — in calculating the total emission level for a source.

EPA's effort to define "potential to emit" under section 120 was interwoven with its efforts to define the same term in rulemaking implementing the section of the 1977

Amendments setting forth standards to prevent significant deterioration of air quality, *see* 42 U.S.C. § 7479(1)(Supp. IV 1980). EPA's original definition in those regulations measured a source's "potential to emit" by what it would emit, when operating at full capacity, *in the absence of air pollution control devices. See* 40 C.F.R. § 52.21(b)(3) (1978). The original definition, in other words, ignored already-installed pollution control equipment in the determination of whether a source was to count as "major." This court rejected the definition, and directed EPA to "look to the facility's 'design capacity' — a concept which not only includes a facility's maximum productive capacity (a criterion employed by EPA) but also takes into account the anticipated functioning of the air pollution control equipment designed into the facility." *Alabama Power Co. v. Costle*, 636 F.2d 323, 353 (D.C.Cir.1979).

* * *

We affirm EPA's definition of "potential to emit." As to the decision to base potential to emit on maximum design capacity, we find it is reasonable in light of the statutory language and the remedial goals of section 120. The very term itself — "potential to emit" — is clear indication that Congress did not intend determinations of whether a source is "major" to be based on actual emissions in day-to-day operations. Sources that generally operate at only a fraction of capacity, if needs or economic conditions change, may suddenly function at a far greater level. If so, they will reap economic benefits of noncompliance concomitant with those of other sources operating at similar levels of capacity, and it is reasonable to penalize them in a similar manner. One of the important goals of section 120 was equalizing the competitive situations of polluters and nonpolluters, and EPA's definition of "potential to emit" advances that goal. Moreover, EPA's definition is consistent with this court's mandate in *Alabama Power* that a determination of whether a source is major for purposes of the PSD requirements should be based on maximum design capacity. 636 F.2d at 353. The flaw in EPA's original PSD regulations was that they ignored pollution control devices built into a source and hence measured the source as it would never be. EPA's section 120 regulations, however, measure the source as it can be at its fullest, and thus reasonably implement the statute.

* * *

III. EXEMPTIONS FROM SECTION 120 PENALTIES

Being in violation of an applicable legal requirement does not automatically subject a source to section 120 penalties, as the statute sets out a number of exemptions to the noncompliance penalties. Five of these exemptions are mandatory, with the burden of proof on the source to show that it is entitled to the exemption it claims. § 120(a)(2)(B)(i)-(v). EPA's regulations implementing two of the five mandatory exemptions are challenged here. The first of these is for noncompliance due solely to an inability to comply with an emissions standard, which inability is "entirely beyond the control of the owner or operator of such source or of any entity controlling, controlled by, or under common control with the owner or operator of such source," and for which inability the source has received a delayed compliance order under the Act. § 113(d); *see* § 120(a)(2)(B)(iv). The second exemption at issue is for noncompliance due solely to conditions by reason of which a temporary emergency suspension is authorized under section 110(f) or (g) of the Clean Air Act, such as one due to a national energy emergency. *See* § 120(a)(2)(B)(v).

In addition to the mandatory exemptions, section 120 authorizes EPA to exempt a source from penalties for a particular instance of noncompliance if it finds that "such instance of noncompliance is de minimis in nature and in duration." § 120(a)(2)(C). In contrast to the mandatory exemptions, this de minimis exemption is permissive only. This exemption is also at issue.

We take up in turn the issues raised by EPA's regulations implementing these exemptions. We find that the regulations overstepped the statutory mandate in one respect when interpreting the "inability to comply" exemption. In all other respects we affirm the regulations' treatment of the section 120 exemptions.

A. *The "Inability to Comply" Exemption*

In passing the Act in 1970, Congress intended to spur the development of air pollution control technology. The Act was technology-forcing: it did not provide exemptions for sources unable to comply with requirements because the technology necessary was as yet undeveloped. When it became clear that optimistic hopes for technological advances in pollution control were not being entirely realized, Congress in the 1977 Amendments provided for delayed compliance orders. § 113. Under these orders, sources making good faith efforts to come into compliance, but faced with immature technology, may continue operation and follow a more protracted schedule of compliance with emission limitations.

In section 120, too, Congress built some flexibility into the penalty scheme for sources unable to meet applicable legal requirements. Such sources are entitled to exemptions if they can show that they meet two conditions: (1) their inability to comply is entirely beyond their control and (2) they have received a delayed compliance order under section 113. § 120(a) (2)(B)(iv). Industry petitioners find flaws in EPA's regulations implementing both of these conditions.

1. Factors Beyond the Control of a Source

Under the inability to comply exemption, a source is exempted from penalties if its failure to comply resulted, *inter alia*, from reasons entirely beyond its control. The statute does not list factors that are to trigger the exemption; it is entirely open-ended. During consideration of section 120, there was some debate over whether to enumerate the factors that would trigger the exemption. EPA had urged confining the list to a narrow set of factors, such as strikes, fires, embargoes, and natural disasters. 1977 House Report at 76, *reprinted in* 4 1977 LEGISLATIVE HISTORY at 2543. The House, however, decided to incorporate "some flexibility" into the exemption, because it was concerned that "[n]ot all possible unforeseen circumstances could be foreseen and expressly provided for in this provision." *Id.* The Senate likewise did not confine the inability to comply exemption to a set list of factors. Both the House and the Senate, however, were insistent that the exemption, like other exemptions, should be narrowly construed.

EPA's regulation implementing section 120 enumerates seven factors that it will consider as beyond the control of a source:

(1) Act of God;
(2) Fire;
(3) Embargo;
(4) Strike;
(5) Inability to obtain capital, if that inability is the result of temporary market conditions;

> (6) Failure of equipment to perform as designed, assuming expectations about performance were reasonable; and
>
> (7) The complete inability of a supplier or contractor to furnish labor or materials.

40 C.F.R. § 66.31(c)(1)-(7)(1981). Only if a source can show that it meets one of these conditions will EPA grant it an exemption for inability to comply.

Industry petitioners object, first, that this list should be expanded to include technological impossibility as a factor. EPA based its refusal to grant a general exemption for technological incapacity on its understanding of the technology-forcing character of the Act. *See* 45 Fed.Reg. 50,096 (1980). EPA recognized, however, the difficulties of assessing a penalty to reflect the economic benefits of noncompliance, when the technology was not yet available to outline the steps to be taken by the source to bring it into compliance. Estimating the costs of pollution control equipment, for example, may be impossible when it is not yet known what equipment will be necessary. EPA thus determined that

> [w]here existing technology has not yet demonstrated compliance, the penalty will be based upon the cost of installing the best available controls as determined on a case-by-case basis, as well as a commitment to an appropriate research and development (R & D) program designed to develop the new means of emission control necessary to achieve the standards. Thus, a source that has taken and is continuing to take all possible steps to achieve compliance, including the installation of the best available controls and, where appropriate, participation in an appropriate R & D program, would be considered to be deriving no economic benefit from its failure to comply ....

Id. EPA's approach, in other words, is to deny an exemption for technological impossibility but to calculate the penalties to ensure that sources doing their best to surmount existing technology will not be assessed any penalties. In EPA's judgment, this approach would provide the best mix of incentives to bring about the goals of the Clean Air Act: sources would be deterred from hiding their inadequate efforts behind the excuse of technological impossibility, and would be encouraged to take advantage of and build upon technological advances as they occur. *Id.* at 50,097.

We agree with EPA that it is reasonable to exclude technological impossibility from the inability to comply exemption. At no time during the debates did Congress consider enumerating technological impossibility as one of the factors triggering the exemption, nor did Congress move towards the more flexible formulation of the exemption in order to incorporate technological impossibility. Indeed, Senator Muskie's explanation of the version of section 120 that emerged from the Senate and House conference stated explicitly that the exemption was not intended to cover a claim that needed technology is unavailable. 3 1977 LEGISLATIVE HISTORY at 347. Congress' emphasis that exemptions should be construed narrowly, to avoid diluting incentives created by the penalty provision, was repeated.

* * *

Industry petitioners' second objection is that EPA erred in enumerating an exclusive list. EPA chose this approach because it was concerned that including a "catch-all" provision would open a loophole and defeat the purpose of the penalty scheme. 45 Fed.Reg. 50,096 (1980). While we agree with EPA that eligibility for this exemption should be determined by regulation rather than by adjudication, we find that in relying on an exclusive list of factors to trigger the exemption, EPA has overstepped Congress' intent.

Although Congress intended the exemption to be narrowly limited, it also required that "some flexibility" be written into the regulations. *See* 1977 House Report at 76, *reprinted in* 4 1977 LEGISLATIVE HISTORY at 2543. EPA argues that this requirement of flexibility is fully met by its power to "expand in the future the list of situations that constitute inability to comply should this become necessary to prevent inequity in a particular case." 45 Fed.Reg. 50,096 (1980). EPA fails, however, to specify whether its power to prevent inequity has prospective application only. We hold that it cannot and that EPA must include in its enumerated factors a provision that allows it, in its discretion, to exempt a source in the first instance in which such circumstances arise. Without such a provision, the regulations lack the flexibility that the Act mandates.

There is no need for this provision to become the loophole EPA fears. The burden of proof is on a source to demonstrate that it meets the conditions of the exemption, which include a showing that the inability resulted from a factor entirely beyond the source's control. This is a heavy burden indeed, not subject to easy exploitation from sources claiming the exemption on spurious grounds.

We therefore remand the regulations to EPA insofar as they strictly enumerate an exclusive list of factors that will trigger the inability to comply exemption. We leave to the agency the fashioning of an additional provision to meet the congressional design.

* * *

CONCLUSION

In 1977, Congress added section 120 to the Act to supplement the system of civil and criminal sanctions enacted in 1970. Section 120 establishes a penalty assessment system whereby sources not in compliance with the applicable legal requirements of the Act are fined in accordance with the economic value of that noncompliance. EPA was directed to and eventually did promulgate a series of regulations implementing this section of the statute.

* * *

It is more than five years since Congress enacted this section; it is certainly time to put into operation the penalty assessment system Congress mandated.

It is so ordered.

NOTES

1. In *Duquesne Light*, the court holds that where EPA misses the statutory deadline for acting on a SIP revision, the noncompliance penalty must be held in abeyance pending final action on the SIP revision by EPA. Recall that in *General Motors Corporation v. United States*, 110 S. Ct. 2528 (1990), the Supreme Court held that EPA retains the authority to enforce an existing SIP, even where it failed to act on a pending SIP within four months. The Court found that the four month deadline did not apply to SIP revisions but that EPA's obligation was nonetheless subject to the requirement of 5 U.S.C. § 555(b), that agency action not be unreasonably delayed. Can *Duquesne Light* be reconciled with the *GMC* decision? Note that the 1990 Amendments specifically allow EPA 12 months to act on revision. § 110(k)(2). What relevance will this change have to the interpretation of these two decisions?

2. How does EPA determine the economic value of delay in compliance? EPA developed a complex mathematical penalty calculation model to perform this task. 40 CFR part 67, appendix A (1991). In a portion of the *Duquesne Light* opinion not reproduced in the casebook, the court rejected several claims made by the petitioners regarding the data assumptions used for this model. 698 F.2d at 483-85.

3. For a comprehensive analysis of § 120 of the Act *see* Orloff, *Butressing the Traditional Approach to Enforcement of Environmental Requirements: Noncompliance Penalties Under the Clean Air Act*, 9 ENV. L. REP. 50029 (ELI, 1979).

PROBLEM #8: INSPECTION AND ENFORCEMENT OF STATIONARY SOURCES

Since 1963, Refined Oil Products of America (ROPA), has operated a small oil refinery near Valley View, Amarillo. In 1996, ROPA received a permit from the State of Amarillo which allows it to emit 1100 tons of SO_2/year, 500 tons of CO/year, and 800 tons of particulate matter/year. The permit was issued by the State in accordance with procedures adopted pursuant to Title V of the Clean Air Act. It is now 1998. For the past two years, ROPA has managed to stay within its permit requirements for CO and particulates, but has exceeded the SO_2 limits established in its permit by about 10%/year. ROPA has determined that the costs associated with bringing its SO_2 levels below the permitted level are prohibitive, and that it will either have to shut down its facility, obtain a revision of its permit, or continue to operate in violation of its permit as it has done for the past two years.

You have been asked to advise ROPA about the risks associated with the latter course of action — continuing to operate in violation of its permit. Review §§ 113, 114, and 120 before attempting to respond. What advantage, if any, might ROPA realize by seeking a revision of its permit? *See e.g.*, § 504(f). Will it matter whether Valley View is a nonattainment area for SO_2? If so, how? Should ROPA consider "opting in" to the Acid Deposition Program? *See* § 410. How might this help ROPA?

11 STRATOSPHERIC OZONE DEPLETION

As discussed previously, tropospheric ozone poses a serious health problem, and control of troposheric ozone pollution is one of the principle themes of the 1990 Amendments. (The troposphere is that portion of the atmosphere below the stratosphere.) Ironically, ozone depletion in the stratosphere poses an even greater threat to public health. The stratospheric ozone layer shields the earth from harmful ultraviolet radiation, and its depletion, which is caused by man-made chemicals, is occurring at a troublesome rate. A fortuitous combination of international concern and the availability of suitable substitutes for ozone depleting chemicals led to the development of a treaty that attempts to confront the problem directly by limiting production of those chemicals thought to pose the most serious problems. Set forth below is an extended excerpt from the treaty known as the Montreal Protocol. This is followed by an excerpt from EPA's proposed regulation which implements Title VI of the Clean Air, which, in turn, was intended to satisfy U.S. obligations under the Protocol. These materials are in chronological order, but the reader who would like more background on the ozone problem may wish to read the proposed rules first.

MONTREAL PROTOCOL ON SUBSTANCES THAT DEPLETE THE OZONE LAYER, 1987 (as amended 1990)

The Parties to this Protocol,

Being Parties to the Vienna Convention for the Protection of the Ozone Layer.

Mindful of their obligation under that Convention to take appropriate measures to protect human health and the environment against adverse effects resulting or likely to result from human activities which modify or are likely to modify the ozone layer,

Recognizing that world-wide emissions of certain substances can significantly deplete and otherwise modify the ozone layer in a manner that is likely to result in adverse effects on human health and the environment,

Conscious of the potential climatic effects of emissions of these substances,

Aware that measure taken to protect the ozone layer from depletion should be based on relevant scientific knowledge, taking into account technical and economic considerations,

Determined to protect the ozone layer by taking precautionary measures to control equitably total global emissions of substances that deplete it, with the ultimate objective of their elimination on the basis of developments in scientific knowledge, taking into account technical and economic considerations and bearing in mind the developmental needs of developing countries,

Acknowledging that special provision is required to meet the needs of developing countries, including the provision of additional financial resources and access to relevant technologies, bearing in mind that the magnitude of funds necessary is predictable, and the funds can be expected to make a substantial difference in the world's ability to address the scientifically established problem of ozone depletion and its harmful effects,

Noting the precautionary measures for controlling emissions of certain chlorofluorocarbons that have already been taken at national and regional levels,

Considering the importance of promoting international co-operation in the research, development and transfer of alternative technologies relating to the control and reduction of emissions of substances that deplete the ozone layer, bearing in mind in particular the needs of developing countries,

Have agreed as follows:

ARTICLE 1: DEFINITIONS

For the purposes of this Protocol:

* * *

4. "Controlled substance" means a substance listed in Annex A or in Annex B to this Protocol, whether existing alone or in a mixture. It includes the isomers of any such substance, except as specified in the relevant Annex, but excludes any controlled substance or mixture which is in a manufactured product other than a container used for the transportation or storage of that substance.

5. "Production" means the amount of controlled substances produced minus the amount destroyed by technologies to be approved by the Parties and minus the amount entirely used as feedstock in the manufacture of other chemicals. The amount recycled and reused is not to be considered as "production."

6. "Consumption" means production plus imports minus exports of controlled substances.

7. "Calculated levels" of production, imports, exports and consumption means levels determined in accordance with Article 3.

8. "Industrial rationalization" means the transfer of all or a portion of the calculated level of production of one Party to another, for the purpose of achieving economic efficiencies or responding to anticipated shortfalls in supply as a result of plant closures.

9. "Transitional substance" means a substance in Annex C to this Protocol whether existing alone or in a mixture. It includes the isomers of any such substance, except as may be specified in Annex C, but excludes any transitional substance or mixture which is in a manufactured product other than a container used for the transportation or storage of that substance.

ARTICLE 2: CONTROL MEASURES

* * *

5. Any Party may, for any one or more control periods, transfer to another Party any portion of its calculated level of production set out in Articles 2A to 2E, provided that the total combined calculated levels of production of the Parties concerned for any group of controlled substances do not exceed the production limits set out in those Articles for that group. Such transfer of production shall be notified to the Secretariat by each of the Parties concerned, stating the terms of such transfer and the period for which it is to apply.

6. Any Party not operating under Article 5, that has facilities for the production of Annex A or Annex B controlled substances under construction, or contracted for, prior to 16 September 1987, and provided for in national legislation prior to 1 January 1987, may add the production from such facilities to its 1986 production of such substances for the purposes of determining its calculated level of production for 1986, provided that such

facilities are completed by 31 December 1990 and that such production does not raise that Party's annual calculated level of consumption of the controlled substances above 0.5 kilogram per capita.

* * *

8. (a) Any Parties which are Member States of a regional economic integration organization as defined in Article I(6) of the Convention may agree that they shall jointly fulfill their obligations respecting consumption under this Article and Articles 2A to 2E provided that their total combined calculated level of consumption does not exceed the levels required by this Article and Articles 2A to 2E.

(b) The Parties to any such agreement shall inform the secretariat of the terms of the agreement before the date of the reduction in consumption with which the agreement is concerned.

(c) Such agreement will become operative only if all Member States of the regional economic integration organization and the organization concerned are Parties to the Protocol and have notified the secretariat of their manner of implementation.

9. (a) Based on the assessments made pursuant to Article 6, the Parties may decide whether:

(i) adjustments to the ozone depleting potentials specified in Annex A should be made and, if so, what the adjustments should be; and

(ii) further adjustments and reductions of production or consumption of the controlled substances should be undertaken and, if so, what the scope, amount and timing of any such adjustments and reductions should be.

(b) Proposals for such adjustments shall be communicated to the Parties by the secretariat at least six months before the meeting of the Parties at which they are proposed for adoption.

(c) In making such decisions, the Parties shall make every effort to reach agreement by consensus. If all efforts at consensus have been exhausted, and no agreement reached, such decisions shall, as a last resort, be adopted by a two-thirds majority vote of the Parties present and voting representing a majority of the Parties operating under paragraph 1 of Article 5 present and voting and a majority of the Parties not so operating present and voting.

(d) The decisions, which shall be binding on all Parties, shall forthwith be communicated to the Parties by the Depositary. Unless otherwise provided in the decisions, they shall enter into force on the expiry of six months from the date of the circulation of the communication by the Depositary.

10. Based on the assessments made pursuant to Article 6 of this Protocol and in accordance with the procedure set out in Article 9 of the Convention, the Parties may decide:

(i) whether any substances, and if so which, should be added to or removed from any annex to this Protocol, and

(ii) the mechanism, scope and timing of the control measures that should apply to those substances;

11. Notwithstanding the provisions contained in this Article and Articles 2A to 2E, Parties may take more stringent measures than those required by this Article and Articles 2A to 2E.

ARTICLE 2A: CFCs

1. Each Party shall ensure that for the twelve-month period commencing on the first day of the seventh month following the date of the entry into force of this Protocol, and in each twelve-month period thereafter, its calculated level of consumption of the controlled substances in Group I of Annex A does not exceed its calculated level of consumption in 1986. By the end of the same period, each Party producing one or more of these substances shall ensure that its calculated level of production in 1986, except that such level may have increased by no more than ten per cent based on the 1986 level. Such increase shall be permitted only so as to satisfy the basic domestic needs of the Parties operating under Article 5 and for the purposes of industrial rationalization between Parties.

* * *

3. Each Party shall ensure that for the twelve-month period commencing on 1 January 1995, and in each twelve-month period thereafter, its calculated level of consumption of the controlled substances in Group I of Annex A does not exceed, annually, fifty per cent of its calculated level of consumption in 1986. Each Party producing one or more of these substances shall, for the same periods, ensure that its calculated level of production of the substance does not exceed, annually, fifty per cent of its calculated level of production in 1986. However, in order to satisfy the basic domestic needs of the Parties operating under paragraph 1 of Article 5, its calculated level of production may exceed that limit by up to ten per cent of its calculated level of production in 1986.
4. Each Party shall ensure that for the twelve-month period commencing on 1 January 1997, and in each twelve-month period thereafter, its calculated level of consumption of the controlled substances in Group I of Annex A does not exceed, annually, fifteen per cent of its calculated level of consumption in 1986. Each Party producing one or more of these substances shall, for the same periods, ensure that its calculated level of production of the substances does not exceed, annually, fifteen per cent of its calculated level of production in 1986. However, in order to satisfy the basic domestic needs of the Parties operating under paragraph 1 of Article 5, its calculated level of production may exceed that limit by up to ten per cent of its calculated level of production in 1986.
5. Each Party shall ensure that for the twelve-month period commencing on 1 January 2000, and in each twelve-month period thereafter, its calculated level of consumption of the controlled substances in Group I of Annex A does not exceed zero. Each Party producing one or more of these substances shall, for the same periods, ensure that its calculated level of production of the substance does not exceed zero. However, in order to satisfy the basic domestic needs of the Parties operating under paragraph 1 of Article 5, its calculated level of production may exceed that limit by up to fifteen per cent of its calculated level of production in 1986.
6. In 1992, the Parties will review the situation with the objective of accelerating the reduction schedule.

ARTICLE 2B: HALONS

1. Each Party shall ensure that for the twelve-month period commencing on 1 January 1992, and in each twelve-month period thereafter, its calculated level of consumption of the controlled substances in Group II of Annex A does not exceed,

annually, its calculated level of consumption in 1986. Each Party producing one or more of these substances shall, for the same periods, ensure that its calculated level of production of the substances does not exceed, annually, its calculated level of production in 1986. However, in order to satisfy the basic domestic needs of the Parties operating under paragraph 1 of Article 5, its calculated level of production may exceed that limit by up to ten per cent of its calculated level of production in 1986.

2. Each Party shall ensure that for the twelve-month period commencing on 1 January 1995, and in each twelve-month period thereafter, its calculated level of consumption of the controlled substances in Group II of Annex A does not exceed, annually, fifty per cent of its calculated level of consumption in 1986. Each Party producing one or more of these of these substances shall, for the same periods, ensure that its calculated level of production of the substances does not exceed, annually, fifty per cent of its calculated level of production in 1986. However, in order to satisfy the basic domestic needs of the Parties operating under paragraph 1 of Article 5, its calculated level of production may exceed that limit by up to ten per cent of its calculated level of production in 1986. This paragraph will apply save to the extent that the Parties decide to permit the level of production or consumption that is necessary to satisfy essential uses for which no adequate alternatives are available.

3. Each Party shall ensure that for the twelve-month period commencing on 1 January 2000, and in each twelve-month period thereafter, its calculated level of consumption of the controlled substances in Group II of Annex A does not exceed zero. Each Party producing one or more of these substances shall, for the same periods, ensure that its calculated level of production of the substances does not exceed zero. However, in order to satisfy the basic domestic needs of the Parties operating under paragraph 1 of Article 5, its calculated level of production may exceed that limit by up to fifteen per cent of its calculated level of production in 1986. This paragraph will apply save to the extent that the Parties decide to permit the level of production or consumption that is necessary to satisfy essential uses for which no adequate alternatives are available.

4. By 1 January 1993, the Parties shall adopt a decision identifying essential uses, if any, for the purposes of paragraphs 2 and 3 of this Article. Such decision shall be reviewed by the Parties at their subsequent meetings.

ARTICLE 2C. OTHER FULLY HALOGENATED CFCs

1. Each Party shall ensure that for the twelve-month period commencing on 1 January 1993, and in each twelve-month period thereafter, its calculated level of consumption of the controlled substances in Group I of Annex B does not exceed, annually, eighty per cent of its calculated level of consumption in 1989. Each Party producing one or more of these substances shall, for the same periods, ensure that its calculated level of production of the substances does not exceed, annually, eighty per cent of its calculated level of production in 1989. However, in order to satisfy the basic domestic needs of the Parties operating under paragraph 1 of Article 5, its calculated level of production may exceed that limit by up to ten per cent of its calculated level of production in 1989.

2. Each party shall ensure that for the twelve-month period commencing on 1 January 1997, and in each twelve-month period thereafter, its calculated level of consumption of the controlled substances in Group I of Annex B does not exceed, annually, fifteen per cent of its calculated level of consumption in 1989. Each Party producing one or more of these substances shall, for the same periods, ensure that its

calculated level of production of the substances does not exceed, annually, fifteen per cent of its calculated level of production in 1989. However, in order to satisfy the basic domestic needs of the Parties operating under paragraph 1 of Article 5, its calculated level of production may exceed that limit by up to ten per cent of its calculated level of production in 1989.

3. Each Party shall ensure that for the twelve-month period commencing on 1 January 2000, and in each twelve-month period thereafter, its calculated level of consumption of the controlled substances in Group I of Annex B does not exceed zero. Each Party producing one or more of these substances shall, for the same periods, ensure that its calculated level of production of the substances does not exceed zero. However, in order to satisfy the basic domestic needs of the Parties operating under paragraph 1 of Article 5, its calculated level of production may exceed that limit by up to fifteen per cent of its calculated level of production in 1989.

ARTICLE 2D. CARBON TETRACHLORIDE

1. Each Party shall ensure that for the twelve-month period commencing on 1 January 1995, and in each twelve-month period thereafter, its calculated level of consumption of the controlled substance in Group II of Annex B does not exceed, annually fifteen per cent of its calculated level of consumption in 1989. Each Party producing the substance shall, for the same periods, ensure that its calculated level of production of the substance does not exceed, annually, fifteen per cent of its calculated level of production in 1989. However, in order to satisfy the basic domestic needs of the Parties operating under paragraph 1 of Article 5, its calculated level of production may exceed that limit by up to ten per cent of its calculated level of production in 1989.

2. Each party shall ensure that for the twelve-month period commencing on 1 January 2000, and in each twelve-month period thereafter, its calculated level of consumption of the controlled substance in Group II of Annex B does not exceed zero. Each Party producing the substance shall, for the same periods, ensure that its calculated level of production does not exceed zero. However, in order to satisfy the basic domestic needs of the Parties operating under paragraph 1 of Article 5, its calculated level of production may exceed that limit by up to fifteen per cent of its calculated level of production in 1989.

ARTICLE 2E. 1,1,1 — TRICHLOROMETHANE (METHYL CHLOROFORM)

1. Each Party shall ensure that for the twelve-month period commencing on 1 January 1993, and in each twelve-month period thereafter, its calculated level of consumption of the controlled substance in group III of Annex B does not exceed, annually, its calculated level of consumption in 1989. Each Party producing the substance shall, for the same periods, ensure that its calculated level of production of the substance does not exceed, annually, its calculated level of production in 1989. However, in order to satisfy the basic domestic needs of the Parties operating under paragraph 1 of Article 5, its calculated level of production may exceed that limit by up to ten per cent of its calculated level of production in 1989.

2. Each Party shall ensure that for the twelve-month period commencing on 1 January 1995, and in each twelve-month period thereafter, its calculated level of consumption of the controlled substance in Group III of Annex B does not exceed, annually, seventy per cent of its calculated level of consumption in 1989. Each Party

producing the substance shall, for the same periods, ensure that its calculated level of production of the substance does not exceed, annually, seventy per cent of its calculated level of consumption in 1989. However, in order to satisfy the basic domestic needs of the Parties operating under paragraph 1 of Article 5, its calculated level of production may exceed that limit by up to ten per cent of its calculated level of production in 1989.

3. Each Party shall ensure that for the twelve-month period commencing on 1 January 2000, and in each twelve-month period thereafter, its calculated level of consumption of the controlled substance in Group III of Annex B does not exceed, annually thirty per cent of its calculated level of consumption in 1989. Each Party producing the substance shall, for the same periods, ensure that its calculated level of production of the substance does not exceed, annually, thirty per cent of its calculated level of production in 1989. However, in order to satisfy the basic domestic needs of Parties operating under paragraph 1 of Article 5, its calculated level of production may exceed that limit by up to ten per cent of its calculated level of production in 1989.

4. Each Party shall ensure that for the twelve-month period commencing on 1 January 2005, and in each twelve-month period thereafter, its calculated level of consumption of the controlled substance in Group III of Annex B does not ensure that its calculated level of production of the substance does not exceed zero. However, in order to satisfy the basic domestic needs of the Parties operating under paragraph 1 of Article 5, its calculated level of production may exceed that limit by up to fifteen per cent of its calculated level of production in 1989.

5. The Parties shall review, in 1992, the feasibility of a more rapid schedule of reductions than that set out in this Article.

ARTICLE 3: CALCULATION OF CONTROL LEVELS

* * *

ARTICLE 4: CONTROL OF TRADE WITH NON-PARTIES

1. As of January 1990, each party shall ban the import of the controlled substances in Annex A from any state not party to this Protocol.

2. As of 1 January 1993, each party shall ban the export of any controlled substances in Annex A to any State not party to this Protocol.

3. By 1 January 1992, the Parties shall, following the procedures in Article 10 of the Convention, elaborate in an annex a list of products containing controlled substances in Annex A. Parties that have not objected to the annex in accordance with those procedures shall ban, within one year of the annex having become effective, the import of those products from any State not party to this Protocol.

4. By 1 January 1994, the Parties shall determine the feasibility of banning or restricting, from States not party to this Protocol, the import of products produced with, but not containing, controlled substances in Annex A. If determined feasible, the Parties shall, following the procedures in Article 10 of the Convention, elaborate in an annex a list of such products. Parties that have not objected to the annex in accordance with those procedures shall ban, within one year of the annex having become effective, the import of those products from any state not party to this Protocol.

5. Each Party undertakes to the fullest practicable extent to discourage the export to any State not party to this Protocol of technology for producing and for utilizing controlled substances.

6. Each Party shall refrain from providing new subsidies, and, credits, guarantees or insurance programs for the export to States not party to this Protocol of products, equipment, plants or technology that would facilitate the production of controlled substances.

7. Paragraphs 5 and 6 shall not apply to products, equipment, plants or technology that improve the containment, recovery, recycling or destruction of controlled substances, promote the development of alternative substances, or otherwise contribute to the reduction of emissions of controlled substances.

8. Notwithstanding the provisions of this Article, imports referred to in paragraphs 1, 1 *bis,* 3, 3 *bis,* 4 and 4 *bis,* and exports referred to in paragraphs 2 and 2 *bis,* may be permitted from, or to, any State not party to this Protocol, if that State is determined by a meeting of the Parties to be in full compliance with Article 2, Articles 2A to 2E, and this Article and have submitted data to that effect as specified in Article 7.

9. For the purposes of this Article, the term "State not party to this Protocol" shall include, with respect to a particular controlled substance, a State or regional economic integration organization that has not agreed to be bound by the control measures in effect for that substance.

ARTICLE 5: SPECIAL SITUATION OF DEVELOPING COUNTRIES

1. Any Party that is a developing country and whose annual calculated level of consumption of the controlled substances in Annex A is less than 0.3 kilograms per capita on the date of the entry into force of the Protocol for it, or any time thereafter until 1 January 1999, shall, in order to meet its basic domestic needs, be entitled to delay for ten years its compliance with the control measures set out in Articles 2A to 2E.

2. However, any Party operating under paragraph 1 of this Article shall exceed neither an annual calculated level of consumption of the controlled substances in Annex A of 0.3 kilograms per capita nor an annual calculated level of consumption of the controlled substances of Annex B of 0.2 kilograms per capita.

3. When implementing the control measures set out in Articles 2A to 2E, any party operating under paragraph 1 of this Article shall be entitled to use:

(a) For controlled substances under Annex A, either the average of its annual calculated level of consumption for the period 1995 to 1997 inclusive or a calculated level of consumption of 0.3 kilograms per capita, whichever is the lower, as the basis for determining its compliance with the control measures;

(b) For the controlled substances under Annex B, the average of its annual calculated level of consumption of 0.2 kilograms per capita, whichever is the lower, as the basis for determining its compliance with the control measures.

4. If a Party operating under paragraph 1 of this Article, at any time before the control measures obligations in Articles 2A to 2E become applicable to it, finds itself unable to obtain an adequate supply of controlled substances, it may notify this to the Secretariat. The Secretariat shall forthwith transmit a copy of such notification to the Parties, which shall consider the matter at their next Meeting, and decide upon appropriate action to be taken.

5. Developing the capacity to fulfil the obligations of the Parties operating under paragraph 1 of this Article to comply with the control measures set out in Articles 2A to 2E and their implementation by those same Parties operating will depend upon the effective implementation of the financial co-operation as provided by Article 10 and transfer of technology as provided by Article 10A.

6. Any Party operating under paragraph 1 of this Article may, at any time, notify the Secretariat in writing that, having taken all practicable steps, it is unable to implement any or all of the obligations laid down in Articles 2A to 2E due to the inadequate implementation of Articles 10 and 10A. The Secretariat shall forthwith transmit a copy of the notification to the Parties, which shall consider the matter at their next Meeting, giving due recognition to paragraph 5 of this Article, and shall decide upon appropriate action to be taken.

7. During the period between notification and the Meeting of the Parties at which the appropriate action referred to in paragraph 6 above is to be decided, or for a further period if the Meeting of the Parties so decides, the noncompliance procedures referred to in Article 8 shall not be invoked against the notifying shall not be invoked against the notifying Party.

8. A Meeting of the Parties shall review, not later than 1995, the situation of the Parties operating under paragraph 1 of this Article, including the effective implementation of financial co-operation and transfer of technology to them, and adopt such revisions as may be deemed necessary regarding the schedule of control measures applicable to those Parties.

9. Decisions of the Parties referred to in paragraphs 4, 6, and 7 of this Article shall be taken according to the same procedure applied to decision-making under Article 10.

ARTICLE 6: ASSESSMENT AND REVIEW OF CONTROL MEASURES

Beginning in 1990, and at least every four years thereafter the Parties shall assess the control measures provided for in Article 2, Articles 2A to 2E, and the situation regarding production, imports and exports of the transitional substances in Group I of Annex C on the basis of available scientific, environmental, technical and economic information. At least one year before each assessment, the Parties shall convene appropriate panels of experts qualified in the fields mentioned and determine the composition and terms of reference of any such panels. Within one year of being convened, the panels will report their conclusions, through the secretariat to the Parties.

ARTICLE 7: REPORTING OF DATA

1. Each Party shall provide to the Secretariat, within three months of becoming a Party, statistical data on its production, imports and exports of each of the controlled substances in Annex A for the year 1986, or the best possible estimates of such data where actual data are not available.

2. Each Party shall provide to the Secretariat statistical data on its production, imports and exports of each of the controlled substances in Annex B and each of the transitional substances in Group I of Annex C, for the year 1989, or the best possible estimates of such data where actual data are not available, not later than three months after the date when the provisions set out in the Protocol with regard to the substances in Annex B enter into force for that Party.

* * *

ARTICLE 8: NON-COMPLIANCE

The Parties at their first meeting, shall consider and approve procedures and institutional mechanisms for determining non-compliance with the provisions of this Protocol and for treatment of Parties found to be in non-compliance.

* * *

ARTICLE 16: ENTRY INTO FORCE

1. This Protocol shall enter into force on 1 January 1989, provided that at least eleven instruments of ratification, acceptance, approval of the Protocol or accession there to have been deposited by States or regional economic integration organizations representing at least two-thirds of 1986 estimated global consumption of the controlled substances, and the provisions of paragraph 1 of Article 17 of the Convention have been fulfilled. In the event that these conditions have not been fulfilled by that date, the Protocol shall enter into force on the ninetieth day following the date on which the conditions have been fulfilled.
2. For the purposes of paragraph 1, any such instrument deposited by a regional economic integration organization shall not be counted as additional to those deposited by member States of such organization.
3. After the entry into force of this Protocol, any State or regional economic integration organization shall become a Party to it on the ninetieth day following the date of deposit of its instrument of ratification, acceptance, approval, or accession.

ARTICLE 17: PARTIES JOINING AFTER ENTRY INTO FORCE

Subject to Article 5, any State or regional economic integration organization which becomes a Party to this Protocol after the date of its entry into force, shall fulfill forthwith the sum of the obligations under Article 2, as well as under Articles 2A to 2E, and Article 4, that apply at that date to the States and regional economic organizations that became Parties on the date the Protocol entered into force.

* * *

ARTICLE 20: AUTHENTIC TEXTS

In witness, whereof the undersigned, being duly authorized to that effect, have signed this Protocol. Done at Montreal this sixteenth day of September, One Thousand Nine Hundred and Eighty-Seven.

ANNEX A — CONTROLLED SUBSTANCES

	Substance	Ozone depleting potential[1]
Group 1	$CFCl_3$ (CFC-11)	1.0
	CF_2Cl_2 (CFC-12)	1.0
	$C_2F_3Cl_3$ (CFC-113)	0.8
	$C_2F_4Cl_2$ (CFC-114)	1.0
	C_2F_5Cl (CFC-115)	0.6
Group 2	CF_2BrCl (halon-1211)	3.0
	CF_3Br (halon-1301)	10.0
	$C_2F_4Br_2$ (halon-2402)	to be determined

[1]These ozone depleting potentials are estimates based on existing knowledge and will be reviewed and revised periodically.

ENTRY INTO FORCE

1. This Amendment shall enter into force on 1 January 1992, provided that at least twenty instruments of ratification, acceptance or approval of the Amendment have been deposited by States or regional economic integration organizations that are Parties to the Montreal Protocol on Substances that Deplete the Ozone Layer. In the event that this condition has not been fulfilled by that date, the Amendment shall enter into force on the ninetieth day following the date on which it has been fulfilled.

2. For the purposes of paragraph 1, any such instrument deposited by a regional economic integration organization shall not be counted as additional to those deposited by member States of such organization.

3. After entry into force of this Amendment as provided under paragraph 1, it shall enter into force for any other Party to the Protocol on the ninetieth day following the date of deposit of its instrument of ratification, acceptance or approval.

NOTES

1. "The Montreal Protocol was the result of research at the frontiers of science combined with a unique collaboration between scientist and policymakers. Unlike any previous diplomatic endeavor, it was based on continually evolving theories, on state-of-the-art computer models simulating the results of intricate chemical and physical reactions for decades into the future, and on satellite-, land-, and rocket-based monitoring of remote gases measured in parts per trillion. An international agreement of this nature could not, in fact, have occurred at any earlier point in history." BENEDICK, OZONE DIPLOMACY, Ch. 2, (1991).

2. What chemicals are included in the Montreal Protocol and how are these chemicals controlled? How does the Protocol restrict trade with non-participating countries?

3. Developing countries are treated separately under the terms of the Protocol. Why was separate treatment necessary? How does separate treatment benefit these countries? See BENEDICK, *supra*, Ch. 12.

4. The European Community increasingly acts in concert on matters affecting its economy and the environment. How is this recognized in the Protocol?

5. The 12 nation European Community, despite its shared political, economic, and environmental values, disagreed with the United States throughout the negotiation of the Montreal Protocol. A catalyst for this disagreement was the fact that European Community industries, being less regulated, were not as prepared as United States industries for the phase out of CFC production. The United Nations Environment Programme (UNEP), a little known extension of the United Nations, continually provided a median of exchange for a world wide arbitration over what may prove to be the most important treaty ever negotiated. The role played by UNEP is extremely important, considering the absolute requirement of a global solution. See *supra*, BENEDICK, Ch. 3 and 4.

6. In June 1990, interested parties convened in London to adopt a more stringent program for the reduction and elimination of ozone depleting chemicals. By that time 58 countries had signed the Protocol representing 99% of world production and 90% of the world's consumption of the regulated chemicals. Today more than 70 countries have signed the Protocol. *See* 56 Fed. Reg. 49,548-01, Sept. 30, 1991. The only significant industrialized countries not to accept the Protocol are China and India.

In the fall of 1991, EPA made the following assessment of the ozone depletion problem and its duties under the 1990 Montreal Protocol and the Clean Air Act Amendments of 1990:

NOTICE OF PROPOSED RULE MAKING — OZONE DEPLETION ENVIRONMENTAL PROTECTION AGENCY

56 Fed. Reg. 49,548-01, September 30, 1991

A. Overview of the Ozone Depletion Problem

Stratospheric ozone shields the earth's surface from dangerous ultraviolet (UV-B) radiation. In response to growing scientific evidence, a national and international consensus has developed that certain human-made halocarbons deplete stratospheric ozone. To the extent depletion occurs, it is believed that penetration of UV-B radiation will increase, resulting in potential health and environmental harm including increased incidence of certain skin cancers and cataracts, suppression of the immune system, damage to crops and aquatic organisms, increased formation of ground-level ozone, and increased weathering of outdoor plastics. (See section C below for more information on the effects of ozone depletion.)

Different chlorine- and bromine-containing substances vary in their potential to deplete stratospheric ozone. The fully halogenated chlorofluorocarbons (CFCs), halons, and carbon tetrachloride, for example, are such stable molecules that they reach the stratosphere largely intact and only there are degraded by high energy solar radiation. The chlorine or bromine from these chemicals is then released in forms (or chemical precursors of forms) which are extremely effective in depleting ozone. In contrast, methyl chloroform has a substantially shorter atmospheric lifetime but is used in such large quantities that it contributes significantly to total atmospheric chlorine levels. Hydrochlorofluorocarbons (HCFCs) also have relatively short atmospheric lifetimes and are only beginning to be introduced as substitutes for fully halogenated CFCs. Future use of HCFCs must be carefully evaluated on the basis of both potential volumes and atmospheric lifetimes.

Most halocarbons that pose a threat to the stratospheric ozone layer are also among the most potent greenhouse gases, which many scientists believe will gradually cause an increase in the surface temperature of the earth. Molecule for molecule, CFCs are thousands of times more powerful greenhouse gases than carbon dioxide, and emissions of CFCs in the last decade have been estimated to constitute 15 to 20 percent of the total greenhouse potential during this period.

B. Scientific Evidence of Ozone Depletion

The initial hypothesis linking CFCs and depletion of the stratospheric ozone layer was published in 1974. A paper by research scientists Molina and Rowland suggested that industrial halocarbons could be stable enough that they would not react with the hydroxyl (OH) radical in the lower atmosphere, but would rise up to the stratosphere largely intact. There they could be broken down by high energy ultraviolet (UV-B) radiation and attack the thin layer of ozone molecules blanketing the earth. The chlorine (Clx) from CFCs would react catalytically with the ozone so that each molecule could destroy thousands of ozone molecules before leaving the stratosphere.

Between 1974 and 1987, the scientific community made remarkable advances in understanding atmospheric processes affecting stratospheric ozone. Several atmospheric models were developed indicating that the ozone layer would begin depleting by the middle of the next century with unabated use of CFCs. In response to this threat, the international community negotiated the Montreal Protocol, which limited the production and consumption of a narrow set of ozone-depleting substances.

Despite the sophistication of the models on which the Protocol was based, scientists were unable to predict the extent of decrease in stratospheric ozone that was observed in the se {sic} and early in this decade. Most dramatically, a seasonal loss of ozone over the south pole, known as the "Antarctic ozone hole," was discovered in 1985. Shortly after the Protocol was signed in 1987, an international team of scientists collected and analyzed evidence linking the ozone hole to CFCs. This report also suggested that some depletion of global ozone levels had already occurred (Ozone Trends Panel Report: Executive Summary, 1988). In response, the Parties to the Protocol agreed to accelerate the assessment process required under article 6 of the Protocol. The results of the Protocol assessment were issued in 1989 and further heightened concern that chlorine- and bromine-containing substances had already led to a greater depletion of stratospheric ozone than had been expected. The most important findings were as follows:

1. Antarctic Ozone Hole

The weight of scientific evidence strongly indicated that human-made halocarbons are primarily responsible for the recently discovered substantial seasonal decreases of stratospheric ozone over Antarctica.

2. Perturbed Arctic Chemistry

While at present ozone loss over the Arctic is not as severe as it is over the Antarctic, the same potentially ozone-destroying processes were identified in the Arctic stratosphere. The degree of any future ozone depletion would likely depend on the particular meteorology of each Arctic winter and future atmospheric levels of chlorine and bromine.

3. Long-Term Ozone Decreases

The analysis of the total-column ozone data from ground-based Dobson instruments showed measurable downward trends from 1969 to 1988 of 3 to 5 percent (i.e., 1.8 to 2.7 percent per decade) in the northern hemisphere (30 to 64 degrees North latitudes) in the winter months that could not be attributed to known natural processes.

4. Model Limitations

The findings listed above led to the recognition of major gaps in theoretical models used to assess rates of ozone depletion. Initial models did not anticipate the polar ozone losses or the winter-time 3 to 5 percent drop over the northern mid-latitudes.

The scientific assessment resulted in a call to strengthen national and international controls on ozone-depleting chemicals. Adjustments adopted by the Parties to the Protocol in June of 1990 and Amendments to the Clean Air Act signed into law in November 1990 require a full phase-out of most or all specified ozone-depleting chemicals by the turn of the century.

New scientific evidence recently released by the National Air and Space Administration (NASA) indicates that stratospheric ozone over the northern mid-latitudes has depleted by three to five percent on an annual basis over the past decade. This is a rate of depletion two to three times greater than past evidence suggested. EPA is very concerned about the health and environmental implications of such a high rate of depletion and is currently reviewing the new evidence. However, any regulatory response to this evidence must await another rulemaking. The Agency is required by section 604(c) to promulgate the rules proposed today by September 15, 1991. Too little time remains before that deadline for EPA to conduct the full scientific assessment necessary to use these data in regulatory action. Therefore, EPA will not consider as part of this rulemaking whether this only recently-announced information requires the Agency to tighten reduction requirements applicable to ozone- depleting substances.

C. Health and Environmental Effects of Ozone Depletion

In its 1987 Risk Assessment of Ozone Depletion, EPA reviewed the effects of increased UV-B radiation resulting from ozone depletion. The risk assessment cited several studies that demonstrated a linkage between UV-B radiation and detrimental health effects, including increased rates of several types of skin cancer, cataracts and actinic keratosis and changes to the immune system. Higher levels of skin cancer could lead to increased fatalities, as well as increased medical costs, decreased productivity, and increased social and economic costs.

Other detrimental health effects brought about by increases in ultraviolet radiation due to depletion of the ozone layer include effects on the immune system and skin.

UV-B radiation reduces the ability of the immune system to respond adequately to disease. Higher UV-B exposures are also associated with increased incidence of actinic keratosis, pre-cancerous lesions that occur as a result of excessive exposure to the sun.

Potential environmental impacts from increased UV-B exposures include risks to marine organisms, risks to crops and impacts due to increased concentrations of tropospheric (ground-level) ozone. Impacts related to the greenhouse gas property of CFCs include effects related to higher temperatures and sea levels.

The increased levels of UV-B radiation that result from stratospheric ozone depletion pose a hazard to various marine organisms. Higher UV-B radiation levels have been shown to cause decreases in fertility, growth, survival, and other functions in a variety of marine organisms, including fish, shrimp, crab, and plants essential to the aquatic food chain (EPA 1987). Although it has also been hypothesized that these effects would likely cause a change in species composition as organisms more resistant to the increase in UV-B radiation predominated, it is not known what the long-term effects of these impacts on the ecosystem might be. Increased UV-B radiation levels are assumed to affect harvest levels for the major commercial fish species, including fin fish and shell fish.

The increase in UV-B radiation at the earth's surface expected to result from ozone depletion is estimated to have two effects on-crops: direct losses in productivity because of UV-B radiation, and secondary losses caused by increase in tropospheric ozone (smog), which also reduces productivity. Direct effects from UV-B radiation could result in losses due to harvest decline. For example, in a number of studies on a variety of crops, UV-B radiation has been shown to adversely affect crop yield and quality (Rowe and Adams, 1987).

In addition, tropospheric ozone, an air pollutant formed as a result of photochemical reactions involving ultraviolet radiation, has been shown to adversely affect human health, agricultural crops, forests, and materials. Human health impacts include alterations in pulmonary function (e.g. chest tightness, lung damage, increased susceptibility to respiratory infection) and extra-pulmonary effects such as effects on the liver, central nervous system, blood enzymes, etc. Agricultural crops and forests experience reduced growth and declines in yield. Materials such as textile fibers and dyes and some paints degrade more quickly (Rowe and Adams, 1987) (Horst, 1986).

D. Past Efforts To Control Ozone-Depleting Substances

1. Aerosol Ban in 1978

Following initial concerns raised by Molina and Rowland in 1974 about possible ozone depletion from CFCs, EPA, the Consumer Product Safety Commission and the Food and Drug Administration acted in 1978 to ban the use of CFCs as aerosol propellants in all but "essential applications" (43 FR 11301, March 17, 1978; 43 FR 11318, March 17, 1978). During the early 1970s, CFCs used as aerosol propellants constituted over 50 percent of total CFC consumption in the United States. This particular use of CFCs was reduced in this country by approximately 95 percent, cutting total United States consumption by nearly half.

In the years following the aerosol ban, CFC use increased significantly in the refrigeration, foam and solvent-using electronics industries. By 1985, CFC use in the United States had surpassed pre-1974 levels and represented 29 percent of global CFC usage.

* * *

1990 Revision of Montreal Protocol

As noted earlier, the Protocol's 1989 scientific assessment confirmed that stratospheric ozone was being depleted more quickly than originally believed. In response to the assessment, the Parties decided at their June 1990 meeting in London to completely phase out by January 1, 2000 the CFCs and halons already subject to the Protocol's control requirements and carbon tetrachloride and the "other" fully halogenated CFCs not originally regulated by the Protocol. They also agreed to phase-out methyl chloroform by 2005. In addition, the Parties decided to shift from July-through-June control periods to calendar year control periods, beginning with the 1993 control period. They provided for an 18-month transitional control period from July 1, 1991 to December 31, 1992 during which Parties would be obligated to limit their production and consumption of the already regulated CFCs and halons to 150 percent of baseline levels. (The controls on the newly regulated chemicals do not take effect until 1993.)

The changes in reduction requirements applicable to the already regulated CFCs and halons were made as "adjustments" to the Protocol and so became binding on the Parties six months after the receipt of formal notification under the terms of the Protocol. The addition of carbon tetrachloride, methyl chloroform and the other CFCs was adopted as an "amendment" to the Protocol which will take effect January 1, 1992 provided a specified number of Protocol Parties ratify the Amendments by that date. Under the Protocol, Amendments bind only the Parties that ratify them. As a result, a nation that is a Party for purposes of the originally regulated CFCs and halons may not be a Party for purposes of carbon tetrachloride, methyl chloroform and the other CFCs.

To encourage all nations to ratify or at least comply with the Protocol and the London Amendments, the Parties also adopted additional trade sanctions against nations that fail to join or comply with all or part of the Protocol. Article 4 originally required that Parties ban imports of controlled substances from non-Parties. Amendments to article 4 require that Parties also ban exports of controlled substances to non-Parties and defines non-Parties for purposes of article 4 as including, with respect to a particular controlled substance, a nation that has not agreed to be bound by the control measures in effect for that substance. Under amended article 4, a nation that is a Party only for the original controlled substances will not be able to import or export the newly regulated controlled substances from other Parties beginning January 1, 1993.

The issue of what nations are operating under article 5 of the Protocol was addressed by the Parties, as well. Article 5 permits any developing country whose consumption of the original controlled substances is less than 0.3 kilograms per capita when it joins the Protocol to delay its compliance with the Protocol's control measures by 10 years. The Parties originally delayed designating article 5 nations on the basis that many countries had not submitted data showing that they were under the 0.3 kilogram cap. At their meeting in Nairobi in June, 1991, however, the Parties agreed on a list of article 5 countries.

At their June, 1990 meeting the Parties also passed a nonbinding resolution regarding the use of HCFCs as "transitional" or interim substitutes for CFCs. As explained above, HCFCs add much less chlorine to the stratosphere than fully halogenated CFCs, but still pose some threat to the ozone layer. The resolution calls for the use of HCFCs only where other alternatives are not feasible, with a phase-out by 2020 if feasible, and no later than 2040 in any case. The resolution also states that where required, HCFCs should be selected and used on the basis of their relative ozone depletion potential.

To encourage greater global participation in the Montreal Protocol and the London revision, the Parties established a fund to provide financial and technical assistance to help developing countries who qualified under article 5 of the Protocol make the transition away from ozone-depleting substances.

8. The Clean Air Act Amendments of 1990

Shortly after the Protocol Parties' London meeting, the United States Congress passed the Clean Air Act Amendments of 1990. The restrictions on production and consumption of ozone-depleting substances found in title VI of the Clean Air Act are similar to those in the London Amendments, although interim targets are more stringent and the phase-out of methyl chloroform is earlier.

The Amendments to the Act also require EPA to promulgate regulations to ensure the "lowest achievable levels" of emissions in all user sectors, to ban nonessential products, to limit the use of harmful substitutes, and to mandate warning labels. Today's notice proposes one of several regulations that will implement the Amendments' title VI provisions.

* * *

[The notice goes on to describe the specific provisions of the Clean Air Act Amendments of 1990 relating to ozone depletion found in Title VI which are intended to implement the Montreal Protocol for the United States.]

* * *

NOTE

As the Administrator suggests in the notice of proposed rule making, significant questions remain about the adequacy of the current timetable for phasing out ozone depleting chemicals. Under § 606 of the Act, EPA is required to accelerate the schedule for phasing out the production and consumption of ozone depleting chemicals if necessary to protect human health and environment or if substitutes become practicably available, or if the Montreal Protocol is modified to require an accelerated schedule. A recent debate in the U.S. Senate on the 1990 London Amendments to the Protocol supported efforts to accelerate the schedule.

SENATE DEBATE: LONDON AMENDMENTS TO THE MONTREAL PROTOCOL

137 Cong. Rec. S18226 (daily ed. Nov. 23, 1991)

Mr. MITCHELL. Mr. President, the Senate ratifies the London amendments to the Montreal protocol on substances that deplete the ozone layer. The Montreal protocols provide for phaseout by the year 2000 of production of chlorofluorocarbons [CFC's], which deplete the earth's protective ozone layer. The London amendments add additional substances to be controlled and provides a financial assistance mechanism for developing countries so that they can more easily comply with the terms of the protocol.

The London amendment adds additional CFC's to the list of substances subject to the phaseout, as well as carbon tetrachloride and methyl chloroform. These substances are important ozone depleters.

The London amendments go into effect on January 1, 1992, if 20 signator nations ratify by that date. The United States should be one of those 20, so I am particularly pleased that we are acting on this amendment today. Only seven other nations have ratified the amendment to date, but I am hopeful that a sufficient number will do so by next year.

While it is necessary that we ratify this amendment, it is already outdated.

* * *

We need to act more expeditiously to protect human health and the environment from depletion of the ozone layer. Fortunately, the 1990 amendments to the Clean Air Act provide the Administrator of the Environmental Protection Agency with authority to accelerate U.S. phaseout of CFC's and other substances that deplete the ozone layer. The science demonstrates that such acceleration is necessary.

* * *

A recent report, commissioned by the United Nations Environmental Programme [UNEP] and the World Meteorological Organization [WMO], contains alarming new scientific information about the extent of ozone depletion. The report found that ozone layer depletion is not limited to the Antarctic and the northern latitudes of the northern hemisphere in winter, but instead occurs in the middle and high latitudes of both hemispheres in spring, summer and winter. But the most frightening part of the report may well be the fact that ozone depletion is occurring at a rate 200 times faster than had ever previously been measured or predicted.

* * *

The Clean Air Act Amendments of 1990 set a timetable for the phase out of CFC's, halons and HCFC's. But section 606 of the Clean Air Act requires the administration to take steps to accelerate the phase out, if and when new data indicates that there is a further threat to health and the environment. Mr. President, I think it is clear that the new evidence demands that the schedule be accelerated.

* * *

LONDON AMENDMENTS TO THE MONTREAL PROTOCOL

Mr. BAUCUS. Mr. President, today we will ratify the 1990 amendments to the Montreal protocol on substances that deplete the ozone layer. These amendments were adopted in London in June 1990, by the second meeting of the parties to the Montreal protocol.

The Montreal protocol, which the United States ratified in 1988, is an unprecedented effort by the nations of the world to protect a critical global environmental resource — the stratospheric ozone layer. It is a carefully constructed and periodically reviewed international effort to heal the Earth's badly frayed ozone layer.

The amendments to the Montreal protocol which we have pending before us today will, when implemented, constitute another major step forward in protecting public health and the environment from the adverse effects of stratospheric ozone depletion. In addition, by controlling the emissions of these chemicals we will also reduce the anthropogenic emissions of greenhouse gases.

* * *

Unfortunately, controls still dangerously lag behind the environmental damage these substances cause.

Under the London amendments, industry still has 9 to 14 more years to continue producing these destructive compounds. Over this period, chemical manufacturers will produce approximately 10 billion more pounds of CFC's and more than 50 percent of the total amount of halons produced to date.

Further, the London amendments fail to address, except on a voluntary basis, the production and consumption of hydrochlorofluorocarbons [HCFC's]. These chemicals are brought into the protocol as transitional substances whose production and consumption must be reported. Parties to the London amendments adopted a nonbinding resolution calling for HCFC's to be phased-out not later than 2040 and if possible, not later than 2020.

Unfortunately, we may not have that much time.

This spring, we were given more bad news about the status of the ozone layer. Scientists at the National Aeronautics and Space Administration released new data which show that between 4 and 5 percent of the ozone layer over North America, Europe and the midlatitudes in both hemispheres has been destroyed in the last decade. This rate is twice as fast as believed earlier by NASA scientists.

The Environmental Protection Agency reported that as a result, some 12 million Americans would develop skin cancer, and more than 200,000 of them would die, over the next 50 years.

And Mr. President, just when things looked bad, we found they were really a lot worse. Last month, international ozone experts working with the United Nations released new data which showed that ozone depletion is not limited to the winter months. For the first time, scientists have found that in the summertime over all of our country, the ozone layer decreases by 2- to 3-percent.

We have substantially increased the risk of skin cancer and crop damage from ultraviolet radiation at precisely the time when schoolchildren are playing outdoors and crops begin to grow.

We and our children and our children's children will be forced to reevaluate our practices of going outside during the summertime months when our exposure to ultraviolet radiation is at a maximum.

In short, we have precipitated through our actions, a major environmental crisis that requires decisive action — both domestically and internationally. Ratification of the London amendments is the next in a series of steps necessary to preserve the ozone layer.

However, while tremendously important, the London amendments do not go far enough toward protecting the Earth's ozone layer. Other actions are needed.

The Clean Air Act Amendments of 1990 require the Administrator of the Environmental Protection Agency to accelerate the phaseout schedule of ozone depleting chemicals more rapidly than the year 2000 deadline, if scientific information suggests it is necessary to protect human health and the environment.

The new data showing the severity of the global ozone depletion demands action by the EPA Administrator.

Mr. President, the United States is far from being the world leader on its phaseout schedule.

All of the other industrialized countries, with the exception of the United States and Japan, have committed to an earlier phaseout of ozone depleting chemicals. Germany and Nordic countries have accelerated their phaseout date to 1995; the European Community, Canada, Australia, and New Zealand are committed to 1997. Interim deadlines would also be quickened. The United States should do no less.

For this reason I have written to President Bush urging more aggressive action.

* * *

Mr. GORE. Mr. President, humankind has entered a new — and disturbing — relationship with planet Earth. Our industrial society — with its excessive consumption and unrelenting pollution of the land and sky — is colliding violently with the planet's delicate life sustaining processes. Our rivers and streams are often foul and lifeless; the air we breathe is thick with smog; our forests are disappearing and thousands of species are vanishing forever.

And yet, somehow we have failed to see and to feel the damage that we are inflicting. But if there is any one of our insults to the earth that has begun to open our eyes, it is the enormous hole that we have torn in the Earth's protective ozone shield. The hole is some four times larger than the size of the continental United States and it continues to grow and it now persists through all seasons of the year.

Just last month, an international team of scientists who have been monitoring and studying the ozone layer sounded a loud alarm. They discovered in April that the depletion is occurring at a rate that is 200 to 300 percent faster than had ever before been detected or predicted and that the depletion is occurring over nearly every part of the globe. But in October they told us that, for the first time, they have found that the ozone layer is impaired not only in winter, but also in the spring and summer months when we are more likely to be outdoors and when crops are at a crucial point in their growing season.

And the damage will continue to intensify. The chlorinated and brominated chemicals that we continue to pump into the atmosphere — even under the limited controls we now have in place — will destroy as much additional ozone as has already been destroyed over the last decade — so, by the turn of the century, we will experience total ozone depletion that is two times as large as that we see today.

In the near term, we may also experience particularly severe spikes in ozone loss because of the violent eruptions of Mount Pinatubo. I have been in close communication with scientists from NASA and NOAA who have been closely monitoring the impact of Pinatubo. Their preliminary findings indicate that Pinatubo may be the largest volcanic eruption this century — 2 to 3 times larger than the El Chichon eruption in 1982. This is a tremendous problem because the scientists suspect that — just as the ice crystals in the polar stratospheric clouds catalyze ozone destruction over the Arctic and Antarctic — sulfur compounds that are emitted in volcanic eruptions catalyze ozone loss over the midlatitudes — that is, over our heads. Because we have continued to pump chlorine into the atmosphere, this means that losses of ozone of up to 30 percent may be experienced over the northern midlatitudes in the fall and winter.

And let us make no mistake — increased exposure to ultraviolet radiation as a consequence of depleted ozone poses a grave threat to human health. The Environmental Protection Agency estimated that the increased ozone loss that the scientists have detected will lead to some 200,000 deaths from skin cancer in the next 50 years in the United States alone. And the international team of experts expects an additional 1.6 million additional cases of cataracts as a result of the depletions.

Moreover, recent studies provide alarming evidence that increased ultraviolet radiation will, as has been suspected, wreak havoc on the human immune system — making us not only more susceptible to skin cancers, but to all infectious diseases. In recent tests, 40 percent of those who were exposed to ultraviolet radiation experienced a failure of their body's ability to fight off harmful substances. And, unlike our increased susceptibility to skin cancer, increased vulnerability to infectious disease affects all human beings — regardless of skin pigmentation.

We know too, that increased exposure to UV-B could disrupt entire ecosystems. Phytoplankton, for example, the small organisms at the base of the oceanic food chain are particularly vulnerable and again, the latest scientific results show that the ability of these organisms to grow is severely impacted by excess radiation. Should plankton populations fail, all other species that feed on plankton are in jeopardy, too.

Mr. President, I have argued that the consequences of ozone depletion require us to do all that we can to end the use of ozone destroying chemicals as quickly as possible. The London Amendments to the Montreal Protocol are an important step forward in that regard, and I urge my colleagues to vote for their immediate ratification.

But, the new scientific findings clearly indicate that phasing out chlorofluorocarbons by the year 2000 as provided for in the London Amendments simply is not fast enough. We must do more; we must move faster. Ozone loss is cumulative and the longer we wait, the more damage we inflict; the more cancers, cataracts and deaths we will suffer.

I therefore hope that, after ratifying the London Amendments, the Senate can move immediately to consideration and passage of S. Res. 95 — a resolution that I introduced in April and that the Senate Foreign Relations Committee reported unanimously last week. That resolution calls on the Administrator of the Environmental Protection Agency to accelerate the phaseout of ozone destroying chemicals as he is required to do under section 606 of the Clean Air Act when there is evidence that the current schedule is not sufficient to protect human health and the environment. The resolution also urges the President to take a leadership role in the international community on this issue and to call on the parties to the Montreal Protocol to accelerate the phaseout that is required under that agreement.

* * *

NOTE

On February 11, 1992, President Bush announced that the United States would, in fact, accelerate the schedule for phasing out CFCs by establishing a new deadline of December 31, 1995, five years earlier than required under the Protocol. *See* 22 ENV. REP. (Current Developments) 2408 (Feb. 21, 1992).

12 MOBILE SOURCES

Motor vehicles are a substantial contributor to the air pollution problem we face today. They are the principal source of hydrocarbons (HC), carbon monoxide (CO), and lead (Pb) in our atmosphere, and they are a major source of nitrous oxides (NO_x) and a lesser source of particulate matter. The mixture of hydrocarbons and NO_x in sunlight forms photochemical oxidants, primarily ozone. Thus, motor vehicles account for a substantial portion of four of the six criteria pollutants — carbon monoxide, lead, nitrous oxides and ozone as well as a smaller amount of particulate matter. Their regulation is thus essential to solving our air pollution problem.

Regulation of motor vehicle use through transportation controls in SIPs is one way in which vehicle emissions are controlled by the law. This was discussed previously in Chapter 6. The Act also prescribes standards for tailpipe emissions from motor vehicles and for fuels and fuel additives that are burned in motor vehicles. These standards are the subject of this chapter.

A. Emission Standards for New Motor Vehicles

1. Emission Standards

Motor vehicle emissions are covered by § 202 of the Act. Section 202(a)(1) directs EPA to promulgate regulations prescribing standards "applicable to the emission of any air pollutant from any class or classes of new motor vehicles or new motor vehicle engines which in [EPA's] judgment cause or contribute to air pollution which may reasonably be anticipated to endanger public health or welfare." These standards apply for the useful life of the vehicle. Before the 1990 Amendments the "useful life" for passenger cars was defined by law as five years or 50,000 miles, whichever occurred first. The 1990 Amendments double the useful life to ten years or 100,000 miles for certain emission standards which become applicable after the 1990 Amendments. § 202(d)(1), *but see also* § 207(c)(4)(C),(5),(6) (Testing, however, for purposes of determining in use compliance is limited to seven years or 75,000 miles.) *Id.* The standards prescribed under § 202(a) take effect following a period determined by EPA to be necessary to permit the development and application of technology, taking into account the cost of compliance within the prescribed period. § 202(a)(2).

In accordance with § 202(a)(1), EPA has promulgated separate standards for light duty passenger vehicles, light duty trucks, heavy duty vehicles and motorcycles. 40 CFR Part 86. The Act requires that standards for carbon monoxide, hydrocarbons, nitrous oxides and particulates reflect "the greatest degree of emission reduction achievable through the application of [available] technology . . . . giving appropriate consideration to cost, energy, and safety factors . . . ." § 202(a)(2).

The 1990 Amcndmcnts mandate substantial reductions in hydrocarbon and NO_x emissions from most passenger cars and light duty trucks. The reductions will be carried out in two phases. Phase I begins with the 1994 model year. § 202(g). Phase II is scheduled to begin in 2003 and could force emission reductions to about one-half of the 1994 levels. § 202(i). Phase II standards will be preceded by a study, however, which must be submitted to Congress by June 1, 1997. Based on this study, EPA must promulgate rules which either implement the standards set out in the law, implement some alternative standards, or delay implementation of more stringent standards. In promulgating these rules, EPA must consider whether further reductions are needed and cost-effective, and whether the technology for meeting the reductions will be available. *Id.*

2. Testing Program

Enforcement of the emission standards is carried out through a testing program. Samples of each new vehicle must be submitted by the manufacturer to EPA for testing. In particular, any emission control device on such vehicles must be tested. § 206(a)(1), (2). A certificate of conformity is issued for vehicles that comply with the regulations. Such certificates of conformity must be obtained before any motor vehicle can be sold in the United States. § 203(a)(1). Penalties up to $10,000 may be imposed for each motor vehicle sold without the required certificate. § 205. EPA may also randomly test new vehicles for which a certificate of conformity has been issued to help insure actual conformity. § 206(b). If all or any part of the vehicles so tested do not conform, EPA may suspend or revoke the certificate of conformity (§ 206(b)(2)), unless the manufacturer pays a nonconformance penalty (NCP). § 206(g)(1). The Act also provides for testing of vehicles during their "useful life." If substantial numbers of any class of vehicles are determined not to conform throughout their useful life, the manufacturer must submit a plan "for remedying the nonconformity." § 207(c)(1). In addition, an individual purchaser may require the manufacturer to remedy a nonconforming vehicle at the manufacturer's cost if such nonconformity occurs during its useful life. § 206(h)(2).

3. Miscellaneous

California has adopted motor vehicle emission standards more stringent than the federal standards. Other states may adopt identical California standards as part of their SIP. *See generally* §§ 177, 209. States may not, however, adopt other vehicle emission standards, even if more stringent than federal standards, unless approved by EPA "to meet compelling and extraordinary conditions." § 209(b)(1).

Several additional new requirements were imposed by the 1990 Amendments. They include the following:

On-board Vapor Recovery: Section 202(a)(6) requires EPA to promulgate rules to address emissions which occur from vehicle refueling.

"Cold Start" Standards: Section 202(j) establishes a special CO standard for "cold starts" (below 20° F) which are to be phased in over three years beginning in 1994.

Summertime "Ozone-prone" Conditions: EPA is required to promulgate hydrocarbon standards to address vehicle emissions during "ozone prone" summertime conditions within 18 months after passage of the law, or report to Congress as to the reasons for the delay. § 202(k).

Hazardous Air Pollutants: Section 202(l) requires EPA to promulgate standards to control hazardous air pollutant emissions from motor vehicles and fuels by mid-1995.

On-board Diagnostics: Section 202(m) requires vehicles to have on-board diagnostics systems to warn of catalytic converter malfunctions and oxygen sensor malfunctions by model year 1996.

Leaded Gas Engines: The Act prohibits the manufacture and sale of any vehicle which requires the use of leaded gas after model year 1992.

Urban Bus Standards: EPA was required to promulgate rules by January 1, 1992 setting PM standards for urban buses at no less than 50% of current standards. These are to take effect in the 1994 model year. § 218(b). Also, if EPA finds that buses are not capable of meeting these standards during their useful life, EPA must require that all buses operated in metropolitan areas with a 1980 population greater than 750,000 use low polluting fuels, such as methanol, ethanol, propane or natural gas. § 218(c)

Clean Fuel Vehicles: States with serious or worse ozone nonattainment areas, or with CO nonattainment areas with populations in excess of 250,000 people, are required to revise their SIPs to establish a clean fuel vehicle fleet program beginning in 1998. §246. This program will be phased in over three years for light duty vehicles (going from 30% to 70%), and is established at 50% for heavy duty vehicles. § 246(b).

NATURAL RESOURCES DEFENSE COUNCIL V. RUCKELSHAUS

21 BNA Envtl. Rep. Cases 1953 (D.D.C. 1984)

PRATT, J:

Plaintiff, a national environmental organization, has brought suit against the Administrator of the United States Environmental Protection Agency (EPA), challenging the latter's failure to promulgate regulations governing the emission of oxides of nitrogen (NO_x) and particulate matter from heavy duty vehicles and engines[1] and providing for non-conformance penalties (NCP's) for vehicles and engines which do not meet such standards. The Administrator's duty to issue these standards arises from the Clean Air Act, 42 U.S.C. §§ 7401 *et seq.* (the Act). Plaintiff has moved this Court for summary judgment pursuant to Rule 56, Fed.R.Civ.P., declaring that defendant has failed to fulfill non-discretionary statutory duties under the Act, and for an injunction requiring defendant to comply with the Act forthwith. Having considered plaintiff's motion, defendant's opposition, plaintiff's reply, and the entire record herein, we grant plaintiff's motion and order defendant's compliance with the Act in accordance with a definite schedule.

DISCUSSION

The Clean Air Act provides for regulation by the EPA, pursuant to certain timetables, of emissions of harmful pollutants from motor vehicles. *See NRDC v. EPA*, 655 F.2d 318, 320-322 (D.C.Cir. 1981). Certain portions of the Act, incorporated by § 224 of the 1977 Amendments, specifically direct the establishment by EPA of standards

---

[1] Heavy duty vehicles are defined by the Act to include a "truck, bus or other vehicle manufactured primarily for use on the public streets, roads and highways . . . which has a gross vehicle weight . . . in excess of six thousand pounds," 42 U.S.C. § 7521(b)(3)(C).

governing the emission of NO_x and particulate matter from heavy duty vehicles and engines. The legislative history of the amendments demonstrates that Congress regarded the specified standards and regulations as a matter of great urgency. *See, e.g.*, H.R.Rep. No. 95-294 at 272, 4 Leg. Hist. at 2739; S.Rep.No. 95-127 at 61, 3 Leg. Hist. at 1441.

The sections of the Act at issue here specify that the EPA Administrator shall prescribe for the 1985 motor vehicle model year standards requiring reduction in NO_x emissions from heavy duty vehicles of at least 75% over the 1979 baseline model year. 42 U.S.C. §§ 7521(a)(3)(A)(i), (ii). The Administrator may deviate from this requirement only by temporarily revising the standards, *id.*, at § 7521(a)(3)(B), or by changing them, *id.*, at § 7521(a)(3)(E), in either case pursuant to notice-and-comment procedures. Moreover, the Administrator must exercise his or her authority to revise or change the standards no later than four years in advance of the 1985 model year. *Id.*

Meanwhile, the Act also mandates that the Administrator prescribe standards for particulates applicable to "classes or categories of vehicles manufactured during and after model year 1981." 42 U.S.C. § 7521(a)(3)(A)(iii). Finally, the Act specifies that the EPA promulgate, no later than one year following enactment of the 1977 amendments — that is, by August 7, 1978 — certain non-conformance penalties. 42 U.S.C. § 7525(g)(3). Those penalties would be paid by manufacturers which sold heavy duty vehicles or engines which do not conform with those applicable emission standards established pursuant to 42 U.S.C. §§ 7521.

Quite apart from the statutory language of the 1977 amendments, it is beyond doubt that Congress deemed the directives contained in the foregoing sections of the Act as mandatory. For example, the Conference Report dealing with the Amendments declared that the standards which "mandate" a 75% reduction of NO_x heavy vehicle emissions over the baseline year will take effect in model year 1985, while the particulate standards "are to become effective as expeditiously as practicable . . . but in no event later than the 1981 model year." H.R.Rep.No. 95-564, 95th Cong., 1st Sess. 163 (1977), 3 Leg. Hist. 543. This mandatory quality of EPA's responsibilities concerning the NO_x regulations has been affirmed by both the Court of Appeals for this Circuit, *NRDC v. EPA*, 655 F.2d at 325, and by the agency itself. *See, e.g.*, EPA "regulatory agendas," Fed.Reg. Pl. 1-9(h) Statement, Exs. E-M.

Despite Congress' determination to establish a specific, unqualified timetable for the promulgation of regulations governing NO_x emissions from heavy vehicles, the EPA has done virtually nothing to establish those prescribed standards. Although EPA issued an Advance Notice of Proposed Rulemaking regarding NO_x standards during the waning days of the Carter Administration, 45 Fed.Reg. 5838, it has done nothing since that time: no promulgation of regulations, no announcement of proposed standards, and no attempt to revise temporarily or change the standards scheduled to be in place by 1985. The same inaction characterizes EPA's treatment of the subject of particulate standards. EPA issued proposed standards on January 7, 1981, 45 Fed.Reg. 1910, which were already too late to apply to vehicles manufactured in 1981, as they were supposed to. Some three and one-half years later, EPA has still not issued final regulations. Finally, with respect to non-conformance penalties, EPA has never issued regulations covering such penalties for NO_x or particulate emissions. Congress specified that such penalties should be promulgated no later than August 7, 1978 — more than six years ago. In each of the foregoing cases, EPA has repeatedly declared that it would shortly issue the required regulations, only to in fact fail to meet any of its self-imposed timetables.

We find no reasonable grounds for the delays thus far incurred, or any future postponement which would attend defendant's proposed timetable. Indeed, other than a somewhat irrelevant discussion of certain steps in the administrative process and the complexity of the issues EPA must address before issuing final regulations, defendant's brief is devoid of justification for the agency's laggard performance of its mandatory duties. It is nothing short of astonishing that the agency seeks additional time to promulgate the required regulations when it offers not one shred of evidence as to why it has thus far failed to issue those standards. We understand the complexity of the issues facing EPA in the area of NO_x and particulate emissions, not to mention the sensitivity of the novel technologies involved. We similarly recognize that EPA must compile an adequate record and explain the reasons for its decisions. We have no reason to doubt that EPA is working "diligently", Def. Mem. at 7, to introduce the new technologies in the production of heavy vehicles. Yet Congress was aware of all these factors when, as the deliberate result of several years of debate, it concluded in the 1977 Amendments to the Clean Air Act that a specific timetable was called for to accelerate the cleanup of this country's air.

Although EPA asserts that it needs more than a year from the present time to promulgate regulations for NO_x and particulate emissions, we well as for non-conformance penalties, Congress has mandated that they already be in place at this time. We concur with another district court which, when faced with a similar case of EPA foot-dragging, noted that '[i]f Congress wanted to leave the Administrator with the flexibility to implement regulation based upon [his] own judgment of the most desirable time schedule, it obviously knew how to do so. Clearly, however, it did not.' *State of New York v. Gorsuch*, 554 F. Supp. 1060, 1064 (S.D.N.Y. 1983).

The only basis on which this court could extend the time for compliance within the Congressionally-mandated time limit — or deny summary judgment for plaintiffs — is if it found that it would be infeasible or impossible for the EPA, acting in good faith, to meet the deadline. The Court of Appeals for this Circuit has established the courts may excuse performance only for reasons of limited staff or budget, or because the agency requires further study of substantive issues. *Alabama Power Co. v. Costle*, 636 F.2d 323, 359 (D.C.Cir. 1980); *NRDC v. Train*, 510 F.2d 692, 712-13 (D.C.Cir. 1975). In such circumstances, the agency, not the complaining party, bears the burden of demonstrating the existence of an impossibility. *Alabama Power*, at 359. Courts must 'scrutinize such claims carefully," Train, at 713, since '[t]he agency's burden in such case is especially heavy.' *Alabama Power*, at 359.

The EPA makes no showing of impossibility or infeasibility. It does not argue that it suffers from any staff or budgetary handicaps. Nor does it present any evidence of need for further study, technical or otherwise, of the major issues involved in NO_x and particulate emissions from heavy duty vehicles and engines. Instead, it merely asserts that if the agency attempted to meet "more pressing schedules than those presently in effect, the Agency probably would be unable to promulgate sound rules, adequately supported by the administrative record." Def. Mem. at 3. When all we have before us is this remarkably abstract and obvious declaration that EPA must have defensible regulations and statements of purpose, we think it is clear that "this evidence does not demonstrate 'impossibility,' but rather a difference in rulemaking philosophy from that evinced by Congress." *State of New York v. Gorsuch*, 554 F. Supp. at 1066. As such, defendants fail to raise an issue of material fact which would preclude the issuance of an order by this court requiring compliance with the Congressional mandate. "To ignore or modify the statutory timetable would be to flout the considered judgment of Congress." *Id.*, at 1063.

* * *

ORDER

Upon consideration of plaintiff's motion for summary judgment, defendant's opposition, plaintiff's reply, and the entire record herein, and having found that there is no genuine issue as to material fact and that plaintiff is entitled to judgment as a matter of law, it is by the court this 14th day of September, 1984,

ORDERED that plaintiff's motion for summary judgment be and the same hereby is granted; and it is

DETERMINED AND DECLARED that defendant has a non-discretionary statutory duty to establish standards for emission of oxides of nitrogen (NO_x) and particulate matter from heavy-duty vehicles and engines pursuant to the Clean Air Act, 42 U.S.C. §§ 7521(a)(3)(A)(i), (iii), and to promulgate regulations specifying penalties to be paid by manufacturers for selling heavy-duty vehicles or engines not in conformity with such emission standards, 42 U.S.C. § 7525(g), and that defendant is in violation of the Act for failing to do so; and it is

ORDERED that defendant comply FORTHWITH with the Act by establishing proposed standards for NO_x and particulate emissions from heavy-duty vehicles or engines and publishing the same in the Federal Register no later than October 15, 1984, and final regulations for the same no later than March 15, 1985; and it is

ORDERED that defendant comply with the Act by publishing proposed generic non-conformance penalty regulations no later than March 15, 1985, and final generic NCP's no later than August 31, 1985; and it is

ORDERED that defendant comply with the Act by publishing proposed specific non-conformance penalty regulations no later than August 31, 1985, and final specific NCP's no later than December 31, 1985; and it is

FURTHER ORDERED that this court shall retain continuing jurisdiction over this matter until defendant has fully complied with the terms of this order.

NOTES

1. The court suggests that EPA had failed to promulgate rules to implement the statutory emission standards for NO_x and particulates, not because of an inability to do so within the statutory time frame, but rather because of a difference of philosophy. Clearly, EPA lacks the authority to override a congressional mandate, but which body is in a better position to set specific standards for tailpipe emissions — EPA or the Congress? Would you be less reluctant to extend greater authority to EPA to prescribe such standards if it were established as an independent regulatory commission such as the Securities and Exchange Commission, the Nuclear Regulatory Commission, or the Federal Trade Commission? Why or why not?

2. As the District Court notes, the Court of Appeals for the District of Columbia Circuit has excused performance by agencies of specific statutory mandates for reasons of limited staff or budget, or because further study is necessary. Under such circumstances, should the court demand that the agency promulgate interim standards based on the best available information?

3. EPA promulgated standards for NO_X and particulates for heavy duty vehicles on March 15, 1985. 50 Fed. Reg 10,606 (1985). NCP rules were published on August 30, 1985. 50 Fed. Reg 35,388 (1985). These latter rules were promulgated through a negotiated rulemaking process or "reg neg" — an innovation which EPA has begun to use in select rulemaking proceedings where consensus decisionmaking among all intended parties seems possible.

NATURAL RESOURCES DEFENSE COUNCIL V. EPA

655 F.2d 318 (D.C. Cir. 1981)

MIKVA, Circuit Judge:

These consolidated cases present a variety of challenges to actions of the Environmental Protection Agency (EPA) in setting standards to govern emissions of particulate matter and oxides of nitrogen from diesel vehicles. The Natural Resources Defense Council (NRDC) argues that the agency's actions do not adequately protect the public health; General Motors Corporation (GM) and Intervenors Mercedes-Benz of North America, Inc., and Volkswagen of America, Inc., assert that the EPA did not give adequate consideration to safety factors, and that, in a variety of ways, the standards are too strict. Finding that the agency has stated adequate reasons for its decisions, and that its actions are consistent with statute, we uphold the challenged regulations in their entirety.

I. THE REGULATORY FRAMEWORK

The EPA is authorized by the Clean Air Act (Act) to regulate emissions of harmful pollutants from motor vehicles. The Act itself specifies the quantity of acceptable emissions from light-duty vehicles for three classes of pollutants: carbon monoxide, hydrocarbons, and oxides of nitrogen. Act § 202(b)(1). Section 202(a)(1) of the Act confers on the EPA Administrator the general power to prescribe by regulation "standards applicable to the emission of any air pollutant from any class or classes of new motor vehicles or new motor vehicle engines, which in his judgment cause, or contribute to, air pollution which may reasonably be anticipated to endanger public health or welfare." These provisions are supplemented and qualified by various specific provisions relating to particular classes of vehicles or pollutants. *E.g.*, Act §§ 202(a)(3)(A)(i), 202(a)(3)(F), 202(b)(6)(A).

The statutory standard for hydrocarbon emissions from light-duty vehicles is an absolute one. For models manufactured from 1977 to 1979, hydrocarbon emissions may not exceed 1.5 grams per vehicle mile; for those manufactured from 1980 on, the standards must require a reduction of at least ninety percent from the emission standards applying in 1970. Act § 202(b)(1)(A). The statutory standards for carbon monoxide and oxides of nitrogen are also absolute, but they are subject to a variety of waivers for certain manufacturers who lack the technological capacity to comply. *See* Act §§ 202(b)(1)(B), 202(b)(5), 202(b)(6).

The emission standards set by the EPA under its general regulatory power, in contrast, are "technology-based" — the levels chosen must be premised on a finding of technological feasibility. Section 202(a)(2) of the Act provides that standards promulgated under section 202(a)(1) shall not take effect until "after such period as the Administrator finds necessary to permit the development and application of the requisite technology."

The requirement that emission standards be technologically achievable highlights the need for the EPA's power to divide the broad spectrum of motor vehicles into classes or categories. *See* Act §§ 202(a)(1), 202(a)(3)(A)(iv). Manufacturers produce a wide variety of motor vehicles of different sizes, some using different engine technologies resulting in unusual emission characteristics. In particular, diesel engines use a different fuel, emit exhaust at a lower temperature, and produce a different distribution of pollutants than traditional gasoline engines. For example, diesel carbon monoxide levels are typically lower than those from gasoline vehicles, *see* 45 Fed.Reg. 5480, 5493 n.192 (1980), but diesel vehicles produce particulate emissions at thirty to seventy times the rate of gasoline vehicles, *see* 45 Fed.Reg. 14,496 (1980), and also produce higher levels of the unregulated pollutants sulfur dioxide and benzo(a)pyrene, *see* 45 Fed.Reg. 5480, 5489 (1980).

The present challenges concern the EPA's promulgation of standards governing particulate emissions from light-duty diesel vehicles and light-duty diesel trucks,[3] and the EPA's waiver of the statutory standard for oxides of nitrogen for light-duty vehicles. The EPA's particulate standard and NO_x decisions are appropriately linked in the present proceeding because current technology creates an unfortunate trade-off between particulate control and control of oxides of nitrogen. The primary technique used today for reducing NO_x emissions is exhaust gas recirculation (EGR). While lowering the NO_x content of the exhaust, EGR increases the particulate content, and "the greater the EGR rate, the greater the increase in particulate emissions." Environmental Protection Agency, Regulatory Analysis [of] Light-Duty Diesel Particulate Regulations 33 (1980) [hereinafter cited as Regulatory Analysis]. Thus the stringency of a technology-based particulate standard depends on the level of the NO_x standard concurrently applied. We consider the EPA's actions and the NRDC and industry challenges in turn.

II. THE PARTICULATE STANDARDS

The EPA announced its intention to promulgate standards for particulate emissions from light-duty diesels on February 1, 1979. *See* 44 Fed.Reg. 6650 (1979). The proposed standards would have limited diesel particulates to 0.60 grams per vehicle mile (gpm) in

---

[3] The statute defines only the term "heavy-duty vehicles": The term "heavy-duty vehicle" means a truck, bus, or other vehicle manufactured primarily for use on the public streets, roads, and highways (not including any vehicle operated exclusively on a rail or rails) which has a gross vehicle weight (as determined under regulations promulgated by the Administrator) in excess of six thousand pounds. Such term includes any such vehicle which has special features enabling off-street or off-highway operation and use. Act 202(b)(3)(C) (added by the Clean Air Act Amendments of 1977, Pub.L.No. 95-95, § 223, 91 Stat. 685). This court held in *International Harvester Co. v. Ruckelshaus*, 478 F.2d 615, 639-40 (D.C. Cir. 1973), that the legislative history of the 1970 amendments demonstrates that the term "light-duty vehicles" as used in section 202(b) is essentially synonymous with "passenger cars." The EPA's current definition of "light-duty vehicles" includes any "passenger car or passenger car derivative capable of seating 12 passengers or less." 40 C.F.R. § 86.077-2 (1980). The definition of "light-duty truck" applicable to the particulate regulations, *see* 45 Fed.Reg. 14,496 n.1 (1980); 40 C.F.R. §§ 86.081-2(a), 86.080-2 (1980), is as follows: "Light-duty truck" means any motor vehicle rated at 8500 pounds (gross vehicle weight rating) or less which has a vehicle curb weight of 6000 pounds or less and which has a basic vehicle frontal area of 45 square feet or less, which is: (1) Designed primarily for purposes of transportation of property or is a derivation of such a vehicle, or (2) Designed primarily for transportation of persons and has a capacity of more than 12 persons, or (3) Available with special features enabling off-street or off-highway operation and use. 40 C.F.R. § 86.079-2 (1980). Thus, some light-duty trucks are heavy-duty vehicles, while other light-duty trucks are neither heavy-duty vehicles nor light-duty vehicles within the meaning of the Act. *See* 44 Fed.Reg. 40,784, 40,784-86 (1979).

model year 1981, and to 0.20 gpm in model year 1983. The agency concluded that a single standard, governing all light-duty vehicles, was the preferable regulatory strategy, although 1979 certification data indicated that diesel particulate performance among those vehicles ranged from the 0.23 gpm achieved by the Volkswagen Rabbit to the 0.84 gpm emitted by the Oldsmobile 350. *Id.* at 6651. Furthermore, these restrictions would have applied equally to light-duty vehicles and light-duty trucks. *Id.* at 6654-55.

After analyzing the comments elicited by its notice of proposed rulemaking, the EPA promulgated as final standards a modification of the rules originally announced. *See* 45 Fed.Reg. 14,496 (1980). The limit of 0.60 gpm was retained, but its effective date was postponed to model year 1982, because the rulemaking process had absorbed so much time that testing and certification of 1981 models was no longer feasible. *Id.* at 14,497. The agency concluded that the technology necessary to make the 0.20 gpm standard feasible would probably not be developed in time for implementation in 1983 model vehicles; 1984 was a more likely goal, but the effective date was postponed to model year 1985 to give sufficient margin for error. *Id.* at 14,498. Finally, the EPA believed that light-duty trucks would not be able to perform as well as light-duty vehicles, and the 1985 standard for light-duty trucks was therefore adjusted to 0.26 gpm. *Id.* at 14,497.

The auto industry petitioners do not challenge the 1982 standard of 0.60 gpm, but they vigorously deny the likelihood that technology will be available to meet the lower standards in 1985. In setting the 1985 standards, the EPA predicted that a currently experimental particulate control device, known as a "trap-oxidizer," would be perfected early enough to allow its mass production and installation in 1985 model diesel vehicles. The manufacturers argue that this prediction lacked a sufficient evidentiary basis, and that the agency's action must therefore be invalidated as failing to meet the requirement of reasoned decisionmaking. They also argue that the EPA gave inadequate consideration to the safety risks involved in trap-oxidizer technology.

NRDC insists that the EPA's entire regulatory strategy is an inadequate response to the agency's statutory mandate to protect the public health. The EPA deliberately set a single standard for all light-duty diesel vehicles, predicting that even the worst performing diesel could meet it. NRDC argues that regulatory choice is inconsistent with the EPA's statutory responsibilities; it urges a variable standard, imposing more rigorous requirements on better performing vehicles. NRDC also urges that the agency failed to consider the risks posed by diesel particulate as a carcinogen, and that in giving "appropriate consideration" to cost as a factor in standard- setting, it should have tried to discourage purchase of polluting vehicles through economic disincentives. Finally, NRDC attacks the postponement of the 0.20 gpm standard from 1984 to 1985 as unnecessary and irresponsible.

* * *

B. *Technological Feasibility*

The EPA's choice of the 0.20 gpm standard for light-duty diesels in 1985 was the result of adjusting current diesel particulate emission data by the percentage of reduction expected from certain technological improvements, most notably the trap-oxidizer. The manufacturers' attack on the standard focuses on the EPA's prediction concerning the probable pace of development of trap-oxidizer technology. Before examining the details of the agency's reasoning and the industry challenges, however, we find it useful to discuss the legal standard that governs our inquiry.

1. *The Standard of Review*

* * *

In the present case, GM attacks the EPA's estimation of the period of time "necessary to permit the development and application of the requisite technology" to achieve compliance with the 1985 particulate standards, *see* Act § 202(a)(2). The agency has determined that the technology will be available in time, and now seeks to defend its conclusion as a product of reasoned decisionmaking. Such predictions inherently involve a greater degree of uncertainty than estimations of the effectiveness of current technology. If we judge the EPA's action by the standard of certainty appropriate to current technology, the agency will be unable to set pollutant levels until the necessary technology is already available.

* * *

This court has upheld the agency's power to make such projections, while recognizing that it is "subject to the restraints of reasonableness, and does not open the door to '"crystal ball" inquiry.'" *International Harvester Co. v. Ruckelshaus*, 478 F.2d 615, 629 (D.C.Cir.1973). The Clean Air Act requires the EPA to look to the future in setting standards, but the agency must also provide a reasoned explanation of its basis for believing that its projection is reliable. This includes a defense of its methodology for arriving at numerical estimates. *Id.*

* * *

The time element in the EPA's prediction affects our reviewing task in three distinct ways. First, it introduces uncertainties in the agency's judgment that render that judgment vulnerable to attack. At the same time, however, the time element gives the EPA greater scope for confidence that theoretical solutions will be translated successfully into mechanical realizations, for "the question of availability is partially dependent on 'lead time', the time in which the technology will have to be available." *Portland Cement Ass'n v. Ruckelshaus*, 486 F.2d 375, 391 (D.C.Cir.1973), *cert. denied*, 417 U.S. 921 (1974). Finally, the presence of substantial lead time for development before manufacturers will have to commit themselves to mass production of a chosen prototype gives the agency greater leeway to modify its standards if the actual future course of technology diverges from expectation.

The relevance of lead time, and of the ability to modify standards in light of future developments, to the degree of justification the agency must offer may be seen in this court's opinion in *International Harvester Co. v. Ruckelshaus*, 478 F.2d 615 (D.C.Cir.1973). That case, despite numerous dissimilarities to the present one, provides a useful point of reference, and all the parties seek to claim it as their own. In *International Harvester*, the court reversed the EPA's refusal to suspend for one year strict new 1975 model year emission standards that had been set by Congress in the 1970 amendments. This court, reviewing in early 1973 an EPA decision of May 1972, stressed the harm that would result from "a relaxation of standards, and promulgation of an interim standard, at a later hour — after the base hour for 'lead time' has been passed, and the production sequence set in motion." *Id.* at 637. Too late a relaxation would penalize technologically advanced firms, like Ford, which would already have begun manufacture of vehicles that achieved better emission control at the expense of road performance. For this and other reasons, the hardship resulting if a suspension were mistakenly denied outweighed the risks from a suspension needlessly granted. Because of that balance of hardships, the court probed deeply into the reliability of the EPA's methodology. The present case is quite different; the "base hour" for commencement of production is relatively distant, and until that time the probable effect of a relaxation of the standard would be to mitigate the consequences of any excessive strictness in the initial rule, not to create new hardships.

The significance of the time factor in *International Harvester* was increased by the fact that the EPA was not predicting future technological advances, but rather was imposing an interpretation on current industry data. That data uniformly indicated that the standards were not being met, yet the EPA claimed that "adjustments" of the data demonstrated the likelihood of compliance. But the court concluded that the agency had failed to demonstrate the reliability of its methodology sufficiently to defend its reinterpretation of apparently adverse data.

* * *

To apply these general considerations to our task of review in the present case, we must examine the nature of the EPA's determination. The agency has predicted that the manufacturers will be able to develop a satisfactory version of the trap-oxidizer in the time remaining. This device was designed specifically for the purpose for which EPA intends it, and prototypes have achieved partial success. GM itself has characterized trap-oxidizers as "[t]he most promising particulate traps," and has admitted that "current program status [would] indicate a possibility of 1985 model year production." General Motors Response to EPA Notice of Proposed Rulemaking 132, 175 (1979) [hereinafter GM Response]. The EPA's decision must be judged in terms of record evidence available in early 1980, allowing a "time frame of 2-2½ years for completion of the design development phase [and] 2- 2½ years of production lead time." 45 Fed.Reg. 48,133, 48,139 (1980).

Given this time frame, we feel that there is substantial room for deference to the EPA's expertise in projecting the likely course of development. The essential question in this case is the pace of that development, and absent a revolution in the study of industry, defense of such a projection can never possess the inescapable logic of a mathematical deduction. We think that the EPA will have demonstrated the reasonableness of its basis for prediction if it answers any theoretical objections to the trap-oxidizer method, identifies the major steps necessary in refinement of the device, and offers plausible reasons for believing that each of those steps can be completed in the time available. If the agency can make this showing, then we cannot say that its determination was the result of crystal ball inquiry, or that it neglected its duty of reasoned decisionmaking.

2. *The Time "Necessary to Permit the Development and Application of the Requisite Technology"*

* * *

The EPA has identified a number of strategies for extracting particulates from diesel exhaust, but the 1985 standard was set in reliance on one preferred method and must stand or fall with the agency's prediction that that method will be available in time. This favored device is the trap-oxidizer, a mechanism that filters out particulates and then periodically incinerates its catch in order to maintain the trapping capacity of the filter.

The trap-oxidizer is essentially a compromise between two other particulate reduction strategies. At one extreme, the vehicle could rely on a mechanical filter alone — but unless that filter were somehow able to maintain its trapping efficiency indefinitely, it would periodically need either replacement or cleaning. At the other extreme, particulates could be continuously incinerated in a catalytic converter — but difficult engineering problems accompany the resulting need to maintain sufficient temperature in the converter (c. 1000° F.) and to keep the particulate matter inside the converter long enough to be burned. Citing the technical barriers to continuous incineration and the behavioral barriers to periodic restoration of a filter by car owners, the EPA recognized the trap-oxidizer as "the preferred method" of particulate control. Regulatory Analysis at 47-50. The trap-oxidizer combines the short-term technical superiority of a filter with the long-term usefulness of a converter.

The EPA has predicted that trap-oxidizers will be available for use in model year 1985 vehicles. As the agency has repeatedly observed, the trap-oxidizer is familiar and unobjectionable as a concept. It is not only theoretically sound experimental data demonstrate that periodic incineration can maintain efficiency for over 10,000 miles. But to date, no filter material has been found that can withstand periodic incineration of the accumulated particulates throughout the 50,000-mile useful life of the vehicle[26] while maintaining a high level of trapping efficiency. The agency noted that

> the best durability of a trap reported to EPA was a metal mesh trap on an Opel vehicle, run on a modified AMA driving schedule with no hard accelerations, hills, or speeds above 45 mph. The trap survived 12,800 miles and at that time had a collection efficiency similar to its zero-mile efficiency of 55 percent.

Regulatory Analysis at 51. Understandably, the EPA has concluded that further research is needed before devices with the appropriate characteristics will be available for use:

> Clearly, more basic research still needs to be done in the areas of regeneration initiation and control, and trap durability. Enough progress has been achieved to convince EPA that a successful trap-oxidizer can be developed, but as of this time, no design has proven to have the required collection efficiency over the desired length of time.

Id. at 52.

Nevertheless, the agency concludes that it is merely a question of time before the trap-oxidizer is perfected. "The improvements that are necessary are engineering problems, and are more a function of the resources allocated to the problem than any scientific or technical breakthrough." 45 Fed.Reg. 14,496, 14,498 (1980). Based on the routine nature of most of the remaining problems, the rapid pace of progress in the field since 1978, and the industry's own forecasts of 1985 as a potential completion date, the agency has determined that the lead time remaining is sufficient for application of the requisite technology.

GM dismisses the agency's conclusion as baseless speculation and charges the EPA with naive optimism about the solution of myriad uncertainties, ranging from the development of a durable filter material to the proper location of the trap on the vehicle itself, *see* GM Brief at 28. GM regards the gaps in present knowledge as vitiating the entire standard-setting endeavor:

> Until further experimental knowledge on these major development needs is obtained, it is totally impossible to specify when a successful system will be developed for passenger cars and light-duty trucks. Thus, any particulate

---

[26] Section 202(d)(1) of the Act sets the useful life of light-duty vehicles and their engines at "five years or fifty thousand miles (or the equivalent), whichever first occurs." In determining compliance with the emission standard, the EPA analyzes the exhaust of vehicles that have accumulated 50,000 miles. *See* 45 Fed.Reg. 14,496, 14,506 (1980). The EPA believes, however, that a trap-oxidizer should last at least 100,000 miles. *See* Regulatory Analysis at 51, 45 Fed.Reg. 48,133, 48,137 n.36 (1980).

> standard which contemplates use of a regenerative trap-oxidizer must be judged premature and not technologically feasible.

GM Petition for Reconsideration of Standard at 8 [hereinafter GM Petition]. Thus, GM believes that no standard can be promulgated, regardless of its effective date, on the current record.

Before analyzing GM's technical objections, we must reiterate the standard of review that governs this case. The EPA is not obliged to provide detailed solutions to every engineering problem posed in the perfection of the trap-oxidizer. In the absence of theoretical objections to the technology, the agency need only identify the major steps necessary for development of the device, and give plausible reasons for its belief that the industry will be able to solve those problems in the time remaining. The EPA is not required to rebut all speculation that unspecified factors may hinder "real world" emission control.

The EPA has identified as the necessary remaining steps in development of trap-oxidizer technology the choice of a durable, efficient filter material, the selection of an incineration method, and the refinement of a control mechanism to bring about automatic initiation of the regeneration process. GM agrees with the agency's specification of these aspects of the trap-oxidizer as the ones requiring further research. GM Brief at 22 ("Three critical issues concerning trap oxidizer feasibility remain unresolved: trap durability, regeneration, and collection efficiency.").

a. *Development of a Durable Filter*

The most vigorously controverted issue in this case concerns durability, which the EPA has recognized as the key remaining problem. "Collection efficiencies and regeneration techniques have progressed to the point where the most critical issue is whether the efficiency and regeneration mechanism can be maintained over the useful life of the vehicle." 45 Fed.Reg. 14,496, 14,498 (1980). Both parties focus on the GM Opel test, in which a metal mesh trap survived over 12,000 miles; the EPA views this test as a stirring demonstration of how far research had progressed in the brief springtime of trap-oxidizer research, while GM sees the 12,000-mile mark as insubstantial compared to the 50,000-to 100,000-mile goal.

The EPA has predicted that the necessary work can be accomplished in time for 1985 model year production. The agency points to the wide variety of materials that have demonstrated appropriate initial efficiencies; several of these are hybrids, suggesting that new combinations of present candidates, rather than hitherto untested substances, may provide the answer. The EPA noted the rapid pace of achievement since attention turned to trap-oxidizers:

> Considerable progress has occurred in the last 1½ years. Initial after-treatment research concentrated on the use of simple traps and gasoline engine catalytic converters, with basic problems of efficiency and backpressure. In the last 1½ years we have seen marked improvements in efficiency and backpressure, and more importantly, a general consensus that the trap-oxidizer can periodically (and possibly even continually) incinerate the particulate matter. Methods for regeneration initiation and control have been investigated and repetitive incineration has been demonstrated for several trap-oxidizers.

45 Fed.Reg. 14,496, 14,498 (1980). The small number of successful tests reflected the recent focus on trap-oxidizers, not a persistent record of failure: "At this time, EPA has limited trap-oxidizer durability data, as researchers have been reluctant to fund durability

testing until other, more basic questions were solved." *Id.* Finally, the manufacturers themselves had projected the possibility of introducing trap-oxidizers in 1985 models. *See* Summary and Analysis of Comments on the Notice of Proposed Rulemaking at 40-41 (1979). The agency fully recognized that no durable, efficient filter material was presently available, but concluded that, based on current progress and past achievements, there were sufficient grounds for believing that one would be developed in time for the 1985 standard.

We conclude that these are plausible reasons for a determination that the industry is capable of solving the durability problem in the allotted time. The EPA could reasonably refuse to be discouraged by the limited initial success, as the project is relatively young. The rapidity of recent progress is a factor that the agency may consider in making a prediction of future capabilities. *See Society of the Plastics Industry, Inc. v. OSHA*, 509 F.2d 1301, 1309 (2d Cir. 1975), *cert. denied*, 421 U.S. 992 (1975). And the industry's own predictions, while not determinative, support the view that success in this kind of research can realistically be expected within the proposed time frame. We conclude that the EPA's durability prediction, though uncertain, is no more uncertain than such estimates inherently must be, and that the EPA has met the requirement of "reasoned decisionmaking."

* * *

[The court then considers GM's objections regarding the collection efficiency of trap oxidizers and the technology for incinerating trapped particles (regeneration). With respect to the first of these objectives, the court suggests that, as with the durability issue, research on this subject is sufficiently promising to support the EPA rule. Regarding the second objection, the Court notes that GM's own tests show some success in achieving the desired results.]

C. *NRDC's Objections to the Particulate Standards*

The NRDC, in contrast to GM, thinks that the EPA's standards for diesel particulates are too lax, and attacks a number of the decisions in their regulatory genesis. We find no merit in the NRDC's objections.

The NRDC's first attack is on the regulatory date, relying on the EPA's suggestion that "there is a strong likelihood that trap- oxidizers will be feasible for vehicle application by 1984," Regulatory Analysis at 53. In view of the uncertainty remaining as to whether even the 1985 date is realistic, we defer to the EPA's determination that a 1984 date would leave too little margin for error.

The second objection is to the EPA's consideration of cost in standard setting. The NRDC notes the EPA's estimate that "[e]ven with the particulate regulations, the overall cost of pollution control from diesels should be less than that from gasoline engines." *Id.* at 120-22. The NRDC argues that the carcinogenic character of diesel particulates makes diesel vehicles so dangerous that "appropriate consideration" to cost would require the EPA to discourage purchase of diesels by making them more expensive. Emission standards should be tightened until the cost of compliance by diesels exceeds the cost of compliance by gasoline vehicles. But the correlation between scientific achievement and research investment is not so mechanical that the EPA could set a dollar figure and then compute the level of emission control it would buy. The agency has projected the probable course of future advances in particulate reduction to the best of its ability, assuming a reasonable range of research investment. The statute requires no more.

The NRDC also charges that the EPA "ignored" the risk of cancer posed by particulates. Even a glance at the record refutes the suggestion that the EPA was *unaware* of the risk, or irresponsibly discounted it. A more temperate rephrasing of this claim is that the regulatory approach would have been stricter if the EPA had focused more strongly on the carcinogenic potential of diesel emissions. In this form, the claim becomes another facet of the NRDC's attack on the choice of worst-performing diesel as the measure of technological feasibility.

* * *

The EPA defends its decision to promulgate a single particulate standard applicable to all light-duty diesel vehicles, rather than a number of standards applicable to various classes of diesels. One reason given is the absence of any apparent parameter on which to base such a classification. Another concern is the paradoxical result that graduated standards, by imposing stricter and more costly requirements on low-polluting vehicles, would skew competition in favor of the more loosely regulated, highly polluting models. Finally, Congress itself has taught this method by example, providing unitary emission standards for all passenger vehicles in both the 1970 and 1977 amendments. We conclude that the adoption of a single particulate standard for light-duty diesel vehicles was within the EPA's regulatory discretion.

Even if a single standard is proper, the NRDC asserts, it ought not to be one that *every* diesel can meet. The NRDC cites a favorable passage in *International Harvester*, in which this court agreed with the Administrator that the Act's technological feasibility provisions required only that the standards permit basic auto demand to be met, "even though this might occasion fewer models and a more limited choice of engine types." 478 F.2d at 640. In this case, however, the EPA viewed the legislative history of the 1977 amendments as justifying a more tolerant attitude toward diesel development in the near future. The availability of waivers of the 1.0 gpm oxides of nitrogen standard for "any class or category" of diesel vehicles that requires them, Act § 202(b)(6)(B) (emphasis added), certainly suggests an interest in exploring the full range of potential benefits of diesel technology. We do not hold that the statute mandates such an approach, but it was well within the EPA's regulatory discretion to impose "standards which provide significant particulate reductions, but which do not force any diesel models out of production." Regulatory Analysis at 32.

* * *

V. CONCLUSION

In the Clean Air Act, Congress encouraged the EPA to set standards for the future without specifying the methodology the agency must follow to determine the probable course of future technological growth. In these circumstances, a reviewing court's role is to make sure that the agency has acted responsibly in formulating a reasoned prediction. It is not our task to decide whether the agency is correct, or to require proof to a mathematical certainty. We must be satisfied if the agency has undertaken its analysis with the degree of precision and clarity that the subject inherently permits. The EPA has done so in this case.

We find no merit in the NRDC's allegations that the EPA granted NO_x waivers unlawfully, at undue risk to the public health. We similarly reject the NRDC's challenges to the particulate standards as inconsistent with the statutory mandate. We uphold the EPA's hydrocarbon testing procedure, and accept as sufficiently reasoned the EPA's prediction of technological availability and the particulate standards based thereupon. The regulations reviewed in this proceeding, in their entirety, are

Affirmed.

[The opinion of Judge Robb, concurring in part and dissenting in part, is omitted]

NOTES

1. EPA has set separate standards for light duty trucks under its general authority at § 202(a)(1) to set emission standards for any class or classes of motor vehicles. Note, however, that some light duty trucks qualify as heavy-duty vehicles while others are neither light-duty or heavy-duty vehicles. *See International Harvester Company v. Ruckelshaus,* 478 F.2d 615 (D.C. Cir. 1973).

2. EPA set particulate standards for light duty vehicles based on what it anticipated could be achieved by the worst-performing vehicle. The court rejects NRDC's challenge to this approach by EPA on the assumption that EPA was required to set standards which reflect the greatest degree of reduction achievable. Note, however, that the court had previously rejected EPA's contention that this standard applied to particulate emissions from light duty vehicles. What was the proper standard against which EPA's particulate standards for light duty vehicles should have been judged? *See* § 202(a)(1). What is the likelihood that the outcome might have been different if reviewed against this other standard?

3. The technology-forcing aspect of the vehicle emission provisions of the Act, described in the *NRDC* case, is tempered by the reality that the government is unlikely to force the entire automobile industry to shut down, even assuming that the industry was not diligent in developing the technology needed to meet EPA's standard. In striking down EPA's decision not to grant the auto industry a one-year suspension of the 1975 vehicle emission standards, Judge Leventhal recognized this reality:

> If in 1974, when model year 1975 cars start to come off the production line, the automobiles of Ford, General Motors and Chrysler cannot meet the 1975 standards and do not qualify for certification, the Administrator of EPA has the theoretical authority, under the Clean Air Act, to shut down the auto industry, as was clearly recognized in Congressional debate. We cannot put blinders on the facts before us so as to omit awareness of the reality that this authority would undoubtedly never be exercised, in light of the fact that approximately 1 out of every 7 jobs in this country is dependent on the production of the automobile. Senator Muskie, the principal sponsor of the bill, stated quite clearly in the debate on the Act that he envisioned the Congress acting if an auto industry shutdown were in sight.

International Harvester Company v. Ruckelshaus, 478 F.2d at 636.

4. On January 24, 1984, the EPA extended for two years the deadline for meeting the light-duty vehicle, diesel engine particulate standard of 0.20 grams per mile. 49 Fed. Reg 3010 (1984); 40 CFR §§ 86.085, 86.087-8 (1986). The decision was based, in part, on a "Trap Oxidizer Feasibility Study" completed by EPA in March, 1982. That study showed that significant progress had indeed been made on trap oxidizer technology and that all of the technical problems had been more or less resolved. EPA nonetheless determined that additional lead time was necessary to develop a prototype or working model of an entire trap-oxidizer system, and to develop production and testing facilities for the system. 49 Fed. Reg at 3010-11.

5. The 1977 Amendments introduced the idea of waivers from meeting the CO and NO_x standards otherwise applicable under the law. The purpose behind these waivers was to "reflect Congress' concern that pollution control standards tailored to the virtues and vices of the traditional gasoline engine might stifle the development of innovative alternative technologies." *NRDC v. EPA*, 655 F.2d at 340. The 1990 Amendments removed the waiver for carbon monoxides and limited the NO_x waiver to vehicles with "innovative power train technolog[ies]." The prior law had included a separate NO_x waiver for diesel engines.

CENTER FOR AUTO SAFETY V. RUCKELSHAUS

747 F.2d 1 (D.C. Cir. 1984)

SCALIA, Circuit Judge:

Section 207 of the Clean Air Act, 42 U.S.C. § 7541 (1982) provides that if the Administrator of the Environmental Protection Agency ("EPA") determines that a substantial number of any class or category of vehicles or engines fail during their statutorily defined useful life to conform to the regulations establishing maximum emission levels, the Administrator shall require the manufacturer to submit a plan for remedying the nonconformity at the manufacturer's expense. The EPA has hitherto implemented this provision by requiring and approving plans that commit the manufacturer to recall and repair the nonconforming vehicles or engines. This case presents the question whether the EPA may implement it instead by approving a plan that commits the manufacturer to "offset" the excessive pollution emitted from nonconforming vehicles or engines by meeting lower than currently permitted emission standards for vehicles or engines to be built in future model years.

I

Until 1970, the EPA enforced motor vehicle pollution restrictions exclusively by testing engine prototypes for compliance with emission standards. Cf. S.Rep. No. 1196, 91st Cong., 2d Sess. 29 (1970), *reprinted in* SENATE COMM. ON PUBLIC WORKS, 93d Cong., 2d Sess. 1 LEGISLATIVE HISTORY OF THE CLEAN AIR ACT AMENDMENTS of 1970, 397, 429 (Comm. Print 1974) ("Leg.Hist."). The experience of the 1960s showed that many vehicles in actual use emitted pollutants at levels far in excess of the tested prototypes and that the discrepancy grew as the vehicles' mileage increased. *Id.* at 29-30, 1 Leg.Hist. 429-30. Proponents of stricter clean air requirements concluded it was essential to "require that new cars meet not only the standards on the production line but also the standards in performance. Unless they do, the whole exercise is useless . . . ." 116 Cong.Rec. 33,093 (1970) (statement of Sen. Muskie). The Clean Air Act Amendments of 1970, Pub.L. No. 91-604, 84 Stat. 1676, addressed this problem by adding § 207, which requires the manufacturer to warrant continuing compliance with emission standards during the vehicle's or engine's useful life, directs the EPA to test for such compliance (if technologically feasible), and provides for the remedying of noncompliance as described above.

As part of its in-use surveillance program, the EPA tested 1979 General Motors ("GM") cars with GM engine family 920S2E. All ten test vehicles exceeded the NO_x emission standard of 2.0 grams per mile, for reasons which neither the EPA nor GM was able to determine. In December 1980, the EPA ordered GM to submit a plan for remedying the nonconformity. In February 1981 GM submitted a proposed remedial plan that called for recall and repair of the nonconforming vehicles. After some discussions with the EPA, GM submitted in May 1981 an alternate plan covering both the 920S2E engine family and the similar 920S4 family which also showed a 100 percent noncompliance rate for NO_x. (The latter was under consideration for a noncompliance order by the EPA, though no formal determination of noncompliance had yet been made.) The new plan proposed not recalling and repairing the nonconforming 1979 vehicles but engineering 1982 and 1983 engine families to meet a target lower than mandatory NO_x standards. The lower emissions from the 1982-83 vehicles would offset the excessive emissions from the 1979 vehicles. GM asserted that this plan would achieve environmental NO_x benefits at least equal to the gain that could theoretically be achieved by a recall if all owners brought in their 1979 vehicles for repair, and far greater than what could realistically be expected given the large number of owners who would in fact not do so. GM claimed that the offset plan would save the company $11.8 million and would save 1979 vehicle owners $25.8 million in fuel costs, since the repair remedy originally proposed would have caused increased fuel consumption.

After negotiations with the EPA, GM submitted a final revised offset plan on July 2, 1982. The EPA accepted it on July 29, and published a Federal Register notice of this decision on August 30. 47 Fed.Reg. 38,189 (1982). On September 3, 1982 the Center for Auto Safety and others petitioned this court for review of the EPA's decision under 42 U.S.C. § 7607(b)(1)(1982).

II

Petitioners challenge the EPA's action as unlawful on the ground that the offset plan does not remedy the nonconformity of the 1979 vehicles within the meaning of Section 207(c). Nothing but recall and repair of the nonconforming vehicles themselves, they say, is an acceptable remedy under the statute.

As in every case involving statutory construction, "our starting point must be the language employed by Congress." *Reiter v. Sonotone Corp.*, 442 U.S. 330, 337 (1979). Section 207(c) provides in relevant part as follows:

> Effective with respect to vehicles and engines manufactured during model years beginning more than 60 days after December 31, 1970 —
>
> (1) If the Administrator determines that a substantial number of any class or category of vehicles or engines, although properly maintained and used, do not conform to the regulations prescribed under section 7521 of this title, when in actual use throughout their useful life (as determined under section 7521(d) of this title), he shall immediately notify the manufacturer thereof of such nonconformity, and he shall require the manufacturer to submit a plan for remedying the nonconformity of the vehicles or engines with respect to which such notification is given. The plan shall provide that the nonconformity of any such vehicles or engines which are properly used and maintained will be remedied at the expense of the manufacturer. If the manufacturer disagrees with such determination of nonconformity and so advises the Administrator, the Administrator shall afford the manufacturer and other interested persons an opportunity to

> present their views and evidence in support thereof at a public hearing. Unless, as a result of such hearing the Administrator withdraws such determination of nonconformity, he shall, within 60 days after the completion of such hearing, order the manufacturer to provide prompt notification of such nonconformity in accordance with paragraph (2).
>
> (2) Any notification required by paragraph (1) with respect to any class or category of vehicles or engines shall be given to dealers, ultimate purchasers, and subsequent purchasers (if known) in such manner and containing such information as the Administrator may by regulations require.

42 U.S.C. § 7541(c) (1982). Respondents Ruckelshaus and EPA, as well as Intervenor GM, argue that the variants of the word "remedy" in this provision should be understood in what they assert is the word's "common law" sense, denoting the means by which a right is enforced or the violation of a right is prevented, redressed or compensated. At common law, they argue, substitutionary relief such as compensation is a basic principle of remedies; and absent evidence of a contrary intent, statutory terms with well defined common law content should be given that meaning.

It seems to us that this argument overlooks the basic principle that, in statutes as elsewhere, a word cannot be construed in isolation from its context. If the common-law meaning that a word has acquired is a specialized one, and if the context of the statute is not the context for which that specialized meaning has been assigned, it would distort rather than effectuate legislative intent to disregard ordinary usage. That is the case here. The "substitutionary" connotation of the term "remedy" for which respondents argue is a specialized one. (When speaking of remedying the problem of international terrorism, for example, one would hardly have in mind the provision of adequate monetary compensation for its victims.) And the common-law context of the specialized meaning is judicial relief for private injury. Since the present statute involves executive rather than judicial action, and is addressed to public needs rather than private entitlements, we think the specialized meaning utterly inapt. Absent evidence of contrary intent, the words in the statute must be presumed to bear their normal meaning of eliminating, rather than merely providing compensation for the effects of, the condition that is to be "remedied." Here that means eliminating the nonconformity of the GM vehicles or engines.

Far from contradicting this ordinary meaning, both the surrounding text of the statute and its legislative history tend to confirm it. Paragraph 207(c)(2) requires that notification of nonconformity be provided by the manufacturer to dealers, ultimate purchasers, and (if known) subsequent purchasers. This expensive procedure is categorically required in all cases — yet it would serve no purpose whatever in those cases (if they existed) where offset was to be the relief. There is no point in notifying owners of a nonconformity that will be "remedied" by making changes in a future model. GM evidently realizes this, so its plan did not envision compliance with the notification procedures. *See* note 1, *supra*. How those statutory requirements could simply be ignored has not been explained.

As for the legislative history: The Senate bill that eventually became the Clean Air Act Amendments of 1970, S. 4358, 91st Cong., 2d Sess. (1970), contained a provision substantially the same as what is before us, requiring the manufacturer to "remedy [the] nonconformity." S. 4358, § 207(e)(3); 1 Leg.Hist. 597. The Senate Committee reporting the bill described this provision as one imposing an obligation "to recall that model or class for the purpose of correcting any nonconformity." S.Rep. No. 1196, *supra*, at 29;

1 Leg.Hist. 429. In the floor debate, Senator McIntyre described the bill as "authorizing the Secretary of Health, Education, and Welfare to have cars road tested and recall those produced if they do not meet standards." 1 Leg.Hist. 389.

It is true, as GM forcefully argues in its brief, that all of the statements we have just cited purport to describe merely what the Administrator *may* require and not what he *must* require. But the point is (as GM might more readily appreciate if it were contesting the Administrator's imposition of a "substitutionary" remedy when it would prefer recall) there is *nothing* to suggest that he *may* impose offset. The mere fact that he has discretion in imposing the only remedy discussed that is authorized by the statute in no way implies that he has discretion to impose other remedies as well. Neither GM nor the EPA has been able to refer us to a single passage in the legislative history indicating that Congress had in mind any remedy other than recall when it enacted § 207(c).

GM and EPA argue that in construing statutes courts must accord deference to the interpretation given by the implementing agency. That is true, but the degree of deference is not uniform. A high degree is appropriate, for example, when the agency's expertise can help in assessing the effects of competing interpretations upon the policies of the statute (and hence assessing the interpretation which a wise Congress should be presumed to have intended). *See, e.g., NLRB v. Hearst Publications, Inc.*, 322 U.S. 111, 130-31 (1944). That is not the case here; the difference between both the nature and the consequences of recall on the one hand and offset on the other is readily apparent to the uninitiated. A high degree of deference is also called for when the text to be interpreted is a statutory provision that directs an agency to apply "a standard of such inherent imprecision ('closely related to banking') that a discretion of almost legislative scope was necessarily contemplated." *Association of Data Processing Service Organizations, Inc. v. Board of Governors of the Federal Reserve System*, 745 F.2d 677, 697 (D.C.Cir.1984). Such a standard is not at issue here. Finally, the degree of deference is also high when the agency presses upon us an administrative construction that is both "contemporaneous" with the statute's enactment (presumably because that is unlikely to have been either informed or coerced by the enacting legislature's genuine intent) and "longstanding" (presumably because, as a matter of stable government, even a minor error regarding the enacting legislature's genuine intent acquires a certain prescriptive right if not corrected by subsequent legislatures). *See Consumer Product Safety Commission v. GTE Sylvania, Inc.*, 447 U.S. 102, 120 (1980). Neither of those conditions is present here. From 1970 until this case, the EPA consistently required recall as the remedy for nonconformity under § 207(c). *See* 47 Fed.Reg. 38,189 (1982). The regulations issued to implement the section continue to be entitled "Recall Regulations," 40 C.F.R. §§ 85.1801-85.1807 (1983), and nowhere suggest that any remedy other than recall might be appropriate. Recall has been assumed to be the exclusive remedy even in litigation before this court involving EPA implementation of § 207(c). *See Chrysler Corp. v. EPA*, 631 F.2d 865, 886-87 (D.C.Cir.), *cert. denied*, 449 U.S. 1021 (1980).

The degree of deference appropriate here, therefore, is modest — no more than that thoughtful respect we should give to the views of the officers of another branch who have been officially presented with the issue and who, like us, have taken an oath to apply the law that Congress enacted. That is not enough to overcome what seems to us the clarity of the statutory analysis set forth above.

We conclude, therefore, that § 207(c) requires recall and repair as the only statutory remedy for nonconformity. Since that is so, the EPA acted unlawfully in proceeding under § 207(c) to accept GM's offset plan as a remedy for the nonconformity

— just as it would have acted unlawfully to require it. We emphasize that this is the only issue presented and decided. Specifically, we do not consider the agency's ability to take account of an offset commitment in the exercise of its enforcement discretion, should it decide in a particular case that such a course is "best calculated to achieve the ends contemplated by Congress and to allocate its available funds and personnel in such a way as to execute its policy efficiently and economically." *Moog Industries, Inc. v. FTC*, 355 U.S. 411, 413 (1958). *See Oil, Chemical and Atomic Workers International Union v. Occupational Safety and Health Review Commission*, 671 F.2d 643, 650 (D.C.Cir.1982), *cert. denied sub nom. American Cyanamid Co. v. Oil, Chemical and Atomic Workers International Union*, 459 U.S. 905 (1982); *State Water Control Board v. Train*, 559 F.2d 921, 927-28 (4th Cir.1977); *Terminal Freight Handling Co. v. Solien*, 444 F.2d 699, 709 (8th Cir.1971), *cert. denied*, 405 U.S. 996 (1972). That is not what has occurred here, but rather a misinterpretation of the statute which would permit systematic substitution of offsets for recalls. That may well be a more effective means of reducing automotive air pollution; but it was not the means envisioned by the Clean Air Act.

The agency's approval of the GM plan, being not in accordance with law, 5 U.S.C. § 706(2)(A) (1982), is set aside. In light of this disposition, we need not consider the petitioners' motion to complete the record.

Petition granted.

NOTES

1. The court employs a broad standard of review in striking down EPA's approval of the GM offset plan, according only "modest" deference to the agency choice. Why? Is the scope of review used here consistent with that required by § 307(d)(9)? *See also* § 307(d)(1)(L). Compare the scope of review used in the *Center for Auto Safety* case with that articulated by the U.S. Supreme Court in *Chevron USA, Inc. v. NRDC*, 467 U.S. 837 (1984), *supra* at Chapter 9. Are the standards consistent? Recall Timothy Dyk's criticism of the *Chevron* decision. On what basis might he support the *Center for Auto Safety* decision?

2. From a policy perspective, was the offset plan truly preferable to the recall which the court determined to be required by law?

3. In February, 1981, GM had submitted a plan which provided for a recall to remedy the nonconforming vehicles. Subsequently, in May, 1981, after discussions with EPA, GM proposed the offset. What does this suggest about effecting change through the administrative process?

4. The test methods and procedures used to determine compliance with the vehicle emission standards are established by regulations. 40 CFR Part 85, Subparts V & W. Those regulations were sustained against a legal challenge by a vehicle manufacturer's organization. *Motor Vehicle Manufacturer's Association v. Ruckelshaus*, 719 F.2d 1159 (D.C. Cir. 1983).

5. Before the 1990 Amendments, vehicle manufacturers were required to warrant to any new or used vehicle purchaser, that the vehicle would conform to federal emissions standards throughout its useful life. As a result of the 1990 Amendments, beginning with the 1995 model year, vehicle manufacturers must warrant the emissions from their vehicles only for a warranty period of two years or 24,000 miles. *Id.* For "specified major emission control components", however, which includes catalytic converters, electronic emissions control units, and onboard emissions diagnostic devices, the warranty period is eight years or 80,000 miles. § 207(i).

6. One problem engendered by the performance warranty provisions of the Act was that vehicle manufacturers were allowed to condition their warranties on the vehicle owner's use of repair parts that were sold and installed by the vehicle manufacturers. In 1977 Congress acted to restore the competitive posture of independent manufacturers of repair parts by establishing a self-certification program, whereby independent manufacturers could certify that their parts would not cause violations of the emission standards. § 207(a)(2). No vehicle manufacturer could deny a warranty claim so long as the vehicle owner used certified parts. Regulations implementing the self-certification program were remanded in part in *Specialty Equipment Marketing Association v. Ruckelshaus*, 720 F.2d 124 (D.C. Cir. 1983). *See also Automotive Parts Rebuilders Association v. EPA*, 720 F.2d 142 (D.C. Cir. 1983) wherein the court considered the validity of regulations which set out the warranty obligations of the vehicle manufacturer where certified and uncertified parts are used to repair automobiles subject to warranty.

7. *High Altitude Provisions.* Due to thin air and a resulting less complete combustion, vehicles in high altitude areas tend to emit greater quantities of CO and HC than the same vehicles at lower altitudes. To accommodate this difference, Congress enacted several provisions in the 1977 Amendments which allowed manufacturers to achieve lower emission reductions in higher altitudes than in lower altitudes. *See* § 202(f). These provisions are of largely historical significance at least as regards light duty vehicles. Technological advances coupled with statutory deadlines have combined to result in identical standards for both high and low altitude light duty vehicles for the years 1984 and beyond. Light duty trucks will have to meet the same standards regardless of altitude beginning with the 1995 model year. § 206(f). 48 Fed. Reg. 7392 (1983); 48 Fed. Reg 48,598 (1983); 40 CFR 86.087-8(g)(1986). Under these regulations light duty vehicles "must be capable of *automatically* controlling emissions to the appropriate levels at both low and high altitudes." 48 Fed. Reg 7393 (1983). Certain limited exceptions apply. EPA estimated that the cost of compliance with these standards would be $13-16 per vehicle. *Id.* at 7392.

8. *Aircraft emissions*. Section 231 of the Act authorizes the EPA to promulgate regulations to issue emission standards for pollutants from aircraft engines which "may reasonably be anticipated to endanger public health or welfare." Unlike other motor vehicle standards, EPA is authorized to regulate emissions from existing as well as new aircraft engines. Any standards promulgated by the EPA under this section may be vetoed by the President upon a finding by the Secretary of Transportation that any such regulation would create a hazard to aircraft safety. The emission regulations are enforced by the Secretary of Transportation through an existing program that requires aircraft to obtain a certificate from the Department of Transportation. § 232(a). Such certificates may be suspended or revoked for noncompliance with emission standards. *Id.* Regulations establishing emission standards for aircraft engines were promulgated by EPA in 1982. 40 CFR Part 87 (1984). For existing aircraft the regulations are limited to emissions of smoke. 40 CFR 87.31. Certain existing gas turbine engines are also prohibited from discharging fuel venting emissions. 40 CFR 87.11. New aircraft engines must meet hydrocarbon standards as well as smoke emission standards. 40 CFR 87.11. EPA chose not to regulate CO and NO_x emissions because they were found not to contribute significantly to ambient air quality violations. *See* 47 Fed. Reg 58,462 (1982).

9. Based on information gathered in 1982-83, EPA ordered the Dynamic Motors Corporation to recall all of its 1979 subcompacts to remedy a nonconformity. The order is issued in 1984 but recall cannot be accomplished until 1985, which is past the useful life of the 1979 vehicles as defined by the statute. Does DMC have to remedy the nonconformity of automobiles which are beyond their useful life? *See General Motors Corp. v. Ruckelshaus*, 724 F.2d 979 (D.C. Cir. 1983).

B. Regulation of Fuels and Fuel Additives

ETHYL CORP. V. EPA

541 F.2d 1 (D.C. Cir. 1976), (en banc), *cert. denied*, 426 U.S. 941 (1976)

J. SKELLY WRIGHT, Circuit Judge:

Man's ability to alter his environment has developed far more rapidly than his ability to foresee with certainty the effects of his alterations. It is only recently that we have begun to appreciate the danger posed by unregulated modification of the world around us, and have created watchdog agencies whose task it is to warn us, and protect us, when technological "advances" present dangers unappreciated — or unrevealed — by their supporters. Such agencies, unequipped with crystal balls and unable to read the future, are nonetheless charged with evaluating the effects of unprecedented environmental modifications, often made on a massive scale. Necessarily, they must deal with predictions and uncertainty, with developing evidence, with conflicting evidence, and, sometimes, with little or no evidence at all. Today we address the scope of the power delegated one such watchdog, the Environmental Protection Agency (EPA). We must determine the certainty required by the Clean Air Act before EPA may act to protect the health of our populace from the lead particulate emissions of automobiles.

Section 211(c)(1)(A) of the Clean Air Act authorizes the Administrator of EPA to regulate gasoline additives whose emission products "will endanger the public health or welfare . . . ." 42 U.S.C. § [7545 (c)(1)(A)].† Acting pursuant to that power, the Administrator, after notice and comment, determined that the automotive emissions caused by leaded gasoline present "a significant risk of harm" to the public health. Accordingly, he promulgated regulations that reduce, in step-wise fashion, the lead content of leaded gasoline. We must decide whether the Administrator properly interpreted the meaning of Section 211(c)(1)(A) and the scope of his power thereunder, and, if so, whether the evidence adduced at the rule-making proceeding supports his final determination. Finding in favor of the Administrator on both grounds, and on all other grounds raised by petitioners, we affirm his determination.

I. THE FACTS, THE STATUTE, THE PROCEEDINGS, AND THE REGULATIONS

Hard on the introduction of the first gasoline-powered automobiles came the discovery that lead "antiknock" compounds, when added to gasoline, dramatically increase the fuel's octane rating. Increased octane allows for higher compression engines, which

† [This section is now codified at 42 U.S.C. § 7545, section 211 of the Act. Subsequent references in the case are omitted to avoid confusion.]

operate with greater efficiency. Since 1923 antiknocks have been regularly added to gasoline, and a large industry has developed to supply those compounds. Today, approximately 90 percent of motor gasoline manufactured in the United States contains lead additives, even though most 1975 and 1976 model automobiles are equipped with catalytic converters, which require lead-free gasoline. From the beginning, however, scientists have questioned whether the addition of lead to gasoline, and its consequent diffusion into the atmosphere from the automobile emission, poses a danger to the public health. As use of automobiles, and emission of lead particulates, has accelerated in the last quarter century, this concern has mounted. The reasons for concern are obvious (and essentially undisputed by petitioners): (1) lead in high concentrations in the body is toxic; (2) lead can be absorbed into the body from the ambient air; and (3) lead particulate emissions from gasoline engines account for approximately 90 percent of the lead in our air. Despite these apparent reasons for concern, hard proof of any danger caused by lead automotive emissions has been hard to come by. Part of the reason for this lies in the multiple sources of human exposure to lead.

Lead is an ubiquitous element. It is found in the land, in the sea, in plants, in animals, and, ultimately, in humans. Traces of lead ranging from 10 to 40 micrograms per 100 grams of blood (10-40 µg/100g) are found in everyone, including those living in environments with almost no atmospheric lead. National Academy of Sciences Committee on Biologic Effects of Atmospheric Pollutants, Airborne Lead in Perspective 118 (1972) (hereinafter NAS Report). Despite its universal presence, however, lead serves no known purpose in the human body, and at higher concentrations is toxic, causing anemia, severe intestinal cramps, paralysis of nerves, fatigue, and even death. Clinical symptoms of lead poisoning appear at blood lead levels of 80-100 µg or higher, and symptomatic lead poisoning may appear at levels of 50-60 µg, particularly in the presence of anemia. EPA's Position on the Health Implications of Airborne Lead (hereinafter Third Health Document) at III-1, Joint Appendix (hereinafter JA) 54-55.

Human body lead comes from three major sources. In most people, the largest source is the diet. EPA estimates daily dietary lead intake for adults to average 200-300 µg per day, with a range of 100-500 µg a day. Third Health Document at V-2, JA 82. Absorption of dietary lead into the bloodstream is estimated at about 10 percent, although in children absorption may be as high as 50 percent. Thus the average adult adds 20-30 µg of lead to his bloodstream daily from his diet alone. This daily intake, which may be highly variable depending on individual diets, NAS Report at 50, is generally regarded as, for all practical purposes, uncontrollable.

A second major source of the body's lead burden, at least among urban children, is regarded as controllable, although effective control may be both difficult and expensive to achieve. Ingestion of lead paint by children with pica (the abnormal ingestion of non-food substances, a relatively common trait in pre-school children, particular ages 1-3) is generally regarded as "the principal environmental source in cases of severe acute lead poisoning in young children." NAS Report at 140. Lead-based paint was widely used in pre-1940 housing, for both interiors and exteriors, so children living in older housing, particularly in urban ghettos where such paint is both present and peeling, are most susceptible to this form of lead poisoning. Limited control has been achieved in that lead paints are now rarely used, and are frequently banned by statute, for interior surfaces. But while some local laws require removal of existing peeling lead paints, and there is federal legislation to aid states and municipalities in such efforts, Lead-Based Paint Poisoning Prevention Act, 42 U.S.C. §§ 4801 *et seq.* (1970), there is no concentrated national effort at removal, and the danger to children living in dilapidated housing will remain for some time.

The last remaining major source of lead exposure for humans is the ambient air. This source is easily the most controllable, since approximately 90 percent of lead in the air comes from automobile emissions, and can be simply eliminated by removing lead from gasoline. While the extent to which such lead actually enters the body is vigorously contested by petitioners and lies at the heart of this appeal, all parties agree that, to some extent at least, airborne lead can be absorbed through the lungs as a person breathes lead-contaminated air and that it can be eaten by children with pica after larger lead particles fall to the ground and mix with dust. Once the lead is in the body, however, its source becomes irrelevant; all lead in the bloodstream, from whatever source, is essentially fungible. Thus so long as there are multiple sources of lead exposure it is virtually impossible to isolate one source and determine its particular effect on the body. The effect of any one source is meaningful only in cumulative terms.

The multiple sources of human exposure to lead explain in part why it has been difficult to pinpoint automobile lead emissions as a danger to public health. Obviously, any danger is caused only by the additive effect of lead emissions on the other, largely uncontrollable, sources of lead. For years the lead antiknock industry has refused to accept the developing evidence that lead emissions contribute significantly to the total human lead body burden. In the Clean Air Act Amendments of 1970, Pub.L. 91-604, December 31, 1970, 84 Stat. 1698-1700, however, Congress finally set up a legal mechanism by which that evidence could be weighed in a more objective tribunal. It gave the newly- created EPA authority to control or prohibit the sale or manufacture of any fuel additive whose emission products "will endanger the public health or welfare . . . ." [Section 211](c)(1)(A)(1970)]. It is beyond question that the fuel additive Congress had in mind was lead.

Given this mandate, EPA published on January 31, 1971 advance notice of proposed rule-making. The Administrator announced he was considering possible controls on lead additives in gasolines, both because of their possible danger to health and because of their incompatibility with the newly-developed catalytic converter emission control system. 36 Fed.Reg. 1486 (1971). Proposed regulations were issued a year later, February 23, 1972, supported by a document *Health Hazards of Lead* [hereinafter First Health Document], prepared by the EPA scientific staff. Comments were invited for a 90-day period, later reopened for an additional 30 days. 37 Fed.Reg. 11786-11787 (1972). At the same time public hearings were held in Washington, D. C., Dallas, and Los Angeles.

On January 10, 1973 the Administrator, while issuing final regulations requiring availability of some lead-free gasoline to allow implementation of the catalytic converter system, 38 Fed.Reg. 1254; approved in *Amoco Oil Co. v. EPA*, 501 F.2d 722 (1974), reproposed the health-based regulations now at issue. 38 Fed.Reg. 1258. The reproposal was supported by a second health document, EPA's *Position on the Health Effects of Airborne Lead* [hereinafter Second Health Document], and was necessitated by a modification of EPA's analysis of the health effects of lead emissions. The Agency concluded, after considering the comments received, that it was virtually impossible to identify the precise amount of airborne lead that will endanger public health. Instead, the control strategy would concentrate on evaluating the cumulative effect of airborne lead on total human lead exposure and the significance of that contribution. 38 Fed.Reg. 1258. The reproposed regulations themselves were similar to the original proposal, requiring a phased cutback to 1.25 grams of lead per gallon of leaded gasoline, but, in recognition of the industry's lead-time problems, pushing the timetable for reduction back one year. The Agency again invited public comment, this time for a 60-day period.

On October 28, 1973, as a result of a motion filed in *Natural Resources Defense Council, Inc. v. EPA*, D.C.Cir. No. 72-2233, this court ordered EPA to reach within 30 days a final decision on whether lead additives should be regulated for health reasons. EPA published its final health document, entitled *EPA's Position on the Health Implications of Airborne Lead*, on November 28, 1973. This document, the Third Health Document, extensively details and reviews the state of knowledge of the health effects of airborne lead. It candidly discusses the various scientific studies, both pro and con, underlying this information, and ultimately concludes that lead from automobile emissions will endanger the public health. The same day, based largely on the conclusions of the Third Health Document, EPA promulgated its final regulations, accompanied by a thorough discussion of its health conclusions, the impact of the regulations, and the alternative courses of action considered and rejected. 38 Fed.Reg. 33734. The final regulations require the same step-wise reduction of lead additives but, in response to the comments of a majority of refiners, calculate the reduction in a slightly different manner. Whereas the original and reproposed regulations set standards for permissible lead use by each refiner on the basis of grams of lead per gallon of *leaded* gasoline produced (leaded pool averaging), the final regulations base the standards on grams of lead per gallon of all gasoline produced (total pool averaging). The quantity of lead emitted into the atmosphere is the same under both systems; EPA simply converted its leaded pool figures into total pool figures. Under the final regulations, lead in all gasoline would be reduced over a five-year period to an average of 0.5 grams per gallon.

Petitioners, various manufacturers of lead additives and refiners of gasoline, appealed the promulgation of low-lead regulations to this court under Section 307 of the Clean Air Act, 42 U.S.C. § 1857h-5. The appeal was heard by a division of the court on September 9, 1974. On December 20, 1974, the division, one judge dissenting, ordered the regulations set aside. The majority and dissenting opinions were published on January 28, 1975. Because of the importance of the issues presented, we granted EPA's petition for rehearing *en banc* on March 17, 1975, vacating the judgment and opinions of the division and setting the case for reargument on May 30, 1975. All parties were invited to submit supplementary briefs addressing the issues raised by the division opinions.

The regulations are challenged by petitioners on a variety of grounds, all of which will be addressed below. Their primary claims, and the ones on which the division majority based its reversal, are that the Administrator misinterpreted the statutory standard of "will endanger" and that his application of that standard is without support in the evidence and arbitrary and capricious.

II. THE STATUTORY REQUIREMENTS

Under Section 211(c)(1)(A) the Administrator may, on the basis of all the information available to him, promulgate regulations that —

> control or prohibit the manufacture, introduction into commerce, offering for sale, or sale of any fuel or fuel additive for use in a motor vehicle or motor vehicle engine (A) if any emission products of such fuel or fuel additive will endanger the public health or welfare . . . .

The Administrator cannot act under Section 211(c)(1)(A), however, until after "consideration of all relevant medical and scientific evidence available to him, including consideration of other technologically or economically feasible means of achieving emission standards under [Section 202]." Section 211(c)(2)(A). Section 202 of the Act allows the Administrator to set standards for emission of pollutants from automobiles (as opposed to standards for the composition of the gasoline that produces the emissions), and is thus the preferred — although not the mandatory alternative under the statutory scheme, presumably because it minimizes Agency interference with manufacturer prerogatives.

The Administrator is also required, before prohibiting a fuel or fuel additive under Section 211(c)(1)(A), to find, and publish the finding, that in his judgment any fuel or fuel additive likely to replace the prohibited one will not "endanger the public health or welfare to the same or greater degree . . . ." Section 211(c)(2)(C). It is significant that this is the only conclusion the Administrator is expressly required to "find" before regulating a fuel or fuel additive for health reasons.

A. *The Threshold Determination*

In making his threshold determination that lead particulate emissions from motor vehicles "will endanger the public health or welfare," the Administrator provided his interpretation of the statutory language by couching his conclusion in these words: such emissions "present a significant risk of harm to the health of urban populations, particularly to the health of city children." 38 Fed.Reg. 33734. By way of further interpretation, he added that it was his view

> that the statutory language . . . does not require a determination that automobile emissions alone create the endangerment on which controls may be based. Rather, the Administrator believes that in providing this authority, the Congress was aware that the public's exposure to harmful substances results from a number of sources which may have varying degrees of susceptibility to control.

* * *

Petitioners argue that the "will endanger" standard requires a high quantum of factual proof, proof of actual harm rather than of a "significant risk of harm." *See* supplemental brief of petitioner Ethyl Corporation [hereinafter Ethyl Supp.Br.] at 20. Since, according to petitioners, regulation under Section 211(c)(1)(A) must be premised upon factual proof of actual harm, the Administrator has, in their view, no power to assess risks or make policy judgments in deciding to regulate lead additives. Moreover, petitioners argue, regulation must be based on the danger presented by lead additives "in and of themselves," so it is improper to consider, as the Administrator did, the cumulative impact of lead additives on all other sources of human exposure to lead. We have considered these arguments with care and find them to be without merit. It is our view that the Administrator's interpretation of the standard is the correct one.

1. *The Precautionary Nature of "Will Endanger."* Simply as a matter of plain meaning, we have difficulty crediting petitioners' reading of the "will endanger" standard. The meaning of "endanger" is not disputed. Case law and dictionary definition agree that endanger means something less than actual harm. When one is endangered, harm is threatened ; no actual injury need ever occur. Thus, for example, a town may be "endangered" by a threatening plague or hurricane and yet emerge from the danger completely unscathed. A statute allowing for regulation in the face of danger is, necessarily, a precautionary statute. Regulatory action may be taken before the threatened harm occurs; indeed, the very existence of such precautionary legislation

would seem to demand that regulatory action precede, and, optimally, prevent, the perceived threat. As should be apparent, the "will endanger" language of Section 211(c)(1)(A) makes it such a precautionary statute.

* * *

Perhaps because it realized that the above interpretation was the only possible reading of the statutory language, petitioner Ethyl addresses this interpretation and argues that even if actual harm is not required for action under Section 211(c)(1)(A), the occurrence of the threatened harm must be "probable" before regulation is justified. Ethyl Supp.Br. 12. While the dictionary admittedly settles on "probable" as its measure of danger, we believe a more sophisticated case-by-case analysis is appropriate. Danger, the Administrator recognized, is not set by a fixed probability of harm, but rather is composed of reciprocal elements of risk and harm, or probability and severity. *Cf. Carolina Environmental Study Group v. United States*, 166 U.S.App.D.C. 416, 419, 510 F.2d 796, 799 (1975); *Reserve Mining Co. v. EPA, supra*, 514 F.2d at 519-520. That is to say, the public health may properly be found endangered both by a lesser risk of a greater harm and by a greater risk of a lesser harm. Danger depends upon the relation between the risk and harm presented by each case, and cannot legitimately be pegged to "probable" harm, regardless of whether that harm be great or small. As the Eighth Circuit found in *Reserve Mining*, these concepts "necessarily must apply in a determination of whether any relief should be given in cases of this kind in which proof with certainty is impossible." 514 F.2d at 520.

* * *

2. *The Administrator's Power to Assess Risks*. Petitioners argue that Section 211 requires the Administrator to make a "threshold factual determination" that automobile emissions "will endanger" the public health, Nalco Supp.Br. at 15- 20; Ethyl Supp.Br. at 24-26, and dispute EPA's claim that the Administrator may make "an essentially legislative policy judgment, rather than a factual determination, concerning the relative risks of underprotection as compared to overprotection." *Industrial Union Department, AFL-CIO v. Hodgson*, 499 F.2d 467, 475 (1974). We must reject petitioners' argument, since the power to assess risks, without relying solely on facts, flows inexorably from the nature of the "will danger" standard. We have already found that Section 211 allows the Administrator to regulate fuel content when he finds that emissions cause a significant risk of harm to the public health. Yet, how can the Administrator determine that a risk is a significant risk if he cannot assess risks? And how can he assess risks if he cannot make policy judgments? Surely reliance on "facts" as contemplated by petitioners will provide little guidance. However, sole reliance on facts was not demanded by Congress.

Originally, it is true, it appeared that Congress would severely restrict the Administrator's ability to assess risks and make policy judgments to protect public health. The bill sent to the floor of the House, and eventually passed by the House, would have allowed EPA to control fuels or fuel additives only if the determination that their emission products would endanger the public health were established —

> on the basis of *specific findings* derived from relevant medical and scientific evidence, including . . . a *finding* that it is not otherwise technologically or economically feasible to achieve the emission standards established pursuant to section 202 of this Act.

H.R. 17255, 91st Cong., 2d Sess. § 210(g)(1) (1970) (Emphasis added). The specific findings requirement had more than procedural significance. It limited the scope of evidence on which the Administrator could proceed, made alternative action under Section 202 mandatory if possible, and was widely interpreted in the House, as the extracts of debate relied upon by petitioners show, Ethyl Supp.Br. at 24; NPRA Supp.Br. at 30; Nalco Supp.Br. at 15, as requiring that any EPA action be based solely on facts. *See also* H.R.Rep. No. 91-1146, 91st Cong., 2d Sess., at 13 (1970), U.S.Code Cong. & Admin.News 1970, p. 5356.

But the House bill did *not* become law. The Senate's preference for less restriction of EPA freedom in regulating fuel additives for health reasons was adopted by the conference committee and ultimately enacted into law. Although the legislative history does not expressly discuss the reasons for the change, the contrast in language is stark. As Section 211 now reads, the only "finding" the Administrator is required to make is that any fuel additive that might replace one that is prohibited does not cause emissions that will pose the same or greater danger to the public health. The substantive impact of the change is clear. All of the requirements for specific findings quoted above are replaced by requirements that the Administrator "consider" the specified evidence. The mandatory deference to Section 202 is removed. And the Administrator may act based on all information available to him. As we recognized in *Amoco*, construing a similar change in parallel Section 211(c)(1)(B), the conference committee's decision "was a deliberated one and was meant to have significance." *Amoco Oil Co. v. EPA, supra*, 501 F.2d at 733.

* * *

Undoubtedly, certainty is the scientific ideal — to the extent that even science can be certain of its truth. But certainty in the complexities of environmental medicine may be achievable only after the fact, when scientists have the opportunity for leisurely and isolated scrutiny of an entire mechanism. Awaiting certainty will often allow for only reactive, not preventive, regulation. Petitioners suggest that anything less than certainty, that any speculation, is irresponsible. But when statutes seek to avoid environmental catastrophe, can preventive, albeit uncertain, decisions legitimately be so labeled?

The problems faced by EPA in deciding whether lead automotive emissions pose a threat to the public health highlight the limitations of awaiting certainty. First, lead concentrations are, even to date, essentially low-level, so that the feared adverse effects would not materialize until after a lifetime of exposure. Contrary to petitioners' suggestion, however, we have not yet suffered a lifetime of exposure to lead emissions. At best, emissions at present levels have been with us for no more than 15-20 years. Second, lead exposure from the ambient air is pervasive, so that valid control groups cannot be found against which the effects of lead on our population can be measured. Third, the sources of human exposure to lead are multiple, so that it is difficult to isolate the effect of automobile emissions. Lastly, significant exposure to lead is toxic, so that considerations of decency and morality limit the flexibility of experiments on humans that would otherwise accelerate lead exposure from years to months, and measure those results. *Cf. Environmental Defense Fund, Inc. v. EPA (Shell)*, 510 F.2d 1292, 1299 (1975).

* * *

Where a statute is precautionary in nature, the evidence difficult to come by, uncertain, or conflicting because it is on the frontiers of scientific knowledge, the regulations designed to protect the public health, and the decision that of an expert administrator, we will not demand rigorous step-by-step proof of cause and effect. Such proof may be impossible to obtain if the precautionary purpose of the statute is to be served. Of course, we are not suggesting that the Administrator has the power to act on hunches or wild guesses. *Amoco* makes it quite clear that his conclusions must be rationally justified. *Amoco Oil Co. v. EPA, supra*, 501 F.2d at 740-741. However, we do hold that in such cases the Administrator may assess risks. He must take account of available facts, of course, but his inquiry does not end there. The Administrator may apply his expertise to draw conclusions from suspected, but not completely substantiated, relationships between facts, from trends among facts, from theoretical projections from imperfect data, from probative preliminary data not yet certifiable as "fact," and the like. We believe that a conclusion so drawn — a risk assessment — may, if rational, form the basis for health-related regulations under the "will endanger" language of Section 211.

* * *

3. *Propriety of the Cumulative Impact Approach*. In addition to demanding that the Administrator act solely on facts, petitioner Ethyl insists that those facts convince him that the emission product of the additive to be regulated "in and of itself," *i. e.*, considered in isolation, endangers health. The Administrator contends that the impact of lead emissions is properly considered together with all other human exposure to lead. *See* page 12 of 541 F.2d *supra*. We agree.

First, Ethyl points to the language of Section 202 allowing regulation of any automobile emission that "causes or *contributes to*, or is likely to cause or to *contribute to*, air pollution which endangers the public health or welfare." Section 202(a)(1) (emphasis Ethyl's in its brief at 18). This is contrasted with Section 211's language allowing regulation of fuels or fuel additives whose "emission products . . . will endanger the public health or welfare." By italicizing the "contribute to" language of Section 202 Ethyl presumably suggests that Section 202 is more lenient, allowing use of the cumulative impact theory while Section 211 does not.

* * *

However they differ, both Section 202 and Section 211 allow regulation of lead additives only on a determination that the resultant polluted air, however composed, endangers the public health. Both provisions leave open the question whether emissions or air pollution can be found to endanger the public health when the endangerment is not caused by that pollution alone.

While Ethyl's comparison suggests no answer, the question is directly raised here. The Administrator found endangerment, but recognized that the national lead exposure problem is caused, not by air pollution alone, but by an aggregate of sources, including food, water, leaded paint, and dust. He believed that regulation was justified because the aggregate was dangerous, and because leaded gasoline was a *significant* source that was particularly suited to ready reduction. 38 Fed.Reg. 33734. To the question whether the Administrator was correct in his belief, comparison with the "contribute to" language of Section 202 provides no guidance.

* * *

4. *Summary of the "Will Endanger" Determination*. In sum, we must reject petitioners' cramped and unrealistic interpretation of Section 211(c)(1)(A). Their reading would render the statute largely useless as a basis for health-related regulation of lead emissions. Petitioners' arguments are rebuffed by the plain meaning of the statute and the Administrator's interpretation of it, by the legislative history and the implications that can drawn from other sections of the same statute, by the relevant precedents, and by the established maxim that health-related legislation is liberally construed to achieve its purpose.

We believe the Administrator may regulate lead additives under Section 211(c)(1)(A) when he determines, based on his assessment of the risks as developed by consideration of all the information available to him, and as guided by the policy judgment inherent in the statute, that lead automobile emissions significantly increase the total human exposure to lead so as to cause a significant risk of harm to the public health. Before so regulating, he must consider the possibility of regulation under Section 202. This interpretation of Section 211 does not allow for baseless or purposeless regulation, but does grant the Administrator the flexibility needed to confront realistically the public health problem presented by massive diffusion of lead emissions from automobiles.

B. *Comparison with Substitute Additives*

Even when the Administrator has determined that a fuel or fuel additive causes emissions which endanger the public health, he is not yet free to prohibit the substance under Section 211. He must first find, and publish his finding,

> that in his judgment such prohibition will not cause the use of any other fuel or fuel additive which will produce emissions which will endanger the public health or welfare to the same or greater degree than the use of the fuel or fuel additive proposed to be prohibited.

Section 211(c)(2)(C).

* * *

After making the "will endanger" determination and the "substitute additives" finding, EPA has complied with the statutory mandate and is free to regulate the fuel or fuel additive under Section 211.

III. THE EVIDENCE

* * *

B. *Overview of the Evidence*

Petitioners vigorously attack both the sufficiency and the validity of the many scientific studies relied upon by the Administrator, while advancing for consideration various studies allegedly supportive of their position. The record in this case is massive — over 10,000 pages. Not surprisingly, evidence may be isolated that supports virtually any inference one might care to draw. Thus we might well have sustained a determination by the Administrator *not* to regulate lead additives on health grounds. That does not mean, however, that we cannot sustain his determination to so regulate. As we have indicated above, we need not decide whether his decision is supported by the preponderance of the evidence, nor, for that matter, whether it is supported by substantial evidence. To the contrary, we must sustain if it has a rational basis in the evidence. Keeping in mind the precautionary "will endanger" standard under which the Administrator acted, we have no difficulty in terming his decision rational.

A word about our approach to the evidence may be in order. Contrary to the apparent suggestion of some of the petitioners, we need not seek a single dispositive study that fully supports the Administrator's determination. Science does not work that way; nor, for that matter, does adjudicatory fact-finding. Rather, the Administrator's decision may be fully supportable if it is based, as it is, on the inconclusive but suggestive results of numerous studies. By its nature, scientific evidence is cumulative: the more supporting, albeit inconclusive, evidence available, the more likely the accuracy of the conclusion. If, as petitioners suggest, one single study or bit of evidence were sufficient independently to mandate a conclusion, there would, of course, be no need for any other studies. Only rarely, however, is such limited study sufficient. Thus, after considering the inferences that can be drawn from the studies supporting the Administrator, and those opposing him, we must decide whether the cumulative effect of all this evidence, and not the effect of any single bit of it, presents a rational basis for the low-lead regulations.

While we have studied the record with great care, we do not discuss it all here; to do so would make this already lengthy opinion completely unwieldy. Instead, we shall briefly review the bases for the Administrator's conclusions that petitioners have singled out for special attack. Before we turn to those issues, however, we should note that some things appear to be uncontested. Thus petitioners seem to concede the following: that lead serves no known purpose in the human body; that lead in sufficiently high quantity is destructive to the body, causing anemia, severe intestinal cramps, paralysis, neurologic damage, and, in sufficient dosage, death, Third Health Document at III-1, 2; that more than 250,000 tons of lead per year are used in production of lead additives, accounting, according to EPA, for approximately 90 percent of all airborne lead, *id.* at Table II-1, JA 46; that lead concentrations in the air over our largest cities are 2,000 times greater than lead concentrations in the air over the mid-Pacific, NAS Report at 205; that lead in the ambient air contributes to body blood lead levels, Nalco Supp.Br. at 37; supplemental brief of petitioners PPG Industries and E. I. duPont de Nemours & Company [hereinafter PPG/duPont Supp.Br.] at 23; and that blood lead levels are a reasonable indication of the body's lead burden. Stripped of their generalized and largely unsubstantiated claims of "bias" and "distortion of the evidence," petitioners principally challenge three EPA conclusions: (1) that, based on a preliminary determination that blood lead levels of 40 µg are indicative of danger to health, elevated blood lead levels "exist to a small but significant extent in the general adult population, and to a very great extent among children," Third Health Document at VII-3; (2) that airborne lead is directly absorbed in the body through respiration to a degree that constitutes a significant risk to public health; and (3) that airborne lead falls to the ground where it mixes with dust and poses a significant risk to the health of urban children.

* * *

C. *Summary of the Evidence*

From a vast mass of evidence the Administrator has concluded that the emission products of lead additives will endanger the public health. He has handled an extraordinarily complicated problem with great care and candor. The evidence did not necessarily always point in one direction and frequently, until EPA authorized research, there was no evidence at all. The Administrator reached his conclusion only after hearings spread over several months, consideration of thousands of pages of documents, publication of three health documents, three formal comment periods, and receipt of hundreds of comments. Each study was considered independently; its worth was assessed only after it was measured against any critical comments. From the totality of the evidence the Administrator concluded that regulation under Section 211(c)(1)(A) was warranted.

In tracking his path through the evidence we, in our appellate role, have also considered separately each study and the objections petitioners make thereto. In no case have we found the Administrator's use of the evidence to be arbitrary or capricious. Having rejected the individual objections, we also reject the overall claim of error. We find the Administrator's analysis of the evidence and assessment of the risks to be well within the flexibility allowed by the "will endanger" standard. Accordingly, we affirm his determination that lead emissions "present a significant risk of harm to the health of urban populations, particularly to the health of city children." 38 Fed.Reg. 33734.

* * *

V. CONCLUSION

The complex scientific questions presented by this rule-making proceeding were "resolved in the crucible of debate through the clash of informed but opposing scientific and technological viewpoints." *International Harvester Co. v. Ruckelshaus*, 478 F.2d 615, 652 (1973) (concurring opinion of Chief Judge Bazelon).

* * *

Because of the importance of the issues raised, we have accorded this case the most careful and exhaustive consideration. We find that in this rule-making proceeding the EPA has complied with all the statutory procedural requirements and that its reasons as stated in its opinion provide a rational basis for its action. Since we reject all of petitioners' claims of error the Agency may enforce its low-lead regulations.

Affirmed.

NOTES

1. The 1977 Amendments to the Act emphatically endorsed the *en banc* panel's majority decision in the *Ethyl Corporation* case. H.R. REP. NO. 95-294, 95th Cong. 1st Sess. 43-50 (1977). To avoid any future misunderstanding regarding the scope of the "will endanger" standard § 211(a)(1)(A) was amended to authorize EPA regulation of the emission products of fuels or fuel additives "which may reasonably be anticipated to endanger the public health or welfare." The House Committee's explanation of the purposes behind this provision reads like a summary of Judge Wright's analysis in *Ethyl Corporation*:

> A. To emphasize the preventive or precautionary nature of the act, i.e., to assure that regulatory action can effectively prevent harm before it occurs; to emphasize the predominant value or protection of public health;
>
> B. To authorize the Administrator to weigh risks and make reasonable projections of future trends; thus, to find a middle road between those who would impose a nearly impossible standard of proof on the Administrator before he may move to protect public health and those who would shift the burden of proof for all pollutants to make the pollution source prove the safety of its emissions as a condition of operation;
>
> C. To assure consideration of the cumulative impact of all sources of a pollutant in setting ambient and emissions standards, not just the extent of the risk from the emissions from a single source or class of sources of the pollutant; to require consideration of cumulative or synergistic effects of multiple pollutants; to mandate evaluations of total body burden of contaminants;
>
> D. To provide the same standard of proof for regulation of any air pollutant, whether that pollutant comes from stationary or mobile sources, or both, and to make the vehicle and fuel industries equally responsible for cleaning up vehicle exhaust emissions;
>
> E. To assure that the health of susceptible individuals, as well as healthy adults, will be encompassed in the term "public health," regardless of the section of the act under which the Administrator proceeds;

> F. To reflect awareness of the uncertainties and limitations in the data which will be available to the Administrator in the foreseeable future to enable him to execute his rulemaking duties under this act, because of the limitations on research resources and the fact that decision making about the risks to public health from air pollution falls on "the frontiers of scientific and medical knowledge"; to provide for adequate judicial review of the reasonableness of the Administrator's judgment in assessing risks, while restraining the courts from attempting to act "as the equivalent of a combined Ph.D. in chemistry, biology, and statistics" or from applying a standard of review which is appropriate only to review of adjudications or formal fact finding.

Id. at 49-50.

2. *Protection of Catalytic Converters.* Other than lead, the primary pollutants associated with automobile exhaust are hydrocarbons, carbon monoxide and nitrous oxides. Virtually all new automobiles in use today employ catalytic converters to oxidize or burn these emissions. The catalyst used in such converters, however, is neutralized by certain substances such as lead, phosphorous, barium or cadmium. Thus, in addition to contributing to airborne lead pollution, leaded gasoline can contaminate the devices used to control other forms of pollution. To address this problem, Congress enacted § 211(a)(1)(B) which authorizes the EPA to control or prohibit fuels or fuel additives if the emissions products of such fuels or additives "will impair to a significant degree the performance of any emission control device or system which is in general use." Pursuant to this provision EPA has adopted regulations which prohibit the introduction of leaded gasoline into automobiles which are marked or designed exclusively for the use of unleaded fuel. 40 CFR § 80.22(a)(1986). Manufacturers of automobiles are required to mark the gas inlet area and the instrument panel so as to inform the driver and the person filling the gas tank of the restriction. 40 CFR § 80.24. In addition, the gas tank inlet must be smaller than the standard nozzle for leaded gasoline pumps. 40 CFR § 80.24(b). In *Amoco Oil Co. v. EPA*, 501 F.2d 722 (D.C. Cir. 1974) the Court sustained EPA's definition of leaded gasoline as gasoline containing in excess of 0.05 grams per gallon of lead, as both necessary and feasible. *Id.* at 742-43. It struck down in part, however, EPA's attempt to impose liability in certain circumstances on refiners or distributors who introduce leaded gasoline into cars designed for unleaded gasoline. *Id.* at 749. Subsequent rules drafted by EPA to incorporate the limitations required by the decision were also struck down as extending liability to refiners and distributors "well beyond the bounds of traditional vicarious liability." *Amoco Oil Co. v. EPA*, 543 F.2d 270, 275 (D.C. Cir. 1976). Professor Currie has criticized the majority opinion in the second *Amoco Oil* opinion for failing to recognize that the common law does not control questions of statutory interpretation, and that the scope of permissible liability had been determined in the first *Amoco* decision. CURRIE, AIR POLLUTION: FEDERAL LAW AND ANALYSIS § 2.44 (Callaghan & Co. 1981).

3. *Registration of Fuels and Fuel Additives.* Section 211(a) of the Act prohibits the sale, offer for sale, or introduction into commerce of any fuel or fuel additive that has not been registered with the Administrator. Section 211(b) further provides that the Administrator shall require the submission of information regarding chemical composition of any additive, its concentration in the fuel, and its purpose. The Administrator may require the manufacturer "to conduct tests to determine potential public health effects" of any fuel or fuel additive and provide other pertinent information. § 211(b)(2)(A). In 1975, EPA promulgated regulations to implement these provisions. 40 Fed. Reg 52,011

(1975). These rules included motor vehicle engine oil used to lubricate the engine within the scope of fuel additives. The basis for EPA's action was that lubricants and additives to them may have effects or emissions similar to the propellants and that those effects may be harmful. *Id.* In *Lubrizoil Corp. v. EPA*, 562 F.2d 807 (D.C. Cir. 1977), a motor vehicle oil manufacturer successfully challenged EPA's inclusion of lubricant oil within the scope of the phrase "fuels or fuel additives." The court accepted the petitioner's argument that Congress intended the common sense meaning of "fuels or fuel additives" as "substances used to *propel* motor vehicles." *Id.* at 816. A mere five days prior to the court's opinion, Congress enacted the Clean Air Act Amendment of 1977. While the Amendments themselves did not contain any clarification of the term "fuels or fuel additives," the 1977 House Report on the Amendments offered the following version of Congress' intent in its prior use of the term:

> [T]he Committee, in repeating the terms "fuel" and "fuel additives" intended that these terms be construed broadly, as with existing Section 211, to include any substance that is intentionally put into a vehicle's motor, either directly or indirectly, and which is combusted in the engine. In terms of the potential effect on pollution control devices or on public health, it matters not whether any such substance makes its way from the engine to the gas tank or is put directly into the engine.

H.R. Rep. No.95-294, 95th Cong., 1st Sess. 309 (1977). Had the court been aware of this language would it likely have reached a different conclusion?

4. Testing of fuels and fuel additives appears to have been made mandatory by the 1977 Amendments to the Act. Section 211(e) now requires EPA to promulgate regulations to implement the Administrator's testing authority for *each* fuel or fuel additive which is currently registered and for any fuels or fuel additives for which an application for registration is later filed. Upon compliance with these provisions the Administrator must register the fuel or fuel additive. *Id.*

5. *Lead Banking.* In 1985 EPA promulgated rules accelerating the schedule for reducing the lead content in gasoline. Under these rules gasoline producers were required to meet a 0.50 gplg standard by July 1, 1985, and a 0.10 gplg standard by January 1, 1986. 50 Fed. Reg. 9386 (1985). In order to ease the burden imposed by these standards EPA allowed producers to "bank" lead credits. Under the rules, producers could obtain credits by reducing their lead usage below the maximum allowed by the rules. These credits could then be used (until December, 1987) by the same producers, or sold to other producers who were unable to meet the standards. *Id.* The sale of leaded gasoline will be banned altogether at the end of 1995. § 211(n).

6. *Manganese.* The 1977 Amendments added a new subsection (f) to § 211 which prohibits the introduction of any new fuel or fuel additive for use in light duty motor vehicles manufactured after model year 1974 that is not substantially similar to existing fuels and fuel additives. The 1990 Amendments extended this prohibition to all motor vehicles. § 211(f)(1)(B). EPA may waive this restriction if it determines that the new fuel will not contribute to the failure of any emission control device. § 211(f)(4). The provision was added after the Senate received testimony regarding the increased use of a fuel additive, MMT, an organomanganese compound. The substance was found to impair the performance of emission control devices. Section 211(f)(2) of the Act expressly prohibits the sale of gasoline with manganese concentrations in excess of 0.0625 grams per gallon.

7. EPA's authority to revoke a waiver issued under § 211(f) was considered by the Court of Appeals for the District of Columbia Circuit in *American Methyl Corporation* *v. EPA*, 749 F.2d 826 (D.C. Cir. 1984). The petitioner, American Methyl, had developed an additive to be used in a methanol/gasoline blend marketed as Petrocoal. Petrocoal can be produced more cheaply than gasoline. In 1981, American Methyl applied for and obtained a waiver of the § 211(f) prohibitions. Shortly thereafter a trade association petitioned EPA to have the waiver reconsidered. A supplemental petition was filed in 1983 with evidence suggesting that Petrocoal caused automobiles to exceed hydrocarbon emission standards. On the basis of this information, EPA proposed to revoke its waiver of § 211(f) claiming inherent authority to do so. American Methyl challenged EPA's authority to revoke the prior waiver under § 211(f). The court held that EPA had no such authority. According to the Court, revocation of a § 211(f) waiver could only be accomplished in accordance with the more cumbersome administrative procedures of § 211(c), which sets out EPA's general authority to regulate and prohibit fuels. *See also Motor Vehicle Mfrs. Ass'n v. EPA*, 768 F.2d 385 (D.C. Cir. 1985), *cert. denied, sub nom., American Methyl Corp. v. Motor Vehicle Mfrs. Ass'n.*, 474 U.S. 1082. (1986).

8. Violations of § 211 are subject to civil fines of $25,000 "for each and every day of such violation and the amount of economic benefit or savings resulting from the violation." § 211(d)(1).

9. Omitted from the excerpt of the *Ethyl Corporation* opinion in the text is the court's lengthy discussion of the technical evidence supporting the Administrator's finding that airborne lead will endanger the public health and welfare. While the evidence before the Court at that time was conflicting, subsequent evidence has proved EPA's determination was correct. *See Small Refinery Lead Phase-Down Task Force v. EPA*, 705 F.2d 506 (D.C. Cir. 1983):

> When EPA first issued lead-content regulations in 1973, there was no firm evidence that gasoline lead was harmful, only a "significant risk" that it was. *Ethyl Corp.*, 541 F.2d at 12. Today, in contrast, there is compelling evidence that gasoline lead is a major cause of lead poisoning in young children. We discuss here only a few of the major pieces of evidence.
>
> i. *The Correlation Between Gasoline Lead and Blood Lead Levels*
>
> Gasoline lead correlates strongly with blood lead levels. A comprehensive study ("NHANES II") by the Centers for Disease Control (CDC) shows that between 1976 and 1980, as gasoline lead use (under the spur of EPA regulation) declined from 105,000 tons per six-month period to 50,000 tons, mean blood levels declined in virtual lockstep from 16 μg/dl to less than 10 μg/dl. The percentage of people with excessive blood lead levels (30 μg/dl or above) showed a similar decline. As Dr. Vernon Houk, Acting Director of CDC's Center for Environmental Health, explained:
>
>> This reduction was real. It was not due to chance, laboratory error, nor sampling of age, sex, race, urban vs. rural areas, income levels, or geographic regions. The most significant environmental change during this time was the reduced amount of lead used in the production of gasoline.... [This data] clearly demonstrates that as we have removed lead from gasoline, we have also removed lead from ourselves and our children.
>
> Other studies show that when gasoline lead use peaks sharply each summer, blood lead levels peak sharply as well.

> Leaded gasoline is the only lead source that can explain this data. Both of the other two major sources of lead (lead paint and food) are roughly constant year-round; thus, neither would produce a summer peak in blood lead levels. Also, neither showed a sharp decline in recent years.
>
> Other evidence also suggests that gasoline lead is a major cause of lead poisoning, through its presence in the air, in dirt, and in dust. Gasoline lead is the source of over 90% of air lead, and there is a well-established relationship between inhalation of air lead and increases in blood lead. Also soil analysis shows that "lead levels . . . in the front yards of urban homes are two to three times greater than . . . in the back yards." Gasoline lead can explain this pattern; the other major sources of dirt and dust lead (lead paint and stationary lead sources) cannot. Moreover, the concentrated lead in dirt and dust can easily produce lead poisoning. An urban child who licks her finger after running it across a table left undusted for several days can consume several times the "safe" daily dose of lead.

Id. at 527-529

10. Ambient concentrations of lead have fallen dramatically since 1975. Environmental Quality, 20th Annual Report, App. E., Table 41 (CEQ 1990), almost entirely due to the restrictions on use of leaded gasoline. As a result of the 1990 Amendments, the sale of leaded gasoline will be prohibited beginning 1996. § 211(n).

11. Although emissions which result from the combustion of vehicle fuels are a significant concern, evaporative emissions from the fuels themselves pose a serious problem as well. In a rulemaking proceeding first proposed in 1987, EPA explained why:

> Evaporative hydrocarbon (HC) emissions from gasoline-related sources are volatile organic compounds (VOC), and as such they contribute substantially to the formation of ozone (and other photochemical oxidants) in the atmosphere. Ozone formation is most active during the summer months because the chemical reactions involved rely on direct sunlight and high ambient temperatures.
>
> Ozone is a powerful oxidant, and as such reacts readily with a wide range of substances. In humans, ozone irritates the respiratory system and reduces lung function and laboratory studies suggest that it may damage lung and other tissue. There is concern that this damage can repair breathing and reduce immunity to disease for people in good health, and the effect may be more severe for people with pre-existing respiratory diseases. Thus, violation of the National Ambient Air Quality Standard (NAAQS) is considered a serious public health concern.
>
> Oxidation by ozone and other photochemical oxidants can impair plant tissue and reduce the yield of some crops, as well as damage materials such as rubber products.
>
> * * *
>
> Despite the imposition of various HC controls, many areas of the nation continue to violate the ozone NAAQS. Based on the latest three-year period for which complete air quality monitoring data are available (1982-84), EPA has determined that 73 urban areas are currently exceeding the ambient standard. Twelve of these areas are located in California. The significance of the nationwide non-attainment problem is clearly indicated by considering the fact that well over 100 million people live in the 73 urban areas which are known to exceed the ozone standard.

52 Fed. Reg. 31,275 (1987). The 1990 Amendments to the Act attempt to address this problem in several ways. For example, as noted in the previous section of this chapter, on-board vapor recovery systems will eventually be required for all light duty motor vehicles § 202(a)(6). Further, EPA is required to promulgate evaporation emissions rules for *all* gasoline-fueled motor vehicles, during operation and over two or more days of non-use, and under "ozone-prone summertime conditions." § 202 (k). A third approach to the problem of evaporation emissions is regulation of vehicle fuels. The amount of evaporation emissions depends on the fuel's volatility. As the EPA has noted:

> [T]he volatility of a liquid is a measure of its tendency to evaporate. Gasoline is composed of a number of hydrocarbon components which are very volatile under most conditions. When these vapors are present in sufficient quantities in the atmosphere on hot, sunny summer days, they can react to form substantial ground-level concentrations of ozone.
>
> Gasoline components vary in their respective volatilities. Since "light-end" hydrocarbons — particularly butane — are the most volatile components in commercial gasoline, they make up the largest part of gasoline vapor. However, evaporated gasoline will also include smaller amounts of heavier hydrocarbons. The aromatic compound benzene is one of these components, and we discuss it further below because it is a known human carcinogen in addition to contributing to ozone formation.
>
> * * *
>
> Although vehicles are able to operate well on a fairly wide range of gasoline volatilities, there are technological upper and lower limits. For the vehicle to start cold, there must be enough fuel vapor in the air reaching the cylinder to ignite — fuel of too low volatility at too low a temperature can cause starting problems. At the other extreme, a fuel whose volatility is too high for the temperature or elevation it is experiencing can actually vaporize inside the fuel system, interrupting the fuel supply ("vapor lock").
>
> * * *
>
> The most common measure of fuel volatility under ambient conditions-which is useful in evaluating vehicle evaporative emissions-is the Reid Vapor Pressure, or RVP. RVP is measured at 100° F, which is in the usual range of temperatures found in vehicle fuel tanks during the summer.

52 Fed. Reg. 31,278. Unfortunately, the trend in fuel production has been toward increased volatility:

> There has been a steady trend upward in the average volatility of commercial gasoline over the past 30 years. Two main factors account for this increase. First vehicle design has over the years become progressively more tolerant of higher RVP fuels primarily due to the increasing availability of fuel injected engines. As vehicle tolerance of higher volatility has increased, the American Society for Testing and Materials has adjusted their recommended RVP limits upward as well. (This last happened in 1970 and could occur again since vehicle technology continues to improve.) Second, there is a strong economic incentive to add as much butane to fuel as vehicles will tolerate since butane is much cheaper than gasoline. The improved vehicle technology has thus allowed refiners to increase the fraction of butane in the fuels they produce, resulting in a substantial increase in the average volatility of fuels available across the country. Whereas in 1970 commercial summertime gasolines averaged around 9.0 psi

> RVP, current gasolines nationwide average about 10.5 psi in the summertime and for the most part have reached the ASTM limits for the areas in which they are sold.

52 Fed. Reg. 31,279. Congress responded in the 1990 Amendments by establishing fuel volatility standards. Section 211(h) requires EPA to promulgate standards making it unlawful to introduce into commerce gasoline with an RVP of more than 9.0 psi. More stringent standards may be established for nonattainment areas, but the rules may not preclude sales of gasolines with an RVP of 9.0 psi in attainment areas unless the area was previously an ozone nonattainment area. These rules are supposed to take effect by the 1992 high ozone season.

11. *Reformulated and Oxygenated Gasolines:* Section 211(k) requires EPA to promulgate standards for reformulated gasoline, which is to be used in the nine worst (extreme and severe) ozone nonattainment areas. § 211(k)(9)(D). Other areas must be included in this program one year after being designated as a severe ozone nonattainment area. Reformulated gasoline is that which meets either a specific formula or a performance standard. § 211(k)(3). Section 211(m) requires that those CO nonattainment areas which exceed a CO design value of 9.5 ppm sell only oxygenated fuels during those times of the year when the area is most prone to high ambient concentrations of CO. This period is to be determined by EPA and cannot be less than four months. § 211(m)(2)(B). Those areas of the country subject to the reformulated and oxygenated gasoline requirements are identified in Garrett & Winner, *A Clean Air Act Primer,* CLEAN AIR DESKBOOK, p.64, Appendix 9B and 9C (Env. L. Inst., 1992)

12. *Low Sulfur Diesel Fuel:* During the debate on the 1990 Amendments, Congress heard testimony that particulate emissions from diesel-equipped engines cause cancer, genetic mutations, and other health related ailments. S.REP. NO. 228, 101st Cong., 1st Sess. 111 (1989). The most cost-effective way of removing particulates from diesel engine exhaust was desulfurization of diesel fuel. This could be accomplished at either the tailpipe or through fuel regulation, but Congress determined that fuel regulation would be far more cost-effective. *Id.* Accordingly, § 211(i) prohibits the sale of diesel fuel with sulfur concentrations in excess of 0.05% effective on October 1, 1993. This compares with a 1986 average sulfur content in diesel fuel of 0.27%.

13 JUDICIAL REVIEW

Most of the cases reviewed thus far in the text were filed under § 307(b)(1) of the Act. Until this point, however, the text avoids any detailed discussion of the limitations and scope of that provision. This section of the book is intended to remedy that omission and to offer some additional insights into § 304, the citizen suit provision of the Act. General administrative law problems arising in the context of judicial review under the Clean Air Act are also considered.

A. Petitions for Review and Rulemaking Proceedings

Before turning to the cases a quick review of the language of selected portions of § 307 should prove helpful.

1. Petitions for Review

Section 307(b)(1) provides for judicial review by petition to the appropriate Circuit Court of all "final actions" of the EPA Administrator. Specifically enumerated as subject to review "only in the United States Court of Appeals for the District of Columbia Circuit" are the promulgation of ambient air quality standards, new source performance standards, emission standards (or other requirements) for hazardous air pollutants, emission standards for new motor vehicles (except HC, CO, and NO_x standards for light-duty vehicles[1]), and aircraft engines, regulations implementing the enforcement requirements at §§ 113, 119, and 120 of the Act, and any other "nationally applicable" regulations or action by the Administrator. Locally applicable actions such as decisions approving SIPs, or "any other final action of the Administrator . . . which is locally or regionally applicable" may be filed only in the circuit that encompasses the locus of the challenged action. If, however, the Administrator determines that any locally or regionally applicable action is "based on a determination of nationwide scope or effect," and he so publishes that determination, review reverts exclusively to the District of Columbia Circuit Court.

---

[1] The express exception from the review provisions of § 307(b)(1) for HC, CO and No_x emissions standards for light duty vehicles does not mean that review of such standards is unavailable; rather, it seems that review of such standards must be obtained in accordance with other general federal statutes that afford jurisdiction, such as 28 U.S.C. § 1331 (federal question jurisdiction). Judicial review would not appear to have been precluded because no intent to do so is expressed in the statute. *See* 5. U.S.C. §§ 701, 702. "A person suffering legal wrong because of agency action...within the meaning of a relevant statute, is entitled to judicial review thereof." The only exceptions to this provision are where a statute precludes judicial review or where the action is committed to agency discretion by law. 5 U.S.C § 706.

Petitions under § 307(b)(1) must be filed within 60 days from the date that notice of the action is published in the Federal Register. Thus, any of the tens of thousands of persons who may be affected by national regulations promulgated by EPA under the Act must file an action within 60 days from the date notice is published in a document they may never even receive, or forever lose the right to challenge the rules. The seemingly harsh result occasioned by this provision is tempered by the fact that a person can always petition an agency to amend, modify or repeal a rule under § 4(d) of the Administrative Procedure Act. 5 U.S.C. § 553(e). If the EPA denies the petition, judicial review of that decision is available.

Nonetheless, Justice Powell has questioned whether the narrow time frame afforded by the law (prior to 1977, a person had only 30 days to file a petition) comports with due process. *Adamo Wrecking Co. v. United States*, 434 U.S. 275, 290-91 (1978) (concurring opinion of Justice Powell). *Compare Holmes Limestone, Inc. v. Andrus*, 655 F. 2d 732 (6th Cir. 1981), *cert. denied*, 456 U.S. 995 (1982) (J.J. White & Blackmun dissenting); *Drummond Coal Co. v. Watt*, 735 F.2d 469 (11th Cir. 1984).

Notwithstanding these restrictions, the Administrative Conference of the United States has recommended that persons be allowed to challenge the validity of a regulation in any enforcement proceeding. 41 Fed. Reg. 56768 (1976) (Recommendation No. 76-4, C.D-1). Do you agree with this recommendation? Where would such actions be filed? Why does the EPA oppose the recommendation?

Judicial review under § 307 is generally on the record made before the agency. Section 307(c) of the Act, however, allows the court, on application of a party, to admit additional evidence if the party demonstrates "to the satisfaction of the court that such additional evidence is material *and* that there were reasonable grounds for the failure to adduce such evidence on the proceedings before the Administrator . . . ."

2. Rulemaking Proceedings Under the Clean Air Act

Many of the actions subject to judicial review pursuant to § 307(b)(1) are rulemaking proceedings to which the procedural standards of § 307(d) apply. Included within this subsection are the promulgation or revision of: (1) ambient air quality standards; (2) SIPs; (3) NSPSs; (4) HAPs; (5) regulations pertaining to the acid deposition program; (6) regulations relating to fuels and fuel additives; (7) aircraft emission standards; (8) regulations pertaining to coal conversion orders, nonferrous smelter orders (but not decisions granting or denying such orders); (9) regulations pertaining to ozone protection; (10) PSD regulations; (11) regulations pertaining to testing of new motor vehicles; (12) regulations pertaining to noncompliance penalties; (13) regulations pertaining to vehicle warranties and compliance; (14) regulations pertaining to interstate pollution; and (15) "such other actions as the Administrator may determine."

The procedures that must be followed in promulgating regulations that fall within this section are more rigorous than the general rulemaking provisions of the APA. Among the more significant requirements is that of § 307 (d)(3) which requires the EPA to provide in any *proposed* rule under this section a statement of its basis and purpose, including — (A) the factual data on which it is based; (B) the methodology used in obtaining the data; and (C) the major legal interpretations and policy considerations underlying the proposed rule.

The scope of review for actions that fall within the ambit of § 307(d) is set out at § 307(d)(9), and is essentially the same as that provided for rulemaking proceedings at § 706 of the APA.

HARRISON v. PPG INDUSTRIES, INC.

446 U.S. 578 (1980)

Mr. Justice STEWART delivered the opinion of the Court.

Section 307(b)(1) of the Clean Air Act (Act) provides for direct review in a federal court of appeals of certain locally and regionally applicable actions taken by the Administrator of the Environmental Protection Agency (EPA) under specifically enumerated provisions of the Act, and of *"any other final action* of the Administrator under [the Act] . . . which is locally or regionally applicable." (Emphasis added.) The issue in this case is whether the Court of Appeals for the Fifth Circuit was correct in concluding that it was without jurisdiction under § 307(b)(1) to entertain a petition for review in which PPG Industries, Inc. (PPG), and Conoco, Inc. (Conoco), the respondents here, challenged a decision of the Administrator concerning the applicability of EPA's "new source" performance standards to a power generating facility operated by PPG. More specifically, we must decide whether the Administrator's decision falls within the ambit of "any other final action" reviewable in a court of appeals under § 307(b)(1).

I

The dispute underlying this jurisdictional question involves a decision of the Administrator under § 111 of the Act, 42 U.S.C. § 7411 (1976 ed., Supp. II). That provision requires the Administrator to publish, and from time to time to revise, a list of categories of any stationary source that he determines "causes, or contributes significantly to, air pollution which may reasonably be anticipated to endanger public health or welfare," § 111(b)(1)(A), and to promulgate regulations establishing standards of performance for "new sources" within the list of those categories, § 111(b)(1)(B). The Act defines a "new source" as "any stationary source, the construction or modification of which is commenced after the publication of regulations (or, if earlier, proposed regulations) prescribing a standard of performance under this section which will be applicable to such source." § 111(a)(2).

In 1971, the Administrator included "fossil fuel-fired steam generators" in his list of stationary sources. 36 Fed.Reg. 5931. Later that year, pursuant to his mandate to promulgate "new source" performance standards, the Administrator established certain emission limits for any "fossil fuel-fired steam generating unit" of more than 250 million Btu's per hour heat input, the construction or modification of which was commenced after August 17, 1971, the date on which the standards were proposed. 40 CFR §§ 60.1-60.15, 60.40-60.46 (1979). These "new source" regulations define the term, "fossil fuel-fired steam generating unit," § 60.41(a), and also create a procedure under which the Administrator, upon request, will determine whether any action taken or planned by the owner or operator of a facility constitutes or will constitute "construction" or "modification" of the facility for purposes of triggering the applicability of the performance standards. § 60.5.

Sometime in 1970, the respondent PPG, a chemical manufacturing corporation, began the planning and preliminary construction of a new power generating facility at its plant in Lake Charles, La. That facility, designed to take advantage of fuel-efficient "cogeneration" technology, was to consist of two gas turbine generators, two "waste-heat" boilers, and a turbogenerator. The dispute between EPA and PPG concerns the applicability of the "new source" performance standards to the waste-heat boilers of this facility. This controversy first arose in 1975, when the respondent Conoco, PPG's fuel supplier, informed EPA that Conoco was switching the supply of fuel to the Lake Charles facility from natural gas to fuel oil. An exchange of correspondence ensued, initiated by EPA's request that PPG submit additional information bearing on whether the waste-heat boilers were covered by the "new source" standards. PPG's submissions revealed that although assembly of the waste-heat boilers had not begun until 1976, the new power facility itself, of which the boilers were an integral component, had been originally designed and partially ordered in 1970, a year before the proposed date of the "new source" performance standards.

On the basis of PPG's submissions, the Regional Director for Enforcement of the EPA notified PPG of his conclusion that the boilers were subject to the "new source" standards, since construction of the boilers themselves had not begun until long after January 14, 1971, the date on which the standards had been proposed. In response, PPG took the position that the boilers were part of an integrated unit, the construction of which had begun in 1970, before the proposed date of the standards. The Regional Director, nevertheless, reaffirmed his initial decision.

Pursuant to the procedure outlined in the "new source" regulations, 40 CFR § 60.5 (1979), PPG then submitted a formal request for an EPA determination that (1) the "new source" standards for "fossil fuel-fired steam generators" do not apply to the type of boilers in question, and (2) in any event since construction of the facility of which the boilers were a part began before the date on which the standards were proposed, the boilers were not "new sources" and thus not subject to the performance standards. In the event that EPA determined that PPG's waste-heat boilers were subject to the standards, PPG also requested a clarification as to how those standards would apply.

Responding to PPG's request, the Regional Administrator notified PPG by letter that he had concluded that the waste-heat boilers were, indeed, subject to the "new source" standards for "fossil fuel-fired steam generators," and rejected PPG's argument that construction of the boilers had begun with the construction of other facets of the Lake Charles facility. Thus, the Regional Administrator affirmed the previous EPA determination that the waste-heat boilers were subject to the "new source" performance standards. With regard to the manner in which those standards were to apply to the waste-heat boilers, the Regional Administrator indicated that since PPG's gas turbine generators were not subject to the "new source" standards, PPG would be held accountable only for those emissions from the waste-heat boilers attributable to the combustion of fossil fuel, not those emissions attributable to waste heat from the gas turbine generators.

PPG then filed a petition in the Court of Appeals for the Fifth Circuit, seeking review of EPA's decision concerning the applicability of the "new source" standards to its waste-heat boilers. Because of its uncertainty regarding the proper forum for judicial review, PPG also filed a complaint for injunctive relief against the Administrator in the United States District Court for the Western District of Louisiana. That suit has been stayed pending the disposition of the present case.

PPG's uncertainty, and the issue in this case, stem from conflicting views as to the proper interpretation of § 307(b)(1) of the Act. Before 1977, § 307(b)(1) provided for exclusive review in an appropriate court of appeals of certain locally or regionally applicable actions of the Administrator under several specifically enumerated provisions of the Act. Actions of the Administrator under provisions not specifically enumerated in § 307(b)(1) were reviewable only in a district court under its federal-question jurisdiction, 28 U.S.C. § 1331. Congress expanded the ambit of § 307(b)(1) in 1977. The Clean Air Act Amendments of 1977, Pub.L. 95-95, 91 Stat. 776, added to the list of locally or regionally applicable actions reviewable exclusively in the appropriate court of appeals both (1) actions of the Administrator under another specifically enumerated provision of the Act, and (2) "*any other final action* of the Administrator under [the] Act which is locally or regionally applicable." (Emphasis added.) Later in 1977, in enacting the Clean Air Act Technical and Conforming Amendments, Pub.L. 95-190, 91 Stat. 1404, Congress added several more provisions to those listed in § 307(b)(1) under which a locally or regionally applicable action of the Administrator is reviewable in the appropriate court of appeals.

It was under § 307(b)(1), as amended, that PPG filed a petition for review in the Court of Appeals for the Fifth Circuit. Despite having filed its petition there, PPG, and Conoco as intervenor, argued that court was without jurisdiction, since the Administrator's decision was not an action taken under one of the provisions specifically enumerated in § 307(b)(1), and could not be properly characterized as "any other final action of the Administrator." The latter phrase, they argued, referred only to other locally or regionally applicable final actions under the provisions of the Act specifically enumerated in § 307(b)(1). In response, EPA argued that the phrase, "any other final action," should be read literally to mean any final action of the Administrator.

The Court of Appeals concluded that the Administrator's decision did not fall within the meaning of "any other final action" under § 307(b)(1). 587 F.2d 237. It was the court's view that "[i]f Congress intended . . . to cast the entire responsibility for reviewing all EPA action under the Act into the courts of appeals, the numeration of specific sections would appear to be redundant." *Id.*, at 243. The "most revealing" aspect of the legislative history of § 307(b)(1), the court thought, was the complete absence of any discussion of such a "massive shift" in jurisdiction. Moreover, the court found it unlikely that Congress could have intended a shift of jurisdiction that would require the courts of appeals to review decisions of the Administrator that simply applied or interpreted his regulations, as in this case. Such a decision, the court noted, is often based on a "skeletal record" that may leave the reviewing court unable to perform meaningful judicial review. Since an appellate court is ill-suited to augment such a record, especially when compared to a trial court in which the tools of discovery are available, the court concluded that "whatever addition to the jurisdiction of the courts of appeals Congress may have contemplated by adding the 'any other final action' language to § 307(b)(1), we assume that section was drafted with the mechanical limitations of the courts of appeals in mind." 587 F.2d, at 245. Accordingly, the Court of Appeals dismissed PPG's petition for lack of jurisdiction under § 307(b)(1). We granted certiorari, 444 U.S. 823 because of the importance of determining the locus of judicial review of the actions of EPA.

II

It is undisputed that the Administrator's decision concerning the applicability of the "new source" performance standards to PPG's waste-heat boilers was locally applicable action under a provision of the Act not specifically enumerated in § 307(b)(1). The question at issue is whether the Administrator's decision falls within the scope of the phrase, "any other final action of the Administrator," so as to make that decision reviewable in a federal court of appeals under § 307(b)(1).

At the outset, we note that the parties are in agreement that the Administrator's decision was "final action" as that term is understood in the context of the Administrative Procedure Act and other provisions of federal law. It is undisputed that the Administrator's ruling represented EPA's final determination concerning the applicability of the "new source" standards to PPG's power facility. Short of an enforcement action, EPA has rendered its last word on the matter. The controversy thus is not about whether the Administrator's decision was "final," but rather about whether it was "any other final action" within the meaning of § 307(b)(1), as amended in 1977.

A

The petitioners argue that the phrase, "any other final action," should be construed in accordance with its literal meaning so as to reach any action of the Administrator under the Act that is "final" and not taken under a specifically enumerated provision in § 307(b)(1). The respondents argue that the statutory language should be construed more narrowly. Relying on the familiar doctrine of *ejusdem generis*, they assert that the phrase, "any other final action," should be read not to reach all final actions of the Administrator, but rather only those similar to the actions under the specifically enumerated provisions that precede that catchall phrase in the statute. The similarity that the respondents discern among the actions under the specifically enumerated provisions in § 307(b)(1) is that those actions must be based on what the respondents refer to as "a contemporaneously compiled administrative record," by which they mean a record "based on administrative proceedings reflecting at least notice and opportunity for hearing." Since the Administrator's informal decision in this case was not based on such a record, the respondents argue that his decision was not "other final action" within the meaning of § 307(b)(1) and thus not within the jurisdiction of the Court of Appeals.

The respondents' reliance on the rule of ejusdem generis is, we think, misplaced in two respects. Under the rule of *ejusdem generis*, where general words follow an enumeration of specific items, the general words are read as applying only to other items akin to those specifically enumerated. Applying this rule to § 307(b)(1), the respondents argue that "any other final action" must refer only to final actions based on an administrative record reflecting at least notice and opportunity for a hearing. The flaw in this argument is that at least one of the specifically enumerated provisions in § 307(b)(1), namely, § 112(c) of the Act, 42 U.S.C. § 7412(c) (1976 ed., Supp. II), does not require the Administrator to act only after notice and opportunity for a hearing. In fact, the respondents themselves recognize that an action by the Administrator under § 112(c) would be based on an administrative record not unlike that involved in this case. Thus, even if the rule of *ejusdem generis* were applied, it would not significantly narrow the ambit of "any other final action" under § 307(b)(1).

The second problem with the respondents' reliance on the rule of *ejusdem generis* is more fundamental. As we have often noted: " 'The rule of *ejusdem generis*, while firmly established, is only an instrumentality for ascertaining the correct meaning of words when there is uncertainty.' " *United States v. Powell,* 423 U.S. 87, 91, *quoting Gooch v. United States,* 297 U.S. 124, 128. With regard to § 307(b)(1), we discern no uncertainty in the meaning of the phrase, "any other final action." When Congress amended the provision in 1977, it expanded its ambit to include not simply "other final action," but rather "any other final action." This expansive language offers no indication whatever that Congress intended the limiting construction of § 307(b)(1) that the respondents now urge. Accordingly, we think it inappropriate to apply the rule of *ejusdem generis* in construing § 307(b)(1). Rather, we agree with the petitioners that the phrase, "any other final action," in the absence of legislative history to the contrary, must be construed to mean exactly what it says, namely, any other final action.

B

* * *

The respondents also rely on what the Committee and the Congress did not say about the 1977 amendments to § 307(b)(1). It is unlikely, the respondents assert, that Congress would have expanded so radically the jurisdiction of the courts of appeals, and divested the district courts of jurisdiction, without some consideration and discussion of the matter. We cannot accept this argument. First, although the number of actions comprehended by a literal interpretation of "any other final action" is no doubt substantial, the number would not appear so large as ineluctably to have provoked comment in Congress. Secondly, it would be a strange canon of statutory construction that would require Congress to state in committee reports or elsewhere in its deliberations that which is obvious on the face of a statute. In ascertaining the meaning of a statute, a court cannot, in the manner of Sherlock Holmes, pursue the theory of the dog that did not bark.

C

The respondents finally argue that, as a matter of policy, the basic purpose of § 307(b)(1) — to provide prompt pre-enforcement review of EPA action — would be better served by providing for judicial review of cases such as this in a district court rather than a court of appeals. It is the respondents' view that since agency action predicated on neither formal adjudication nor informal rulemaking is apt to be based on a record too scant to permit informed judicial review, the district court is the preferable forum, since the tools of discovery are there available to augment the record, whereas in a court of appeals a time-consuming remand to EPA might be required.

This is an argument to be addressed to Congress, not to this Court. It is not our task to determine which would be the ideal forum for judicial review of the Administrator's decision in this case. *See, e.g.,* Currie & Goodman, *Judicial Review of Federal Administrative Action: Quest for the Optimum Forum,* 75 Colum.L.Rev. 1 (1975). Rather, we must determine what Congress intended when it vested the courts of appeals with jurisdiction under § 307(b)(1) to review "any other final action." The language of the statute clearly provides that a decision of the sort at issue here is reviewable in a court of appeals, and nothing in the legislative history points to any different conclusion.

We add only that, as a matter of policy, this conferral of jurisdiction upon the courts of appeals is not wholly irrational. The most obvious advantage of direct review by a court of appeals is the time saved compared to review by a district court, followed by a second review on appeal. It may be seriously questioned whether the overall time lost by court of appeals remands to EPA of those cases in which the records are inadequate would exceed the time saved by forgoing in every case initial review in a district court. But whatever the answer to this empirical question, an appellate court is not without recourse in the event it finds itself unable to exercise informed judicial review because of an inadequate administrative record. In such a situation, an appellate court may always remand a case to the agency for further consideration.

For the reasons stated, we hold that the Court of Appeals erred in dismissing the petition for want of jurisdiction. Accordingly, the judgment is reversed, and the case is remanded to the Court of Appeals for further proceedings consistent with this opinion.

It is so ordered.

Mr. Justice REHNQUIST, dissenting.

The effort to determine congressional intent here might better be entrusted to a detective than to a judge. The Court rejects the application of the traditional canon of *ejusdem generis* to the phrase "any other final action" on the grounds that (1) there is no uncertainty as to the meaning of that phrase, *ante*, at 1895, and (2) at least one of the provisions now included in § 307(b)(1), 42 U.S.C. § 7607(b)(1) (1976 ed., Supp. II) — i. e., § 112(c), 42 U.S.C. § 7412(c) (1976 ed., Supp. II)—does not require the Administrator to act after notice and opportunity for comment or hearing, supra, at 1895. While I agree with the Court that the phrase "any other final action" may not by itself be "ambiguous," I think that what we know of the matter makes Congress' additions to § 307(b)(1) in the Clean Air Act Technical and Conforming Amendments of 1977 no less curious than was the incident in the Silver Blaze of the dog that did nothing in the nighttime. If I am correct in this, we must look beyond the language of the phrase "any other final action" in ascertaining congressional intention. The Court did just that in *Chemehuevi Tribe of Indians v. FPC,* 420 U.S. 395 (1975).

Before 1977, § 307(b)(1) granted exclusive jurisdiction to courts of appeals to review only a limited class of actions taken by the Administrator. *District of Columbia v. Train,* 533 F.2d 1250, 1254 (1976); *Utah Power & Light Co. v. EPA,* 553 F.2d 215, 217 (1977). The EPA was required to provide for notice and an opportunity for hearing or comment with respect to all such actions. These procedural requirements generally result in the creation of an administrative record that is more susceptible of judicial review by courts of appeals than actions such as the one in this case in which no notice and opportunity for comment are required. Indeed, it has been stated: "The requirements that interested persons have an opportunity at least for written comment and that the agency provide a general statement of reasons virtually assure that an appellate court will have a meaningful record to review. While it is true that in many instances informal adjudication also produces an administrative record, the nature and scope of the records vary widely from one type of action to another and cannot provide the same assurance that appellate review will be feasible." Currie & Goodman, *Judicial Review of Federal Administrative Action: Quest for the Optimum Forum,* 75 Colum.L.Rev. 1, 57 (1975). Thus the grant of exclusive jurisdiction to courts of appeals in pre-1977 § 307(b)(1) actions fully comports with the traditional role of appellate courts in reviewing agency decisions that are based on development of factual issues by means of an administrative record. * * *

[I]n adding the phrase "any other final action" Congress gave no indication whatsoever that it intended to make reviewable in the courts of appeals actions that differed substantially in character from those authorized by § 120 and the other sections listed in § 307(b)(1). Instead the limited legislative history on the subject suggests that the amendment was aimed at resolving problems of venue under the section, not at effecting a major jurisdictional shift from the district courts to courts of appeals.

* * *

In my view, absent any clear indication to the contrary, the statute should not be construed as creating a broad expansion of the jurisdiction of the federal courts of appeals. Such an approach is quite appropriate in this case because the jurisdictional expansion wrought by the Court is thoroughly inconsistent with the traditional role of appellate courts. Indeed, I think it is difficult to believe that Congress would adopt a massive shift in jurisdiction from the district courts to the courts of appeals without any comment whatsoever.

* * *

In a case where the construction of legislative language such as this makes so sweeping and so relatively unorthodox a change as that made here, I think judges as well as detectives may take into consideration the fact that a watchdog did not bark in the night.

[The concurring opinions of Justices Powell and Blackmun, and the dissenting opinion of Justice Stevens are omitted.]

NOTES

1. How does the majority respond to Justice Rehnquist's contention that appellate review may not be feasible in some instances of informal agency action because the administrative record will not be adequate? From a policy perspective which view makes the most practical sense?

2. Are administrative enforcement actions such as the issuance of notices of violation and compliance orders subject to judicial review under § 307(b)(1)? Consider *Union Electric Co. v. EPA*, 593 F.2d 299 (8th Cir. 1979), which was decided after the 1977 Amendments, but before the Supreme Court's decision in *Harrison v. PPG Industries, supra* at Chapter 10.

3. *The Silver Blaze,* alluded to by Justice Stewart in his majority opinion and referred to specifically by Justice Rehnquist in his dissenting opinion, is a short story written by Sir Arthur Conan Doyle. In the story, Sherlock Holmes deduces that a crime must have been committed by an insider because a dog kept in the stable did not bark on the night of the crime. "I had grasped the significance of the silence of the dog, for one true inference invariably suggests others." Sir Arthur Conan Doyle, *The Adventure of the Speckled Band and Other Stories of Sherlock Holmes*, p. 167 (Signet, 1965).

B. Citizen Suits

The broad review afforded under § 307(b)(1) may be had *only* in the appropriate court of appeals. Is review under § 307 (b)(1) thereby intended to be exclusive? If so, what remains of the provision for citizen suits which are filed in the federal district courts under § 304 of the Act? One obvious distinction is that the citizen suit provision authorized private rights of action against individuals who violate the law. § 304 (a)(1) and (3). In addition, however, § 304(a)(2) authorizes action against the Administrator where there is "an alleged failure of the Administrator to perform any act or duty under this [Act] which is not discretionary . . . " Section 304(a)(2)'s reference to "a failure . . . to perform any [nondiscretionary] act" most obviously suggests a situation where the Administrator fails to meet a statutory deadline, as occurred, for example, in a case involving EPA's failure to promulgate NO_x and particulate standards for heavy duty vehicles within a time frame specified by law. *Natural Resources Defense Council v. Ruckelshaus*, 21 BNA Env. Rep. Cases 1953 (D.D.C. 1984), *supra* at Chapter 12.

It is not difficult, however, to hypothesize many other nondiscretionary actions of the Administrator, which fall within the scope of § 307(b)(1). Thus, for example, where the Administrator approves a SIP which violates the law one can say that the Administrator failed to perform his nondiscretionary duty to disapprove a SIP which violates the law. The possible overlap between § 304(a)(2) and § 307(b)(1) is the subject of the following cases.

ENVIRONMENTAL DEFENSE FUND V. THOMAS

870 F.2d 892 (2d Cir. 1989)

WINTER, Circuit Judge:

This appeal involves the Clean Air Act, 42 U.S.C. §§ 7401 et seq. (1982 and Supp. IV 1986) ("the Act"), and in particular its bifurcated jurisdictional scheme for judicial review of decision making by the Environmental Protection Agency ("EPA"). The Act provides that suits to compel the Administrator to perform non-discretionary duties may be brought only in district courts, while petitions seeking review of the Administrator's discretionary actions must be brought in the Court of Appeals for the District of Columbia. *See, e.g., Citizens for a Better Env't v. Costle,* 515 F.Supp. 264, 268 (N.D.Ill.1981). Jurisdiction under the Act thus turns on the threshold question of whether the Administrator's challenged action (or inaction) is discretionary or non-discretionary.

In the instant appeal, a number of environmentalist groups, along with six states, have challenged the Administrator's failure to revise the "National Ambient Air Quality Standards" ("NAAQS") for sulphur oxides ("SO_x"). SO_x are causative agents of both acid rain and dry acid deposition — phenomena we will refer to collectively as "acid deposition." Judge Edelstein held that the Administrator's authority to revise those NAAQS is discretionary and that the district court therefore did not have jurisdiction to entertain the suit. *Environmental Defense Fund v. Thomas,* 85 Civ. 9507, 1988 WL 36332 (S.D.N.Y. April 19, 1988). Although we agree that the Administrator has discretion to decide on the precise form and substance of the NAAQS at issue, we believe that under the circumstances the Administrator has a non-discretionary duty to make some formal decision whether to revise those NAAQS. Subsequent published actions by the Administrator have begun the process of decision making, however, and we remand so the district court may enter an order that the rulemaking be continued to final decision.

BACKGROUND

The Clean Air Act was first passed in the 1960's and has since undergone two major legislative overhauls. The first of these overhauls, in 1970, established a multi-stage process for EPA evaluation of potential air pollutants. In the first stage, the EPA was, after scientific study, to publish "criteria" for the evaluation of any given potential pollutant. Section 108 of the Act, 42 U.S.C. § 7408 (1982). After the establishment of these "criteria," the EPA was to publish two types of initial NAAQS pursuant to Section 109 of the Act, 42 U.S.C. § 7409 (1982): (i) primary ambient air quality standards, designed to "protect the public health"; and (ii) secondary ambient air quality standards, designed to "protect the public welfare from any known or anticipated adverse effects associated with the presence of [a given] air pollutant in the ambient air." 42 U.S.C. § 7409(b).

The 1970 amendments distinguished between pollutants for which criteria had been announced before 1970 and pollutants for which criteria were announced after 1970. In the case of pollutants for which criteria had been announced before 1970 (which included SO_x), Sections 109(a)(1)(A) and (B) required the EPA to issue proposed initial primary and secondary NAAQS within 120 days of the passage of the 1970 amendments. In the case of pollutants for which criteria were announced after 1970, the amendments required the EPA to issue proposed initial primary and secondary NAAQS simultaneously with its publication of "criteria." The 1970 amendments added that both primary and secondary NAAQS "may be revised in the same manner as promulgated." 42 U.S.C. §§ 7409(b)(1) and (2).

The 1970 amendments also introduced into the statute a bifurcated jurisdictional scheme. In Section 307 of the Act, the 1970 amendments vested the Court of Appeals for the District of Columbia with exclusive jurisdiction to review a variety of rule promulgations and other "final actions" by the Administrator. 42 U.S.C. § 7607(b) (1982). In addition, Section 304 of the Act, the so-called "Citizen Suits" provision, permits any person to bring a civil action in a district court "against the Administrator where there is alleged a failure of the Administrator to perform any act or duty under this chapter which is not discretionary with the Administrator...." 42 U.S.C. § 7604(a)(2) (1982).

The second statutory overhaul occurred in 1977. These amendments added Section 109(d) concerning the "review and revision" of NAAQS, which provides that: [n]ot later than December 31, 1980, and at five-year intervals thereafter, the Administrator shall complete a thorough review of the criteria published under Section 108 ... and promulgate such new standards as may be appropriate.... The Administrator may review and revise criteria or promulgate new standards earlier or more frequently than required under this paragraph. 42 U.S.C. § 7409(d) (1982). It is this section that plaintiffs seek to enforce by this action under Section 304.

The pollutants involved in this appeal, SO_x, are causative or acid deposition and belong to the class of pollutants for which criteria had been issued before the 1970 amendments. In 1971, the Administrator promulgated primary and secondary NAAQS for SO_x. 36 Fed.Reg. 8186. The secondary NAAQS were reviewed by the Court of Appeals for the District of Columbia and were thereafter remanded to the Administrator with instructions to elaborate on their justification. *Kennecott Copper Corp. v. EPA,* 462 F.2d 846 (D.C.Cir.1972). On that remand, the Administrator modified the secondary NAAQS. 38 Fed.Reg. 25679 (1973). The secondary NAAQS as modified were not designed to protect against the deleterious effects of SO_x associated with acid rain and dry acid deposition — deleterious effects on water quality, wildlife, soils and forests, and corrosive effects of SO_x on building materials, monuments and products. 38 Fed.Reg. 25680 (1973). Neither the primary SO_x NAAQS as promulgated in 1971, nor the modified secondary SO_x NAAQS of 1973, have been revised since.

In 1979, the Administrator undertook a review of the air quality criteria for SO_x in response to the passage of Section 109(d)(1) in 1977. 44 Fed.Reg. 56731 col. 2 (1979). In 1982, that review resulted in the publication of new criteria both for SO_x and for particulate matter, another pollutant, which includes forms of SO_x, listed under Section 108. The new criteria described in some detail the ill effects associated with acid deposition. The Administrator did not, however, issue revised NAAQS for SO_x. Indeed, the Administrator took no official public action, neither revising the existing standards nor formally declining to revise them. In 1984 and 1985, the EPA issued a three-volume "Critical Assessment" on the acid deposition effects of SO_x. This did not constitute a formal revision of the SO_x criteria, and the Administrator again took no action in conjunction with the issuance of this "Critical Assessment."

In 1985, appellants brought the instant case in the District Court for the Southern District of New York, pursuant to Section 304, the "Citizen Suits" provision of the Act, to compel the Administrator to promulgate revised NAAQS for SO_x. Their complaint alleged that the revised criteria of 1982 and the "Critical Assessment" of 1984 and 1985 constituted a formal finding that SO_x caused acid deposition threatening to the public health and welfare. Appellants claimed that those findings imposed on the Administrator a non- discretionary duty to revise the NAAQS for SO_x, pursuant to Sections 109(b) and 109(d), in order to combat such health and welfare effects. Judge Edelstein disagreed. Looking to the language of Section 109(d), he concluded that the section created a mandatory duty only to revise pollutant criteria — an action the Administrator had taken in 1982. The Administrator, he held, had discretion not to revise the SO_x NAAQS if he so chose. Because the duty to revise the NAAQS was discretionary, he concluded that the district court lacked jurisdiction over the dispute and dismissed the complaint.

One week after Judge Edelstein's decision, the EPA issued a "Proposed Decision Not To Revise the National Ambient Air Quality Standards for Sulfur Oxides (Sulfur Dioxide)." 53 Fed.Reg. 14926 (April 26, 1988). In that "Proposed Decision," the Administrator announced that he was formally "propos[ing] not to revise [the primary and secondary] standards" for sulfur oxides, 53 Fed.Reg. at 14926 col. 1, and invited comments. However, the Administrator expressly excluded the problem of acid deposition from the list of welfare effects for which no revision of the secondary SO_x NAAQS was necessary:

1. Based upon the current scientific understanding of the acid deposition problem, it would be premature and unwise to prescribe any regulatory control program at this time.
2. When the fundamental scientific uncertainties have been reduced through ongoing research efforts, EPA will craft and support an appropriate set of control measures.

Id. at 14936 col. 1. In light of this EPA action, appellants have narrowed their claim on appeal. Rather than challenging both the primary and secondary NAAQS, they abandoned the challenge to the primary NAAQS, which the Administrator has formally proposed not to revise in his "Proposed Decision," and limited their appeal to a challenge to the secondary NAAQS, the revision of which the Administrator has declared to be "premature and unwise."

DISCUSSION

Section 304 grants jurisdiction to district courts to compel the Administrator to perform non-discretionary statutory duties. *Cf. Council of Commuter Org. v. Metropolitan Transp. Auth.,* 683 F.2d 663, 665 (2d Cir.1982). Section 307 grants exclusive jurisdiction to the Court of Appeals for the District of Columbia over "final" and other actions of the EPA. Because Section 307 embodies a grant of exclusive jurisdiction, it appears that if the District of Columbia has jurisdiction over the present action, the district court does not. *New England Legal Found. v. Costle,* 666 F.2d 30, 33 (2d Cir.1981). If the District of Columbia Circuit does not have jurisdiction, however, then either the district court has jurisdiction or appellants have no forum in which to assert their claims.

Appellants take the position that the district court has jurisdiction and must order the Administrator to revise the secondary NAAQS. Appellees argue that the Administrator may stand pat, deciding neither to revise the NAAQS nor to make a public decision that revision is unnecessary. In their view, such a non-decision is unreviewable by the Court of Appeals for the District of Columbia under Section 307 because it involves no decision or other agency "action" and is also invulnerable to challenge in district courts under Section 304 because it is discretionary. We disagree with both parties.

In view of the revised criteria and "Critical Assessment," we believe the Administrator must make some decision regarding the revision of the NAAQS that is thereafter reviewable under Section 307 in the Court of Appeals for the District of Columbia. Because the duty to make some decision is nondiscretionary, it is enforceable under Section 304 in the district courts. Appellants argue that in the present case a revision is mandatory and should be ordered by the district court. The substance of the Administrator's decision is beyond the power of the district court, however, its authority being limited to ordering the Administrator to make a formal decision. Were we to order a revision, we would have to set out criteria governing that revision, and the district court would potentially have to apply those criteria in an enforcement proceeding. An order to revise would thus plunge the district court into the merits, matters that are the exclusive province of the District of Columbia Circuit. We appreciate that this distinction is somewhat artificial but believe it is necessary to confine the district court's authority and to defer to the authority of the District of Columbia Circuit. The April 26, 1988 "Proposed Decision Not To Revise," however, has begun the formal process of decision making, and we remand for entry of an order directing that process to continue.

Our analysis begins with an examination of the jurisdiction of the Court of Appeals for the District of Columbia. In *Oljato Chapter of Navajo Tribe v. Train,* 515 F.2d 654 (D.C.Cir.1975), that court held that "a challenge to the Administrator's refusal to revise a standard of performance is in effect a challenge to the standard itself and so can be brought only in this court under Section 307(b)(1) of the Clean Air Act...." *Id.* at 656. This language suggests that the District of Columbia Circuit has exclusive jurisdiction over the instant matter. The categorical language of *Oljato* is, however, misleading. *Oljato* involved Section 111 of the Act, which, at that time, included language permitting, but not requiring, the Administrator to revise the "standards of performance" for new stationary sources of air pollution. Because the statute included no stated deadlines for revision of the standards in question, the *Oljato* court could reasonably treat the decision to revise or not to revise as one wholly within the discretion of the Administrator. Since *Oljato*, however, the District of Columbia Circuit has distinguished between those revision provisions in the Act that include stated deadlines and those that do not, holding that revision provisions that do include stated deadlines should, as a rule, be construed as creating non-discretionary duties. *Sierra Club v. Thomas,* 828 F.2d 783, 791 (D.C.Cir.1987). Section 109(d), the provision at issue here, includes a stated deadline of "[n]ot later than December 31, 1980, and at five-year intervals thereafter." *Oljato* thus does not apply.

The District of Columbia Circuit has also held that it may review agency inaction under the Administrative Procedure Act where the agency has unreasonably delayed in performing a duty over which the District of Columbia Circuit would have jurisdiction after final action under the Act. *Sierra Club,* 828 F.2d at 795-96. Thus, the District of Columbia Circuit arguably has jurisdiction on the grounds that the EPA has unreasonably delayed its decision whether or not to revise the secondary NAAQS for SO_x. The District of Columbia Circuit was careful in *Sierra Club*, however, to limit its exclusive jurisdiction to cases involving "a right the denial of which we would have jurisdiction to review upon final agency action but the integrity of which might be irreversibly compromised by the time such review would occur." *Id.* at 796. Appellants' claimed right in the instant case is not one whose integrity is likely to be "irreversibly compromised." We therefore conclude that the instant action does not raise a claim within the exclusive grant of jurisdiction to the District of Columbia Circuit under Section 307.

Having determined that the District of Columbia Circuit does not have exclusive jurisdiction, we now address what mandatory or, as the case may be, discretionary duties are created by the following language of Section 109(d) of the Act. To repeat, that section states in pertinent part: [n]ot later than December 31, 1980, and at five-year intervals thereafter, the Administrator shall complete a thorough review of the criteria published under section 108 ... and promulgate such new standards as may be appropriate.... The Administrator may review and revise criteria or promulgate new standards earlier or more frequently than required under this paragraph. Clearly this section includes both mandatory ("shall complete," "required") and non-mandatory language ("as may be appropriate"). Appellees rely on the phrase "as may be appropriate," arguing that Judge Edelstein was correct in holding that that language confers on the Administrator a wholly discretionary authority to revise the NAAQS, not to revise them, or simply not to address the issue with a formal public opinion. Appellants argue that, as a matter of statutory construction, Section 109(d) must be interpreted in light of the mandatory language of Sections 109(a) and (b). Section 109(a), which requires the initial promulgation of NAAQS, contains clearly mandatory language directing the Administrator to issue NAAQS within 120 days for those pollutants for which criteria had been published before 1970 and to issue proposed NAAQS simultaneously with the publication of criteria for newly identified pollutants. Appellants argue that Section 109(d) should be read in light of this clearly mandatory language.

We find this argument unpersuasive. Section 109(d) contains no cross-reference to Section 109(a). Moreover, it is difficult to perceive why the standard for the promulgation of initial NAAQS should be identical to that for revised NAAQS. Congress could have repeated the mandatory language of Section 109(a) in Section 109(d), but did not do so. Appellants also argue that Section 109(d) should be read in light of Section 109(b)(2), which declares that secondary NAAQS "shall specify a level of air quality the attainment and maintenance of which in the judgment of the Administrator ... is requisite to protect the public welfare...." Section 109(d) does include a cross-reference to Section 109(b). Because Section 109(b)(2) expressly entrusts the substance of secondary NAAQS to the "judgment of the Administrator," it is difficult to read it as imposing non-discretionary duties. Furthermore, that section adds that secondary NAAQS "may be revised in the same manner as promulgated" (emphasis added). This permissive language suggests that, contrary to appellants' contention, the Administrator has discretion not to follow the procedures for issuing initial NAAQS when revising NAAQS. Harmonizing Section 109(d) with Section 109(b) thus does nothing to further appellants' case.

Appellants also contend that language of Section 109(d) itself, read in isolation, imposes a mandatory duty to revise the NAAQS. The phrase "as may be appropriate," they argue, is subject to the section's command that the Administrator "shall make ... revisions." Under this view, the district court has jurisdiction to order the Administrator to make appropriate revisions in the NAAQS — power in short to issue orders affecting the substance of revised NAAQS. Again we disagree. The words "as may be appropriate" clearly suggest that the Administrator must exercise judgment and the presence of "shall" in the section implies only that the district court has jurisdiction to order the Administrator to make some formal decision whether to revise the NAAQS, the content of that decision being within the Administrator's discretion and reviewable only in the District of Columbia Circuit. *Cf. Natural Resources Defense Council v. New York State Dept. of Envtl. Conservation,* 700 F.Supp. 173 (S.D.N.Y.1988).

Appellants advance a final argument, based on our caselaw. Conceding arguendo that the "as may be appropriate" language creates only discretionary authority, they contend that the district court has jurisdiction to compel the Administrator to revise its secondary NAAQS, the content of the revision being left to the Administrator. Under this view, the Administrator does not have power to decide not to revise. This argument is based on *Natural Resources Defense Council v. Train,* 545 F.2d 320 (2d Cir.1976), which involved Section 108 of the Act. Section 108 requires the Administrator to evaluate potential air pollutants and then to publish a list of those which "endanger public health or welfare," employing the following language: (a)(1) For the purpose of establishing national primary and secondary ambient air quality standards, the Administrator shall within 30 days after December 31, 1970, publish, and shall from time to time thereafter revise, a list which includes each air pollutant—(A) emissions of which in his judgment, cause or contribute to air pollution which may reasonably be anticipated to endanger public health or welfare.... In *Train*, the EPA had evaluated lead, and conceded that lead met its standard for pollutants that "endanger [the] public health or welfare." It refused, however, to include lead on its list of pollutants. The *Train* plaintiffs brought suit, under Section 304, the "Citizen Suits" provision, seeking to compel the EPA to include lead on its pollutant list. In agreeing with the plaintiffs, we reasoned that the EPA had a non-discretionary duty to list lead, noting that the language of Section 108 was clearly mandatory and that the EPA had concededly found lead to "endanger public health or welfare." Because the duty to list lead was not discretionary in light of the finding of harmfulness, we held that the district court had jurisdiction to hear the suit and ordered the Administrator to include lead on his list of pollutants.

Appellants contend that *Train* requires a similar result in the instant case. They observe that the EPA's revised criteria of 1982 and its "Critical Assessment" of 1984-1985 both acknowledge the adverse effects of SO_x-caused acid deposition. The published acknowledgements of those adverse effects are, appellants argue, the equivalent of the EPA's explicit concession in Train concerning the adverse effects of lead. The 1982 criteria and the "Critical Assessment" constitute, in effect, a formal declaration that revision of the SO_x NAAQS is "appropriate" according to the terms of Section 109(d). In their view, the Administrator has thus already exercised his discretion, impliedly found revision to be "appropriate," and now has a non-discretionary duty, enforceable in the district court, to revise the NAAQS in line with his revised criteria.

This argument did not persuade Judge Edelstein, and it does not persuade us. Even if we were to treat the EPA's revised criteria of 1982 and its "Critical Assessment" of 1984-1985 as equivalent to the concession of the harmful effects of lead that underlay our holding in *Train* — and it is far from clear that we should do so, *cf. National Resources Defense Council, Inc. v. Thomas,* 689 F.Supp. 246, 254-56 (S.D.N.Y.1988)—*Train* is still distinguishable from the present case. The duty at issue in *Train* was a thoroughly ministerial one. We did no more than affirm an order compelling the EPA to include "lead" on a list and to issue some NAAQS for lead. We did not, however, specify the content of those NAAQS. *Train,* 545 F.2d at 328. *Train* thus stands solely for the proposition that the district court has jurisdiction, under Section 304, to compel the

Administrator to perform purely ministerial acts, not to order the Administrator to make particular judgmental decisions. An order in the instant case to the Administrator to revise the NAAQS for SO_x would be essentially meaningless and unenforceable unless it also directed that he revise those NAAQS in a particular manner. Formulating the details of substantive NAAQS, however, clearly requires the sort of scientific judgment that is the "hallmark" of agency discretion, *Kennecott Copper Corp., Nevada Mines v. Costle,* 572 F.2d 1349, 1354 (9th Cir.1978); *Lead Industries Ass'n v. EPA,* 647 F.2d 1130, 1146 (D.C.Cir.), *cert. denied,* 449 U.S. 1042 (1980), and is exclusively within the jurisdiction of the District of Columbia Circuit.

However, if *Train* does not justify all of the relief that appellants seek, that is not to say that it does not justify any relief at all. Although the district court does not have jurisdiction to order the Administrator to make a particular revision, we cannot agree with appellees that the Administrator may simply make no formal decision to revise or not to revise, leaving the matter in a bureaucratic limbo subject neither to review in the District of Columbia Circuit nor to challenge in the district court. No discernible congressional purpose is served by creating such a bureaucratic twilight zone, in which many of the Act's purposes might become subject to evasion. The 1982 criteria and the 1984-1985 "Critical Assessment" triggered a duty on the part of EPA to address and decide whether and what kind of revision is necessary. The district court thus does have jurisdiction to compel the Administrator to make some formal decision as to whether or not to revise the secondary NAAQS. *Cf. Natural Resources Defense Council v. New York State Dep't of Envtl. Conservation, supra.*

* * *

Accordingly, we hold that, while the district court did not have jurisdiction to compel the Administrator to revise the NAAQS, it did have jurisdiction to compel the Administrator to take some formal action, employing rulemaking procedures, *see Thomas v. State of New York,* 802 F.2d 1443 (D.C.Cir.1986), either revising the NAAQS or declining to revise them.

However, the Administrator's "Proposed Decision Not To Revise" of April 26, 1988, inviting comments on his determination that a decision as to the advisability of revising the secondary NAAQS for acid deposition "would be premature and unwise," is a required procedure in the course of reaching a formal decision. If this process continues, and a formal decision is rendered, appellants will have obtained all the relief to which they are entitled in a Section 304 action. Whether the decision when reached is wrong on the merits — even egregiously wrong — will be for the District of Columbia Circuit to resolve. We remand so the district court can enter an order directing the Administrator to continue the rulemaking to formal decision.

Reversed and remanded.

[The dissenting opinion of Judge Mahoney, which viewed the *Oljato* case as controlling, is omitted.]

NATURAL RESOURCES DEFENSE COUNCIL v. EPA
512 F.2d 1351 (D.C.Cir. 1975)

BAZELON, Chief Judge:

Natural Resources Defense Council, Inc., (NRDC) brought this action following the publication of final regulations by EPA pursuant to section 211 of the Clean Air Act, as amended. As initially proposed, the regulations had required gasoline retailers to carry at least one grade of unleaded gasoline and had also laid down standards governing the use of lead additives in all grades of gasoline. In final form, they contained only the lead-free brand requirements. Before briefs were filed, NRDC filed a Motion for Prehearing Conference, Summary Reversal, or Expedited Hearing, urging the immediate need for across-the-board controls on lead additives. This motion was denied without prejudice to its renewal if EPA did not take final action in deciding whether to promulgate such controls within 60 days. Subsequent delays by the agency resulted in an order by this court on October 29, 1973, directing EPA to reach a final decision within thirty days. On November 28, 1973, EPA informed the court that it had decided to issue the regulations in question. NRDC now petitions to withdraw its appeal and for an award of costs and attorneys' fees against EPA under section 304(d) of the Act.

The principle of sovereign immunity precludes the award of costs and fees against the United States "in the absence of a statute directly authorizing it ...." In 1966 Congress revamped 28 U.S.C. § 2412 to provide:

> Except as otherwise specifically provided by statute, a judgment for costs ... may be awarded to the prevailing party in any civil action brought by or against the United States or any agency or official of the United States acting in his official capacity ....

But "fees and expenses of attorneys" were specifically excluded from the "costs" which courts were authorized to award. This limitation seems, on its face, inconsistent with the broad principle which led to the revision of section 2412 in the first place: "It is fundamental that the law should be uniform in its application." It also presents a significant impediment to the implementation of the "private-attorney-general" theory, as federal agencies are defendants in a large percentage of public interest cases. Having registered these concerns, however, we are left to determine whether Congress has made a specific grant of attorneys' fees covering this case.

I.

Section 304 of the Clean Air Act Amendments authorizes the award of costs and attorneys' fees "whenever the court determines [that] such [an] award is appropriate." This authorization goes specifically to suits brought under section 304(a), which recognizes actions against the Administrator "where there is alleged a failure ... to perform any act or duty under this chapter which is not discretionary" and grants the district courts jurisdiction to hear these suits and issue appropriate relief. NRDC's action, however, was initiated in this court under section 307(b), which directs petitions for review of specified actions by the Administrator to the circuit courts of appeals. EPA urges us to conclude, therefore, that the provisions of section 304(d) are inapplicable and that in the absence of any other express authorization for the award of fees, NRDC's petition must be rejected.

The same question was considered by the First Circuit in *NRDC v. EPA*. In that case, the court determined that section 304(a) provided the authorization for suits against the Administrator, whether brought in district court or in an appeals court under section 307. Section 307 simply directed that certain actions authorized by section 304(a) be brought in one forum rather than the other. NRDC's appeal was thus an action pursuant to section 304(a) and section 304(d) was applicable. Reluctantly, we find ourselves unable to follow the path by which the First Circuit reached this result.

* * *

Although the major emphasis throughout the development of section 304 was on its role as a vehicle for enforcement of established standards, courts have read it to cover the Administrator's failure to take other steps required of him, such as the promulgation of implementation plans or standards within a specified time. But the language and history do not provide a basis for holding, as a general matter, that section 304 encompasses suits against the Administrator for taking steps alleged to be misguided or uninformed. Review of the Administrator's exercise of judgment, or "discretion," of course, is available under section 307, which establishes exclusive jurisdiction in the courts of appeals for actions within its compass. We conclude, contrary to the First Circuit, that sections 304 and 307 contemplate distinct groups of cases.

Another problem with the view adopted by the First Circuit is simply that the conditions for bringing actions under each section are inconsistent. This point, which is not addressed by the court in NRDC v. EPA, rests on the requirement of section 304(b) that no action may be brought pursuant to section 304(a) prior to sixty days after notification of a Administrator. Section 307 requires that appeals be brought within 30 days of the Administrator's action. NRDC urges that these conflicting requirements must be read functionally. The requirement of section 304(b) has the purpose of allowing the Administrator, and other officials, to rectify inaction. No similar requirement is necessary with regard to suits contemplated under section 307, which covers actions which have already been taken. The notice provisions of section 304(b), NRDC concludes, should not be read as a "stone wall" separating one jurisdiction from the other. We find this argument unconvincing, particularly as it would lead to a rather tortured reading of section 304, whereby a section 307 appeal would be considered an action pursuant to section 304(a) for purposes of subsection (d) but not for purposes of subsection (b).

II.

Having come this far, however, we acknowledge a peculiar and for us somewhat troubling aspect of this case. Although brought under section 307, and properly so, NRDC's appeal also resembles in important respects the class of cases contemplated by section 304(a). This resemblance raises the possibility at least that the suit falls within the intended reach of section 304(d), if not within its literal terms. This possibility was not explored by the parties but is significant enough in our view to warrant a brief discussion.

From one point of view, NRDC sought review of "action of the Administrator in promulgating" final regulations which omitted the controls that NRDC thought were immediately necessary. This is the characterization on which our jurisdiction is premised, and it retains validity even though at the time the administrator issued the rules which provoked NRDC's appeal, he continued to consider the promulgation of across-the-board restrictions at some later time. As we said in *Environmental Defense Fund, Inc. v. Hardin,* the line between action and inaction sometimes disappears, particularly where, as here, the deferral of a ruling involves potentially irreversible consequences for human health. Our jurisdiction over the appeal, as within section 307, is suggested further by the national scope of the regulation involved: as we have indicated, the designation of this court as the exclusive forum for appeals from standard-setting actions by the Administrator was to ensure uniformity in decisions concerning issues of more than purely local or regional impact.

From another point of view, however, NRDC's suit was directed at the "failure of the Administrator to perform [an] act or duty ... which is not discretionary ...," i. e., refusal to promulgate controls which, given the information available to him on the health effects of airborne lead, he had no choice but to promulgate. This characterization may rest on an overly broad reading of what Congress intended by "not discretionary," but it was seriously advanced by EPA itself in initially disputing the power of this court to hear and decide the case. The agency urged that NRDC was required to proceed in district court under section 304(a).

It is the fundamental purpose of section 304(d) to encourage meritorious litigation in furtherance of the goals of the Act. But this formulation does not explain why Congress failed to extend the availability of fees to suits brought under section 307. Perhaps Congress understood that affected industries could be counted on to force review of regulations under the Act, attorneys' fees or no, but that the same concerns would not police the sort of nonregulation addressed by section 304(a). Private citizens and public interest groups could be expected to perform that task-but only if steps were taken to mitigate the high costs of suits involving complex questions. These considerations suggest that the purpose of section 304(d), even construed in its strictest sense, is well-served by the availability of fees in this case and a small group of section 307 actions like it.

We are tempted on this analysis to award fees to NRDC notwithstanding our rejection of the First Circuit's construction of the statute. But to do so would strain the limits of our interpretive function, pressing in a direction contrary to a still vital common law principle. It could also impede the development of clear and workable guidelines for the administration of sections 304 and 307 as the Act's basic jurisdictional grants. We decline to bend the statutory framework to accommodate our good intentions, and leave the matter where it belongs, with Congress.

Leave to withdraw the appeal is granted; in all other respects, petitioner's motion is denied.

J. SKELLY WRIGHT, Circuit Judge (concurring and dissenting):

While I concur in Part I of the court's opinion and in much of the analysis in Part II, I am forced to dissent from the court's decision to deny attorneys' fees in this case.

Judge Bazelon has well outlined the reasons for and against awarding attorneys' fees to the Natural Resources Defense Council (NRDC). I am persuaded by the reasons for awarding fees. The litigation here at issue, while apparently properly brought before this court under Section 307 (1970), could, in my judgment, have been brought in District Court under Section 304 (1970), as well. Of course, so far as this motion is concerned the difference is crucial; Section 304 authorizes attorneys' fees while Section 307 does not. I do not think, however, that the congressional purpose in allowing fees under Section 304 should be frustrated where an action, cognizable under Section 304, is brought under Section 307 instead. I think this is particularly so because the courts have been of so little help to litigants attempting to discern the parameters of Sections 304 and 307. While the courts play jurisdictional badminton with these provisions, batting one case back to the District Court under Section 304 while taking another identical one under Section 307, litigants should not be denied substantial rights because of uncertainty created by courts and Congress. *Compare Sierra Club v. Ruckelshaus,* D.D.C., 344 F.Supp. 253, *affirmed on the basis of the District Court opinion,* 4 BNA Env.Rep.Cas. 1815 (1972), *affirmed by an equally divided Court,* 412 U.S. 541 (1973), *with Anaconda v. Ruckelshaus,* 10 Cir., 482 F.2d 1301 (1973), *reversing* D.Colo., 352 F.Supp. 697 (1972).

I believe NRDC is an innocent victim of this badminton game. When the evidence before the Administrator proved that lead emissions from automobiles endangered the public health, I believe he had no choice but to regulate those emissions. His failure to perform that nondiscretionary duty created District Court jurisdiction over NRDC's claim under Section 304 while his simultaneous promulgation of related lead regulations created jurisdiction in this court under Section 307. I do not believe NRDC should be penalized for suing under Section 307. Since Congress intended that private citizens bringing such public interest litigation should be rewarded with attorneys' fees and since the law is so unsettled as to which section NRDC should properly have utilized, I would award fees to NRDC. My conclusion that the attorneys' fees provision of Section 304 should be read broadly is buttressed by the impossibility of awarding fees on other theories. *Alyeska Pipeline Service Co. v. Wilderness Society,* 421 U.S 240 (1975).

Accordingly, I respectfully dissent from the judgment of the court.

NOTES

1. As Judge Bazelon notes in his majority opinion, the First Circuit reached a different conclusion on similar facts. *Natural Resources Defense Council v. EPA*, 484 F.2d. 1331 (1st Cir. 1973). The court's reasoning in that case was quite simple:

> While the statutory language is confusing, both common sense and the legislative history lead us to conclude that a petition for review is to be regarded as an action pursuant to § 304(a). Section 307 designates the forum; it goes no further. The authorization for, and conditions of, suit are contained in § 304(a). The legislative history reveals that § 307 does no more than direct that some proceedings must be brought in the circuit courts.

Id. at 1336. The court fails, however, to address one of Judge Bazelon's chief concerns — that an action under § 307(b)(1) had to be filed within 30 days (now 60 days) from the date of the Administrator's action, while a citizen suit could not be filed until 60 days' prior notice had been afforded. The Court of Appeals for the Fifth Circuit sided with the D.C. Court in a third case involving the interplay between §§ 304 and 307. *Natural Resources Defense Council v. EPA*, 538 F.2d 1068 (5th Cir. 1976).

2. In 1977, Congress amended § 307(b) of the Act so as to provide expressly for awards of legal fees in cases brought under that section. In describing its action the Senate Report states as follows: "The purpose of the amendments to Section 307 is to carry out the intent of the committee in 1970 that a court may, in its discretion, award costs of litigation to a party bringing a suit under Section 307 of the Clean Air Act. The law has been interpreted otherwise . . . ." S.REP. NO. 95-127, 95th Cong., 1st Sess. 99 (1977).

3. One interesting question raised by these cases, and the subsequent legislative history, is their impact on cases arising under analogous judicial review provisions of other environmental statutes which are patterned after the Clean Air Act of 1970. For example, both the Clean Water Act, 33 U.S.C. §§ 1251 *et set.*, and the Surface Mining

Control and Reclamation Act, 30 U.S.C. §§ 1251 *et seq.*, bifurcate judicial review with separate citizen suit and petition for review provisions which are patterned after those contained in the 1970 Clean Air Act. Neither statute has been amended, however, to provide for fee recoveries in the manner of § 307 of the Clean Air Act. Should a court award fees in cases involving petitions for review under the water and mining statutes? The Court of Appeals for the District of Columbia Circuit answered that question in the negative in a case under the Clean Water Act on the theory that by amending § 307 Congress evinced an intent to award fees on a petition for review only after the law was amended to so provide. *Montgomery Environmental Coalition v. Costle*, 646 F.2d 595 (D.C. Cir. 1981). Is this decision sound in light of the legislative history on the 1977 Amendment to § 307?

4. *Attorney Fees*. Entitlement to attorney fees in cases under the Clean Air Act has received increasing attention by the courts and the Congress. In a landmark case, *Ruckelshaus v. Sierra Club*, 463 U.S. 680 (1983) the Supreme Court construed § 307(f) of the Act, which provides that "the Court may award costs of litigation (including reasonable attorney and expert witness fees) whenever it determines that such an award is appropriate." In a 5-4 decision the Court held that this language, which is identical to language contained in 16 other federal statutes, authorized an award only to parties who prevail in litigation. In a subsequent case under the Civil Rights Act, the Court held that a "partially prevailing plaintiff" is entitled only to a partial award. *Hensley v. Eckerhart*, 461 U.S. 424 (1983). *See also Newman v. Piggie Park Enterprises*, 390 U.S. 400, 402 (1968), where the Court held that normally a prevailing party is entitled to a fee award if a statute authorizes such awards.

5. In 1980, Congress amended 28 U.S.C. § 2412 to authorize awards to parties who prevail in litigation against the United States even where the underlying statute does not otherwise authorize awards. Awards under this law, called the Equal Access to Justice Act, are limited to circumstances where the position of the government is substantially unjustified. The maximum hourly rate for an award to attorneys under this law is $75 (plus cost of living increases).

6. Unlike § 307(b), § 304 of the Act requires 60 days' prior notice to the Administrator, and where appropriate, to the state and alleged violator, before any citizen suit may be filed. § 304(b). The purpose of this provision is to afford the alleged violator an opportunity to correct the violation and thus obviate the need for litigation. *Friends of the Earth v. Potomac Electric Power Co.*, 546 F.Supp. 1357 (D.D.C. 1982). Failure to provide proper notice will probably lead to dismissal of the action, *City of Highland Park v. Train*, 519 F.2d 681 (7th Cir. 1975), but the cases are not uniform in requiring such dismissal. *See e.g., Metropolitan Washington Coalition For Clean Air v. District of Columbia*, 373 F.Supp. 1089 (D.D.C. 1974), *remanded on other grounds*, 511 F.2d 809 (D.C. Cir. 1975) where the court held that the purpose of § 304(b) was met merely by staying the action for 60 days to give the Administrator time to act. 373 F.Supp. at 1092.

7. Another important attorney fee case which arose under the Clean Air Act was *Pennsylvania v. Delaware Valley Citizens' Council for Clear Air,* 478 U.S. 546 (1986); 483 U.S. 711 (1987). In that case the Citizens' Council successfully sued the State of Pennsylvania to compel implementation of a vehicle emission, inspection, and maintenance program required by the SIP. The Council then sought an award of fees which included time spent on administrative proceedings necessary to the litigation. The Council also claimed that the award should be enhanced on the basis of the superior quality of counsel's performance and to account for the risk of no fee award. In two split opinions the Court ruled: (1) that fees could be awarded for administrative work necessary to vindicate the Council's rights; (2) that an award should not be enhanced on the basis of counsel's superior performance absent a showing that counsel had not been adequately compensated; and (3) that fees might be enhanced to account for the risk of loss but not on the facts of this case. This last holding, which addresses the sole issue involved in the Court's second opinion, was supported by four justices who would have allowed enhancement for risk of loss on the facts of the case, and one justice, O'Connor, who would allow an enhancement in an appropriate case but not on the facts of this case. Four justices would allow an enhancement only in exceptional cases "where the need and justification for enhancement are readily apparent and supported by evidence in the record and specific findings by the courts." 483 U.S. at 728.

8. *Standing.* One unique aspect of the Clean Air Act's citizen suit provision is that it appears to confer standing on "any person" whatever their interest in the controversy. Most citizen suit provisions in analogous statutes limit standing to persons with an interest which is or may be adversely affected. *See e.g.*, § 520 of the Surface Mining Control and Reclamation Act, 30 U.S.C. § 1270. The apparent "universal standing" provision in the Act should, however, be viewed with circumspection. The Supreme Court has, on a number of occasions, suggested that the Article III "case or controversy" requirement of the constitution limits standing to persons who are injured by the action of which they complain. *See e.g., Warth v. Selden*, 422 U.S. 490, 499 (1975). This constitutional limitation on the broad standing provision of § 304 was applied by the U.S. District Court of Columbia in *New York v. Thomas*, 613 F.Supp. 1412 (D.D.C. 1985), *rev'd on other grounds*, 802 F.2d 1443, (D.C. Cir. 1986); *see also* Berger, *Standing to Sue in Public Actions: Is it a Constitutional Requirement?* 78 YALE L.J. 816 (1969).

III
BEYOND THE CLEAN AIR ACT

14 GLOBAL CLIMATE CHANGE

CHANGING BY DEGREES
STEPS TO REDUCE GREENHOUSE GASES

Office of Technology Assessment, U.S. Congress, OTA-O-483 (1991)

CLIMATE CHANGE AND GREENHOUSE GASES

The first photographs from space brought home the fact that Earth is an integrated and isolated system. Concern that human impacts could be changing the equilibrium of this system grew in the 1970s as theories about ozone depletion and the "greenhouse effect" developed. The concept of the Earth changing over various time scales was not new: solar and astronomical cycles, the waxing and waning of ice ages, and seasonal changes have long been recognized. What was new was the realization that humans can have a lasting and far-reaching impact on Earth's natural fluctuations and cycles.

Potential human impacts on climate are linked to the globally increasing emission of "greenhouse gases"[1] through activities such as burning fossil fuels (coal, oil, natural gas); deforestation; fertilizing croplands; and heating, air-conditioning, and lighting buildings. Greenhouse gases, like other atmospheric gases, allow sunlight to reach and warm the Earth's surface; unlike other atmospheric gases, however, they trap much of the heat and keep it from escaping back into space. Such gases, therefore, aid in warming the surface of the Earth. Some of them — the chlorofluorocarbons (CFCs) and halons—also react with sunlight in the upper atmosphere to destroy the ozone layer around the Earth. In industrialized countries, greenhouse gas emissions are primarily related to energy use. In developing countries, current greenhouse gas emissions are tied primarily to changes in land use practices (e.g., deforestation).

We cannot yet predict the magnitude of climatic effects from greenhouse gas emissions with accuracy. But it is clear that the decision to limit emissions cannot await

---

[1] The main greenhouses gases are carbon dioxide (CO_2), methane (CH_4), nitrous oxide (N_2O) and chlorofluorocarbons (CFCs). The increase in these gases over natural levels is largely due to actions of humankind; CO_2 levels are rising in the atmosphere at a rate 30 to 100 times faster than observed in the climatic record; CH_4 concentrations are increasing 400 times faster than historically. Most scientists anticipate the global average temperature will increase 2 to 8 °F over the next century if current emission trends continue. Changes in weather, wind and ocean circulation patterns, and sea level are expected, leading to unpredictable changes in agriculture, forests, and human settlements.

the time when the full impacts are evident. The lag time between emission of the gases and their full impact is on the order of decades to centuries;[2] so too is the time needed to reverse any effects. Today's emissions thus commit the planet to changes well into the 21st century. And the lag times between identification of policy options, legislation of controls, and actual implementation can also be considerable. For example, the recent reauthorization of the Clean Air Act took 10 years; implementation of the Act will begin now and continue over the next 10 to 20 years.

Among individual countries, the United States is the leading contributor of greenhouse gases. With 5 percent of the world's population, the Untied States accounts for about 20 percent of the world's warming commitment. U.S. CO_2 emissions (20 percent of the global total) originate almost exclusively from fossil fuel combustion. Anthropogenic sources of methane in the United States account for about 6 percent of global emissions from all sources; among the anthropogenic sources, landfills, coal mining, and domestic animals account for most of the U.S. total. The United States also consumes between 20 and 30 percent of the world's CFC-11 and CFC-12, the two most damaging chlorofluorocarbons in terms of global warming. Roughly 60 to 70 percent of these CFCs are used in air-conditioning or in the production of thermal insulation; these gases are scheduled to be phased out by the year 2000 under the revised Montreal Protocol. U.S. nitrous oxide emissions (roughly 15 to 20 percent of the manmade global total) originate primarily from fertilizer breakdown and high-temperature fossil-fuel combustion. Greenhouse gas emissions are closely entwined in the United States with energy use; currently, America uses about 15 times more energy per person than does the typical developing country.

The warming commitment or "radiative forcing" caused by the different greenhouse gases is not equal. It depends on the absorbing characteristics, concentration in the atmosphere, and the lifetime of each gas. Although the other gases are more potent on a per molecule basis, currently CO_2 accounts for an estimated 55 percent of the commitment to global warming. This is largely due to the fact that so much CO_2 has been emitted worldwide (6 billion metric tons of carbon in 1988) as to swamp the higher radiative forcings per unit of the other gases. Still, CFCs are responsible for 24 percent of the current commitment to global warming; CH_4 is responsible for 15 percent and N_2O for 6 percent.

Recently, public interest and concern over global changes intensified with the discovery of the annual ozone hole over Antarctica, thinning ozone over the Arctic, the severe drought of 1988, and recent abnormal weather patterns in Europe. International concern was demonstrated by the recent rapid renegotiation of the Montreal Protocol to completely phase out CFCs and assist developing countries in achieving that goal. Many industrialized countries, principally in Europe, have further called for a 20-percent reduction in CO_2 emissions from the developed world by 2000 or shortly thereafter; several have pledged to freeze or reduce emissions whether or not the rest of the world participates.

Meanwhile, there is a debate here as to whether and when a freeze or a 20-percent reduction in U.S. greenhouse gas emissions could be achieved in the near-term. A 20-percent reduction in U.S. CO_2 and less than a 2-percent decline in current worldwide

---

[2] The atmospheric lifetime of CO_2 is 50 to 200 years; N_2O about 150 years; CFCs and halons, from 60 to 400 years; and CH_4 10 years. CFC replacements allowed under the Montreal Protocol for the next several decades have lifetimes of less than 40 years.

emissions of all greenhouse gases. More importantly, however, even if a 20-percent cut by all developed Nations could be achieved, it would not be enough to stabilize the atmosphere at today's level, let alone to reduce greenhouse gases to pre-industrial levels. To stabilize the atmosphere, which the Intergovernmental Panel on Climate Change and the Environmental Protection Agency (EPA) suggest, would require much more — up to an 80-percent global reduction in CO_2 emissions from current levels as well as significant reductions in the other greenhouse gases. To achieve this under the combined pressures of economic and population growth, nonfossil fuel technologies such as solar or nuclear power would be needed to replace much of today's fossil fuel use.

Energy conservation is the logical first step for the Unites States if it wishes to reduce its own CO_2 emissions below present levels over the next 25 years. For comparison, if no actions are taken, emissions of CO_2 will likely rise 50 percent during the next quarter century. Under a set of modest policies designed to encourage people to choose technologies that are cost-effective, emissions of CO_2 probably will rise about 15 percent over the next 25 years. This policy package is labeled OTA's "Moderate" scenario.

OTA also identified an energy conservation, energy-supply, and forest-management package that can achieve a 20- to 35-percent emissions reduction. This package is labeled OTA's "Tough" scenario. While difficult to achieve, major technological breakthroughs are not needed. Existing equipment would not have to be instantly scrapped and replaced with untested prototypes. The requisite energy-related technologies are either already available or are demonstrated and close to commercialization today. Most of the forestry-related practices also are proven and already commercialized. OTA's Tough scenario thus does not represent "maximum technological potential." Although it could be argued, for example, that there is a "technical potential" for a massive return to nuclear power by 2015, we assume that this is not feasible for the United States, given lead times and current public concerns. Likewise, we assume that a massive penetration of solar based electricity generation will not take place by then. Nor will most people be driving 80 mile per gallon (mpg) cars, although prototypes are available today. In each of these cases, though, increased research, development, and demonstration (RD&D) could bring substantial benefits within a half-century.

In the OTA analysis of energy-related activities, only those technical options that would result in CO_2 emissions reductions without loss of comfort or convenience were examined. If implemented, the energy conservation options discussed in our Moderate scenario would likely save consumers money over the lifetime of, for example, an energy-using appliance, given today's energy costs. Greater reductions are quite feasible, as our Tough scenario shows, with technologies that are either technically challenging or more expensive.

* * *

NOTES

1. Like stratospheric ozone depletion, global climate change is caused by the total emissions of certain gases throughout the world. Thus, the problem lends itself to a similar world-wide solution. Unfortunately, a consensus has yet to develop over the appropriate solution. In particular, the United States has been reluctant to commit to establishing CO_2 emissions at 1990 levels by the year 2000 as had originally been proposed for the Earth Summit in Rio de Janeiro, Brazil, in 1992. Why does global warming pose a more difficult problem for international resolution than stratospheric ozone depletion?

2. Global climate change, and the impacts of CO_2 on this phenomenon, received much discussion during the debate over the 1990 Amendments. Ultimately, however, Congress settled for a provision which requires "all affected sources subject to title V of the Clean Air Act [to] . . . monitor carbon dioxide emissions. . . ." Clean Air Act Amendments of 1990, § 821(a). EPA is required to incorporate data from all such sources in a computer data base and make the "aggregate annual data" available to the public. *Id.* at § 821(b).

3. The day after the 1990 amendments were signed into law, President Bush signed the Global Charge Research Act of 1990, P.L. 101-606, 104 Stat. 3096. The purpose of this law is to coordinate and promote research on global change issues in the United States and abroad. The Act also establishes a Global Charge Research Information Office, whose purpose is to disseminate information throughout the world "which would be useful in preventing, mitigating or adapting to the effects of global change." *Id.* at § 204.

4. The options discussed in the OTA report are set out after the following excerpt from an EPA report which describes some of the impacts that might be anticipated from global climate change.

THE POTENTIAL EFFECTS OF GLOBAL CLIMATE CHANGE ON THE UNITED STATES

Report to Congress, EPA-230-05-89-050 (1989)

Scientific theory suggests that the addition of greenhouse gases to the atmosphere will alter global climate, increasing temperatures and changing rainfall and other weather patterns. In 1979, the National Academy of Sciences estimated the most probable global warming from a doubling of carbon dioxide concentrations over preindustrial levels to be between 1.5 and 4.5°C. In 1985, the World Meteorological Organization (WMO), the United Nations Environment Programme (UNEP), and the International Council of Scientific Unions (ICSU) reaffirmed these estimates. Such a climate change could have significant implications for mankind and the environment: it could raise sea level, alter patterns of water availability, and affect agriculture and global ecosystems.

Although there is consensus that increased greenhouse gas concentrations will change global climate, the rate and magnitude of change are not certain (see box entitled "Climate Change"). Uncertainties about climate feedbacks from clouds, vegetation, and other factors make it difficult to predict the exact amount of warming that a given level of greenhouse gases, such as doubled carbon dioxide (CO_2) concentrations, would cause. How quickly climate may change also is not known, because scientists are uncertain both about how rapidly heat will be taken up by the oceans and about some climate feedback processes. Generally, scientists assume that current trends in emissions will continue and that climate will change gradually over the next century, although at a much faster pace than historically. At this rate, the full effect of the equivalent doubling of CO_2 concentrations probably would not be experienced until after 2050. It is possible, however, that sudden changes in ocean circulation could cause abrupt changes in global climate. Indeed, if climate changed more rapidly than estimated, adapting to the effects would be more difficult and more costly. Furthermore, continued emissions of greenhouse gases could raise atmospheric concentrations beyond doubled CO_2 causing greater and more rapid climate changes, and larger effects.

CLIMATE CHANGE

A panel of experts convened by the National Academy of Sciences (National Research Council, 1987) recently gave the following estimates of scientific confidence in predictions of the climate response to increased greenhouse gas concentrations. This table summarizes only their conclusions concerning "the possible climate responses to increased greenhouse gases." The full report should be consulted for the details.

Large Stratospheric Cooling (virtually certain). The combination of increased cooling by additional CO_2 and other trace gases, and reduced heating by reduced ozone, "will lead to a major lowering of temperatures in the upper stratosphere."

Global-Mean Surface Warming (very probable). For an equivalent doubling of CO_2, "the long-term global-mean surface warming is expected to be in the range of 1.5 to 4.5° C."

Global-Mean Precipitation Increase (very probable). "Increased heating of the [Earth's] surface will lead to increased evaporation and, therefore, to greater global mean precipitation. Despite this increase in global average precipitation, some individual regions might well experience decreases in rainfall."

Reduction of Sea Ice (very probable). This will be due to melting as the climate warms.

Polar Winter Surface Warming (very probable). Due to the sea ice reduction, polar surface air may warm by as much as 3 times the global average.

Summer Continental Dryness/Warming (likely in the long term). Found in several, but not all, studies, it is mainly caused by earlier termination of winter storms. "Of course, these simulations of long-term equilibrium conditions may not offer a reliable guide to trends over the next few decades of changing atmospheric composition and changing climate."

To explore the implication of climate change and ways to control it, Congress asked the U.S. Environmental Protection Agency (EPA) to undertake two studies on the greenhouse effect: the first study was to address "The potential health and environmental effects of climate change including, but not limited to, the potential impacts on agriculture, forests, wetlands, human health, rivers, lakes estuaries as well as societal impacts;" and the second study was to examine "policy options that if implemented would stabilize current levels of greenhouse gas concentrations." The second study, "Policy Options for Stabilizing Global Climate," is a companion report to this document.

EPA responded to this request by first holding workshops with atmospheric scientists to discuss the use of global climate change models for impact analyses and then meeting with ecologists, hydrologists, geographers, and forestry and agricultural specialists to identify topics for this study. A major purpose was to bridge the gap in our ability to relate a rise in average annual surface temperatures to regional climate changes. Based on these and other discussions, EPA decided to use common scenarios of climate change to analyze the sensitivities of coastal resources, water resources, and electricity demand to climate change on regional and national scales. These systems were chosen for analysis because they are sensitive to climate and significantly affect our quality of life. EPA decided to conduct regional analyses for the Southeast, the Great Plains, California, and the Great Lakes, because of their climatological, ecological, hydrological, and economic diversity. Leading academic and government scientists in the relevant fields used published models to estimate the impacts on both the regional and national scales. As a common base for conducting these analyses, they used the scenarios specified by EPA.

After consulting with scientific experts, EPA developed scenarios for use in effects analysis. Regional data from atmospheric models known as General Circulation Models (GCMs) were used as a basis for climate change scenarios. The GCMs are large models of the ocean-atmosphere system that simulate the fundamental physical relationships in the system. GCMs provide the best scientific estimates of the impacts of increased greenhouse gas concentrations on climate. Yet they use relatively simple models of oceans and clouds, both of which will be very critical in influencing climate change. The GCMs generally agree concerning global and latitudinal increases in temperature, but they disagree and are less reliable concerning other areas, such as regional changes in rainfall and soil moisture. The GCM data were compared with historic meteorologic data. In addition, the decade of the 1930s was used as an analog for global warming.

* * *

NATIONAL FINDINGS

Natural Systems

The location and composition of various plants and animals in the natural environment depend, to a great extent, on climate. Trees grow in certain areas and fish exist in streams and lakes because the local climate and other conditions are conducive to reproduction and growth. A major focus of this report was to identify what may happen to plants and animals, as a result of climate change — whether they would survive in their current locations or be able to migrate to new habitats, and how soon these ecosystems could be affected. The following descriptions of impacts on natural systems are subject to uncertainties about climate change and the responses of natural systems to such change.

Natural Systems May Be Unable to Adapt Quickly to a Rapid Warming

If the current trends continue, climate may change too quickly for many natural systems to adapt. In the past, plants and animals adapted to historic climate changes over many centuries. For example, since the last ice age 18,000 years ago, oak trees migrated northward from the southeastern United States as the ice sheet receded. Temperatures warmed about 5° C (9° F) over thousands of years, but they rose slowly enough for forests to migrate at the same rate as climate change. In the future, the greenhouse effect may lead to similar changes in the magnitude of warming, but the changes may take place within a century. Climate zones may shift hundreds of miles northward, and animals and especially plants may have difficulty migrating northward that quickly.

Forests

Forests occupy one-third of the land area of the United States. Temperature and precipitation ranges are among the determinants of forest distributions. Forests are also sensitive to soils, light intensity, air pollution, pests and pathogens, disturbances such as fires and wind, and management practices.

Several approaches were used to examine geographic shifts in forests. Potential ranges of forests were estimated for eastern North American using temperature and precipitation correlations from pollen data. Changes in composition and abundance of particular forests were estimated for particular sites in the Great Lakes and Southeast using site-specific models. These regions were chosen to represent a diversity of forest types and uses. Finally, the ability of trees to migrate to new habitats was analyzed using shifts in climate zones from GCMs and historic rates of tree migration. This study focused on several species that are widely dispersed across the northeastern United States. The direct effects of CO_2, which could change water-use efficiency, pest interactions, and the competitive balance among plants, were not modeled, nor were reforestation or the suitability of soils and sunlight considered. It is not clear how these results would have been affected if such factors had been included.

The Range of Trees May Be Reduced

* * *

[C]limate change could move the southern boundary of forest ranges northward by 600-700 km (approximately 400 miles), while the northern boundary would move only as fast as the rate of migration of forests. Assuming a migration rate of 100 km (60 miles) per century, or double the known historic rate, the inhabited ranges of forests could be significantly reduced because the southern boundary may advance more quickly than the northern boundary. Even if climate stabilizes, it could take centuries for migration to reverse this effect. If climate continues to warm, migration would continue to lag behind shifts in climate zones. If elevated CO_2 concentrations increase the water-use efficiency of tree species and pest infestations do not worsen, the declines of the southern ranges could be partially alleviated. Reforestation could help speed the migration of forests into new areas.

Changes in Forest Composition Are Likely

Climate change may significantly alter forest composition and reduce the land area of healthy forests. Higher temperatures may lead to drier soils in many parts of the country. Trees that need wetter soils may die, and their seedlings could have difficulty surviving these conditions. A study of forests in northern Mississippi and northern Georgia indicated that seedlings currently in such areas would not grow because of high temperatures and dry soil conditions. In central Michigan, forests now dominated by sugar maple and oak may be replaced by grasslands, with some sparse oak trees surviving. These analyses did not consider the introduction of species from areas south of these regions. In northern Minnesota, the mixed boreal and northern hardwood forests could become entirely northern hardwoods. Some areas might experience a decline in productivity, while others (currently saturated soils) might have an increase. The process of changes in species composition would most likely continue for centuries. Other studies of the potential effects of climate change in forests imply northward shifts in ranges and significant changes in composition, although specific results vary depending on sites and scenarios used.

Changes May Begin in 30 to 80 Years

Forest change may be visible in a few decades from now. This would involve a faster rate of mortality among mature trees and a decline in seedlings and growth of new species. The studies of forests in Southeast and Great Lakes indicate that these forests could begin to die back in 30 to 80 years.

* * *

At the same time in Minnesota, for example, sugar maple could become more abundant. These forests appear to be very sensitive to small changes in climate, because dieback starts to become noticeable after an approximate 1 to 1.5° C warming. Once this process starts, major dieback may occur rapidly. The timing of a decline is sensitive to the rate of climate change; a warming slower than that assumed in the scenarios would delay the dieback.

* * *

Biodiversity

Biological diversity can be defined as the variety of species in ecosystems, and the genetic variability within each species and the variety of ecosystems around the world. Over 400 species of mammals, 460 species of reptiles, 660 species of freshwater fishes, and tens of thousands of invertebrate species can be found in this country, in addition to some 22,000 plant species. About 650 species of birds reside in or pass through the United States annually. Biological diversity is needed to provide food, medicine, shelter, and other important products.

This report examined the impacts of climate change on specific plants and animals by using climate change scenarios and models of particular species or systems within a region. Analyses have been performed for impacts on finfish and shellfish in the Apalachicola Bay in the Florida Panhandle, fish in the Great Lakes, and marine species in San Francisco Bay. Additional information on potential impacts in biodiversity was gathered from the published literature.

Extinction of Species Could Increase

Historic climate changes, such as the ice ages, have led to extinction of many species. More recently, human activities, such as deforestation have greatly accelerated the rate of species extinction. The faster rate of climate warming due to the greenhouse effect, absent an active program to preserve species, would most likely lead to an even greater loss of species. The uncertainties surrounding the rate of warming, the response of individual species, and interspecies dynamics make it difficult to access the probable impacts, although natural ecosystems are likely to be destabilized in unpredictable ways.

* * *

Impacts on Fisheries Would Vary

Freshwater fish populations may grow in some areas and decline in others. Fish in such large water bodies as the Great Lakes may grow faster and may be able to migrate to new habitats. Increased amounts of plankton could provide more forage for fish. However, higher temperatures may lead to more aquatic growth, such as algal blooms, and decreased mixing of lakes (longer stratification), which would deplete oxygen levels in shallow areas of the Great Lakes, for example, Lake Erie, and make them less habitable for fish. Fish in small lakes and streams may be unable to escape temperatures beyond their tolerances, or their habitats may simply disappear.

* * *

Sea Level Rise

A rise in sea level is one of the more probable impacts of climate change. Higher global temperatures will expand ocean water and melt some mountain glaciers, and may eventually cause polar ice sheets to discharge ice. Over the last century, global sea level has risen 10 to 15 cm (4 to 6 inches), and along the U.S. coastline, relative sea level rise (which includes land subsidence) has averaged about 30 cm (1 foot). Published estimates of sea level rise due to global warming generally range from 0.5 to 2.0 meters (1.5 to 7 feet) by 2100. Sea level rise could be greater than or less than this range because uncertainties exist regarding the rate of atmospheric warming, glacial processes, oceanic uptake of heat, precipitation in polar areas, and other variables.

* * *

Protecting Developed Areas May Be Expensive

Given the high property values of developed coastlines in the United States, it is likely that measures would be taken to hold back the sea along most developed shores. Preliminary estimates suggest that the cumulative capital costs (including response to current sea level rise) of protecting currently developed areas would be $73 to $111 billion (in 1988 dollars) through 2100 for a 1-meter global rise (compared with $4 to $6 billion to protect developed areas from current trends in sea level rise). A 1-meter sea level rise would lead to a cumulative inundation of 7,000 square miles of dryland — an area the size of Massachusetts. If the oceans continue to rise at current rates, approximately 3,000 square miles of dryland would be lost.

Most Coastal Wetlands Would Be Lost

Historically, wetlands have kept pace with a slow rate of sea level rise. However, in the future, sea level will probably rise too fast for some marshes and swamps to keep pace. Although some wetlands can survive by migrating inland, a study on coastal wetlands estimated that for a 1-meter rise, 26 to 66% of wetlands would be lost, even if these losses would be in the South (see Table 2). Efforts to protect coastal development would increase wetland losses, because bulkheads and levees would prevent new wetlands from forming inland. If all shorelines are protected, 50 to 82% of wetlands would be lost.

The loss of woodland area would have adverse ecological impacts, with the ability of ecosystems to survive a rising sea level depending greatly on how shorelines are managed. For many fish and shellfish species, the fraction of shorelines along which wetlands can be found is more important than the total area of wetlands. This fraction could remain at approximately present levels if people do not erect additional bulkheads and levees. In Louisiana, with 40% of U.S. coastal wetlands, large areas of wetlands are already being converted to open water as a result of natural subsidence and the effects of human activities, and most could be lost by 2030 if current trends continue.

Estuaries May Enlarge and Become More Saline

Although future riverflows into estuaries are uncertain, a rise in sea level would increase the size and salinity of estuaries and would increase the salinity of coastal aquifers. For example, sea level rise may result in a more saline and enlarged Sacramento-San Joaquin Delta, and Miami, New York, and other coastal communities would have to step up current efforts to combat salinity increases in surface water and groundwater supplies.

Agriculture

The temperate climate and rich soils in the United States, especially in the Midwest, have helped make this country the world's leading agricultural producer. Agriculture, a critical component of the U.S. economy, contributed 17.5% of the gross national product in 1985, with farm assets totaling $771 billion. Crop production is sensitive to climate, soils, management methods, and many other factors. During the Dust Bowl years of the 1930s, wheat and corn yields dropped by up to 50%, and during the drought of 1988, corn yields declined about 40%.

The agricultural analyses in this report examined potential impacts on crop yields and productivity from changes in climate and direct effects of CO_2. (Higher CO_2 concentrations may increase plant growth and water-use efficiency.) The studies used high estimates of the beneficial effects of CO_2 on crops. Changes in dryland and irrigated corn, wheat, and soybean yields and in irrigation demand were estimated for the Southeast, Great Plains, and Great Lakes regions using widely validated crop growth models. Crop yield changes were estimated for California using a simple agroclimatic index. The studies did not examine effects on yields of introduction of crops, such as citrus, into new areas; changes in week growth caused by higher CO_2 concentrations; or new technologies, such as biotechnology. Some of these changes could enhance the ability of agriculture to adapt to global warming.

The estimated yield changes from the four regional crop modeling studies and runoff changes from the GCMs were used in a nationwide agricultural economic model to estimate regional and national changes in crop production, land use, and demand for irrigation. The economic model did not consider the introduction of new crops, changes in government policies on agriculture, uses, and global agricultural changes. Both a modeling study and a literature review were used to estimate changes in plant-pest interactions. An agricultural runoff and leaching model was used to estimate potential changes in water quality in the Great Plains. Some farm-level adjustments, including the effects of changed planting dates and various studies, and the potential national implications on livestock were analyzed using modeling studies and a literature review.

Yields Could Be Reduced Although the Combined Effects of Climate and CO_2 Would Depend on the Severity of Climate Change

In most regions of the country, climate change alone could reduce dryland yields of corn, wheat, and soybeans, with site-to-site losses ranging from negligible amounts to 80%. These decreases would be primarily the result of higher temperatures, which would shorten a crop's life cycle. In very northern areas, such as Minnesota, dryland yields of corn and soybeans could increase as warmer temperatures extend the frost-free growing season. The combined effects of climate change and increased CO_2 may result in net increases in yields in some cases, especially in northern areas or in areas where rainfall is abundant. In southern areas, however, where heat stress is already a problem, and in areas where rainfall is reduced, crop yields could decline.

Productivity May Shift Northward

Under all the scenarios (with and without the direct effects of increased CO_2), the relative productivity of northern areas for the crops studied was estimated to rise in comparison with that of southern areas. In response to the shift in relative yields, grain crop acreage in Appalachia, the Southeast, and the Southern Great Plains could decrease, and acreage in the northern Great Lakes States, the northern Great Plains, and the Pacific Northwest could increase. A change in agriculture would affect not only the livelihood of farmers but also agricultural infrastructure and other support services.

The National Supply of Agricultural Commodities May be Sufficient to Meet Domestic Needs, But Exports May Be Reduced

Even under the more extreme climate change scenarios, the production capacity of U.S. agriculture was estimated to be adequate to meet domestic needs. Only small to moderate economic losses were estimated when the climate change scenarios were modeled without the beneficial effects of CO_2 on crop yields. When the combined effects of climate and CO_2 were considered, results were positive with a relatively wetter climate change scenario and negative with the hotter, drier climate change scenario. Thus, the severity of the economic consequences that occurs and the ability of the direct effects of CO_2 to enhance yields. A decline in crop production would reduce exports, which could have serious implications for food-importing nations. If climate change is severe, continued and substantial improvements in crop yields would be needed to fully offset the negative effects. Technological improvements, such as improved crop varieties from bioengineering, could be helpful in keeping up with climate change. These results could be affected by global changes in agriculture, which were not considered in the analysis.

Farmers Would Likely Change Many of Their Practices

Farm practices would likely change in response to different climate conditions. Most significantly, in many regions, the demand for irrigation is likely to increase as a result of higher temperatures. If national productivity declines, crop prices may rise, making irrigation more economical and increasing the use of it. Irrigation equipment may be installed in many areas that are currently dryland farms, and farmers already irrigating may extract more water from surface and groundwater sources. Changes in competing demands for water by municipal and industrial users, which could raise the cost of irrigation, were not considered. Farmers may also switch to more heat- and drought-resistant crop varieties, plant two crops during a growing season, and plant and harvest earlier. Whether these adjustments would compensate for climate change depends on a number of factors, including the severity of the climate change. Under extreme climate change conditions, some farms could be abandoned.

Ranges of Agricultural Pests May Extend Northward

Warmer temperatures may result in the northward extension of the range of diseases and pests that now afflict livestock in the South, and could make conditions more favorable for the introduction of new livestock diseases into the southern United States. This extension could reduce crop yields and affect livestock.

Shifts in Agriculture May Harm the Environment in Some Areas

Expansion of irrigation and shifts in regional production patterns imply more competition for water resources, greater potential for surface water and groundwater pollution, loss of some wildlife habitats, and increased soil erosion. A northward migration of agriculture would increase the use of irrigation and fertilizers on sandy soils, thus endangering the quality of underlying groundwater. Chemical pesticide usage may change to control different crop and livestock pests. Thus, climate change could exacerbate environmental pollution and increase resource use from agriculture in some areas.

Water Resources

The United States is endowed with a bountiful supply of water, but the water is not always in the right place at the right time or of the right quality. In some regions, such as the Great Basin and the Colorado River Basin, the gap between demand and supply of water is narrow. In these basins, such offstream uses as irrigation and domestic consumption often conflict with each other and with other needs, such as maintaining flow to preserve environmental quality.

Although global precipitation is likely to increase, it is not known how regional rainfall patterns will be affected. Some regions may have more rainfall, while others may have less. Furthermore, higher temperatures would most likely increase evaporation. These changes would likely create new stresses for many water management systems.

To discuss the potential impacts of climate change on water resources, this report studies water resources in California, the Great Lakes, and the Southeast, estimated the demand for irrigation in the Great Plains, and drew on information from the literature. These studies focused on changes in runoff and, for California and the Southeast, considered management responses. The studies examined the water management systems as they are currently configured and did not examine new construction. Among other factors not considered were changes in demand for water resources (which would most likely lead to greater changes in water management systems) and changes in vegetation due to climate change and increased CO_2, which could affect runoff. The studies did not estimate impacts on groundwater.

The Direction in Some Water Bodies Can Be Estimated, but Total Impacts in the United States Cannot Be Determined

Results of hydrology studies indicate that it is possible in some regions to identify the direction of change in water supplies and quality due to global warming. For example, in California, higher temperatures would reduce the snowpack and cause earlier melting. Earlier runoff from mountains could increase winter flooding and reduce snowpack combined with potentially higher evaporation could lower lake levels (although certain combinations of conditions could lead to higher levels). In other areas, such as the South, little snowcover currently exists, so riverflow and lake levels depend more on rainfall patterns. Without better rainfall estimates, we cannot determine whether riverflow and lake levels in the South would rise or fall.

Water Quality in Many Basins Could Change

Changes in water supply could significantly affect water quality. Where riverflow and lake levels decline, such as in the Great Lakes, there would be less water to dilute pollutants. On the other hand, where there is more water, water quality may improve. Higher temperatures may enhance thermal stratification in some lakes and increase algal production, degrading water quality. Changes in runoff and leaching from farms and potential increases in the use of irrigation for agriculture could affect surface and groundwater quality in many areas.

Water Use Conflicts May Increase

In some regions, decreased water availability and increased demand for water, such as for irrigation and powerplant cooling, may intensify conflicts among offstream uses. Conflicts between these offstream uses and instream uses such as flood control and wildlife habitat also may be intensified.

Electricity Demand

The demand for electricity is influenced by economic growth, by changes in industrial and residential/commercial technologies, and by climate. The principal climate-sensitive electricity end uses are space heating and cooling and, to a lesser degree, water heating and refrigeration. These uses of electricity may account for up to a third of total sales from some utilities and may contribute an even larger portion of seasonal and daily peak demands.

This report analyzed potential changes in the national demand for electricity in 2010 and 2055, for several major utility systems. The study estimated changes in demand due to nonclimate factors, such as increases in population and GNP. The impacts of climate change are expressed as an increase over non-climate growth, and results are given on nationwide and regional bases. The study did not consider changes in technology and improvements in energy efficiency; the impacts of higher temperatures on the demand for natural gas and oil for home heating, which will most likely decrease; changes in electricity supplies, such as hydropower; or changes in demand for electricity for such uses as irrigation.

National Electricity Demand Would Rise

Global warming would increase annual demand for electricity and total generating capacity requirements in the United States. The demand for electricity for summer cooling would increase, and the demand for electricity for winter heating would decrease. Annual electricity generation in 2055 was estimated under the transient scenarios to be 4 to 6% greater than without climate change. The annual costs of meeting the increase due to global warming, assuming no change in technology or efficiency, was estimated to be $33-73 billion (in 1986 dollars). These results differ on a regional basis. States along the northern tier of the United States could have net reductions in annual demand of up to 5%, because decreased heating demand would exceed increased demand for air conditioning. In the South, where heating needs are already low, net demand was estimated to rise 7 to 11% by 2055.

Generating capacity requirements are determined largely by peak demand, which occurs in the summer in all but the far northern areas of the country. By 2010, generating requirements to meet increased demand could rise by 25 to 55 gigawatts (GW), or by 9 to 19% above new capacity requirements, assuming no climate change. By 2055, generating requirements could be up by 200 to 400 GW, or 14 to 23% above non-climate-related growth. The cumulative cost of such an increase in capacity, assuming no change in technology or improvements in energy efficiency, was estimated to be between $175 and $325 billion (1988 dollars). The South would have a greater need than the North for additional capacity. Increases in capacity requirements could range from 0 to 10% in the North, to 20 to 30% in the South and Southwest. U.S. emissions of such greenhouse gases as CO_2 could increase substantially if additional powerplants are built to meet these capacity requirements, especially if they burn coal. Improvement in the efficiency of energy production and use would reduce these emissions.

Air Quality

Air pollution caused by emissions from industrial and transportation sources is a subject of concern in the United States. Over the last two decades, considerable progress has been made in improving air quality by reducing emissions. Yet high temperatures in the summer of 1988 helped raise tropospheric ozone levels to all-time highs in many U.S. cities. But air quality is also directly affected by other weather variables, such as windspeed and direction, precipitation patterns, cloud cover, atmospheric water vapor, and global circulation patterns.

A literature review of the relationship between climate and air pollution was conducted for this report. In addition, air quality models were used for a preliminary analysis of the changes in ozone levels in several regions. The latter analysis did not consider reduction in emissions of air pollutants due to enforcement of the Clean Air Act.

Climate Changes Could Increase Air Pollution, Especially Smog

A rise in global temperatures would increase man-made and natural emissions of hydrocarbons and man-made emissions of sulfur and nitrogen oxides over what they would be without climate change. Natural emissions of sulfur would also change, but the direction is uncertain. Although the potential magnitude of the impacts of the increased emissions on air quality is uncertain, higher temperatures would speed the reaction rates among chemicals in the atmosphere, causing higher ozone pollution in many urban areas than would occur otherwise. They would also increase the length of the summer season, usually a time of high air pollution levels.

* * *

[P]reliminary analyses of a 4°C temperature increase in the San Francisco Bay area (with no changes in other meteorologic variables, such as mixing heights), assuming no change in emissions from current levels, suggest that maximum ozone concentrations would increase by 20%, and that the area exceeding the National Ambient Air Quality Standards would almost double. Studies of the Southeast also show expansion of the areas violating the standards, but they show smaller changes in levels. Although the impacts of higher temperatures on acid rain were not analyzed, it is likely that sulfur and nitrogen would oxidize more rapidly under higher temperatures. The ultimate effect on acid deposition is difficult to assess because changes in clouds, winds, and precipitation patterns are uncertain.

Health Effects

Human illness and mortality are linked in many ways to weather patterns. Weather affects contagious diseases such as influenza and pneumonia, and allergic diseases such as asthma. Mortality rates, particularly for the elderly and the very ill, are influenced by the frequency and severity of extreme temperatures. The life cycles of disease-carrying insects, such as mosquitoes and ticks, are affected by changes in temperature and rainfall, as well as by habitat, which is itself sensitive to climate. Finally, increased air pollution, which is related to weather patterns, can heighten the incidence and severity of such respiratory diseases as emphysema and asthma.

Both expert judgment and modeling were used to study the potential impacts of climate change on human health. A literature review and workshop were conducted to identify potential changes in vector-borne diseases caused by ticks, fleas, and mosquitoes (such as dengue and malaria). Models were used to estimate potential geographic shifts in the prevalence of Rocky Mountain spotted fever and malaria. Potential changes in mortality from heat and cold stress were quantitatively estimated, although such estimates did not consider changes in air pollution levels. The total impacts of climate change on human health are difficult to assess; these analyses looked at a limited number of potential effects and are only indicative of possible changes in mortality and morbidity.

Summer Mortality Could Increase, While Winter Mortality Could Decrease

Global warming may lead to changes in morbidity and increases in mortality, particularly for the elderly during the summer. Morbidity and mortality may decrease because of milder winters, although net mortality may increase. If the frequency or intensity of climate extremes increases, mortality is likely to rise. If people acclimatize by using air-conditioning, changing their workplace habits, and altering the construction of their homes and cities, the impact on summer mortality rates may be substantially reduced.

Regional Morbidity Patterns Could Change

Changes in climate as well as in habitat may alter the regional prevalence of vector-borne diseases. For example, some forests may become grasslands, thereby modifying the incidence of vector-borne diseases. Changes in summer rainfall could alter the amount of ragweed growing on cultivated land, and changes in humidity may affect the incidence and severity of skin infections and infestations such as ringworm, candidiasis, and scabies. Increases in the persistence and level of air pollution episodes associated with climate change would have other harmful health effects.

Urban Infrastructure

The value of municipal infrastructure in the United States, excluding buildings and electric power production, probably approaches one trillion dollars. The majority of the nation's investments are in water supply, wastewater transport and treatment facilities, drainage, roadways, airports, and mass transit facilities. Like the regions studied for this report, urban areas would feel a variety of impacts from climate change. This report examined the potential impacts of climate change on Cleveland, New York City, and Miami. These areas encompass a diversity of climates and uses of natural resources.

Much of the current inventory in urban infrastructure will most likely turn over in the next 35 to 50 years. A warmer global climate would require changes in the capital investment patterns of cities for water supplies, peak electric generating capacity, and storm sewer capacity. Urbanized coastal areas might have to invest additional billions of dollars into coastal protection to defend developed areas from a rising sea. In Miami, for example, this could imply an increase of 1 to 2% in the city's capital spending over the next 100 years. Generally, northern cities such as Cleveland may fare better, since reductions in the operating and maintenance costs associated with heating public buildings, snow removal, and road maintenance should offset increasing costs for air-conditioning and port dredging.

* * *

FINAL THOUGHTS AND POLICY IMPLICATIONS

Because this is the most comprehensive study to address the issue of the environmental effects of climate change in the United States, we expect that a sizeable debate will follow its publication. Considerable additional research and analyses are likely to amplify, improve, and challenge these findings. We expect further research to develop new insights into the role of climate, but precise forecasts must await more advanced climate models, which may require many years to develop. For some time to come, our ability to provide national and local officials with guidance may be limited to effects driven primarily by temperature and sea level changes.

Apart from strategies to limit emissions of greenhouse gases, policymakers should consider policy options for adapting to global warming. Consideration of these options is complicated by the uncertainties identified in this report by delays in the onset of climate change, and by the pressure to solve today's problems. Many adaptations would undoubtedly occur as climate changes, but some decisions being made today have a long enough lifetime and sufficient risk to support consideration of the potential range of impacts of the greenhouse effect. These decisions should be made if they make economic and environmental sense for today's conditions and are sufficiently flexible to handle changing climate. Given the uncertainty about the timing, magnitude, and regional scope of climate change, we cannot plan for specific climate conditions in the future, but we can strive to be ready to respond to significantly changed climate conditions in the future.

Conversely, natural resource management should not assume that climate will not change. All managers of natural resources that are sensitive to climate should consider the vulnerabilities of their systems to climate change and whether anticipatory action would be needed — the systems can be adjusted and adapted as climate changes. In other areas, where long-term decisions on sensitive systems may result in irreversible impacts, anticipatory actions to mitigate these potential effects may be required. It may make sense in some instances to change the rules under which long-term planning is done, such as zoning laws, to allow for consideration of climate change in private-sector decisions. Finally, research and education are needed in many areas to improve our ability to respond to these changes. In any case, managers should reexamine their systems to consider ways to improve the flexibility and resiliency of the systems to handle these and other changes. The criteria to guide decisions should include consideration of the following factors:

- the uncertainties in the magnitude and timing of effects;
- whether the lifetime of the plan, project, or policy is long enough to be affected by climate change;
- whether effects of climate change are irreversible;
- whether the policy or project will increase flexibility and resilience or restrict future options;
- the uniqueness of the ecosystems or manmade structures that may need protection; and
- whether the impacts would be greater if no anticipatory action were taken.

The U.S. government is strongly supporting the Intergovernmental Panel on Climate Change (IPCC) under the auspices of the United Nations Environment Programme and the World Meteorological Organization. The IPCC has established a process for governments to follow when reviewing scientific information and policy options. The federal government is conducting other activities on global climate change. The Global Climate Protection Act of 1987 calls for a scientific assessment of climate change, which is to be completed by 1989. This work will be sponsored by EPA and other federal agencies such as the National Aeronautics and Space Administration, the National Oceanic and Atmospheric Administration, and the National Science Foundation, and coordinated through the IPCC. Also, the Department of Energy and EPA have been asked to report to Congress on policy options for reducing CO_2 emissions in the United States. In addition, various federal agencies conduct significant research programs on climate. These research efforts on climate change are coordinated by the National Climate Program Office and the Committee on Earth Sciences. The latter has produced a plan called Our Changing Planet: A United States Strategy for Global Change Research, which outlines federal research activities.

The federal government can also take the lead in pursuing prudent policies in anticipation of climate change, and many agencies can play a role in preparing the country for the impacts. These include the Departments of the Interior, Energy, Health and Human Services, and Agriculture; the U.S. Environmental Protection Agency; and the U.S. Army Corps of Engineers (see box on "Federal Activities"). However, adaptation should not occur just at the federal level, for there will likely be a need to involve other nations, state and local governments, industry and even individuals. The regional studies in this report demonstrate that climate change cuts across manmade and natural systems, geographic boundaries, and government agencies. Research, technical guidance, planning, and creative approaches to resource management will be needed in the future to prepare for the impacts of climate change on the United States.

FEDERAL ACTIVITIES THAT SHOULD CONSIDER CLIMATE CHANGE

Sample questions relating to climate change impacts that federal agencies should consider:

Agency	Policy Question
U.S. Environmental Protection Agency	How should current wetlands protection programs be modified to accommodate future sea level rise and precipitation changes?
U.S. Department of the Interior	Should national parks and wildlife refuges purchase land to accommodate the migration necessitated by climate change?
	Are current activities increasing the vulnerability of species that might be threatened by climate change?

U.S Department of the Interior	Should the U.S. Geological Survey produce coastal area maps with finer contour intervals? How will climate change alter projected ground-water levels?
	Will current water policies in the West prove to have been ill-advised if the climate changes?
U.S. Department of Agriculture	Do price support programs help or hinder the adjustments that climate change may necessitate?
	To what extent could irrigation be increased on a sustainable basis if climate became drier?
	What actions would be necessary to maintain national forests as the climate changes?
U.S. Army Corps of Engineers	How does a consideration of future climate change alter the relative merits of alternative approaches to coastal protection, flood control, and navigation?

The enormity of the potential global warming problem has led to much debate over a possible solution. Set forth below is a discussion of the options, as identified by the Office of Technology Assessment, from the report that introduced this chapter.

CHANGING BY DEGREES
STEPS TO REDUCE GREENHOUSE GASES

Office of Technology Assessment, U.S. Congress, OTA-O-483 (1991)

* * *

OPTIONS FOR REDUCING U.S. EMISSIONS

The major options available or likely to be available for **reducing** CO_2 emissions in the near term fall into three categories:

1. increasing energy conservation and efficiency in end-use technologies.
2. changing use patterns to conserve energy, and
3. shifting energy supply away from high CO_2-emitting fuels.

Additional options to **offset** CO_2 emissions are primarily forestry-related or agricultural. If Congress chooses to pursue any of these options, it obviously will also seek to assure continuous economic progress.

When choosing policy options Congress must consider **two** interdependent components: the universe of possible **technical** (or in some cases, behavioral) changes and the policy **instruments** (e.g., taxes, regulations, financial incentives) available to require or encourage the technical change. One policy option, for example, would be to reduce CO_2 emissions through regulations (i.e., a policy instrument) to require more fuel-efficient autos (i.e., a technical option). An alternative or perhaps complementary policy option would be to use a high "gas guzzler" tax (i.e., policy instrument) to stimulate purchase of fuel-efficient autos.

Technical Options

This report identifies a range of CO_2-reducing technical options available or likely to be available to the Nation over the next 25 years, and what their contribution might be. There are a large number of technical options to pick from and many targets of opportunity within each sector. Significant progress in reducing U.S. CO_2 emissions will require that most of these options be pursued simultaneously.

Presently available energy "supply" options for achieving major CO_2 reductions over the 25-year timeframe of this assessment include: replacing high carbon-emitting fuels (e.g., coal) with lower carbon-emitting fuels (e.g., natural gas); using high-efficiency gas turbines or cogeneration); and using nonfossil fuels.

While nonfossil energy offers the greatest long-term potential for achieving deep cuts in CO_2 emissions, we cannot count on **large-scale** use of nonfossil energy sources to replace fossil fuels within 25 years. These sources do not yet offer the performance, costs, or social acceptance needed to fully displace fossil fuels in such a relatively short period of time. Only three nonfossil sources are presently being used on a significant scale in the United States: hydroelectric power, biomass, and nuclear light-water reactors (LWRs). Because of a combination of low baseload demand growth, cost and environmental and social problems, no orders for new LWRs have been initiated in over a decade and there are no plans underway to build new reactors in the United States. Environmental factors set an upper limit on the number of potential new dam sites for hydroelectric facilities and on biomass production.

On the energy "end use" side, the technical options available today are primarily more efficient technologies or changes in energy use patterns. The first requires time and investment, whether for old equipment to be replaced or new equipment to be purchased. Changing energy use can include immediate (but reversible) changes such as fewer miles driven, lights dimmed, etc. In addition to the currently available technical options there is a large menu of additional options that could be developed over time. A diverse suite of energy R&D is ongoing, but what it will make available in the next quarter century depends greatly on Federal funding for demonstration.

Several technical options are available in the forestry sector to provide some **offsets** of CO_2 emissions. Increasing forest productivity and planting new trees can result in increased carbon storage that offsets fossil-fuel related emissions. Planting short-rotation tree crops for use as biomass fuels can partially replace the use of fossil fuels in some situations. These and other forestry options have attendant uncertainties and difficulties. For example, attempts to increase productivity focus on the timber component of forests (i.e., the commercially valuable portion). However, it is unclear whether increases in timber productivity actually indicate whether or not productivity in the entire forest has increased.

Policy Instruments

Policy instruments are the means government uses to require or encourage a desired technical or behavioral response. Many potential targets exist within each sector to achieve CO_2 emissions reductions. Whatever the CO_2 reduction goal, Congress will have to use a variety of policy instruments to stimulate a diverse set of decisionmakers to use the appropriate fuels, technologies, and forestry and agriculture practices and to adopt energy use patterns that conserve energy.

Identifying the relevant decisionmakers will be critical to selection of appropriate policy instruments. Within the energy system, for example, appliance and lighting use patterns represent the collective decisions of nearly all Americans. In contrast, utility fuel choices are made within a relatively small community of decisionmakers (e.g., utility executives, State regulators, and segments of the financial community).

Certain generalizations nonetheless can provide guidance:

- Decisionmakers generally prefer lower cost options and many individuals prefer low first-cost options over low life-cycle cost options.
- Highly efficient "cutting edge" technologies often have relatively lower life-cycle costs but higher front-end costs.
- Historically, fragmented decisionmaking reinforces the preference for low first costs, especially in the buildings sector — decisions relevant to efficiency are made by developers and builders, not by the occupants who will be paying the energy bills.

A wide range of possible policy instruments could be used to influence decisionmakers. [These can be broken down] into six generic categories:

1. taxes;
2. financial incentives;
3. marketable permits;
4. regulations;
5. research, development, and demonstration (RD&D); and
6. information and public education.

Just as there is no single technical option that is a cure-all, many policy instruments will be needed. The synergisms possible among taxation, regulation, incentives, information, and RD&D programs are key to significantly reducing emissions. Taxes, if properly set, can be used to adjust prices to tilt purchase decisions. Regulation (codes and standards) can be used to remove the least efficient equipment, appliances, and buildings from the market. Incentives and information programs can be used to clarify cost information and help create a market for improved energy performance. Education programs also provide consumers with the knowledge and information needed to make wiser energy choices. Government-sponsored RD&D can help provide producers and consumers with new technical options that can be used to reach national goals, as well as reduce, by cost-sharing, the risk to industry of developing these new options.

Taxes

Taxes offer a way to make high CO_2-emitting technical options more expensive than lower CO_2-emitting options. If Congress so desires, new tax monies could help fund incentive programs, offset the budget deficit, or replace other existing taxes.

Three possibilities include: 1) a general energy tax, 2) a carbon tax, and 3) initial purchase taxes. A general energy tax is levied on the energy (i.e., Btu) content of fuels. A carbon tax is set to reflect the fact that some fuels emit more carbon per unit of energy than do others. Both of these are thus "fuel" taxes. An initial purchase tax is levied on energy-consuming **technologies**, rather than fuels; the tax would be based on estimates of lifetime energy use or carbon emissions.

Financial Incentives

Through financial incentives (e.g., tax incentives, low cost loans, and direct payment subsidies), the government pays part of the costs of utilizing desirable fuels, technologies, or practices. Tax incentives can be powerful instruments for stimulating desired actions by corporations and individual taxpayers looking for ways to reduce tax liabilities; however, tax incentives have little effect on those who pay low or no taxes.

* * *

Marketable Permits

Marketable permits and carbon taxes are closely related. Under a marketable permit system, policymakers fix the amount of carbon that can be emitted. The government then issues the allowed number of permits to emit a given amount of carbon. Permits can be bought and sold by energy users just like fuels. For example, for every 1 million Btu's of **coal** purchased, the user must also own (or purchase) permits to emit 57 pounds of carbon. To burn 1 million Btu's of **natural gas**, the user must own or purchase permits to emit 32 pounds of carbon. If demand for energy rises, the price of a carbon permit will rise to reflect the cost of lowering emissions. Some holders of permits will find ways to lower emissions (e.g., purchase more efficient equipment, switch from coal to natural gas) so that they can sell their permits (at a profit) to others. Theoretically, the effective price of fossil fuels will rise just high enough to meet the allowed carbon emission target. Just how high prices will rise, however, is difficult to forecast.

Marketable emission permits is the current U.S. method for enforcing the Montreal Protocol and controlling CFC emissions. A marketable permit system also is the regulatory mechanism for limiting emissions of sulfur dioxide to control acid rain under the new Clean Air Act Amendments (Public Law 101-549).

Marketable permits could be required for all fossil fuel users or only for large users such as electric utilities, factories, and even large commercial installations. Permits could be required for wholesalers who **sell** gasoline, rather than for individual drivers.

Regulations

Regulations are policy instruments that can eliminate inefficient and/or high CO_2-emitting activities from the market. They can take the form, for example, of performance standards and building codes. Performance standards can be established for many diverse types of technologies (e.g., lighting standards) and applied nationwide; they are currently used for automobile efficiency and appliance efficiency. Building codes traditionally have been the province of local governments and their effective use depends on enforcement at that level.

Research Development and Demonstration (RD&D)

Through RD&D, government can search for and fine-tune technological fixes to the greenhouse gas emissions problem. **In fact, climate change can only be effectively addressed over the long-term with the development and worldwide use of better nonfossil energy sources.** Government can speed the process of testing and commercializing many energy-supply and end-use technologies. However, only about 5 percent of the $2.7 billion national budget for energy technology R&D in 1990 was devoted to renewables (including biomass energy) and only 7 percent to energy conservation. Fossil fuels had 25 percent of the research budget, nuclear fusion 12 percent, and nuclear fission 9 percent.

Information

Information as a policy instrument has the potential to change the awareness level and perceptions of decisionmakers. Information programs rest on the assumption that if decisionmakers are better informed they will make better decisions. The most common goal of information programs is to stimulate decisionmakers to opt for least cost (life-cycle) savings, as opposed to initial-purchase savings, in their energy decision. For example, although the most efficient model of an appliance usually costs more initially, energy savings accrue over its useful life.

* * *

NOTES

1. During hearings before the House Energy & Commerce subcommittee, John Rowe, President and Chief Executive Officer of the New England Electric System endorsed a $2/ton carbon tax. The Bush administration opposed the tax, however, claiming that the tax would have to be $140/ton to stabilize CO_2 emissions at 1990 levels. 4 *Environment Week* No. 49 at 3 (December 12, 1991).

2. EPA's scientists have determined that "global surface warming" is very probable. Moreover, since the atmospheric lifetime of greenhouse gases ranges from 10 to 400 years, some impacts are likely even if emissions of all such gases are stopped immediately. For this reason, any strategy to address the problem must consider both how our society will cope with the likely changes, and what ought to be done to arrest the problem. How would you balance these two approaches?

15 INDOOR AIR POLLUTION

With the exception of smoking regulation, indoor air pollution has largely escaped state and federal control. Recent events, however, have spurred administrative as well as legislative efforts in this area. A report from the General Accounting Office explains why indoor air pollution has begun to attract more attention.

INDOOR AIR POLLUTION: FEDERAL EFFORTS NOT EFFECTIVELY ADDRESSING A GROWING PROBLEM

U.S. General Accounting Office, GAO/RCED-92-8

With the increased emphasis on energy conservation in the 1970s, and the identification of radon and asbestos as causing serious health problems, public concern about indoor air pollution has increased. Elevated levels of indoor pollutants — such as second-hand tobacco smoke, formaldehyde used in pressed wood products, molds in ventilation systems, and paint strippers and other solvents containing methylene chloride — can cause headaches, fatigue, respiratory diseases, and cancer. In the early 1980s the Congress began funding Environmental Protection Agency (EPA) programs to identify indoor air pollution sources — in addition to radon and asbestos — and conduct research on the health effects of such pollutants. In 1986 the Congress enacted title IV of the Superfund Amendments and Reauthorization Act (SARA), which directed EPA to develop an indoor air research program, disseminate the results of the research, establish an advisory committee comprised of federal agencies to assist EPA in carrying out the program, and report to the Congress on federal indoor air activities.

* * *

RESULTS IN BRIEF

* * *

Federal agencies other than EPA have programs that affect indoor air quality, and title IV of SARA required EPA to work with these agencies to address indoor air issues. The Interagency Committee on Indoor Air Quality[1] (CIAQ) was established for this purpose, but there has been limited commitment from the other agencies. Furthermore, CIAQ has not been as effective as it could be primarily because it lacks a clear charter how the agencies will work together to address indoor air issues. Without such a charter, some indoor air activities are not being accomplished because a national agenda has not been established for indoor air that determines what projects need to be completed, which agencies should be responsible for the projects, and what the time frames are for their completion.

---

[1] The Committee on Indoor Air Quality is composed of sixteen (16) federal agencies. The Committee outlined current research efforts, including case studies on radon and formaldehyde, and a research strategy for the future in a 1984 report entitled "Comprehensive Indoor Air Quality Research Strategy."

Most of the states with active programs that we contacted concentrate on mitigating indoor air pollution through increased ventilation. Six of the state programs we visited were in the two EPA regions that work actively with the states to develop indoor air programs. Given the success of such programs, EPA plans to initiate indoor air programs in its eight other regional offices.

BACKGROUND

In the 1970s increased emphasis on energy conservation measures, such as using more energy-efficient building materials and reducing the air exchange rates of ventilation systems, resulted in increases in indoor air pollution in offices and homes. For example, energy efficiency measures sometimes result in lower air exchange rates for ventilation systems and cause pollutants, such as second-hand tobacco smoke, dust mites, carbon monoxide, benzene, and pesticides, to remain indoors and contribute to indoor air problems.

Additionally, certain materials used in carpets, insulation, and home office furniture contribute to the overall indoor air problem by giving off chemical emissions. Therefore, the elevated levels of such pollutants increase health risks — headaches, fatigue, respiratory diseases, and cancer — for building occupants when such materials, along with air exchange rate reductions, are employed.

By the early 1980s research began demonstrating the significance of indoor air pollution, and between fiscal years 1984 and 1986, the Congress appropriated approximately $2 million annually for EPA to conduct indoor air research. However, according to EPA there was considerable debate and uncertainty among federal agencies about the appropriate government role. For example, questions were raised about whether federal agencies could implement policies or regulations that would infringe on the rights of citizens in private residences.

As concern over the risks to human health from indoor air pollutants increased, the Congress enacted title IV of SARA in 1986. Title IV directed EPA to develop an indoor air research program, disseminate the results of the research, establish an advisory committee comprised of federal agencies to assist EPA in carrying out the program, and report to the Congress on federal indoor air activities. One reason for establishing the advisory committee was that a number of federal agencies, other than EPA, have programs affecting indoor air quality. Federal agencies with the largest indoor air program responsibilities, other than EPA, are the Consumer Product Safety Commission (CPSC), National Institute of Occupational Safety and Health (NIOSH), Occupational Safety and Health Administration (OSHA), and Department of Energy (DOE). For example, NIOSH estimates that about 30 percent of its health and safety inspections involve indoor air problems. Furthermore, DOE is conducting research on the impact on indoor air quality of energy conservation materials and reduced air exchange rates of ventilation systems.

* * *

In 1989 and 1990 indoor air legislation was introduced in the Congress that called for a more direct focus on indoor air by establishing a national program to reduce the human health threat caused by such pollution. Although the Senate passed its indoor air bill, the Congress did not enact any of the proposed legislation. Similar legislative proposals were introduced in both houses of Congress in 1991. These legislative proposals go beyond research, requiring more emphasis on source control and mitigation of indoor air pollution.

* * *

EPA'S EMPHASIS ON INDOOR AIR POLLUTION IS NOT COMMENSURATE WITH THE HEALTH RISKS

Even though EPA recognizes that indoor air pollution represents a serious health risk with symptoms ranging from eye irritation, headaches, and fatigue to respiratory diseases and cancer, funding levels have not been commensurate with these health risks. In its *Unfinished Business* report, EPA ranked indoor air pollution fourth among 31 environmental problems in terms of the risk it poses to human health and the environment, based on the opinions of a task force of 75 EPA scientists, engineers, and managers. Similarly, in a 1990 study EPA's Science Advisory Board advised EPA to give higher priority to funding high-risk environmental problems, such as indoor air pollution.

EPA's indoor air program budget for fiscal year 1991 was $6.6 million, less than 4 percent of EPA's overall air program budget. EPA's overall budget has remained essentially level for over a decade, but its program responsibilities have increased significantly. According to EPA officials, one of the primary reasons that indoor air programs have not received more funding is that they compete in EPA's constrained budget process with other air quality programs that have legislative mandates. For example, EPA's air quality programs with legislative deadlines, such as those aimed at regulating toxic air emissions, attaining national air quality standards, and reducing automotive emissions, are given higher priority when budget decisions are made. Although title IV of SARA requires EPA to establish an indoor air research program, it does not set time frames or require EPA to take any specific measures to control indoor air pollution. In contrast, programs that have legislative mandates, such as attaining national air quality standards, ranked 22nd in EPA's *Unfinished Business* report, are given higher funding. Funding for the national air quality standards was $18.4 million, more than four times greater than the $4.3 million for indoor air research.

* * *

RECOMMENDATIONS TO THE ADMINISTRATOR, EPA

We recommend that the Administrator, EPA, examine the agency's indoor air research budget to ensure that funding for the indoor air pollution program is consistent with its high health and environment risk. To elevate the attention given to indoor air pollution and to leverage EPA's influence with other federal agencies, we recommend that the Administrator work with other members of CIAQ to develop a clear charter that capitalizes on the indoor air expertise of each federal agency and clearly defines the roles and responsibilities of each agency to improve coordination and information sharing among EPA and the other agencies responsible for indoor air issues.

MATTER FOR CONSIDERATION BY THE CONGRESS

Legislative proposals to strengthen the federal response to indoor air pollution have been introduced in both houses of the Congress. We believe that strengthening CIAQ will help EPA and other agencies focus their indoor air efforts even without additional legislative authority. Nevertheless, given the many priorities of the other federal agencies that have roles in addressing indoor air pollution and the increasing competition for limited funding, the Congress, in debating the Indoor Air Quality Act of 1991, may wish to consider giving other federal agencies more specific mandates in this area. The mandates could require these agencies to take more active roles in addressing indoor air pollution issues within the purview of their existing program objectives and coordinate their indoor air efforts with other federal agencies.

NOTES

1. As noted in the GAO report, legislation has been introduced to combat the health risks and problems associated with indoor air pollution. The Indoor Air Quality Act of 1991 would require the EPA to: (1) expand and strengthen indoor air research, and establish a technology demonstration program; (2) conduct an assessment of indoor air quality in schools; (3) develop health advisories on indoor air contaminants which may occur in indoor air at levels which may reasonably be expected to have an adverse impact on human health; (4) prepare a response plan using existing regulatory authorities and other specified nonregulatory authorities to reduce exposure to indoor air contaminants; (5) make grants to states to develop and implement indoor air pollution strategies; (6) prepare a report on multiple chemical sensitivities, and expand its research program to address the effects of indoor air pollutants on those who suffer from multiple chemical sensitivities; (7) conduct an assessment of indoor air problems in buildings housing child care facilities; (8) conduct research with the Department of Transportation on indoor air pollution in public and private transportation; (9) establish a program to address the role of ventilation in protecting the public from indoor air contaminants; and (10) provide an assessment of indoor air monitoring and mitigation services provided by private firms. The bill also expands the authority of the National Institute of Occupational Safety and Health to conduct assessments of buildings that are declared "sick". 137 Cong. Rec. S16022, 16030-31 (daily ed. Nov. 6, 1991) (Indoor Air Quality Act of 1991.)

2. The regulation of smoking has become more commonplace than regulation of other forms of indoor air pollution. In one of the more interesting cases, prison inmates successfully challenged forced exposure to second-hand tobacco smoke. *Avery v. Powell*, 696 F. Supp. 632 (D. N. H. 1988). In that case, Clifford Avery, an inmate incarcerated in the New Hampshire State Prison ("NHSP"), filed a civil rights action under 42 U.S.C. § 1983 against NHSP officials alleging that continuous exposure to passive tobacco smoke as a condition of confinement violated the Fifth, Eighth, and Fourteenth Amendments to the U.S. Constitution. Avery, a nonsmoker, was one of approximately two hundred inmates incarcerated in the Medium North and Medium South Units of the New Hampshire State Prison. The Medium North and Medium South Units share a common air flow system which circulates air and heat between the pods. Avery argued that the tobacco smoke contained toxic substances which had a long-term pernicious effect on his health. In support of his contention Avery cited a 1986 Surgeon General report. That report reached three major conclusions: (1) that involuntary smoking is a cause of disease, including lung cancer, in healthy nonsmokers; (2) that the children of parents who smoke compared with the children of non-smoking parents have an increased frequency of respiratory infections, increased respiratory symptoms, and slightly smaller rates of increased lung function as their lungs mature; and (3) that the simple separation of smokers and nonsmokers within the same air space may reduce, but does not eliminate, the exposure of nonsmokers to environmental tobacco smoke. The court, in denying the prison's motion to dismiss, found that exposure to environmental tobacco smoke was not merely discomforting and that conditions of Avery's confinement could constitute punishment cognizable under the Eighth Amendment.

3. The Civil Aeronautics Board regulates smoking on interstate, overseas and foreign air transportation. In *Action on Smoking and Health (ASH) v. Civil Aeronautics Board (CAB)*, 699 F.2d 1209 (D.C.C. 1983), ASH challenged a CAB regulatory change which had relaxed the protections afforded nonsmokers from the tobacco smoke of fellow passengers aboard aircraft. The Air Transport Association of America and Transamerica Airlines, Inc. intervened to argue that the Board lacked the authority to regulate smoking altogether. In ruling on the intervenor's claim, the court found the agency's authority to regulate smoking aboard international aircraft less compelling than its authority to regulate interstate aircraft, but nonetheless sustained the CAB's authority in both cases.

4. The widespread discovery of radon contamination in homes, and its significant health effects, has spurred federal legislation. In 1988, Congress amended the Toxic Substances Control Act to address specifically indoor radon abatement. 15 U.S.C. §§ 2661 *et seq.* This law establishes a goal of assuring that radon levels in buildings "be as free of radon as the ambient air outside of buildings." The statute requires EPA to publish and make available, "A Citizen's Guide to Radon." *Id.* at § 2663. In addition, EPA must develop construction standards and techniques for controlling radon, and provide technical and financial assistance to the states to develop radon programs. *Id.* at §§ 2664-66. Finally, the law supports studies of radon in schools and federal buildings, and, in the case of schools, offers some technical assistance to help abate radon problems. Despite these efforts, some members of Congress continue to support stronger radon programs. The following are comments of Senator George Mitchell explaining the need for new legislation —

> Radon is a naturally occurring element found in soil and rock containing granite, shale, and uranium. In its gaseous form, radon can seep into homes and other structures through cracks in foundations and basement floors. Radon contamination of homes and other buildings is a deadly serious problem. Exposure to radon poses a significant threat of lung cancer, second only to cigarette smoking. The Environmental Protection Agency estimates that radon causes between 8,000 and 40,000 lung cancer deaths throughout the country each year.
>
> Over the past several years, the EPA has conducted screening tests for radon in homes in 34 States. The EPA found that 20 percent of homes tested had radon above the EPA action level. In some States, over half the homes tested had high radon levels. For the Nation as a whole, EPA estimates that 10 percent of homes have average, annual radon levels above the EPA action level.

137 Cong. Rec. S4230-4231 (daily ed. April 9, 1991)

5. Most urban residents spend 19-23 hours each day indoors, including 14 to 16 hours at home. *See* Sexton, *Indoor Air Quality: An Overview of Policy and Regulatory Issues*, SCIENCE, TECHNOLOGY & HUMAN VALUES (Winter, 1986) at 53. Yet, for some pollutants, indoor exposures regularly exceed outdoor exposures set for them. *See Indoor Air Pollution*, CONSUMER REPORTS October, 1985). Why then has the government imposed a multi-billion dollar program to clean up outdoor air but been slow to act to address indoor air pollution?

GLOSSARY

Affected Sources: A source subject to the acid deposition control program under Title IV of the Act. Affected sources may contain one or more "affected units". A unit is a fossil fuel-fired combustion device. § 402(1),(2),(15).

AQCR: Air Quality Control Regions. Regions within one or more states designated by the EPA or the Governor of the state with EPA approval, for the purpose of providing for the attainment and maintenance of the NAAQSs.

AQRV: Air Quality Related Values. The term used to describe those values that federal land managers must protect when considering the impacts of major emitting facilities on class I areas. § 165(d).

Area Source: ". . . [A]ny stationary source of HAPs that is not a major source." § 112(a)(2).

BACT: Best Available Control Technology. An emission limitation based on the maximum degree of reduction which the permitting authority determines is achievable taking into account energy, environmental and economic impacts and other costs. § 169(3). BACT must be used by any new or modified major emitting facility in a PSD area.

BART: Best Available Retrofit Technology. The best available technology for reducing or eliminating visibility impairment taking into consideration costs, energy and non-environmental impacts, the remaining useful life of the source, existing pollution control technology in use at the source, and the degree of improvement that may reasonably be expected from use of the technology. § 169A(g)(2). BART must be used by major stationary sources that adversely affect the visibility of specially designated federal Class I areas.

Baseline Concentration. "The term 'baseline concentration' means, with respect to a pollutant, the ambient concentration levels which exist at the time of the first application for a permit in an area subject to this part, based on air quality data available in the Environmental Protection Agency or a State air pollution control agency and on such monitoring data as the permit applicant is required to submit. Such ambient concentration levels shall take into account all projected emissions in, or which may affect such area from any major emitting facility on which construction commenced prior to January 6, 1975, but which has not begun operation by the date of the baseline air quality concentration determination. Emissions of sulfur oxides and particulate matter from any major emitting facility on which construction commenced after January 6, 1975, shall not be included in the baseline and shall be counted against the maximum allowable increases in pollutant concentrations established under this part." § 169(4).

CEMS: Continuous Emissions Monitoring System: Monitoring equipment "used to sample, analyze, measure, and provide on a continuous basis a permanent record of emissions and flow...." § 402(7). Such equipment is required for all "affected sources" under Title IV of the Act, unless it can be shown that an alternative monitoring system will provide information with the same precision, reliability, accessibility, and timeliness as CEMS. § 412.

Criteria Pollutants: Air pollutants which the EPA has determined endanger the public health or welfare *and* which result from numerous and adverse sources. § 108(a). EPA must establish national primary and secondary ambient air quality standards for each such pollutant. In conjunction with the establishment of these standards, EPA must also issue *air quality criteria* for each of these pollutants which reflect the latest scientific knowledge regarding their impact on the health and welfare of the public. § 108(a)(2).

CTG: Control Techniques Guidance: Guidance documents issued by EPA describing those techniques available to limit air emissions subject to various control standards under the Act. At the time of the 1990 Amendments, EPA had promulgated 29 CTGs. Section 183(a) requires EPA to issues CTGs for 11 additional sources of VOC emissions by November 15, 1993.

Designated Pollutants: Pollutants which are neither criteria pollutants nor hazardous pollutants but for which standards have been established for categories or classes of facilities under the NSPS program.

GACT: Generally Available Control Technology: A substitute for MACT that EPA may impose in lieu of MACT for area sources of HAPs. § 112(d)(5)

GEP: Good Engineering Practice. The principle used to ascertain appropriate stack heights for stationary sources of air pollution. "Good engineering practice means...the height necessary to insure that emissions for the stack do not result in excessive concentrations of any air pollutant in the immediate vicinity of the source..." § 123(c). Stack heights may not exceed two and one-half times the height of the source unless the owner of the source demonstrates to EPA that such heights is necessary as a GEP. *Id.* Emission limits for a source are set based on a stack height no higher than the GEP stack height.

HAP: Hazardous Air Pollutant: Any of 189 pollutants initially listed at § 112(b)(1) of the Act. This list may be revised to add or delete pollutants by petition, or in the discretion of EPA. Any pollutant which is know to cause or may be reasonably anticipated to cause adverse human health effects, or adverse environmental effects must be listed. § 112(b)(3)(B).

Integral Vista: "[A] view perceived from within a mandatory Class I Federal area of a specific landmark or panorama located outside the boundary of the mandatory Class I Federal area." 40 CFR 51.301 (n). EPA rules provide for limited protection of these integral vistas from major sources of air pollution so long as such vistas are identified at least six months prior to submission of the permit application for the new source. *See* 40 CFR 51.30 (b).

LAER: Lowest Achievable Emission Rate. The rate of emissions which reflects the most stringent emission limitation which is contained in the implementation plan of any State (unless the operator demonstrates that such limitations are not achievable) or, the most stringent emission limitation achieved in practice, whichever is more stringent. § 171(3). No new or modified major stationary source can be located in a nonattainment area unless, among other things, it can achieve LAER.

MACT: Maximum Achievable Control Technology: The basis upon which EPA must set emissions standards for sources of HAPs. For categories of existing sources, EPA must set the standard as least as stringent as the best performing 12%. For categories of new sources, MACT can be no less stringent than the best performing source. MACT can be more stringent than these standards. § 112(d)(3).

Major Source: "...[A]ny stationary source or group of stationary sources ... that emits or has the potential to emit 10 tons per year or more of any HAP or 25 tons per year or more of any combination of HAPs." § 112(a)(1).

Major Stationary Source and Major Emitting Facility. Any stationary facility or source of air pollutants which directly emits or has a potential to emit, one hundred tons per year or more of any pollutant (including any major emitting facility or source of fugitive emissions of any such pollutant, as determined by rule by the Administrator). CAUTION: For purposes of PSD and visibility protection these terms have different meanings. *See* §§ 169(1); 169A(g)(7).

mmBtu: One million British thermal units. A Btu is the amount of heat required to raise the temperature of one pound of water one degree Fahrenheit at or near 39.2°F.

Modification. "The term 'modification' means any physical change in, or change in the method of operation of, a stationary source which increases the amount of any air pollutant emitted by such source or which results in the emission of any air pollutant not previously emitted." § 111(a)(4).

NAA: Nonattainment Area. ACQRs, or portions thereof, for which one or more of the ambient air quality standards have not been met.

NAAQS: National Ambient Air Quality Standards. Primary and secondary NAAQSs are established for all criteria pollutants. Primary standards are considered the minimum standards necessary to maintain public health with an adequate margin of safety. Secondary standards are those necessary to promote the public welfare.

NESHAP: National Emission Standards for Hazardous Air Pollutants. Special standards established under § 112 of the Act to control emissions of those air pollutants which might reasonably be expected to result in an increase in mortality or other irreversible or incapacitating illness.

NCP: Noncompliance Penalties. Penalties which are *required* for (1) all major stationary sources violating any emission limit, or any emission standard or schedule established by a SIP; (2) *any* stationary source violating a standard established under the NSPS or NESHAP programs; (3) any stationary sources which are violating their NSPS. Limited exemptions apply to this penalty requirement. Any penalty imposed under this section must at least equal the economic value of noncompliance. § 120(d).

Nonconformance Penalties. Penalties issues under § 206(g) to manufacturers of motor vehicles or engines which fail to meet tailpipe emission standards established under § 202(a).

NSPS: New Source Performance Standards. NSPSs are *emission* standards for new or modified *stationary* sources. They must also include a percentage reduction in emission limitation and percentage reduction achievable through the application of the best technological system of continuous emission reduction which the EPA determines has been adequately demonstrated, taking into account costs, other health and environmental impact, and energy requirements. § 111 (a)(1)(C). In accordance with § 111 of the Act these emission standards are established for various categories and classes of facilities.

NSR: New Source Review. The preconstruction review requirements for parts C (PSD) and D (nonattainment) of the Clean Air Act. New source review requirements also apply to major stationary sources which might adversely affect visibility in Class I areas. 40 CFR § 51.307.

Offsets. The principle which prohibits the construction of major new sources of air pollution in nonattainment areas unless the proponent of the new source can obtain reductions in pollution within the area that will more than compensate for the pollution contributions to be made by the new source.
§ 173 (1)(A).

PSD: Prevention of Significant Deterioration. PSD is a federal policy established by § 169 of the Act to protect the quality of those areas of the country that currently meet or exceed the NAAQSs.

RFP: Reasonable Further Progress. Annual incremental reductions of emissions of criteria pollutants in nonattainment areas, as necessary statutory standards, or as may reasonably be required by the EPA. § 171(1).

RACM: Reasonably Available Control Measures. Those measures required to be taken in any nonattainment area to abate air pollution as specified in the nonattainment plan. § 172(c).

RACT: Reasonably Available Control Technology. Devices, systems, process modifications, or other apparatus or techniques, the application of which will achieve emission limitations established by EPA, taking into account the necessity of imposing such limitations to maintain air quality standards, the social and economic impacts of imposing such limitation and alternative meaning available for achieving the air quality standards. 40 CFR 51.1 (o). Existing stationary sources in nonattainment areas are required, at a minimum, to use RACT to achieve reductions in air emissions.

RVP: Reid Vapor Pressure. A term used to describe the volatility of fuel. The higher the pressure, the more volatile the fuel. § 211(h) prohibits the sale of gasoline during the high ozone season that exceeds an RVP of 9.0 psi (pounds per square inch).

SIP: State Implementation Plan. SIPs are plans developed by the states subject to EPA approval for achieving and maintaining the NAAQS for that state. If a state fails to adopt an adequate SIP, EPA must devise and implement a SIP for that state.

VMT: Vehicle Miles Traveled. § 182(d) attempts to limit ozone pollution in severe and extreme nonattainment areas by requiring offsets emissions growth that results from growth in the VMT.

VOC: Volatile Organic Compounds. Hydrocarbon substances that mix with NOx and sunlight to form ozone. EPA has recently promulgated rules defining VOC for purposes of ozone pollution control. *See* 57 Fed. Reg. 3941 (1992).

INDEX

accidental release program 57, 272

acid deposition 58-59, 81, 93, 301-326
    affected sources/units 59, 250, 347
    allowances 59

air quality maintenance plans (AQMP) 127

air quality related values (AQRV) 193

baseline concentrations *(see prevention of significant deterioration)*

best available control technology (BACT) *(see prevention of significant deterioration)*

best available retrofit technology (BART) *(see prevention of significant deterioration)*

carbon dioxide 81, 449-472

carbon monoxide 6-7, 49, 116

chemical safety and hazard investigation board (CSHIB) 57, 272

chlorofluorcarbon (CFC) 368-370, 375-383, 450

citizen suits 339, 435-448

common law remedies 29-45
    federal common law 37-45
    nuisance 29-34
    trespass 35

continuous emission monitoring system (CEMS) 59

control techniques guidance (CTG) 121

designated pollutants 221

economic issues 15-27
    emissions banking
    bubble policy 58, 183-185, 187
    economic and technological
feasibility 96-105, 395-400
    emissions charges 15-18
    emissions reduction credits (ERC) 58
    emissions trading 57-58, 115, 281-300
    lead banking 421
    netting 58
    offsets 58, 115

enforcement 337-364
    civil and criminal penalties 60, 338
    compliance certifications 60
    compliance order 337, 342-347
    criminal penalties 61, 339, 348-352
    emergencies 339
    jury trial 347
    federal enforcement 337-338
    noncompliance penalties 338, 353-364
    notice of violation 337, 342-347
    state implementation plans

extremely hazardous air pollutants 57

federal facilities 90

fuels and fuel additives 409-425
    catalytic converters 420
    low sulfur diesel fuel 425
    oxygenated gasoline 425
    reformulated gasoline 425
    Reid vapor pressure (RVP) 424

fugitive emissions 186, 194-200

generally available control technology (GACT) *(see hazardous air pollutants)*

global climate change 81, 449-472

good engineering practice (GEP) 94

hazardous air pollutants (HAP) 56-57, 260-280
- area sources 57, 254
- early reduction program 57, 272
- generally available control technology (GACT) 57, 271
- listing 271
- major source 57, 254, 250
- maximum achievable control technology (MACT) 57, 271
- motor vehicles 390
- residual risk 57, 272

hydrocarbons *(see also volatile organic compounds)* 10, 83-89

indoor air pollution 473-477

inspections 60, 327-337

international air pollution 150-157

interstate air pollution 127-149

judicial review
- citizen suits 339, 435-448
- petitions for review 427-435
- state implementation plans 163-169

lead 63-65, 67-78, 81, 409-419, 422-423

lowest achievable emissions rate (LAER) *(see nonattainment areas)*

major emitting facilities (MEF) 54, 188

major source *(see hazardous air pollutants)*

major stationary source (MSS) 54

maximum achievable control technology (MACT) *(see hazardous air pollutants)*

modifications of stationary sources 53, 55, 221-222, 225-234

monitoring and modeling 176, 186-187, 217-232

Montreal Protocol 365-376

mobile sources 387-409
- aircraft emissions 408
- clean fuel vehicles 389
- "cold start" CO standards 388
- hazardous air pollutants 388
- motor vehicle emission standards 387-409
- nonconformance penalties 389-393
- on-board vapor recovery 388
- summertime "ozone-prone" conditions 388
- useful life 387
- warranty 407-408

national ambient air quality standards (NAAQS) 48, 63-82

new source performance standards (NSPS) 53, 217-225, 233-241

new source review 54-55, 225-234, 241-249

nitrous oxides 11, 59

nonattainment areas 49, 105-127
- emissions offsets
- lowest achievable emissions rate (LAER) 49, 111-116
- milestones 110
- nonattainment area plans 116-127
- reasonably available control measures (RACM) 106, 116

reasonably available control technology (RACT) 106, 114, 116-121
reasonable further progress (RFP) 106, 116

noncompliance penalties *(see enforcement)*

nonconformance penalties *(see mobile sources)*

oxygenated gasoline *(see fuels and fuel additives)*

ozone (tropospheric) 67, 78, 107-110, 116

particulate matter 3-6, 49, 116

permits and preconstruction requirements 51-53, 233-326
monitoring requirements 52
operational flexibility 254
permit fees 52, 253
permits for acid deposition program 253
permits for hazardous air pollutants 252
permit shield 52, 254
PSD permits *(see also, new source review)* 255-259
EPA veto authority 254

photochemical oxidants 11

prevention of significant deterioration (PSD) 50-51, 173-215, 234-243
administrative review 188-189
baseline concentrations 50, 181-183
best available control technology (BACT) 50, 188
best available retrofit technology (BART) 206-207
class I, II, & III increments 178-179, 189-193
integral vistas 207
top-down 188-189
visibility protection 201-215
visibility transport regions 215

reasonably available control measures (RACM) *(see nonattainment areas)*

reasonably available control technology (RACT) *(see nonattainment areas)*

reasonable further progress (RFP) *(see nonattainment areas)*

reformulated gasoline *(see fuels and fuel additives)*

state implementation plans 83-172

stratospheric ozone 365-385

sulfur dioxide 7-8, 59, 67, 82, 90-93

tall stacks 93-96

technology-forcing 105

top-down *(see prevention of significant deterioration)*

visibility protection *(see prevention of significant deterioration)*

volatile organic compounds (VOC) 49, 89, 107-108, 423-424

wood stoves 19